Latin American
Politics and Development

Latin American Politics and Development

SIXTH EDITION

Edited by

Howard J. Wiarda, *University of Georgia*
Harvey F. Kline, *University of Alabama*

A Member of the Perseus Books Group

Find us on the World Wide Web at www.westviewpress.com.

Westview Press books are available at special discounts for bulk purchases in the
United States by corporations, institutions, and other organizations. For more
information, please contact the Special Markets Department at the Perseus Books
Group, 11 Cambridge Center, Cambridge MA 02142, or call (617) 252-5298 or
(800) 255-1514, or e-mail special.markets@perseusbooks.com.

Designed by Trish Wilkinson
Set in 10.5-point Adobe Caslon

Library of Congress Cataloging-in-Publication Data
    Latin American politics and development / edited by Howard J. Wiarda [and]
Harvey F. Kline. — 6th ed.
        p.   cm.
    Includes bibliographical references and index.
    ISBN-13: 978-0-8133-4327-3 (paperback : alk. paper)
    ISBN-10: 0-8133-4327-5 (paperback : alk. paper) 1. Latin America—Politics
and government. I. Wiarda, Howard J., 1939– II. Kline, Harvey F.
F1410.L39 2006
980—dc22   2006003512

07 08 09 / 10 9 8 7 6 5 4 3 2 1

Contents

Tables and Maps

Acronyms

AID	Agency for International Development
GATT	General Agreement on Tariffs and Trade
GDP	Gross Domestic Product
GNP	Gross National Product
ISI	import-substitution-industrialization
IADB	Inter-American Development Bank
IAF	Inter-American Foundation
IMF	International Monetary Fund
ALASI	Latin American Integration Association
NAFTA	North American Free Trade Agreement
NGOs	nongovernmental organizations
OAS	Organization of American States

Preface to the Sixth Edition

The first edition of this book was published in 1979, the second in 1985, the third in 1990, the fourth in 1996, the fifth in 2000, and now the sixth in 2007. The issues we have sought to examine in all six editions include why Latin America is different from the United States, why it lagged behind economically and politically, how societies cast historically in a medieval and semifeudal mode have gone about achieving modernization and development, what paths of national development the distinct countries of the area have followed (evolutionary or revolutionary; authoritarian, Marxist, or democratic; capitalist, socialist, or statist), and the evolution and difficulties of democracy in the area. These are large, meaty issues; their importance goes beyond the geographic confines of Latin America.

Each of the six editions of the book has reflected the major dynamic changes occurring in Latin America itself. The decade of the 1970s was a period of authoritarianism and repression in much of the region, widespread human rights abuses, and interpretation about the area—corporatism, dependency theory, and bureaucratic-authoritarianism—that reflected scholars' pessimism about Latin America's future. The 1980s were a period of democratization throughout Latin America, greater optimism about the area's political future (even though the economic prospects continued to be poor), and newer interpretations that stressed transitions to democracy.

In the early 1990s there was considerable agreement (labeled the "Washington consensus") between the United States and Latin America on goals for the region: democracy, economic liberalization, and free trade. By this point most of the authoritarian regimes of the area had given way and, with the collapse of the Soviet Union, Marxism-Leninism had become less attractive; democracy and liberalism seemed the only viable option. But by the end of the 1990s and continuing into the twenty-first century, although democracy, economic reform, and freer trade were still high on the agenda, a number of cracks had appeared in the prevailing consensus. Democracy was still limited and not working well in quite a few countries; much of Latin America had achieved electoral democracy but not liberal or participatory democracy. Economic reform continued, but the neoliberal agenda had resulted in widespread unemployment and privation in many countries. Trade barriers continued to fall in Latin America, but in the United States protectionist political pressures prevented bold new trade initiatives.

While Latin America over this forty-year period has gone through its political and economic ups and downs, its society has been massively transformed. These are no longer the "sleepy," "backward," "underdeveloped" countries of cartoon and movie stereotypes. Since 1960 Latin America as a whole has gone from 70 percent rural to 70 percent urban and from a 70 percent illiteracy rate to 70 percent literacy. These figures reflect the massive social changes underway throughout the area as well as the transformation from a peasant-agricultural economy to a more modern, industrial, and diversified one. In the mid-1970s seventeen of the twenty countries were authoritarian, but today nineteen of the twenty (all except Cuba, and even there major changes are likely soon) are democratic—incomplete democracies, but certainly better than the human rights-abusing regimes of earlier decades. Economically quite a number of the countries are booming, with miraculous or East Asian-level growth rates, but others are still mired in poverty. At the same time a host of new issues—rising crime and insecurity, social inequality, and globalization—have come to the fore. So, as always, Latin America reflects a mixture of successes and failures, of traditional and modern features of mixed and often crazy-quilt regimes in an always-changing, dynamic context.

No longer a group of backward, underdeveloped countries, Latin America is one of the most exciting regions of the globe for the comparative study of economic, social, and political change. In previous decades the choice of developmental models seemed wide open, representing diverse routes to modernization, but by now the democratic-mixed economy route seems the only one conceivable, although with great variation still among the countries of the region. Virtually every social, economic, and political issue, process, and policy present in the world can be found in Latin America. It remains an exciting, innovative ever-changing, endlessly fascinating living laboratory for study, travel, and research.

Not only is Latin America an interesting area to study, but it has become increasingly important to the United States. Mexico is now the United States' second largest (after Canada) trading partner in the world. Hispanics have become the largest minority in the United States and are voting in increasing numbers. On a host of new, hot issues—drugs, trade, immigration, tourism, pollution, investment, the environment, democracy, human rights—the United

States and Latin America have become increasingly intertwined and interdependent. Yet conflict persists in U.S. relations with Cuba, Venezuela, and other countries. At the same time both Europe and Asia are also increasing their trade with and interest in Latin America and are often competing with the United States for influence.

This book offers in its introduction to the area a broad, region-wide overview of the patterns and processes of Latin American history, politics, society, and development. It then proceeds to a detailed country-by-country treatment of all twenty Latin American countries. (The smaller former British and Dutch colonies of the region are not included, and of the former French colonies only Haiti is considered.) Major countries like Argentina, Brazil, Chile, Colombia, Mexico, Peru, and Venezuela receive extended coverage, and the smaller countries receive complete but somewhat briefer treatment. Each country chapter is written by a leading specialist in the field. To facilitate comparisons between countries we have asked each of our authors as far as is feasible to use a common outline and approach. We emphasize throughout both the unique features of each country as well as the common patterns and processes that exist; instructors thus have maximum flexibility in the selection of which countries to study and which themes or developmental models to emphasize.

Latin American Politics and Development has throughout its previous editions emerged as one of the most durable yet innovative texts in the field, and we hope that this sixth edition will intrigue new students of Latin America as it has stimulated two generations of earlier ones. Many of these students have now gone on to careers in business, academia, private agencies, or foreign policy, and it is always rewarding to meet, hear from, or run into these former as well as current students. We hope that some of our enthusiasm for the subject continues to rub off on them.

The editors wish to thank their wives and families, for whom this book has over the years become almost another addition to the household. Thanks also to our contributors, both new and old; in each edition we have tried to bring in new faces, new ideas, and more women and minority contributors. Finally, we wish to thank acquisitions editor Karl Yambert of Westview Press for encouraging this new edition and shepherding it through the publication process.

Howard J. Wiarda
Harvey F. Kline

PART I

The Latin American Tradition and Process of Development

Howard J. Wiarda
Harvey F. Kline

1

The Context of
Latin American Politics

Profound social, economic, cultural, and political transformations are sweeping through Latin America, affecting all institutions and areas of life. Accelerated economic and social change, democratization, and globalization are having an impact on all countries, often incompletely and unevenly. Latin America still has abundant poverty, malnutrition, disease, poor housing, and the worst distribution of income in the world; its economic and political institutions often fail to work well or as intended; and social and political reforms are still strongly needed. However, at least some of the countries—generally the larger, more stable, and richer ones—are making what appears to be a definitive breakthrough to democracy and development, and many of the small nations are modernizing as well.

We speak of "Latin America" as if it were a single, homogeneous region, but in fact the area is exceedingly diverse, and because of this diversity we need to understand each country individually as well as the common patterns. The Latin American countries share a common basis in law, language, history, culture, sociology, colonial experience, and overall political patterns that enables us to discuss the region in general terms, while also recognizing that each country is different and becoming increasingly more so. Unity amid diversity is a theme that runs throughout this book, so in Part 1 we survey the general patterns before going on to the individual countries in Part 2.

Throughout Latin America's history its leaders and people have debated their heritage and future: Western or non-Western; feudal, capitalist, or socialist; First World (developed nations) or Third World (developing ones); evolutionary or revolutionary change. Conflict over these issues has often delayed development.

Now at last a consensus seems to be emerging: democracy in the political sphere, a modern mixed economy, and greater integration with the rest of the world. Authoritarianism seems to be on the decrease in Latin America, although when the economy declines and instability results, the authoritarian temptation is still often present. Marxism-Leninism is similarly in decline, even while social democracy and populism are still attractive options for many political leaders. More and more of Latin America is becoming middle class and centrist. The old extremes are no longer attractive; the range of political and economic options has narrowed.

Driving these changes are democratization and globalization. Democracy is overwhelmingly the preferred form of government of Latin America, even though democracy does not always work well or quickly enough; it takes forms that are often different from that of the United States; and it is still threatened by upheaval, corruption, and vast social problems. Globalization affects Latin America in all areas of life: culture (movies and television), society (behavioral norms), politics (democracy), and above all economics. Latin America is now part of a global market economy. It has little choice but to open its markets to global trade and investment. With the Cold War over, and the war on terrorism concentrated elsewhere, there is little foreign aid, and Latin America can no longer play the superpowers against each other. It must have private investment and become globally competitive or it will sink. If a country deviates from the path of democracy or free markets, that all-important investment will simply go elsewhere. All political leaders and economic sectors in Latin America now recognize these hard facts, even though they may still rail against them in populist fashion or still disagree on the precise balance between authority and democracy, between statism and free markets, and between unfettered capitalism and social justice. The Latin American countries vary greatly in how they manage development policy, but they no longer have much choice about the basic model to follow.

As Latin America has become more democratic and its economies more open, it has, in its own way, balanced outside pressures and domestic, often traditional, ways of doing things. Modernity and traditions often exist side by side in Latin America—the most traditional agricultural methods alongside the most modern skyscrapers—reflecting the mixed, often transitional nature of Latin American society. Patronage considerations often remain as important as merit and electoral choice. Moreover, as democracy has come to the area, it has often been a more centralized, executive-centered form of democracy rather than one of separate and equal legislative and judicial branches. At the same time, despite privatization and neoliberalism, the state has remained a strong force in the economic and social programs, closer to the European tradition than to the U.S. laissez-faire model. Modernization in Latin America has represented a fascinating blend of U.S., European, and historic Latin American ways of doing things.

A Quick Snapshot

For the purposes of this book, Latin America consists of eighteen Spanish-speaking countries, one Portuguese-speaking country (Brazil), and one French or patois-speaking country (Haiti). Including South America, Central America, Mexico, and the Caribbean islands, it encompasses 8 million square miles (21 million square kilometers), about one fifth of the world's total land area. Its population is over 500 million, almost twice that of the United States. The former Dutch and British colonies in the area are also interesting and worthy of study and are part of the geographic region of Latin America, but they are not culturally, socially, religiously, or politically "Latin" American, and therefore they are not included in this book.

The social and racial composition of Latin America is exceedingly diverse and complicated. At the time of Columbus's "discovery" of America in 1492, some areas (Mexico, parts of Central America, the western area of South America) had large numbers of indigenous people, whereas other areas did not; even today the assimilation and integration of indigenous people into national life remains one of the great unsolved problems of these countries. Where there were few Indians or they died out, and when the climate was right for plantation agriculture (the Caribbean islands, northeast Brazil, some coastal areas), large numbers of African slaves were brought in. White Europeans formed the upper class and Indians and blacks were slaves, peasants, and subsistence agriculturists. Once the Indians had died off or had been eliminated, social and race relations in the Caribbean islands and northeast Brazil would be written in terms of the relations between whites and blacks; on the rest of the mainland the major socio-racial components were white and Indian. The cultures of the Spanish colonies in the Caribbean and the Portuguese in Brazil, because of the African influence, were often different from those in the other Spanish-speaking countries. In some countries all three major racial strains (Indian, black, white), as well as Asian and Middle Eastern, are now present.

In contrast to North America, where the colonists took their wives and families along to settle and farm, the conquest of Latin America was viewed as a military campaign (no women initially), and widespread miscegenation between whites and Indians, whites and blacks, blacks and Indians, and all of their offspring took place right from the beginning. Hence a mulatto (white and black) element in the Caribbean and Brazil and a *mestizo* (white and Indian) element in the mainland countries of the Spanish empire emerged, with endless gradations based on color, hair, and facial features. Although there is racial prejudice, because of the many variations and gradations, Latin Americans tend not to typecast people as "black," "white," or "Indian" based solely on color as North Americans do. Indeed, in many of the Central American and Andean countries of South America, one is an *indio* or *indígeno* only if he or she dresses like a native American and speaks a language other than Spanish. Moving to a city, wearing Western clothes, and speaking Spanish probably means that the person would no longer be called an "Indian," although of course there has been no change of ethnic background.

The racial situation in Latin America is generally more fluid and permeable than it is in the United States; in addition, higher education, wealth, the clothes one wears, and comportment tend to make one "whiter." Because being viewed as whiter is pragmatically seen by most Latin Americans as being easier and/or better, it has long been hard to launch Indian or black rights or power movements, although this is changing as well. Endlessly fascinating, racial/social relations in Latin America are very different from those in the United States.

Richard C. Williamson, in *Latin American Societies in Transition*, suggests that in broad ethnic terms the countries of Latin America could be classified into four major groups (although many countries had regional variations):

1. Countries in which a *mestizo* population dominates;
2. Countries overwhelmingly European in character;
3. Countries with conspicuous Indian groupings, generally inhabiting the highlands; and
4. Countries dominated by African admixtures.[1]

The first group of countries includes the South American countries of Venezuela and Colombia, as well as Nicaragua, El Salvador, Honduras, and Panama in Central America and Mexico. The predominantly European countries are Argentina, Chile, Uruguay, and Costa Rica, and the countries with large Indian groups are Guatemala, Ecuador, Peru, Bolivia, and Paraguay. Finally, the countries dominated by African admixtures are Brazil and the Caribbean countries of Cuba, the Dominican Republic, and Haiti.

The economies of the area are similarly diverse. Few countries (Argentina, Brazil, Uruguay, Venezuela) have vast, rich agricultural lands comparable to the American Midwest; in most of the others subsistence agriculture has predominated. Because of climate few countries can grow the kind of grains grown in more temperate climates; hence sugar, coffee, cacao beans, and fruits have predominated. Mexico and the larger, South American countries have considerable mineral wealth and some have oil, but other countries have few natural resources and are likely to remain poor, regardless of whether they call themselves capitalist or socialist. Based on their resources, some countries—generally the bigger ones with large internal markets (Argentina, Brazil, Chile, Mexico)—are "making it" in the global economy and becoming competitive with the most efficient countries. Another group of Latin American countries is doing moderately well economically and improving their condition. However, a handful of countries (Bolivia, Ecuador, Haiti, Honduras, Nicaragua) are not doing well at all and are mired at the lower end of the rankings with the world's poorest nations.

The Latin American countries differ not only in people and economics but also in terms of geography. The continent contains the world's second highest mountain range (over 20,000 feet), the Andes, which runs like a vertical spine up and down the Pacific Coast. Latin America also has some of the world's largest river systems (Amazon, Orinoco, Plate), but few of these connect major cities with agricultural areas or provide the internal transportation networks formed by the rivers and Great Lakes of North America. In many countries mountains come right down to the sea, leaving little coastal land for settlement and agricultural development. Much of the interior land is similarly unsuitable for cash crops, and although some countries have iron ore, few have coal, making it difficult to produce steel, one of the keys to early industrial development. Hence, although nature has been kind to Latin America in some resources, it has been stingy in others, and although a few countries are resource-rich, others are stunningly poor.

One of the most startling features of South America is the vast Amazon basin, stretching nearly 2,000 miles in all directions. Largely uninhabited until recently, the Amazon rain forest produces upward of 40 percent of the world's oxygen supply. Environmentalists seek to preserve this environment, but Brazil and other countries on its perimeter see the Amazon's resources as the keys to their future development. Note from the map in Part 2 that most of South America's great cities are located on the ocean coast; only in recent decades have efforts been made to populate, develop, and exploit the vast interior.

Geographically Latin America is a land of extremes: high mountains that are virtually impassable; lowlands that are densely tropical and also difficult to penetrate; and such extremes of heat, rainfall, and climate that make living and working difficult. Latin America largely lacked the resources that the United States had during its great march to modernization in the nineteenth century, one of the key reasons it lagged behind. The mountainous, chopped-up terrain also made internal communications and transportation difficult, dividing Latin America into *patrias chicas* (small, isolated villages) and making national integration extremely difficult. Only now, with the advent of modern communications and transportation, have the Latin American countries begun to become better integrated and develop their vast potential.

The Economies

The Latin American economies were founded on a basis that was rapacious and exploitative. Under the prevailing economic theory of mercantilism, colonies such as those of Spain and Portugal existed solely for the benefit of the mother countries. The considerable gold, silver, and other resources of the colonies were drained away by the colonial powers. Ironically Latin America's precious metals benefited the mother countries not at all but flowed through Spain and Portugal to England and Holland, where they helped launch the Industrial Revolution. As in the Americas, the north of Europe then forged ahead while the south fell farther behind.

The most characteristic feature of colonial Latin America was the feudal or semifeudal estate, patterned after the European model, with Spaniards and Portuguese as the overlords and Indians and blacks as peasants and slaves. Even after independence Latin America remained mainly feudal; only slowly did capitalism and an entrepreneurial ethic develop. Under feudalism the land, wealth, and people were all exploited; there was almost no effort to plow back the wealth of the land into development or to raise living standards. In accord with the feudal ethic and then-prevailing values, the total social product was fixed, and people had a duty to accept their station in life. Land, cattle, and peasants, then as now, were to the wealthy elites symbols of status and not necessarily to be used for productive purposes. However the economic situation of the colonies varied considerably: The Caribbean islands and northeast Brazil were areas of large-scale sugar plantations, and Mexico, Central America, Colombia, Peru, Bolivia, and other areas of Brazil were valued for their mineral wealth. Argentina, Uruguay, and other farm areas were settled later because at the time there were better ways than agriculture to get rich quick.

Once the readily available precious metals were exhausted, the vast territory of Latin America was divided up among the Spanish and Portuguese conquerors, mostly into huge estates that were the size of U.S. states or counties and resembled medieval fiefdoms. Along with the land came the right to exploit the Indian labor living on the land. Each Spanish and Portuguese conquistador could live like the feudal nobility: haughty, authoritarian, exploitative, avoiding manual labor. These large estates were mainly self-sufficient, with their own priests, political authority (the landowners themselves), and social and economic life. Few areas in Latin America (Costa Rica comes closest) were founded on the productive, family-farm basis that the New England colonies were.

It was only in the last half of the nineteenth century that these feudal estates began to be converted into more capitalistic enterprises producing more intensively for a world market as well as home consumption. Sugar and tobacco in the Caribbean; bananas and coffee in Central America and Colombia; rubber in Brazil; and beef, hides, and wool in Argentina and Uruguay were the new crops being produced for profit. The old feudal estates began to modernize and become export-oriented enterprises. Foreign investment stimulated this conversion process. Latin America went through the first stages of economic development, but in the process many Indians and peasants were exploited even more than in the past or pushed off their communal lands into the infertile hillsides. The result was class polarization and, in Mexico, a violent revolution in 1910.

Production for the export market resulted in an economic quickening throughout Latin America that led to further growth later on, but it also brought Latin America into the world economy for the first time, with both positive and negative consequences. Greater affluence led to greater political stability and new economic opportunities, but it also made Latin America subject to global economic forces over which it had no control. Particularly in countries where 60 percent or higher of export earnings depended on one crop, if that crop (sugar, coffee, bananas) suffered a price decrease on world markets, the entire national economy could go into a tailspin. That is precisely what happened in virtually every price fluctuation and especially during the 1929–1930 world market crash, when not only did the bottom drop out of all the Latin American economies but their political systems collapsed as well. Almost every country of the area had a military coup d'état associated with the depression; Colombia and Mexico were exceptions.

Industrialization began in Latin America in the 1930s precisely because the countries had no export earnings to purchase imported manufactured goods and therefore had to produce them on their own. Most of the heavy industry—steel, electricity, petroleum, manufacturing—was established as state-owned industries, reflecting the weakness of entrepreneurialism and the history of mercantilism. The system was called state capitalism in order to distinguish it from the laissez-faire capitalism of the United States. This was the beginning of Latin America's large but often bloated, inefficient, and patronage-dominated state sector.

During World War II and the postwar period Latin America developed rapidly on the basis of this import-substitution-industrialization (ISI) model. However, growing demand for new social programs outstripped the countries' ability to pay for them, and then came the massive oil price increases of the 1970s and the debt crisis of the 1980s. Latin America was unable to pay its obligations and many countries slipped into near bankruptcy. Economic downturn again helped produce political instability in the 1960s and 1970s as it had in the 1930s.

In the 1990s and continuing in the new millennium, the Latin American economies began to recover, but in many countries the growth was anemic and debt continued to be a burden. Nevertheless there was recovery throughout the region and many countries began to reform their economies. In an effort to become competitive in the global economy many countries sold off inefficient public enterprises, opened previously protected economic sectors to competition, emphasized exports, and sought to reduce or streamline inefficient bureaucratic regulation. They also tried to diversify their economies internally and sought a wider range of trading partners. However, their reform efforts often produced mixed results because, although it was economically rational to reduce the size of the state, that conflicted with social justice requirements and the political patronage demands of rewarding friends and supporters with cushy state jobs.

Chile, Brazil, and Mexico were the chief leaders and beneficiaries of the new, free-market economic policies. Several countries did moderately well as middle-income countries, but others remained poor and backward, as shown in Table 1.1.

Classes and Social Forces

During the colonial period Latin America was structured on a fundamentally two-class basis. There was a small, white Hispanic or Portuguese elite at the top and a huge mass of Indians, black slaves, and peasants at the bottom, with almost no one in between. The two-class system was a reflection of feudal Spain and of the medieval Christian conception of each person fixed and situated in his or her station in life. This strict social hierarchy was assumed to be immutable and in accord with God's ordering of the universe; in Latin America the rigid class structure was reinforced by racial criteria. Over time, as miscegenation went forward, a considerable number of mulattos and *mestizos* emerged, often forming the small middle class.

The onset of economic growth in the late nineteenth century and industrialization in the twentieth century eventually gave rise to new social forces, although for a long time did not change the basic two-class structure of society. In the early stages of modernization in the nineteenth century a new business-commercial class began to emerge alongside the traditional landed elite, but this new class thought like the old elite, intermarried with it, and adopted the same aristocratic, haughty ethos. Similarly, as a large middle class of shop owners, small businesspeople, government workers, and professionals began to emerge in the 1930s and thereafter, it too acquired conservative attitudes, disdained manual labor, and often allied with a repressive military to prevent left-wing and lower-class movements from acquiring power. Emerging new social movements were co-opted by the elites and the two-class society was generally preserved.

During the 1930s as industrialization began, a working class also developed in Latin America; by the 1950s and 1960s peasant groups were being mobilized; and in the 1970s and thereafter women, indigenous elements,

Table 1.1 Indices of Modernization in Latin America, 2004

Country	Population	Population growth rate*	GNI per capita	GDP growth rate*	Inflation*	Life expectancy**	Infant mortality***
Argentina	36,771,840	1	3,810	9	11	74	17
Bolivia	8,814,158	2	900	2	5	64	5
Brazil	176,596,256	1	2,720	–0	13	69	33
Chile	15,774,000	1	4,360	3	4	76	8
Colombia	44,584,000	2	1,810	4	8	72	18
Costa Rica	4,004,680	2	4,300	6	8	79	8
Cuba	11,326,000	1	..	..	..	77	..
Dominican Republic	8,738,639	1	2,130	–0	27	67	29
Ecuador	13,007,942	2	1,830	3	9	71	24
El Salvador	6,533,215	2	2,340	2	2	70	32
Guatemala	12,307,091	3	1,910	2	6	66	35
Haiti	8,439,799	2	400	0	25	52	76
Honduras	6,968,512	2	970	3	9	66	32
Mexico	102,290,976	1	6,230	1	6	74	23
Nicaragua	5,480,000	3	740	2	6	69	30
Panama	2,984,022	1	4,060	4	1	75	18
Paraguay	5,643,097	2	1,110	3	18	71	25
Peru	27,148,000	1	2,140	4	..	70	26
Uruguay	3,380,177	1	3,820	2	18	75	12
Venezuela	25,674,000	2	3,490	–9	37	74	18
Latin America	**532,743,840**	1	3,280	2	..	71	28

Source: World Bank. World Development Indicators 2004. http://devdata.worldbank.org/data-query/
  * Annual percentage.
 ** Life expectancy at birth (years).
*** Per 1,000 live births.

community and neighborhood groups, and other social movements and civil society also organized. At first the elite groups (oligarchy, church, army) that had long dominated Latin America tried to co-opt these groups as they had others in the past, or sent the army out to repress, kill, and intimidate them. The co-optation/repression or carrot-and-stick strategies worked initially when these new groups were small, heading off revolution or even democracy and enabling the old power structure to survive. However, as the labor movement, peasant elements, and other civil society groups grew in power, the old techniques of co-optation/repression proved less successful. These processes produced a variety of outcomes in Latin America: dictatorships in some countries, democracy in others, revolution in still others, and in most alternation or muddling along between rival alternatives.

Latin America today is much more pluralistic than before. There is still an old, landed, oligarchic class in most countries, but it has been largely supplanted by business, banking, industrial (including agri-industrial), and commercial groups. There is now a larger middle class that, depending on the country, may number 20 to 40 percent of the population. In many countries the business and middle classes, no longer the old oligarchies, dominate. These groups tend to favor a stable democracy both because it serves their interests and because the global international community now demands it.

At lower-class levels important changes are also occurring. Labor is organizing; peasants are mobilizing and sometimes marching on private lands; new neighborhood and community groups are forming; Protestantism is growing, especially evangelical groups; and women's organizations, racial and ethnic groups, and many nongovernmental organizations (NGOs) are becoming more active. At grassroots levels many of these groups have organized to get things done, often bypassing the traditional political parties, bureaucratic agencies, and patronage systems. In many countries, however, there are rivalries between these newer, more pluralistic civil society groups and the traditional, patronage-dominated ones. We must also remember that Latin America's pluralism is still more limited than is the chaotic hurly-burly of U.S. interest group pluralism, still more top-controlled, and therefore less participatory and democratic. The number of plural groups is small, the elites and/or the state still try to co-opt and control them, and interest group lobbying as seen in the U.S. system is often absent. Nevertheless, Latin America is sufficiently pluralist that it is harder now to govern dictatorially, and that means a stronger base for democracy's survival.

Changing Political Culture

Political culture—the basic values and ideas that dominate in a society—varies from country to country and from region to region. Political culture represents a composite view of a society's beliefs as represented by its religious orientation, historical experience, and standard operating procedures. Political culture can be determined and analyzed using literature, music, other variables that shape the general culture and, most importantly, public opinion surveys. In speaking of political culture we want to avoid stereotyping; at the same time, when carefully used, political culture can be an important explanatory tool. Remember also that political culture may change (usually slowly) over time, there may be two or more (elite versus mass, left versus right) political cultures within a given society, and the diverse views and orientations that compose political culture may be in conflict.

Whereas the political culture of the United States is mainly democratic, liberal (believing in the classic freedoms of the Bill of Rights), and committed to representative government, that of Latin America has historically been more elitist, authoritarian, hierarchical, corporatist, and patrimonial. Latin American elitism stems from the Iberian tradition of nobility, from the feudal landholding system, and from a powerful tradition in Spanish-Portuguese political theory that society should be governed by its "natural" elites.

Authoritarianism in Latin America derived from the prevailing elitist power structure, biblical precepts and medieval Christianity's emphasis on top-down rule, and the chaotic and often anarchic conditions in Latin America that seemed to demand strong government.

The notion of a hierarchy among people similarly derived from early Christian political ideas as well as the social/power structure of medieval Spain and Portugal that was carried over to Latin America. God was at the top of this hierarchy, then archangels, angels, and so on until we reach mankind. Rulers received their mandate from God; land, cattle, military prowess, and high social and political status were similarly believed to derive from the "Great Chain of Being," God's unchanging design for the universe. Proceeding down through society, one eventually reaches workers and peasants, who have some, but limited, rights. In the New World, Indians and Africans were thought to be barely human. After a long debate the Roman Catholic Church decided that Indians had souls; as a result they were given to Spanish conquerors in *encomiendas*, through which they would work for the Spanish, who had the duty of "civilizing" and "Christianizing" the less-fortunate Indians. The Church fathers initially decided, on the other hand, that Africans did not have souls and could therefore be enslaved, having no rights at all. It is obvious that this hierarchical conception is profoundly inegalitarian and undemocratic.

Another feature of Latin American political culture and institutions is corporatism, the organization of the nation's interest group life under state regulation and control, not on the basis of freedom of association. The main corporate groups in Latin America have been the church; the armed forces; the landed and business elites; and, more recently, the trade union movement, peasants, women, and indigenous elements. Corporatism, which is largely unknown in U.S. politics, is a way of both organizing and controlling interest group activity. Corporatism is thus often associated with authoritarianism and an illiberal society, and it reinforces the other undemocratic traits previously mentioned.

One other feature of traditional—and continuing—Latin American society and politics is patronage. Historically in Latin America this has been based on a system of mutual obligation: a favor for a favor. This is also a quasi-feudal concept with its roots in Greek and Christian philosophy: If I give you a gift, then you owe me a gift in return. Patronage manifests itself in various ways: votes in return for gifts or money, votes in return for a government job, friends or relatives rewarded with government contracts, special access to those with good connections, sometimes whole programs or government offices doled out in return for critical political support. At high levels patronage verges on and is corruption; at low levels it constitutes the "grease" that keeps the machinery of government working.

These features of historic Latin American political culture—elitism, authoritarianism, hierarchy, corporatism, and patrimonialism—remained largely intact over three centuries of colonial rule and became deeply embedded in the customs and political processes. However, when Latin America became independent in the nineteenth century a new political culture based on representative institutions emerged, even while the old political culture remained strong. The result was two political cultures, one authoritarian, the other nascently liberal, existing side by side and vying for dominance through all of the nineteenth century and much of the twentieth. The two political cultures also had different social bases: the more traditional one centered in the church, the landed elite, the military, and the conservative peasantry; the newer, liberal one concentrated in urban areas among intellectuals, students, the emerging middle class, and some business elements. With no one single political culture dominant, unlike the situation in the United States after the Civil War when the liberal-democratic ethos definitively triumphed, Latin American politics was often unstable and torn by frequent civil war between the two ways of life.

A third tradition—socialist, Marxist, social-democratic—emerged in the 1930s, particularly among students, trade unionists, and intellectuals. Some of these groups favored a full-scale Marxist-Leninist regime, others wanted a redistribution of wealth, and still others advocated greater social welfare. The common themes of these groups included a strong role for the state in directing change, a leftist ideology, and anti-American nationalism. Fidel Castro, the Nicaraguan Sandinista revolution, and recently Hugo Chávez galvanized these leftist groups, which in the past often looked to the Soviet Union and/or China for support. However, the collapse of the Soviet Union and of Marxist-Leninist movements and regimes worldwide led to a severe drop in support for Marxist solutions. By now this third alternative is fading, although in an updated social-democratic or populist form it may be possible for the left to come back to power.

Meanwhile the historic political culture, or at least some of its aspects, is fading. No one believes anymore that one must stay poor and one's children must have bloated bellies because God or Saint Thomas has willed it that way and one must accept one's station in life. The older notions of authority, hierarchy, and elitism, although still often present, are no longer the dominant political culture. At the same time the groups that were the strongest proponents of the traditional political culture (the church, the landed oligarchy, the army, the conservative peasantry) are either changing internally or are losing influence. However, patronage and patrimonialism seem as strong as ever.

Latin America has modernized, democratized, and become part of the global economy; it is no longer the same Latin America portrayed in earlier editions of this book. Rising literacy, urbanization, social change, immigration, globalization, and democratization are all changing the appearance and culture of Latin America. Polls tell us that 60, 70, even 80 percent of the public in most countries support democratic rule; none of the other alternatives (authoritarianism, Marxism-Leninism) have much support. It may be that the historic conflict over political culture in Latin America is finally ending and that the democratic option with a modern mixed economy has finally emerged as triumphant.

And yet these same polls show Latin Americans want an effective government, one that delivers real social and economic reform. Democracy and economic liberalism (or neoliberalism) are still weak and unconsolidated in Latin America. They could still be upset in some of the weaker and poorly institutionalized countries. Moreover—and this is what makes Latin America so interesting—the form that democracy takes there is often quite different from democracy in the United States. It is more organic, centralized, and with still powerful patronage and corporatism features. Latin America now has formal, electoral democracy; whether it has genuinely liberal democracy may be quite another thing. Although the changes have been vast, the continuities from Latin America's past are still powerful.

An Assessment

Latin America's geography, economic underdevelopment, socio-racial conditions, and traditions of political culture have historically retarded national unity, democracy, and development. However, the great forces of twentieth-century change—urbanization, industrialization, modernization, democratization, and now globalization—are breaking down the historic barriers and altering the foundations of traditional Latin American society. Latin America is experiencing many of the same revolutionary transformations that the United States, Western Europe, and Japan went through in earlier times. Latin America has also commenced the process, but in Latin America the time period is much more telescoped and the outcome is still likely to be a great variety of political systems rather than some pale imitation of the United States. To us that is healthy, invigorating, challenging, and interesting.

Although the changes have been immense and often inspiring, many problems remain. Poverty, malnutrition, and malnutrition-related disease are still endemic in many areas; too many people are ill-housed, ill-fed, ill-educated, and just plain ill; wages are too low, the economies and democracies are often fragile; and the gap between the rich and the poor is greater than in any other area in the world. The political systems are often corrupt and ineffective; the standards of living of the rural and urban poor are woefully inadequate; and crime, violence, drug activity, and general personal insecurity are increasing. Frequently social and economic change occurs faster than political systems can handle them; fragmentation, ungovernability, and collapse are still lurking.

Three recent changes command special attention. The first is the dramatic shift to democracy in all but one (Cuba) country of the area. The second is the new consensus on economic policy emphasizing free markets, reform of the state, export-led growth, and integration. Some of these economic reforms are still weak and limited, and in some countries democracy is fragile, has not been consolidated, and could still be reversed. Nevertheless, the degree of progress over the previous two decades is often breathtaking.

The third profound change is the impact of globalization on Latin America in all its dimensions (cultural, political, economic), which has broken down Latin America's traditional isolation and forced all countries to become integrated into the modern world, mostly for good but damaging to marginal groups such as small farmers.

There is, overall, strong economic, social, and political reform; a growing realization that Latin America must take charge of its own future; and great eagerness to enter the modern global community of developed nations. Later chapters detail which countries have made this great leap forward; examine how they have done so; and consider the successes, failure, and future prospects of all the Latin American nations.

Note

1. Robert C. Williamson, *Latin American Societies in Transition* (Westport, CT: Praeger, 1997), 127.

2

The Pattern of Historical Development

Whereas the United States was founded during the seventeenth and eighteenth centuries, when modernization was beginning (capitalism, liberalism, pluralism, the Enlightenment, the Industrial Revolution), Latin America was founded in an earlier time when feudal and medieval practices and institutions still held sway. If the United States was "born free," Latin America was "born feudal," and these differences still account for many of the contrasts between the two areas. To a degree unknown in the United States, Latin America has long been dominated by a political, social, and economic structure that had its roots not in modernity but in medievalism. Much of Latin America's recent history involves the efforts to overcome or ameliorate that feudal past. Because this feudal legacy remains so strong, because the heavy hand of ancient history hangs so oppressively over the area, we must come to grips with Latin America's past to understand its present and future.

The Conquest

The conquest of the Americas by Spain and Portugal was the extension of a reconquest of the Iberian Peninsula that had been occurring in the mother countries for the preceding seven centuries. In the eighth century AD the armies of a dynamic, expansionist Islam had crossed the Strait of Gibraltar from North Africa and conquered most of present-day Spain and Portugal. In the following centuries the Christian forces of Spain and Portugal had gradually retaken these conquered lands, until the last of the Islamic Moors were driven out in 1492, the same year that Columbus discovered America. Because of the long military campaign against the Moors, which was also a religious crusade to drive out the Islamic "infidels," Spanish and Portuguese institutions

17

tended to be authoritarian, intolerant, militaristic, and undemocratic. These same practices and institutions were carried over to Latin America.

The conquest of the Americas was one of the great epic adventures of all time; its impact was worldwide. The encounter with the New World vastly expanded humankind's knowledge, exploration, and frontiers; led to a period of prolonged European world dominance; and helped stimulate the Industrial Revolution. It also led to the brutalization, death, and isolation of much of the indigenous population.

At the time of Columbus's landing in America there were only three million indigenous people in all of North America but some thirty million in Latin America. The Indians in Latin America were often organized into large civilizations—Aztec, Maya, Inca—of five to seven million persons each, as compared with the generally smaller tribal, nomadic basis of most North American Indians. Whereas in North America, the Indians were often eliminated, pushed farther west, or confined to reservations, in Latin America the large numbers and organization of indigenous groups called for a different strategy. The Spanish tactic was usually to capture or kill the Indian chiefs, replace them with Spanish overlords, and rule (and enslave) them by dominating their own power structure, meanwhile seeking to Christianize, Hispanicize, and assimilate them into European ways. That has been the strategy for over five hundred years, but recently Indian groups in such countries as Mexico, Guatemala, Colombia, Ecuador, and Bolivia have been raising the issue of indigenous rights and seeking new degrees of autonomy from the nation-states that Spain and Portugal left in their wake.

The degree of colonial influence varied from place to place. The first area to receive the impact of Spanish colonial rule was Hispaniola, an island in the Caribbean that later was divided between the two independent countries of Haiti and the Dominican Republic. Here Spain carried out its first experiments in colonial rule: a slave-plantation economy, a two-class and caste society, an authoritarian political structure, and a church that served as an arm of the conquest. But Hispaniola had little gold and silver and, as the Indian population was decimated, largely by disease, Spain moved on to more valuable conquests.

Next came Cuba and Puerto Rico, but when the scarce precious metals and Indian labor supply were exhausted there also, Spain moved on to conquer Mexico and explored Florida and the North American Southeast. The conquest of Mexico by Cortéz was fundamentally different from the earlier island conquests. First, Spain found a huge Indian civilization, the Aztecs, with immense quantities of gold and silver and a virtually unlimited labor supply, and second, Mexico's huge mainland territory finally convinced the Spaniards that they had found a new continent and not just scattered islands on the outskirts of Asia. Mexico therefore became a serious and valuable colony to be settled and colonized by Spain, not just some way station en route to somewhere else.

From Mexico Cortéz's lieutenants fanned out to conquer Central America and the American Southwest. In the meantime Balboa had crossed the Isthmus of Panama to gaze out upon the Pacific, and other Spanish conquistadores had explored both the east and west coasts of South America. From Panama in the 1530s the Pizarro brothers, using the same methods Cortéz had used in Mexico, moved south to conquer the vast Inca empire that stretched from southern Colombia in the north, through Ecuador and Peru, to Chile in the south. Meanwhile Portugal had gained a foothold on the coast of Brazil that sticks out toward Africa. Other Spanish explorers spilled over the Andes from Peru to discover and subdue Bolivia and Paraguay and sailed all the way down river to present-day Buenos Aires, which had been explored in the 1530s but was not settled until the 1580s. Meanwhile Chile, where the Indian resistance was especially strong, was conquered in the 1570s, and other previously unconquered territories were then explored and subdued.

In less than a hundred years from the initial discovery, Mexico, the Caribbean, Central America, and all of South America, east to west and north to south, had been conquered. Spain had most of the territory, Portugal had Brazil. It was a remarkable feat in a short period of time, especially when one considers that it took North American settlers almost three hundred years to cross the continent from the Atlantic to the Pacific.

Colonial Society: Principles and Institutions

The institutions that Spain and, less aggressively, Portugal brought to the New World reflected the institutions that had developed in the mother countries during their centuries-long struggles against the Moors and their efforts to form unified nation-states out of disparate social and regional forces. These institutions included a rigid, authoritarian political system, a similarly rigid and hierarchical class structure, a statist and mercantilist economy, an absolutist church, and a similarly closed and absolutist educational system.

In the New World the Spanish and Portuguese conquerors found abundant territory that they could claim as feudal estates; abundant wealth that enabled them to live like grandees; and a ready-made "peasantry" to exploit, in the forms of the indigenous Indian population or imported African slaves. The men who accompanied Columbus and other explorers to the New World were often the second and third sons of the Spanish and Portuguese aristocracy, and under Spanish law they were prohibited from inheriting their father's land, which went to the first son. But in the New World they could acquire vast territories and servants and live like feudal overlords. The oligarchies of Latin America, then as now, were haughty, aloof, authoritarian, and disdainful of manual labor and those forced to work with their hands. This aristocratic ethos and power structure has been a very powerful force in Latin America even to this day.

The institutions established by Spain and Portugal in Latin America reflected and reinforced the medieval system of the mother countries. At the top was the king, who claimed absolute power; his authority came from God (divine-right monarchy) and was therefore unquestionable. Below the king was the viceroy (literally "vice king"), similarly with absolute power and serving as the king's agent in the colonies. Below the viceroy was the captain-general, also absolute within his sphere of influence; next came the landowner or *hacendado,* who also enjoyed absolute power within his own estate.

The economy was feudal and exploitative; the wealth of the colonies, in accord with the prevailing mercantilism, was drained off to benefit the mother countries and not used for the betterment of the colonies themselves. Similarly, the social structure was basically feudal and two-class, with a small group of Spaniards and Portuguese at the top, a large mass of Indians and Africans at the bottom, and almost no one in between. Democracy cannot be based on such a strict two-class structure, which was not only social and economic but also racist.

The Roman Catholic Church reinforced royal authority and policy in the colonies and was similarly absolutist and authoritarian. Its role was to Christianize and pacify the indigenous population and thus serve the Crown's assimilationist policies. Some individual clergy sought to defend the Indians against enslavement and maltreatment, but the church was primarily an arm of the state. Intellectual life and learning, monopolized by the church, was scholastic, based on rote memorization, deductive reasoning, and unquestioned orthodoxy.

It is not surprising that Latin America was founded on this feudal-absolutist basis in the early sixteenth century; that was before the onset of modernization, and most countries were still organized on that basis. What is surprising is that this system lasted so long: through the centuries of colonial rule, only slightly modified by the Latin American independence movements, and on into the twentieth century. Most Latin American countries are still struggling to overcome this feudal past.

The founding principles and institutions of Latin America were essentially medieval, pre-1500. In contrast, by the time the North American colonies were established the back of feudalism had been broken in England and Holland, and hence the thirteen colonies that would later form the United States were organized on a more modern basis. By that time the idea of limited government rather than absolutism had emerged, the Protestant Reformation

Table 2.1   Contrasting Foundations of Latin and North American Society

Institutions	Latin America, 1492–1570	North America, Seventeenth Century
Political	Authoritarian, absolutist, centralized, corporatist	More liberal, early steps toward representative and democratic rule
Religious	Catholic orthodoxy and absolutism	Protestantism and religious pluralism
Economic	Feudal, mercantilist patrimonialist	Emerging capitalist, entrepreneurial
Social	Hierarchical, two-class, rigid	More mobile, multiclass
Educational and intellectual	Scholastic and deductive	Empirical

had destroyed the older religious orthodoxy and given rise to religious and po-litical pluralism, the Industrial Revolution was occurring, mercantilism was giv-ing way to commerce and entrepreneurship, the scientific revolution was breaking the hold of the old scholasticism, and a new multiclass society was be-ginning to emerge. Founded on these principles and changes, North Ameri-can society was modern from the start, whereas Latin America continued to be plagued by feudalism. These differences also explain why from the start the United States was destined to forge ahead while Latin America lagged be-hind. Table 2.1 summarizes these contrasting foundations of U.S. and Latin American society.

Spanish and Portuguese colonial rule lasted for over three centuries, from the late fifteenth through the early nineteenth centuries. It was a remarkably stable period, with few revolts against the colonial system, a testimony to its efficiency even if it was unjust. However, in the late eighteenth century the first serious cracks began to appear in this monolithic colonial structure. Un-der the impact of the eighteenth-century Enlightenment, ideas of liberty, freedom, and nationalism began to creep in; the examples of the American (1776) and French (1789) revolutions also caused tremors in Latin America. In addition a rising Latin American commercial class sought to break the monopolistic barriers of Spanish mercantilism so as to trade freely with other countries. One of the main sources of independence sentiment was the grow-ing rivalries between creoles (persons of Spanish background born in the colonies) and peninsulars (officials sent out by the Spanish crown to govern the colonies). The creoles had growing economic and social influence, but the peninsulars monopolized all administrative positions. Denied the political power to go along with their rising prominence, many creoles began to think of doing away with the inconvenience of Spanish colonialism and moving toward independence.

The immediate causes of Latin American independence were precipitated by events in Europe. In 1807 to 1808 the forces of Napoleon Bonaparte invaded the Iberian Peninsula, occupied both Spain and Portugal, ousted the reigning monarchs, and placed Napoleon's brother Joseph on the Spanish throne. The Latin American creoles opposed this usurpation of royal authority by Napoleon's army and, operating under longtime medieval doctrine, moved to hold power until the legitimate king could be restored. This was, in effect, an early declaration of independence. A few years later Napoleon's forces were driven from the peninsula and the Spanish and Portuguese monarchies restored. However, when the Spanish king accepted the principle of limited monarchy and a liberal constitution, the conservative creoles in Latin America moved for independence.

The independence struggles in Latin America waxed and waned for nearly two decades before succeeding in the 1820s. The first revolt in Argentina in 1807 was quashed by Spanish authorities, but independence fervor was also growing in Colombia, Mexico, Venezuela, and other countries. Independence sentiment waned for a time after 1814 when the Spanish monarchy was restored but resumed again in 1820 as a result of the king's shortsighted policies.

Simón Bolívar, the "George Washington of Latin America," led the struggle against Spanish forces in Venezuela, Colombia, and Ecuador. José San Martín liberated Argentina, then crossed the Andes to drive the Spanish forces from Chile. The key to the independence of the rest of South America was Lima, Peru, one of the most important Spanish viceroyalties and home of a sizable Spanish garrison. Bolívar came south overland and San Martín north by ship, and in the key battle of Ayacucho they defeated the royalist forces, ending Spanish authority in South America. The other main viceroyalty was Mexico City, but by 1821 independence forces were in control there, also. Once Mexico was freed, Central America, as part of the same administration, was liberated without much actual fighting. By 1824 all Spanish forces and authority were removed from mainland Latin America. The two exceptions were Cuba and Puerto Rico, which remained Spanish colonies until 1898. For all of the nineteenth century their nationalism was frustrated by the lack of independence, which would also shape twentieth-century politics on the two islands.

Haiti and Brazil were also special cases. In Haiti a successful slave revolt in 1795 drove out the French colonial ruling class, destroyed the plantations, and established Haiti as the world's first black republic, unloved and unwelcome by the rest of the world (including the United States), which still practiced slavery. Haiti's economy went into decline and its political system since then has alternated between repressive dictatorships and chaotic upheaval.

Brazil was a different story. When Napoleon's troops occupied Portugal, the royal family fled to Rio de Janeiro, the first reigning monarchs to set foot in Latin America. In 1821 the king, Dom João, was called back to Lisbon, but he left his son Pedro in charge of the kingdom of Brazil. The following year Pedro was also called back to Portugal, but he refused to go and declared Brazil an independent monarchy. Thus Brazil gained independence without the upheaval and destruction of the other countries and was a monarchy for the first seventy years. Brazil escaped the tumult that soon enveloped its Spanish-speaking neighbors.

The independence movements in Latin America had almost all been conservative movements of separation from the mother countries rather than full-scale social or political revolutions. Led and directed by the white, aristocratic, creole elite, they were aimed at holding power for the disposed monarch and in defense of the old social hierarchy. After they later became movements for independence, they retained their elitist, conservative orientation. When social revolution raised its head, it was either isolated and despised as in Haiti or brutally repressed as in Mexico, where large-scale Indian protest had been part of the independence struggle.

The same conservative orientation was present in the laws, constitutions, and institutions established in the new republics. The franchise was extremely limited: only literates and property owners (less than 1 percent of the population) could vote, if and when there were elections. Thus, the feudal landholding and class system was kept intact, before and after independence. The church was given a privileged position, and Catholicism in most countries remained the official religion. However, a new, similarly conservative power force was added: the army, which replaced the crown as the ultimate authority and became almost a fourth branch of government. Although Latin America adopted constitutions modeled after the United States, in reality, checks and balances, human rights, and separation of powers existed mostly in theory. The laws and constitutions of the new Latin American states enshrined the existing power structure and perpetuated paternalistic, top-down, elite rule.

During the three-hundred-plus years of colonial rule Latin America had had no experience with self-government, lacked infrastructure, and had none of the "web of sociability" (neighborhood, community, religious, civic, social groups) that nineteenth-century theorist Alexis de Tocqueville identified with U.S. democracy. With independence the Latin American economies also went into decline, and the social structure was severely disrupted. It should not be surprising, therefore, that after independence Latin America fell into chaos and that the disintegrative forces set loose by independence continued. The former viceroyalty of New Granada split up into the separate nations of Colombia, Ecuador, and Venezuela; the viceroyalty of Rio de la Plata divided into the separate countries of Argentina, Paraguay, and Uruguay; and the Central American Confederation disintegrated into the small "city-states" (too small to be economically viable) of Guatemala, El Salvador, Honduras, Nicaragua, and Costa Rica. Within the new nations further fragmentation and confusion occurred. Only Brazil under its monarchy and Chile under a stable oligarchy escaped these divisive, disruptive, and disintegrative early postindependence forces.

Deprived of their Spanish markets but still lacking new ones, many of the countries slipped back to a more primitive barter economy and living standards plummeted. Similarly, the old Spanish/Portuguese social-racial categories were formally abolished in most countries but were resurrected informally; at the same time the level of education, literacy, integration, and assimilation was so low (in many countries the majority of the population did not speak the national language, participate in the national economy, or even know that they were a part of a nation-state) that pluralist and participatory democracy seemed only a distant dream. In the absence of political parties, organized interest groups, civil society, or well-established institutions of any kind, the Latin American countries sank into either dictatorship or anarchy, usually alternating between the two. Internationally Latin America was isolated and cut off from the modern, Western world. Hence the immediate post-independence period, from the mid-1820s until the mid-1850s, was in most countries a time of turbulence and decline.

Early Stirrings of Modernization

By the 1850s a degree of stability had begun to emerge in many Latin American countries. Some of the more vexing questions of early independence—sovereignty and borders, federalism versus unitarianism, church-state relations—had been resolved. By this time also the first generation of post-independence dictators (Juan Manuel de Rosas in Argentina, Antonio López de Santa Anna in Mexico) had passed from the scene. Agriculture began to recover; a degree of order returned.

With increased stability at midcentury came foreign investment and greater productivity. The first banks in the region were chartered. British capital invested in the area provided a major stimulus to growth. New lands were opened to cultivation and new exports (sugar, coffee, tobacco, beef, wool) began to restore national coffers. The first highways, railways, and port facilities were built to transport the exports to foreign markets. The telephone and telegraph were introduced. The opportunities available in Latin America began to attract immigrants from Europe, who often brought knowledge and entrepreneurial skills with them. They opened small shops and started farms and prospered; often this new wealth intermixed with older landed wealth.

As Latin America's prospects began to improve, the area attracted other investors: France, Germany, Italy, and most important, the United States, which began to replace England as the largest investor in the area. These changes, beginning at midcentury but accelerating in the 1870s and 1880s, represented the first stirrings of modernization in Latin America after nearly four centuries of stagnation. They brought prosperity for the landed and business elites and stimulated the growth of a middle class, but often peasant and Indian elements were left behind or had their lands taken from them for the sake of greater production for global markets.

Economic growth also increased political stability, although not in all countries. Three patterns may be observed. The first, in Argentina, Brazil, Chile, Peru, and other countries, involved the consolidation of power by an export-oriented landed oligarchy whose leaders rotated in the presidential palace over a thirty- to forty-year period. The second, in Mexico, Venezuela, and the Dominican Republic, involved the seizure of power by strong authoritarian dictators, no longer the simple men on horseback of the past but leaders who provided both long-term stability and development. A third pattern emerged slightly later, in the first decades of the twentieth century, in the smaller, weaker, resource-poor countries of Central America and the Caribbean. It involved U.S. military intervention and occupation and the carrying out by the Marines of many of the same policies as the order-and-progress oligarchs and dictators: pacification, infrastructure development (roads, communication, port facilities), and overall nation-building.

Two subperiods are discernible here. The first, 1850 to 1890, established the preconditions for Latin America's takeoff: greater stability, banks, investment, population increase, and infrastructure development. The second, 1890 to 1930, was the economic takeoff itself, the most stable and prosperous period in Latin American history. Under more stable regimes and exporting for the first time for a world market, Latin America began its development process, not at the rapid rate of the United States and Europe during the same period, but slowly and steadily.

Although Latin America's development was often impressive, it came under nondemocratic leadership: oligarchs, order-and-progress dictators, and U.S. military occupations. Hence the potential for future problems was also present even amid the growing prosperity. Three applecarts were upset even before the 1930s market crash caused the entire edifice to come crumbling down. In 1910 the order-and-progress dictator Porfirio Díaz was overthrown in Mexico, precipitating a bloody ten-year social revolution out of which Mexico's present political system emerged. In 1912 in Argentina and in the early 1920s in Chile a rising middle class challenged and eventually wrested political power away from the old oligarchs. These changes in some of the more advanced countries of Latin America provided a foretaste of what would occur in the other countries in later decades.

Upheaval and Restructuring

When the stock market crashed in the United States in 1929 and in Europe the following year, the effects were global. The bottom dropped out of the market for Latin America's exports, sending the economics of the area into a tailspin and crashing their political systems as well. Between 1930 and 1935 there were governmental overthrows in fourteen of the twenty Latin American countries, not just the usual substitution of one colonel for another but real transforming revolutions. The immediate causes of this collapse were economic, but deep-rooted social and political issues were also involved. By this time Latin America had a business class, a middle class, and a restless trade union movement, but power was still monopolized by the old landowning oligarchs and something had to give. The chasm between the traditional holders of power and the new social and political forces clamoring for change had grown wider; the new forces were demanding change and democratization while the older elites clung to their privileges at all costs. The 1930s Depression was the catalyst that collapsed the prevailing political as well as economic structure.

Once Humpty Dumpty (the Latin American political systems) had fallen off the wall, the question was how to put him back together again. A variety of solutions was tried—an important turning point to remember because this is the time when most of our country-by-country analyses begin. Some countries, after a brief interruption in the early 1930s, reverted by restoring oligarchic rule. In others new, tough dictatorships (Fulgencio Batista in Cuba, Anastasio Somoza in Nicaragua, Rafael Trujillo in the Dominican Republic, Jorge Ubico in Guatemala) brought the new business and middle classes into power and stimulated development, but under authoritarian auspices. (It is getting ahead of the story only a little bit to note that all these countries that had brutal right-wing dictatorships produced left-wing revolutions later on.) Mexico replaced the old regime with a one-party authoritarian/corporatist regime that monopolized power for the next seventy years.

In Argentina and Brazil the regimes of Juan Perón and Getúlio Vargas, respectively, borrowed some semifascist features from Mussolini's Italy in an effort to bring labor unions into the system even while imposing strict controls over them. Other countries borrowed selectively from European corporatism and fascism while maintaining a democratic facade. Populism was still another option, whereas other countries—Chile and Uruguay followed by Costa Rica, Colombia, and Venezuela—moved toward democracy. The revolutionary alternative (as in Cuba) came later.

The 1930s were thus, in David Colliers's and Ruth Berins Colliers's words, a "critical juncture" in Latin American history, a period in which a variety of alternative developmental models—authoritarian, quasi-fascist, populist, single party, democratic—were tried out and came to power in the various Latin American countries.[1]

Some countries rotated among several of these options or tried to combine them. Many countries are still strongly shaped by the choices made and the directions taken during this period. The Depression years of the 1930s and the later war and postwar years of the 1940s were thus a time of both uncertainty and upheaval; although the old, stable, oligarchic order had come crashing down, what would replace it was not altogether clear and, eighty years later, is still not clear in quite a number of countries.

As the demand for their products rose again during World War II, the Latin American economies began to recover from the devastation of the Depression; they were also stimulated by industrialization. The postwar period continued this economic growth, enabling some countries to move toward greater prosperity and democracy while others continued under dictatorship. Although gradual economic growth was occurring throughout the region in the 1940s and 1950s and stimulating further social change, the political systems of Latin America remained divided, full of conflict, and often unstable.

A key turning point in the region and in U.S.-Latin American relations was the Cuban revolution of 1959. Cuba became the first openly socialist country in Latin America, the first to ally itself with the Soviet Union, and the first to openly turn its back on the United States. The revolution initiated improvements in health care, education, and other social programs, although over time its economic policies proved a failure and its political system was hardly democratic (see chapter 17 for details), but here we are concerned with the broader, region-wide impact of Cuba. First, Cuba added a new "model," a new option to the Latin American landscape, one that stood for armed revolution and a Marxist-Leninist political structure. Second, the Cuban revolution divided and thus hurt the prospects for democratic development and social reform in Latin America by splitting the reform groups into pro- and anti-Castro factions. Third, although the Cuban revolution forced the United States to pay closer attention to Latin America (the Peace Corps, the Alliance for Progress), it skewed U.S. policy by making the prevention of "another Cuba" (Marxist-Leninist, allied with the Soviet Union, housing missiles aimed at the United

States) virtually the only goal of U.S. policy. This was the "lesser evil" doctrine: When faced with the choice between a usually wobbly Latin American democracy that believed in freedom even for leftists and a tough, anti-Communist military regime, the U.S. government almost always opted for the military regime. But the policy polarized Latin America even more and led in the 1960s and 1970s to a series of civil conflicts and wars that tore several countries apart.

After a brief democratic interlude in the late 1950s and early 1960s, by the late 1960s and throughout the 1970s Latin America had succumbed to a new wave of militarism. By the mid-1970s fourteen of the twenty countries were under military-authoritarian rule, and in three others the military was so close to the surface of power that authoritarianism ruled even if civilians were still technically in office. That left only Colombia, Costa Rica, and Venezuela as democracies, and even they were elite-directed regimes.

The causes of this throwback to military authoritarianism were basically two: economic and political. By the 1960s Latin America's economies had become less competitive in global markets, the strategy of import-substitution-industrialization (ISI) was not working, the terms of trade had turned unfavorable (it costs Latin America more exports of sugars, bananas, coffee, whatever to pay for its imports than before), and the economies of the area could not pay for all the programs its citizens were demanding. Politically, the 1960s was a period when workers, peasants, and left-wing guerrillas were all mobilizing; the traditional wielders of power (elites, military) felt threatened by the mass mobilization and they thus turned to the army to keep the lower classes in check. This was called "bureaucratic-authoritarianism": rule by the institutional armed forces and their civilian supporters, as distinct from the man-on-horseback leaders of the past.

By the late 1970s the steam had gone out of most of these military regimes, and Latin America began to reverse course and return to democracy. The armed forces had often proved just as corrupt and inefficient at running governments as their civilian predecessors, they were notorious human rights abusers and thus despised by their own people, and the international community led by the United States put pressure on them to return to the barracks. There followed one of the most amazing transformations in all of Latin American history: By the turn of the millennium nineteen of the twenty Latin American countries were ruled democratically, with Cuba as the lone holdout. Latin America was the main arena of the "third wave" of democratization that affected the entire world and surely constituted one of the most significant events of the late twentieth century.

Many of these new democracies are still weak and not very well institutionalized. They lack strong and independent legislatures, judiciaries and court systems, bureaucracies, political parties, interest groups, and local government.

They are often not very effective in carrying out public policies. They are referred to as "electoral democracies" (formal elections are held) but not "liberal democracies," in the sense of being open, pluralistic, and egalitarian. Many regimes in the area are still partial or limited democracies, designations that indicate links to Latin America's past. Nevertheless, even partial democracies are better than no democracies at all, no one doubts that an important breakthrough has been made, and certainly the human rights situation in virtually every country is far better now that it was a decade or two ago.

A Framework for Thinking

The 1930s was a critical juncture, a key turning point, maybe *the* key turning point in Latin American history. In that period, give or take a decade or two depending on the country, Latin America's old oligarchic, feudal, and medieval social, economic, and political structures began to collapse, in some cases collapsing altogether, in others hanging on but in attenuated form. What replaced the old order was then uncertain, often unstable, frequently alternating between one type of regime and another. But of the fact that Latin America had begun a profound transformation leading to modernization there could be no doubt. At present, after decades of confusion and upheaval, what seems finally to be emerging is a system of democracy and freer markets; but this process is still incomplete, shows many continuities with Latin America's past, and remains fragile.

As we begin to probe more deeply into Latin America's political institutions and processes, and as we go through the county-by-country analyses, readers should keep in mind the following framework for assessing the changes occurring. How much has changed in each country, what are the emerging patterns, what outcomes are likely? This approach will not only give us a deeper understanding, it is also fundamental to the comparative analysis that is at the heart of this book.

Changes in Political Culture

Until the 1930s Latin America still had been often feudal and medieval in its thinking, but then education increased; literacy expanded; and radio, television, and VCRs brought new ideas even to the most isolated areas. The old fatalism and passivity faded, people were mobilized, and new and challenging ideas (democracy, socialism) arose. The Catholic Church, long a supporter of the traditional political culture, began to change; Protestantism as well as secular ideas made strong inroads. The fundamental beliefs, ideas, and orientations by which people order their lives began changing. So in each country we will want to know among which groups these ideas are changing, how deep and extensive the changes are, what impact a changing, more democratic and participatory political culture has had on institutions and policy.

Economic Change

Latin America's economies are now more diversified toward business, industry, services, manufacturing, tourism, mining, and agri-industry and are no longer the subsistence and plantation agriculture of the past. The economies are larger, more complex, and integrated into world markets. Most of them are now moving away from the statism and mercantilism of the past toward a system of open markets, freer trade, greater efficiency, less corruption, and neoliberalism. These changes are creating greater affluence (although the wealth is unevenly distributed), creating new jobs and opportunities, and giving new dynamism to the economies of the area. However, there are also lags, uneven development, and some groups and countries doing much better than others. In addition all of these changes, the positive and the negative, carry important political and policy implications that vary from country to country.

Social Change

The economic changes just outlined have also accelerated social change. The old landed oligarchy is giving way to a more diverse panoply of business, industrial, commercial, banking, and other new elites. A sizable middle class has grown up in every country, ranging from 20 to 40 percent of the population, whose size and political orientation help determine whether democracy survives. Labor unions have organized, peasant groups are mobilizing, and urban unemployed slum dwellers are becoming politicized. In addition there are new women's groups, community organizations, civil society, and indigenous movements. Some of the older groups such as the church and the military are also undergoing change (more middle class, less elitist), and Roman Catholicism is being challenged in many countries by Protestant evangelicalism, which often involves quite different values and attitudes toward work and the role of the family. In a forty-year period Latin America has gone from being mostly rural to two-thirds urban. All these social changes and the far greater social pluralism force us to ask if political pluralism (which usually means democracy) can be far behind.

Political Institutions

Along with the political-cultural, economic, and social transformations in Latin America have also come changes in political institutions. First, political parties in most countries tend to be better organized, with a real mass base and real programs and ideology, as compared with the small, personalist, and patronage-based parties of the past, which still exist in some countries. Second, and reflecting the greater societal pluralism, there are far more interest groups, NGOs, and civil societies than ever before, whose agendas need to be satisfied—although U.S.-style lobbying is still seldom practiced in Latin America. Third, government agencies and institutions are being forced to modernize, increase efficiency, reduce corruption, and deliver real goods and services. Elections have become more honest and are recognized as the only legitimate route to power; legislatures, court systems, the police, and local government are all being modernized in various ways.

Public Policy

Not only are Latin American political processes and institutions modernizing, but so are public policy programs. In the past, governments in Latin America had few functions, but now government is being called upon to provide a host of new public policy programs: agrarian reform, family planning, education, economic development, the environment, housing, health care, and dozens of others. Moreover, with an aroused population, these programs are demanded as a matter of course, and governments in this new era of democracy have to deliver or they will be voted out. Rather than jobs, patronage, and handouts, public institutions in Latin America are called upon to provide real public goods and services.

The International Environment

For centuries Latin America was isolated from the world, but now it is becoming closely integrated into it—politically, culturally, and economically. Globalization has come to Latin America. Politically Latin America is becoming democratic, and if a country deviates from that course, the full weight of international sanctions comes down on it. Culturally Latin America is being swept up in the world political culture of jeans, rock music, Coca Cola, and consumerism; values, especially of young people, are becoming like those everywhere else (democratic, less authoritarian, less religious, less traditional). Economically Latin America is now a part of the global economy, with mostly good consequences (increased trade, commerce, jobs, affluence) but sometimes negative ones (currency uncertainties, fluctuating market demands, capital flight). Latin America can no longer choose among other economic options because foreign aid is meager and no other country is about to bail it out: It must join the global economy, compete with everyone else, and adopt neoliberal economic policies. It must do so not just because outside pressures force it to but also because its own businesspeople, middle classes, and governments also recognize that they have no other choice.

All of these long-term modernizing and globalizing changes have had a profound effect on Latin America, but they vary between countries and within institutions and even individuals, which continue to show complex mixes of traditional and modern attitudes and practices. As Latin America enters a new millennium, we will want to know in general for the region and for individual countries just how democratic they are. Have the societies modernized sufficiently to provide a firmer basis for pluralism and democracy? How successful are the new reforms in favor of free trade and open markets, and will they pay off in terms of improved living standards? How strong are political parties, interest groups, and government institutions? Now that the Cold War is over, can U.S.-Latin American relations be put on a normal, more mature basis, and what of Latin America's relations with the rest of the world? These are some of the crucial questions that this book tries to answer.

In the next three chapters we examine the nature and role of interest groups and political parties in Latin America, describe government institutions and public policy, and analyze the overall political process and how it is changing. We then examine individual countries to see how they conform to these overall patterns.

Note

1. David Collier and Ruth Berins Collier, *Shaping the Political Arena: Critical Junctures, the Labor Movement, and Regime Dynamics in Latin America* (Princeton, NJ: Princeton University Press, 1991).

3

Interest Groups and
Political Parties

L atin American political parties and interest groups, as suggested in the
last chapter, are involved in the current transition of the area from its
corporatist, historic past to a newer system based on pluralism and democracy. During the 1990s the conflict was between two different views of what
the political rules of the game should be. On the one side are the new forces
that desire majority rule, human rights, and freedom of association. On the
other side are those that favor traditional ways of doing things, where the emphasis was often on creating an administrative state above party and interest-
group politics, and in which such agencies as the church, the army, the
university, and perhaps even the trade unions were often more than mere interest groups, forming a part of the state system and inseparable from it.

Of particular importance is the degree of government control over interest
groups. Although this traditionally ranged from almost complete control to
almost complete freedom, as under liberalism, the usual pattern involved considerably more state control over interest groups than in the United States,
and this helped put interest-group behavior in Latin America in a different
framework than was the case in the United States. Throughout the area there
is considerably less control over interest groups, although there is still great
variation among the nations.

At least until the 1980s Latin America, as Charles Anderson has suggested,[1]
never experienced a definitive democratic revolution—that is, a struggle resulting in agreement that elections would be the only legitimate way to obtain
public power. In the absence of such a consensus, political groups did not necessarily work for political power by seeking votes, support of political parties, or
contacts with elected representatives. The groups might seek power through
any number of other strategies including coercion, economic might, technical

expertise, and controlled violence. Any group that could mobilize votes was likely to do so for electoral purposes, but because that was not the only legitimated route to power, the result of any election was tentative. Given the varying power of the competing groups and the incomplete legitimacy of the government itself, the duration of any government was uncertain. Without a definitive term of office for any government, political competition became a constant, virtually permanent struggle and preoccupation.

Further, group behavior in Latin America was conditioned by a set of unwritten rules, called by Anderson the "living museum" effect. Before a new group could participate in the political system, it had to demonstrate tacitly both that it had a power resource and that it would respect the rights of already existing groups. The result was the gradual addition of new groups under these two conditions but seldom the elimination of the old ones. The newest, most modern groups coexisted with the oldest, most traditionalist ones.

A related factor was the practice of co-optation or repression. As new groups emerged as potential politically relevant actors, already established actors (particularly political parties or strong national leaders) sometimes offered to assist them in their new political activities. The deal struck was one mutually beneficial to both: The new group gained acceptance, prestige, and some of its original goals, and the established group or leader gained new support and increased political resources. The co-opted group dropped some of its original goals, leading many observers to be critical of the system as not providing for enough change. Those leaders and observers who preferred stability to more fundamental change saw the co-optation system as beneficial to the political system.

In some circumstances, new groups—often more radical—refused to be co-opted, rejecting the rules of the game. Instead, they took steps indicating to established groups and leaders that they might act in a revolutionary fashion against the interests of the established elites. In the case of a group that violated the ground rules by employing mass violence, for example, an effort was made by the established interests to repress the new group, either legally by refusing it legal standing or in some cases through the use of violence. Most commonly, such repression proved successful, and the new group, at least for the time being, disappeared or atrophied, accomplishing none of its goals. The general success of repression made co-optation seem more desirable to new groups, because obtaining some of their goals through co-optation was preferable to being repressed.

In a few cases the result was quite different. The established political groups failed to repress the emergent groups, and the latter came to power through revolutionary means, proceeding to eliminate the traditional power contenders. These are known as the "true," genuine, or social revolutions in

Latin America and include only the Mexican Revolution of 1910–1920, the Bolivian Revolution of 1952, the Cuban Revolution of 1959, and the Nicaraguan Revolution of 1979. Examples of the reverse process—utilization of violence and repression to eliminate the newer challenging groups and to secure in power the more traditional system—were Brazil in 1964 and Chile in 1973. Both led to the elimination of independent political parties, student associations, and labor and peasant unions as power groups.

Before the late 1980s we viewed the politically relevant groups of Latin America in this context of a historically patrimonial, corporative, and cooptive tradition. Now that system is being replaced with liberal democracy. Because some individuals and groups favor the new regime while other people and organizations prefer the historical one, throughout Latin America there is conflict between the new supporters of democracy and the supporters of the traditional system. The chapters on Peru and Guatemala hold special interest in this regard, as both show cases in which presidents tried to govern within the old, unwritten rules rather than the new, written ones incorporated in constitutional and democratic precepts.

The Traditional Oligarchy

After independence three groups, often referred to as the "nineteenth-century oligarchy," were predominant in Latin America: the military, the Roman Catholic church, and the large landholders. Through the process of economic growth and change new groups emerged: first commercial elites; later industrial elites, students, and middle-income sectors; then industrial labor unions and peasants; and most recently groups representing indigenous people, women, consumers, nongovernmental organizations, and many others. Throughout the process, political parties have existed. Particularly since the end of the nineteenth century, the United States has been a politically relevant force in the domestic politics of the Latin American countries. During the Cold War years of conflict with Communist countries the U.S. government seemed most interested in keeping Latin America out of the enemy camp; today in absence of international enemies, U.S. governmental concerns have more to do with democracy, human rights, and drugs. Other foreign countries and international actors are now active in Latin America as well.

The Armed Forces

During the wars for independence, the Spanish American countries developed armies led by a great variety of individuals, including well-born creoles, priests, and people of more humble background. The officers did not come from military academies but were self-selected or chosen by other leaders. Few of the officers had previous military training, and the armies were much less professional than the armies we know today.

Following independence the military element continued as one of the first important power groups. The national army was supposed to be preeminent, and in some countries national military academies were founded in the first quarter century after independence. Yet the national military was challenged by other local or regional armies. The early nineteenth century was a period of limited national integration, with the *patrias chicas* or regional subdivisions of the countries often dominated by local landowners or *caudillos,* men on horseback who had their own private armies. One aspect of the development of Latin America was the struggle between the central government and its army on the one hand and the *patrias chicas* and local *caudillos* on the other, with the former winning out in most cases. One of the unanswered questions about Latin American politics even at the beginning of the new millennium is the extent to which outlying areas of the countries, in the mountains or jungles, are effectively covered by the laws made in the national capitals.

The development of Brazil varied somewhat from the norm because of the different colonizing power (Portugal) and because of the lack of a struggle for independence. The military first gained prominence in the Paraguayan War (1864–1870). Until 1930 the Brazilian states had powerful militias, in some cases of comparable strength to the national army.

Although Latin American militaries varied in the nineteenth century, a study of them reveals two general themes. First, various militaries, including the national one, became active in politics. At given times they were regional or personal organizations; at others, they were parts of political parties that were the participants in the civil wars frequently waged between rival factions. However, second, the national military often played the role of a moderating power, staying above factional struggles, preferring that civilians govern, but taking over power temporarily when the civilians could not effectively rule. Although this moderating power did not emerge in all countries, it was seen in most, especially in Brazil, where, with the abdication of the emperor in 1889, the military became the chief moderator in the system.

As early as the 1830s and 1840s in Argentina and Mexico, and later in the other Latin American countries, national military academies were established. Their goal was to introduce professionalism into the military, requiring graduation rather than elite family connections for officer status. These academies were for the most part successful in making entry and promotion in the officer corps proceed in a routinized manner, and by the 1950s a Latin American officer was named a general, with potential political power, only after a career of some twenty years.

Through professionalization the military career was designed to be a highly specialized one that taught the skills for warfare but eschewed interest in political matters. Officership would supposedly absorb all the energy of its members, and this functional expertise would be distinct from that of politicians. Civilians were theoretically to have complete control of the military, which would stay out of politics. However, this model of professionalism, imported from Western Europe and the United States, never took complete root in Latin America. Usually in the absence of strong civilian institutions, the military continued to play politics and to exercise its moderating power, and coups d'état continued.

By the late 1950s and early 1960s a change had occurred in the nature of the role of the military in Latin America. The success of guerrilla revolutions in China, Indochina, Algeria, and Cuba led to a new emphasis on the military's role in counterinsurgency and internal defense functions. In addition, Latin American militaries—encouraged by U.S. military aid—began to assume responsibility for civic-action programs, which assisted civilians in the construction of roads, schools, and other public projects. This led to a broader responsibility for the military in nation-building.

The new professionalism, with its emphasis on counterinsurgency, was a product of the Cold War and may have been more in keeping with the Latin American political culture than the old professionalism had been. Military skills—management, administration, nation-building—were no longer viewed as separate or different from civilian skills. The military was to acquire the ability to help solve those national problems that might lead to insurgency, which was, in its very essence, a political rather than an apolitical task. The implication of the new professionalism was that, besides combating active guerrilla factions, the military would take care that social and economic reforms necessary to prevent insurgency were adopted if the civilians proved incapable of doing so. Although the new professionalism was also seen in the developed Western world and in other parts of the Third World, it was particularly prevalent in Latin America. Professionalism in Latin America led to more military intervention in politics, not less.

The end result of this process was called "bureaucratic authoritarianism,"[2] the rule of the military institution on a long-term basis. Seen especially in Argentina, Brazil, Chile, Peru, and Uruguay, this new form of military government was of the institution as a whole—not an individual general—and was based on the idea that the military could govern better than civilians. The military often governed repressively and violated human rights. The bureaucratic-authoritarian period lasted from the mid-1960s through the late 1970s, when the military in many countries was replaced by elected civilian governments.

The Latin American militaries, from the mid-1980s to the end of the 1990s, began transitions to constitutionalism, subservience to civilian control, and support of democratically elected presidents. The transformation has had its difficulties, including support for a president who dismissed congress and the courts (Peru), playing a key role in overthrowing a president who attempted the same maneuver (Guatemala), putting down coups d'état against chief executives (Venezuela), helping civilian groups to depose unpopular presidents (Ecuador), and failing to intervene although key elements of public opinion and the U.S. ambassador apparently favored getting rid of the elected president (Colombia). In general the Latin American militaries are now in the process of learning a new role, that of "democratic sustainment," or support for civilian democracy, something that the U.S. Army is trying to help them learn.

It has always been difficult to compare the Latin American militaries cross-nationally. Trying to distinguish "civilian" from "military" regimes was similarly a meaningless task at times or at best a difficult one. Often military personnel temporarily resigned their commissions to take leadership positions in civilian bureaucracies or as government ministers. Frequently they held military and civilian positions at the same time. In some cases an officer resigned his commission, was elected president, and then governed with strong military backing. In almost all instances, coups d'état were not just simple military affairs but were supported by groups of civilians as well. It was not unheard of for civilians to take a significant part in the ensuing governments. Sometimes civilians actually drew the military into playing a larger political role. In short, Latin American governments were often coalitions made between certain factions of the militaries and certain factions of civilians in an attempt to control the pinnacles of power of the system.

We suggest that several dimensions of military involvement in politics be considered in the chapters about individual countries that follow. The first is whether the military still forcefully removes chief executives, an activity that in the new millennium seems to be becoming a thing of the past in most countries. The second is the extent to which the military leaders have a say in nonmilitary matters. Although in the past generals have protected their large-landowner friends and relatives, that phenomenon might also be passing. The final question is to what extent the moderating power of the military still obligates it to step in and unseat an incompetent president or one who has violated the rules of the game.

Considering this very complicated question, Peter Smith classifies all Latin American countries in 2000 into four types:

1. Military control;
2. Military tutelage: in the case of crisis of the civilian government the armed forces supervise civilian authorities and play key roles in decision-making;
3. Conditional military subordination: the armed forces keep careful watch over civilians, protecting military prerogatives; and
4. Civilian control.

Table 3.1 Patterns of Civil-Military Relations in 2000

Military control	Military tutelage	Conditional military subordination	Civilian control*
None as of 2000 (with the possible exception of Guatemala)	Ecuador	Bolivia	Costa Rica
	El Salvador	Brazil	Mexico
	Guatemala	Chile	Haiti
	Venezuela	Colombia	Panama
		Dominican Republic	Argentina
		Honduras	Uruguay
		Nicaragua	
		Paraguay	
		Peru	

Source: Peter H. Smith, *Democracy in Latin America: Political Change in Comparative Prospective* (New York: Oxford University Press, 2005), 103.

*Grouped in this way because of structural variations.

How Smith classified the Latin American countries is shown in Table 3.1.[3]

Besides the degree of military influence in the political system, several other interrelated questions should be kept in mind during the reading of the country chapters. These include the reason for military involvement in politics, what the results of military rule were, and how the military was internally divided. The military was one of the traditional pillars of Latin American society, with rights (*fueros*), responsibilities, and legal standing that can be traced back to colonial times. This meant the military played a different role than it did in the United States. Although this seems to be a matter of the past, the cases of Peru (1992) and Guatemala (1993) show that, in some countries, the generals still play very important roles in politics.

The Roman Catholic Church

All Latin American countries were nominally Catholic, although the form of that religion varied from country to country. The Spanish and Portuguese came to "Christianize the heathens" as well as to seek precious metals. In areas of large Amerindian concentrations, religion became a mixture of pre-Columbian and Roman Catholic beliefs. To a lesser degree, Catholicism later blended with African religions, which also existed on their own in certain areas, especially in Brazil and Cuba. In contrast, religion in the large cities of Latin America was similar to that in the urban centers of the United States and Western Europe. However, in the more isolated small towns, Roman Catholicism was still of fifteenth-century vintage.

The power of the church hierarchy in politics also varies. Traditionally the church was one of the main sectors of Spanish and Portuguese corporate society, with rights and responsibilities in such areas as care for orphans, education, and public morals. During the nineteenth century the church was one of the three major groups in politics, along with the military and the landed interests. Yet during the same century some laypeople wanted to strip the church of all its temporal power, including its lands. Generally speaking, the conflict over the role of the church had ended in most countries by the first part of the twentieth century.

In the 1960s to the 1980s the church changed, especially if by "church" we mean the top levels of the hierarchy that control the religious and political fortunes of the institution. These transformations were occasioned by the new theologies of the past hundred years, as expressed through various papal encyclicals, Vatican II, and the conferences of the Latin American bishops at Medellín, Colombia, in 1968 and Puebla, Mexico, in 1979. Significant numbers of bishops (and many more parish priests and members of the various orders) subscribed to what was commonly called liberation theology. This new theology stresses that the church was of and for this world and should take stands against repression and violence, including the "institutionalized violence"—the life-demeaning and -threatening violence—experienced by the poor of the area. Liberation theology also stressed the equality of all believers—laypeople as well as clerics and bishops—as opposed to the former stress on hierarchy. The end result, in some parts of the area, was new popular-level People's Churches, with lay leadership and only minimal involvement of priests.

It would be a mistake, however, to assume that all, or even most, members of the Latin American clergy ever subscribed to liberation theology. Many believed that the new social doctrine had taken the church more into politics than it should be. Some were concerned with the loss of traditional authority that the erosion of hierarchy has brought. As the various countries of Latin America differ substantially in church authority and adherence of the bishops to liberation theology, we raise this issue now.

The result of the changes is a clergy that is no longer uniformly conservative, but rather one whose members differ on the role that the church should play in socioeconomic reform and on the nature of hierarchical relations within the church. At one extreme of this conflict is the traditional church elite, usually with social origins in the upper class or aspirations to be accepted by it, still very conservative, and with close connections to other supporters of the status quo. At the other end of this intraclergy conflict are those priests, of various social backgrounds, who see the major objective of the church as assisting the masses to obtain social justice. In some cases these priests have been openly revolutionary, fighting in guerrilla wars. Other priests fall between these two extremes of political ideology, and still others favor a relaxing of the rigid hierarchy, giving more discretion to local parish priests.

The church still participates in politics to defend its interests, although in most cases its wealth is no longer in land. Certain church interests are still the traditional ones: giving religious instruction in schools and running parochial high schools and universities, the cost of which has traditionally made higher education possible only for people of middle income or higher, and occasionally attempting to prevent divorce legislation and to make purely civil marriage difficult. At times the church has been a major proponent of human rights, especially when military governments deny them. A touchier issue has been that of birth control, and in most cases the Latin American hierarchies have fought artificial methods. However, in the face of the population explosion many church officials have assisted in family-planning clinics, turned their heads when governments have promoted artificial methods of birth control, and occasionally even assisted in those governmental efforts.

Some analysts feel the Roman Catholic church in Latin America is no longer a major contender. They argue that on certain issues its sway is still considerable, but that the church is no longer as influential politically as the army, the wealthy elites, or the U.S. Embassy. Modernization, urbanization, and secularism have also taken their toll on church attendance and the political power of the church. Other analysts, pointing to the liberation theology of People's Churches, argue, on the contrary, that the church or individual clerics connected to it are powerful as never before.

One of the most interesting phenomena in Latin America in recent decades has been the explosive growth of Protestant religious groups. In some countries Protestants number upward of 25 to 35 percent of the population; in Guatemala a Protestant general became dictator for a time. The fastest growing of these sects were the evangelical Christians, not the older mainline churches. Protestantism was associated with middle-classness, making it socially attractive. Protestantism was identified with a strong work ethic, obliging its members to work hard and save. Until recently the Protestant groups, however, have generally not become politically active.

Large Landowners

In all the countries of Latin America, save Costa Rica and Paraguay, the colonial period led to the establishment of a group of large landowners who had received their lands as royal grants. With the coming of independence these latifundistas (owners of large land tracts called latifundios) were more powerful than before and developed into one of the three major power groups of nineteenth-century politics. This was not to say that they operated monolithically; in some cases they were divided against each other.

In recent times such rifts have remained among the large landowners, usually along the lines of crop production. They might disagree on a governmental policy favoring livestock raising to the detriment of crop planting. However, the major conflict has been between those who have large tracts of land and the many landless peasants. In those circumstances the various groups of large landowners tend to coalesce. In some cases there is an umbrella organization to bring all of the various producer organizations together formally; in other cases the coalition is much more informal.

In the 1960s the pressures for land reform were considerable, both from landless peasants and from foreign and domestic groups who saw this type of reform as a way to achieve social justice and to avoid Castro-like revolutions. In some countries, such as Mexico, land reform had previously come by revolution; in others, such as Venezuela, a good bit of land had been distributed by the government to the landless; in still others, the power of the landed, in coalition with other status quo groups, led to the appearance of land reform rather than the reality. In many of the Latin American countries, especially those in which the amount of arable land is limited and where the population explosion has led to higher person-land ratios, the issue of breaking up large estates will continue for the foreseeable future. Given the historic power of the landed elite, change is likely to be slow in the absence of something approaching a social revolution.

Since the 1960s, with Latin America rapidly urbanizing and in some cases even industrializing, the rural issue has become less important. The traditional landowners still dominate in some countries, but in others power has passed to newer commercial and industrial elites. Although land reform may still be necessary in some areas, with large percentages of the population moving to the cities, many of the main social issues have become urban rather than rural.

Other Major Interest Groups

Commercial and Industrial Elites

Although not part of the traditional oligarchy, commercial elites have existed in Latin America since independence; one of the early political conflicts was between those who wanted free trade (the commercial elites and allied landed interests producing crops for export) and those who wanted protection of nascent industry (industrial elites with allied landed groups not producing for export). In recent decades the strength of these commercial and industrial groups has steadily grown.

With the exception of Colombia, the real push for industrialization in Latin America did not come until the Great Depression and World War II, when Latin America was cut off from trade with the industrialized world. Before those crises industrial goods from England and the United States were cheaper, even with transportation costs and import duties, than locally produced goods.

Between the mid-1930s and the mid-1980s, Latin American countries experienced industrialization of the import substitution type—that is, producing goods that formerly were imported from the industrialized countries. This was the case in light consumer goods; in some consumer durables, including assembly of North American and European automobiles; and in some other heavy industries such as cement and steel. Because import substitution necessitated increased foreign trade to import capital goods, there was no longer much conflict between commercial and industrial elites: Expanded trade and industrialization go together.

Since the 1980s the push of neoliberal presidents in Latin America has been for more foreign commerce in a world with trade barriers that are lower or do not exist at all. In this "internationalization" of the Latin American economies, foreign trade is of utmost importance. Hence so are the commercial elites. Mexico entered a free trade association with the United States and Canada in 1994 through the North American Free Trade Agreement (NAFTA), Central America and the Dominican Republic in 2005 through the Central American Free Trade Association (CAFTA), and the goal is to have a free trade association covering all of the Americas, from Alaska to Tierra del Fuego.

A complicating factor in the consideration of the industrial elite is its relationship with the landed elite. In some countries, such as Argentina, the early industrialists were linked to the landed groups; later, individuals who began as industrialists invested in land. The result was two intertwined groups, a marriage of older landed and newer moneyed wealth, with only vague boundaries separating them and some families and individuals straddling the line. All these groups were opposed to agrarian reform.

Industrialists and commercial elites are highly organized in various chambers of commerce, industrial associations, and the like; they are strategically located in major cities of Latin America; and generally they favor a status quo that profits themselves. They are often the driving forces in Latin American economic development; for this reason and because they are frequently represented in high official circles, no matter what government is in control, they are very powerful. Neoliberalism and globalism have made these groups even more essential to the functioning of the economy, and hence also to the political system.

The Middle Sectors

Although the Latin American countries began independence with a basically two-class system, there have always been individuals who fell statistically into the middle ranges, neither very rich nor abjectly poor. These few individuals during the nineteenth century were primarily artisans and shopkeepers and, later, doctors and lawyers. The emergence of a larger middle sector was a twentieth-century phenomenon, associated with urbanization, technological advances, industrialization, and the expansion of public education and the role of the government.

All of these changes necessitated a large number of white-collar, managerial workers. New teachers and government bureaucrats constituted part of this sector, as did office workers in private businesses. In addition, small businesses grew, particularly in the service sector of the economy. Many of these new nonmanual professions have been organized: teachers' associations, small-business associations, lawyers' associations, organizations of governmental bureaucrats, and so forth. Military officers, university students, political party officials, and even union and peasant group leaders are usually considered middle class.

The people who filled the new middle-sector jobs were the product of social mobility, with some coming from the lower class and others as "fallen aristocrats" from the upper class. They lacked a prolonged, common historical experience. This, together with their numerous and heterogeneous occupations, temporarily impeded the formation of a sense of common identity as members of a middle class. Indeed, in some of the countries of Latin America this identification has yet to emerge. In Latin America the middle-class ideal is still to be a part of "society," preferably high society.

In those countries of Latin America in which a large middle-sector group has emerged, certain generalizations about its political behavior can be made. In the early stages of political activities, coalitions tended to be formed with groups from the lower classes against the more traditional and oligarchic groups in power. Major goals included expanded suffrage, the promotion of urban growth and economic development, a greater role for public education, increased industrialization, and social-welfare programs.

In the later political evolution of the middle sectors the tendency has been to side with the established order against rising mass or populist movements. In some cases the middle-class movements allied with landowners, industrialists, and the church against their working-class partners of earlier years; in other cases, when the more numerous lower class seemed ready to take power on its own, the middle sectors were instrumental in fomenting a middle-class military coup, to prevent "premature democratization"[4] (a democratic system that the middle sectors could not control). Over the years, then, middle-class movements changed dramatically.

Because the status of the middle class varies greatly in Latin America, a number of factors should be considered when reading the chapters about individual countries, including the size of the middle-income group, its cohesion and relationships with political parties, and the degree of self-identification as members of a "middle class." Only time will tell if the middle sectors will act differently because of the years of bureaucratic authoritarianism, whether the middle sectors will serve as a new, invigorated social base for democracy or whether they will continue to ape and imitate the upper class and thus perpetuate an essentially two-class and polarized social structure. While in the 1990s the middle class favored stability at all costs and saw democracy as the best way of achieving and continuing stability, in the new millennium many have become impatient with the failure of democracy to produce better economic conditions.

Labor Unions

From its inception, organized labor in Latin America has been highly political. Virtually all important trade union groups of the area have been closely associated with a political party, strong leader, or government. On some occasions labor unions have grown independently until they were co-opted or repressed. In other cases labor unions have owed their origins directly to the efforts of a party, leader, or government.

Three characteristics of the Latin American economies have favored partisan unionism. First, unions came relatively early in the economic development of the region—in most cases earlier than in the United States and Western Europe. Second, the labor pool of employables has been much larger than the number who can get the relatively well-paid jobs in industry. An employer in that situation could almost always find people to replace striking workers unless they were protected by a party or by the government. Finally, Latin American unionism was influenced by ideological currents that came from Southern Europe, including anarchist and Marxist orientations. Further, inflation has been a problem in Latin America in recent decades, making it important for unions to win the support of other political groups in the continual renegotiation of contracts to obtain higher salaries, which often need governmental approval.

The Latin American legal tradition required that unions be officially recognized by the government before they could collectively bargain. If a group could not obtain or retain this legal standing, it had little power. Labor legislation, in addition, varied greatly, including codes making it mandatory that labor organizers be employed full time by the industry that they were organizing, limiting the power of unions lacking leaders who were paid full salaries to spend part of the working day in union activities. This was only one of the many governmental restrictions placed on labor unions. In general, there is now a movement away from corporate or state control of unions toward greater freedom of association, and often conflict arises between the state and the free unions.

Some union organizations were co-opted by the state; others remained outside the system. Key questions to consider when reading the country chapters include the extent to which workers are organized, how the labor code is used to prevent or facilitate worker organization, the nature of the relationships between labor and the political parties or between labor and the government, and the extent to which unions have been co-opted or repressed. Are the unions a declining or growing interest in Latin America?

Peasants

The term peasants refers to many different kinds of people in Latin America. Some prefer the Spanish term *campesinos* (people who work in the *campo*, the countryside) rather than the English term with its European-based connotations. The major groups of campesinos, who vary in importance from country to country, include indigenous groups who speak only their native language or who are bilingual in that language and Spanish; workers on the traditional hacienda tilling the fields in return for wages or part of the crops, with the owner as a patrón to care for the family or, more frequently, a manager-patrón who represents the absentee owner; workers on modern plantations, receiving wages but remaining outside of the older patrón-client relationship; persons with a small landholding (minifundio), legally held, of such a size that a bare existence is possible; persons who cultivate small plots, with no legal claim, perhaps moving every few years after the slash-and-burn method and the lack of crop rotation deplete the soil; and persons who have been given a small plot of land to work by a landowner in exchange for work on the large estate.

What all of these campesinos have in common, in the context of the extremely inequitable distribution of arable lands in Latin America, is a marginal existence due to their small amount of land or income and a high degree of insecurity due to their uncertain claims to the lands they cultivate. It was estimated in 1961 that over five million very small farms (below thirty acres—twelve hectares) occupied only 3.7 percent of the land, while, at the other extreme, 100,000 holdings of more than 1,500 acres (607 hectares) took up some 65 percent of the land. Three decades later, the situation had changed little. At least eighty million people still lived on small landholdings with insufficient land to earn a minimum subsistence, or they worked as agricultural laborers with no land at all. For many of these rural people their only real chance of breaking out of this circle of poverty was by moving to an urban area, where they faced another—in some ways even worse—culture of poverty. For those who remained on the land, unless there was a dramatic restructuring of ownership, the present subhuman existence was likely to continue. Moreover, as commercial agriculture for export increased in many countries, the campesinos were increasingly shoved off the fertile lands into the sterile hillsides, where their ability to subsist has become more precarious.

Rural peasant elements have long been active in politics, but only recently as independent, organized interest groups. The traditional political structure of the countryside was one in which participation in national politics meant taking part in the patronage system. The local patrones, besides expecting work on the estate from the campesino, expected certain political behavior. In some countries this meant that the campesino belonged to the same political party as the patrón, voted for that party on election day, and, if necessary, served as cannon fodder in its civil wars. In other countries the national party organizations never reached the local levels, and restrictive suffrage laws prevented the peasants from participation in elections. In both patterns, for the peasants there was no such thing as national politics, only local politics, which might or might not have national party labels attached to the local person or groups in power.

This traditional system still exists in many areas of Latin America. However, since the 1950s signs of agrarian unrest and political mobilization have been more and more evident. In many cases major agrarian movements were organized by urban interests: political parties, especially those of the Marxist left. Some of these peasant movements have been openly revolutionary, seeking to reform and improve the land tenure system and to significantly reform the entire power structure of the nation. They have employed strategies that include the illegal seizure of land, the elimination of landowners, and armed defense of the gains thus achieved. We could call these movements ones of revolutionary agrarianism. Less radical were the movements that sought to reform the social order partially through the elimination of a few of the most oppressive effects of the existing power structure that weighs on the peasant subculture, but without threatening the power structure as such.

The peasants, still a large group in Latin America, remain politically weak, a characteristic that is likely to continue as their numbers dwindle through urbanization. Their weakness comes chiefly because the peasant sector is largely unorganized. Because of the diversity of land and labor patterns, the dispersed nature of the countryside, and high illiteracy, it is difficult to mobilize a strong peasant movement. Their distance from the urban centers of power also makes it hard for peasants to effect change. At the same time, millions of peasants are leaving the land, migrating to cities or the United States, and thus weakening the peasant movements still more.

The United States

Another important power element in Latin American politics is the United States. This influence usually has been seen in at least three interrelated ways: U.S. governmental representatives, U.S.-based private business, and U.S.-dominated international agencies. At times these groups work in harmony, and at times they operate at cross-purposes. The U.S. government has been interested in the area since Latin America's independence. Its first concern, that the new nations not fall under the control of European powers, led to the Monroe Doctrine in 1823. Originally a defensive statement, the doctrine was later changed through various corollaries to a more aggressive one, telling the Latin Americans that they could not sell lands to nonhemispheric governments or businesses (if the locations were strategic) and that the United States would intervene in Latin America to collect debts owed to nonhemispheric powers (the Roosevelt Corollary).

At various times the U.S. government has set standards that must be met before full diplomatic recognition was accorded to a Latin American nation. This de jure recognition policy, most memorable in the Wilson, early Kennedy, and Carter administrations, favored elected democratic governments, exclusion of the military from government, and a vision of human rights that should be applied in Latin America. At other times the United States has pursued a de facto recognition policy, according full diplomatic standing to any government with effective control of its nation's territory.

Whatever recognition policy was followed, the U.S. ambassador to a Latin American country usually has had impressive powers. One ambassador to pre-Castro Cuba testified that he was second only to the president in influence in the country. This ambassadorial power has typically been used to support or defeat governments, to focus governmental policy of the Latin American countries in certain directions, and to assist U.S.-based corporations in the various countries. In Central America during the 1980s a number of U.S. ambassadors played this strong proconsular role, as did the ambassador to Colombia during the government of Ernesto Samper (1994–1998), because of the president's suspected ties to drug groups.

From their early beginnings, particularly in agribusiness (especially sugar and bananas), U.S.-based corporations in Latin America have grown dramatically. In addition to agribusiness, corporations later entered the extractive field (petroleum, copper, coal, iron ore), retailing, the services industry (accounting firms, computer outfits), and communications (telephones, telegraphs, computers). The most recent kind of U.S. corporation introduced to Latin America was the export-platform variety—that is, a company that takes advantage of the low wages in Latin America to produce pocket calculators in Mexico or baseballs in Haiti, mainly for export to the industrialized world.

U.S. corporations in Latin America often enter into the politics of their host countries. Some of the instances have been flagrant: bribing public officials to keep taxes low or threatening to cut off a country's products if certain policies were approved by its government. However, most political activities of U.S. corporations currently are much less dramatic. Almost always Latin Americans in the host countries buy stock in the U.S. corporations and hold high managerial positions in them. In many cases, U.S. businesses purchase Latin American corporations, the leaders of which then work for the new owners. The result is that the U.S. corporation develops contacts, obligations, and political influence similar to those possessed by domestic interest groups. In the 1980s there were some indications that the era of large U.S. corporate holdings and hence influence in Latin America might be in decline. Many U.S. corporations, as a result of the recession in Latin America and the debt crisis, pulled up stakes, withdrew their capital, and moved on to more profitable and stable areas. Yet by the end of the 1980s the business climate had improved: Latin American governments rescinded restrictions on maximum profits and repatriation. Once again U.S. capital began to flow into the area; in the 1990s, as Latin American economies recovered, massive U.S. capital flowed into the area.

Most foreign-aid and international lending organizations have been dominated historically by the United States. These agencies, especially active during the 1960s, when aid to Latin America began in large quantities, include the U.S. Agency for International Development (AID), which administers most of U.S. foreign aid; the World Bank; the International Monetary Fund (IMF); the Inter-American Development Bank, and a variety of others. The World Bank and the IMF were international agencies, results of post–World War II agreements between the countries of the West. However, the representation of the United States on the governing boards of both has been so large (based on the amount of money donated to the agencies), and the convergence of interests of the two with those of the U.S. government has been so great, that they can be considered U.S.-oriented groups. So can the Inter-American Development Bank (IADB). Although urged to do so by Latin American leaders who wanted a lending agency less dominated by the United States, in effect the IADB cannot lend to countries if the U.S. government does not want it to. Because economic development has been a central goal of the Latin American states for the past fifty years; loans for that development have come predominantly from AID, the World Bank, and the IADB; and those loans were contingent many times on a monetary policy judged healthy by the IMF, the officials of these four groups have much influence in the day-to-day policies of the governments of the area.

This power of the lending agencies was probably greatest during the 1960s, and then again during the debt crisis of the 1980s. AID had most leverage or "conditionality" during the Alliance for Progress. This foreign-aid program, initiated by the Kennedy administration, attempted to change Latin America dramatically in a decade. Even though it failed, it did lead to large loans from the U.S. government, substantial progress in some fields, and much influence for the local AID head in the domestic politics of some Latin American countries. Some AID representatives sat in on cabinet meetings and wrote speeches for and gave advice to the local officials with whom they worked, and others largely ran the agencies or even ministries of the host government to which they were assigned.

The Alliance for Progress was terminated by the Nixon administration. Further, the power of the World Bank waned in the wake of the crisis of the industrialized economies of the West following the Arab oil embargo of 1973–1974 and with the growing power of OPEC. Then the private banks, recycling petrodollars, filled many of the needs of the Latin American countries. However, with the debt crisis of the 1980s the IMF, and its Bretton Woods partner the World Bank, regained much of their lost power.

In the meantime the economies of Latin America were undergoing crisis while protectionist measures rose in the importing nations. The Latin American nations were clamoring for access to U.S. markets, and they were likely to be partially successful in that quest. The U.S. government also initiated a new massive assistance program for Central America and the Caribbean designed to restore solvency and preserve stability. More recently, foreign aid has dwindled while direct private investment has multiplied.

The influence of U.S.-directed and -oriented groups—diplomatic, business, foreign-assistance—in Latin America is considerable. This does not mean that the power has been equal in all the Latin American countries. When a Latin American country is strategically important to the United States and when U.S. private investors have established a large investment in the economy (Cuba before Castro), U.S. elements are extremely powerful in domestic Latin politics. This does not mean that the United States cannot have considerable influence in domestic politics in distant countries with relatively little private investment by U.S. corporations, as the example of Allende's Chile showed. With the end of the Cold War, U.S. foreign policy interest in Latin America, with the exception of a few countries, has waned; private transactions are more important than official ones.

New Groups

Many new groups have appeared in Latin America in recent decades. Three that seem of particular importance are indigenous groups, women's groups, and nongovernmental organizations (NGOs).

Indigenous Groups

Indigenous peoples constitute about 8 percent of the total population of Latin America, or an estimated forty million people. In some four hundred distinct groups, they are concentrated in southern Mexico, parts of Central America, and the central Andes of South America. In these states they make up between 10 to 70 percent of the population. Some individual language groups have more than one million members. A dozen groups have more than a quarter million members, making up some 73 percent of the total indigenous population of the region. Finally, two groups have less than one thousand members.

In the 1970s Amerindian populations in Latin America began to mobilize politically in unprecedented ways to protect their lands and cultures from the increasing influence of multinational companies, colonists, the state, and other intruders. In the 1980s they placed a greater emphasis on the recuperation of ethnic identities and the construction of a pan-indigenous cultural identity. In ways that vary throughout the region, Latin American indigenous peoples share the common goal of ending ethnic discrimination and the assimilationist policies of Latin American governments.

Contemporary Latin American indigenous organizations seek equal and legitimate status for their cultures, forms of social organization, laws, and the means to facilitate and control their economic development. Their ultimate goal is the transformation of what they view to be a discriminatory, homogeneous state into a "plurinational state," one whose institutions reflect the cultural diversity of society. In the 1990s seven Latin American states—Bolivia, Colombia, Ecuador, Mexico, Nicaragua, Peru, and Paraguay—recognized a milder version of this claim, declaring their societies "pluricultural and multiethnic." At the same time many individuals of indigenous background continue to follow the traditional assimilationist strategy of seeking to integrate themselves into Hispanic (Catholic, Spanish- or Portuguese-speaking, Western) culture.

The main component of rising indigenous nationalism is the struggle for territorial, political, economic, and cultural autonomy. Until 1987 only the Kuna of Panama enjoyed what could be described as territorial and political autonomy. In 1987 the Nicaraguan government established two multiethnic autonomous regions to accommodate claims of the Miskitu and other smaller groups, who had joined the anti-Sandinista counterrevolutionary guerrilla movement supported by the United States. Although the autonomous regions were largely a failure in terms of indigenous peoples' aspirations, their establishment inspired indigenous organizations throughout Latin America to make similar claims.

Only Colombia's indigenous population has achieved politico-territorial autonomy. The 1991 Colombian constitution elevated indigenous reserves (resguardos) to the status of municipal governments; recognized indigenous traditional leaders as public authorities and, with some restrictions, indigenous customary law as public and binding; and provided guaranteed representation in the national senate. The governments of Bolivia, Ecuador, Guatemala, and Mexico have recently considered some type of politico-territorial autonomy arrangements following constitutional reforms or peace agreements with armed groups concluded in the 1990s.[5]

The most notable cases of members of indigenous groups taking part in national politics were in Peru in 2001, where Alejandro Toledo was elected president, and in Bolivia in 2006 when Evo Morales was elected president. While the Toledo presidency was troubled (see chapter 10), it is too soon to conclude how Morales will do.

Women's Groups

There is little doubt that women in Latin America are making progress in ascending to leadership positions in government, politics, and civil society. A 1999 study concluded that, although their numbers remain low, the percentage of women in national congresses and cabinets in Latin America (15 and 11 percent, respectively) is second only to the Nordic countries of Europe (36 and 35 percent) and is higher in the congress but lower in cabinets than in the United States (12 and 21 percent).[6]

More politicized women's groups emerged in the 1970s and 1980s, playing a prominent role in the struggles against authoritarian rule, raising hopes that the return to democracy would generate greater opportunities for women in the region. The consolidation of democracy was expected to promote greater participation of women in the formulation and execution of laws governing their lives. Although in the 1990s the presence of women in leadership positions remained low, their situation does appear to be improving. In that decade women's presence in the public spheres of politics, the economy, and society grew. Such growth is a reflection of social changes such as women's entry into the labor force, rising educational levels, and changing attitudes about the role of women. Most notably, three women were elected presidents in their countries: Violeta Barrios de Chamorro in Nicaragua in

1990, Mireya Moscoso de Gruber in Panama in 1999, and Michelle Bachelet in Chile in 2006.

Figures on women's representation in politics show that their opportunities to exercise leadership are greater outside the main centers of power, in the lower levels of organizational hierarchy, outside the capital city area, and in less powerful governmental agencies. For example, women's presence in the judicial branch of government shows that they make up 45 percent of the trial judges but only 20 percent at the appellate court level, and virtually zero at the supreme court level.

One important consequence of women's organizing has been the adoption of quota laws, intended to increase women's representation in political office. After pressure from organized women's groups, Argentina, Bolivia, Brazil, Costa Rica, the Dominican Republic, Ecuador, Panama, and Peru have passed national laws requiring political parties to reserve 20 to 40 percent of candidacies for women. Of course, that women are nominated does not necessarily mean that they are elected. Colombia enacted a law making it mandatory that mayors have women as one-third of their appointed officials, a law that is not always followed.

Despite the growth of women's representation, the women's movement has appeared to some observers to be increasingly fragmented and to have lost its visibility and capacity for political intervention. One reason for this is the weakening of cross-class links between middle-class feminists and working-class women's groups. In an important sense this is a consequence of democracy: As the access of middle-class women to power has increased during democracy, their connections with the lower classes seems to have grown weaker. Another split is between more traditional, social service-oriented women's groups and their often more militant, younger, feminist sisters.

In conclusion, the obstacles to women's full participation in Latin American democracies and economies stem from women's weaker social position, traditional gender roles and cultural expectations and stereotypes built around these roles, and blatant sex discrimination. Few Latin American countries have made efforts to make motherhood and work compatible. No Latin American country has a comprehensive child care policy. Although most countries have laws that require businesses that employ twenty or more women to have on-site day care facilities, these laws are rarely enforced. Pregnancy discrimination is widespread in the region, some companies requiring a pregnancy test or a sterilization certificate as a condition of employment. Some fire women once they become pregnant. Although both actions are against the law, once again the laws are seldom enforced. Although cultural changes coming from women's improving position will help erode such discriminatory barriers, this is likely to happen only in the very long run.

Nongovernmental Organizations

Another newer type of group is the nongovernmental organizations (NGOs), which are increasingly important actors in Latin American politics. Although some are specific for individual countries, others are based on a general theme and have offices in many Latin American countries. Some NGOs are transnational, with headquarters in one country and activities in many countries. Amnesty International, the Environmental Defense Fund, and the Red Cross are transnational NGOs that have influenced recent events in Latin America. Local NGOs are shaping contemporary politics, too. For example, NGOs are providing community services in Mexico, raising racial consciousness in Brazil, extending credit to poor people in Colombia, defending indigenous peoples in Bolivia, and asserting women's rights in Argentina. Unlike interest groups, NGOs do not focus their activities exclusively on governments. They also work to change the policies of international institutions such as the World Bank, the practices of private businesses and entire industries, and the behavior of individuals and society as a whole.[7]

Political Parties

In Latin America political parties have often been only one set of groups among several, probably no more (and perhaps less) important than the army or the economic oligarchy. Elections were not the only legitimate route to power, nor were the parties themselves particularly strong or well organized. They were important actors in the political process in some of the more democratic countries, representing the chief means to gain high office. But frequently in other countries the parties were peripheral to the main focal points of power and the electoral arena was considered only one among several. Many Latin Americans have viewed political parties as divisive elements and hence they are not held in high esteem. This increasingly seems to be the case in recent years as candidates use the mass media rather than parties to get elected.

Many of the groups described earlier in this chapter have often joined into political parties in their pursuit of governmental power. As a result there have been a myriad of political parties in the history of Latin America. Indeed, someone once quipped that to form a political party all you needed was a president, vice president, secretary-treasurer, and rubber stamp. (If times were bad, you could do without the vice president and the secretary-treasurer!) Peter Smith shows that during the period of democracy since 1978 there are more political parties in most Latin American countries than during the 1940–1977 period.[8] Nevertheless, there have been certain characteristics common to parties, although the country chapters that follow show great national variation.

The first parties were usually founded by elite groups in competition with other factions of the elite. Mass demands played only a small role, although campesinos were sometimes mobilized by the party leaders, often to vote as they were instructed or to serve as cannon fodder. In many cases the first cleavage was between individuals in favor of free trade, federalism, and anticlericalism (the Liberals) and those who favored protectionism for nascent industry, centralism, and clericalism (the Conservatives). In most countries these original party divisions have long since disappeared, replaced by other cleavages.

With accelerating social and economic change in most countries of Latin America the emergence of new social strata in the 1920s and 1930s led to the founding of new political parties. Some of these attracted the growing middle sectors, who were quite reformist in the early years but later changed as they became part of the system. In other cases new parties were more radical, calling for a basic restructuring of society and including elements from the working classes. Some of these originally radical parties were of international inspiration; most of the countries have had Communist and socialist parties of differing effectiveness and legality. Other radical parties were primarily national ones, albeit with ideological inspiration traceable to Marxism.

One such party, founded in 1923 by the Peruvian Víctor Raúl Haya de la Torre, was the American Popular Revolutionary Alliance (APRA). Although APRA purported to be the beginning of a new international association of like-minded democratic-left individuals in Latin America, this goal was never fully reached. At the same time, inspired by Haya and APRA, a number of similar national parties were founded by young Latin Americans. The most successful APRA-like party was Democratic Action (AD) in Venezuela, but many of the same programs have been advocated by numerous other parties of this type, including the Party of National Liberation (PLN) in Costa Rica and the National Revolutionary Movement (MNR) in Bolivia, as well as parties in Paraguay, the Dominican Republic, Guatemala, Honduras, and Argentina. Only in Venezuela and Costa Rica did the APRA-like parties come to power more than temporarily, and in a much less radical form. They favored liberal democracy, rapid reform, and economic growth. In most cases the APRA-like parties were led by members of the middle sectors, and they received much of their electoral support from middle- and lower-class ranks. APRA came to power in Peru in 1986, although founder Haya was no longer living.

A newer group of political parties was the Christian-Democratic ones, particularly successful in Chile, Venezuela, Costa Rica, Nicaragua, and El Salvador. These parties often call for fundamental reforms but are guided by church teachings and papal encyclicals rather than Marx or Engels, even though they are nondenominational and open to all. The nature of the ideology of these parties varies from country to country.

Other parties in Latin America have been based on the leadership of one or few persons, and hence do not fit into the neat party spectrum just described. Quite often the "man on horseback" was more important than the program of a party. This tradition of the *caudillo* was seen in Brazil, where Getúlio Vargas founded not one but two official political parties; in Ecuador, where personalistic parties have been strong contenders for the presidency; and in Communist Cuba, where in the 1960s the party was more Castroist than Communist. In Venezuela former military coup leader Hugo Chávez personalized not only a presidency but an entire change of government structure.

The system of co-optation further complicates the attempt at classification. How is one to classify a political party, traditional in origin, that includes at the same time large landowners and the peasants tied to them, as well as trade union members organized by the party with the assistance of parts of the clergy? How does one classify a party such as the Mexican Institutional Revolutionary party (PRI), which until the mid-1990s made a conscious effort to co-opt and include all politically relevant sectors of the society?

With the increasing number of popularly elected governments in Latin America in the 1990s, political parties generally became more important than before. Democracy only exists if there is real competition between candidates, and throughout the world political parties have been the organizations that have presented such rival candidates. However, in some Latin American countries (Peru and Venezuela, for example) political parties are held in such low esteem that attempts have been made to have democracy without parties.

In addition to the traditional questions posed about parties in Latin America (the number of major parties, their programs and policies, the nature of electoral laws, the relationships between parties and the military) we need to ask questions posed all over the world in democracies. How are parties funded? Do they come up with programs and follow them after the elections? Are voters well informed about political party activities by the mass media? Are those countries that are trying to have democracy without parties having any success?

Conclusions and Implications

The preceding discussion has indicated that there have been many politically relevant groups in Latin America and that they use various means to secure and retain political power. Yet at least two other themes should be introduced that tend to complicate the picture.

First, it should be noted that the urban poor—outside the labor unions— have not been included in the discussion. This shows one of the biases of the system. Traditionally, a necessary first step in attaining political relevance is being organized. This means that potential groups, especially poorly educated and geographically dispersed ones like the peasants and the urban poor, face difficulties in becoming politically relevant because they have difficulties in organizing themselves or being organized from the outside. These tend to be the weakest groups in politics although they are often numerically the largest.

Second, not all politically relevant groups fall into the neat categories of this chapter. Anthony Leed's research in Brazil has shown (at least in small towns, probably larger cities, and even perhaps the whole nation) a politically more relevant series of groups to be the patronage and family-based panelin-has ("little saucepans").[9] The same kind of informal family-based networks exist in other countries. These groups are composed of individuals with common interests but different occupations—say, a doctor, a large landowner, surely a lawyer, and a governmental official. The panelinha at the local level controls and endeavors to establish contacts with the panelinha at the state level, which might have contacts with a national panelinha. Of course, at the local level there are rival panelinhas, with contacts with like-minded ones at the state level, with contacts in the national patronage system as well. As is generally the case with such patrimonial-type relations, all interactions (except those within the panelinhas themselves) are vertical, and one level of panelinha must take care to ally with the winning one at the next higher level if it wants to have political power.

Similar research in other countries has revealed a parallel pattern of informal, elitist, familial, patronage politics. Whether called the panelinha system as in Brazil or the camarilla system as in Mexico, the process and dynamics are the same. The aspiring politician connects himself with an aspiring politician at a higher level, who is connected with an aspiring . . . and so forth on up to an aspiring candidate for the presidency. If the person in question becomes president, the various levels of camarillas prosper; if he remains powerful without becoming president, the camarillas continue functioning in expectation of what will take place at the next presidential election; but if the aspiring candidate is disgraced, is dismissed from the official party, or dies, the whole system of various levels of camarillas connected with him disintegrates. The camarilla system operates outside of but overlapping the formal structure of groups and parties described here.

This discussion of panelinhas and camarillas raises the question of whether U.S.-style interest groups and political parties are operating and are important in Latin America, or if they are operating in the same way. The answer is: They are and they aren't. In the larger and better-institutionalized systems, the parties and interest groups are often important and function not unlike their North American or European counterparts. However, in the less-institutionalized, personalistic countries of Central America (and even behind the scenes in the larger ones), family groups, cliques, clan alliances, and patronage networks frequently are more important, often disguised behind the appearance of partisan or ideological dispute. One must be careful therefore not to minimize the importance of a functional, operational party and interest-group system in some countries, while recognizing that in others it is often the less formal network through which politics is carried out.

Notes

1. Charles W. Anderson, *Politics and Economic Change in Latin America: The Governing of Restless Nations* (New York: Van Nostrand, 1967), especially chapter 4.

2. See David Collier, ed., *The New Authoritarianism in Latin America* (Princeton, NJ: Princeton University Press, 1979).

3. Peter H. Smith, *Democracy in Latin America: Political Change in Comparative Prospective* (New York: Oxford University Press, 2005), 103.

4. José Nun, "The Middle Class Military Coup," in *The Politics of Conformity in Latin America*, ed. Claudio Véliz (London: Oxford University Press, 1967), 66–118.

5. This section is based on Donna Lee Van Cott, "Latin America: Indigenous Movements," in the *Encyclopedia of Nationalism*, vol. 2 (San Diego: Academic Press, 2000). Our thanks go to Dr. Van Cott for her assistance in this section.

6. Mala N. Htun, "Women's Political Participation, Representation, and Leadership in Latin America," in *Women's Leadership Conference of the Americas*, Issue Brief, http://www.iadiaglo.org/htunpol.html, 9/22/99. All of the analysis that follows is based on this source.

7. This section is based on suggestions from Dr. Vanessa Gray. Our thanks go to Dr. Gray for her assistance in this section.

8. Smith, 176.

9. Anthony Leeds, "Brazilian Careers and Social Structure: A Case History and Model," *American Anthropologist* 66 (1964): 1321–1347.

4

Government Machinery, the Role of the State, and Public Policy

Neither the classic Marxian categories nor the theory of liberalism gave more than secondary importance to the role of the state. In the Marxian paradigm the state or governmental system was viewed as part of the superstructure that was shaped, if not determined, by the underlying structure of class relations. In the liberal model the state was generally conceived as a referee, umpiring the competition among the interest groups while not itself participating in the game—a kind of "black box" intermediary into which the "inputs" of the system go in the form of competing interests and pressures and from which come "outputs" or public policies. Neither of these two classic models adequately explains the Latin American systems.

In Latin America the state historically held an importance that it lacks in the classic models. The state was viewed as a powerful and independent agency in its own right, above and frequently autonomous from the class and interest-group struggle. Whether in socialist regimes such as Cuba's or capitalist ones like Brazil's, it was the state and its central leadership that largely determined the shape of the system and its developmental directions.

The state did not merely reflect the class structure but rather, through its control of economic and political resources, itself shaped the class system. The state was viewed as the prime regulator, coordinator, and pacesetter of the entire national system, the apex of the Latin American pyramid from which patronage, wealth, power, and programs flowed. The critical importance of the state in the Latin American nations helped explain why the competition for control of it was so intense and sometimes violent.

Related to this was the contrasting way citizens of North America and Latin America tended to view government. In North America government has usually been considered something of a necessary evil requiring elaborate checks and balances. Political theory in Iberia and Latin America, in contrast, viewed government as good, natural, and necessary for the welfare of society. If government was good, there was little reason to limit or put checks and balances on it. Hence, before we fall into the trap of condemning Latin America for its powerful autocratic executives, subservient parliaments, and weak local government, we must remember the different assumptions on which the Latin American systems are based.

With the neoliberal changes of the 1990s and at present, there has been a change in the procedures about which much of Latin American politics revolve. The fundamental issues are still who controls the state apparatus and the immense power, patronage, and funds at its disposal, and the ongoing efforts of the state or strong presidents to expand their power. However, now there are also issues of how much of the old corporatist structure will be retained, if any; how neoliberal or civil society dominates the political and economic systems; and how the historically powerful role of the state can be harmonized with the new demands for limited government, privatization, and democracy.

The Theory of the State: Constitutions and Legal Systems

After achieving independence early in the nineteenth century, the Latin American nations faced a severe legitimacy crisis. Monarchy was a possibility (and some nations did consider or experiment briefly with monarchical rule), but Latin America had just struggled through years of independence wars to rid itself of the Spanish imperial yoke, and monarchy had been discredited. Liberalism and republicanism were attractive and seemed the wave of the future, but Latin America had no prior experience with liberal or republican rule.

The solution was ingenious, though often woefully misunderstood. The new nations of Latin America moved to adopt liberal and democratic forms, while at the same time preserving many of the organic, elitist, and authoritarian principles of the colonial tradition. The liberal and democratic forms provided goals and aspirations toward which society could strive; they also helped present a progressive picture to the outside world. But these principles were circumscribed by a series of measures, authoritarian in content, that were truer to the realities and history of the area and to its existing oligarchic power relationships.

Virtually all the Latin American constitutions have provided for the historical three-part division of powers among executive, legislature, and judiciary. However, in practice the three powers are not coequal and were not intended to be. The executive is constitutionally given extensive powers to bypass the legislature, and judicial review until recently has been largely outside the Latin American legal tradition. The same kinds of apparent contradictions exist in other areas. Although one part of the constitution may be devoted to civilian institutions and the traditional three branches of government, another may give the armed forces a higher-order role to protect the nation, preserve internal order, and prevent internal disruption. However, the legislative branch is now increasing in power in many countries.

The same is true of human rights. Even though all the Latin American constitutions contain long lists of human and political rights, these same constitutions also give the executive power to declare a state of siege or emergency, suspend human rights, and rule by decree. The same applies to privilege. Although one section of the constitution may proclaim democratic and egalitarian principles, other parts may give special privileges to the church, the army, or the landed elites, and although representative and republican precepts are enshrined in one quarter, authoritarian and elitist ones are legitimated in another. Increasingly, however, human rights and democratic precepts are being incorporated into Latin American basic law.

None of this is meant to imply approval of human-rights violations or of overthrows of democratic governments; it is only to point out how these have often been perceived differently in Latin America. Hence, the real questions may concern the degrees of military intervention or limits on legislative authority and how and why these actions are taken. It has not simply been a matter of the military usurping the constitution, because it was often the constitution itself that gave the military the right—even obligation—to intervene in the political process under certain circumstances. Similarly, when human-rights violations are reported we must understand this within the Latin American constitutional and legal tradition as well as our own. Human rights have not been conceived as constitutional absolutes, and frequently there is a constitutional provision for their suspension. Recently, however, human rights as well as democracy in Latin America are being viewed more and more according to universal standards.

The most important issues of Latin American politics involve the dynamics of change and process from the Latin American as well as a global perspective. We cannot understand the region if we look only at the liberal and republican side of the Latin American tradition while ignoring the rest; nor should we simply condemn some action from the point of view of the North

American constitutional tradition without seeing it in the Latin American context. If the civil and military spheres are not strictly segregated as in the U.S. tradition, then what are their dynamic relations in Latin America, and what are the causes of military intervention? If strict separation of powers is not seen in the same light in Latin America and if the branches are not equal, what are their respective powers and interrelations? If hierarchy, authority, and special privilege have long been legitimated principles along with democratic and egalitarian ones, then how are these reconciled, glossed over, or challenged—and why? And how are these relations all changing as Latin America enters a more democratic era?

The Latin American constitutions are misunderstood in another way that has to do with their sheer number. The number of constitutions (thirty or more in some countries) ignores the fact that in most of the countries a new constitution is generally promulgated whenever a new amendment is added or when a major new interpretation requires official legitimization. The facts are, first, that the Latin American constitutional tradition has been far more stable than the number of constitutions implies, and second, that in most countries of the area there are only two main constitutional traditions, the one more centralized and even authoritarian and the other liberal and democratic, with the trend now increasing toward the democratic side. The many constitutions, then, signify the repeated alternations between these two basic traditions, with variations.

These perspectives on the constitutional tradition also provide hints as to the distinct legal tradition of Latin America. Whereas in the United States laws and constitutions are based on a history and practice derived from British common law, those of Latin America derive from a code-law tradition. This difference has several implications. Where the U.S. legal system is founded on precedent and reinterpretation, the Latin American codes are complete bodies of law allowing little room for precedent or judicial reinterpretation. The codes are fixed and absolute; they embody a comprehensive framework of operating principles; and unlike the common-law tradition with its inductive reasoning based upon cases, enforcement of the codes implies deductive reasoning. One begins not with facts or cases but with general truth (the codes or constitution) and then deduces rules or applications for specific circumstances from this.

Although one should not overstress the point and although mixed forms exist throughout Latin America, an understanding of the code-law system and its philosophical underpinnings carries us a considerable distance toward understanding Latin American behavior. The truths embodied in the codes and constitutions and the deductive method have their origins and reflection in the Roman, medieval, and Catholic-scholastic tradition. The authoritarian, absolutist nature of the codes also finds reflection in (and helps reinforce) an absolutist, historically authoritarian political culture. The effort to cover all contingencies with one code or to engage in almost constant constitutional engineering to obtain a "perfect" document tends to rule out the logrolling, compromise, informal understandings, and unwritten rules that lie at the heart of U.S. or British political culture. Because courts and judges, in their role as applicators and enforcers of the law rather than creative interpreters of it, are bureaucrats and bureaucratic agencies, they do not enjoy the respect their counterparts do in the United States, thus making judicial review and even an independent judiciary difficult at best. These precepts and practices are changing as Latin America becomes more democratic and as U.S. legal precepts are incorporated in Latin American law.

Executive-Legislative-Judicial Relations

Power in the Latin American systems has historically been concentrated in the executive branch, specifically the presidency. Terms like continuismo (prolonging one's term of office beyond its constitutional limits), personalismo (emphasis on the person of the president rather than on the office), to say nothing of machismo (strong, manly authority) are all now so familiar that they form part of our own political lexicon. The present-day Latin American executive is heir to an imperial and autocratic tradition stemming from the absolute, virtually unlimited authority of the Spanish and Portuguese crowns. Of course, modern authoritarianism has multiple explanations for its origin (a reaction against earlier mass mobilization by populist and leftist leaders, the result of stresses generated by modernization, and the strategies of civilian and military elites for accelerating development) as well as various forms (caudillistic and more institutionalized arrangements). In any case the Latin American presidency has long been an imperial presidency in ways that no president of the United States ever conceived.

The formal authority of Latin American executives is extensive. It derives from a president's powers as chief executive, commander in chief, and head of state, and from the broad emergency powers to declare a state of siege or emergency, suspend constitutional guarantees, and rule by decree. The presidency has been a chief beneficiary of many twentieth-century changes, among them radio and television, concentrated war-making powers, and broad responsibility for the economy. In addition many Latin American chief executives serve simultaneously as heads of state and presidents of their party machines. If the potential leader's route to power was the army, the president also has the enormous weight of armed might for use against foreign enemies and domestic foes. Considerable wealth, often generated because the lines between private and public wealth are not so sharply drawn as in North American political society, may also become an effective instrument of rule.

Perhaps the main difference lies in the fact that the Latin American systems, by tradition and history, are more centralized and executive oriented than those in the United States. It is around the person occupying the presidency that national life swirls. The president is responsible not only for governance but also for the well-being of society as a whole and is the symbol of the national society in ways that a U.S. president is not. Not only is politics concentrated in the office and person of the president, but it is by presidential favors and patronage that contracts are determined; different clientele are served; and wealth, privilege, and social position are parceled out. The president is the national patrón, replacing the local landowners and men on horseback of the past. With both broad appointive powers and wide latitude in favoring friends and those who show loyalty, the Latin American president is truly the hub of the national system. Hence, when a good, able executive is in power, the system works exceedingly well; when this is not the case, the whole system breaks down.

Various gimmicks have been used to try to limit executive authority. Few have worked well. These range from the disastrous results of the experiment with a plural (nine-person government-by-committee) executive in Uruguay to the varied unsuccessful efforts at parliamentary or semiparliamentary rule in Chile, Brazil, Cuba, and Costa Rica. Constitutional gimmickry has not worked in limiting executive rule because it has been an area-wide tradition and cultural pattern that is, in effect, not just some legal article. Spreading democracy in Latin America is now forcing most presidents to work within a constitutional framework.

The role of the congress in such a system has not historically been to initiate or veto laws, much less to serve as a separate and coequal branch of government. Congress's functions can be understood if we begin not with the assumption of an independent branch but with one of an agency that has historically been subservient to the president and, along with the executive, a part of the same organic, integrated state system. The congress's role was thus to give advice and consent to presidential acts (but not much dissent), to serve as a sounding board for new programs, to represent the varied interests of the nation, and to modify laws in some particulars (but not usually to nullify them). The legislature was also a place to bring some new faces into government as well as to pension off old ones, to reward political friends and cronies, and to ensure the opposition a voice while guaranteeing that it remained a minority. In recent years, however, the congress in several Latin American countries has acquired newfound power and autonomy.

In some countries (Chile, Colombia, Costa Rica, Venezuela) the congress has long enjoyed considerable independence and strength. A few congresses have gone so far as to defy the executive—and gotten away with it. In 1992–1993, congresses in both Brazil and Venezuela removed the president from office for fiscal improprieties. The congress may serve additionally as a forum that allows the opposition to embarrass or undermine the government, as a means of gauging who is rising and who is falling in official favor, or as a way of weighing the relative strength of the various factions within the regime.

Many of the same comments apply to the courts and court system. First, the court system has not historically been a separate and coequal branch, nor was it intended or generally expected to be. Many Latin American supreme courts would declare a law unconstitutional or defy a determined executive only at the risk of embarrassment and danger to themselves, something the courts have assiduously avoided. Second, within these limits the Latin American court systems have often functioned not entirely badly. Third, the courts, through such devices as the writ of *amparo* (Mexico and Argentina), popular action and *tutela* (Colombia), and *segurança* (Brazil), have played an increasingly important role in controlling and overseeing governmental action, protecting civil liberties, and restricting executive authority even under dictatorial regimes.

The court system had its origins in the Iberian tradition. The chief influences historically were Roman law; Christianity and the Thomistic hierarchy of laws; and the traditional legal concepts of Iberia, most notably the Siete Partidas of Alfonso the Wise. In Latin America's codes, lists of human rights, and hierarchy of courts, the influence of the French Napoleonic Code has been pronounced. In the situation of a supreme court passing (in theory at least) upon the constitutionality of executive or legislative acts, the U.S. inspiration is clear. At present the courts in various countries are increasing in power and beginning to assert themselves, but they often face problems of incompetence, corruption, and lack of adequate training.

It should be remembered, however, that what has made the system work is not so much the legislature or judiciary but the executive. The formally institutionalized limits on executive power in terms of the usual checks and balances are still not extensive and frequently can be bypassed. More significant has been the informal balance of power within the system and the set of generally agreed upon understandings and rules of the game beyond which even the strongest of Latin American presidents goes only at severe risk to his regime's survival. Nevertheless, the growing importance of congress and courts in many countries is a subject for further study.

Local Government and Federalism

Federalism in Latin America emerged from exactly the reverse of the situation that existed in the United States. In the United States in 1789 a national government was reluctantly accepted by thirteen self-governing colonies that had never had a central administration. In Latin America, by contrast, a federal structure was adopted in some countries (Argentina, Venezuela, Mexico, Brazil) that had always been centrally administered.

Although these four nations were federal in principle, the central government reserved the right to "intervene" in the states. As the authority of the central government grew during the 1920s and 1930s its inclination to intervene also increased, thereby often negating the federal principle. Over a long period these major countries were progressively centralized with virtually all power concentrated in the national capital. Nevertheless, the dynamics of relations and tensions between the central government and its component states and regions, who still have some independent autonomy, make for one of the most interesting political arenas. Recently there have been pressures to decentralize, but in all countries the central state remains dominant.

The Latin American countries are structured after the French system of local government, with virtually all power concentrated in the central government and its ministries and authority flowing from the top down. Local government is ordinarily administered through the ministry of interior, which is also responsible for the national police. Almost all local officials historically were appointed by the central government and served as its agents at the local level.

Local governments have almost no power to tax or to run local social programs. These activities are generally administered by the central government according to a national plan. This system of centralized rule is also a means of concentrating power in oftentimes weak and uninstitutionalized nations.

Yet even though the theory has been that of a centralized state, the reality in Latin America has always been somewhat different. The Spanish and Portuguese crowns had difficulty enforcing their authority in the interior, which was far away and virtually autonomous. With the withdrawal of the Crown early in the nineteenth century centrifugal tendencies were accelerated. Power drained off into the hands of local landowners or regional men on horseback, who competed for control of the national palace. With a weak central state and powerful centrifugal tendencies a strong de facto system of local rule did emerge in Latin America, contrary to what the laws or constitutions proclaimed.

Thereafter, nation-building in Latin America often consisted of two major tendencies: populating and thus "civilizing" the vast empty interior and extending the central government's authority over the national territory. Toward the end of the nineteenth century national armies and bureaucracies were created to replace the unprofessional armed bands under the local *caudillos*, national police agencies enforced the central government's authority at the local level, and the collection of customs duties was centralized. Authority became concentrated in the central state, the regional isolation of the patria chica broke down as roads and communications grids were developed, and the economy was similarly centralized under the direction of the state.

In most of Latin America the process of centralization, begun in the 1870s and 1880s, is still going forward. Indeed, that is how development is often defined throughout the area. A developed political system is one in which the central agencies of the state exercise control over the disparate and centrifugal forces that comprise the system. In many countries this process is still incomplete, so that in the vast interior, in the highlands, in diverse Indian communities, and among some groups (such as landowners, large industrialists, the military, and big multinationals), the authority of the central state is still tenuous. Even today isolated areas (especially those in the rugged mountains or tropical jungles) often have little governmental presence. Local strongmen—sometimes guerrillas or drug traffickers—may be more powerful than the national government's representatives. Indeed, the efforts of the central government to extend its sway over the entire nation constitute one of the main arenas of Latin American politics. Conversely, the local units (be they regions, towns, parishes, or Indian communities) still attempt to maintain some degree of autonomy. Centralization and decentralization are often going forward at the same time.

Fourth Branch of Government: The Automous State Agencies

One of the primary tools in the struggle to centralize power in Latin America from the 1930s to the 1980s was the government corporation or the autonomous agency. The growth of these agencies in many ways parallels that of the "alphabet agencies" in the United States, giving the central government a means to extend its control into new areas. These agencies became so large and so pervasive that they could be termed a separate branch of government. Some Latin American constitutions recognized them as such.

The proliferation of these agencies was such that in some countries they numbered in the hundreds. Many were regulatory agencies, often with far broader powers than their North American counterparts, with the authority to set or regulate prices, wages, and production quotas. Others administered vast government corporations, among them steel, mining, electricity, sugar, coffee, tobacco, railroads, utilities, and petrochemicals. Still others were involved in social programs: education, social security, housing, relief activities, and the like. Many more participated in the administration of new services that the state had been called upon to perform, such as national planning, agrarian reform, water supplies, and family planning.

The purposes for which these agencies were set up were diverse. Some, such as the agrarian-reform or family-planning agencies, were established as much to please the U.S. government and to qualify a country for U.S. and World Bank loans as to carry out agrarian reform or family planning. Others were created to bring a recalcitrant or rebellious economic sector (such as labor or the business community) under government control and direction. Some were used to stimulate economic growth and development, to increase government efficiency and hence its legitimacy, or to create a capitalist structure and officially sanctioned entrepreneurial class where none had existed before. They also enabled more job seekers to be put on the public payroll.

The common feature of these myriad agencies was that they tended to serve as agents of centralization in that historic quest to "civilize" and bring order to what was, in the past even more than now, a vast, often unruly, near-empty territory with strong centrifugal propensities. The growth of these agencies, specifically the government corporations, meant that the degree of central state control and even ownership of the means of production increased significantly as well. As a result it is a fundamental mistake to think of the Latin American economies as private enterprise-dominated systems. It is not just Cuba that had a large public sector; in fact, all the Latin American economies were heavily influenced by the state.

This phenomenon had important implications. It meant the stakes involved in the issue of control of the central government, with the vast resources involved, were very high. It also implied that very rapid structural change was readily possible. In countries where between 40 and 60 percent of the GNP (far higher than in the United States) was generated by the public sector and where so much power was concentrated in the central state, the transformation from a state-capitalist to a state-socialist system was relatively easy and could happen almost overnight (as in Cuba or Peru, for a time). All that was required was for a left or socialist element to capture the pinnacles of these highly centralized systems. At present this process is being reversed, as many Latin America countries move toward privatization.

The growth of all these centralized state agencies had another implication deserving mention. Although established as autonomous and self-governing bodies, the state corporations had in fact become heavily political agencies. They provided a wealth of sinecures, a means to put nearly everyone on the public payroll. They were giant patronage agencies by which one rewarded friends and cronies and found places for (and hence the loyalty or at least neutrality of) the opposition. Depending on the country, 30 to 50 percent of the gainfully employed labor force worked for the government. Many of the agencies were woefully inefficient, and the immense funds involved provided nearly endless opportunities for private enrichment from the great public trough. In performing these patronage and spoils functions, the state agencies preserved the status quo because large numbers of people, indeed virtually the entire middle class, were dependent upon them for their livelihood and opportunities for advancement. It is not surprising that a significant part of the debt problems faced by many Latin American countries came from state agencies—not the national governments—receiving foreign loans.

Today the Latin American countries are trying to solve the problems of corruption, inefficiency, and over-centralization. With the neoliberal reforms of the 1990s, and continuing today, governments have reduced the number and role of decentralized agencies. Many that were in productive activities have been privatized. In the process the benefits for poorer people in the countries have been reduced, as well as the number of jobs available to be passed out to political supporters.

Public Policy and the Policy Process

By public policy we mean the actions of groups and leaders in authority to implement their decisions. No political system is completely successful in accomplishing what it wishes, certainly the case in those societies that are underdeveloped politically and economically like the Latin American countries. Further, there are certain uniquely Latin American traits, over and above the area's underdeveloped character, that militate against effective public policies.

Major Issues of Public Policy

Most of the historic issues of the nineteenth century—the role of the church, centralism or federalism, free trade or protectionism—have been resolved or at least placed on the back burner in post–World War II Latin America. Although from time to time these old issues reemerge in some countries, the newer issues of economic development, agrarian reform, urban reform, and population growth largely replaced them in the last third of the twentieth century.

Economic Development.   One goal of almost all sectors in the Latin American political process is economic development, although the individual countries still sometimes disagree on its nature and the best way to obtain it. For some, economic development means no more than a growth in the national economy, with a resulting larger gross domestic product. In this conception the nature and structure of the economy would not change at all, only the size. The kinds of products would remain the same, and the nature of trade relations with the outside world would vary only slightly, albeit expanded in amount.

Other Latin Americans define economic development as the industrialization and diversification of their economies. Traditionally, Latin American countries have produced agricultural or other primary goods that are traded with the more developed countries of the North for industrial goods. Many Latin American countries have concentrated on only one such primary good. Although they might have comparative advantage in those primary products, the national economies suffered when there was a world oversupply of them and were also vulnerable to crop failures and to quotas fixed by the industrial nations.

By the early 1960s it became evident that there was a general decline in the relative value of all such primary goods. The long-term trend was for industrial articles to go up in price more rapidly than primary goods. Although a frost in Brazil might mean a short-term increase in the price of Colombian coffee, by the 1960s a tractor imported to Colombia from the United States cost more bags of coffee beans than it had twenty years before. Although this example did not pertain to Venezuelan oil between 1973 and 1982, almost all other Latin American countries lost income from the declining terms of trade.

The middle position on economic policy, then, would call for two major policies of an economic nature: industrialization and diversification. The former would be for the purpose of import substitution. Rather than importing industrial goods, the Latin American country imports capital goods and technology, which it then uses to produce the goods that formerly were imported. Further, to lessen the dependence on one crop, a government makes tax and credit decisions that will encourage production of goods other than the traditional one for export. This vision of a new, economically developed society is one in which more goods of greater variety are produced for export, while fewer manufactured goods are imported. Increased trade is an important facet of this policy, because hard currency is needed for the purchase of these capital goods.

By the late 1980s a new "neoliberal" policy emerged in many Latin American countries. To a certain extent it was like the traditional one, emphasizing products in which a nation had a comparative advantage. However, it also included privatization of government-owned enterprises and ending subsidies for the poor through pricing products at international levels. In the short run, at least, these new policies led to more unemployment and a greater disparity of income. The neoliberal leaders urged patience, but some politicians paid more attention to the cries of large numbers of suffering people. Hence, in recent years the new conflict (but in some ways much like the struggle of the 1930s) was between the Neoliberals and the supporters of the government-controlled economy.

Economic policy is often more complex than the preceding discussion indicates. What about inflation? Latin American countries have experienced "stagflation" (the combination of a stagnant economy and high inflation) for at least three decades, in its most acute form in the first half of the 1980s. Is this to be solved by monetary measures as the Neoliberals suggest (printing less money, balancing budgets, maintaining a balance of trade between imports and exports), or is the real cause for inflation a structural one, based on the declining terms of trade and the concentration of economic power in the small group at the top in most of the Latin American countries? If the reason is structural, more dramatic public policies are needed.

Another key question is: Who is to develop industry? The supporters of a strong role of the government suggest that national enterprise do it, whereas Neoliberals encourage foreign investment and multinational corporations. How will the generally negative balances of payment be redressed? What kinds of laws, if any, are needed to encourage the importation of capital goods and infrastructure materials while discouraging the purchase of consumer goods from foreign countries? If national industry is to be developed, how is capital to be generated? Is this to be done by stopping capital flight, by reducing consumption by the lower and middle classes through forced savings, or by some combination of techniques?

After October 1973 a new economic issue arose: the value of petroleum. For the oil-exporting countries (Venezuela, Mexico, Ecuador), the question became how best to use the new wealth while keeping inflationary pressures at a minimum and protecting national industry. For the petroleum importers the questions revolved around how to keep economic growth going while using more of the scarce hard-currency export earnings and reserves to purchase needed oil. Later, when oil prices declined, these economies also went into a tailspin.

By the early 1980s, whether these policy issues were successfully resolved or not, the question changed to how the debt crisis could or would be resolved. This crisis was caused by the energy crisis in two ways. First, all Latin American countries found, by the late 1970s, that private banks, recycling petrodollars invested by OPEC members, were willing to lend money at real interest rates (corrected for inflation) that were near or even below zero. The debts were impossible to repay, however, because recession in the industrial world in the early 1980s resulted in fewer Latin American exports being bought. Second, the oil-exporting countries (especially Mexico and Venezuela) contracted debts under the assumption that the price of petroleum would continue increasing. By 1982, however, the oil glut led to much lower prices for their exports.

By the late 1980s the new agenda revolved around the Neoliberal proposals to open markets, free trade, cut budgets, and have less protectionism. As in
the struggle between the traditional and democratic models of government
(see Chapter 5), the economic contest became one between individuals and
groups who had benefited from the old mercantilist system and those who
thought that they would benefit more from the Neoliberal one. At this writing it is not clear that where there is democracy the majority of the people
will consistently choose Neoliberal leaders.

More recently the issue has become globalization. With the end of the
Cold War and the decline in foreign aid, the Latin American economies are
on their own as never before. They must compete in global markets because no
one is there to give them aid or bail them out any more. Inefficiency, corruption, and patronage politics must all be tamed because they are costly and
make Latin America noncompetitive. Hence it is not just the United States or
the international lending agencies anymore that are pushing Latin America to
modernize and streamline, but often their own business sectors and educated
persons. Latin America must become a part of the global, competitive economy because it no longer has any choice in the matter.

Agrarian Reform.   A second major issue is that of the ownership of land,
which is very inequitably distributed, with a small number of very large landholders and a great number of landless, illegal squatters and owners of very
small holdings. Only in a few countries are there substantial numbers of middle-class farmers. During the 1960s, in large part because of the influence of
the United States and fear of an agrarian revolution (such as the Cuban one
was perceived to have been), many countries of Latin America set up agencies
to deal with the problems of land. Yet only in Nicaragua, Venezuela, and
Mexico were there significant land reforms, and even there very limited advances. Even though land reform is not the issue today that it had been in the
1960s, the problem still exists: Land ownership is very unevenly distributed,
and over eighty million Latin Americans live in the countryside under subhuman conditions. Guerrilla movements took root in many Latin American
countries because of the land problem, and in one—Nicaragua—the agrarian
problem was one of the reasons for the victory of the Sandinistas in July
1979. Since then some Latin American governments, often supported by the
AID, have continued to support land reform as a way to prevent revolutions.

One very important reason that more dramatic land reforms have not occurred is the power of the large landowners, who have been adept at preventing what they see as an attack on their property. In some countries, however,
the landowners have given up a little land—again the co-optation strategy—
to avoid giving up a lot. Another reason for the failure of land reform is the

lack of good technical information about who owns what land and what it is being used for. If the land were divided among peasants, would production go up or down? What would be the best crops? Which kinds of seeds and fertilizers would be best? What does the peasant need in addition to land?

Further, there are economic reasons for not breaking up the large tracts of land. The latifundios vary greatly in their use and economic output. If a sizable estate is not used or is used very inefficiently, any granting of the land to campesinos would lead to increased agricultural production for either national consumption or export. If, however, the estate is effectively utilized by the large landowner, the goals of land reform and increased agricultural production are, at least for the short run, in conflict. Moreover, there are certain agricultural products that have economies of scale—that is, they cannot be successfully grown on a family-sized farm. In this case agrarian reform means long-term lower production unless the land holdings are held collectively. There are both Spanish (the ejido) and Amerindian traditions of collective ownership of lands, and the Peruvian case shows such traditions being used through communal ownership. The Cuban case shows that state farms— those owned by the government with campesinos receiving wages for work— can be another alternative, although so far not a successful one.

Meanwhile, the agrarian issue has faded in importance. The fact is that Latin America is now more urban than rural, a reversal of the situation forty to fifty years ago when land reform was first offered as a solution. There are still immense social, economic, and political inequalities and inefficiencies in the Latin American countryside that need to be addressed, as the Brazilian Landless Movement illustrates. The appearance of the Zapatista National Liberation Army (Ejército Zapatista de Liberación Nacional, EZLN) in Chiapas, Mexico, in the mid-1990s demonstrated that there are still areas within Latin American countries in which the land issue still has major importance.

Nonetheless, with more and more people moving to the cities the land problem is not as important as it was, and it is unlikely that we will see any new agrarian revolutions succeeding in seizing national power. There are too few peasants for that to happen, and many of them are too unorganized to form a strong political movement. The peasants who would presumably stand to benefit from agrarian reform are themselves "thinking with their feet" by moving to the cities—or abroad.

Urban Reform.   With few jobs or little future in the rural areas, many people have left the countryside to seek a better life in the cities. There are both push and pull factors accounting for this internal migration. Some campesinos are pushed off the land, either because there are more children than the land can support or because the large landowners have mechanized production. Others are pulled to the cities by the better life that they believe will be found there. The movement has been dramatic: It is estimated that every year from 1970 to 1985 a population of some 8.75 million persons was incorporated into the cities of Latin America, and in the 1985–2000 period this increased to between 11 and 12 million per year. This urban growth affects the major cities, many of which doubled or tripled in size during the 1990s and continue their accelerated growth today.

Cities in Latin America were not prepared for such rapid growth; this was true of U.S. cities during similar growth periods at the end of the nineteenth century and the beginning of the twentieth. However, there are important differences. Unlike that of the United States and West Europe, Latin American urbanization was not accompanied by a surge of industrial growth. Not many of these new urbanites received jobs in industry. Only the lucky ones did, with others settling for hand-labor construction work and many more underemployed or unemployed. The political dimension was also different in Latin America, given the greater centralization of the state. Policies to meet the new problems of the cities were more likely to come from national than from city governments.

The problems that these national governments face are numerous and difficult. One is housing. Although some of the urban migrants rent rooms in large old houses where certain public utilities already exist, even more build makeshift homes in the open areas in and around the cities. Most of these new slums are built illegally on private or state-owned land and are completely devoid of such urban services as water, sewerage facilities, electricity, roads, and effective police and fire protection. Some studies have shown that the life expectancy is lower for the dwellers of these shantytowns than for the campesinos. Cities such as Mexico City, Rio de Janeiro, and São Paulo, among the very largest in the world, suffer from extreme pollution, rampant lawlessness, and other characteristics that make them unlivable for many residents.

Urban reform has so far failed to occur, partly because the urban poor have not yet developed effective political movements. Explanations offered for this situation include:

1. The new urban poor are too busy in the day-to-day attempt to make enough money to feed themselves and their children to have time for political activities.
2. People often develop a sense of community in the shantytowns that seems to provide considerable security.
3. Additional security is received from the extended family and from the ceremonial kinship relationship in which people slightly higher in the social structure are godparents of a person's children.

4. Close contact is maintained between the urban poor and the rural areas from which they came, allowing a possibility of returning if things get extremely bad economically.
5. A high percentage of the urban poor are engaged in service work and petty commercial activities, such as street vending, forming an atomized labor force without association with others like themselves.
6. Many who do obtain factory jobs work in very small factories, often of the cottage variety, with the owner filling the traditional patrón function.
7. Business people, industrialists, and governments participate in strategic activities designed to give the urban poor a bit of what they want.
8. The same elite groups participate in sanctions against the urban poor, who often have jobs in which they can be easily replaced by the unemployed if they engage in political activities.
9. Whether they will live longer or not, the new urban poor perceive themselves to be better off—or at least their children to be better off—than they have been in the countryside.

Whatever the precise reasons for lack of political influence of these lower-class urban residents, the flow of people into the cities has continued unabated.

Population Policy.   Another issue of Latin American politics is population growth. During the last quarter of the twentieth century Latin America had the highest growth rate in the world. Although the birthrate is higher in certain parts of Asia and Africa, death rates are lower in Latin America, and the result is a population growth rate for the area of roughly 3 percent per year. This of course varies from country to country. Argentina and Uruguay both increase in population at about 1.0 percent a year, roughly comparable to the United States. Other countries, such as Brazil and Mexico, grow at between 2 and 3 percent a year, which means that the population doubles every twenty-four to thirty-six years.

Population growth is related to another issue previously discussed. Economic growth must be at least equal to population growth for a country just to stand still in per capita income terms. If an increase in per capita income is a target, then it must be greater than the population growth rate. The Alliance for Progress of the 1960s led to impressive growth in the GDPs, but the GDP per capita gained only slightly in the face of population growth. Later, in the 1980s, population growth had slowed, but it came at the time of the "Lost Decade" of the economies, which grew very little.

One of the key reasons for population growth is increasing life expectancy and lower infant mortality rates, which have changed dramatically since

World War II. These improved rates are the result of better health care; education; more doctors; better sanitary conditions; and the eradication of some diseases, such as smallpox and malaria, through public-health programs. In many places the birthrate did not decrease dramatically, and life expectancy kept rising. The way to slow this growth, therefore, has to be through some control of the high birthrate.

Some countries (even strongly Catholic Colombia) have developed family-planning programs. Further, it has become evident that even in those countries that lack effective programs the birthrate has begun to fall. This decline seems related to increased urbanization, education, and knowledge concerning ways to limit family size, not necessarily to organized family-planning programs. After all, it may make some sense for a rural peasant to have lots of children, both to put to work in the fields and to take care of the parents (in nations that have few effective social-security programs) in their old age. However, for the urban poor the argument for more rather than fewer children makes less sense, and it is precisely in the urban areas that the population growth rate has begun to fall.

Constraints in Latin American Policymaking

In the previous section some of the major issues of Latin American public policy were considered. The aim of this section is to outline some of the constraints—conditions that affect political decisions as well as those that impede effective transition from policy outputs to policy outcomes.

Underdevelopment. The key feature of economic underdevelopment is that even a government wishing to change many things seldom has the revenue to do so. All allocative policies have money costs. If the governing coalition of a Latin American country decides that economic development through agrarian reform, urban reform, and birth control are desirable, there might not be enough money adequately to fund all policies.

In some instances in Latin America policymakers honestly cannot do all that they would like; in other cases legislation creates programs that are never funded. Governmental policy in Latin America, therefore, should be analyzed not only by studying established law but by looking at the actual expenditures of governmental revenues.

Yet another feature of underdevelopment, more political than economic, is the lack of bureaucratic expertise. Bureaucracies in Latin America have had one very important purpose: to provide white-collar, nonmanual employment for the members of the middle sectors, especially those who, in the absence of such employment, would be likely to join the political opposition. Because of this co-optive and patronage function, the bureaucracies of the area many times were not efficient in the day-to-day running of governmental programs. They contain people who have jobs only because of personal connections, people who do not have the necessary educational background, and people who hold multiple bureaucratic jobs, working only briefly or not at all in any one.

For this reason some governments of Latin America went the route of decentralized agencies set up for specific policies in an attempt to insulate them from the more corrupt regular bureaucracy. But in many countries even this has failed to produce an effective bureaucracy. Therefore, even in the case of a policy that is accepted by the ruling coalition and adequately funded, the policy consequence might not be what was intended.

The Neoliberals have called for smaller, more efficient, less corrupt bureaucracies. To a certain extent that has happened in many Latin American countries, albeit with considerable difficulties. No politician wants to cut his supporters out of the state bureaucracy; nor do most want to increase unemployment by laying off large numbers of bureaucrats. This is especially dangerous because most are highly educated and fairly well paid. Hence, they could contribute to the opposition with both money and technical expertise.

The Political System.   The rules of the traditional Latin American political game were described in Chapter 3. Here it is sufficient to repeat that a new group entering into the accepted circle of power groups traditionally needed to demonstrate that it would not do anything to harm already existing groups. This meant that many alternatives were closed for public policy by the rules of the game. In most countries of Latin America there were two possible ways to solve this dilemma. First, governmental policy could work in such a political system if the economy was expanding and steadily increasing governmental income. In such a case new revenues could be allocated to public policies in a distributive fashion—that is, by dividing up the bigger pie. Governments still had difficulties with such distributive policies because industrialists, for example, preferred that the new revenue used for urban reform, which benefited them little, be employed for infrastructure improvements (roads and railroads) that helped them economically.

However, the controversy over distributive policies was much less than that over redistributive ones—that is, policies that would take something away from one group and give it to another. For this reason land reform encountered many difficulties. It was not surprising that before the falling prices that accompanied the oil glut of the early 1980s, Venezuela had one of the most successful reformist governments in Latin America, made possible by governmental taxes on foreign oil producers (and after 1976 by profits made by the government oil enterprise), and one of the most successful agrarian reforms, using lands that the government already owned.

Yet not all the governments of Latin America had the luxury of participating in only distributive policies; many required redistributive policies as well. If the economy was stagnant or, even worse, if it was shrinking, there could hardly be any governmental programs at all. So a second possibility was a case-by-case, eclectic policy situation in which one group won on one policy issue, another group on another issue, and so forth. Although politically this was good short-run strategy, the long-term result often had contradictory effects, with detrimental ramifications for the economy, the people, and even the political system. Venezuela in the 1990s discovered that low prices for petroleum meant that a government that had long used distributive policies had to shift to redistributive ones. As the chapter on Venezuela shows, the shift was accompanied by mass dissatisfaction, bloodshed, attempted military coups d'état, the end of the political parties that had successfully brought democracy to the country for the first time in its history, the election of a populist president who had led a military coup d'état, and a constituent assembly to reform its democracy.

This dilemma of policymaking in the Latin American context was most evident in those countries where almost all individuals had organized into groups that had accepted the rules of the game. This was the case in Mexico,[1] and Argentina was at worst a situation of almost complete governmental stalemate or at best one of very eclectic and contradictory policies. Because all groups were politically relevant and involved and had agreed not to harm the interests of others, practically no agreed upon policy was possible.

It remains to be seen if the new movement to democracy in Latin America has changed this dilemma of policymaking. It might be that strong political parties will develop, with the result that majority rule will mean effective presidential-congressional collaboration with successful redistributive policies. On the other hand democracy might lead to executive-legislative gridlock, like the United States has had in recent years. In the 1990s Argentina seemed to have solved the problem to a considerable extent, while it remained to be seen what would happen in Mexico with increased democratization. Other countries seemed to alternate between sometimes effective policymaking and paralysis that led to gridlock.

The United States and the International Political Economy.   A third set of constraints on Latin American public policymaking relates to the position of these countries in a hemisphere dominated politically and economically by the United States and to their position in the international political economy. Some of the constraints on policymaking are dramatic, appearing on the front pages of newspapers. Guatemala in 1954 demonstrated that a Central American government could not enact a dramatic land reform adversely affecting U.S. business interests or launch a general social revolution backed by the local Communist Party without prompting a CIA-sponsored overthrow of the government. Eleven years later the case of the Dominican Republic showed that the U.S. government might intervene militarily even if a coalition about to come to power only appeared dangerous from a U.S. security ("another Cuba") point of view. Chile in the 1970s illustrated that no matter how geographically remote and economically unimportant a country might be to the United States, the "giant of the north" can intervene through both governmental and private business agencies. The obvious exception to these generalizations is Cuba, where U.S. opposition was foreseen and, through planning and the clear leadership of Fidel Castro the revolution survived. In Peru and Venezuela major U.S. properties were nationalized without provoking a Marine intervention. So far, however, these cases are the exceptions and not the rule. Nicaragua during the Sandinista regime (1979–1990) is another case of a country constrained in its policy options by U.S. intervention.

There are other, more subtle ways in which the United States manipulates Latin America. The AID uses its leverage to push certain programs: land reform in the 1960s, birth control in the 1970s, and private-sector initiatives in the 1980s and 1990s. Within these areas and elsewhere, AID officials often assist the Latin American governments in operational plans, although AID influence is much less now than it was thirty years ago. Likewise, international agencies, in part dominated by the United States, such as the World Bank, the IMF, and the IADB, traditionally encourage the Latin American governments to follow austerity-based economic and fiscal policy decisions. For example, the IMF might push a Latin American government to devalue its currency and tighten its belt. If the country refuses, World Bank and IADB loans become unlikely, AID will be hesitant to offer credit to the country, and even the private banks of the United States and Western Europe will be reluctant to extend credit.

During the 1970s and early 1980s, many Latin Americans accepted the argument of "dependency," that they were underdeveloped because the United States had exploited their resources, and therefore they needed to break the hold of this dependency on the United States. Regardless of the arguments of the dependency theorists, however, most Latin American governments recognize pragmatically that they must deal realistically with the United States. For better or worse, the United States is the major political and economic power in the hemisphere. Latin America is stuck in a dependency position, but it also desperately needs U.S. and other capital if it is to develop. Hence, the real question is not whether Latin America can dispense with the United States but whether the Latin American countries can reap some advantages from this re-lationship. Can they get the necessary capital and help from the United States without losing their sovereignty? That is the trick. To try to achieve that goal, clever Latin American presidents manipulate the U.S. Embassy as adeptly as the Embassy does the politics of the Latin American countries, particularly if they have commodities or strategic assets that the United States must have.

Conclusions and Implications

In the previous pages, we have generalized about the issues and constraints of public policy in Latin America. Although there are great commonalities among the Latin American countries on these matters, there are also notable differences. We suggest that the following questions be considered when reading the chapters about individual countries:

1. What are the major issues of public policy in the individual Latin American countries?
2. Which of these issues lead to governmental policies and which do not, and why?
3. What kinds of policies-distributive or redistributive-are designed?
4. What does the nature of the governing coalition suggest about which issues become policies?
5. How effective is the bureaucracy in translating official policy outputs into policy outcomes?
6. What are the major constraints on policymaking?
7. Who benefits from public policy: elites? the public?
8. How have globalization, trade, and economic interdependence changed the operating procedures and rules of the game?

We should warn that definitive answers to these questions should not al-ways be expected. The study of public policy in Latin America is primarily one of the last twenty years. The authors of the individual chapters have often been hindered by lack of empirical studies on which to base their conclusions, a condition that, it is hoped, will soon be rectified as new and better studies become available.

Note

1. Raymond Vernon, *The Dilemma of Mexico's Development* (Cambridge, MA: Harvard University Press, 1963).

5

The Struggle for Democracy in Latin America

In the preceding chapters we have made reference to how Latin America is becoming more democratic. While we maintain that position, we also feel that it is important to draw attention to the characteristics of democracy, a term that is really quite complex, and to the difficulties that Latin American countries have had in achieving and maintaining constitutional governments.

Democracy: A Simple Concept or a Complex One?

There is no doubt that, both in the world in general and in Latin America, the 1980s brought remarkable change. Communism collapsed in the Soviet Union, which then had elections and disappeared as a political system, replaced by a smaller Russia. In some countries of Asia and Africa dictatorships disintegrated and elections ensued. In Latin America the changes might have seemed less dramatic, although in the 1980s military dictatorships ended in Brazil, Ecuador, Bolivia, Argentina, Uruguay, Chile, and several of the Central American countries.

In Nicaragua internationally monitored elections saw the defeat of the candidate of the ruling Sandinista party, and even more remarkably that revolutionary party allowed the opposition candidate Violeta Barrios de Chamorro to take office. In Panama, albeit with the assistance of an intervention of the United States, strongman Manuel Antonio Noriega fell and the previously elected Guillermo Endara, whom Noriega had not allowed to take power, occupied the presidency. Finally, in Paraguay, Alfredo Stroessner—longest in power of the Latin American *caudillos*—fell to a military coup that immediately called for elections.

By 2006, of the twenty Latin America countries, only Cuba did not have an elected chief executive, which suggested that democracy had finally arrived as the dominant political system in Latin America. However, although elections are necessary for a country to be called a democracy, elections alone are not sufficient. Various Latin American dictators, including Anastasio Somoza Debayle in Nicaragua, had already shown that a nice electoral facade could make a country appear to be democratic, although fraud made it far from that.[1]

The history of elected governments in Latin America surely warns against assuming that having elections means that there is necessarily a democracy. Elections are often a good first step, but they are not the whole story. Within a cultural tradition that favored strong leadership more than institutional constraints on power, the region has often had elections without having democracy. Historically this has come about for four basic reasons: the limitation of suffrage on gender, educational, economic, or racial grounds; the restriction of voting rights of parties opposing the one in power; the qualification of the power of the elected executive by some other body, usually the military or foreign governments and multilateral institutions; and excessive executive power. But even if those four conditions are taken care of, a consolidated democracy means much more than elections, as will be discussed below.

In the first case, suffrage was sometimes restricted by race, but more often by either literacy or property ownership. Of course, in many countries the landless and uneducated tended to be Indians, blacks, mulattos, and *mestizos*, but there were also many whites who had the misfortune to fall into that category. As for the question of female suffrage, Latin American countries tended to be later than the United States in enfranchisement of women. However, by the 1960s there were few, if any, Latin American countries in which suffrage was not at least theoretically open to all.

Second, there have been many Latin American cases in which the vote was denied on the basis of political loyalties. At times this has been done by not allowing members of one political party to vote, while allowing members of another the prerogative to vote more than once (Colombia in the 1950s). In other cases the ability to vote as one pleases was constrained when the voting process was watched closely by the military (Venezuela in the early 1950s). Likewise, there have been instances when press freedoms were so restricted that opposition parties could not effectively get their views out to the electors (Nicaragua and El Salvador in the 1980s).

Third, there were countries in which all citizens apparently had the right to vote and there were few constraints on any candidate during the electoral process. However, afterwards the elected president was greatly restricted in his policy options by the military. Hence, in the 1960s, the Guatemalan military allegedly informed President Julio César Méndez Montenegro that he could do anything that did not affect either the military or the large landowners. In the 1990s the Sandinistas in Nicaragua placed similar restrictions on Violeta Barrios de Chamorro, protecting Sandinista labor unions and the military upon agreeing to let her take the presidency after her election in 1990. Sometimes the constraint might come from some foreign government or international organization. The 1960s were filled with events in which Latin American governments were constrained in their economic policies, especially those having to do with foreign businesses, by either the U.S. government, the World Bank, or the IMF, or the combination of the three. The most notable instance in the 1970s was the government of Salvador Allende in Chile, but the same limits, albeit in a different form, were seen in Argentina during the first years of the new millennium.

In the 1990s the constraints of that decade had more to do with the continuation of democracy. In 1992, for example, the United States reduced aid to Peru after President Alberto Fujimori suspended the congress and the judicial system. This policy was tempered in the new millennium, especially after terrorism became a priority of the U.S. government. However, the Organization of American States used its influence at times to maintain democracy, as seen in the cases of Ecuador and Paraguay.

Another aberration of democracy has been caused by excessive power of the president, with no real separation of powers or checks and balances. Hernando de Soto and Deborah Orsini were writing about Peru before the presidency of Alberto Fujimori (although it could be about other Latin American countries):

> The only element of democracy in Peru today is the electoral process, which gives Peruvians the privilege of choosing a dictator every five years. Rule making is subsequently carried out in a vacuum, with the executive branch enacting new rules and regulations at a clip of 134,000 every five years (an average of 106 each working day) without any feedback from the population.[2]

De Soto and Orsini argued that the contradictions in the political and economic systems impeded change in Peru. Those incongruities came from the presence of strong, entrenched interests, defended by a tiny minority of the population, which effectively prevented the majority from taking part in decision making.

The gridlock of this system led President Alberto Fujimori to disband congress and the courts in 1992, leading to international condemnation for ending "democracy." Guatemalan President Jorge Serrano tried to do the same in

1993. In this case the president failed for lack of support from the armed forces and was removed from power by them. Both cases show that, even though excessive executive power detracts from democracy in Latin America, on occasion the chief executive has attempted to increase his already overwhelming power.

Traditionally almost all Latin American countries have had constitutional ways for the president to acquire more power. Whether called "state of siege" or "state of emergency," these stipulations allow presidents to decree policy, in many cases without conferring with the congress or having the decrees subject to judicial review. Although the democratic idea of limited power is found in the constitutions of Latin American, so also are means for the chief executive to rule with almost unlimited authority.

The Definition of Democracy

Although elections are a necessary condition for a country to be considered a "democracy," they alone are not sufficient. Scholars disagree on what other characteristics a regime must have to meet that standard, although we would suggest the following characteristics that should exist for democracy to exist.[3]

First, constitutionally elected officials must effectively control government decisions. Second, the elections for those officials must be frequent and fair. Coercion cannot exist on a large scale if the criterion of free elections is going to be met.

Third, almost all adults must have the right to vote in these elections and, fourth, likewise they must have the right to run in them. There must be no danger in either voting or running for public office.

Fifth, citizens must have the right to express themselves about politics without fear of punishment. Sixth, they also must have the right to seek alternative sources of information, and such sources must exist and be protected by law. This suggests that the media must be allowed to publish and broadcast, unlike many cases in the past when states of siege or emergency have led to censorship.

Seventh, citizens must have the right to form independent organizations and groups, including political parties, civil societies, and interest groups. The stipulation of "independent" suggests that the government should not favor certain interest groups over others (as was characteristic of the ones that had been successfully co-opted), and should neither reward some with financial assistance nor punish some by using violence against them.

Eighth, the officials who are elected must be able to govern constitutionally without the veto power of unelected officials, such as the military. Ninth, the same officials must be able to act independently without outside constraints.

Tenth, power must not be controlled by one branch of government alone; rather, there should a system of checks and balances.

These constitute institutional requirements for democracy. However, some argue that a full democracy should also have a considerable degree of egalitarianism, a sense that all people are full citizens, not victims of class, racial, or gender discrimination. All should have a sense of participation, social and economic programs that are more or less just, and a certain civic consciousness that all people deal with each other in fair, impartial, and just ways. So although some of the Latin American countries may have the institutional apparatus of democracy, in many respects they are still far from having democratic societies.[4]

It is doubtful that any political system meets the ten institutional requirements perfectly. However, for purposes of comparison in the chapters that follow, it seems useful to measure how close the political systems of the Latin American countries come to them.

Consolidation of Democracy

A democracy is consolidated when people consider it "the only game in town." This means that, no matter how bad things get, the only option is to behave in a "democratic" way—that is, wait for the next election, contact representatives in government, use (if available) other constitutional methods such as recall elections. It does not mean occupying key roads and bridges (as happened in Argentina in 2000–2002), using the military to overthrow a president who is disliked (Ecuador several times in the first decade of the new millennium), or using economic power to get rid of a president, or at least pressure him to change policies (Venezuela in 2002).

A consolidated democracy is also one in which human rights are respected, there is true freedom of the media, and the government has effective law enforcement abilities. When all of these criteria are combined, just a few Latin American countries are "consolidated democracies," perhaps including in 2006 no more than Chile, Argentina, Uruguay, Brazil, and Costa Rica.

Challenges to Democracy

Constructing and maintaining a democracy is not an easy matter anywhere. As the Latin American countries face a possible democratic future, difficulties are likely to arise from a political tradition unfavorable to limited government, serious inequities of income distribution, the aftereffects of recent civil wars, and the absence of governments that can effectively implement policies for the nation as a whole.

The Political Tradition

Heralding the demise of Latin America's elitist, authoritarian, top-down, often antidemocratic political tradition, Mario Vargas Llosa, the Peruvian novelist and unsuccessful presidential candidate in 1990, called for

> the will to modernize, to clean up, and to cut the state down to the proper size for ensuring order, justice, and liberty. It means fostering the right to create wealth in an open system, based on merit, without bureaucratic privileges and interference. It also means that the state must assume responsibility for ensuring that each generation will enjoy that which, together with liberty, is the basis for democratic societies—namely, equality of opportunity.[5]

It might be anticipated that the groups that benefited from the old system would resist democracy, and if Latin American history of the 1970s and 1980s is any guide, the two major groups uncomfortable with the new rules of the game will likely be the military and the economic elite. Although evidence suggests that the civilian elites now see democracy as the best hope for stability, it still seems possible that, if elected governments in Latin America face serious economic difficulties, some members of the military will think of the traditional way of disposing of misbehaving governments—the military coup. There were two attempts to overthrow the elected president of Venezuela in the early 1990s, and the New York Times reported in January 1994 that many Brazilians were ready for the military to return to power because of economic problems and rampant corruption among civilian politicians. Yet with the passing of each year the probability of a military coup seems lower. In the first five years of the new millennium this happened in Ecuador, Bolivia, and Paraguay.

Pockets of Underdevelopment

Although very modern in many ways, all Latin American countries have large pockets of people living in abject poverty. The neoliberal economic changes, the end of protective tariffs, the privatization of state-owned industries, the reduction of support for the poor now occurring in the area are likely, at least in the short run, to increase the number of poor people through the unemployment caused when previously protected industries go bankrupt. In addition, some people with slightly higher living standards, such as owners of small businesses and bureaucrats, may oppose further change because they once benefited from the traditional state-capitalist economic system.

Even before the recent changes, socioeconomic inequalities seemed to some to make democracy unlikely in Latin America. Robert Wesson, for example, after listing the problems of ethnic divisiveness, low standards of living, disdain for politics, a weak or unfree press, poorly organized and narrow parties, unfair elections, politically powerful armies, weak institutions of higher education, traditions of strong leadership, the paternalistic state, and clientelist politics, argued that "one basic condition may account for most of the rest, and it is probably a sufficient condition to explain the difficulty of democracy in Latin America, although by no means the sole cause. This is inequality, the separation of the rich from poor or top from bottom, of educated from ignorant or illiterate, or refined and proud elite from despised masses."[6] The difficulty that this inequality creates for democracy is that "to expect the cultured and well-off would accede to major social changes because they are outnumbered and outvoted in elections of dubious honesty by the ignorant and impoverished—many of whom are undernourished and diseased—is unrealistic. That would require a society of saints with an unlikely degree of loyalty to democratic principles."[7] Ironically, since the Neoliberals see democracy and economic reform as interdependent, the poor and others who benefited from the mercantilist system may use the new democratic political regime to elect presidents and members of national congresses that are opposed to neoliberalism. This seems to have happened in the 1993 Venezuelan election of Rafael Caldera and the 1999 election of Hugo Chávez. Alternatively, the poor may turn to guerrilla violence, as Indians did in a post–Cold War revolutionary Zapatista National Liberation Army in early 1994, in Chiapas, Mexico.

The paradox of democracy lies in pitting representativeness against governability. Democracy implies an unwillingness to concentrate power in the hands of a few, and therefore subjects leaders and policies to mechanisms of popular representation and accountability. To be stable, however, a democracy must be able to act, sometimes quickly and decisively. Representativeness requires that parties and leaders speak to and for these conflicting interests; to be able to govern, parties must have sufficient autonomy to rise above them.[8]

A related contradiction of democracy likely to be important in Latin America is between consent and effectiveness. Democracy means literally "rule by the people." To be stable a democracy must be deemed legitimate by the people; they must view it as the best, most appropriate form of government for their society. This legitimacy requires a profound moral commitment and emotional allegiance, but these develop over time and partly as a result of effective performance. "Democracy will not be valued by the people unless it deals effectively with social and economic problems and achieves a modicum of order and justice."[9] This has been a problem in many Latin American countries as the neoliberal removal of customs barriers leads to large-scale unemployment of individuals who had jobs under the old, protected economies. The 2000 presidential elections in Mexico, for example, demonstrated how this could be a political issue. Even within the party in power opposition arose to the neoliberal changes, as their effects on the poor of the country became obvious.

The Legacy of Civil Wars

In many Latin American countries thousands have died in recent civil wars. Tension exists between conflict and consensus in any democracy, by its nature a system of institutionalized competition for power. As Diamond argues, "Hence the paradox: Democracy requires conflict—but not too much; competition there must be, but only within carefully defined and universally accepted boundaries. Cleavage must be tempered by consensus."[10] Many Latin American countries have suffered years of war before learning this lesson. Nowhere has the problem of conflict been more serious than in Mexico (albeit not since the 1920s) and Colombia, where there have been bloody civil wars between parties. Other countries have had civil wars at the beginning of their independent history but then moved on to less violent modes of competition. In the 1960s Marxist guerrilla groups chose armed conflict instead of electoral competition, and the resulting civil wars created a series of related problems for Latin American democracies.

It is especially difficult for a democratic government to deal with revolutionaries with different ethical standards. As Gustavo Gorriti has argued about countries with guerrilla challenges,

> The authorities in the threatened countries must confront the nightmarish realities that any Third World democracy faces when battling a determined group of ruthless insurgents. A well-planned insurgency can severely test the basic assumptions of the democratic process. While they provoke and dare the elected regime to overstep its own laws in response to their aggression, the insurgents strive to paint the very process they are trying to destroy as a sham. If ensnared in such perverse dynamics, most Third World democracies will find their legitimacy eroding, and may eventually cease to be democracies altogether.[11]

Democracy is abandoned altogether when a government under this pressure becomes involved in a "dirty war." A number of countries have had such wars, in which thousands of people have been murdered or simply "disappeared." In Argentina and Chile in the 1970s, in El Salvador in the 1980s, and in Colombia and Peru in the 1980s and 1990s, and still in Colombia today, the government, or at least the military, has been involved. Once the dirty war is over and democracy is restored, the question becomes to what extent violators of human rights in the previous period should be punished. Punishing the guilty (from the military, predominantly) may in turn threaten the democracy. As did Raúl Alfonsín in Argentina, many civilian presidents may pardon putative violators of human rights rather than risk making the military so angry as to intervene again.

Although during the 1960s most Latin American countries faced guerrilla threats, by 2006 only Colombia remained. Sendero Luminoso still existed in Peru, albeit with much less importance than before; and guerrillas still existed in the southern part of Mexico. Hence insurrections still existed. Where civil wars have only recently ended, the difficult task is to achieve consensus among erstwhile enemies. As has become apparent in El Salvador and Colombia, even though a government may grant amnesty to guerrillas, the people who suffered at their hands may not be ready to forgive and forget.

The Ability to Govern

As relatively poor countries with serious problems of transportation and communication, many Latin American countries have never been able to ensure the rule of law for the entire nation. Although quite democratic in the way in which their leaders are elected and their laws are written, they at best govern only the major cities. This weakness of government was exacerbated in Latin American countries with the emergence of the drug trade. Especially affected in this regard were Colombia, Peru, Bolivia, and Mexico. The ways in which the drug trade distorted democracy in her native Colombia have been described by María Jimena Duzán, herself a personal victim of it:

> Today in Colombia, we have had to take a stand against drug trafficking. Colombians, especially journalists, who deal with these themes know that at such times our democracy itself is at stake in the form of our freedom of expression and our right to dissent. . . . This is a terrorized political class that has delivered itself to the designs and money of the drug dealers. Those who stand up to the bosses and challenge them have fallen victim.[12]

In Peru the Marxist Sendero Luminoso (Shining Path) and the drug interests of the Upper Huallaga valley destabilized politics for ten years. In Bolivia one military dictator had very close connections to the coca-growers syndicate. Mexico, given its size and apparent stability, at times seemed less affected. However, its location made it a transit point to the United States, and some think that drug interests have infiltrated its government as much as they have in Colombia.

Conclusions

Peter Hakim and Abraham Lowenthal consider the Latin American countries to be generally ones in which "few nations have yet managed to develop strong representative institutions that can maintain the rule of law, protect the rights of all citizens, effectively respond to popular demands, and give ordinary people a continuing, active voice in public policy decisions."[13] Others would point out different obstacles to the transition to democracy. Racial, religious, and other minorities have a history of being victims of discrimination and lacking effective organizations to represent them. Women have typically been the casualties of a male-dominated system, although they are a majority of the Latin American population.

Optimists like Hakim and Lowenthal argue that even Colombia, with its serious drug-trafficking and guerrilla problems, continues to demonstrate resilience in its democracy. If they are right about a country that has been attacked by Marxist guerrillas since the early 1960s and threatened by the strongest and wealthiest drug organizations in the world, then perhaps democracy is solidly entrenched in Latin America for the first time. Perhaps this was best stated by Scott Mainwaring: "To put it simply, I am more struck than most observers by the positive political achievements of the past 20 years, and by the resilience of Latin America's elected governments in the post-1978 period. Since 1978, a sea change that has not been sufficiently appreciated has occurred in Latin American politics."[14]

Mitchell Seligson was also optimistic in suggesting three reasons that the current wave of democracy is likely to be stronger than previous ones. First, the record of the military during the bureaucratic-authoritarian period, during which human rights were violated as never before, makes it less likely that civilians will invite the generals back. Second, during that period the military showed that it was at least as inept as civilians. Economies were not well managed, and national debts soared beyond control. Third, civilian governments have taken power at a time that per capita income and literacy have reached the minimum necessary level in almost all countries of the region.[15]

More pessimistic observers would stress that all the Latin American countries face serious challenges; that corruption is rampant throughout the area; and that, although the military has been out of power in most Latin American countries for at least a decade, that is not long from the perspective of most nations. Decades or perhaps even generations will have to pass before we can conclude definitively that Latin America has joined the democratic world. Julio María Sanguinetti, president of Uruguay during its 1985–1989 transition from dictatorship to democracy, has compared contemporary Latin America to Europe after World War II:

> We in Latin America now face a somewhat similar challenge. Our success or failure will depend on us. At times we remain skeptical, as when we see social groups making unrealistic demands, parties splitting up, leaders assuming messianic pretensions, and drug dealers challenging the state itself. Yet we are also optimistic, because we feel that as a hemisphere born in liberty, we are not condemned to a lesser share of stability and prosperity than the rest of the world.[16]

Yet there are likely to be many obstacles along the path to democracy in Latin America. Richard Millett might have been predicting what would happen in many countries, including Venezuela in 1999 (in which Hugo Chávez, a colonel who had participated in an abortive military coup d'état, was elected president and called for a constituent assembly to write a new constitution amid economic problems), when he argued,

> Today, the greatest threat to democracy comes not from the military, not from domestic radicals, not from foreign intervention, but from the potential loss of faith in the process by a nation's own population. Despair, fueled by mounting economic and social problems, by government gridlock and rampant corruption, undermines efforts at democratic consolidation. Lack of opportunity, mass poverty, and deteriorating infrastructures threaten the social order in major urban centers. Frustration with the paralyzed judicial system, combined with rising levels of personal insecurity, makes citizens willing to consider a return to patterns of official oppression.[17]

Millett's conclusion was substantiated by a 2002 survey of 18,643 persons in eighteen countries. While 57 percent said that they preferred democracy over any other system of government, of these people 48.1 percent said that they preferred economic development over democracy and 44.9 percent said that they would be prepared to support an authoritarian regime if it was able to resolve the country's economic problems.[18]

As the following chapters of this book demonstrate, many Latin American countries have a coexistence of democracy and the "old system" of Creole politics. To the extent that the former system exists, the paradigm suggested by Charles Anderson (and presented here in Chapter 3) is still useful. To the extent that democracy has become the dominant system, a new paradigm for interpreting Latin America must be developed.

In assessing the process of democratization in the Latin American countries considered here, it will be helpful to focus on the following dimensions of democracy:

1. Constitutionally elected officials must control government decisions. They must be able to govern constitutionally without the veto power of unelected agents such as the military, and must be able to act independently without outside constraints.
2. Elections must be frequent and fair.
3. Almost all adults must have the right to vote.
4. Almost all adults must have the right to become candidates for public office without fear for their lives or their property.
5. Citizens must have the right to express themselves about politics without the fear of punishment.
6. Citizens must have the right to seek alternative sources of information, and such sources must exist and be protected by law.
7. Citizens must have the right to form independent organizations and groups, including political parties and interest groups, and the government should not favor certain interest groups over others.
8. All political power should not be concentrated in one person or group; rather, there should be separation of powers.
9. The human rights of people, especially the right to life, must be respected.

Notes

1. Calling anything with elections democracy, despite fraud, was labeled "electoralism" by Philippe C. Schmitter and Terry Lynn Karl, "What Democracy Is . . . And Is Not," *Journal of Democracy* 2, no. 3 (Summer 1991): 78.

2. Hernando de Soto and Deborah Orsini, "Overcoming Under-Development," *Journal of Democracy* 2, no. 2 (Spring 1991): 106.

3. This is stated quite clearly in Schmitter and Karl, "What Democracy Is," 81, quoting Robert Dahl, *Dilemmas of Pluralist Democracy* (New Haven, CT: Yale University Press, 1982), 11.

4. A study of Latin America that added other criteria to the institutional ones of democracy was Jorge I. Domínguez and Abraham F. Lowenthal, eds., *Constructing Democratic Governance: Latin America and the Caribbean in the 1990s* (Baltimore: Johns Hopkins University Press, 1996).

5. Mario Vargas Llosa, "The Culture of Liberty," in *The Global Resurgence of Democracy*, ed. Larry Diamond and Mark F. Plattner (Baltimore: Johns Hopkins University Press, 1993), 86.

6. Robert Wesson, *Democracy in Latin America: Promise and Problems* (New York: Praeger, 1982), 125.

7. Ibid., 130–131.

8. Larry Diamond, "Three Paradoxes of Democracy," *Journal of Democracy* 1, no. 3 (Summer 1990): 49.

9. Ibid.

10. Ibid.

11. Gustavo Gorriti, "Latin America's Internal Wars," *Journal of Democracy* 2, no. 1 (Winter 1991): 86–87.

12. María Jimena Duzán, "Colombia's Bloody War of Words," *Journal of Democracy* 2, no. 1 (Winter 1991): 105.

13. Peter Hakim and Abraham F. Lowenthal, "Latin America's Fragile Democracies," *Journal of Democracy* 2, no. 3 (Summer 1991): 26.

14. Scott Mainwaring, "The Surprising Resilience of Elected Governments," *Journal of Democracy* 10, no. 3 (July 1999): 101.

15. Mitchell A. Seligson, "Democratization in Latin America: The Current Cycle," in *Authoritarians and Democrats: Regime Transition in Latin America*, ed. James M. Malloy and Mitchell A. Seligson (Pittsburgh: University of Pittsburgh Press, 1987), 9–10.

16. Julio María Sanguinetti, "Present at the Transition," in *The Global Resurgence of Democracy*, ed. Larry Diamond and Mark F. Plattner (Baltimore: Johns Hopkins University Press, 1993), 59.

17. Richard L. Millett, "Is Latin American Democracy Sustainable?" *North-South Issues* 2, no. 3 (1993): 6.

18. United Nations Development Programme, *Democracy in Latin America: Towards a Citizens' Democracy* (New York, United Nations, 2005), 52. http://www.undp.org/democracy_report_latin_america/Ideas_and_Contributions.pdf. Last visited January 16, 2006.

PART II

The Political Systems of South America

NICARAGUA

Caribbean Sea

CANAL AREA

COSTA RICA

PANAMA

Medellín

Bogotá ★

Cali

COLOMBIA

★ Caracas

VENEZUELA

GUYANA

Georgetown ★

SURINAM

Paramaribo ★

FRENCH GUIANA

Cayenne ★

ATLANTIC OCEAN

Quito ★

ECUADOR

PERU

Lima ★

La Paz ★

BOLIVIA

★ Sucre

BRAZIL

Fortaleza ●

Recife ●

Salvador ●

★ Brasília

Belo Horizonte ●

PARAGUAY

Asunción ★

São Paulo ●

Rio de Janeiro ●

PACIFIC OCEAN

Pôrto Alegre ●

CHILE

Santiago ★

URUGUAY

Buenos Aires ★

Montevideo ●

ARGENTINA

Falkland Islands
(Islas Malvinas)

SOUTH AMERICA

6

Argentina in the Twenty-first Century

Linda Chen

Argentina began the twenty-first century in political and economic chaos. Its president had resigned in December 2001 after losing the support of his coalition partner and for failing to arrest the country's economic decline. What had been viewed as one of the most culturally advanced nations in Latin America, with a large middle class, high literacy rates, low rates of infant mortality, and beef a staple of nearly everyone's diet, was wracked by massive unemployment, rising levels of poverty, and the specter of hunger among its population. Buenos Aires, where over a third of Argentina's population lives, once viewed as the "Paris" of Latin America, with a thriving nightlife and cosmopolitan culture and where safety was never an issue, saw its inhabitants plagued by crime and kidnappings for ransom.

Politically, fully twenty years after its last military dictatorship ended in 1983, Argentina's attempt at democratic institutionalization was still a work in progress. Raul Alfonsín, Argentina's first civilian president elected in the post-1983 era, left office early. Carlos Menem, his successor, manipulated constitutional changes to allow his reelection to a second term. Fernando de la Rúa, elected in 1999 to lead Argentina into the millennium, was ignominiously forced from office just two years later. What followed was a succession of three presidents elected by the Congress, all in the space of two weeks. Teetering near total collapse, Eduardo Duhalde was selected as president in January 2002 and served until 2003. The current president, Néstor Carlos Kirchner appears to have an excellent chance of serving out his term. Still, political stability remains a concern.

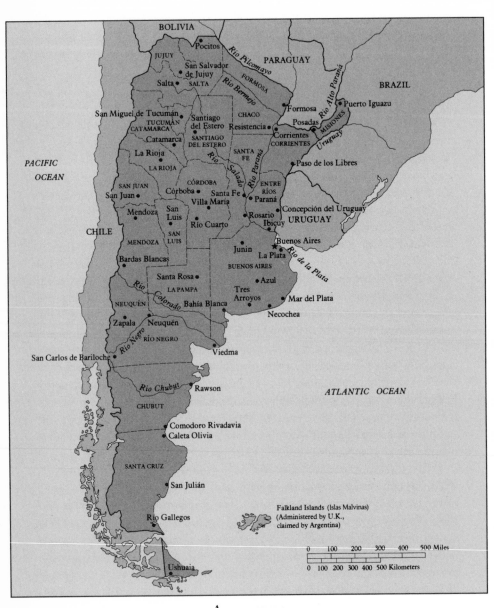

ARGENTINA

In the three years since the economic meltdown of 2001–2002 Argentina's economic indicators show a turn toward recovery. Real growth rates have averaged 8 percent in the past two years and, although this is expected to slow, growth is projected to stay on the positive side for the remainder of the decade. Inflation has been contained to single digit figures. Per capita income is now at $12,400, but the proportion of the population living below the poverty line is 44 percent. Unemployment, while decreasing from record high levels in the 2000–2002 period, stands at 13 percent in 2005. Whether this recovery can be sustained remains an open question.

The Land

Argentina's size (1.1 million square miles, or 2.77 million square kilometers) makes it about four times the size of Texas. Located in the southernmost part of South America in the area known as the Southern Cone, it faces the Atlantic Ocean to the east and has the Andean Mountains at its back. Its northern border, which it shares with Paraguay and Bolivia, is mostly tropical. Its southern area, which includes Patagonia, Tierra del Fuego, and (according to Argentine claims) a part of Antarctica, lies in the subpolar and polar zones.

Embracing so many climates as it does, Argentina is easily divided into many different regions, each with its own economic and social character. Most of the population and economic activity are found on the Pampa, a flat, open plain of rich soil, moderate rainfall, and temperate climate lying along the Atlantic coast and running into the country's midsection. This is where Argentina's principal exports—wheat, corn, and beef—are produced. It is also where Argentina's major cities and industries are located. Buenos Aires, the nation's federal capital and chief port, is an extensive metropolis of over thirteen million people. It dominates the rest of the country politically, economically, financially, and culturally. The porteños, as the residents of Buenos Aires are known, consider themselves much superior to their fellow citizens in the provinces, and indeed to all of Argentina's neighbors. Whatever may be the accuracy of such a claim, it is certain that Buenos Aires does tend to draw in much of the talent of southern South America. In addition to Buenos Aires, the Pampa includes other large industrial hubs such as La Plata (approximately 650,000 people), the capital of Buenos Aires Province; Córdoba (about 1.5 million), where much of the automobile industry is located; and Mar del Plata (about half a million), a popular beach resort on the Atlantic.

North of the Pampa lies another fertile plain, known as the Littoral because it lies between the Paraná and Uruguay Rivers. It is slightly warmer than the Pampa but still produces beef and grain crops. Having been settled later in time than the Pampa, it exhibits more evidence of planned colonization in the sense that there are fewer large estates and more medium-sized farms. The city of Rosario (about 1.3 million), situated on the Paraná River, is another major industrial center with a number of important oil refineries.

Beyond the Littoral is the tropical Northeast, much of it a frontier region only recently settled. The population is a mixture of Paraguayans, with their unique Guaraní language and customs, and Europeans. Traditionally, the economic mainstay of this region was yerba maté, a bitter green tea grown on large plantations that is very popular in southern South America. More recently, however, cotton and citrus crops have been introduced.

Proceeding west from the Pampa the traveler encounters a range of low mountains, similar to the Appalachians, in the western part of Córdoba province. Beyond these is the desert, as the land falls increasingly under the rain shadow of the Andes Mountains. There are oases lying due west, however, in a region known as Cuyo. The main city here is Mendoza (approximately one million), and the principal economic activities are wine growing and the cultivation of olives. Much of this is done by small producers, many of them Italian immigrants.

North of Cuyo the Andes Mountains spread out to form the Bolivian altiplano. This is Argentina's most backward and impoverished region, cut off by the mountains from the Pacific coast and too far from the Atlantic. Much of the population is ethnically and culturally similar to Bolivians and lives on isolated farms in the mountain valleys. In the lowlands of Salta province, along the Bolivian border, there is some oil industry. Tiny Tucumán province, just south of Salta, was once the sugar-growing center of Argentina, but antiquated practices and the withdrawal of government subsidies caused this industry to go into a sharp decline, much of it moving to more modern plantations in Salta's lowlands.

Going south from the Pampa brings one to Patagonia, Argentina's largest, coldest, and emptiest region. Upper Patagonia is a transitional zone in which cooler-temperature fruit such as apples and pears can be grown. Farther down in Patagonia, however, the land becomes a bleak, windswept plateau, often buffeted by Antarctic storms. With the exception of oil fields located along the coast in Comodoro Rivadavia and against the Andes Mountains in Neuquén, this area's economic activity is limited to fishing, mining, and the raising of sheep for wool on enormous estancias, Argentina's sheep and cattle ranches. Mining consists of exploiting mainly low-grade coal and iron deposits.

The People

Argentina's population of just over thirty-nine million is overwhelmingly urban (90 percent), with approximately one third living in the greater Buenos

Aires metropolitan area. It is also overwhelmingly of European descent—mainly Spaniards and Italians—and overwhelmingly Roman Catholic, at least nominally. Argentines are relatively healthy, although some deterioration in living standards due to the economic crisis of 2001–2002 has been evident. Infant mortality stands at sixteen per one thousand live births, life expectancy is seventy-two years for males and seventy-nine years for females, and the literacy rate is 97 percent for Argentines fifteen years and older (schooling is compulsory until age fifteen).

Argentina's ethnic mix (97 percent European, 3 percent *mestizo* and others) is a product of its unusual pattern of settlement. As a colony it produced little wealth for the Spanish crown and therefore remained sparsely settled. The Indian population was made up of small, nomadic, hostile tribes that were gradually driven off the Pampa by the settlers, down into Patagonia. By the end of the nineteenth century they were practically eliminated. At the same time Argentina's cattle-raising culture required little importation of African slaves to work the estancias. In the last two decades of the nineteenth century there was an enormous influx of European migrants, drawn by the attraction of vast tracts of cheap land, that significantly reconstituted the population. Today, Italian, French, German, English, Irish, Slavic, Jewish, and Arabic last names are common, as are Spanish.

Social structure in Argentina has allowed for movement upward and downward. The upper classes consist of two kinds of elites. First is the traditional large rancher/farmer *estanciero* elite. Although very wealthy, this is by no means a closed aristocracy. Many successful immigrants joined it during the late nineteenth and early twentieth centuries. Alongside it, and overlapping with it, is the more modern group of bankers, merchants, and industrialists. The two elites mingle socially in the highly prestigious Jockey Club and tend to congregate in the fashionable neighborhood of Barrio Norte in Buenos Aires.

The middle classes range from a very well-to-do upper stratum that is positioned just below the elites to a petit bourgeoisie consisting of small farmers and businesspeople, white-collar professionals, and lower-level bureaucrats. Top military officers, Catholic clergy, lawyers, doctors, and managers of corporations form the upper middle class. Sometimes their control of the government may make some of them as powerful as the elites.

The upper levels of the working classes consist of white-collar workers (*empleados*) and the skilled laborers (*obreros calificados*). Skilled laborers often make more money than white-collar workers, but they lack the latter's social status. *Empleados* go to work in a coat and tie and, although they may own only one of each, they do not get their hands dirty. *Obreros* do sweaty work. Most working-class parents dream of getting their children enough education to move them up the social scale from *obrero* to the *empleado* category, if indeed not into the middle class. Below these two groups are the semi and unskilled urban workers, and below them are the unskilled rural workers. Joining them are the members of the informal labor force, or *"cuentapropistas."* These are un-registered workers who work, part- or full-time in economic activities that of-ficial statistics do not capture. The ranks of workers in the informal economy have exploded in the past twenty years. Some estimates are that they now con-stitute nearly half of all workers in the country.

The Economy

Argentina has a sophisticated economy based on plentiful natural resources (especially oil), a highly skilled labor force, an efficient, export-oriented agri-cultural sector, and a great variety of industries. Its exports consist mainly of wheat, corn, soy, beef, and oilseeds. Argentina's chief trading partners are Brazil, the United States, and Italy. In 1991 it joined Brazil, Paraguay, and Uruguay to form a regional trading bloc called MERCOSUR, which has proved to be an important boost to foreign trade. Economic growth in the early 1990s averaged between 6 and 8 percent a year, following a period in the 1980s of economic contraction and hyperinflation. Unfortunately that period also left Argentina saddled with a huge foreign debt that continues to plague the Argentine economy. The Argentine recovery of the early 1990s did not last, as structural problems, international crises, and domestic policies all worked to undermine Argentina's ability to grow and prosper. By the late 1990s the economy was in recession and the years 2000–2002 saw the Argen-tine economy contract and economic crises take hold. The situation began to improve starting in 2003 as the administration of Néstor Carlos Kirchner managed to arrest Argentina's decline and steer it on the road to recovery.

The Argentine economy has a long history of "stagflation": a combination of stagnant growth and runaway inflation. The causes were structural and arose mainly from excessive government intervention in the economy. Pop-ulist administrations, beginning in the 1940s, based their electoral support on a combination of heavy social spending, trade protectionism, and ubiquitous economic regulation. Such an inward-oriented, "hothouse" economy was de-signed to guarantee high living standards for labor and to subsidize a large number of small, labor-intensive businesses that would provide plenty of jobs.

Traditionally, Argentina's economy was characterized by the dominance of large *estancias* in the countryside and small businesses in the towns and cities. Naturally, there were many exceptions to this general rule. Small and medium-sized farms and ranches produced profitably for the market, and there were even well-off tenant farmers. In certain industries, such as automobiles, pharmaceuticals, and rubber—any large enterprise requiring heavy capital inputs and advanced technology—big foreign companies dominated. The state was in control of "basic" or militarily strategic industries (energy, transportation, mining, oil, armaments, utilities). Often that meant the armed forces' direct ownership and management. The domestic private sector tended to concentrate on manufacturing light, nondurable consumer goods, such as food products, textiles, home furnishings, and small appliances. In addition, domestic private capital controlled most wholesale and retail commerce, as well as the service sector. With a few notable exceptions these locally owned private companies were small, employing fewer than ten people on the average. Many simply worked with their own, unpaid family members. In short, Argentina had an urban economy of mainly small capitalists, a "shopkeeper society."

This society began showing signs of breaking down in the 1960s. Argentine industry was inefficient, and its products were therefore both costly and, often, shoddy. Protected by tariffs and manipulated exchange rates, however, it had a captive market to exploit. Because most people lived in the cities and depended directly or indirectly on this industry, politicians hesitated to challenge it. The money to support public services came mainly from sales taxes, tariffs on foreign goods, and tariffs levied on Argentina's agricultural exports. The tariffs were greatly resented by the farmers and ranchers, but because they were only a minority of the population they were unable to change the policy. Nonetheless, these added costs were pricing Argentine beef and grains out of world markets, and as they did so the government's treasury began running low on foreign exchange.

By the 1980s Argentina was in a real crisis: deeply in debt, with banks and businesses failing, agriculture stagnant, and capital fleeing the country. Population trends added to the crisis. Like many other socially advanced countries Argentina's birthrate had fallen greatly, to a little over 1 percent—not enough to replenish itself. Young people with skills were leaving for Europe or the United States while the elderly and retired were becoming an increasingly large portion of the population. A slight increase of women in the workforce helped to alleviate the situation somewhat, but with the growing recession and unemployment there was little incentive to seek regular work. On the other hand, the informal economy, where people worked for below minimum wages, evaded social security payments and payroll taxes, and flouted most other labor laws, grew rapidly. By the end of the 1990s it was believed to account for at least 60 percent of all economic activity, although no records exist to prove that assertion.

Following the election of President Carlos Menem in 1989 the old system came under full-scale attack. In January 1991 Menem's economic minister,

Domingo Cavallo, announced a radical package of neoliberal economic reforms that effectively opened the country to foreign competition and investment, forced the government to cut back on its spending, and began a rapid process of divesting the state—including the military—of its enterprises. The impact on Argentina's urban middle and working classes was devastating. Stripped of protection and subsidies, many small businesses disappeared, gobbled up by larger foreign and domestic companies. Within a few years the "shopkeeper society" was transformed into one dominated by large private conglomerates. Because these were capital-intensive rather than labor-intensive, unemployment rose in the working classes as well, especially among women and youth.

The lynchpin of Menem's neoliberal economic project was the "convertibility plan" that pegged the peso's value to the dollar so that one peso equaled one dollar. While early results from the convertibility plan were positive and international creditors and lending agencies were impressed, the structural flaws in such a plan began to take hold after 1994. The overvaluation of the Argentine peso meant that Argentine goods were not competitive on the world market. This plan also depended on access to available credit, a situation that would turn sour after the Mexican financial crisis of 1994 caused a shrinking of external investment. Along with problems of political corruption, infighting in Menem's government, profligate spending by the provincial governments, and the chronic problem of tax evasion, the Argentine economy headed toward crisis by the end of the 1990s.

In 2001 Argentina defaulted on its US$100 billion debt, plunging the country into economic and political chaos. Neoliberal reforms were in a shambles. The next two years saw the unprecedented contraction of the economy and severe impoverishment of the Argentine population. Between 1999 and 2002 the GDP shrank by 20 percent, unemployment reached record-high levels of 18 percent; and over 50 percent of the population saw their lives descend into poverty. International lending agencies all but abandoned the country.

The economic situation began a recovery in 2003 with the election of Peronist Néstor Kirchner. Rejecting the advice of the International Monetary Fund, Kirchner embarked on an economic course that insisted that reducing the foreign debt had to take a back seat to relieving the population out of its misery. Adopting a nationalist stance, Kirchner has seen early successes in pulling the economy back from the brink. The GDP has grown impressively in 2003 and 2004; unemployment has decreased, and the poverty rate fell 10 percent from 2002 to 2004. Particularly impressive was Kirchner's success at negotiating a debt swap with 80 percent of the holders of Argentina's external debt, that effectively wipes out two thirds of the money owed to private creditors. Inflation has remained stable and the exchange rate of the peso has stabilized.

Fueling much of the economic recovery has been Argentina's ability to increase exports, especially of commodities, fuels, and processed agricultural goods. In addition, Kirchner has been able to increase tax revenues, and foreign investment is once again flowing into the economy. Spending is under control and a budget surplus now exists. In 2005 Argentina appeared steady in its economic recovery. Whether this economic recovery will succeed remains an open question halfway through the first decade of the twenty-first century.

Argentina's Early Development

Argentina's history has been shaped by conflict and division. Once Spanish rule was overthrown the leaders of the independence movement quickly fell out among themselves over what sort of government they would have. The city of Buenos Aires, the former capital of the old Viceroyalty of La Plata, wanted a centralized government and advocated for a form of liberalism that emphasized free trade, encouraging European immigration, promoting modernization, and reducing the power of the Catholic Church. Led by Bernardino Rivadavia, they created a Unitary Party and sought to concentrate power in a central government dominated by Buenos Aires. Opponents from the interior provinces of Argentina bridled under the dominance of Buenos Aires. Their interests were basically local, and what united them was a desire to promote their own interests and limit the power of a central government. Aside from this, among the federalists many disagreements would arise. For instance, while the interior provinces were open to foreign trade, each wanted to do so on its own terms by encouraging inland navigation by foreign ships. Buenos Aires federalists were opposed to this idea. Still, when Buenos Aires *caudillo* Juan Manuel Rosas sought to unify the country under a "federalist scheme," many of the provinces went along. A federalist scheme, even if promoted by a *caudillo* from Buenos Aires, was better than anything the Unitaries advocated.

A powerful *estanciero* who represented the cattle interests, Rosas had adopted the ways of a gaucho and had gained prestige in a series of frontier wars against the Indians. With his own cavalry, in 1829 he drove the Unitaries out of the country and from then to 1852 he ruled as the *caudillo* dictator of Buenos Aires. Rosas ruled as a strong nationalist and all aspects of liberalism were repressed. The Catholic Church was given control over education, censorship suppressed any criticism, and those suspected of Unitary sympathies were intimidated—and sometimes murdered—by a paramilitary organization known as the Mazorca. Most people with liberal opinions went into exile.

Rosas was defeated in 1852 by a combination of rebellious *caudillos* and exiles. The following year the Argentine Federation adopted a constitution patterned closely after that of the United States. Its liberal principles included the separation of powers, checks and balances, the right to private property, and the guarantees of free speech and free press. It also encouraged the government to foster immigration. Because it provided for a federal system, however, the city of Buenos Aires would not accept it. Armed clashes followed. In 1862 Buenos Aires finally agreed to join the federation and in 1880 the city itself was detached from the province and made a federal district.

From 1852 to 1916 Argentina was ruled by a "liberal oligarchy" who believed that governing should be left in the hands of the educated and the propertied. To control electoral outcomes various provincial gentry formed a single official party, the National Autonomist Party (Partido Autonoma Nacional, PAN) and ruled by fraud and corruption. Under the liberal oligarchy, Argentina's foreign trade grew rapidly and the proceeds were plowed into internal developments: roads, bridges, ports, and an excellent system of public education. New methods of agriculture were adopted; cattle breeding and pasturage were improved; and new lines of production were introduced: grain-growing and sheep-raising. Foreign capital brought in the railroads, the telephone and telegraph, gas and electric power, the refrigerated steamship, modern meatpacking, and modern sanitation. With the commercial boom came an increase in banking, insurance, and construction. The port of Buenos Aires became one of the busiest in the world, and the city was transformed from a dull colonial-looking town into a modern European-type capital whose broad boulevards and imposing buildings reminded travelers of Paris.

Along with these radical changes came a huge wave of immigration from Europe. Many came originally as seasonal farm workers, saved their earnings, and bought their own farms out on the expanding frontier. Others moved to Buenos Aires or smaller cities, where they started small factories, commercial shops, and services to meet the growing demands of a rapidly rising population. Between 1869 and 1895 Argentina's population had more than doubled, from 1.7 to 3.9 million. By 1914 it would more than double again, to over 7.8 million. About half the gain was due to immigration. Most of the immigrants settled on the Pampa or in the Littoral. In that same period the city of Buenos Aires grew from only about 100,000 inhabitants to over 1.5 million. Fully half of the latter were foreign-born. The massive influx of immigrants had far-reaching consequences. To begin with, it greatly increased the size of Argentina's middle classes. In 1914 the economic census showed that two thirds of all the proprietors of industrial establishments and three-fourths of owners were foreign-born. The vast majority of these were small-scale, averaging fewer than seven workers. Nevertheless, industry and commerce were beginning to take their place alongside agriculture as important economic activities, and a new entrepreneurial class was emerging. Rising in tandem with these small capitalists was a new urban industrial working class. The same 1914 census found that half of all industrial workers were foreign-born. Many of them had experience in Europe's socialist, anarchist, or syndicalist movements.

These new elements would soon tear apart the liberal oligarchy's monopoly on government. In 1889 the Civic Union (later called the *Unión Cívica Radical*, or Radical Party) launched as a reform party, called for universal suffrage, honest elections, and good government. Its leaders were progressive members of the oligarchy, but the bulk of its following came from the middle classes. The Radicals attempted to overthrow the oligarchy on two occasions, in 1890 and 1905, but failed. Their leader, Hipólito Yrigoyen, denounced PAN's continual resort to fraud. At the same time, the labor movement divided into a moderate socialist wing and a revolutionary anarchist wing. The liberal oligarchy, now organized under the Conservative Party, sought to repel these pressures from below. However, progressive members, including Roque Sáenz Peña, accepted the need for reform. In 1910 Sáenz Peña won the presidency and pushed through Congress an electoral law (that bears his name) granting suffrage to all males who performed a year of military service, and institution of the secret ballot. It also included a new electoral law, called the "incomplete list" system under which the party with the most votes in a district would receive two-thirds of the representatives, while the one coming in second would get the other third. The era of mass politics had begun.

Mass Politics

The election of 1916 brought Yrigoyen to power and ushered in fourteen years of rule by the Radical Party. Yrigoyen and his successors did little to transform the economic priorities of the era. The economic interests of the elites, still concentrated in the export cattle industries, were little threatened under Radical rule. Even so, elements of the conservative elites grew increasingly unhappy sharing power with middle class interests. The Radicals did not have a particularly good relationship with the rising ranks of the working classes either. While Yrigoyen seemed to tolerate the socialist-oriented unions, he had disdain for the anarchists. A number of labor strikes during Yrigoyen's presidency were met with police force and repression. In 1919 labor repression reached an all-time high with the events of the "Tragic Week," when the police, the army, and armed groups of members of a right-wing paramilitary organization called the Patriotic League attacked strikers at a steel mill and then proceeded to the Barrio Once, where many workers and Jews lived, killing an estimated one thousand. Two years later the army crushed an anarchist-led strike in Patagonia, executing over two thousand workers and torturing many more.

With the Great Depression of 1929 the era of the Radicals came to an end. Conservative elite interests, who had never been supportive of "opening up the political system," saw their chance to oust Yrigoyen, who had been re-elected for a second term but who seemed incapable of handling the economic dislocation brought about by the Depression. Agitation among the military, who had their own grievances against the Radicals, led to a military coup that deposed Yrigoyen in 1930.

The leader of the coup was army general José F. Uriburu, an admirer of Benito Mussolini, who advocated an ultranationalist state that favored elite rule under a corporatist state. Ousted after two years in power, he was replaced by General Agustín P. Justo, who had the support of a broader array of interests—Conservatives, dissident anti-Yrigoyen Radicals, and maverick socialists. Economic policymaking in the 1930s led to inroads in industrialization. The Great Depression laid bare the vulnerabilities of Argentina's dependence on commodity exports and the small industrial base began to expand. Bereft of markets from which to import manufactured goods, urban middle-class entrepreneurs began production of light manufactured goods. Argentina's industrial base expanded under this import-substitution-industrialization model. Foreign investors played a key role in this expansion.

The 1930s were also a time of social upheaval. European immigration had ended with World War I, never again to reach its former volume, but now came a great wave of migrants from Argentina's rural interior to the cities, pushed off the land by the Depression and pulled into urban centers in search of factory jobs. Metropolitan Buenos Aires alone doubled its population to over six million. Most of the newcomers were unskilled and could not find steady work; instead, they scrambled for low-paying peripheral jobs. Nor were they welcomed by the older working class. The latter were Europeans or their descendants, and looked down on these rural, dark-skinned migrants. The "little blackheads" (*cabecitas negras*), as they called them, had no interest in the foreign-sounding ideologies like communism and socialism, then dominant in the labor movement. They would take any work at any pay, and thus avoided the labor unions, who also avoided them. So the Argentine working classes divided: the relatively well-off skilled workers with their Marxist-oriented unions, on one side, and a much larger, un-unionized , unskilled, insecure mass of recent migrants, living in sprawling, squalid, makeshift slums on the city's edge, on the other. This was the soil from which Peronism would emerge.

The Peronist Watershed

The political scene in Argentina in the early 1940s was dominated by the external events of World War II. The army, many of whose officers were

German-trained, supported an alliance with the Axis powers. A group of high-level officers conspired to implant a government modeled after Mussolini's Italian fascist regime. Calling themselves the Group of United Officers (GOU), they successfully took power in 1943. Among its members was a little known army colonel named Juan Domingo Perón. When the events of World War II made it clear that the Axis powers were losing, the military establishment in power began a search for an exit strategy.

Meanwhile, in 1943 Juan Domingo Perón had asked to take over the management of the Secretariat of Labor and Social Welfare. Previously he had served as Minister of War, a position he used to build a support base within the army. As minister of labor Perón began to settle disputes in labor's favor. He reversed longstanding antilabor legislation and actively promoted legislation to improve workers' lives. Old-age pensions, accident and health insurance, annual paid vacations, factory safety codes, minimum wage and maximum hour legislation—all were expanded and enforced. Labor unionists were given positions in his ministry; others were freed from jail. Employers who had fought the creation of labor unions were now forced to accept them. Perón's support base among labor grew.

Some within the military began to view with alarm the policies of Perón. The conservative elites and industrial groups were also resentful and suspicious of Perón's courting of workers. The growing opposition to Perón led a group of officers to oust him from all government posts and put him under arrest on a naval base in the La Plata River. What happened next is still the stuff of Peronist legend. Labor unions and workers' organizations mobilized to protest the jailing of Perón. Thousands of workers descended on the capital of Buenos Aires and converged on the Plaza de Mayo demanding Perón's release. Not having an alternative, the military finally agreed to release Perón. On October 17, 1945, Perón appeared on the balcony of the Casa Rosada (Government House) and saw the results of his hard work of organizing the working classes. Gesturing in victory to thousands of workers cheering him, it was clear that the working classes had forced their way into the political arena. The Peronist Era had begun.

The election of 1946 passed the mantle of power and legitimacy to Perón. In the run-up to the election Perón organized his own political party, the Labor Party, which organized his many supporters under his leadership. He had the solid support of the labor unions, many of which had organized within the past three years; of factions of the military from whose ranks he came; and of the Catholic Church, for which Perón had promised to retain their right to control education and to prevent divorce legislation. Opposed to Perón were the Conservative Party, landed elites, urban industrialists, middle-class radicals, and an array of socialists and communists. Nevertheless, Perón's victory in the 1946 election was decisive: 1,479,517 votes for the Labor Party and 1,220,822 for the opposition Democratic Union, a coalition of anti-Peronist interests. Perón's allies also swept the two houses of Congress, the provincial governorships, and all but one of the provincial legislatures.

Perón came to power with a number of factors in his favor. He had won a fair and open election with the support of a broad coalition of groups, including elements of the military and the Catholic Church. The state treasury was full as Argentina had been able to capitalize on the sale of supplies to the Allies during World War II. International prices of food and raw agricultural materials were rising relative to industrial goods. His development policies focused on expanding basic industrialization, expanding social welfare benefits, a certain redistribution of wealth, and promoting nationalism.

Perón continued to pursue his prolabor policies by promulgating legislation covering all aspects of workers' lives. Real wages and fringe benefits went up. Under the Secretariat of Labor and Prevision, Perón created an extensive network for the administration of labor affairs. He gradually concentrated labor matters under the General Direction of Labor and Direct Social Action (DGTASD). All aspects of labor relations, including collective bargaining, labor law enforcement, union registrations and dues, workplace conditions, and employer-union conflicts came under the purview of the DGTASD. To ensure labor compliance with Peronist policies the General Confederation of Labor (CGT) was given a monopoly of control over labor unions. The CGT was the only legally recognized labor confederation in the country and any union that wished to be legally recognized had to fall under its control and oversight. In classical corporatist fashion the CGT was the vehicle by which Perón transmitted his policies down to labor rank and file.

Perón's prolabor policies were part of his economic project to further industrialization. Profits from the agricultural sector were transferred to the industrial sector. Agriculturalists were forced to sell all their commodity exports to a government agency called the Argentine Institute for Production and Trade (*Instituto Argentino de Producción y Intercambio*, IAPI) at government-set prices. The idea was for IAPI to buy at the lowest possible price and then sell the goods on the world market at the highest possible price. The profits would then be used to finance industrialization.

Perón's industrial project sought to expand import substitution industrialization. To that end he nationalized the central bank, the railroads, telephone, electricity and gas, and urban transport. The state began development of an aviation industry and a steel industry. Compensation for the nationalizations came from state treasury funds, leading to a severe depletion of state funds for promoting industrialization beyond that of light manufactured goods. Capital intensive industrialization never really took off. Parallel to the CGT controlling labor, Perón set up the General Economic Confederation (CGE) to represent industrialists, merchants, and agriculturalists.

Perón's political style was clearly populist as he continued to direct his words and deeds to the working classes. With his wife, Eva Duarte, Perón sought to elevate the working classes from their historic second-class status. Eva Perón (Evita), in particular, served as an effective interlocutor between Perón and the people. Her own biography, emphasizing her illegitimate upbringing in a dusty provincial town and her rise to political fame, served as an inspiration to millions of working-class and poor Argentines. Adopting a glamorous style, Eva Perón took an active part in dispensing social welfare funds to the working class and poor.

Perón's populism, though, also had its authoritarian side. Soon after taking office he renamed the Labor Party as the Peronist Party so as to solidify his own personal power base. He and his allies set about purging Argentine politics and society of anyone who opposed Perón, whether they were independent-minded labor leaders or newspaper publishers. Political parties other than the Peronist Party were harassed and repressed. Censorship and outright strong-arm Mafioso brutality were tactics Perón used to reinforce his power. Political corruption also was endemic as the Peróns surrounded themselves with relatives and friends, many of whom saw access to the Peróns as an invitation to seek personal and material gains.

From 1946 to 1949, the Peronist project produced economic growth and a substantive improvement in people's lives. The real incomes and quality of life of Argentine workers and the middle classes increased and for all the loathing the economic elites expressed toward Perón, they did not suffer much under his redistributive policies. Still, industrialization did not lead to sustained economic growth and by 1950 the state treasury was running out of monies to continue supporting its own state-run, inefficient industries and its expanded social welfare expenditures. When Eva Perón died in 1952 from cancer, Perón's decline began.

Facing pressure from a deteriorating economic situation, Perón sought even greater controls over society. He attacked the Catholic Church, an early Perón supporter, when they refused to canonize his wife as a saint, despite popular demonstrations on her behalf. Then the clergy provoked a confrontation when it began to organize Christian Democratic trade unions in competition with Perón's. Perón went on the attack, forbidding religious processions and expelling priests. Street clashes escalated until finally, on the night of June 16, 1955, Peronist fanatics set fire to several downtown churches, including the Cathedral and the Archbishop's Palace. At the same time, anti-Peronist opposition had been growing in the military. The navy always had been a center of resistance, but now the army, one of Perón's main pillars of support, was restive. Its professionalism was insulted by mandatory courses in Peronist political indoctrination at the Academy and by the regime's new program of encouraging the sergeants and enlisted men to join the Peronist Party. The officers feared that their own men would be encouraged to spy on them. With the Catholic Church and important factions of the military allied against Perón, a military coup, led by General Eduardo Lonardi, forced Perón from office in September 1955. Perón took refuge initially in Paraguay and ultimately made his way to Spain. The first Peronist experiment was over.

The legacy Perón left Argentina in 1955 was expanded group interests vying for political power. Alongside the agricultural elites, the armed forces, the urban middle class interests, and industrialists, the Peronist Party-supported labor unions, and working classes vied for political power. To the state he left a huge bureaucracy with responsibilities to nationalized industries and social welfare policies. To the economy he left a depleted state treasury and a shaky industrial base. Perón neither destroyed the power of the traditional economic elites nor did his government gain enough strength to check their power. Rather, the next eighteen years would see attempts to defeat Peronism, all of which would fail at high social and political cost.

Peronism in Exile

The military coup of 1955 opened a period of political and economic turmoil in Argentina. The military regime, led first by coup leader Lonardi and then by General Pedro Aramburu, set about de-Peronizing Argentine society. It outlawed the Peronist Party and purged the labor union leadership of all Peronists. Strikes by workers were quashed as well. De-Peronization also involved attacking the symbols and historical memory of the Peróns. Aramburu embarked on a campaign to expose the excesses and corruption of the Peróns by displaying the material goods amassed by them. He was also responsible for kidnapping Evita's body and having it sent to Milan, Italy, so as to deny the Peronist movement of a "sacred" symbol.

Aramburu was committed to returning the government to civilian rule, and so in 1958 elections were called. Aramburu had hoped that a resurrected Radical Party would lead the country out of its Peronist nightmare. Unfortunately for him the Radicals split internally and a left-wing faction, led by Arturo Frondizi, attempted to win the support of the labor unions by advocating a populist platform very similar to Perón's. The Peronist Party was denied the right to field candidates. Because voting was and is obligatory, Perón, from his place in exile in Venezuela, ordered his followers to cast blank ballots in the provincial elections that were a prelude to national elections. A full 25 percent of the votes cast were blank, attesting to Frondizi and everyone else the popular support Perón still enjoyed.

So as to ensure his success in the presidential election, Frondizi entered a pact with Perón to legalize Peronism in return for Peronist votes. Frondizi won in a landslide and initially promoted prolabor policies. This stance would not last, however, and for the next four years Frondizi sought to carve out a middle position between Peronism and anti-Peronism. He failed and managed to alienate both Peronists and anti-Peronists. When Frondizi attempted to adopt a mediating stance with the Cuban Revolution, the military ousted him from power. The next Radical experiment would be Arturo Illia, who represented the right-wing faction of the Radicals. An elderly doctor from Córdoba province, Illia was ineffectual and in 1966 was replaced by a military coup. Factions of the military decided to give up on civilian rule and take power themselves for the long term.

General Juan Carlos Onganía took power in 1966, and like most of his military colleagues no longer viewed democracy as viable for Argentina. Peronism still remained strong, a fact that was viewed as preventing Argentina from addressing its most pressing economic problems. According to the military Argentina suffered from "stagflation," a combination of stagnant production and inflation. Free market reforms that included austerity, competition, privatization, and reducing unemployment were needed, all of which would result in social unrest. Only a military dictatorship could enforce such harsh policies.

Onganía's economic policies were successful for the first two years. Inflation dropped from 40 to 5 percent, productivity rose, and exchange reserves were at their highest level in years. The unions were forced to suffer a wage freeze, and their strikes were brutally repressed. The press was censored and the universities were placed under tight control. Then, in mid-1969, workers in the city of Córdoba struck and were joined by university students. Four days of urban warfare left more than a dozen people dead. Known as the "cordobazo," this event inspired antigovernment demonstrations throughout the country. That same year a leading collaborationist labor leader, Augusto Vandor was assassinated and a group of urban guerillas, the Montoneros, kidnapped former President Aramburu and executed him. Onganía, having lost control of the political situation, was forced from office.

For the next few years political forces converged to enable Perón to return to power. Political violence became commonplace as left-wing terrorism was met with right-wing terrorism. The military was finding it increasingly difficult to repress Peronism; labor unions continued to overwhelmingly support Perón; the Montoneros wanted Perón's return; and other classes in society viewed Perón's return as a way out of the chaos and violence plaguing society. After a bit of political machination Perón returned triumphant, once again, to Argentina in 1973. This time, his wife was Maria Estela (Isabel) Perón.

Now a frail old man, Perón could not manage the forces he had supported from exile. The Montoneros who had demanded his return as a condition for ending their violent tactics were rejected by Perón once he returned to power. Within his own inner circle Perón was very much dependent on his personal secretary, José López Rega. A confidant of Isabel Perón, López Rega became minister of social welfare, which gave him control of a large budget that he used to build a private terrorist army of his own, known as the Argentine Anticommunist Alliance (AAA). It targeted left-wing guerilla movements, including the Montoneros, who responded in kind with their own violence.

Perón's death in 1974 brought further violence and chaos to Argentina. His widow, Isabel, who had been his vice president, was incapable of running a government, much less able to deal with Argentina's serious social and economic problems. Erratic economic policymaking, the rising militancy of the labor unions, and the increasing fears of the military brought an end to Isabel's regime. Once again, the military stepped into power. On March 26, 1976, to most Argentines' relief, Isabel was removed from power in a military coup.

Military-Sponsored Terror

The coup of March 1976 that heralded a return to military rule would be a departure from past military interventions. Calling its mission the "Process of National Reorganization," the military junta, made up of representatives of the army, navy, and air force, with Army General Jorge Rafael Videla as its head, committed itself to ending the political chaos and to setting the economy on a stable course. To achieve the former the military undertook draconian measures to purge Argentine society of subversive elements that were impeding Argentina's development. It was not enough to route the guerilla forces that had plagued Argentine society for the past decade; what was needed was to attack the root causes of Argentina's political instability. According to the military junta Argentina's woes went beyond the problems of Peronism and an intransigent labor movement. To the military junta the entire fabric of Argentine life had been poisoned and diseased by leftist subversion, leading to a sick society rent with chaos and corruption. The solution was a concerted campaign to purge Argentina of those subversive elements and to reassert the "true" values of Argentine life. One of the self-proclaimed mottoes of the military junta was "Tradition, Family, and Property," borrowed from the ultraconservative Catholic Opus Dei organization that was popular with some in the military. The Argentine Catholic Church hierarchy became a staunch supporter of the junta.

The methods used by the military junta are by now famous. Green Ford Falcons with no license plates chauffeured by nondescript men sped through the streets of Buenos Aires both day and night in search of specific individuals believed to be subversives. Illegal detention centers were set up all over the country, equipped with both sophisticated and primitive means of torture. Basic civil liberties were severely restricted as Argentine society found itself gripped in fear and terror by the military junta's actions. All groups representing civil society (political parties, labor unions, civic associations) were repressed and their leadership went underground.

No sector of Argentine society was immune from this war against subversion; the hardest hit were the working classes, students, labor-movement activists, and urban professionals. The words "*los desaparecidos*" entered the Argentine lexicon to signify that persons were "being disappeared" by shadowy forces rather than disappearing of their own accord. Most of the disappeared were never found (all told, 30,000 persons lost their lives between 1976 and 1983), although mass graves are periodically uncovered in contemporary Argentina, filled with skeletons that show signs of violent deaths such as bullet holes, bashed in skulls, and broken bones. In addition to dumping torture victims in mass graves, people were burned alive in ovens, and others were thrown into the La Plata River, in hopes their bodies would be eaten by sharks. Some remains, however, would end up on the Uruguay beaches of the river.

Among those who were kidnapped and disappeared in this "Dirty War" were women who were pregnant. It is estimated that approximately 400 babies were born in captivity of women who were subsequently killed upon giving birth. The babies were "adopted" by the families of military men or were sold on the black market. The whereabouts of these children of the disappeared continues to play out in contemporary Argentina.

Although all sectors of Argentine society were repressed, it is noteworthy that a group of women whose children were disappeared organized to defy the military junta's policies. The Mothers of the Plaza de Mayo captured the imagination of the international media beginning in 1977, when a few brave women decided to demonstrate publicly against the repressive policies of the regime. Covering their heads with white scarves and holding up placards with pictures of their missing children, the Mothers held weekly marches around the Plaza de Mayo, calling attention to the regime's human rights abuses. Several of the original founders of the group were themselves disappeared, but the group persevered and were an important voice in ensuring that the human rights abuses of the junta not be ignored once it left power.

Part of the motivating drive for the repression was the military junta's economic priorities. Under the direction of José Martínez de Hoz, Argentina's economy was to be "reorganized" so as to promote growth, competitiveness, and global integration. Argentina's economy suffered from too much state intervention and the dominance of trade unions. In order to fix Argentina's economy, labor unions needed to be tamed and state-run industries needed to be privatized. In these ways foreign investment could be attracted to restart the Argentine economy.

With respect to the organized labor movement, the military junta attacked the central labor confederation, the CGT, and jailed many prominent labor leaders. Factory floors were occupied by military men to coerce workers to work. Trade union activity was banned, union elections were disrupted by the military, and control over union dues reverted to the government. Organized labor's fortunes were also eroded due to the free-market policies of the regime that led to the closing of state-run and inefficient industries, thereby causing massive unemployment.

The long-term impact of Martínez de Hoz's policies were a disaster. Neither economic growth nor inflation were tamed, and by 1980 the days of Martínez de Hoz were numbered.

As the economic situation took a downturn the military junta sought ways to maintain power. In 1981 General Videla ceded power to General Roberto Viola, who in turn was replaced by General Leopoldo Galtieri at the end of the year. By this time human rights groups in Argentina and newly radicalized labor unions began to agitate against the military regime. To quell the rising domestic discontent Galtieri took Argentina into the ill-conceived war against Great Britain for control of the Falklands—or the Malvinas, as the Argentines call this group of islands in the South Atlantic. It was hoped that enflaming a longtime conflict with Great Britain would rally Argentine nationalism toward the regime. What Galtieri did not bargain for was Great Britain's response in sending its famed naval fleet and Royal Air Forces to retake the islands. Argentina's defeat led to the hurried exit of the military junta from political power.

Transition to Democracy

The election of Raul Alfonsín to the presidency in December 1983 was a watershed event in Argentina's political history. For the first time in a freely contested election the Peronists did not win. The people's preference for the Radical Civic Union candidate, who himself had been jailed under the military, signaled a desire for a fresh start in Argentine politics, one that was a clear repudiation of past authoritarian regimes. During the electoral campaign Alfonsín promised to bring the Proceso's top military officers to trial for violating human rights, a promise he made good once elected. Alfonsín appointed a special investigative commission whose report was used as the basis for the trial held in 1985. For several months in early 1985 victims and families of victims testified to the extent of the human rights violations. General Videla was handed a life sentence and the other junta leaders were given long prison sentences. The military, fully discredited due to the disastrous performance in the Falklands War, had little recourse to protest. However, when courts and prosecutors began to indict lower level officers, military rebellions occurred. Three military rebellions took place between 1987 and 1988, events that led to the curtailing of the human rights prosecutions. The "due obedience" law that passed in 1987 absolved from prosecution those who were "just following orders." The "full stop" law limited the time period for when cases could be brought to the courts, all but stopping prosecutions against military personnel. Human rights organizations, including the Mothers of the Plaza de Mayo, vigorously opposed this legislation.

In the area of the economy Alfonsín and his economic team embarked on a number of strategies to curb rampant inflation, which had reached a yearly rate of 6,900 percent by 1985. He introduced a reform package called the Austral Plan that consisted of wage and price freezes, spending cutbacks, and raises in utility rates. Although the plan had initial successes, Alfonsín's failure to follow through on all his promises soon led to a resurgence of hyperinflation. Attempts at fixing the Austral Plan came to nothing, and in the 1987 congressional elections the Radicals were roundly defeated by the Peronists. Two years later Alfonsín himself would leave office early due to his government's inability to manage the economic crisis. At the time of his resignation in June 1989, inflation had roared back to 4,900 percent, the GDP had contracted, real wages had fallen, and the external debt had reached a record $63,314 million in U.S. dollars.

Peronism Without Perón

Carlos Menem, governor of La Rioja province, had campaigned as an old-fashioned Peronist *caudillo,* promising to be the champion of the lower classes, but on taking office he shifted his stance so as not to end up as Alfonsín had. Instead of populist economics he embraced a very orthodox neoliberal formula. Foreign capital, free trade, and privatization were promoted with vigor. To keep government spending within budgetary limits the peso was pegged to the dollar at an exchange rate of one to one, and the Treasury was allowed to print only as many pesos as there were dollars in the Central Bank. Called the "convertibility plan," such measures soon brought inflation down to single digits, and economic growth climbed to around 9 percent. However, the social costs of these reforms were high. Thousands of government workers lost their jobs, as did workers in Argentina's inefficient industries. Local companies, long protected from competition, were either bought by foreigners or were absorbed into Argentine conglomerates. About a third of the economically active population was officially classified as living in poverty. Menem had reinvented the terms of debate with regards to the Argentine economy.

While Menem revolutionized the economy, his style of governance in other ways resembled aspects of Peronist caudillismo. Seeking to maximize his power, Menem sought a number of changes to Argentine institutional arrangements. He expanded the Supreme Court to nine members from the original five, and thereby set about packing the court with his allies. Under pressure from the military, he granted pardons to convicted military leaders. While these moves enabled Menem to successfully reduce the size of the military ranks from around 100,000 to 20,000, he engendered the enmity of human rights organizations. He succeeded in instituting legislation that severely weakened the labor movement, including abolishing collective bargaining, enabling employers to have greater flexibility in hiring and firing, and breaking the labor unions' control over social welfare funds. Perhaps Menem's most important political maneuver was to have the constitution amended to allow his reelection as president. Instead of one six-year term, in 1994 the constitution was changed to allow for a four-year presidential term but with reelection possible.

Menem's early success in controlling the economic situation enabled him to make many of the changes cited above and he easily won reelection in 1995. However, his administration was increasingly beset by scandals (many related to the sale of state-run industries) and allegations of political corruption. Menem's highly public divorce from his wife, his penchant for consorting with movie stars and celebrities, and his use of family members as political advisors, who were accountable to no one, further compromised his reputation. As the economic situation began to decline, so did Menem's political fortunes.

The election of 1999 brought about Peronism's defeat once again, this time at the hands of a coalition consisting of the Radical Civic Union and the Front for a Country in Solidarity (*Frente del Pais Solidario, FrePaso*). The latter was a political party formed in 1994 of disaffected Peronists and persons from left-of-center political parties. Calling themselves the "*Alianza*," Fernando de la Rúa (head of the Radicals) was elected on a platform of promising to end political corruption and to ameliorate the suffering of millions of Argentines whose economic livelihoods were destroyed by the neoliberal policies of the 1990s. The Alianza was shortlived as political differences between the Radicals and FrePaso led to a fracturing of the alliance and instability in the de la Rúa coalition. Economic policymaking failed to arrest the deepening decline of economic productivity, and poverty rates increased. By the end of 2001 the political and economic situation was chaotic. De la Rúa resigned from the presidency, thereby plunging Argentina into its worst political crisis since the era of military rule. A succession of three presidents were selected by Congress in a two-week period. Finally, Eduardo Duhalde, a Peronist Party boss from Buenos Aires Province, was elected president in early 2002. Instead of calling for early elections, Duhalde opted for elections in 2003 (what would have been the end of de la Rúa's full term).

The 2003 presidential election brought Néstor Carlos Kirchner, Peronist governor of Santa Cruz Province, to office. An ally of Eduardo Duhalde at the time, Kirchner won the presidency with only 22 percent of the popular vote after his closest rival, former President Carlos Menem, dropped out of second-round balloting. Kirchner set about stabilizing the economy and by 2005 it appeared that economic growth, reductions in unemployment, and a reduction in poverty rates were taking hold. Embracing a populist and nationalist stance, Kirchner has been able to pressure international lending agencies and creditors to allow greater flexibility in meeting Argentina's debt obligations. Enjoying record approval ratings at the midpoint of his presidency in 2005, Kirchner's party increased its seats from forty to one hundred in the lower house.

Along with espousing an economic populism that is somewhat reminiscent of traditional Peronism, it appears that Kirchner is governing in a typical *caudillo* fashion. He consults very little with his cabinet and has been accused of governing by fiat and decree. He and his once close ally Eduardo Duhalde are engaged in a long drawn-out struggle over control of the Peronist Party and who gets selected to run for influential seats in the legislature and provincial governorships. He has also been criticized for his aversion to dealing with foreign leaders and business executives who come to Argentina, usually with economic interests in mind, but whom he then snubs by refusing to meet. The long-term solvency of Kirchner's administration remains to be seen.

Argentina's political history in the first decade of the twenty-first century has weathered a number of crises. It is perhaps significant that the military has not played a leading role in resolving any of them. This may indicate that Argentina has reached a certain degree of institutionalization of democratic norms and processes. Still, problems such as hyperpresidentialism, the lack of political accountability, and political corruption continue to be endemic in Argentina's political system.

The Government

The 1853 constitution, which though revised is still basically the law of the land, was modeled after that of the United States. It provides for a federal republic with twenty-three provinces and a federal district. The national government is divided into three branches: the executive, a bicameral Congress, and a judiciary. There is a strict separation of powers and a classic system of constitutional checks and balances. The constitution also contains a lengthy section outlining citizens' rights and guarantees, including the rights of petition, assembly, free speech, and free press. Freedom of religion is guaranteed, as is the right to own private property. An individual may not be arrested without a warrant, may not be forced to testify against himself or herself, and has a right to a lawyer and to a speedy and fair trial. The sanctity of the home and personal privacy are to be protected.

There is often a wide gap, however, between the written constitution and how Argentina actually is governed. For example, rights and guarantees may be suspended in times of emergency. Serious internal commotion or the threat of a foreign attack may be used by the president to justify declaring a state of siege. He is supposed to get the Senate's approval, which is given only for a limited period of time and only for specific purposes, but in practice both dictatorial and democratic governments have found it relatively easy to evade these restrictions, especially if the president has a congressional majority.

By the same token, Argentina's federal system is a great deal more centralized than a formal reading of the constitution would indicate. The federal government has specific, enumerated powers; the provinces are left with unspecified "reserve" powers, which in practice are quite whittled down. Provinces are referred to in the constitution as "the natural agents of the Federal Government, to see that the laws of the land are obeyed." Federal law and treaties always trump provincial law. The real sources of provincial weakness, however, are their financial dependence on the federal government and the latter's right to intervene in a province to maintain order. Concerning finances, the provinces are restricted in their ability to levy taxes. By contrast, the federal government has the revenues derived from the port of Buenos Aires and other (mostly indirect) taxes. Even those are hardly sufficient to cover its responsibilities, given the widespread practice of tax evasion, so there is little left over for revenue sharing with the provinces. As for the federal government's power of intervention, this frequently has been abused. Citing electoral fraud or financial mismanagement, past presidents have often replaced opposition party governors or provincial legislatures with their own hand-picked interveners.

Despite the tripartite division of powers at the national level, the president dominates the political system. As we noted at the start of this chapter, neither Congress nor the courts have been allowed to develop as powerful, independent institutions. At various times both have been abolished, suspended, or ignored. Even under democratic rule a president whose party enjoys a comfortable majority in both houses of Congress usually has no trouble getting any legislation he wants passed. And if the Supreme Court threatens to declare his acts unconstitutional, he can either get Congress to remove opposition justices through impeachment or increase the number of justices and pack it. Currently, the Supreme Court consists of nine justices, up from five when Menem first took over. They are appointed by the president, upon approval by the Senate, to serve for life, on condition of good behavior.

Congress consists of two houses: a Senate and a Chamber of Deputies. Every province, plus the city of Buenos Aires (the federal district), has three senators, for a total of seventy-two. They are directly elected for six years, with one third of the Senate up for reelection each two years. The Chamber of Deputies will vary in size after each census, with every province and the federal district allocated one deputy for every 33,000 inhabitants. Currently, there are 257 members of the Chamber, directly elected for four-year terms, with one half up for reelection every two years. Seats are distributed by proportional representation. An innovation begun in 2005 called for open primaries to select candidates for political party slates. The primary was designed to allow greater voter input into the candidate selection process. As in the United States, participation in the first open primaries was low.

Legislation may originate in either house, except for bills dealing with taxes or appropriations, which must start in the Chamber of Deputies. Bills must pass both houses, after which they go to the president for his approval. If he signs them, they become law, but if he vetoes them in whole or in part (he has the line-item veto), only a two-thirds majority of both houses can override him.

The president and vice president are directly elected by the voters for a four-year term. The president may be reelected once. His patronage powers are wide ranging: judges, ambassadors, cabinet officers, and the top military posts require Senate approval, but lower administration officials are appointed by him alone. Beyond that, he is charged with seeing that the laws are faithfully executed, acting as commander-in-chief of the armed forces, and opening each annual session of Congress with a state-of-the-union message. But the real source of his dominance lies in certain extraordinary powers, which presidents traditionally have interpreted in such a way as to overwhelm the other branches of government. First, there is the state-of-siege power, which can temporarily release a president from constitutional restraints. Second, the power to intervene in the provinces has enabled presidents in the past to cancel the mandates of their opponents. Third, the president may issue rules and instructions that are "urgent and necessary" for the execution of the laws. This innocuous phrase has been the source of presidents' increasingly common use of executive orders to bypass the regular legislative process. Some of the most controversial economic reforms of the Menem administration were put into effect in this way. Nor does the Congress usually act as a watchdog over such overexpansion of executive power. For President Kirchner, his coming to office in the midst of one of Argentina's worst economic crises enabled him to demand—and get—from Congress extraordinary emergency powers to issue legally binding decrees.

The 1994 constitutional reforms contained two noteworthy innovations. Beneath the president and vice president there is now a chief of the Cabinet, a kind of senior coordinating minister who represents the president before Congress during its debates (but without a vote) and presides over the Cabinet in the president's absence. The other new post is the elective mayor of the city of Buenos Aires, which previously had been governed by an intendant appointed by the president.

Political Parties and Pressure Groups

Argentina has been an essentially two party system since popular elections were introduced in 1912. This does not preclude minor parties, some of which may have considerable local strength, but traditionally between 70 and 80 percent of the electorate identifies with one of the two major parties. That is especially true in presidential election years; in off-year elections minor parties may make a better showing. Since Perón came on the political scene the Peronist Party has constituted one of the two major parties. Today, it is officially known as the Justicialist Party (JP), after justicialismo, which stands for "social justice" or the idea that wealth ought to be redistributed. Peronism's principal rival is the Radical Civic Union (UCR), or Radical Party, whose origins go back to 1889. As we have seen, the Radicals began as reformers, advocating "good government" and the expansion of suffrage, and thus became the party of the middle classes. By contrast, Peronism's mass base was in the labor movement.

Both of the major parties have experienced factional divisions. During the 1920s the Radicals were split between those who followed Argentina's first populist caudillo, Hipólito Yrigoyen, and the so-called Anti-Personalistas, who wanted a more pluralistic society. During the following decades, Radicals argued over whether the party should move toward the left and adopt a position of democratic national-socialism, or remain simply a moderate liberal democratic party. The UCR split into distinct parties in 1957, when Arturo Frondizi, the leader of the socialist wing, broke with the party leadership and led his Intransigent Radical Civic Union (UCRI) to victory the following year. After Frondizi was overthrown in 1962, however, his party went into a steady decline and eventually disappeared. The mainline Radicals, led by Ricardo Balbín, regained control of the party organization only to face another factional struggle during the 1970s. Balbín's conservative leadership came under increasing attack by the party's youth, who supported Raul Alfonsín, a human rights lawyer. After Balbín died Alfonsín took control of the UCR and steered it to victory in 1983, when democracy was restored. Under Alfonsín it established a close working relationship with the European social democratic parties. The debacle of Fernando de la Rúa seriously compromised the fortunes of the Radicals, but the party shows some recovery and currently enjoys the status of the leading minority party in the Congress.

Justicialismo's institutional development was marked by the fact that it began as Perón's personal vehicle, the Peronist Party. Even so, the party has often been a coalition of various interests. Besides the trade union movement, its membership consisted originally of dissidents from the Radicals who liked Perón's statist program, as well as right-wing authoritarians with fascist leanings. When Perón granted women the vote, Evita helped form a feminine wing to the party. Translated into practical terms, Justicialismo was a version of the corporate state, in which business, farmers, labor, the professions, and students were required to belong to officially sanctioned organizations. Its highly regulated economy, which aimed at national self-sufficiency, encouraged the growth of three powerful interests that became the permanent basis for the Peronist coalition: a highly centralized trade union movement, a class of rent-seeking capitalists living off state subsidies and protection, and a large government bureaucracy. These interests survived Perón's fall in 1955 and continued to resist all attempts by successive governments to eradicate Peronism. In the 1970s the left-wing Montonero guerrillas added themselves temporarily to the Peronist coalition, so that ideologically its supporters ran the entire political spectrum, from extreme left to extreme right. In the 1990s President Carlos Menem moved the Justicialist Party decisively to the right with his neoliberal program, at the cost of alienating a large number of working-class supporters. President Kirchner has resurrected some traditional Peronist populist rhetoric during his two years in office. Adopting a nationalist tone, Kirchner has called for Argentina's external creditors to take a back seat while he deals with the internal suffering of its citizens. Backed by policies that appear to be working, Justicialismo has recovered some of its leftist roots.

Both the UCR and the Justicialists are ideologically diverse and seek a broad appeal. Still, they must share the field with a number of minor parties. To the left there is the Front for a Country in Solidarity (*FrePaso*), a coalition of left-of-center parties that was elected in a coalition with the Radicals in the 1999 elections. Heralded as a new political phenomenon, *FrePaso* never could overcome its status as a protest party and, while still alive, has not been able to capitalize on its early electoral successes. More recently there is the Alternative for a Republic of Equals (ARI) led by Elisa Carrío, who is trying to mount another campaign for the presidency in 2007. ARI's platform revolves around ending political corruption. On the right, there is the Federal Recreate Movement (RECREAR) led by Ricardo López Murphy who represents business interests, and the Interbloque Federal (IF), a broad coalition of center-right parties.

All of Argentina's parties are poorly articulated. Factionalism and personalities within the parties usually count for more than ideology and procedures. In the run-up to the October 2005 legislative elections, which were considered a prelude to the 2007 presidential elections, infighting within the Peronist Party held center stage. Current Peronist President Néstor Carlos Kirchner is at serious odds with his predecessor, Eduardo Duhalde, over who should be placed on the Justicialist Party's slate of candidates for the legislative seats representing Buenos Aires. All the other parties hope that a split within the Peronist ranks will rebound to their benefit.

Pressure groups used to fill the political vacuum left by an unstable government based on weak parties. The old populist system, with its protected "hothouse" economy, nurtured well-organized interests—the military, labor, and business—that had an important stake in affecting government policy. Business bribed, labor struck, and the army rolled out the tanks. All that has changed. The military's horrible human rights record under the Proceso and its equally awful mismanagement of the economy left it without friends in any quarter. Labor split under the Menem regime between those who continued to vote Peronist and those who rejected the turn toward neoliberalism. More importantly, changes in Argentina's leading capitalist enterprises, which are no longer labor-intensive, have reduced the size of the blue-collar workforce. Fewer workers are unionized and more are self-employed. Unemployment and underemployment also keep wages depressed and discourage labor militancy. Finally, downsizing the state and selling off its many companies has undermined the position of those businesspeople who previously depended on government subsidies and contracts. Others have prospered in the new globalized economy, building huge conglomerates and squeezing out their smaller competitors. Like labor, businesses prosper or decline according to which sector of the economy they are in, and whether they can compete in an open economy.

Future Prospects

Since the transition to democracy in 1983 Argentina has experienced periods of political stability marked by free and open elections, the transition of power from one political party to another, and after some initial tensions, military willingness to be subordinated to civilian power. At the same time, Argentina has at times seemed to seesaw out of control, as the political crisis of 2001 that led to the resignation of Fernando de la Rúa illustrates.

The economic stability of Argentina has been even more problematic. Hyperinflation, massive external debt, defaulting on the foreign debt, and monetary and fiscal crises have all plagued the Argentine economy for years. The economic meltdown of 2001–2002 caused massive unemployment, impoverishment, and the contraction of the economy. The much vaunted reforms of neoliberalism championed by Carlos Menem failed, and the economic crises it precipitated served to reverse decades of development in Argentina. Perhaps one of the lessons of the recent past is that neither neoliberal or left-leaning, state-driven redistributive policies are the answers to Argentina's quest for sustained economic growth. Néstor Carlos Kirchner is offering up his own brand of populist social welfarism by emphasizing the need to respond to citizens' suffering before the debt is paid off. International lending agencies and creditors have for the time being been willing to negotiate on Kirchner's terms. It is important to note that he has not rejected negotiating with international lending agencies but wants to work with them on more equal terms.

Perhaps all that can be done at this particular moment is to adopt a wait-and-see attitude about Argentina's future prospects for continued development. Its current political and economic recovery remain very fragile. Argentines have weathered the most severe economic crises of their lives and, while their disaffection with recent political leaders has been high, their commitment to democracy remains strong. Kirchner, for his part, is enjoying record levels of support from the public, but Argentines have suffered much in the recent past from ineffectual leaders, and a negative turn in the economic recovery could unleash demands for someone else to take power. For now Argentines are casting their eyes toward the 2007 presidential elections. The continuing commitment to regularly contested elections is perhaps a sign that Argentina still sees democracy as the best hope for promoting change and progress.

Suggestions and Further Reading

Anderson, Martin. *Dossier Secreto: Argentina's Desaparecidos and the Myth of the "Dirty War"*. Boulder, CO: Westview Press, 1993.

Calvert, Susan, and Peter Calvert. *Argentina: Political Culture and Instability*. Pittsburgh, PA: University of Pittsburgh Press, 1989.

Corradi, Juan. *The Fitful Republic, Economy, Society, and Politics in Argentina*. Boulder, CO: Westview Press, 1985.

Crassweller, Robert D. *Perón and the Enigmas of Argentina*. New York: W. W. Norton & Co., 1987.

Epstein, Edward. *The New Argentine Democracy: The Search for a Successful Formula*. Westport, CT: Praeger, 1992.

Fraser, N., and M. Navarro. *Eva Perón*. New York: W. W. Norton & Co., 1980.

Gibson, Edward. *Class and Conservative Parties: Argentina in Comparative Perspective*. Baltimore: Johns Hopkins University Press, 1996.

Gillespie, Richard. *Soldiers of Perón: Argentina's Montoneros*. Oxford: Oxford University Press, 1982.

Lewis, Paul H. *The Crisis of Argentine Capitalism*. Chapel Hill: University of North Carolina Press, 1990.

Mazetti, Luigi. *Institutions, Parties, and Coalitions in Argentine Politics*. Pittsburgh: University of Pittsburgh Press, 1993.

McGuire, James. *Peronism without Perón: Unions, Parties, and Democracy in Argentina*. Stanford, CA: Stanford University Press, 1997.

Moyano, Maria Jose. *Argentina's Lost Patrol*. New Haven, CT: Yale University Press, 1995.

O'Donnell, Guillermo. *Bureaucratic Authoritarianism*. Berkeley: University of California Press, 1988.

Page, Joseph. *Perón: A Biography*. New York: Random House, 1983.

Potash, Robert A. *The Army and Politics in Argentina*. 3 vols. Stanford, CA: Stanford University Press, 1969–1996.

Ranis, Peter. *Argentine Workers: Peronism and Contemporary Class Consciousness*. Pittsburgh: Pittsburgh University Press, 1992.

Rock, David. *Argentina, 1516–1987*. Berkeley: University of California Press, 1987.

Tedesco, Laura. *The State of Democracy in Latin America: Post-transition Conflicts in Argentina and Chile*. New York: Routledge, 2004.

7

Brazil

The Disorders of a Progressive Democracy

Iêda Siqueira Wiarda

The commemoration of its 500 years of existence in 2000 was followed by the euphoria of the 2002 elections when a barely literate but heroic union leader, Luiz Inácio Lula da Silva, fifty-eight, won an overwhelming popular mandate over the government-supported candidate.[1] Proclaiming a "Brasil: Um País de Todos" (Brazil, a Country for Everybody), Lula, as he likes to be called, celebrated not only his electoral victory but also the promises inherent in an embrace of a multiethnic society. To most seasoned observers in and out of Brazil the following months demonstrated Lula as an adept national and international politician. He moved beyond his left basis toward the center, chose a good cabinet, and signed a number of well received international economic and diplomatic agreements.

As is often the case in the history of this enormous country, the promising first two years of Lula's presidency were quickly overcome by the spreading stain of major corruption linked to some of the of the president's closest associates in the spring of 2005. It is thus possible to repeat one of Brazil's proverbs, "A Country of the Future—Where the Future Never Arrives," or to replace Brazil's motto of "Order and Progress" for one that more closely reflects reality: "Disorders of Progress."[2]

Yet, it is well to remember that both the promises and the disappointments, the renewal of well placed hope and the travails of everyday life did not start with Lula but reflect the vast panorama of Brazil's multifaceted resources, both human and geographic, and a history both intriguing and unique in Latin America. It is thus incumbent to examine the cultural and political

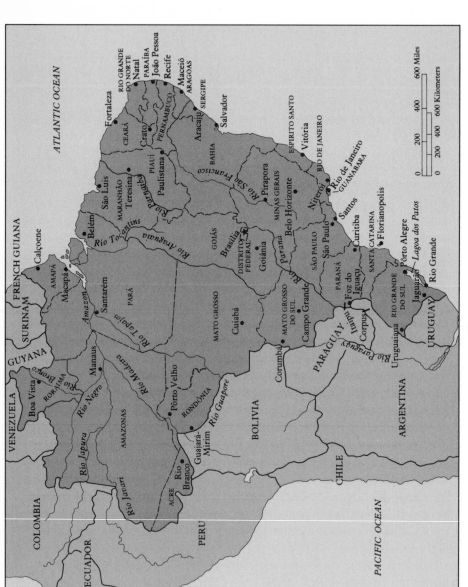

BRAZIL

underpinnings as we begin to assess whether this giant of a country, richly endowed in so many ways, will ever be able to indeed achieve what it senses it deserves—respect and weight within world councils.

The largest of Latin American countries, Brazil covers nearly half of South America and is the fifth largest country in the world. Except for a few islands, it consists of one single, unbroken land mass. Given its size, it is not surprising that Brazil has distinct regions and that Brazilians enjoy touting their state of origin as the best.

Historically, its population ranges from those living at the level of the Stone Age to those who are comfortable in the great metropolises of the world. Throughout this largest Portuguese-speaking country in the world, the language is surprisingly uniform. While different accents are detectable, Brazilians of all classes, all colors, and all regions understand each other. Thus, although Brazil faces many complex problems, a high degree of cultural integration among the overwhelming majority of its citizens remains a major source of strength. "A Country of All," indeed.

Brazil's 4,500-mile Atlantic coast facilitates trade with the world. Its population, approaching 180 million,[3] concentrated along that coast, has now slowed its growth to around 1 percent per year (1998–2002), thus giving the country the fifth most populous nation, a relatively low demographic density in comparison to other countries. Most of its citizens live on 10 percent of the land, in a 200-mile-wide zone bordering the Atlantic from Fortaleza to the Uruguayan border. The country shares borders with all South American countries with the exception of Ecuador and Chile. Controlling the world's eighth largest market-based economy, Brazil was the economic miracle from the mid-1960s through the mid-1970s, until the economic disaster of the 1980s. Hyperinflation in the early 1990s was tamed by the ambitious "Real Plan" of the late 1990s. Inflation is estimated around 10 percent (1998–2002). Globalization has meant that Brazil's products can be found everywhere, from orange juice, coffee, bran and oils, soybeans, cocoa, and beef to transport equipment and parts, metallurgical products. Brazilian engineers and technicians supervise and complete major construction projects in Africa and the Middle East. São Paulo's stock exchange, Bovespa, is quoted in the economic sections of most newspapers. The Internet and the World Wide Web have enmeshed the country with the rest of the world, as seen in the linkages formed between human rights groups and indigenous councils.

Globalization has meant that Brazil has had to divest itself of its long-held protectionist garb. More liberal and flexible interpretations of 1988 constitution restrictions have served as inducements for greater foreign capital participation. Under former President Fernando Henrique Cardoso, Brazil strengthened its economic ties with Argentina, Paraguay, and Uruguay under the Southern Common Market, (MERCOSUL); Chile and Bolivia became associate members.

Early in 2005 Brasília was the site of a South American and Arab country summit; this was another indication that President Lula had gone beyond traditional ties to Portuguese-speaking African countries to Muslim countries and China in particular. The heightened economic and international profile gave Brazilians a renewed sense of direction and cause for nationalistic pride. But this sense was tempered by the realization that the riches of Brazil have not as yet been fully and humanely explored and that corruption seemed even more rampant than ever. The country's entrepreneurs, among the most highly paid in the world, have failed to turn much of their abundance toward the improvement of some of the most impoverished people in the world.[4]

In short, Brazil is now a major player in the economic and strategic worlds, but social and political problems persist and fester. The promise of democracy and of reform, so firmly held when power passed into civilian hands after decades of military regimes, has not delivered a better life for many Brazilians. Thus as Brazil has celebrated 500 years of existence, its citizens rightly ask about their past and speculate about their future. It is to this past history and speculation about the new millennium that this chapter is devoted.

History, Background, and Political Culture

Brazil, bigger than the forty-eight contiguous states of the United States, stretches across three time zones, and the Atlantic island of Fernando de Noronha territory lies in a fourth. Most of the country's landmass is east of the United States; the Equator crosses Brazil's northern border, and the area south of Rio de Janeiro is outside the Tropical Zone. Mountains, geologically old and not very high, moderate the climate, and nights are relatively cool. Rainfall is generally plentiful, but precipitation in the Northeast is irregular, and that region, plagued by droughts, is the poorest in Brazil.

Some twenty mountains are higher than 5,000 feet, but none is as high as 10,000 feet. Half of the country is a plateau running from 500 to 3,000 feet above sea level. The Amazon carries more water into the ocean than any other river in the world; the immense river can be plied by oceangoing vessels as far as Peru, and many of its tributaries are navigable by major ships. Despite having no great lakes, Brazil contains one fifth of the world's fresh water. For a country that has only recently found much oil it is fortunate that Brazil has great hydroelectric potential and that it boasts the world's largest hydroelectric power plant at Itaipú; less fortunate is the fact that the country's overall energy production is considered inefficient and expensive compared with that of other countries.

Brazilians usually divide their country into five regions: North, Northeast, Southeast, South, and West Central. The North, stretching across the northern third of Brazil, is the largest (42.07 percent of the area) and least populated region (7 percent of the 2001 population). It is dominated by the Amazon and is an area of legendary wealth and potential, mostly still untapped. Manaus and Belém are the major cities in the largest rain forest in the world.

The Northeast, with 18.2 percent of the land and 28 percent of the population in 2001, occupies the eastern bulge and has become notorious in recent years for recurring droughts and human hardship. It is tropical in climate and has a narrow coastal plain where traditional crops such as sugarcane and cacao have been grown for centuries. It is a region of old Portuguese names and proud political traditions, but, poor and far away from the center of power, it is often labeled "Brazil's Bangladesh."[5]

The densely populated Southeast represents 10.86 percent of Brazil's territory and close to half (43 percent) of the nation's population. It has long been the political and economic center of the country, contributing more than 60 percent of the country's gross national product (GNP). Large numbers of Japanese, Italians, Lebanese, and impoverished Northeasterners have come to São Paulo and often prospered, making that city and the state the cosmopolitan heart of Brazil. Industry in this region has attracted millions, and its mild climate and abundant rainfall have reinforced it as a magnet. The highlands, rugged and mined for gold and precious and semiprecious stones in colonial days, are now mined for high-grade iron ore and other minerals.

The South, stretching from Paraná to Rio Grande do Sul, has attracted a large number of North European immigrants. Containing 14 percent of the population, the South occupies 6.79 percent of the national territory. Important agriculturally, and the home of national political leaders such as presidents Getúlio Vargas and General Ernesto Geisel, the South has for decades been a haven for separatist ideas. The climate is temperate with occasional frosts that damage the coffee crop.

The West Central region includes the states of Mato Grosso (North and South), Goiás, and the federal district. This region has grown tremendously since the establishment of Brasília as the country's capital in 1960 and the development of lucrative agribusiness. Rainfall is sometimes sparse, and the climate is tropical to mild in the highlands. In the north the region resembles the Amazon area, with dense forests and heavy rains, but its savannas are ideal for cattle-raising. Some rivers flow north toward the Amazon, whereas others run south to join the Plata Basin. With 22.08 percent of the territory and 8 percent of the population of the country, the West Central region is now contributing relatively more than previously (now slightly over 6 percent) to the GNP. It is reminiscent of the American Far West, with extensive cattle ranches, sparse population, and a wealth of minerals.

The Southeast and the South have composed the undisputed economic and political heartland for decades. São Paulo, a state with a population larger than Argentina, has a GDP second only to all of Mexico. The Northeast is the proverbial land of history, poverty, and drought. The North is the Amazon land of jungle and promise, and the West Central is the brash political and growing agribusiness center. What links these varied regions is the Portuguese language and, progressively, a national communications grid. Railroads are scarce, highways are somewhat less so, and rivers are used when not interrupted by falls; airplanes now link most cities throughout the country, as do television, the telephone, the Internet, and radio.

Brazil's history sets it apart from Spanish America.[6] Brazil can be said to have existed before it was formally discovered by the Portuguese explorer Pedros Álvares Cabral in 1500. In 1494 the Pope, in an attempt to avoid subsequent disputes between the then-major empires of Spain and Portugal, divided the South American continent into an eastern portion, to belong to Portugal, and a larger western portion, to belong to Spain. Before long it was clear that the Pope's Tordesilhas line would be breached and the Portuguese would proceed to colonize the Brazilian landmass and impart to it their own Iberian traditions and language. The Tordesilhas line had granted Portugal only the easternmost bulge of today's Brazil, but Portuguese and later Brazilian explorers pushed the line westward to the present borders. Seldom did land wars erupt between the Portuguese and the Spanish colonizers and their heirs. Often expansion occurred naturally as Brazilian pioneers went beyond the Tordesilhas line—in fact, most of them had never heard of any such line—to settle new land and populate new areas, and their offspring moved even farther west. Thus, from the beginning of its history Brazil's concept of a "living frontier" has been a major aspect of its existence as a nation and has defined the character of its relations with other South American countries.

In the very early decades, however, the Portuguese seldom ventured beyond a few scattered outposts on the Atlantic shore. Portugal, in contrast to Spain, was more interested in its lucrative trade with India than in exploring a primitive land where early promises of gold and precious stones had gone unfulfilled. The only attraction of the new colony seems to have been a red wood that produced a brilliant red dye. From this red wood—the color of glowing coals, and thus *brasil* wood in Portuguese—came the name of Brazil. In the middle of the sixteenth century the French twice tried to settle near present-day Rio de Janeiro and were driven off, but their bold challenge proved to be the catalyst to Portugal's interest, and João III finally decided that he needed to secure Cabral's discovery. The king parceled out the coastline in the form of fourteen royal grants (*capitanias*) to wealthy Portuguese. The *capitanias* gave Brazil its first formal shape and laid the basis for the country's enduring federalist tradition.

The *capitanias* grew slowly and became less stagnant only as the Portuguese started raising sugarcane later in the sixteenth century. Sugar, however, required a great deal of labor in its production, and Brazilian Indians were not well-suited to this strenuous labor, preferring death to slavery. The Portuguese therefore captured blacks at trading posts along the African coast and took them to tend the sugarcane fields and refineries. For the next three centuries over three million young blacks were forcibly brought to the colony. Intermarriage between Portuguese, Indians, blacks, and the growing number of Brazilians (i.e. Portuguese subjects born in Brazil) was not uncommon, and the basis for Brazil's racial mixture was established.

Jesuit missionaries attempted to protect the Indians by gathering them into villages organized around a church, with the aim of Christianizing and educating them. Although the missionaries' intentions may have been good and they did save the Indians from enslavement and slaughter, most of the Indians died from European diseases to which they lacked immunity such as smallpox, measles, tuberculosis, and the common cold. Their unique culture was largely lost or slowly blended with the culture of the far more numerous blacks and whites. Today only around two hundred thousand Indians remain in Brazil.

A sense of Brazilian national identity first emerged with the expulsion of the Protestant Dutch. For two decades they had controlled the northeastern coast, but Portuguese and Brazilians drove them out in 1654, a triumph for the Catholic Church and for a Portuguese Brazil. The event that brought about the opening the interior, however, was the discovery of gold and plentiful precious and semiprecious stones just before the onset of the eighteenth century. In Minas Gerais (literally "general mines") the development of the interior was given a major thrust by the exploits of the daring *bandeirantes*, mostly pioneers from São Paulo. These descendants of Portuguese and Indians traveled in bands and brought along flags (*bandeiras*), families, cattle, and Indian slaves. If confronted by the Jesuits, they were likely to pillage the missionaries' villages. Cruel and energetic, they ventured far from the coast and established the first settlements of the present-day states of Goiás and Mato Grosso. Diamantina in central Minas Gerais, now almost unknown outside of Brazil, was at one time the diamond capital of the world. It was these early mining towns that saw the first stirrings toward independence from Portugal, tragic and abortive attempts to emulate the North American independence movement and the republican form of government.

Brazil's independence came about in a different way from that of its Spanish neighbors. The other South American countries rebelled against Spain and eventually formed separate republics, but Brazil stayed intact and its "war" of independence does not merit that label. Historically speaking, Brazil owes its independence to the fact that Napoleon's army invaded Portugal in

1807, and under British pressure and protection the Portuguese court moved to Brazil. João VI enjoyed the colony so much that he raised it in rank to a kingdom within the Portuguese empire and stayed in Rio de Janeiro long after the Napoleonic threat was past. When the British finally persuaded him to return to Lisbon he left his son Pedro I as his regent. Shortly afterward in 1822 Dom Pedro proclaimed Brazil's independence, and this Portuguese prince became Brazil's first monarch.

After this rather uneventful independence Brazil experienced minor civil wars, slave rebellions, and attempts at secession, including some in the South in favor of a republican form of government, but the former Portuguese colony somehow managed to survive all struggles intact. The best explanation is that Brazil, in contrast to the rest of Spanish America, did not struggle through a protracted and divisive war of independence. The Portuguese House of Bragança ruled until 1889, and even today there are Bragança pretenders to head the Brazilian government.

The 1988 constitution allowed voters to choose a monarchical form of government, if they wished, in 1993. Although Brazilians rejected monarchy, many debated its merits. In the 1993 referendum 12 percent of the participants voted in favor of a monarchical parliamentary system. The easy separation from the colonial power and the long period of relative stability gave Brazil a strong feeling of national unity and nearly a century of enlightened rule. In fact, it can be argued that it was the farsightedness of Brazil's second emperor, Pedro II, that brought his reign to a close. His daughter's approval of the abolition of slavery in 1888 robbed Pedro II of the crucial support of the landed gentry, and shortly thereafter a republic was proclaimed and the heartbroken king went into exile.

However, other forces helped bring about the republic, many of them nurtured by the king's policies. A greater opening to the world made it possible for the Brazilian elite to become familiar with democratic and republican forms of government elsewhere, and a trip by the emperor to the United States, fully reported back home, made educated people familiar with the thriving republic to the north. In the meantime, especially during Pedro II's prolonged reign, people in the southern portion of the country were feeling neglected by the government in Rio de Janeiro. Of even greater significance, younger military men were becoming increasingly politically involved and restless under the emperor's rule. Brazil's war against Paraguay, which lasted from 1864 to 1870, was fought with a mixture of pride and shame because it pitted a giant against a determined but extremely weak opponent. Paraguay was ruined for decades by the consequences of the war and even though Brazil and its allies, Argentina and Uruguay, were victorious, the war had been expensive and divisive for them.

The war debt, the doubts about the war itself, a desire for greater say in the form of government, and the abolition of slavery converged to make change a foregone conclusion. Yet Pedro II was personally respected, and the overthrow of the monarchy came as a surprise to most Brazilians. Benjamin Constant and Marshal Floriano Peixoto, who represented affected military elements, engineered it with the crucial blessing of Marshal Deodoro da Fonseca, a longtime friend and supporter of Pedro II. On November 15, 1889, the Republic of Brazil was proclaimed. The emperor departed for Europe with his family and a few friends, refusing to accept the substantial compensation that the revolutionaries offered. His wife died shortly thereafter, and Pedro himself died two years later.

Pedro's long reign provided Brazil with decades of stability, but at the turn of the century the country was almost empty; its sparse population was mostly illiterate and divided into a minuscule rich elite, a large poor class, and a nearly nonexistent middle class. The freed people were hardly better off than they had been as slaves. Wealthy Brazilians sent their sons to Europe, mostly to France to get an education, because Pedro II's legendary love of learning had not been translated into the establishment of even a basic educational system. The few schools that did exist were run by the Catholic Church, and most offered only a rudimentary education to the children of the elite.

From 1889 to today the form of government has been that of a federal republic, but Brazil has never had a truly federal system. The president has traditionally been stronger than governors or mayors, checks and balances have not always applied, and the republican system itself has been tempered by a degree of authoritarianism. The 1988 constitution attempted to give greater power to Congress. Although the 1992 impeachment of the first president to be democratically elected seemed to indicate new congressional authority, the corruption surrounding major congressional leaders in the 1990s and 2000s ran counter to constitutional intentions. In reality the possibility of impeachment for corruption remains alive, but it reflects less congressional power than the weakness of the party system.

The military, a power behind the throne during the monarchy, is still influential, and between 1964 and 1985 it governed the country with very few challenges. Revealingly, the latent powers of the military to intervene were not fully eliminated in the liberal constitutional charter of 1988. In the 1990s political turmoil and the weakness of congresses, presidents, and political parties have caused many Brazilians to look again to the military as the ultimate stabilizer. It is to the credit of the military that, so far at least, it has not taken advantage of the situation to reenter the political arena as it did in the chaos of 1964.

The middle class has expanded, especially since the 1930s, but it cannot compete in terms of sheer political and economic power with the military and economic elites. The poor still form the largest group, and they have gained some welfare protection since the 1930s. The 1988 constitution extended and expanded many of their protections and welfare entitlements, but again, many promises remained on paper. The 1993–1994 constitutional revisions sought to review the plight of the poor pragmatically and find the money to implement social justice provisions. Sophisticated Brazilians in the 1990s liked to joke that they live in "Belindia," a juxtaposition of Belgium and India. The 1988 constitution contained the promise of a less disparate Brazil, but the reality has been far less generous.

The lingering economic gap is somehow bridged—even transcended—by Brazil's vibrant culture. Television viewers worldwide are familiar with the spectacular pageant of carnival in Rio de Janeiro, in which the most daring and imaginative (as well as expensive) displays are staged by slum dwellers. Popular music, similarly highlighted during carnival, reaches many countries in toned-down versions of samba and bossa nova transformed into the all-pervasive Muzak. Brazilian movies have competed well in world festivals and in box office appeal; television shows are technically advanced and innovative; and a great many *novelas* (soap operas), first shown in Brazil, are routinely seen in Portugal, in Lusophone, Africa, and even throughout Spanish America and Spain itself.[7]

From an international perspective it is not far-fetched to consider Brazil the cultural center of the Portuguese-speaking world because of its vastly superior number of writers, actors, painters, and artists in comparison with other Lusophone countries. Jorge Amado, whose works fictionally depicted life in Bahia and the Northeast, saw several of his novels, among them *Gabriela* and *Dona Flor*, become best sellers and then movies in the United States. The visual arts are noteworthy; some of their best-known interpreters reflect the ethnic mix of the country. Candido Portinari's murals in São Paulo portray the suffering of Northeastern migrants and urban poor; the paintings of Manabu Mabe, another *paulista*, are viewed around the world. The cities of Salvador and Ouro Preto feature some of the hemisphere's best examples of Baroque architecture by early artisans. Brasília is well known for its futuristic design, and its architecture has been emulated on all continents.

Sports, particularly soccer, occupy an important position in Brazilians' lives. Life comes to a stop when the World Cup soccer competition takes place every four years, and politicians vie with each other to show their devotion to a winning team. Volleyball, water sports, track and field, basketball, car racing, and tennis are other major sports in which Brazilians have done well in international meets.

A love of *novelas*, a penchant for emotional and earthy sambas, a cynical approach to religion and other ponderous matters, and a perennial optimism in the face of daily disappointments seem to characterize the Brazilian personality. In the words of Elizabeth Bishop, a Pulitzer-prize winning writer who made Brazil her home for decades,

> Brazilians are very quick, both emotionally and physically. Like the heroes of Homer, men can show their emotions without disgrace. Their superb futebol players hug and kiss each other when they score goals, and weep dramatically when they fail to. Brazilians are also quick to show sympathy. One of the first and most useful words a foreigner picks up is *coitado* ["poor thing"] . . . [There is the great] Brazilian belief in tolerance and forbearance . . . [with] the greatest tolerance . . . extended to love, because in Brazil that is always the most important emotion. Love is the constant element in almost every news story, street scene, or familiar conversation.[8]

Few Brazilians would quarrel with the poet's understanding of their soul.

When Bishop wrote, she had in mind a mostly rural country; by the 2000s more than 70 percent of the population had become urban. Greater Brasília, which many thought would never amount to more than a backwater capital, now has a population over two million and is a major magnet in the West Central region. Porto Alegre, with three million inhabitants, is the major center in the South. Urban growth has been spectacular; it has aided economic development and brought more people to work in the great and expanding industries, but has created serious social and political problems. The major cities are chronically short of funds to provide even the most rudimentary services, such as water and sewer facilities. Yet, various attempts to lure the peasants back to the land have been dismal failures.

Whether in the cities or in the countryside four major groups make up the Brazilian population: the indigenous Indians; the Portuguese, who began colonizing in the sixteenth century and who again came in large numbers after their own "revolution" in the 1970s; Africans, who were brought as slaves to work on the plantations and in the mines; and the various European, Middle Eastern, and Asian immigrants, who have settled since the middle of the nineteenth century, particularly in the Southeast, where they have made São Paulo one of the most cosmopolitan cities in the world. The states of Santa Catarina and Rio Grande do Sul have been havens for waves of German immigrants, once prompting the unfounded fear that they might subvert Brazil to Hitler's cause. It is conservatively estimated that about five million Europeans settled in Brazil between 1875 and 1960, and millions of Japanese and Middle Easterners have come to Brazil to find a land of opportunity. These immigrants struggled for a long time but eventually succeeded beyond all expectations. Many highly placed politicians, professionals, and entrepreneurs are second- and third-generation hyphenated Brazilians. Most immigrant families have become fully integrated, having adopted the Portuguese language and often the Catholic religion as well. The sense of being Brazilian is strong; ethnic strife is minor, and when it does occur openly it is not condoned officially and is ridiculed and condemned by the media. President Lula's "Um País de Todos" (A Country for Everybody) is not an empty slogan.

Most Portuguese explorers usually came without their families and often intermarried with Indians and later with African slaves. Thus, although the basic ethnic stock of Brazil was once Portuguese, miscegenation and the subsequent waves of immigrants have resulted in a rich ethnic and cultural heritage. Traditionally, Brazilians are adamant in denying any racial or ethnic prejudice. It is true, however, that the farther one progresses up the socioeconomic and political ladder, the whiter one is likely to be (although not necessarily carrying a Portuguese name, as presidential candidate Paulo Maluf and presidents Juscelino Kubitshek and Ernesto Geisel attest). By the same token, attempts to organize black movements have not been very successful and, perhaps revealingly, the labels used in these attempts are not Portuguese but imported from abroad, and the leadership is as likely to be foreign as Brazilian.

The Indians have been far less fortunate than blacks or immigrants. Located mainly in the northern and western border regions and in the upper Amazon Basin, there are now only around two hundred thousand Brazilian Indians and they are considered an endangered group. Their numbers have been declining for years, but recently increased contact with the outside world, the expansion of agribusiness, and road projects have accelerated the process. Although the government has programs to establish reservations and to provide assistance, it has promoted or at least condoned the expansion of roads, mining, and commerce onto hunting and tribal lands, with disastrous results for the dwindling numbers of indigenous people. Tragic stories of farmers and miners despoiling Indian villages are not unusual. Meanwhile, the efforts of private groups and the Catholic Church to help the Indians survive are subject to controversy, and most Brazilians feel that the Indians should "integrate"— or else.

The fact that the few Indians who have survived often cannot communicate in Portuguese has not helped their cause because the Indian languages are wholly foreign to the vast majority of Brazilians. In fact, Portuguese is one of the main strands that holds the overwhelming majority of Brazilians together. It is true that Brazilians who live near the borders can communicate in Spanish and that educated Brazilians know English, but Portuguese is the language of Brazil. North American-Brazilian cultural centers are popular, and a knowledge of English is avidly sought as a key to professional, business, and social betterment. With the economic recession of the early 1990s some professionals went to the United States, Portugal, and Japan seeking better opportunities, only to find themselves unwelcome aliens; many returned to their native country disillusioned. With the advent of the Internet and global communications most groups have established links with similar ones in the United States, Europe, and Asia.

Another main cultural strand is the Roman Catholic Church, but this largest Catholic country in the world is one in which Catholic tenets have traditionally been lightly respected and in which the number of religious vocations has never been high. Protestant churches, notably charismatic and fundamentalist ones, have grown tremendously in recent years, especially among the poorer urban dwellers. By now Protestants have their own informal *bloque* in Congress, and a governor of Rio de Janeiro, an *evangélico*, has the very Brazilian name of Anthony William Garotinho Matheus de Oliveira. Many Brazilians, even if nominally Catholic, are devoted to various spiritualist and voodoo rituals. There are Jewish groups, mostly in Rio de Janeiro and São Paulo; Moacyr Scliar, a well-known novelist and essayist from Porto Alegre, has written extensively on Brazil's Jewish community and its role in national life. Overall, religious tolerance is the norm and persecution for one's beliefs has been rare, although the Catholic Church is accorded a special place in religious festivals, family traditions, and everyday life.

Interest Groups, Parties, and Political Organizations

With its size and economic, political, and regional diversity, it is not surprising that Brazil has always had a variety of interest groups, parties, and organizations; but this variety has become more pronounced in recent decades. Because Pedro II's empire represented stability and provided for a great deal of freedom, the transition from monarchy to republic in 1889 did not bring about an outcropping of popular groups overnight. Indeed, the republic emerged as a continuation of oligarchic rule, one in which the landed interests were the most powerful, the states of São Paulo and Minas Gerais continued their preeminence, and the top military officers exerted the moderating power (*poder moderador*) that the emperor had represented. Outstanding civilians such as the great jurist Rui Barbosa were sometimes brought to the fore, and it was he, rather than the military leaders, who wrote the decree that brought about the separation of church and state in 1890.

World War I brought the first major challenge to the Brazilian rulers. The loss of European markets was disastrous; farmers were unable to sell their crops, and only toward the end of the European conflict did trade improve somewhat as the warring nations sought to import foodstuffs. Brazil officially opted to side with the Allies in 1916, and this choice helped the country's trade situation, but even this improved trade was not enough to cure festering problems. The coffee plantations, which had supplanted sugar plantations as the major export activity, were overproducing, and prices continued to drop. More ominous, the southern states, which long had felt alienated from Rio de Janeiro, were becoming more restless, and the old dream of secession persisted.

Issues of civilian-military relations were a constant source of aggravation to people in and out of government. Although civilians managed to keep the military out of the presidency, discontent within the army was a concern for all presidents. The impact of the Great Depression was acutely felt early on in Brazil as exports continued to drop. Influential Brazilians, powerful farmers, and young military officers began to look for a forceful president as the 1930 election approached. The incumbent president contributed to the search for alternatives by favoring a presidential candidate from his own state of São Paulo in defiance of an informal tradition whereby presidents from São Paulo and Minas Gerais had taken turns. This proved to be the catalyst for *mineiros'* support of another candidate, Getúlio Vargas, a popular governor from the southern state of Rio Grande do Sul. When the official candidate won the election many Brazilians felt that Vargas had been deprived of a legitimate triumph, and he was urged to rebel. Feeling that he had enough military and popular support to succeed, Vargas and his followers moved by train toward the capital. Support grew as he traveled north, and by the time he reached Rio de Janeiro the president had fled and Vargas was able to assume power with a minimum of force.

Between 1930 and his resignation in 1945 Vargas ruled with a combination of cunning; ever-changing political coalitions; a vaguely corporatist Estado Novo concept; and a brand of populism that endeared him to many Brazilians, who came to call him "the father of the poor." With little regard for rules Vargas instituted extraconstitutional policies and programs and was not averse to ruthless suppression of people who opposed him. Power was centralized, and federalism, already weak, was practically abolished when he used his powers to intervene in the states, appointing his own governors. Education became centralized and controlled, censorship was imposed, and the legislative assembly was not convened. Although many of Vargas's decrees were softened in their application, other policies he instituted were to have lasting effects. His social security system, a novelty in Brazil that made him very popular with workers, still forms the core of today's social welfare system. He garnered a great deal of support from nationalists of different political stripes with extensive nationalization of economic institutions and natural resources. Characteristically calling himself "apolitical," he presided over a regime that lacked a coherent ideology and even political parties. He counted on the support of labor but made sure it had little independent strength.

During World War II, after some initial hesitation, Brazil joined the Allied side in 1942 and contributed troops and officers who saw action in Italy alongside U.S. forces. The United States was allowed to use Brazilian bases in the Northeast, and the country prospered because of the great demand for its products. Yet World War II, fought for the preservation of democracy, had the unsurprising effect of calling into question Vargas's authoritarianism. In October 1945 military officers, responding to popular demands for a freer system, stepped in and sent Vargas home to Rio Grande do Sul. The second republic, with a former minister of war, General Eurico Gaspar Dutra, as president, was ushered in during January 1946.

In September 1946 a new constitution was adopted and, although it guaranteed free elections and civil liberties, it preserved the greatly enlarged executive built up by Vargas and his centralized institutions. President Dutra continued investments in public works and further expanded the health and transportation systems. Inflation, however, was a constant menace. Brazil expected greater trade and economic help from the United States, especially in view of Brazil's role in World War II, but these expectations were disappointed. Even more disappointing was that the massive European Marshall Plan for economic reconstruction was not paralleled in Latin America. Vargas was popularly elected to the presidency in 1951 as the candidate of the Labor Party, but he no longer commanded the respect or the affection he had enjoyed during his earliest years in power. He had lost much of his popular appeal and was unable to deal with economic problems any more successfully than had Dutra. Charges of corruption involved some of his closest associates, and when one of his aides appeared to have been directly involved in an assassination attempt against an opposition journalist and the death of an air force major, the armed forces seemed prepared to push Vargas to resign. Faced with the possibility of a coup, or perhaps in an effort to avoid possible bloodshed, Vargas committed suicide.

The election of 1955, in which Juscelino Kubitshek was chosen as president and former Vargas minister of labor João Goulart vice president was made possible by the military's willingness to play its *poder moderador* role to the hilt and serve as the guarantor that the duly elected officials could take office. Kubitshek, who had been one of the most popular governors of Minas Gerais, vowed to give Brazil "fifty years of progress in five," and in many ways he fulfilled his promise, but at a heavy price. He pushed for the hasty completion of hydroelectric plants and a variety of public works, the establishment of several new universities, medical schools, and economic institutions, and the opening of major highways and airports. He launched Brazil's automobile and aircraft industries and built the long-planned new capital, Brasília, in the central state of Goiás. All of these projects could be justified as serving as the building blocks for a modern Brazil, but they were pushed too hastily and involved tremendous cost overruns. By the time he left office Juscelino (as he preferred to be called) was still a very popular man, but inflation had become a major burden. The successful presidential candidate in 1960, the former mayor and governor of São Paulo Jânio Quadros, ran on a pledge to balance the budget, end inflation, protect Brazil from foreign greed, curb corruption, and launch an independent foreign policy.

Quadros was elected with the largest plurality in the history of Brazil, but he soon ran afoul of Congress and alienated even some of his strongest supporters by his aloof and erratic behavior. He did push for measures designed to reform exchange controls, end consumer subsidies, and curtail the printing of worthless money, but these measures took away much of his support among the poor people and others most negatively affected. He publicly praised the Soviet Union, even though little trade was possible between the two countries and a communist system held little appeal for most Brazilians. He pinned a medal on Fidel Castro, even though it was common knowledge that the Cuban dictator had just presided over a period of terrorism and indiscriminate killings at the infamous *paredón* (wall).

Quadros became an even more enigmatic figure as he exhibited a number of eccentricities, among them wearing a uniform and requiring others around him to wear them too to ward off "germs." His economic measures did not seem to be working, his popularity evaporated, and his peculiarities led people to believe he was unstable. No longer adulated as a savior, he resigned abruptly and left Brazil before completing a year in office. His irresponsible tantrum was to cost Brazil's democracy dearly.

Quadros's vice president, João Goulart, had been picked for that position almost as an afterthought and because it was felt he would bring to the ticket whatever remained of the old Vargas machine. Goulart, like Vargas, was from the South, a landowner and a politician with close ties to labor. At the time of Quadros's unexpected resignation Goulart happened to be in the People's Republic of China. Politicians favorable as well as unfavorable to him counseled that he return to Brazil by a long route so that the military, Congress, and other influential groups could work out a compromise that would enable him to become president. The eventual compromise created the post of prime minister who would share power with Goulart (and probably be close to the people who most objected to him), and Goulart became president. But almost from the very start the relations among the president, the military, and the old-line politicians were strained. Goulart prevailed in getting rid of the prime minister, but this was a Pyrrhic victory.

For the people who were already suspicious of his intentions it confirmed their fear that Goulart wanted to become a second Vargas, only more so: more populist, more to the left, and more demagogic. His populist economic policies proved more inflationary than beneficial, and unable or unwilling to control his one base of support, the unions, he allowed strikes and threats of strikes to become a daily occurrence. For many Brazilians, who traditionally had opted for their flag's motto *Ordem e Progresso* (Order and Progress), the spectacle of a demagogic president unable to provide at least a measure of economic and political certainty engendered a longing for a more stable president.

Much has been written about the U.S. involvement in the coup that eventually drove Goulart form the presidency. A fair appraisal would conclude that many North Americans felt uneasy about the turn of events. This uneasiness was compounded by Goulart's vague, inflammatory threats against "foreign powers" and by the suggestion that some of his more radical advisers may have had links to Brazil's small Communist Party. However, to conclude that the United States engineered the coup is to be blind to the realities of Brazilian traditions and politics in 1964. The United States probably knew about and did not discourage a coup. For a variety of good and not so good reasons the U.S. embassy was supportive of the people who wanted to get rid of Goulart. After all, a number of highly placed North Americans in Brazil were close friends of influential Brazilians who were active in the opposition, especially those in the military.[9]

The actual unraveling is beyond dispute. The final catalyst came from Goulart himself when he seemed to undermine military discipline by siding with groups of mutinous soldiers. With the growing middle class already bitter because of inflation and the daily uncertainties caused by strikes, the military was urged to fulfill its constitutional duty to act as the *poder moderador* and make sure that "order and progress," as well as discipline, prevailed. Unhappy governors of powerful states such as Minas Gerais joined with generals in insisting that Goulart resign or face the prospect of a protracted civil war.

The "revolution" of March 31, 1964, was virtually bloodless. There was practically no support for Goulart and even his base, the labor unions, failed to rise in his favor. Most political leaders regarded military rule as the only alternative to strikes fomented by the president, mutinies, and daily chaos. The army chief of staff, Marshal Humberto Castelo Branco, who had seen combat duty in Italy alongside U.S. forces, was chosen president. A quiet, intellectual man, he sincerely believed that his term in office would be a mere transition to another, more reliable civilian president. But Castelo Branco was in the minority among his fellow officers, most of whom—along with a great many civilians in Brazil—felt otherwise and thought that the country needed a strong "apolitical" government. The military was destined to rule Brazil for over twenty years, and even in the liberal 1988 constitution its traditional power as a moderating force was not eliminated.

Castelo Branco himself never doubted that he had acted constitutionally. The 1946 constitution had given the armed forces the responsibility of maintaining law and order and ensuring the normal functioning of government. In the military men's eyes—as in the eyes of many Brazilians—the civilian president had violated his own mandate. Goulart had trampled on the constitution and had violated the military's code of conduct by siding with mutinous troops against their officers.

Whatever the debate about the constitutionality of the military takeover there was little anticipation of what came after the coup. Instead of a transitional regime the military consolidated its power. Even those politicians who had initially sided with the officers were banned from politics or sent into exile. The still-popular Kubitshek was among those who were proscribed. At first, political parties were considered unnecessary or a nuisance, and thus the thirteen that did exist were abolished. Eventually the military saw the need to promote a more "popular" image, and two political organizations, the progovernment National Renovating Alliance (ARENA) and the opposition Brazilian Democratic Movement (MDB) were formed under government auspices. As their names indicate they were coalitions of parties and ideological factions rather than political parties in the U.S. sense.

For a time, especially between 1968 and 1972, the military leaders in power were prone to disdain any effort at democratization. Their idea seems to have been to provide an economic miracle that would, in turn, expand the economic pie and eventually the number of pieces that could be given away to the populace. The emphasis was on technocratic rather than political advice, on economic development rather than preparation for democracy and popular participation. Censorship was the order of the day; the regime in power was not hesitant to show who was boss and to use threats and outright brutality if it felt they were needed to "sanitize" the system.

As long as economic expansion continued and inflation was kept fairly low, demands that the military give up power were muted, but the oil shock of 1973 changed the situation. Coming from outside and completely out of the control of the government, the skyrocketing oil prices meant a drastic reduction of the economic forecasts. The economic miracle was no more, the pie was no longer growing, and the people who were demanding more than the merest of crumbs were becoming less intimidated and more vocal. With the economy faltering the military leaders saw the wisdom of moving for an *abertura*, an opening toward the eventual resumption of democratic forms.

Under an administration-sponsored bill, Congress abolished the two-party system and a multiparty system was put into place. Five parties were recognized under the party reorganization law; two of them were actual continuations of those allowed previously. The opposition MDB became the Brazilian Democratic Movement Party (PMDB), based in part on the old Brazilian Labor Party (PTB) and a few smaller political groupings, as well as whatever remained of the more progressive elements of President Dutra's Social Democratic Party (PSD). In its new incarnation the PMDB counted among its supporters the expanding urban middle class, intellectuals, and workers. Its program called for greater control of the economy, income redistribution to help disadvantaged groups in society, full political democracy, and direct elections.

The pre-1964 PTB suffered much infighting in its attempt to regain its preeminence, and out of the struggle emerged the Democratic Workers' Party (PDT). The PDT was most active in the state of Rio de Janeiro, where it was led by Governor Leonel Brizola. The governor, closely associated by family, state, and political ties with the deposed Goulart, sought to model the party on the European social-democratic parties, but most observers saw the PDT as a personalistic vehicle for the ambitious governor rather than an ideological one. Another party in search of the labor vote was the Worker's Party (PT), which competed primarily with the PMDB and the PDT for the votes of industrial workers and for the ideological backing of urban intellectuals.

The Liberal Front Party (PFL) was led by former Vice President Aureliano Chaves of Minas Gerais, who split from the PSD in the 1984 presidential campaign to support the PMDB and fellow *mineiro* presidential candidate Tancredo Neves. In fact, most of the PFL, which in 1985 became a junior partner in President José Sarney's democratic alliance, was composed of politicians who had been elected in 1982 on the Democratic Social Party ticket but who had subsequently broken away from that party to support Neves. With capable young leaders, the PFL nonetheless fared poorly in the 1986 election, giving rise to the joke that it was a party of great leaders and a tiny following. Its modest strength lay in small and rural enclaves, and this support worked to its disadvantage in a country increasingly urban and urban oriented.

President Sarney himself had been one of the original PFL leaders before he formally joined the PMDB to become Neves's new running mate. The PMDB-PFL coalition enabled Neves to upset most predictions and defeat the government-backed PSD opponent, Deputy Paulo Maluf of São Paulo, in 1984. Neves commanded a wide margin in the electoral college and was a popular, grandfatherly figure. He had accomplished the nearly impossible task of assembling a variety of ideological groups intent upon replacing the military and launching a democratic system. For its part the military had stacked the game to favor Maluf but, faced with the popularity of Neves, opted to accept Neves as someone too politically cunning to attempt radical progress without a good measure of order. All prognostications came to naught when Neves fell fatally ill on the eve of his inauguration.

With Neves near death the specter of a military coup or the passing of the presidency to Ulysses Guimarães, the congressional leader, were only two of many possibilities. But Guimarães, a longtime opposition leader, could not count on the goodwill of the military, and vice president elect Sarney had, after all, been a former president of the promilitary Democratic Social Party. After a great deal of political maneuvering Sarney was confirmed as the new president. He had the support of the PSD and the PFL, but he was not a popular figure. The military did not fully trust him because he had switched sides instead of supporting its candidate, Maluf; the democratic forces that had so enthusiastically supported Neves could not forget that Sarney had been added to the ticket as a last-minute gesture toward people who had supported the military but were now willing to jump onto the civilian bandwagon.

Opposition to Sarney came mainly from the left, from the PDT of Rio de Janeiro and the PT of São Paulo. The PDT mixed populism and machine politics as part of Leonel Brizola's perennial struggle to attain the presidency; the PT, on the other hand, had really been an umbrella for a variety of socialist groups, often based on unions and on the Catholic Church's liberation-theology wing. Both the PDT and the PT assumed that worsening economic problems would bring them victory. Their calculations, however, initially backfired because of the short-term maneuvers of the president and his supporters. The early success of the economic Cruzado Plan, launched in February 1986, buoyed Sarney's popularity and ensured an easy victory for those aligned with him. It mattered little in the election campaign that the Cruzado Plan proved to be an ephemeral respite and that it had to be abandoned shortly after the 1986 elections; in fact, cynics said that the plan worked only long enough to ensure the socialists' defeat in those elections.

By 1988, however, Sarney no longer could hide the economic debacle or even buy or influence many voters. In the November election for mayors and municipal assemblies Sarney's policies were overwhelmingly rejected. Sarney and the old-line politicians, including presidential hopefuls Maluf and Guimarães, were the great losers, and the undisputed great winner was the PT, closely followed by Brizola's PDT. It could also be said that the 1988 election, in which an unpopular and arguably illegitimate government paid the price for an inflation rate of more than 700 percent in the preceding year, reestablished populist Brizola and socialist Luís Inácio da Silva (better known as Lula) as serious candidates for the presidency in 1989. The possibility of either man's winning the elections was viewed with deep misgivings by the armed forces and the conservative business establishment, and both the other alternatives were not much more reassuring for an orderly transition to democracy and a renewal of "progress."

As it turned out, the 1989 contest proved the volatility of a large, young, and inexperienced electorate. More than twenty candidates waged a vigorous campaign. Some of them were old political names, not only Brizola but also Maluf, Guimarães, and Chaves. Others represented the new forces of organized labor and liberation theology; Lula probably found his greatest strength here. Just days before the elections, all polls were rendered meaningless when a popular television star announced his candidacy and immediately became one of the front-runners. In a twist of the proverbial *jeito* (a creative maneuver), the supreme electoral court found him ineligible to run. That left Lula and Brizola as the major contenders, along with Fernando Collor de Mello, a young former governor of one of Brazil's smallest states.

Disdaining to affiliate with any major party, Collor came out of nowhere to lead the race. He survived the first ballot contest and narrowly edged out Lula in the runoff elections in December 1989—53 percent to 47 percent. Collor had come to prominence when as governor of Alagoas he led a campaign against highly paid civil servants. He turned this campaign into a national crusade against corruption and incompetence. His vigorous denunciation of Sarney struck a responsive chord among Brazil's poorest, the rural population, and also business people fed up with the state's dominance of the economy. With the backing of the powerful Globo news network, Collor succeeded in undermining Lula's appeal. Most of Brazil's intellectuals supported Lula and agreed with his Marxist prescription for curing the country's ills. Collor called for a vague modernizing and restructuring of the economy.

Collor (a young president, forty years of age) promised to bring back some order and progress to the economically troubled nation. His program included cutting the inflation rate, which ran at a record 1,800 percent in 1989; prosecuting tax evaders; cutting the number of ministries in half; and selling money-losing state companies. He hoped that foreign creditors would not take the 1988 constitutional restrictions too seriously but would be willing to swap their debt titles for shares in Brazilian companies and that the debt could be renegotiated so that service payments could be capped at $5 billion a year. However, to enact even a portion of this ambitious plan Collor needed the cooperation of a powerful and hostile Congress. Lula, Brizola, and other disappointed presidential hopefuls counted on increasing their supporters' share of the congressional seats in the October 1990 elections. In fact, the PMDB obtained 21 percent of the vote, the PFL 17 percent, the PDT 9 percent, the PSD 8 percent, the PRN (National Reconstruction Party) 7.9 percent, and the PTB and the PT 7 percent each, with "other" making up 23.1 percent of the 503 seats. In the federal Senate the results gave the PMDB twenty-seven seats, the PFL fifteen seats, the PDS ten seats, the PTB eight, and the PDT five, and the "other" pertained to sixteen seats. In so fractionalized a Congress, much of it bitterly frustrated by Collor's victory, the goal was not greater order and progress but more chaos and confrontation.

As fate would have it, Collor played into the hands of his enemies and thoroughly disgraced himself even in the eyes of those who had supported him. By early 1992 it became clear that the president who had come into government under the banner of austerity and probity, was deeply enmeshed in a scandal of corruption and favoritism. Slowly but surely, Congress moved to remove the president through an unprecedented impeachment process, with the result that by December 29, 1992, Collor was removed from the presidency in disgrace. In his place Itamar Franco, the physical, political, and generational antithesis of Collor, became president.

The specter of a coup lurked in the wings. The military, some members of which opposed both Lula and Brizola, had been uneasy over Collor's proposal to abolish the National Information Service (SNI), Brazil's foreign and domestic intelligence agency, and to shut down Brazil's nuclear program. At the other end of the spectrum two small Communist parties, illegal during the military regimes, were eager to discredit both the youthful Collor and the avuncular Franco but with the dissolution of the former Soviet Union, Marxist parties were having a hard time justifying their own existence. At most, thirty thousand Communists were said to exist in Brazil; of far greater relevance was the fact that social-democratic ideas and ideals were embraced by a large percentage of the population. A small Green Party objected to Collor's development plans, but a wide variety of ecologically minded groups received a world forum during the proceedings of the Earth Summit in 1992, which garnered a great deal of praise for the Collor government's ability to hold a major international gathering.

Overall, the exuberant political ferment of the 1980s had some positive results. Since 1985 Brazilians, regardless of their ideological leanings, have fully participated in vigorous partisan politics, informed by media reporting that reflects a broad range of political views and ideologies. One can speculate, however, that the two dozen or so political parties will eventually coalesce into three to five major fronts or umbrella organizations that fit into the pattern of right, center, and left, with Brazil's political center being considerably to the left of the U.S. one. Less speculative are polling results that show increasing disenchantment in the 2000s with all political parties and politicians, so much so that those vying for leadership roles are careful to stress their "independent" and nonpartisan credentials. For example, the PMDB, if literally translated, is the Party of the Brazilian Democratic Movement, but its adherents stress "movement" rather than "party."

In summary, the political system is notable for the fragmentary nature of parties; governments struggle to keep their own supporters in line. For a time during 2003–2005, the PT, which had a minority in both houses of Congress, was able to obtain the support of center-left parties and particularly the powerful centrist PMDB. With the tainting of several ministers and congress-people in the growing corruption scandal of the mid-2005, the president found it ever harder to push for his party's agenda in Congress. A more vigorous opposition was emerging as both Lula became tainted and the 2006 presidential election approached.

In addition to the political parties, a number of interest groups compete for popular support. Some of these groups predate the latest democratic opening and even go back to the Vargas era, when the president subsidized and assisted such groups in exchange for political support. Among them is labor, whose members first banded together in mutual aid societies in the very early years of industrialization. It was not until Vargas's first term as president in the late 1930s and early 1940s, however, that these workers were organized into unions that received benefits from the government while avoiding strikes and other destabilizing tactics. In effect, labor rights and social security provisions were provided at the price of collaboration or, at the very least, apathy.

After the 1964 coup the military abolished the largest labor confederation, the General Worker's Command (CGT), which had been a major supporter of Goulart, himself a former labor minister under Vargas. Under all the military administrations the labor unions were strictly controlled and subject to government intervention. Union leaders were chosen by the government to ensure industrial peace because it was essential to the military's plan for attracting domestic and foreign investment that labor not agitate for raises or go on strike.

While the economy was booming in the late 1960s and early 1970s, coinciding with the most stringent military controls, the system of state-imposed industrial peace worked well in that strikes seldom took place, much less succeeded. After the downturn in the late 1970s labor was not as easily tamed, and about this time the military itself was beginning to question the wisdom of remaining in power indefinitely. Eventually, new unions and new leaders emerged outside of government control or, at the very least, with tacit acceptance by the military administration. After the *abertura*, which also began in the late 1970s, it was possible to strike even though strikes could still be ruled illegal. In 1980 metalworkers in São Paulo managed to shut down the powerful automobile industry there for several weeks. Their leader, Lula, was jailed, but the strike showed that workers were again willing to take risks. From this fairly successful strike action emerged the new PT, the Workers' Party, which remained the most coherent opponent of the government. It takes an anticorruption stance and espouses state-led economic development, but it continues to be plagued by internal strife and, on occasion, charges of corruption.

Brazilian businesspeople, either as individuals or through their organizations, encouraged or welcomed the 1964 coup. They had reason to fear Goulart's increasing sympathy for labor's demands; and they had disliked the general economic and political uncertainty, which made investment planning difficult if not impossible. Their euphoria over getting rid of Goulart, however, proved short-lived, because the military proceeded to consolidate the government's role in the economy. Military and civilian technocrats moved into various new economic areas without consulting the private sector, and the old tradition of having the government protect weak companies was rendered obsolete by the government's determination to achieve economic growth as fast as possible. Foreign companies were lured to invest in Brazil, often at the expense of less-efficient Brazilian enterprises, and the lowering of tariffs made it easier to import certain items than to produce them at home. Tax collection was tightened and thus another traditional way of financing business was removed. Their growing disappointment with and even resentment of the military made businesspeople, for their own reasons, ready to welcome and support the *abertura* just as the workers and old-line politicians were doing.

Business support for an end to the military regime coalesced with that of other groups that had challenged the authoritarian system for years. One of these groups was the Catholic Church. Brazil is the most Catholic country in the world in terms of the number of church members, and the Church has a special position as an interest group. In contrast to many Spanish-speaking countries in Latin America, Brazil has not experienced long and bitter fights in relation to the Catholic Church. The first republican constitution in 1891, under the inspiration of Positivism, took away the Church's special privileges without causing major trauma. For decades after the advent of the republic the Brazilian Catholic hierarchy concentrated on running schools for the Brazilian elite and performing its theological and pastoral duties. Vatican II, between 1962 and 1965, moved the Church toward greater involvement in social and political matters but this was not a radical departure because, especially in the 1940s and 1950s, a number of lay and Catholic groups had become active among students, workers, and even clearly political organizations. Vatican II did give a new impetus to this refocusing of the Church, however, and it gave Brazilian theologians the opportunity to advocate liberation theology and greater attention to the poor.

In the early 1960s this refocusing coincided with President Goulart's call for populist measures such as agrarian reform and expansion of the welfare system. At the time of the 1964 coup the Church was deeply divided, with some members of the clergy supporting Goulart and others seeking to undermine him. Some supported his populism but others saw it simply as a demagogic appeal. Many people feared that the Church's growing political involvement would entangle it in matters that were not crucial to it as an institution and as a church. Large parades in the major cities often had the tacit approval and support of the Church, with parishioners calling for moral renewal and decrying the chaos of everyday life. In the Northeast priests were among those who helped landless peasants take over large and often unused tracts of land. The possibility of a divided Church did not help Goulart's cause.

After the advent of the military regime in 1964 this split continued. At first many people continued to be wary of what they perceived as the politicization of the Catholic Church. Others, however, increasingly denounced government repression and accused the government of failing to conform to Brazilian tradition by refusing to return to the barracks and give power back to civilians. By the 1970s much of the Brazilian Church hierarchy was behind the effort to organize popular Catholic base communities to obtain greater social justice and respect for human rights, and the churches were providing sanctuary for striking workers being pursued by the military. With the *abertura*, Church leaders and laypeople alike were involved in the formation of political parties and eventually in the drafting of the new constitution. Perhaps not by coincidence, the greater political involvement of the Catholic Church occurred simultaneously with a growing challenge to Catholicism by a variety of Protestant churches, especially the more charismatic and evangelical ones and those concentrating their proselytizing efforts on the poor, the illiterate, and the displaced in the urban areas.

Besides the churches, the unions, the military, the business sector, and the political parties, a number of other organizations acted as pressure groups, with varying degrees of success. The Brazilian Order of Lawyers was active during the military regimes in seeking the restoration and enforcement of legal protections. The Brazilian Press Association opposed censorship and publicized, especially abroad, the plight of persecuted journalists. A number of women's organizations emerged, particularly after the 1975 International Women's Year. The National Student Union, abolished at the time of the coup, continued to operate underground and sometimes even fairly openly. A novelty in Brazil, race-based groups emerged and began to demand "real" versus theoretical equality for all. With the *abertura* and the holding of elections, literally hundreds of issue-, policy-, and candidate-focused groups emerged and began to compete, although most of them were transitory. More focused and militant African-Brazilian groups have coalesced in more recent years. Benedita da Silva Sampaio, a former PT federal senator and vice-governor of Rio de Janeiro at the end of the 1990s, is probably the best known voice for these groups.

One organization that continues to exert influence is the Superior War College (ESG). Founded in 1949, the ESG has been a center for training military and civilian elites. Somewhat similar to a think tank except that it is sponsored and subsidized by the government, it trained several presidents, including Castelo Branco, Geisel, and the presidential adviser Golbery do Couto e Silva. The ESG's slogan, "Security and Development," became a banner for anticommunism during the military regimes, but the organization goes far beyond mere anticommunism. It has been at the forefront of a great deal of sophisticated economic and strategic planning, and because it stresses that it aims to educate and inspire leaders, whether military or civilian, it is likely to remain a formidable institution. Its extensive network of alumni serves as a recruiting source for both government and private enterprises; many male and female ESG alumni are in key positions.

Government Institutions, Bureaucracy, Main Policy Issues

Russell H. Fitzgibbon, one of the most astute observers of Latin America, has said that "the organization of the Brazilian political system is largely distinguished by its federalism, which provides a backdrop for the performance of various political functions."[10] It has also been said that Brazil is the most federal of Latin America's regimes, but these statements do not mean that it is "really" federal in terms of the U.S. model.

Given the size and diversity of Brazil, federalism made sense to the people who drafted the first republican constitution in 1891. The Rio de Janeiro government was weak and unwilling to challenge powerful regional centers and, although the central government remained vulnerable, for the next three or four decades the states had a great deal of freedom. São Paulo, Minas Gerais, and Rio Grande do Sul showed so much independence that they maintained diplomatic relations with foreign governments, displayed their state flags above the national one, and called their state governors "presidents."

The Vargas era lessened these centrifugal pulls. The 1934 constitution gave preeminence to the national executive, state flags and anthems were abolished, and most economic functions were handled by the national government. Vargas's Estado Novo strengthened and reinforced centralization to the extent that even after his departure in 1945 the national government's powers far outstripped states' rights. Only during the turbulent and short Goulart years did some states again act on their own, perhaps secure in the knowledge that the federal government had enough other problems and could not worry about states' initiatives. Governor Leonel Brizola of Rio Grande do Sul, without a clear mandate to do so, expropriated U.S.-owned utilities in that state, and an economic development organization in the Northeast, SUDENE, managed to receive funds directly from AID (Agency for International Development). Military units based in Rio Grande do Sul, Minas Gerais, and São Paulo were also crucially involved in the civilian-military coup that deposed Goulart in 1964.

From 1964 to 1985 the military regimes revised the constitution with institutional acts and decrees; sometimes these gave the national executive carte blanche in the restructuring of the government and in the proclamation of all types of policies. The taxing powers of the federal government ensured that all governors and mayors, even those of powerful states and metropolises, would comply with the wishes of the president if they hoped to get any funding for essential services. Even after the ushering in of a civilian regime, the president holds a great deal of power: he chooses and heads a cabinet, he coordinates the actions of all ministries, and he selects thousands of positions.

In an attempt to curb some of the presidential powers and to meld federalist and antifederalist impulses the 1988 constitution became a monstrous hybrid. It promised greater freedom and power to states and local administrations but it did not truly reverse the decades-old trend toward centralization. It gave Congress greater power than ever before and strengthened civil liberties, labor rights, and social benefits. Its proclamation, in October 1988, abolished the authoritarian charter of 1967. It ensured the right to strike, set the voting age at sixteen, abolished censorship, and gave more power and income to state and municipal governments.

Under the new constitution, Brazilians in November 1989 elected a president by direct popular vote for the first time since 1960. In what turned out to be a major source of domestic and international wrangles, questions concerning the international debt were debated by the entire Congress, and the president and the minister of finance were no longer able to settle by themselves on a course to resolve Brazil's international obligations. Since 1992 major amendments have been adopted, mostly pertaining to economic issues. Many of the more restrictive clauses in the constitution have been implemented in a more liberal way so as to make possible both privatization of state-owned enterprises and greater influx of foreign investors. However, unless and until the constitution is fully revised the possibility of interference by federal and/or state government in business ventures is still very much alive, as seen in the actions of a state governor who challenged not only the constitutionality of some contracts but even the payment of governmental debts. In the political realm a 1997 constitutional amendment permitted the president and vice president, who are elected for four-year terms, to serve a second consecutive term.

Under the constitution Brazil remains a federative republic composed of twenty-six states and a federal district where the capital of the country, Brasília, is located. Each state has its own government; their structures mirror the federal ones, with powers that are not reserved for the federal government or assigned to municipal councils. Governors are elected by direct popular vote and the state legislatures are unicameral. The state judiciary similarly mirrors the federal model, and its jurisdiction is defined to avoid conflicts with federal courts. Brazil has some 5,560 municipalities, and their councils handle local affairs.

While the political fighting continues as a daily occurrence, the revision of the 1988 charter has been piecemeal and sporadic. Ambiguity continues to surround the role of the military as the guarantor of the constitutional order. The left complains that the proposed changes further protect large private landowners and undermine the sputtering efforts to distribute plots to landless peasants at a time when 5 percent of the country's population owns half the arable land. In the growing corruption scandal of 2005 no level of government or of society has escaped the enveloping taint.

Regardless of the constitutional tinkering and the travails of a disordered democracy, some structural mainstays are not likely to change. Thus, traditionally, Brazilian ministries have been very large bureaucracies with a plethora of subcabinets, councils, and other agencies—many of them powerful in their own right—plus institutes, autonomous agencies, and the like attached directly or indirectly to the ministries themselves. In this bureaucratic maze personal and political linkages are of great importance and often override considerations of merit, efficiency, or organizational rationalism. With so many people involved, many of them moving toward contradictory goals and policies, it is not surprising that Brazilian bureaucracy is notorious for its *papelada* (red tape), unpredictability, and penchant for corruption. Antibureaucratic czars have been appointed, to no avail.

Throughout the system, from top to bottom, the sheer dead weight of a myriad of legal rules and enacted codes that have long ago outlived their usefulness remains untouched. Systematic inefficiency and the opportunity for favoritism are not mitigated when presidents, members of Congress, and governors themselves routinely appoint cronies and family members to important posts, regardless of their qualifications. Thus, with little relevance to the constitution du jour, only the proverbial ability of the Brazilian bureaucrat to bend the rules just a little, apply a little humor or a *jeito*, so that some business can be transacted daily, has kept the whole machinery of government from coming to a grinding halt.

A conservative estimate places the federal civil service at three-quarters of a million people. This figure is meaningless because it does not take into consideration the countless independent and semi-independent bureaucracies and the many civil servants who have more than one full-time job. Presidents Collor, Cardoso, and Lula have applied regimes of austerity and tried to shrink the federal payroll, with some success. Mostly, longtime employees lost one of their many jobs, but most of those who dropped from the rolls did so because they were entitled to generous pensions and retirement benefits. The Foreign Ministry (Itamaraty) is one of the better-run ministries, with a reputation for well-trained career officers, some continuity, and a relative insulation from political vagaries. Interestingly, it is also the ministry that is the least popular, with Brazilians and foreigners alike complaining about its inflexibility and its mind-numbing respect for the most minute and meaningless detail.

Brazil has traditionally had a bicameral legislature, and this tradition remained unchallenged in the 1988 constitution. Although the number of legislators has varied, the usual provision calls for three senators from each state and the federal district for a total of eighty-one members. The Chamber of Deputies, 513 strong, is chosen on a population basis and favors the least-populated rural states. The chambers have legislative committees, but their staffing patterns vary a great deal, and thus their ability to draft legislation is hard to predict. Throughout history the president has been the chief legislator, and the legislation proposed by the executive branch has almost always been approved by Congress by overwhelming margins. This has been somewhat moderated by the 1988 charter, which gave greater powers to the Congress and denied the presidency its former wide decree powers. It was no longer possible for a strong dictatorial president to dismiss the legislature, as had been done several times in the past. The realities, however, have remained far more powerful than any constitutional provisions. The presidency was weakened when President Collor was impeached for malfeasance; old-timers recalled that his father had, with impunity, killed a fellow senator in chambers. Congress has been discredited when many of its members are tarnished by grand larceny, rampant favoritism, and even the crude elimination of estranged wives and inconvenient enemies.

The legislature under the 1988 constitution can sanction the president, alter the national budget, and determine international treaties. The text of the constitution was sufficiently ambiguous concerning the power of Congress that it made it possible for the legislative branch to assert itself against a president and vice versa. In the presidential debacle of 1992, with the removal of President Collor, there was little doubt that Congress was preeminent. But in reality congressional powers ebb and flow. To obtain the constitutional amendment that allowed for a second presidential term, President Fernando Henrique Cardoso had to barter power and funds with legislators and governors. His initiatives toward fiscal reforms were stymied by congressional objections, but Congress was equally frustrated in obtaining presidential implementation of some of its adopted measures. The weakness of the political parties ensures that neither president nor representatives will be able to count on the loyalty of most of their partisans.

Even the constitutions have not proven safe from outright rigging in day-to-day implementation. Thus, the overly long and detailed 1988 charter proved unworkable and was discarded in favor of a shorter version. To the credit of the 1988 charter one should not forget that it was under its aegis that the first presidential direct election in decades took place, and the same popularly elected president lost his job when he was implicated in criminal activities. To Brazilians' surprise—and pride—the removal of Fernando Collor and his replacement by Vice President Itamar Franco were accomplished without bloodshed. By the same token, the voters in 1993 showed a marked preference for the continuation of the presidential over the parliamentary and monarchical forms of government.

Government structure and policymaking up to the beginning of the 2000s have seen small and major adjustments, but there is a rising skepticism about the benefits of democracy, and a constant despair over the inability of politicians to govern. Yet, if one relies on history and tradition as guides, the 1988 constitution, like the others that preceded it, will be "reformed" through its daily encounters with Brazilian realities just as policymaking, regardless of the mountains of regulations and decrees, will ultimately remain at the mercy of the most skilled bureaucrat or the most imaginative Brazilian's *jeito*.

But even a new constitution and the proverbial *jeito* have not been able to ameliorate some of the country's policy issues. On the one hand the risk of armed conflict per se is low and no guerrilla groups pose a threat. More worrisome are the threats posed by private militias that are hired by landowners to deter the MST (Landless Worker Movement) members from encroaching on their properties or the very well armed groups that protect one or more of the many drug lords. A great deal of international attention was focused upon the killing of an American nun in the Amazon region. It is likely that her assassins had been paid off by those who wanted to continue clearing the rain forest, which she opposed. The government has promised to investigate and punish, but most Brazilians are skeptical.

On an earlier occasion, international attention followed the September 11, 2001, terrorist event in New York City. The mayor and some of the citizens of a border Southern town celebrated the occasion with fireworks, leading the Brazilian and American governments to surmise that the remote and mostly unguarded locality harbored terrorist sympathizers.

In reality, far more problematic for Brazil is the rising level of crime, especially in major cities such as São Paulo and Rio de Janeiro. The growing incidence of poverty and the increased occurrence of drug abuse and commerce are often reflected in the kidnapping of tourists and wealthy Brazilians. The country's police force, for its part, remains badly trained and poorly paid, which helps promote corruption and deficiencies in law enforcement.

In long range terms, the policy areas that concern Brazilian governments the most have been the weaknesses inherent in Brazil's educational system. Indicators tend to compare Brazil unfavorably to its neighbors Argentina and Uruguay, and farther away, Chile. Presidents Cardoso and Lula have promoted greater funding and attention to primary education. At the upper end, Brazil does have an excellent system of public universities but most students able to meet stringent entrance requirements come from middle- or upper-class families.

Poor health indices reflect poverty, inadequate sanitation, low levels of education, ecological degradation. The constitution provides for many health benefits but these mostly remain on paper. More promising has been the government's proactive programs toward Brazil's HIV-AIDS population that have been hailed as one of the most successful efforts of its kind in the world.[11]

The International Arena

Even in colonial times Brazil's relations with its neighbors were characterized by accommodation and expansion: accommodation in the sense that Brazil seldom went to war with its neighbors (the major exception being its war with Paraguay); and the expansion government's indifference or lukewarm encouragement meant that Brazil's borders, initially marked off by the Tordesilhas line, now contain more than twice as much territory as originally envisaged by the Pope who drew the imaginary line. In more recent years Brazil has been a leader among the Latin American nations and has played a prominent role in security efforts and in economic cooperation within the Western Hemisphere. During World Wars I and II Brazil aligned itself with the Allies, and in the 1940s Brazilian soldiers played a distinguished and decisive role in the Allied victory at Monte Castelo, Italy. Many of the generals behind the 1964 coup were involved in that campaign and formed close professional and personal relations with their North American counterparts. A man who later became president, Castelo Branco, shared a tent with the American Vernon Walters, and the two men became lifelong friends.[12]

Brazil is a signatory of the Rio Treaty, the Inter-American Treaty of Reciprocal Assistance, and the Organization of American States (OAS), which is sometimes headed by a Brazilian diplomat. Brazilian career foreign officers have distinguished themselves in international bodies, and some of them have been chosen to head such organizations, as was the case in the World Health Organization a few years ago. More recently Brazil has given priority to strengthening its ties with other South American states and has become a member of the Amazon Pact and the Latin American Integration Association (ALASI). President Sarney and Argentine President Raúl Alfonsín overcame the traditional enmity between their two countries with several understandings and protocols to ensure cooperation in a number of areas, including nuclear armaments and research. Brazil is a charter member of the United Nations and has been an active participant in several of its specialized agencies. It has contributed troops to UN peacekeeping efforts in the Middle East, in the former Belgian Congo (now Democratic Republic of Congo), Cyprus, Mozambique, and Haiti. Brazil helped mediate the resolution of the Angolan civil war.

Brazil's booming economy, trade, and international debt have caused it to become increasingly involved in international politics and economics. It is a member of the General Agreement on Tarriffs and Trade (GATT), the Committee of Twenty of the International Monetary Fund (IMF), several World Bank organizations, the Inter-American Development Bank (IADB), and many international commodity agreements. The United States, Western Europe, and Japan are the primary markets for Brazilian exports and the main sources of foreign lending and investments. In value Brazil is the third-leading trade partner of the European Economic Community (EEC). Brazil's earlier dependence on imported oil had forced it to strengthen its ties with the oil producing nations in the Middle East, and a number of technical barter arrangements have been worked out whereby Brazilian technicians and laborers exchanged their expertise and their work for oil from Middle Eastern countries, especially Iraq. The Gulf War, for example, found thousands of Brazilian contractors stuck in a variety of jobs in Iraq. In a pragmatic if not a principled way, Brazil has often voted with Arab countries rather than with Israel in international organizations.

Beginning in the 1970s Brazil expanded its relations with black African countries. In 1986 it introduced a proposal at the UN General Assembly to establish a zone of peace and cooperation in the South Atlantic. Because of its own large black population and its longstanding integrationist record, Brazil consistently voted for resolutions calling for the end of apartheid in South Africa. With the democratization of that country, Brazil has joined and might lead in the formation of a South Atlantic security and economic zone.

Brazil has diplomatic relations with most countries in the world, among them the former Soviet Union, all the East European countries, and Cuba. The country's relations with the United States are unique. The United States was the first country to recognize Brazil's independence in 1822. Dom Pedro II admired Abraham Lincoln and visited the United States during the 1876 centennial. President Dwight Eisenhower was given a hero's welcome when he visited Brazil in 1960, and presidents Franklin Roosevelt and Harry Truman were cordially received. President Jimmy Carter visited in 1978, but at the time there were major strains between the two countries on questions of human rights, and Brazilians were incensed by the attempts of the United States to interfere in Brazil's nuclear program. President Ronald Reagan visited Brazil in 1982, and President Sarney was in the United States 1986. President Bill Clinton visited Brazil in 1997 and has maintained warm relations with former President Cardoso, whom he entertained at Camp David and in the White House. President Lula has met with President Bush.

In the 1950s and 1960s Brazil received about $2.4 billion in U.S. economic assistance through AID, PL480 (Food for Peace), and the Peace Corps. During the military administrations the Peace Corps and the International American Foundation (IAF) were accused of interfering in domestic affairs and were told to leave the country; IAF has since resumed its large program. After 1972 U.S. aid efforts emphasized, among other programs, the training of young Brazilian technicians and social scientists in graduate schools in the United States. In view of Brazil's economic development and its ability to obtain loans and technical assistance from private and multilateral sources, the U.S. assistance programs were phased out in the 1970s. Major AID activities ceased in 1979, and the Peace Corps ended its work in Brazil in 1980. The department of State and other departments have small contingents in Brazil that collaborate on science and technology projects; respond to endemic diseases, emergencies, and natural disasters; and may be of technical assistance in family-planning efforts.

The United States is still Brazil's most important commercial partner; in 2001 the United States exported approximately $15 billion to Brazil. By 2003 Brazil's world trade surplus stood at $17.3 billion and the overwhelming presence of the United States had lessened. Indeed, the trading relations have become less friendly since Brazil actively sought other partners and refused to open its markets to U.S. products, particularly certain types of computers. Nationalism and simple tradition reinforced Brazil's insistence on continuing export subsidies and protectionism; nowhere were these clearer than in the 1988 constitutional provisions that actively discriminated against foreign investors and, in effect, closed certain industries to foreign firms. By the 1990s tradition and protectionism, shaken by the cold realities of tough global competition, were giving way to privatization and a friendlier response to international economic overtures. The Cardoso and Lula administrations have been characterized by higher international profiles. Both have vigorously pursued expanded relations within South America and have promoted an expansion of the Southern Common Market to include free trade agreements (FTA) with Chile (1996) and with Bolivia (1997) and closer relations with Venezuela. Both have campaigned for Brazil to become a permanent member of an enlarged UN Security Council and have heightened Brazil's presence in the Inter-American Bank and World Bank.

The more formal agreements between Brazil and the United States include a treaty of peace and friendship; an extradition treaty; a joint participation agreement on communication satellites; and scientific cooperation, civil aviation, and maritime agreements. The two countries exchange academic personnel under Fulbright and other scholarly programs and carry out university cooperation projects. Under the popular Partners of the Americas Program, several U.S. states have active exchanges with their counterparts in Brazil. Increasingly, Brazil has sponsored artistic groups to enable them to visit the United States and other countries to promote better relations and publicize Brazil's cultural achievements.

With respect to this international debt, there are both encouraging signs and signs that do not seem to augur well. On the plus side, in September 1988 President Sarney formally ended the country's nineteen-month-old moratorium on payments on its then $121-billion foreign debt. At the time the Brazilian president warned that Brazil could not permanently export capital and called on creditors to do their part as Brazil was doing its part. Brazil's return to orthodox strategies and its rapprochement with the IMF marked the end of a roller-coaster period of economic experiments that included a wage and price freeze, a promising boom, and the moratorium on payments enacted shortly after the 1986 elections.

The 1988 constitution has complicated the picture by giving Congress wide powers to decide on external payments and policies affecting Brazil's relations with international banking institutions. Those developments were but the most recent chapters in the long-simmering dispute between Brazil and its creditors. The oil shocks of the 1970s and 1980s, and the world recession that followed were keenly felt in Brazil because of its crucial need to maintain ever-higher levels of exports to finance its economic development. Through the oil shocks and vagaries of international markets over which it had little or no control, Brazil has sought to work out mutually satisfactory banking relations that would, in effect, let the country stretch its payments on the interest and, in the meantime, count on eventual forgiveness of the huge principal. Not surprising, at times U.S. banks have felt that they are hostages to Brazil's economy and, worse, Brazil's sense of nationalism in the late 1980s. By the 1990s and 2000s, with the cold realities of fewer investors and a growing unwillingness of the international financial institutions to continue their generosity, Brazilians are less inclined to rail against foreign lenders and multinationals, and the investment climate is considered "good".

Many of the 1988 constitutional restrictions have been formally set aside, and the investment climate has become more forthcoming. Unfortunately, if constitutionally the climate has become more propitious for investment, the political stability leaves much to be desired. New constitutional guarantees and enticements can do little to dispel the sense that the *papelada* remains and that political uncertainty and corruption are long-term problems.

In a broader sense, relations between Brazil and the United States have had an uneven track record in the 1990s. Although tensions and disagreements remain on charges that Brazil "dumps" (i.e. sells below cost) such products as steel, both countries became more engaged in day-to-day consultations after Cardoso took office. On the U.S. side, there seems to be a realization that the health of the Brazilian economy is vital to the overall health of South American economies while, on the Brazilian side, given the stiff competition linked to globalization, there has been a corresponding realization that the United States is too big a customer to be annoyed with obsolete nationalistic posturing. However, old attitudes do not change easily. Presidential aspirants denounced Cardoso and Lula's more liberal economic policies. They echo the popular sentiment that the United States is the country that could—but does not—help this significant (in resources and strategic terms) partner in the hemisphere to overcome its economic and international problems, and has appeared to prevent Brazil from becoming a world power and serving in the UN Security Council. At the very least, investments are routinely labeled "Trojan horses" that enrich foreigners at the expense of ordinary Brazilians.

Brazil's relations with other North and South American countries have their own uniqueness. Brazil and Mexico agreed in 1983 to complete a barter deal that would provide for the exchange of up to $1 billion of goods each way. Brazil has concluded agreements for hydroelectric dam systems in the Plata Basin, and the Itaipú Treaty, signed with Argentina and Paraguay, makes Brazil the owner of the largest hydroelectric dam in the world. Better relations now exist between Argentina and Brazil after decades of suspicion on both sides. President Sarney advocated a common market between the two countries and, although this idea is probably far from realization, they are trading much more than before, with Brazil exporting a wide variety of manufactured goods in exchange for agricultural products. Nearly one quarter of Brazil's capital goods exported to Latin America in the late 1980s went to Argentina.

Brazil was never a major partner with the former Soviet Union, but it has remained interested in increasing its exports to that region. The Soviet Union was quite active in promoting cultural exchanges at all levels, and a number of young, promising Brazilians were provided with scholarships to study in Moscow.

Overall, Brazil has been pragmatic in the conduct of its foreign affairs. Unless a clear benefit can be derived, Brazilians seldom take the lead. Brazil is content with and comfortable in pursuing its own interests without unnecessarily antagonizing the countries it deeply depends upon, but it will stand firm when it feels that its nationalism and sovereignty are not being given the attention they deserve. The best example, in this instance, was Brazil's strong stand in obtaining nuclear technology from West Germany in spite of President Carter's insistent and eventually counterproductive pressure.

The overly specific and detailed provisions in the 1988 constitution might have affected Brazil's conduct of foreign policy to a greater extent than they actually did, given Brazil's internal political disarray and governmental turnovers. It is clear that for the time being and in the prolonged period of transition Congress will have much more to say in this area than before. Once a popularly elected and determined president comes upon the scene, however, the pendulum may swing again toward the executive as the major player.

Conclusion

Brazil's growing sense of importance and impact on the world scene goes beyond mere posturing. If it were not so diverse, so potentially rich, and so culturally integrated, its assertiveness would be empty indeed. A longtime observer of Brazil put it best:

> Brazil is the unstoppable colossus of the south; a major regional power already; the first big third-world country knocking on the door of the club of developed democracies; and a potential United States in the next century. . . . Brazil's long-term prospects are glowing; its very bravado is one of the main reasons why it can look forward to the future much as, say, bankers, investors, potential migrants and, not least, governments ought to be looking at Brazil as carefully as their precursors did at the United States in its early maturity. . . . Brazil has reached major power adulthood, although not yet the responsibility—and caution—of middle age.[13]

In fact, most careful observers usually echo this correspondent's conclusions. They agree that despite Brazil's present economic and political problems, it is not too rash to predict that the next decades will witness Brazil's rise first to an unchallenged status within Latin America, then to a predominant status within the South Atlantic community, and finally to major world power status.

The potential is there, but so also are the burdens of a chaotic and overly bureaucratized system, constitutional arrangements still untried, and a fragile and discredited democracy. One military president expressed his misgivings: "The country is doing well, the people not so well." In spite of over a decade of democracy this assessment is still mostly true because although in the 1990s a new order was indeed taking shape, progress has often been slow and fitful. If anything, because in the 2000s it is a maturing democracy, more is expected of Brazil, of its leaders and its system, by the average Brazilian. This is the same average Brazilian who is indeed proud of seeing fellow Brazilians reach international pinnacles in sport, culture, and fashion, but who has to deal with the daily indignities of unemployment, corrupt civil servants, a chaotic party system, and inadequate health and educational institutions. In the new millennium, will the average Brazilian see the potential and the reality finally meld into one? Will Brazilians no longer be, at one and at the same time, among the poorest and richest people in Latin America? Time alone will tell.

Suggestions for Further Reading

Ames, Barry. *The Deadlock of Democracy in Brazil: Interests, Identities, and Institutions in Comparative Politics.* Ann Arbor: University of Michigan Press, 2001.

Baaklini, Abdo. *The Brazilian Legislature and Political System.* Westport, CT: Greenwood, 1992.

Baer, Werner. *The Brazilian Economy: Growth and Development.* 5th ed. Westport, CT: Praeger, 1999.

Cardoso, Fernando Henrique and Mauricio A. Font. *Charting a New Course: The Politics of Globalization and Social Transformation.* Boulder, CO: Rowan and Littlefield, 2001.

Eakin, Marshall C. *Brazil: The Once and Future Country.* New York: St. Martin's Press, 1997.

Font, Mauricio A. and Anthony Peter Spanakos, eds. *Reforming Brazil.* Lanham, MD: Lexington, 2004.

Gordon, Lincoln. *Brazil's Second Chance: En Route Toward the First World.* Washington, D.C.: The Brookings Institution, 2001.

Ireland, Rowan. *Kingdom Comes: Religion and Politics in Brazil.* Pittsburgh: University of Pittsburgh Press, 1991.

Roett, Riordan. *Brazil: Politics in a Patrimonial Society.* 5th ed. Westport, CT: Praeger, 1999.

Roett, Riordan, ed. *Mercosur: Regional Integration, World Markets.* Boulder, CO: Lynn Rienner, 1999.

Skidmore, Thomas E. *Brazil: Five Centuries of Change.* New York: Oxford University Press, 1999.

Telles, Edward E. *Race in Another America: The Significance of Skin Color in Brazil.* Princeton, NJ: Princeton University Press, 2004.

Notes

1. The votes of 110 million Brazilians for 367,271 candidates were counted flawlessly across Brazil by electronic machines. Lula's impressive victory was proclaimed within hours of closing of the polls.

2. "Disorders of Progress," *The Economist*, March 27, 1999, 3–18.

3. Statistics and indices can be found in World Bank, *Little Data Book* (Washington, D.C.), and various publications by the Economist Intelligence Unit (London) as *Country Report: Brazil* (June 2005), *Country Profile* (2004), and *Latin America at a Glance* (2003).

4. Alex Bearak, "Poor Man's Burden," *New York Times*, June 27, 2004, 30–35, 50, 56–57; 1–7.

5. Greg Victor, "First and Third Worlds Coexist Uneasily as Brazil Lurches Toward Global Prominence," *Pittsburgh Post Gazette*, March 24, 2002.

6. Thomas E. Skidmore, *Brazil: Five Centuries of Change,* (New York: Oxford University Press, 1999).

7. G. Harvey Summ, ed. *Brazilian Mosaic: Portrait of a Diverse People and Culture* (Wilmington, DE: Scholarly Resources, 1995). Michael Kimmelman, "The Last of the Moderns," *The New York Times*, May 15, 2005, 60–67.

8. Elizabeth Bishop, excerpt from *Brazil* (*New York Times*, 1963), 12–13.

9. Much has been written on this issue. One of the best and shortest pieces is the analytical article by Glaucio Ary Sillon Soares, "The Rise of the Brazilian Military," *Studies in Comparative International Development* 21, no. 2 (Summer 1986), 34–62. Alfred Stepan, ed., *Democratizing Brazil* (New York: Oxford University Press, 1989).

10. Russell H. Fitzgibbon and Julio A. Fernandez, *Latin America: Political Culture of Development* (Englewood Cliffs, NJ: Prentice-Hall, 1981), 270.

11. "AIDS: No Carnival" and "Roll Out, Roll Out," *The Economist*, July 30, 2005, 71–72.

12. Brazilian Embassy, *Brazil and the USA: What Do We Have in Common?* (Washington, DC, 1999).

13. Robert Harvey, "Brazil: Unstoppable," *The Economist*, April 25, 1987, 3.

8

Chile

Paul E. Sigmund

What is it about Chile that is so fascinating to the foreign observer? A long (2,600-mile, 4,200-kilometer) "string bean" of a country of fourteen million inhabitants squeezed between the Andes and the sea, it is one of the most important copper producers in the world. It exports fine fruits and wine and has a literate, relatively large middle class. Evidence of its cultural sophistication is the substantial number of world-class Chilean writers and poets, including two Nobel prizewinners. Its topography is varied, ranging from deserts in the north to a fertile 600-mile (966-kilometer) Central Valley, not unlike the valley of the same name in California, to heavily wooded mountains and fjords in the farthest southern regions. Chile's strategic value is limited, except for its control of the Strait of Magellan. None of these factors accounts for foreigners' extraordinary fascination with the country.

Chilean politics is the reason for the great interest in that country. Until the 1973 coup it was one of the oldest constitutional democracies in the world. Since 1833, with only two interruptions—a short but bloody civil war in 1891 and a period of military intervention and plebiscitarian rule between 1925 and 1932—its political system followed regular constitutional procedures, with civil liberties, the rule of law, and periodic contested elections for a bicameral legislature and a directly elected president.

In recent decades successive governments have attempted to implement a variety of approaches to address Chilean underdevelopment. Between 1958 and 1964 a conservative government headed by President Jorge Alessandri tried to resolve Chile's problems of inflation, unemployment, and slow growth by emphasizing market incentives along with government programs in the areas of housing and limited agrarian reform. The Christian Democratic

CHILE

government of Eduardo Frei (1964–1970) initiated a Chileanization program for a partial government takeover by purchase of the U.S.-owned copper mines, adopted a much more radical agrarian reform law, promoted programs to organize and benefit peasants and "marginalized" sectors, and cooperated actively with the U.S.-sponsored Alliance for Progress in attempting to carry out what Frei called a "Revolution in Liberty." A three-way election in 1970 led to the victory of Salvador Allende, the candidate of the Marxist-dominated Popular Unity coalition. Allende tried to initiate a "transition to socialism" involving takeovers—sometimes of questionable legality—of industry and agriculture, income redistribution, and accelerated class polarization.

In 1973 the three armed services and the national police (*carabineros*) overthrew Allende, and what had begun as an institutional coup to save democracy from Marxism soon became a personalist dictatorship under General Augusto Pinochet, the head of the army. Pinochet closed down the political system but allowed a group of free-market-oriented economists, many of whom (known as "los Chicago boys") had been trained at the University of Chicago, to open up what had been a highly protected economy and drastically reduce government intervention in a controversial experiment in economic—but not political—libertarianism. In 1980 Pinochet appealed to Chilean legalism and constitutionalism to legitimate his power by calling and winning a snap plebiscite on a constitution that enabled him to continue in office until 1989 but required another plebiscite on a new mandate for an additional eight years. On October 5, 1988, he lost that plebiscite by a vote of 55 percent to 43 percent.

In the elections that followed, a multiparty, anti-Pinochet coalition (the *Concertación por la Democracia*) elected a Christian Democrat, Patricio Aylwin, to a four-year term ending in March, 1994. His successor, Eduardo Frei Ruiz-Tagle, the son of the former Christian Democratic president, was elected for a six-year term and, after a very close election that required a second round of voting, Ricardo Lagos, a Socialist, became president on March 11, 2000. All three *Concertación* presidents maintained an open market economy, but combined it with much larger expenditures on health, education, and social welfare. Despite the narrowness of his electoral mandate, Lagos proved to be a very popular president, maintaining the economic policies of his predecessors while increasing educational expenditures, establishing an unemployment insurance program, and substantially expanding health coverage. He was succeeded in March 2006 by another Socialist, Michelle Bachelet, Lagos's minister of health and defense and the daughter of an Air Force general who had opposed the coup and died in prison.

The contrasting approaches to development adopted by successive Chilean governments have produced a large and controversial literature. Conservatives, reformists, revolutionaries, and authoritarians have cited the accomplishments and failures of the various Chilean governments to defend or attack more general ideological approaches to Third World politics. The Allende experiment in particular has spawned an enormous literature—probably one thousand books in many languages—but the other governments also have both their defenders and their critics. The Pinochet dictatorship was characterized by a dramatic opening of the economy, accompanied by violations of human rights that drew worldwide attention. The policies of the post-Pinochet democratic governments that have combined economic growth based on private and foreign investment, export promotion, and low inflation with increased social equity and a dramatic reduction in poverty have been seen as a model for the rest of Latin America.

Citizens of the United States have reason to be interested in Chilean politics because of the deep involvement of the U.S. government in that country between the 1950s and the 1990s. Because Chile had the oldest and, outside of Cuba, the largest Communist party in the Western Hemisphere, the United States began in the 1950s to take a strong interest in its political life. The United States supported, overtly and covertly, the reformist Christian Democratic regime in the 1960s; opposed, overtly and covertly, the Allende government in the early 1970s; and was ambivalent about the Pinochet regime—repelled by its human rights violations (which led to a cutoff in 1976 by the U.S. Congress of all military aid and sales to Chile) but supportive of Chile's free-market approach to development and willingness to respect its international economic obligations. Beginning in the mid-1980s, for both ideological and pragmatic reasons, the Reagan administration began to promote a democratic transition in Chile and an end to the Pinochet dictatorship. Before the 1988 plebiscite the U.S. Congress went even further, appropriating one million dollars to support free elections in Chile. Since the return of democracy in 1990 U.S.-Chilean relations have improved dramatically, and in 2004, after many years of negotiation, the two countries signed a free trade agreement.

Interest in Chile revolves around three general questions. First, how is it that, in contrast to most other Latin American countries, Chile has been able to develop and maintain pluralist civilian constitutional rule throughout most of its history? Second, why did what appeared to be a strong, stable democracy give way to repressive military rule in 1973, and what was the role of the U.S. government before and after the coup? And third, what lessons can be drawn from the contrasting approaches of recent Chilean governments for achieving a successful combination of democracy, economic growth, and social justice?

Political History to 1973

To answer the first question we must look at Chile's history and political culture and at the self-image held by the Chileans themselves. Most accounts of the origins of Chile's constitutionalism begin with the early postindependence struggles for control of the government between the conservative *pelucones* ("bigwigs") and the more liberal *pipiolos* ("upstarts"). After the autocratic ways of "the Liberator," Bernardo O'Higgins, had led to his resignation in 1823, a period of conflict ensued that ended with the triumph of the *pelucones* in the Battle of Lircay. The 1833 constitution adopted under their auspices created a strong role for the president, elected by property holders for a five-year term with the possibility of reelection for a second term, but it also gave the Congress a role in approving the budget. To this day Chilean conservatives look back to the 1830s, when Diego Portales established a strong centralized state operating under the rule of law, as a governmental ideal that is still valid. They argue that the strong presidency and state not only continued cultural patterns inherited from the Spanish monarchy but also maintained the rule of Castillian-Basque landowners in a way that prevented the breakdown of authority and military intervention that characterized many other newly independent Latin American states. Others maintain that the development of civilian constitutionalism owes more to the presidency of Manuel Bulnes (1841–1851), the hero of the 1837 war with Peru and Bolivia, than to Portales. Bulnes sharply reduced the size of the army and built up a civilian-based national guard as a counterweight to it while strengthening the state bureaucracy so that it provided effective administration and loyalty to the institutions of the state. In addition, he was willing to work with Congress even when it opposed his plans; he relied on changes in his cabinet to keep in touch with elite opinion; and, most important, though still personally popular, he left office in accordance with the constitutional timetable.

In the two-term, ten-year presidency of Bulnes's successor, Manuel Montt (1851–1861), the Liberals reemerged, now reinforced by the influx of progressive ideas from the Europe of the liberal revolutions of 1848. As in other Latin American countries the Liberal-Conservative split focused on centralism versus federalism and the relations between church and state. The federalist tendencies of the Liberals reflected the opposition of the mining interests of the north and the medium-sized landholders of the south to the political dominance of the large landowners of the Central Valley around the capital, Santiago. Revolts against Santiago domination in 1851 and 1859 were put down, but what Chileans call the Oligarchic Republic (1830–1861) gave way to the Liberal Republic (1861–1891), in which factions of the elite combined and recombined in the Congress and the presidency to open the system by limiting the presidency to five years (1871) and abolishing the property requirement for voting (1874). A small but expanding middle class found political expression in the founding in 1861 of the Radical Party, which was committed to Freemasonry, reducing church influence, promoting public education, and establishing universal male suffrage. However, Conservative control of elections in the countryside in what was still largely a rural country meant that the large landowners were able to use electoral democracy to maintain their dominance rather than resorting to military intervention to stem the effects of increased popular participation. Church-state issues, such as who should control clerical appointments, cemeteries, and education, still divided the political class; but after 1859 all groups now agreed on elections and peaceful competition rather than on the use of force to resolve their differences.

The Liberal-Conservative split was papered over during the War of the Pacific (1879–1883) against Peru and Bolivia. Chile's victory gave it a one-third increase in territory involving the rich copper and nitrate areas of the north, but it also led to border disputes with Peru (which were resolved only as late as 1929) and with Bolivia, over its access to the Pacific (still an issue today). The victory vastly increased government revenues from export taxes and produced not only a period of economic prosperity but also the beginnings of an inflation problem that was to continue for almost a century. When President José Manuel Balmaceda (1886–1891) began to take measures to end currency depreciation, promote small landholding, and establish state control over the largely British-owned nitrate deposits, he encountered fierce resistance from landowners and foreign interests. When Congress refused to approve his budget he attempted to rule alone, and a civil war ensued in which ten thousand Chileans died, including Balmaceda himself, who committed suicide after his forces were defeated.

The Chilean constitutional system was fundamentally transformed as a result of the 1891 Civil War. During the period of the Parliamentary Republic (1891–1920), power passed from the president to Congress, and the center of political attention shifted to the local bases of the notables who controlled the Congress National governments (a total of 121 cabinets between 1891 and 1924), which rose and fell depending on shifting congressional majorities, while weak presidents presided over unstable coalition governments.

Following the end of the War of the Pacific in 1883 a Prussian captain, Emil Körner, was invited to organize the Chilean Academy of War, and he began a program to professionalize the army along Prussian lines. (The goose step and the army's strict hierarchical structure and professionalism mark the continuing effects of the original Prussian influence.) So effective was Körner that Chilean military missions were subsequently invited to train armies in Colombia and El Salvador.

In the economy, nitrate, coal, and copper mining expanded (in the last case, by U.S. companies), and labor agitation increased. Labor began to organize, and the massacre of two thousand nitrate workers and their families at Iquique in 1907 became a part of the collective memory of the labor movement. Luis Emilio Recabarren, a labor leader, was elected to Congress in 1906 but was not allowed to take his seat. In 1912 Recabarren founded the Socialist Workers' party, which in 1921 became the Communist Party of Chile. The expanding middle class found its political expression in the Radical Party, which, in addition to its traditional endorsement of the separation of church and state, began to adopt programs favoring social welfare legislation.

The development of cheap synthetic nitrate during World War I dealt a serious blow to Chilean prosperity, which had been based on mineral exports. The election of 1920 brought to the presidency a new populist leader, Arturo Alessandri Palma. Although Alessandri's supporters secured a majority in the congressional elections of 1924, Congress resisted his proposals for social legislation and labor rights. These proposals were adopted only under pressure from young reformist military men in the galleries—the so-called "rattling of the sabres." Alessandri left the country in protest against military intervention but returned in 1925 to preside over the writing of the 1925 constitution. The constitution provided for a strong president, elected for a six-year term but denied the possibility of immediate reelection. Members of Congress were elected at a different time and for different terms (four years for the Chamber of Deputies and eight years for the Senate), and Congress was obliged to choose between the top two presidential candidates if no single candidate received an absolute majority in the popular election. Legislators were elected according to a system of proportional representation that accentuated the proliferation of parties that had already begun to take place. Church and state were separated, and labor and social welfare guarantees were included in the constitution. Chile was thus well ahead of most other Latin American countries in the establishment of the welfare state.

Alessandri resigned three months later, and his successor was forced out by Colonel Carlos Ibáñez, who ruled by plebiscite and decree until 1931. Following a series of short-lived military governments Chile returned to elected governments in late 1932. The military largely withdrew from politics, and four decades of civilian rule ensued.

One of the many unstable governments in the period from 1931 to 1932 was a military-dominated "Socialist Republic" that lasted one hundred days from June to September 1932. Marxist intellectuals, students, and military men then joined to form a new leftist party, the Socialist Party of Chile, which was formally established in April 1933. In late 1932 Arturo Alessandri returned as president, but he now followed a much more conservative policy than earlier. The period that followed has been described by some Chilean writers as *el Estado de Compromiso* (the compromise state)—that is, one in which there was something for everyone and no interest group was directly threatened. The combination of staggered elections and proportional representation meant that it was difficult to get a stable majority for any program, especially if it involved fundamental reforms.

In 1938 Pedro Aguirre Cerda, the candidate of a Popular Front coalition of Radicals and Socialists with Communist support, won the presidential elections. He faced a hostile legislative majority, and the coalition lasted only two years. The Popular Front succeeded in securing the passage of a few social welfare laws, but its principal accomplishment was the establishment of the Chilean Development Corporation (CORFO), which provided the legal basis for a larger state role in the economy. The period from 1938 to 1952 was characterized by the dominance of the Radical Party, which governed through shifting coalitions and policies along with generous patronage to the party faithful. One such shift was from an alliance with the Communists in 1938 to the outlawing of the party by the Radical-sponsored Law for the Defense of Democracy in 1948. (The Communists were legalized again in 1958.)

When the country looked for an alternative to the Radical Party in 1952 it turned to none other than the old military strongman Carlos Ibáñez, who won by a landslide under the symbol of a broom to sweep out the corrupt and ineffective Radicals. Ibáñez did not deliver on his promises, however, and the traditional parties returned to the fray in 1958. A new party, the Christian Democrats, which had been formed by successive reformist splits from the Conservatives, made a surprising showing in the 1958 elections. The Christian Democrats divided the centrist vote with the Radicals, while the leftist alliance of the Socialists and Communists came close to electing Salvador Allende as president. Allende was narrowly edged out by Arturo Alessandri's son, Jorge, the candidate of the Liberals and Conservatives. (There were no longer any significant differences between the Liberals and Conservatives, since the church-state issue had been settled in 1925, and overlapping rural and urban interests in both parties rendered obsolete the old divisions between the landowner and merchant classes.) The 1958 election, with its three-way split between left, center, and right, marked the beginning of a recurrent problem in Chilean politics—how to get majority support for presidents and parties when the electorate was divided into "the three thirds" (*los tres tercios*).

When it looked as if the 1964 presidential elections might give Allende a chance to win by a plurality in a multi-candidate race (and thus, by tradition, to be elected in the congressional runoff), the right threw its support to the charismatic Christian-Democratic candidate, Eduardo Frei, whose program for a "Revolution in Liberty" was offered as a democratic response to the challenge of the Cuban Revolution. Frei won the popular election with the first absolute majority in modern Chilean history—55 percent to Allende's 39 percent. But when he began to implement his program of accelerated agrarian reform, expanded welfare legislation, and higher taxes, the right withdrew its support.

Frei's reforms had strong U.S. backing inasmuch as they coincided in aims and methods with the Alliance for Progress, but they ran into congressional opposition (because of staggered elections, the Christian Democrats never controlled both houses) and created inflationary pressures. After a successful first three years Frei faced an increasingly hostile Congress, and in 1969 he had to put down a local military revolt, the first since the 1930s. The right was optimistic that it could win the 1970 presidential elections with Jorge Alessandri, now eligible to run again, since the Christian Democrats had lost support and did not put forward a strong candidate. On the left, meanwhile, the Socialist-Communist alliance backing Allende was broadened to include a left splinter group from the Christian Democrats as well as the main body of the Radical Party (which had also split).

The result was a narrow victory by Allende (36.2 percent, lower than his vote in 1964) over Alessandri (34.9 percent) with the Christian-Democratic candidate a distant third with 27.8 percent. Chile was thrown into a constitutional, political, and economic crisis as Congress, which was over two-thirds non-Marxist, was asked to elect a Marxist as president in the constitutionally mandated runoff between the top two candidates. The crisis was intensified by U.S. covert efforts to create turmoil in the economy and to promote a military coup, and by the assassination by a rightist group of the army commander-in-chief. It is a testimony to the legalism and constitutionalism of the Chilean military and people that after lengthy negotiations, the constitutional tradition was followed, and in November 1970 Salvador Allende became president.

In the case of the Allende government, the pattern of three good years followed by three bad ones that had characterized previous administrations was telescoped into eighteen months for each period. In 1971 the U.S.-owned mines were completely nationalized by a widely supported constitutional amendment (although the compensation procedures, which in most cases amounted to confiscation, immediately got the Allende government into trouble with the United States and the copper companies); a boom, produced by the granting of large wage raises while price controls were strictly enforced, buoyed the economy; and the Allende coalition received nearly 50 percent support in the municipal elections. However, by 1972 runaway inflation had set in; violence was increasing in the countryside; shortages of foodstuffs and essential goods occurred; and class polarization, encouraged by a government that was trying to broaden its base of support among the lower classes, exacerbated personal and political relations. Using among other "legal loopholes" legislation from the 1932 Socialist Republic, the government took over and "intervened" or "requisitioned" five hundred firms, and industrial and agricultural production dropped. Further exacerbating the economic problems, opposition-dominated professional and occupational groups (*gremios*) called strikes that paralyzed the country in October 1972 and again in July 1973.

Despite several attempts at negotiations with the Christian Democrats, Allende was not able to work out an agreement with the opposition-dominated Congress. (The left wing of his Socialist Party opposed any agreement, as did the right wing of the Christian Democrats.) By the time the congressional elections of March 1973 took place, the three-thirds had become two intransigent pro- and anti-Allende blocs. The center-right Democratic Confederation won 55 percent of the congressional vote, compared with 43 percent for Allende's Popular Unity Federation, but the division of the country only intensified. Violence increased as extremists on both sides (the Movement of the Revolutionary Left [MIR] and the rightist *Patria y Libertad)* carried out assassinations, blackouts, and bombings. To the concerns of the military over the collapse of the economy and the breakdown of law and order (symbolized by a widely circulated picture of a policeman being beaten by a masked and helmeted revolutionary) were added fears of Marxism as the government announced that all schools would be required to give government-mandated courses in socialism.

Yet the army still considered itself to be "professional, hierarchical, obedient, and non-deliberating" as required by the 1925 constitution. The armed forces did not move until the Supreme Court had written open letters to Allende protesting the government's refusal to carry out court orders to return seized property, the Congress had passed a resolution accusing the government of "habitually" violating the constitution and the law, and the other army generals had forced out their constitutionalist commander-in-chief, Carlos Prats (later assassinated in exile by Chilean intelligence agents).

On September 11, 1973, the army, air force, navy, and national police overthrew the Allende government in a one-day coup that included the bombing of La Moneda, the presidential palace (the traditional symbol of civilian rule), and the suicide of Allende (following the example, which he often cited, of President Balmaceda in 1891), as army troops stormed the burning palace.

Despite reports, never proven, of CIA involvement in the coup (a 1975 U.S. Senate investigation concluded that between 1971 and 1973 CIA money supported the opposition media, some of the strikers, an extreme-right group, and anti-Allende propaganda among the military), the coup was an authentically Chilean product. The armed forces moved only when it became clear that the civilian politicians were unable to run the economy or to maintain a constitutional consensus and that the military monopoly on the instruments of coercion was being threatened by armed groups. Allende had been able to use the constitution to defend himself against military intervention as long as the economy was functioning and law and order prevailed. But once it appeared that the legality and constitutionalism that Allende had proclaimed as essential to the *via chilena* to socialism no longer existed, the armed forces broke with their tradition of nonintervention. Many factors contributed to the breakdown of constitutional democracy, but the most important ones seem to have been the sharp increase in violence and polarization, and the collapse of the economy.

Military Rule

Most observers had assumed that if the armed forces intervened, it would be for a short period during which they would outlaw the Marxist parties, stabilize the economy, and call new elections. They were wrong. It is now clear that 1973 was a turning point in Chilean history. The leaders of the coup—especially General Augusto Pinochet, who used his position as head of the senior branch of the armed services to centralize political power in his hands—were determined to change the pattern of Chilean politics. They spoke of eradicating the "cancer of Marxism," creating a "protected democracy" that would not be subject to the demagoguery of the politicians, and making sure that the breakdown of law and order as well as the threats to national security that occurred during the Allende administration would never be repeated.

Yet as clear as their determination to change Chilean political culture might have been, the specifics of how to do so were not evident at the outset. The leftist parties were outlawed, the Communist Party headquarters was burned, and the other parties were declared "in recess." Thousands of suspected leftists were rounded up, tortured, and in many cases killed. (The best-known case is that of Charles Horman, a U.S. citizen. It is the subject of the book and film *Missing*, which accurately portray the atmosphere of postcoup Chile, although the basic thesis of *Missing*, that Horman was killed because "he knew too much" about the U.S. role in the coup, is incorrect.) Many of the leaders of the left went into exile or took refuge in foreign embassies. Those who did not were transported to Dawson Island in the frigid south and were later allowed to go into exile as well. The constitution, in the name of which the coup had been carried out, was simply ignored as the government began to function in accordance with a series of decree-laws that gave legislative and constitutional power to the four-person junta and executive power to its head, Augusto Pinochet. (At the time of the coup there had been discussion of rotating the presidency of the junta among the armed forces, but it was soon clear that Pinochet intended to stay in that post, and a decree-law in June 1974 made him President of the Republic and Supreme Chief of the Nation.) The judiciary remained in place and supinely recognized the legal validity of the decree-laws, refusing to issue writs of habeas corpus (*recursos de amparo*) for all but a minuscule number of the thousands who were arrested. A committee of conservative jurists was appointed to revise the constitution, but it worked very slowly and did not report out a draft until five years later.

The effort to remove what the military viewed as the sources of subversion meant not only that the parties that were members of Allende's Popular Unity Federation were outlawed but also that the universities were put under military rectors and leftist professors were purged; the newspapers and magazines of the left were closed (along with the theoretical journal of the Christian Democrats); labor unions, many of which had been Marxist-led, were dissolved; and peasant organizations were disbanded. Foreigners who had been assisting the Allende government were expelled and, in a few cases, tortured or killed. Diplomatic relations were broken with Cuba and the Soviet Union (but not with China, a principal customer for Chilean copper).

The most important change, in terms of its lasting impact on Chilean society, was the opening of the economy carried out under the auspices of "los Chicago boys." Departing from the usual statist tendencies of the Latin American military, the junta decided to entrust economic policy to a group of free-market-oriented civilian economists, most of whom had received graduate training in economics at the University of Chicago. Reacting to the socialist interventionism of the Allende years, their program called for opening Chile to internal and external competition by relying on private enterprise, competition, and market forces. It removed price controls, reduced tariffs dramatically, expanded exports, moved toward the establishment of more realistic exchange rates, and returned landholdings and businesses that had been illegally seized. (The copper nationalization was not reversed both because it had been carried out by a constitutional amendment and because part of the foreign exchange earnings of copper was earmarked for military purchases.) At first the program was adopted in a gradual fashion; two years later it was applied in a drastic "shock treatment."

The junta's Declaration of Principles, published in March 1974, spoke of organizing "a great civilian-military movement based on decentralized vehicles of participation." However, no effort was made to create a government party or movement, inasmuch as the regime's main aim was the depoliticization of Chile—and Pinochet may have seen such a movement as a possible rival center of power. The declaration spoke of property rights as an example of the principle of subsidiarity endorsed by Catholic social thought, ignoring the substantial limits that the papal social encyclicals place on individual property rights. It also stated that although the government respected human rights, it could not allow that "in the name of a misunderstood pluralism, a naive democracy could permit organized groups within it to promote guerrilla violence or, pretending to accept the rules of democracy, support a doctrine or morality whose objective is the construction of a totalitarian state. Consequently Marxist movements and parties will not be admitted again to civic life."

It was clear from the outset that human rights were not respected by the new regime. Military missions moved to the north and the south to carry out summary executions of leftists. The report of the National Commission on Truth and Reconciliation in February 1991 and subsequent investigations identified by name 3,197 Chileans who had been killed or had disappeared between 1973 and 1990, most of them victims of "agents of the state or persons in its service." The reports of the National Commission on Political Imprisonment and Torture, chaired by Bishop Sergio Valech, published in 2004 and 2005, listed 28,456 cases, often involving physical abuse, rape, electric shock, and other forms of torture.

The violation of human rights in Chile led to a serious deterioration in relations with the United States, and in 1976 the United States Congress imposed a ban on Chilean arms aid and purchases—a ban that was not lifted until 1990. Relations worsened when President Jimmy Carter made human rights a central element of U.S. foreign policy. In the United Nations, reports to the General Assembly about Chile were prepared each year by a special rapporteur, and the UN Human Rights Commission continued to discuss Chilean abuses.

Within Chile Pinochet managed to transform what had been an institutional coup by the four services into a personal dictatorship. The system of promotions and retirements was altered so that his protégés could remain beyond retirement age while those who were a possible threat to his power could be retired. The intelligence branches of the armed services were consolidated into a single National Intelligence Service (DINA), which established computerized files and conducted a national system of terror. DINA killed General Prats, in exile in Argentina, and wounded Bernardo Leighton, a Christian Democrat with good relations with the left, in Rome. Its most heinous crime was to blow up the car of Allende's former ambassador to the United States, Orlando Letelier, in the heart of Washington, D.C. The U.S. investigation that followed led to the extradition and conviction of the immediate perpetrator, a rightist U.S.

citizen who had been living in Chile, and continuing pressure on Chile to extradite the higher-ups involved.[1] After the return of democracy the head of DINA, Manuel Contreras, was tried and sentenced to seven years in prison for ordering Letelier's death. (After his release he was tried and sentenced to life imprisonment for other human rights crimes.)

As a result of the Letelier investigation, Pinochet removed Contreras and reorganized DINA as the National Information Center (CNI), which wielded less independent power than DINA had exercised. In 1978 when General Gustavo Leigh, the air force member of the junta, began to call for more rapid progress toward civilian rule, Pinochet removed him and appointed a low-ranking air force general as his successor. This action led to the resignation or forced retirement of eighteen air force generals. With his triumph over Leigh, Pinochet's personal control of the armed forces was complete.

Meanwhile, the economy, which had suffered a drastic contraction as a result of the shock treatment, was now beginning to be described as the "Chilean economic miracle." From 1977 until 1981 it expanded at rates of 6 to 8 percent a year. With tariff rates down to 10 percent (from an average of 100 percent during the Allende period), cheap foreign imports flooded the country. The exchange rate was fixed at 39 pesos to the dollar, and nontraditional exports such as fruit, lumber, and seafood reduced the share of copper in earning foreign exchange from 80 percent to less than 40 percent. It was possible to take out dollar loans at the overvalued exchange rate, and Japanese cars and scotch whiskey could be purchased more cheaply in Chile than in their countries of origin. It was in this heady atmosphere that a plebiscite was held on a new constitution.

The 1980 Constitution

In late 1978 the Committee for the Study of a New Constitution produced a draft that was submitted to the advisory Council of State, which had been created by Pinochet in 1976. On July 1, 1980, the Council submitted a revised draft that proposed a five-year transition, with an appointed Congress until 1985 and a full return to civilian rule at that time. In the next month Pinochet and his advisers completely rewrote the transitional provisions of the draft to produce a quite different timetable that would enable Pinochet to remain in power until at least 1990, and possibly until 1997. With only one opportunity for public criticism—a public meeting at which Frei spoke and leftist slogans were chanted (by CNI agents, some said)—the draft was submitted to a vote on the seventh anniversary of the coup, September 11, 1980, and the government-controlled media announced that it had been approved by a 67 percent vote. Later there were charges that the vote had been artificially inflated in the more remote areas, with more votes reported than there were voters. (The voting rolls had been destroyed after the coup, and there were no independent poll watchers to check on the voting.)

One of the transitional provisions added in July 1980 was that approval of the constitution also constituted election of General Pinochet for an eight-year presidential term beginning March 11, 1981. The transitional articles also called for a plebiscite in late 1988 on an additional eight-year term for a presidential candidate nominated by the junta. In the event that the junta candidate lost the plebiscite (as in fact happened), competitive elections for the presidency and for Congress were to be held in late 1989, with the elected government taking office on March 11, 1990.

The 1980 constitution attempted to remedy the defects of the 1925 constitution by providing for the simultaneous election of the president and the Congress (thus removing the adverse effects of staggered elections) and establishing a two-round runoff system for the popular election of the president (so that he would have the mandate of a popular majority—a system that almost certainly would have led to the election of Jorge Alessandri in 1970). The constitution also created a strong Constitutional Tribunal with the power to "control" (that is, review) the constitutionality of all important laws and to make definitive judgments on all constitutional disputes. The Chamber of Deputies was to have 120 members elected for four-year terms, and there would be 26 senators (later increased to 38), elected for eight-year terms, with half chosen every four years. In addition, all ex-presidents who had served six years were to be senators for life, and there were to be nine appointed senators—two former members of the Supreme Court, one ex-controller general, one former university rector, one ex-cabinet member, and one former commander from each of the four armed service. (The nonelected senators were abolished in August 2005, but in the initial years of the transition to democracy they gave the right the power to block government legislation in the upper house.)

In the Declaration of Principles the junta had announced its commitment to administrative and governmental decentralization and it had reorganized the country into numbered regions that replaced the provinces as intermediate governmental bodies. The regions were governed by a presidentially appointed *intendente* (usually a military man), and the mayors of the local municipalities were replaced by presidential appointees.

The "Modernizations"

With the apparent success of the government's economic policy Pinochet's advisers began to extend the principle of free choice to the area of social policy by means of the so-called "modernizations." Labor unions were now permitted, but they were restricted to the local firm or factory, and their right to strike was limited. The National Health Service was reorganized and decentralized, and private health services were authorized to receive payments from the compulsory health insurance deduction, leading eventually to the enrollment of about 30 percent of Chileans in private health plans. Private universities and educational institutions were authorized, and tuitions were raised, which could be financed by low-interest loans that were immediately payable if a student failed or was expelled from the university (e.g., for political activities). Local education was reorganized on the basis of contracts between the municipality and private educational corporations, so that teachers ceased to be civil servants and lost tenure rights. Housing policy was reoriented to encourage private contractors to build low-cost housing, and the government provided low-interest loans and grants to the poor only if they had saved enough to make a small down payment.

The most fundamental shift was the privatization of the complicated and bankrupt social security system. A reduction in premiums persuaded Chileans to place their compulsory social security deductions in publicly-regulated but private and competitive pension funds resembling the individual retirement accounts (IRAs) in the United States. Unlike IRAs, however, the pension funds replaced rather than supplemented the public social security program. The government still maintained a basic social security safety net for those people who, for reasons such as poor health or insufficient contributions, could not participate in the system. Over the next several years, however, the government's responsibility for most of the social security program ended.

The "modernizations" and the opening of the economy to internal and external market forces were part of a broader view that was influenced by economically conservative (Latin Americans would call them "neoliberal") thinkers in the United States and Europe. Friedrich Hayek and Milton Friedman visited Chile, and think tanks and publications began to project a vision of a new Chile with a consumer-oriented and prosperous economy like those of South Korea and Hong Kong, gradually moving toward democratic and decentralized politics that would replace the statism and socialism of the past.

In March 1981 when Augusto Pinochet entered the newly reconstructed presidential palace as "constitutional" president of Chile, he was able to feel secure. The original legitimization of the coup (the prevention of a Marxist takeover) was no longer viable, but it had been replaced by a constitution that had the support of the armed forces and of many members of the upper and middle classes—and the new prosperity of the "economic miracle" was even beginning to trickle down to the lower classes as employment and wages began to rise and inflation declined. A state of emergency in various degrees and a limited curfew were still in force, and police roundups in the poor areas and occasional political murders of leftists still occurred. But some opposition magazines and books (although not newspapers or television) were tolerated and the more visible aspects of the repression were no longer evident.

The Protests

The sudden collapse of the Chilean economy in 1982 shattered this optimistic view of the prospects of the regime. External factors such as excessive indebtedness at rising interest rates and a low price for copper exports, combined with internal weaknesses such as an overvalued exchange rate and the existence of underfinanced paper financial empires involving interlocking banks and industries, led to a wave of bankruptcies and widespread unemployment. As unemployment figures rose to include nearly a third of the workforce (including those enrolled in the Minimum Employment Program) Chileans began to engage in public protests against the government for the first time since 1973. Beginning with the copper workers' union in May 1983 and soon joined by the illegal but newly revived parties, the protests escalated monthly until August, when President Pinochet had to call out 17,000 members of the regular army to keep order.

Pinochet, however, was able to keep his hold on power by pointing to the timetable outlined in the constitution and appealing to fears of disorder and violence. (The Manuel Rodríguez Patriotic Front [FPMR], a terrorist movement associated with, but more committed to violence than the Communist Party, had begun to engage in acts of sabotage, bombings, and blackouts.) In 1986 Pinochet's position was strengthened when large arms deposits destined for the FPMR were discovered, and the group carried out an unsuccessful assassination attempt against him.

As a result of the protest movement the political parties—though still technically illegal—began to be active. The threefold division of the pre-coup period was still evident, but there was a significant broadening of the center, as the "renovated" wing of the Socialist Party began to work with the centrist parties in the newly-formed Democratic Alliance. The Communists, who were illegal and had adopted a policy that included "all forms of struggle," including violence, were not invited to join. With the recognition that protests alone could not force Pinochet out of office, particularly as the economy began to rebound from the crash of the early 1980s, the party leaders were compelled to decide whether or how to participate in the plebiscite scheduled for late 1988.

The 1988 Plebiscite

In contrast to the plebiscite on the 1980 constitution, the 1988 plebiscite was organized well in advance. Laws were published concerning electoral registration, recognition of political parties, and the method of carrying out the plebiscite itself. The problem for the opposition was to decide whether, by participating, they would give implicit recognition to the 1980 constitution, the legitimacy of which they had always questioned. The Communist Party called for a boycott, but later, under pressure from its membership, it permitted its adherents to register. The Christian Democrats eventually complied with the legal requirements for party registration, and the Socialists had it both ways by refusing to seek recognition while registering a Party for Democracy (PPD), which was open to all who opposed the regime.

The conservative parties, the center-right National Renovation Party, and the pro-Pinochet Independent Democratic Union (UDI), had already been recognized, and they urged their members to register and vote. The government pressured the military and public employees to do the same. At the beginning of 1988, when it was rumored that Pinochet was urging the junta to call a plebiscite in March, it looked as if he could get a new eight-year term without difficulty. However, several factors turned the situation around.

First, sixteen opposition parties from the center and the left (minus the Communists) formed a unified Command for the No, published a program calling for a return to democracy and an end to ideological proscriptions, and insisted that a democratic government would respect private property and the economic rules of the game. Second, church-related groups conducted massive registration drives throughout the country, resulting in the registration of 92 percent of the eligible voters by the time the electoral registries were closed. Third, the Constitutional Tribunal ruled that the opposition must be given access to the state-owned television—and fifteen minutes of prime time were given free of charge to the opposition for twenty-seven days. With the assistance of the Center for Free Elections (COPEL) of the Organization of American States and the U.S. National Endowment for Democracy, the opposition developed an effective television campaign as well as poll-watching and vote-counting techniques that made fraud almost impossible. The result was that, despite massive government propaganda arguing that a "no" vote would mean a return to the chaos and communism of the Allende period, Pinochet was defeated by a vote of 55 percent "no" to 43 percent "yes" on his continuation as president for another eight-year term.

The Return to Democracy

On December 14, 1989, Chile elected Patricio Aylwin, a Christian Democrat, the candidate of the center-left *Concertación por la Democracia* to a four-year term (later lengthened to six years for his successors and cut again to four years in 2005), who took office on March 11, 1990. Pinochet continued as

army commander for an eight-year term as permitted by the transitional provisions of the 1980 constitution. Along with the heads of the other armed
services, he also had a seat on the National Security Council and thereafter, as
an ex-president, he could be a senator for the rest of his life.

Thanks to their years of exile in Europe and the United States, the Aylwin
cabinet contained the largest number of ministers and deputy ministers with
graduate degrees of any modern government. The government announced
that it would give priority to primary education and job training. Government
spending on education, adjusted for inflation, doubled between 1990 and
1997. Health spending increased by 75 percent, although substantial inequalities between the public and private health care sectors remained. Between
1990 and 1997 foreign investment and exports doubled, and inflation and unemployment dropped to 6 percent. Economic growth averaged 7 percent a
year in the same period, with an 11 percent growth rate in 1992. The percentage of the population living in poverty dropped from 39 percent in 1987 to 23
percent in 1994, and the living standards of all groups rose as average wages
increased by 22 percent, although income distribution remained highly
skewed. The U.S. embargo on military aid was lifted, and negotiations for free
trade agreements with the United States, Canada, and Mexico were begun.

The Aylwin government moved quickly in the area of human rights. To
investigate human rights abuses Aylwin appointed a Commission on Truth
and Reconciliation, headed by Raúl Rettig, a former Radical senator, and including Gonzalo Vial, a conservative historian and former education minister
in the Pinochet government. The Commission had no judicial powers and
did not identify the perpetrators, but it listed the victims by name and called
for moral and monetary reparations to the families of the victims. In April
1991 an additional politically-inspired murder was added to the list with the
assassination by the leftist Manuel Rodríguez Patriotic Front of Senator
Jaime Guzman, the founder of the rightist UDI party.

The Aylwin government was pressured by members of the Socialist and
PPD parties, as well as by the Association of Families of the Detained and
Disappeared (AFDD), to take further action in the human rights area. Political cases were moved from military to civilian courts, nonviolent political prisoners were released, and the Communist Party was legalized, but Pinochet
continued to insist that he would protect "my people" (*mi gente*) from prosecution. In December 1991 he issued a low-level mobilization ("call to quarters")
that was intended to deliver a message to the government. Cases that involved
murders and disappearances that had taken place after the amnesty declared
by Pinochet in 1978, as well as the Letelier murder in Washington that, at
U.S. insistence, had been exempted from that amnesty, proceeded at a slow
pace through the court system.

The human rights cases were among the first problems of the new administration of Eduardo Frei Ruiz-Tagle, who took office on March 11, 1994, following a record win—with 58 percent of the votes—over Arturo Alessandri, a nephew of the former president. In retrospect, it now appears that the jurisdiction of the civilian courts over human rights cases involving the military was finally established in November 1993 with the sentencing of retired General Manuel Contreras, the former head of the DINA intelligence agency, and his assistant, Pedro Espinoza, for their part in the Letelier assassination. After many months of resistance, including a stay at a military hospital by Contreras, the two former officers began in September and October 1994 to serve their sentences in a specially-constructed jail for members of the military. In March 1993 fifteen members of the national police and one civilian were also sentenced to jail terms for the kidnapping and murder of leading leftist leaders in 1985—the so-called case of the *degollados* ("throat-slitting"). Earlier Allende's body had been reburied in the part of the General Cemetery reserved for former presidents, and later in the decade a memorial to the disappeared was erected in the cemetery, and a park with the names of the murdered created at the former location of the Villa Grimaldi torture center.

Alessandri, the candidate of two right-wing parties, had received 24 percent of the presidential vote in a six-candidate field, but the rightist parties received nearly 40 percent of the vote in the Senate and 36 percent in the Chamber of Deputies, and the continuation of the terms of the appointed senators as well as an electoral system that exaggerated the representation of the second-ranking party or coalition (there are two seats in each senatorial or congressional district) enabled the right to maintain its control of the upper house.

The Pinochet Case

In accordance with the 1980 constitution Pinochet went out of office as commander-in-chief of the army in March 1998 and decided to accept his seat as a senator for life. There were protests at his swearing-in, as well as an unsuccessful attempt by Socialist, PPD, and some Christian Democratic members of Congress to deny him his seat. His only significant legislative activity was involvement in the resolution of a dispute over ending the status as a legal holiday of September 11th, the anniversary of the coup, by replacing it with a Day of National Unity on the first Monday in September.

In October Pinochet went to London for back surgery, and on October 16, while he was recovering in a hospital, he was arrested by Scotland Yard in response to warrants issued by a Spanish judge requesting that he be extradited for trial for the murder of Spanish citizens, as well as for acts of "geno cide, terrorism, and torture." On October 28 a three-judge panel of the Queen's Bench Division of the High Court ruled that the warrants were invalid because, as a former head of state, Pinochet was "entitled to immunity in relation to criminal acts performed in the course of exercising public functions." On appeal a five-member panel of the Law Lords ruled by a vote of 3–2 on November 28 that torture and hostage-taking could not be considered acts of state, but the House of Lords vacated that decision on the ground that one of the judges was connected to Amnesty International, a human rights organization that had long opposed Pinochet. A rehearing by a seven member panel of the Law Lords led to a decision on March 28, 1999, dismissing most of the charges because they were not crimes under British law at the time they were committed, but upholding the charge of torture for acts carried out after December 8, 1988, the date that Britain ratified the International Convention against Torture. Following lengthy hearings in which the Chilean government (arguing that he should be returned to Chile to face charges there) and international human rights organizations participated, the Magistrates Court ruled on October 8, 1999, that Pinochet could be extradited to Spain to stand trial on charges of torture and conspiracy to torture after December 8, 1988, adding a gratuitous additional argument that the continuing "mental torture" of survivors and relatives caused by earlier murders and disappearances meant that earlier cases could be considered as well.

In August and September Pinochet's health (he was now eighty-three) deteriorated with a series of minor strokes, and he was reported to be suffering as well from diabetes, asthma, circulatory problems, and depression. The Chilean government had already appealed to the British Home Secretary to return him to Chile on humanitarian grounds, and after a government-appointed board of doctors declared him unfit to stand trial in January 2000 he was returned to Chile on March 4, 2000. Awaiting him were fifty-eight cases of human rights abuses being considered by a Chilean judge.

The Frei government, made up of opponents and in some cases victims of Pinochet, had argued for his return, claiming that Chile as the country in which the crimes had been committed had original jurisdiction. That claim was initially unconvincing because of the slow pace of human rights cases in the Chilean courts, Pinochet's congressional immunity as a senator, and the amnesty that he had declared in March 1978 for crimes committed between 1973 and the date of the amnesty. However, during his detention in England there had been a turnaround in the personnel and actions of the Chilean courts, as the Pinochet appointees began to retire. The judges began to take up more and more of the human rights cases, including those committed before 1978, which were now considered capable of being tried under the novel judicial doctrine that if the bodies of the disappeared had not been found, a crime of "ongoing kidnapping" (*secuestro permanente*) was still being committed. Cases such as the infamous "Caravan of Death"—the murders of political prisoners in central and northern Chile in October 1973 about which a best-selling book had been written—the assassination of a leading labor leader in 1982, and the 1974 murder of General Prats in Buenos Aires began to be pursued actively in the Chilean judicial system, and military commanders were called upon to testify.

Pinochet's successor as army commander protested against the new judicial activism and reinterpretations of the law, but took no further action. Frei's minister of defense organized a series of dialogues on human rights that included both members of the military and human rights activists, but there was no talk of military action. Clearly Pinochet's arrest and detention had changed the nature of politics in Chile.

The 1999–2000 Presidential Election

Proof that the Pinochet era had been left behind came with the presidential elections of December 1999 and January 2000. Ricardo Lagos, a Socialist who had been education minister and public works minister in the Aylwin and Frei governments, won the *Concertación* primary election (a new feature of Chilean politics), resoundingly defeating the Christian Democratic candidate. The rightist Alliance for Chile, made up of the National Renovation Party (RN) and the Independent Democratic Union (UDI), nominated Joaquín Lavín from the more conservative UDI. Lavin had become nationally visible because of his innovative administration as mayor of Las Condes, the upper-class suburb of Santiago, where he had promoted public works, health clinics, housing for the poor, and centers for the elderly. Neither Lavín's earlier association with the Pinochet government nor Lagos's participation in the Allende government was discussed in the campaign, which focused principally on issues of education, health care, public safety, and the economy. Lavín was able to point to his record as a "doer" (*cosista*) and to benefit from the dissatisfaction with the incumbent government because of a sudden increase in unemployment to 11 percent resulting from the downturn in the economy caused by the economic difficulties of Chile's Asian markets. After a well-financed campaign in which he projected a image of youth, vigor, and charisma (and outspent the *Concertación* by a reported U.S. $50 million to U.S. $10 million) Lavín came within 34,000 votes of defeating Lagos in the December 12, 1999 elections, winning a majority of the women's vote and carrying many of Chile's regions. He lost the January 16, 2000 runoff by 2.6 percent, and political observers attributed Lagos's margin to the votes of some or all of the 3 percent who had voted for the Communist candidate in the first round, and to a shift to Lagos in the women's vote as a result of the organization of women voters by the popular Christian Democratic minister of justice, Soledad Alvear, whom Lagos appointed as his campaign manager for the second round. Lavín's final tally of 48.7 percent, however, was far above the usual vote for conservative candidates, and indicated that he had become a major figure in Chilean politics and a likely standard bearer of the right in the next presidential election.

Lagos appointed a cabinet that included, besides his Socialist/PPD fellow party members, a significant number of Christian Democrats, especially at the assistant minister level, and a minister of finance who had been a director of the International Monetary Fund. His administration lost electoral ground in the 2001 congressional elections when the ultraconservative UDI replaced the Christian Democrats as the largest party in Chile, but by the end of his six-year term the right had received a series of setbacks that undercut what had appeared to be the near certainty of a victory of its leader, Joaquín Lavín, in the 2005 presidential election.

The economy, adversely affected by the world crisis of the latter 1990s, recovered dramatically with growth rates around 6 percent in 2005 and 2006. Foreign investment poured in, copper prices rose to all time highs, and Chile became the world's second largest exporter of salmon. Chile signed free trade agreements with the European Union, South Korea, and the United States, adding them to those with Canada and Mexico concluded under the previous administration. While Chile's distribution of income remained among the most inequitable in the world, with the top 10 percent of the population receiving 42 percent of income and the bottom 20 percent only 3.3 percent, the expanding economy led to a further decline in poverty to 18 percent and to a reduction in unemployment. While other Latin American countries suffered inflation, government instability, and budget deficits, Chile's budgets and balance of payments remained in surplus, its price levels stable, and its level of corruption the lowest in Latin America.

The Lagos government modernized the judicial system, replacing the inefficient "inquisitorial" system in which the judge also carries out the investigation and indictment, with the adversarial system in use in the United States and Britain. Augusto Pinochet's senatorial immunity was lifted after he returned from Great Britain and a number of judges ruled that he was fit to stand trial, despite his illnesses, although no actual trials took place.

Beginning in late 2004 the fortunes of the right took a decided turn for the worse. In the municipal elections of October the UDI lost ground and the Christian Democrats regained their position as the largest party in Chile. In

November the commander of the army accepted the institutional responsibility of the army for the human rights abuses of the Pinochet period. At the end of the month the Commission on Political Imprisonment and Torture, headed by Bishop Sergio Valech gave gruesome and detailed accounts of the tortures inflicted as a matter of policy on tens of thousands of Chileans by the Pinochet regime. Its report and a later follow-up demonstrated that over 28,000 Chileans has been subjected to rape, torture, and physical abuse. It proposed that the victims receive health and education benefits as well as a pension equivalent to $180 a month.

In 2004 and 2005 a subcommittee of the U.S. Senate investigating money laundering found evidence that the Riggs Bank has assisted Pinochet in setting up fictitious accounts to hide dollar deposits. Further investigation revealed that the Pinochet family had 125 bank accounts holding in excess of $17 million in nine American banks under false names. Legal proceedings against the family included the arrest of Pinochet's wife and one of his sons, who were accused of involvement in the cover-up as well as income tax evasion.

The political and social consequences of these developments were considerable. Lavín lost support and the conservative vote was split as the other rightist party, National Renovation, nominated as its presidential candidate Sebastian Pinera, a wealthy businessman who had voted against Pinochet in the 1988 plebiscite. In contrast, the *Concertación* avoided a primary fight when Soledad Alvear, the Christian Democratic candidate, bowed out in view of the commanding lead in the polls of Michelle Bachelet, the Socialist/PPD nominee. The fact that both candidates were women was an indication of the cultural liberalization that had taken place in Chile.

In August 2005 Congress passed a series of constitutional amendments removing the antidemocratic provisions of the 1988 constitution, such as the nonelected senators and the prohibition of presidential removal of military commanders without the consent of the National Security Council, and returning the national police *(carabineros)* to the Ministry of the Interior. It also shortened the presidential term to four years, thus assuring that henceforth the president, the Chamber of Deputies, and half the Senate would be elected simultaneously. However, it was not able to agree on abandoning the "binominal" congressional electoral system of two-member districts.

The *Concertación* candidates received 52 percent of the vote in the December 11, 2005 legislative elections, assuring them control of both houses of Congress. There were four presidential candidates, Michelle Bachelet, Sebastian Pinera, Joaquín Lavín, and Tomas Hirsch, a member of the tiny Humanist Party running on behalf of a coalition dominated by the Communists. Bachelet received 46 percent, Pinera 26 percent, Lavín 23 percent, and Hirsch

5 percent. Since Bachelet had not received an absolute majority, a runoff second round between Bachelet and Pinera took place on January 15, 2006. After a campaign in which Pinera attempted unsuccessfully to draw Christian Democratic votes by contrasting his "Christian humanism" with Bachelet's agnosticism, Bachelet defeated Pinera by a margin of 7 percent, thus becoming the first woman president of Chile.

Bachelet promised a reform of the largely privatized pension system, democratization of the electoral system, and the creation of a nationwide system of day care centers. Her economic program, developed by a team of internationally-known economists, continued to combine a market-friendly economic policy with social measures designed to reduce proverty and inequality. She also promised that half of her cabinet would be women.

Political Parties

The Right

Before 1973 the right was dominated by the National party, which had been formed in 1966 by a fusion of the old Liberal and Conservative parties. The National Party declared itself dissolved after the coup, and during the 1980s two center-right parties were formed—the Independent Democratic Union (UDI), which was initially based on the anti-Allende *gremialista* movement at the Catholic University, and the Party of National Renovation (RN), which is somewhat more secular in inspiration and less committed to the personal and institutional defense of Augusto Pinochet. The electoral system encouraged the two parties to present joint candidates for the presidency and congress. Joaquín Lavín's near-victory in 1999–2000 seemed to make the UDI the dominant party of the coalition, but strong personal enmities between the leaders of the two parties and the discrediting of those like Lavín associated with Pinochet (a result of the revelations of 2004–2005 concerning Pinochet's secret bank accounts and the systematic use of torture by his regime) led them to present separate presidential candidates in 2005.

The Center

The most significant centrist party is the Christian Democratic party of Chile. The government party in the 1960s, it maintained its internal structure and youth, student, labor, and women's branches during the period of military rule. Drawing its welfare state-human rights-mixed economy political philosophy from Catholic social thought, the Christian Democrats are the largest party in Chile in most elections, although their share of the vote has declined in recent years. Having abandoned the policy of going it alone (*camino propio*) that it pursued in the 1960s, the party is strongly committed to working with other parties in order to maintain stable progressive governments in Chile. The Christian Democrats were the most important group in bringing about the Democratic Alliance in 1983, the formation of the sixteen-party Command for the No in 1988, and the creation of the Coalition (*Concertación*) of Parties for Democracy in 1989.

The Christian Democratic Party is supported by the Chilean middle class, but it has an important labor component. The party has long since abandoned the communitarian socialism with which it briefly flirted during the Allende period, and it now accepts the importance of the market as an allocator of resources, although it criticized the regressive social effects of the economic policies of the Pinochet regime. The Christian Democratic government of the 1960s adopted a strong agrarian reform law, but the party now advocates other means (e.g., technical assistance and access to credit) to raise living standards and production in the countryside. It supports the encouragement of foreign investment and the promotion of exports, but combines this with strong commitment to the expansion of educational opportunity, health care, and the reduction of poverty.

The Radical Party, now renamed the Radical Social Democratic Party, was once the fulcrum of the Chilean center, but it has been seriously weakened by frequent splits on the left and right. Although there are still Radical supporters in the provincial towns and rural areas, and the party has international recognition as, for example, a member of the Socialist International, it has received less than 5 percent of the vote in recent elections.

The Left

In the past the left has been dominated by the Socialist and Communist parties, which were allied in the Popular Action Front (FRAP) between 1957 and 1970 and formed the core of Allende's Popular Unity coalition between 1970 and 1973. In the late 1960s the Socialists adopted an increasingly radical position so that, during the Allende period, they represented the most "revolutionary" party in Allende's coalition, often taking positions to the left of Allende himself. After the coup most of the Socialist leaders went into exile in Europe. By the late 1970s a split had emerged between those (mainly in Western Europe) who favored a more moderate position similar to the positions of the French and Spanish Socialists and those (mainly in Eastern Europe and the Soviet Union) who favored continued close cooperation with the Communists and commitment to Marxism-Leninism. With the opening of politics in Chile the two groups united to reestablish the Chilean Socialist party, which abandoned Marxism, becoming an important partner in the electoral coalitions and governments of Aylwin and Frei, and nominating the successful presidential candidates of the *Concertación* in 2000 and 2006, Ricardo Lagos and Michelle Bachelet.

When the more moderate wing of the Socialists decided to form the Party for Democracy (PPD) as an "instrumental" party to defeat Pinochet in the 1988 plebiscite, its president, Ricardo Lagos, achieved national prominence denouncing Pinochet on television. (Lagos ran as the presidential candidate of both the Socialists and the PPD in 1999.) The PPD has abandoned its quasi-Marxist roots and emphasizes the need to modernize Chilean economics, politics, and society. It continues to field its own candidates but cooperates closely with the Socialist Party.

The Communist Party was outlawed after the coup and many of its leaders persecuted and murdered, but it continued to be active among workers and in the shantytowns. Although it endorsed the *via pacífica* to power between 1957 and 1973, in 1980 it began to advocate "all forms of struggle," including "acute forms of violence." For this reason the other parties were unwilling to work with the Communists against Pinochet, although they supported its right to participate in the democratic process by nonviolent means. After the party was legalized in the 1990s it only secured 3 to 6 percent of the vote, compared with the 15 to 18 percent that it had received before 1973, although in alliance with other leftist groups it has received more votes in municipal elections. The Communists still have strength among the trade unions and in university student politics. The Manuel Rodríguez Patriotic Front, an offshoot of the party, carried out violent actions in the 1980s, but it split in the early 1990s on the issue of the continued use of violence, and it is no longer significant. In the December 2005 presidential election the Communists helped to form a coalition that presented a candidate from the Humanist Party who received 5 percent of the vote.

After fifteen years of democratic government the classic "three-thirds" division of the Chilean parties into left, center, and right no longer describes the Chilean political scene. It has been replaced by a bipolar division between the governing *Concertación*, composed primarily of the Christian Democrats, the Socialists, and the PPD, and the conservative opposition, made up of National Renovation (RN) and the Independent Democratic Union (UDI). That division has been encouraged by the electoral system for the Congress that in effect only allots seats to the first- and second-ranking parties or coalitions, but there is now considerable support for a return to a modified proportional representation system that is considered more democratic.

The Armed Forces

It has been said that Chile has a British navy, a U.S. air force, and a Prussian army. The navy has an aristocratic tradition, the army and air force draw many of their officers from the upper-middle class, and members of the national police often come from lower-middle-class backgrounds. There were tensions among the services within the junta, especially over Pinochet's dominance and even concerning the advisability of his candidacy in 1988, but he was able to use his control of the army and, after 1980 the military tradition of legalism and constitutionalism to maintain a facade of unity and support. He remained as army commander until March 1998, and when his intelligence agency, the National Information Center (CNI), was dissolved in January 1990 many of its members and activities were transferred to the army intelligence unit.

As long as Pinochet was army commander the threat of military action could not be discounted. After his arrest and detention in October 1998, however, a much younger group took power and accepted the legitimacy of civilian control of the military. With the official apology in 2004 by the army commander for its institutional involvement in human rights abuses of the dictatorship, the break from the Pinochet-dominated past was complete.

Business and Agriculture

Chilean industry and business have long been formally organized into the Society for the Promotion of Manufacturing (SOFOFA) and the Confederation for Production and Commerce. Chilean industry was fundamentally altered by the policies of the Pinochet government. Inefficient companies protected by high tariffs went bankrupt while new export-oriented businesses handling everything from kiwi fruit to rosehip tea flourished. Ownership became concentrated in a few financial-industrial *grupos* after the sell-off of state enterprises following the coup. Some of the largest groups went bankrupt and were taken over by the government in 1982. They and most other state enterprises (except the copper industry) were privatized later in the decade, sometimes through dubious transactions that enriched Pinochet supporters.

In agriculture, too, a process of restructuring has taken place. Seized lands were returned to their owners after the coup, and the land that had been distributed into cooperatives under the 1967 agrarian reform law was divided into individual holdings. Many of the small holdings were later sold to agrobusiness entrepreneurs, resulting in a process of reconcentration—though often under owners different from the traditional landowner families. The landowners are organized into the National Agricultural Society (SNA), one of Chile's oldest interest groups. Other groups such as shopkeepers, truckers, etc., are represented by organized occupational groups—as are lawyers, doctors, nurses, and architects. However, their legal right to set rules for the professions was withdrawn in the late 1970s, and their influence has diminished since the return to democracy.

Other Groups

The Roman Catholic Church

Seventy-six percent of Chileans claim to be Catholic, although the percentage of Chileans who actively practice that faith is much lower, and 12 to 15 percent are Protestant. There are significant numbers of Lutherans descended from earlier German immigration, a small Jewish colony, and a rapidly expanding number of evangelicals and fundamentalists. Although church and state have been separated since 1925, the Catholic Church retains considerable national influence. Several of the elite private secondary schools are church-related, and the Catholic universities in Santiago and Valparaiso are important educational institutions. Church publications are influential, and the declarations of the Chilean Bishops' Conference are given wide publicity by the media. The bishops repeatedly criticized the human rights abuses of the Pinochet government, and the Church-sponsored Vicariate of Solidarity actively assisted the victims of repression. In the past a progressive majority dominated the Bishops' Conference, but more recent Vatican appointments have substantially increased conservative influence. Opus Dei, the conservative lay Catholic group, has become influential with its own university, secondary schools, and in the case of Joaquín Lavín, presidential candidate. The Church opposed efforts initiated by Christian Democratic legislators to enact a divorce law to replace the existing fraudulent annulment procedure, but after many years of debate, legal divorce became possible in 2005. Abortion is illegal in Chile, and Michelle Bachelet, as a presidential candidate, indicated that she did not intend to propose legislation to permit it.

Labor Organizations

The Marxist-dominated Unitary Labor Central (CUT) was dissolved after the coup, and its leaders were persecuted, but the Christian-Democratic labor leaders were treated less severely. In the late 1970s limited union activity was permitted, and in the early 1980s a National Labor Command (CNT) was organized, later renaming itself the CUT. With the return of democracy new legislation expanded the rights of labor, but the labor movement is much weaker than before 1973, with only 16 percent of workers enrolled as union members. The Lagos government reintroduced collective bargaining, but there are still limits on the right to strike.

Students and Intellectuals

Reflecting a worldwide trend, Chilean students have become increasingly apathetic and even hostile to politics—a striking change from their earlier activism. Chilean intellectuals were highly critical of the Pinochet government. Two Chilean novels—*La Casa de los Espíritus* (*The House of the Spirits*), by Isabel Allende, the niece of the former president, and José Donoso's *Desesperanza* (*Curfew*)—were international best-sellers that attacked the dictatorship; Ariel Dorfman's play, *Death and the Maiden,* concerning torture under the Pinochet regime, has been presented in many countries. *Machuca,* a fictionalized account of the impact of the Allende government on an exclusive private school, is the most successful Chilean film in recent years.

Foreign Influences

Chileans have always tried to overcome their geographical isolation by keeping up with developments in Europe and the Americas through the media or, if they can afford it, foreign travel. There are significant foreign colonies in Chile as well as English, French, and German schools. With the opening of the Chilean economy foreign banks and financial institutions established branches in Chile, and foreign investment soared. Nearly all the economic technocrats of the Pinochet and *Concertación* governments were trained at American universities. There are major UN regional offices in Chile, the most important of which is the UN Economic Commission for Latin America and the Caribbean (CEPAL is its Spanish acronym). The Chilean left was an active participant in the rethinking of radical, especially Marxist, ideology that occurred in Europe in the 1970s, and the Chilean right, also influenced by international ideological currents, moved from a traditionalist hierarchical corporatism to more modern libertarian and economically-oriented modes of thinking.

Governmental Structure

The 1980 constitution was clearly designed to limit the power of Congress. The president can call a plebiscite on constitutional amendments rejected by Congress. Presidential budgets must be voted on within sixty days or they automatically go into effect. New expenditures must be matched by new taxes, and the Central Bank may not borrow money. All takeovers of property must be compensated in cash at full value. The Constitutional Tribunal automatically reviews important legislation, and its decision is final. And, to reinforce the Pinochet government's intention to keep Congress out of the way, a new Congress building was constructed in Valparaiso, an hour and a half from Santiago. (The Congress will return to the capital in the near future).

In addition, local government has been strengthened, taxing power has been given to the *comunas* (municipalities), education and health care have been decentralized and partially privatized, and social security has been turned over to private pension funds, although a safety net exists for what turned out to be a large number of Chileans who were not able to participate. The number of state enterprises has been reduced from five hundred at the time of the coup to fewer than twenty, and even the state-owned copper mines have been opened to joint ventures with foreign capital.

Toward the Future:
The Lessons of Chile

Many lessons have been drawn from the Chilean experience. An obvious conclusion is the importance of maintaining the institutional and constitutional consensus and the willingness to compromise that characterized Chile for so many years. Chile's civilian political leaders have learned from the sad recent history of their country the desirability of avoiding the ideological dogmatism of the right, the left, and even the center that characterized the politics of the 1960s and early 1970s and ultimately led to military intervention.

A second general lesson is the importance of maintaining a healthy growing economy that in recent years has meant opening Chile to foreign investment and integrating it economically into regional and global markets, even if this means an increased dependence on economic decisions made elsewhere.

However, an open economy is not enough, Chile tells us. Both for ideological and pragmatic reasons it is necessary to improve education on all levels and to upgrade living standards through health, housing, and social security programs, often involving collaboration between the public and private sectors. Unemployment is still relatively high, educational opportunity has expanded but is still limited, and a regressive distribution of income remains the Achilles' heel of what appears to be a thriving economy.

In the twentieth century Chile experienced more than its share of political and economic upheavals. It became a laboratory for the application of the models of development proposed by liberals, radicals, and conservatives, as often providing negative lessons as positive ones. It has modernized and globalized its economy, carried out a peaceful transition from military rule, and moved in the direction of greater social justice, tolerance, and democracy. No institutional model is perfect, but Chile seems to have found a successful combination of democracy, economic growth, and social equity.

Suggestions for Further Reading

Arriagada, Genaro. *Pinochet: The Politics of Power.* Boston: Unwin Hyman, 1988.

Barahona de Brito, Alexandra. *Human Rights and Democratization in Latin America: Uruguay and Chile.* New York: Oxford University Press, 1997.

Barros, Robert. *Constitutionalism and Dictatorship: Pinochet, the Junta, and the 1980 Constitution.* New York: Cambridge University Press, 2002.

Borzutsky, Silvia. *Vital Connections: Politics, Social Security, and Inequality in Chile.* Notre Dame, IN: University of Notre Dame Press, 2002.

Branch, Taylor, and Eugene M. Propper. *Labyrinth.* New York: Penguin, 1983.

Cavallo, Ascanio. *La historia oculta de la transicion: Chile 1990–1998.* Santiago: Ediciones Grijalbo, 1998.

Cavallo Castro, Ascanio et al. *La historia oculta del regimen militar.* 2nd ed. Santiago: Editorial Antartica, 1989.

Chile, Comision Nacional sobre Prision Politica y Tortura (Valech Commission) *Informe.* (www.gobiernodechile.cl/comision valech), 2004.

Chile, National Commission on Truth and Reconciliation. *Report.* Trans. Phillip E. Berryman. Notre Dame, IN: University of Notre Dame Press, 1994.

Collier, Simon. *Chile: the Making of the Republic, 1830–1865.* New York: Cambridge University Press, 2003.

Constable, Pamela, and Arturo Valenzuela. *A Nation of Enemies: Chile Under Pinochet.* New York: W. W. Norton, 1991.

Davis, Madeleine, ed. *The Pinochet Case.* London: Institute of Latin American Studies, 2003.

Davis, Nathaniel. *The Last Two Years of Salvador Allende.* Ithaca, NY: Cornell University Press, 1985.

Dinges, John. *The Condor Years: How Pinochet and his Allies Brought Terrorism to Three Continents.* New York: New Press, 2004.

Ensalaco, Mark. *Chile under Pinochet: Recovering the Truth.* Philadelphia: University of Pennsylvania Press, 2000.

Falcoff, Mark. *Modern Chile, 1970–89: A Critical History.* New Brunswick, NJ: Transaction Books, 1989.

Francischet, Susan. *Women in Politics in Chile.* Boulder, CO: Lynn Rienner, 2005.

Garreton, Manuel A. *Incomplete Democracy: Political Democratization in Chile and Latin America.* Chapel Hill: University of North Carolina Press, 2003.

Hauser, Thomas. *Missing: The Execution of Charles Horman.* New York: Touchstone Books, Simon and Schuster, 1983.

Hawkins, Darren G. *International Human Rights and Authoritarian Rule in Chile.* Lincoln: University of Nebraska Press, 2002.

Israel, Ricardo. *Politics and Ideology in Allende's Chile.* Tempe: Arizona State University Press, 1989.

Kornbluh, Peter. *The Pinochet File.* New York: New Press, 2003.

Loveman, Brian. *Chile: The Legacy of Hispanic Capitalism,* 3rd ed. New York: Oxford University Press, 2001.

Meller, Patricio. *The Unidad Popular and the Pinochet Dictatorship: A Political Economy Analysis.* New York: St. Martin's Press, 2000.

Moran, Theodore. *Multinational Corporations and the Politics of Dependence: Copper in Chile.* Princeton, NJ: Princeton University Press, 1974.

Nunn, Frederick. *The Military in Chilean History.* Albuquerque: University of New Mexico Press, 1976.

Pollack, Marcelo. *The New Right in Chile, 1973–97.* New York: St. Martin's Press, 1999.

Remmer, Karen. *Party Competition in Argentina and Chile, 1890–1930.* Lincoln: University of Nebraska Press, 1984.

Roberts, Kenneth. *The Modern Left and Social Movements in Chile and Peru.* Stanford, CA: Stanford University Press, 1998.

Schamis, Hector. *Re-forming the State: The Politics of Privatization in Latin America and Europe.* Ann Arbor: University of Michigan Press, 2002.

Scully, Timothy. *Rethinking the Center: Politics in Nineteenth- and Twentieth-Century Chile.* Stanford, CA: Stanford University Press, 1992.

Sigmund, Paul E. *The Overthrow of Allende and the Politics of Chile, 1964–1976.* Pittsburgh: University of Pittsburgh Press, 1977.

———. *The United States and Democracy in Chile.* Baltimore: Johns Hopkins University Press, 1993.

——— (ed.). *Chile 1973–1998: The Coup and its Consequences.* Princeton, NJ: Princeton University Program in Latin American Studies, 1999.

Silva, Edward. *The State and Capital in Chile.* Boulder, CO: Westview Press, 1996.

Smith, Brian H. *The Church and Politics in Chile.* Princeton, NJ: Princeton University Press, 1982.

Stallings, Barbara. *Class Conflict and Economic Development in Chile, 1958–1973.* Stanford, CA: Stanford University Press, 1978.

U.S. Senate. Staff Report on the Select Committee on Intelligence Activities: *Covert Action in Chile.* Washington, D.C.: Government Printing Office, December 18, 1975.

Valdes, Juan Gabriel. *Pinochet's Economists: The Chicago School of Economics in Chile.* New York: Cambridge University Press, 1996.

Valenzuela, Arturo. *The Breakdown of Democratic Regimes: Chile.* Baltimore: Johns Hopkins University Press, 1978.

Verdugo, Patricia. *Chile, Pinochet and the Caravan of Death.* Miami: North-South Center Press, 2001.

Weeks, Gregory. *The Military and Politics in Postauthoritarian Chile.* Tuscaloosa: University of Alabama Press, 2003.

Whelan, James R. *Out of the Ashes: Life, Death, and Transfiguration of Democracy in Chile, 1833–1988.* Washington, D.C.: Regnery/Gateway, 1989.

Note

1. For the details of this real-life James Bond tale, see Taylor Branch and Eugene M. Propper. *Labyrinth.* New York: Penguin Books, 1983.

9

Colombia

A Resilient Political
System with Intransigent Problems

Harvey F. Kline and Vanessa Joan Gray

Not many Latin American countries have had a stronger tradition of civilian government, fewer military coups, or more elections held with few incidents than Colombia. Nevertheless, Colombian democracy has long been compromised by endemic violence, the uneven application of the rule of law, and severe inequalities. Despite having impressive and advanced attributes, the Colombian democratic regime possesses great weaknesses.

Every dimension of politics in Colombia is affected by violence, particularly beyond Bogotá (the national capital) and a few other major cities. When President Álvaro Uribe Vélez took office on August 7, 2002, guerrilla violence had gripped the Colombian countryside for roughly forty years. Long before the two principle guerrilla organizations (the Armed Forces of the Colombian Revolution, FARC, or *Fuerzas Armadas Revolucionarias de Colombia*) and the Army of National Liberation (ELN, or *Ejército de Liberación Nacional*) were founded in the 1960s, the country had suffered over a century of intermittent civil war directed by the two traditional political parties, the Liberals and the Conservatives.

The violence also stems from the fact that the Colombian government has never managed to establish effective rule in all parts of its territory. Landowners historically used private armies to further their interests, and in recent decades to defend themselves from guerrillas. Though some paramilitary forces were legally sanctioned from the early 1960s to the late 1980s, they are

Map labels:

Caribbean Sea

0 50 100 150 Miles
0 50 100 150 Kilometers

Santa Marta
Riohacha
Barranquilla
ATLÁNTICO
LA GUAJIRA
Cartagena
SIERRA NEVADA
DE SANTA MARIA
CÉSAR
Sincelejo
NORTE
DE
SANTANDER
Montería
SUCRE
CÓRDOBA
Cúcuta
Turbo
Pamplona
Río Arauca
Río Atrato
Río Cauca
BOLÍVAR
Bucaramanga
Arauca
ARAUCA
VENEZUELA
ANTIOQUIA
SANTANDER
Medellín
Quibdó
Río Magdalena
PACIFIC OCEAN
RISARALDA
Tunja
BOYACÁ
Río Meta
CALDA
Pereira
Manizales
CUNDINAMARCA
VICHADA
CHOCÓ
Armenia
Bogotá
ORINOCO PLAINS
Ibagué
Río Upía
Buenaventura
QUINDÍO
Villavicencio
Puerto López
Río Guaviare
VALLE DEL CAUCA
TOLIMA
Cali
META
DISTRITO
ESPECIAL
GUAINÍA
Neiva
CAUCA
HUILA
Río Guainía
Popayán
VAUPÉS
NARIÑO
Río Vaupés
Pasto
ANDES MOUNTAINS
Ipiales
CAQUETÁ
PUTUMAYO
AMAZON REGION
ECUADOR
Río Caquetá
BRAZIL
AMAZONAS
Río Putumayo
PERU
Leticia

COLOMBIA

major perpetrators of Colombia's violence. In 1997 paramilitary leader Carlos Castaño organized the United Self-Defense Groups of Colombia (AUC, or *Autodefensas Unidas de Colombia)* to represent the political interests of hundreds of the paramilitary groups operating nationally.

A third type of violent actor, drug traffickers, emerged in the late 1970s. A lack of effective law enforcement in certain regions, intense foreign demand for marijuana and cocaine, and chronic rural unemployment combined to allow drug trafficking to flourish in Colombian territory. During the 1980s the Medellín cartel waged a terrorist bombing campaign to force the suspension of extraditions to the United States. Drug traffickers also helped to create and continue to finance paramilitary groups, further escalating that form of violence. Finally, "common" crime compounds the problem of violence in Colombia, so much so that the country has one of the highest rates in the world of (nonpolitical) homicides and kidnapping.

Statistics from the National Planning Department give a picture of the dismal panorama President Uribe inherited upon taking office. From the last two years of the presidency of Ernesto Samper (1996–1998) to the end of the presidency of Andrés Pastrana (1998–2002) murders rose from 25,039 a year to 26,891 a year, kidnapping increased from 2,068 to 3,106 per year, terrorist attacks increased from 744 to 944, attacks on towns went from 90 to 130, the number of massacres went up from 114 to 176, and the number of massacre victims increased from 607 to 1,013. Most dramatically, the number of internal refugees increased from 3,907 a year during the last two years of the Samper government to 41,355 a year during the four years of the Pastrana presidency.[1]

In Latin American terms Colombia is a middle-income country. The purchasing power parity per capita in 2003 was estimated at U.S. $6,300 per year. The highly uneven distribution of income, however, leaves a significant portion of the population quite poor. In 2004 the United Nations reported that 8 percent of the Colombian population lived in extreme poverty on an income of U.S. $1 a day or less. Two out of every three Colombians lived in poverty. Overall, the bottom 20 percent of the population had just 2.7 percent of the national income, while the top 20 percent had 61.8 percent. Most live without government medical insurance, social security or unemployment benefits, or any kind of welfare. Politics are dominated by individuals of the middle- and upper-income groups, with poor people having the right to vote but only for candidates chosen by the upper-income groups.

In this chapter we describe the longstanding features of Colombian politics, the multiple and complex challenges to the political system, and the Uribe government's response to the challenges. It remains to be seen whether Uribe's strategy can install the kind of order required by an advanced industrial capitalist economy and polity.

Background

Colombia is a country of spectacular geographic diversity. Influenced by climate patterns from two oceans and two continents, Colombian territory includes three ranges of the Andes Mountains, plains of the Orinoco River basin, large expanses of Amazonian forest, and coasts on the Caribbean Sea and the Pacific Ocean. Among the diverse habitats found in Colombia are mangroves, deserts, rain forests, cloud forests, and snow-capped mountains. In fact, Colombia is one of the most biologically rich places on the planet: it has more bird species than any other nation and ranks second in number of amphibian species and vascular plants. The only nation to surpass Colombia in its endowment of biodiversity, Brazil, is seven times larger.

The national territory is the fifth largest in Latin America. The Andean region contains 75 percent of the population and, along with the Caribbean cities of Barranquilla and Cartagena, most of the nation's economic and political activity. Climate varies widely with altitude. Bogotá, at 8,530 feet (2,600 meters), is known for cool nights and abundant rain, though average temperatures have risen in the capital, consistent with the massive growth of this metropolis and the resulting heat-island effect. Medellín, at 4,852 feet (1,479 meters), calls itself the "city of eternal spring," with year-round temperatures in the sixties at night and the low eighties during the day. Cali and Bucaramanga, at slightly lower elevations, are hot. The hottest cities are located at sea level: on the coasts of the Caribbean and the Pacific, in the plains of the Orinoco, or in the Amazon basin.

Agricultural products also vary with elevation: the highest areas produce grains and potatoes; the middle altitudes grow coffee and flowers; and the lowlands favor tropical crops such as sugarcane and bananas. (The cut-flower industry also has massive operations at higher elevations now, thanks to state-of-the-art facilities.) Large-scale production in the Orinoco plains (*llanos*) includes cattle ranching, rice and palm oil plantations, and petroleum extraction. Major emerald deposits are mined in the Andes and coal is mined in the Guajira Peninsula. The Amazon region and the Pacific Chocó, formerly centers of rubber production and small-scale mining, became colonization frontiers and the focus of logging, fisheries, and vacation resorts. Coca is cultivated and processed in the lowlands of the Orinoco and Amazon, marijuana cultivation is concentrated on the Atlantic coast, and the opium poppy is grown high in the Andes. In the 1990s petroleum extraction and drug-crop cultivation intensified in frontier regions, as did the establishment of new agribusiness and resource extraction ventures.

The diversity of Colombia's geography is matched by the diversity of its people, who number forty-five million, the third largest population in Latin

America. The main indigenous group at the time of the arrival of the Spanish, the Chibchas, had reached a relatively high level of civilization, albeit less advanced than that of the Aztecs or the Incas. Spanish colonization and enslavement, along with European diseases and livestock, led to widespread loss of life and, subsequently, the nearly complete assimilation of the Chibchas. Their descendants continue to inhabit the central Andean region, but they speak Spanish and dress no differently from people of Spanish or mixed *(mestizo)* background of the same social standing.

Other indigenous cultures survive in the southern departments of Nariño and Cauca, and in parts of the Chocó, the Amazon, and the Guajira Peninsula. In the Sierra Nevada de Santa Marta, some 45,000 Kogui and Arauco continue to speak languages other than Spanish, practice their traditional faiths, and maintain ancient practices for growing food and weaving textiles. In 2003 indigenous Colombians numbered roughly 800,000, but their communities are increasingly besieged by developers, petroleum interests, drug traffickers, colonists, guerrillas, miners, and government troops. Their continued survival is far from assured.

Africans were brought to Colombia as slaves to labor on plantations during the colonial era. Today their descendants comprise a large portion of the population in Colombia's coastal areas, in the Chocó, and in the Cauca Valley region. While the societies of regions with a large Afro-Colombian population tend to differ from those of the *mestizo* areas, throughout Colombia African influences can be heard in the music and observed in popular forms of dance.

Ethnically, the majority of Colombians are a mixture of European and indigenous, European and African, African and indigenous, or all three groups. In affluent, powerful circles one finds Colombians of pure Spanish ancestry that take pride in their *abolengo* (pedigree). Descendants of more recent arrivals from Europe and the Middle East are also prominent in the economic and political elite. At the other end of the socioeconomic spectrum are Colombians of pure Indian or African descent. Race has not been the salient issue that it is in the United States, despite there being a strong correlation between race and poverty and the fact that the Colombians who enjoy the greatest wealth and power almost never have dark skin or non-European features. In recent years both indigenous groups and Afro-Colombians have formed identity-based organizations that have achieved limited material and political gains.

Colombian society remains highly stratified. A division exists between those engaged in manual labor and those who are not. Among nonmanual groups, further stratification is based on wealth, race, and *abolengo*. At the top are people with the "best" of all three criteria, although there are notable cases of "fallen aristocrats," who no longer have the extensive wealth of the past, and *nuevos ricos* (drug dealers, for example), who have great wealth but no pedigree. Colombia's egregious disparities of income, living standards, and access to health care and education mean that for the average person, life is difficult and the prospects for betterment are slim. It cannot be overemphasized that Colombia consistently ranks among the three countries worldwide with the worst inequality.

For years Colombia had one of the fastest-growing populations in the world, increasing from 17.5 million in 1964 to 27.3 million in 1980. The population boom, combined with massive migration to the cities, fed a meteoric urbanization process. Colombia went from being a nation of *campesinos* to one in which over 70 percent are city dwellers. The number of Bogotá residents soared from 1.5 million in 1968 to 5 million in 1980. Other major cities grew in a similarly rapid and chaotic manner. Air quality, transportation, waste management, social interaction, and personal security in the megacities are notably poor, though since the late 1990s innovative Bogotá mayors have achieved significant improvements in the capital. At the same time, violence in the rural sector continues to expel millions of people, many of whom end up in the shantytowns that ring Bogotá and other big cities. Conditions are miserable in these places: while infrastructure and services are lacking, armed militias and criminal gangs abound.

The Colombian economy occupies a middle tier in global terms. In foreign trade Colombia has diversified away from production of a single crop. In 2003 the largest export was petroleum (26 percent), followed by coal (11 percent), basic chemicals (7 percent), coffee (6 percent), flowers (5 percent), and apparel (5 percent). These figures represent a dramatic change from Colombia's former dependence on coffee, which made up 79 percent of exports in 1964, 42 percent in 1975, and 32 percent in 1987. No longer do fluctuations in world coffee markets cause major shocks in Colombia. Another key shift was the rise of marijuana and cocaine trafficking, which by 1979 brought more foreign currency into the country than all legal export earnings combined. Since then the drug trade has continued to grow, despite the government's vigorous antinarcotics campaigns and the massive U.S. assistance for those efforts.

Colombia is Latin America's third largest oil exporter, after Venezuela and Mexico. In the mid-1970s the country ceased to be an exporter of petroleum and was forced to import that essential product. New policies, however, provided foreign corporations with more favorable terms, resulting in the discovery of extensive oil reserves. By 1985 Colombia was once again a petroleum exporter, and it later became a major supplier of coal as well. From the U.S. perspective, Colombia's importance as an oil producer has risen significantly as supplies from other nations, such as Venezuela and Iraq, have become less reliable.

Consistent with Colombia's position in the global economy, Colombian policymakers have grappled with chronic balance-of-payments problems. Before the 1970s the strategy to meet the trade imbalance was import-substitution-industrialization (ISI). Numerous manufactured goods—food products, clothing, and consumer durables such as cars, stoves, and refrigerators—were produced in Colombia, either by Colombian firms or U.S.- and European-based corporations. The "cheap" dollar brought by coffee and drug exports, however, undermined efforts to promote industry within Colombia, as did the weak enforcement of contraband laws. By the early 1980s the Colombian government sought to curb inflation by keeping the exchange rate artificially low and easing the purchase of consumer goods. Colombian manufacturers were consequently exposed to withering competition. At the urging of the International Monetary Fund (IMF) the government of Belisario Betancur (1982–1986) began a series of mini-devaluations.

In the 1990s the Colombian government began an "opening" of the economy, with lower tariffs on imports. In 2005, as the Colombian government sees it, the free trade agreement between the Andean countries and the United States is an international treaty that, once implemented, will regulate the trade and investment relationship between the parties in a comprehensive manner, with the aim of increasing trade and investment flows and contributing to the economic and social development of the signatory countries. In 2004 and 2005 Colombia and the United States negotiated a mutual free trade agreement.

From the early 1950s to the 1980s the Colombian economy expanded at an impressive rate, with GDP growing at 6 percent per year during some periods. Real per capita GNP gains were made. When the recession of the 1980s gripped Latin America Colombian growth rates slowed, but the economy did not experience the profound reversals suffered by its neighbors. Colombia maintained creditworthiness with international lenders and received new loans without an IMF standby loan. An Inter-American Development Bank report released in 1988 stated that in the previous five years Colombia had had the lowest rate of inflation in Latin America, one of the five highest per capita GDP growth rates, and the lowest foreign debt per capita overall.

The comparative strength of the Colombian economy during this period can be attributed to a relatively stable political regime that was less subject to the populist and military demands for expenditures that distorted macroeconomic policymaking in other Latin American nations. One can also credit Colombian technocrats who, in addition to being relatively insulated from political pressures, had the skill, foresight, and consensus to pursue policies that encouraged investment and growth while avoiding excessive indebtedness, protectionism, or economic openness. Examples of Colombia's economic policy successes are the early application of a crawling-peg devaluation, an export-led growth strategy, and the development of national coal and petroleum resources through joint ventures.

Nevertheless, in the 1990s economic performance was insufficient to mitigate the intense pressures straining the political system. The Colombian political class faced a crisis of legitimacy as the economy foundered and then sunk into one of the worst recessions in the nation's history. Economic policymakers accelerated the implementation of neoliberal reforms, lowering tariff barriers and privatizing government-controlled sectors. Early in the new millennium the economy was somewhat improved. In 2003 real economic growth had more than doubled to 3.7 percent from 1.6 percent the previous year. Unemployment had declined somewhat (to 14.1 percent), and inflation was down from 7 percent in 2002 to 6.5 percent during 2003. Net international reserves increased slightly, despite an expected decline of about U.S. $200 million, and the external current account deficit held steady at 1.8 percent of GDP in 2003, as exports performed well and family remittances from abroad rose by over 20 percent.

History to 1930

During the Spanish colonial period Colombia was neither a backwater nor an administrative or economic center like Mexico or Peru. Precious metals were less abundant, although there was a substantial amount of gold. For most of the period Colombia was part of the viceroyalty of Peru, but in 1739 Bogotá became the center of a new viceroyalty that also included present-day Venezuela, Panama, and Ecuador. The struggle for independence in Colombia was waged by *criollos* of the very highest standing. The battles were fierce and there were various reversals and historic treks through the rugged mountains on horseback. Independence finally came after the Battle of Boyacá (1819), and the victorious army, led by Simón Bolívar, went south to help liberate Ecuador, Peru, and Bolivia.

For the first ten years of the postcolonial era Colombia was part of Gran Colombia, a confederation with Venezuela and Ecuador. Regional differences among the three countries undermined the union. Bolívar once remarked that Venezuela was a military garrison, Ecuador a convent, and Colombia a debating society, a fairly apt characterization of national inclinations in those years. In 1830 the three nations went their separate ways, and Colombia (called Nueva Granada and including a province that would later become Panama) was on its own.

The chaos found in newly independent republics throughout Latin America also prevailed in Colombia for a time, but by 1850 the new country had settled into patterns that characterize the nation even today. In striking contrast to most other Latin American countries, and for reasons about which historians disagree, the norm became civilian partisan politics. By 1849 there were two political parties, one calling itself Liberal and the other Conservative, and the programs of the two were not dramatically different. These were elite-instigated parties (like most in Latin America at the time) rather than ones arising from popular demands. Despite differences over the desired level of federalism and free trade, or the role of the Roman Catholic hierarchy in society and politics, the two parties shared the same fundamental ideology regarding the social and economic order.

In the nineteenth century a change of party in the presidential palace would result in policy shifts, particularly in trade and relations with the Church. More importantly, one party's victory over the other entailed the replacement of one vertically integrated network of patrons and clients by another. Party competition was not restricted to the ballot box; there were six civil wars between the two parties, some of which were lengthy and involved many deaths. These civil wars consisted of party elites mobilizing *campesinos* as their troops, people who were economically and socially dependent on party bosses. A *campesino* was a Liberal or Conservative due to his ties to his patron, not because of interests that could objectively be called his own.

Repeated civil war fueled intense partisan hatreds among *campesinos*. The wars produced "martyrs," family members who had been killed by people from the other party. Colombians came to be "born with party identification cards attached to the umbilical cord," as one Colombian sociologist described it.[2] Not only were they born into the party of their parents, but they were socialized to hate members of the other party. Because the population was torn into two antagonistic camps, other cleavages—social, economic, ethnic or regional—were secondary in importance to political party affiliation.

The masses took party differences seriously while the elite elements of the parties reaped the benefits and ruled. There were periods of one-party hegemony, such as when the Liberals monopolized power from 1861 to 1886 and the Conservatives did from 1886 to 1930. When the elites of the two parties disagreed so sharply that civil war resulted, it was *campesinos* that supplied virtually all of the casualties. Elite factions also collaborated across party lines. In nine instances before 1930 and three cases thereafter all or part of the elite of one party formed an electoral and/or governing coalition with members of the elite of the other party. In roughly twenty-eight of the eighty years between 1850 and 1930 there were such coalitions. These alliances typically formed in response to a strong antiparty executive in the aftermath of a civil war, or toward the end of a period of party hegemony.[3]

Before 1930 Colombia's economic development was slow, and few new social groups sought access to the political system. A small middle class was created by the growth of government and private industry, but it never banded together to form a new political party. Members of middle-income groups identified first and foremost as Liberals or Conservatives based on their family loyalties. Their political weight was felt within the traditional parties, not as an external challenge to them.

Political History Since 1930

Toward the end of the 1920s the hegemony of the Conservative Party ran into difficulties caused by the Great Depression, the degeneration of the party from within, and the challenge of a growing labor union movement, to which the incumbent government responded with brute force. When the new president, Enrique Olaya Herrera, was elected in 1930 by a coalition of Liberals and Conservatives, civil war broke out between Liberal and Conservative peasants. This time the violence was only partly directed by the leaders of the parties. The conflict was also fueled by the modernization of the agrarian sector, which tended to consolidate land holdings, intensify struggles over arable land and water rights, and usurp access by the poor.

Other important developments marked the period. A key faction of the Liberal Party had adopted a stance called "new liberalism," in which the state was to take an activist role in economic development. This group of Liberals dominated the party during Alfonso López Pumarejo's "Revolution on the March" (1934–1938), when various reforms were attempted, including social welfare legislation, agrarian reform, and ISI. Labor organization was encouraged and López Pumarejo was instrumental in the creation of the first national labor federation, the Confederation of Colombian Workers (CTC), in 1935. In 1946 the Conservatives responded by promoting the Church-formed Union of Colombian Workers (UTC). Hence, in a pattern typical of politics in Colombia, organized labor gained legal access to the political arena via institutions heavily influenced by one or the other of the two traditional parties.

In reaction to Liberal activism a faction of the Conservative Party led by Laureano Gómez took an extremist stance, evoking as its model the Spain of Ferdinand and Isabella, that is, traditional Spanish corporatism. Centrists in the leadership of both parties joined a coalition with the Gómez Conservatives and thwarted the reforms of the López Liberals. López ultimately left office before completing his second term as president (1942–1945). In the election of 1946 two Liberals were opposed by a single Conservative, Mariano Ospina Pérez. Following Ospina's election, partisan violence broke out in rural areas. Much of the violence was elite-instigated, by Conservatives to consolidate their power and to win a majority in the congressional elections of 1948, and by Liberals to prevent the same things. Conservative *campesinos* were also spontaneously seizing lands that had been taken from them by Liberals sixteen years earlier, believing correctly that the government in Bogotá would support them.

The civil war that resulted, *la violencia*, greatly exceeded previous wars in both its scope and intensity. Aggravated by the April 9, 1948, assassination of Jorge Gaitán—a populist Liberal who had lost the 1946 election but later become head of the party and the odds-on favorite to win the 1950 presidential election—the violence engulfed the entire Andean region (with the exception of Nariño); the *llanos* of the Orinoco region; and, to a lesser extent, the Caribbean coastal region. The war was most intense in areas already experiencing land conflicts. Over the next twenty years more than two hundred thousand Colombians (in a country of ten million) lost their lives. In some parts of Colombia, practically everyone became a victim, a perpetrator, or a first-hand witness to horrific carnage. Throughout the country an entire generation grew up hearing vivid accounts of atrocities.

Despite its partisan origins, the war evolved into distinct forms: politicides and economic plunder were carried out on behalf of the powerful; ruthless bandits of lower-class origins prospered; vicious personal vendettas cycled back and forth; and self-defense forces were organized among persecuted Liberals and communists. (The guerrilla groups founded in the 1960s have origins in the armed resistance groups of the so-called "independent" or "red" republics.)

The violence precipitated the only military dictatorship of the twentieth century, that of Gustavo Rojas Pinilla, from 1953 to 1957. Vowing to end the violence, Rojas came to power supported by all factions of the two traditional parties except the Gómez Conservatives (it was the presidency of Laureano Gómez [1950–1953], that the coup terminated). Rojas carried out economic infrastructure improvements and promised social reforms. The combination of military force and populist spending employed by Rojas succeeded at pacifying areas affected by partisan violence, banditry, and blood feuds, but where the peasantry was radicalized, pockets of resistance survived. Moreover, the public works projects fell far short of a nation-building effort. Much of Colombia remained isolated and without formal governance. Rojas grew increasingly repressive and began to show interest in remaining in power.

The leaders of the two historic parties responded by joining forces to oust Rojas and implement a power-sharing agreement. In 1957 Rojas was replaced by a caretaker military regime, and a year later the most significant bipartisan coalition government in Colombian history, the National Front, was installed.

Though the National Front was approved by the Colombian electorate in a plebiscite and by the national congress in a constitutional amendment, it was largely the creation of two men. One was Alberto Lleras Camargo, the former president (Liberal, 1945 to 1946) who completed López's second term, and the other was the Conservative ex-president Laureano Gómez. The agreement stipulated that for the sixteen-year period from 1958 to 1974:

1. The presidency would alternate every four years between the two traditional parties (*alternación*).
2. All legislative bodies (National Congress, departmental assemblies, municipal councils) would be divided equally between the Liberals and the Conservatives regardless of electoral results within a district (*paridad* [parity]). Within each of the traditional parties, seats would be assigned by a list of proportional representation.
3. The same rule of party parity would apply to all high administrative appointments, such as the president's cabinet, governors, governors' cabinets, and mayors.
4. No new political parties could participate in elections during the period.
5. The lower-level, nonappointive bureaucrats would be chosen not on the basis of partisan affiliation but on merit in a proposed civil service system. This stipulation was to end the pre-National Front practice of wholesale turnovers of bureaucratic personnel whenever the party in power changed.
6. All legislation in the National Congress had to be passed by a two-thirds majority.

During the National Front two Liberals were president (Alberto Lleras Camargo, 1958–1962; Carlos Lleras Restrepo, 1966–1970), and so were two Conservatives (Guillermo León Valencia, 1962–1966; Misael Pastrana Borrero, 1970–1974). The arrangement quelled the violence in about six years, but in some rural areas discontent and radicalism, as well as small bands of guerrillas, were never completely eliminated.

In essence, the National Front was an elite pact designed to divide political power equally between the two traditional parties. It established a restricted form of democracy that limited voters' options to candidates supported by one of the traditional parties. Political competition was legally restricted to the two traditional parties, and these did not actually compete with each other in elections. New groups participated in elections, but they could not call themselves "political parties" until a constitutional reform in 1968 made it possible for them to do so. Parity prevailed until the 1968 constitutional amendment reopened competitive elections for departmental assemblies (roughly the equivalent of state legislatures in the United States but with considerably less power) and town councils in 1970.

The National Front enabled elites from the two parties to monopolize power for sixteen years and to exclude alternative political actors. At the same time it severely restricted a president's ability to implement change. The arrangement ultimately served to reduce the capacity of the state to govern the nation effectively. During the Front and its aftermath party organization languished and millions migrated to the cities, weakening the parties' traditional bases of power. Political elites failed to incorporate new groups into the system or to diminish structural unemployment. As a result, conditions were propitious for the growth of guerrilla movements, drug trafficking, and a black-market economy during this period.

On August 7, 1974, the National Front ostensibly ended with the inauguration of Liberal Alfonso López Michelsen, who obtained 56 percent of the popular vote. Yet the new president was still constrained by rules outlined in the constitutional reform of 1968, which determined how the National Front would be dismantled. During López Michelsen's term full parity continued: all cabinet ministers, governors, mayors, and other administrative positions not part of civil service were divided equally between Liberals and Conservatives. After the López Michelsen presidency, government offices were divided between the parties "in such a way that gives adequate and equitable participation to the major party distinct from that of the president" (though if the other party declined to participate in the administration, the president was free to name the officials in any way he chose).

Both President Julio César Turbay Ayala (Liberal, 1978–1982) and President Belisario Betancur Cuartas (Conservative, 1982–1986) offered to the other party what they considered "adequate and equitable participation" in the appointive positions. Closely allied with the Reagan administration in Washington, Turbay pursued a hardline, repressive approach to Colombia's social problems. His policies did not curb the growth of narcotrafficking, leftist insurgency, or the underground economy. In contrast, Betancur shifted Colombia toward a nonaligned foreign policy, and negotiated amnesties, truces, and the reincorporation of guerrillas into society.

One outcome of the Betancur peace process was the founding of a political party, the Patriotic Union (UP, or *Unión Patriótrica*) by former insurgents who had laid down their weapons. The UP attracted followers from the unarmed left as well as community organizers, idealists, and young people, but the party soon became the target of death squads. After thousands of its members were systematically murdered by paramilitary groups with links to elements within the Colombian armed forces, the party faded from relevance. Betancur also instituted major democratization reforms, which unfolded during subsequent presidencies, but many were unsuccessful. Betancur's peace program lacked support from domestic elites, his policies were financially constrained by unfavorable global economic trends, and his government faced structural impediments to mobilizing popular support.

In 1986 the Conservatives refused to accept the three cabinet positions offered by the newly elected Liberal, Virgilio Barco (1986–1990), thus marking the end of the National Front system. During the Barco years, violence escalated, eventually causing more deaths per capita than during *la violencia*. All three types of irregular armed actor—guerrilla, drug trafficker, and paramilitary—expanded forces in this period. In the election to succeed Barco, three presidential candidates were assassinated.

During the presidency of César Gaviria Trujillo (1990–1994) the Colombian government negotiated with guerrilla groups and drug traffickers. Major traffickers, most notably Pablo Escobar of the Medellín group, did surrender and plea bargain, and some members of paramilitary groups also turned themselves in. The government also held elections to select a constituent assembly. The assembly debated and eventually wrote a new constitution. Nevertheless, at the end of the Gaviria's term the level of violence in Colombia was higher than before it began.[4]

The presidency of Ernesto Samper Pizano (1994–1998) was incapacitated by a scandal arising from the accusation (originally made by his opponent in the presidential campaign, Andrés Pastrana) that the Cali drug group had donated U.S. $4 million to Samper's electoral campaign. Although the Colombian House of Representatives did not impeach Samper, the U.S. government considered him guilty and poor relations between the two countries further debilitated the Samper government. Under Samper almost all of the leaders of the Cali cartel either surrendered or were captured, but other traffickers assumed their places, and cocaine production continued to rise. The Colombian drug trade also diversified to include heroin production and distribution. Despite rumors of a military coup, Samper was able to finish his presidency.

The Samper government did not pursue a policy of negotiating with guerrilla groups, whose numbers, victories, and territory grew substantially during the period. The growth of the guerrilla organizations was largely due to their burgeoning finances from protection and extortion of Colombia's booming drug trade and energy sector. The guerrillas continued to attract many volunteers without offering material compensation other than meals, but the majority of Colombians ceased to express any sympathy for leftist insurgents.

The military strength of guerrilla forces alarmed Colombian political elites and the U.S. government. Large economic interests, both national and foreign, complained bitterly about soaring security costs, and foreign investors began to turn away from Colombia. The policy response of Samper's successor, Andrés

Pastrana (1998–2002), was to seek peace via negotiations with guerrilla groups. As part of the talks with the FARC, the Pastrana government granted the FARC guerrilla forces control of an area the size of Switzerland. Apparently FARC leaders were not inclined to cede much of anything in return, presumably because their treasury, arsenal, and troops were larger than ever. Meanwhile, the FARC's worst adversaries, the paramilitaries, also dramatically increased their forces and significantly improved their public image. The Pastrana government did not pursue policies that reined in the power of the paramilitaries. To paraphrase Colombian Nobel laureate Gabriel García Márquez, Pastrana's peace program might be called a "chronicle of an announced failure." Despite all the effort, all the rhetoric, all the well-written documents, and all the meetings, in the end the bargaining failed miserably. Fighting in the countryside remained as before, and attacks on cities increased.

Traditional Political Groups

The Colombian political system has demonstrated a great deal of resiliency, with the two predominant political parties being the most important political actors since the mid-nineteenth century. Large landowners, industrialists, and other upper-income groups are very well organized and effective in advancing their interests. Labor unions are organized in both political parties (and elsewhere), but represent only a small fraction of Colombian workers. Organized attempts by *campesinos* and the urban poor to seek social justice have been frustrated by internal divisions, state repression, the closed nature of the political system, and the assassination of countless leaders.

Political Parties

Colombia's most important political organizations have traditionally been the Liberal and Conservative parties. Dominant for over a century, the two parties did not resemble the "mass party" model, nor did they need such a structure to mobilize votes. Party leaderships often split into factions, sometimes along programmatic lines, other times along more personalist ones. Today the ideological differences of the party elites are about as great (or meager) as those of the Democrats and Republicans in the United States.

Throughout the twentieth century public opinion polls confirmed that the majority of the Colombian electorate identified with the Liberal Party. During the National Front period, more people voted for Liberals for Congress than for Conservatives (although parity rules awarded each of the parties 50 percent of the seats). López Michelsen, in his successful 1974 presidential campaign, received 56 percent of the vote in a contest against two principal opponents and several minor ones. Turbay Ayala received a smaller majority over Betancur in 1978. A Conservative president was elected in 1982 when the Liberals had presented two candidates, Alfonso López Michelsen and Luis Carlos Galán, which allowed Conservative Belisario Betancur to win with 46.6 percent. When Betancur became the first Conservative to be elected in a competitive election since 1946, it exemplified the historic tendency for the minority party to win when the majority party splits into factions and fields separate candidates. In 1986 and 1990, with the Liberals once again united, Virgilio Barco and César Gaviria won overwhelmingly.

After the constitution of 1991 required an absolute majority for election to the presidency, the elections of 1994 and 1998 each went to a second round. In 1994 Liberal Ernesto Samper defeated Conservative Andrés Pastrana, and in 1998 Pastrana won over Liberal Horacio Serpa. Although the framers of the constitution thought that the new rules would help mitigate the dominance of the Liberals and Conservatives, this did not occur in presidential elections until 2002.

Third-party movements, however, are now more common than before. When in 1961 the ex-dictator Gustavo Rojas Pinilla founded the National Popular Alliance (ANAPO), calling it a "party" would have made it ineligible for elections, so it was a "movement" that offered both Liberal and Conservative candidates for legislative bodies at all levels. ANAPO had its greatest success in 1970, when it garnered 14 percent of the national Liberal vote and 21 percent of the national Conservative vote. Rojas lost the presidential election to Conservative Misael Pastrana by a margin of only 3 percent. The fortunes of ANAPO declined after becoming a party in 1971 and with the end of the National Front in 1974. ANAPO was a personalist vehicle with little organization or leadership beyond the Rojas family. As Rojas's health declined, leadership shifted to his daughter, María Eugenia Rojas de Moreno Díaz, who ran for president in 1974. She received only 9.4 percent of the popular vote, finishing a poor third to the two traditional party candidates.

The party that emerged from the Betancur government's democratic opening, the Patriotic Union (UP), was founded by the Communist Party and by demobilized FARC guerrillas. The 1986 elections became the first in Colombia in which a leftist coalition ran a presidential candidate. While the UP candidate, Jaime Pardo Leal, received only 4 percent of the vote, the party did elect twelve members to the Congress as well as scores of local officials. In the following presidential campaign in 1990, Pardo was assassinated. It is possible that over time the UP might have developed in a pattern similar to that of the Brazilian Workers Party (PT), gaining experience by governing at the municipal level and gradually building a mass membership. It is impossible to say what future direction the UP might have taken had its ranks not been decimated by death squads: over six thousand of its leaders were murdered, effectively ending its role in politics.

The demobilization of the M–19 guerrilla group in 1990 produced another leftist party, the Nineteenth of April Democratic Alliance (AD M–19). Despite losing a presidential candidate to yet another assassination in 1990, the AD M–19 finished second in the elections for the Constituent Assembly later that year, winning nineteen delegates and playing an important role in the writing of the new constitution. The party's showing in the 1990 presidential election (13 percent of the vote) was impressive, but the party's strength faded as the decade wore on.

Today several trends are evident in Colombian party politics. The two largest parties in Congress are still the Liberals and Conservatives, but there are seventy-four other political parties, sixty-eight of which have won congressional seats. Party discipline in the legislature continues to be weak and voter enthusiasm for the traditional parties continues to decline. The traditional parties are rife with internal divisions.

In 2005 individuals from various parties discussed creating an Uribista party, that is, one to support the reelection of Uribe in 2006. The president of the national directorate of the Conservative Party, Carlos Holguín, announced his support for the reelection of Liberal Álvaro Uribe, declaring that the Conservative party should not run a presidential candidate in 2006. Conservatives were thus divided between those who, like Holguín, favored conceding to Uribe because no Conservative had much chance of defeating him, and others, such as former president Andrés Pastrana, who vehemently opposed such a strategy.

Deep divisions marked the Liberal party, too. In June 2005 President Uribe accused former president César Gaviria, a Liberal and the former secretary general of the Organization of American States, of being "sectarian." Uribe also criticized the economic policies of Gaviria's presidency, particularly the privatization of the public sector. Liberal Party leaders responded by denouncing Uribe for "flagrant" intervention in politics and called on the attorney general to take action against the president. Shortly after, the Liberal party declared its formal opposition to Uribe's reelection.

In contrast to the disunity of the traditional parties, the leaders of two leftist parties—the Independent Democratic Pole (*Polo Democrático Independiente*, PDI), and the Democratic Alternative (*Alternativa Democrática*, AD)—began meeting in April 2005 to join forces. Unification efforts followed the 2003 election of the PDI's Luis Eduardo "Lucho" Garzón, a former communist union leader, as the mayor of Bogotá. Another PDI candidate won the mayoralty in the petroleum-refining city of Barrancabermeja, and a third candidate linked to the PDI won in Bucaramanga, the capital of the Santander department. The Colombian Communist Party (PCC) also represents the electoral left. The new party appears to have programmatic consensus, but wrangles over electoral lists. On March 12, 2006, Carlos Gavinia defeated Antonio Navarro Wolff (formerly an M–19 guerrilla) to be the presidential candidate of the Polo Democrático. Gavinia will be the first presidential candidate of a united left in Colombian history.

Other Traditional Groups

In addition to the traditional political parties, the most powerful groups in the formal Colombian political system are those representing or allied with economic elites. Industrialization has been a goal of Colombian presidents for half a century, especially since the National Front. The National Association of Industrialists (ANDI), founded in 1944, has more than five hundred of the largest industrial enterprises affiliated with it throughout the country. Its influence comes from the wealth and prestige of its members, its active role in policymaking, and the overlapping of its interests with those of large agricultural producers.

A second powerful interest group is the National Federation of Coffee Growers (FEDECAFE). Founded in 1927, this private association tends to be dominated by the larger coffee producers and/or exporters. Relations between the coffee growers and the government are close. The present head of FEDECAFE, for example, previously served as ambassador to the United States and as presidential advisor. Meanwhile, Colombian society is replete with other interest groups at the upper- and middle-income levels: large agrarian interests, retailers, teachers, doctors, and so forth. Most any professional is represented by an organization that has *personería juridical,* which essentially is a license to exist and the formal right to a measure of input into the political process.

Historically, the Roman Catholic Church in Colombia was among the most powerful in Latin America, partly because of the religious fervor of the masses, and partly because of the Church's extensive landholdings and explicit alliances with political and economic elites. Until the beginning of the National Front the relationship between the Church hierarchy and the Conservative party was especially close. During *la violencia,* for example, bishops threatened to excommunicate anyone who voted for Liberal candidates, and some parish priests refused the sacraments, including burial, to Liberals. This attitude is exemplified in a 1949 bishops' statement forbidding Catholics to vote for Liberal candidates because they might "wish to implant civil marriage, divorce, and co-education, which would open the doors to immorality and Communism."⁵ (All of these things did come to Colombia, with divorce arriving last with the constitution of 1991.)

Urbanization and secularization have eroded Church power, and the Church hierarchy is no longer unified in support of the status quo (if, indeed, it ever was). More priests now come from the middle and lower sectors, but the upper hierarchy is still dominated by sons of the wealthy. There have been cases of radical priests, the most dramatic one being that of Camilo Torres, a sociologist from an affluent Bogotá family. In the 1960s Torres concluded that to be a good Christian in Colombia required working for fundamental change. After frustrating experiences trying to promote substantive reform first as a priest and then as a government official in the agrarian reform agency, Torres left the clergy and joined the guerrillas. Soon afterward he was killed in combat. A more recent example of a radical priest is Manuel Pérez Martinez, a defrocked Spanish priest who from the 1970s until his death in 1998 was a leader of the ELN guerrillas.

Military

The Colombian military has been one of the least interventionist in Latin America, and civilian control of the armed forces is relatively high. During the nineteenth century each party controlled its own army. The "national army" supported the party in power while the opposition party maintained a separate army. The Colombian military did not become a professional institution until the early twentieth century. The military and naval academies were founded in 1907, and a war college followed two years later.

Colombian presidents cannot, of course, ignore military interests. The military has a share of the national budget (which historically was one of the lowest per capita in Latin America) and the government must share its autonomy over internal decisions within the military. Since the 1980s military elites have increasingly sought to influence national policy toward the guerrillas. History offers examples of the military taking independent actions under presidents that encroached on military prerogatives. In the 1930s López Pumarejo, during his "Revolution on the March," transferred military officers who opposed him to remote posts and promoted those who supported him. During his second term he was briefly taken prisoner in a coup attempt.

More recently, two presidents have faced situations when, according to accusations, the military has acted without presidential approval. One was in November 1985, when the M–19 guerrilla group seized the Palace of Justice and took its occupants hostage. The military stormed the palace, defeating a band of guerrillas but also killing over a hundred innocent people (including all the justices of the Supreme Court) and totally incinerating the contents of a building that housed a vital branch of government. In another incident, in December 1990 the military attacked guerrilla headquarters in Meta, on precisely the same day as the nation was electing a Constituent Assembly. Many Colombians question whether the presidents in the two cases (Betancur in the first and Gaviria in the second) actually gave their approval for the actions the military carried out.

One cannot categorically reject the possibility of a military coup in the future. From 1946 to 1953 Conservative presidents Ospina and Gómez greatly politicized the military, probably contributing to the military coup of 1953. The National Front significantly lowered the partisan identification of the military, but beginning in 1962, with the aid of the U.S. government, the army began employing its personnel, equipment, and skills in social and economic projects. The military has subsequently developed expertise in a number of development areas, in some cases exceeding that of the civilian bureaucracy. During the "dirty war" of the 1980s, many civilian leaders feared that military officers would seize power; they did not. Similarly, they did not remove Samper despite urging from retired military leaders. Since the late 1990s the trend has been for the Colombian military to grow much stronger—relative to the national police force and also relative to civilian agencies—under the auspices of the U.S.-funded Plan Colombia.

The power of organized labor in Colombia has never matched that of its counterparts in some Latin American societies. First, industrialization arrived later than in the Southern Cone. More importantly, Colombia's first two labor federations were largely the creation of the traditional political parties and thus the labor movement was divided along partisan lines. The Confederation of Colombian Workers (CTC) was founded in 1935 under the auspices of the Liberal government of López Pumarejo. The Union of Colombian Workers (UTC), closely linked to the Conservative party and the church, was formed in 1946 under Conservative Mariano Ospina Pérez, and on the eve of *la violencia*. By the late 1950s the UTC had become Colombia's largest labor federation.

Also fragmenting the labor movement is the fact that many union locals are not affiliated with any of the three national federations (a third federation, the Syndical Confederation of Workers of Colombia (CSTC), had surpassed the UTC by the 1980s). In addition, Colombian law requires labor leaders to be full-time workers in their industries, a requirement that, when enforced, impedes unionization. Repression has also been a limiting factor. Though Colombia's political elite has long accepted active unions, and massive strikes have been waged over the years, the government does not refrain from using force when a union has Communist ties or mounts actions contrary to dominant interests. Since the 1990s transnational labor groups have been providing support to Colombian unionists in various ways: by publicizing the high number of Colombian labor activists murdered by paramilitary forces, by exposing links between paramilitary violence and some of the foreign corporations operating in Colombia, and by providing resources and temporary asylum to Colombian unionists receiving death threats.

The political parties, large economic groups, the church, the military, and organized labor are the political actors that enjoy a legitimate role in the Colombian political system. The great majority of Colombians—the *campesinos* and the urban poor—have little formal access to power and have not been well organized. The National Association of Land Users (ANUC) provides about five hundred thousand small farmers with limited government services, and the National Agrarian Association, an affiliate of the UTC, claims to represent one hundred thousand *campesinos*. These organizations, however, are elite-instigated, divided along traditional party lines, and reach only a small portion of their potential constituency. No mass organization exists that lobbies for the interests of the urban poor.

Civil society groups proliferated in Colombia during the 1990s, but their impact on politics is weak compared to that of some of their counterparts elsewhere in Latin America. Tens of thousands of rural Colombians have repeatedly marched on provincial capitals in protest of the aerial spraying of herbicides in the drug war, to no avail. Peace activists organize mass demonstrations in the large cities, and human rights workers bravely document the unending atrocities, but the influence of such groups on the government is at an all-time low. Indeed, President Uribe has referred to human rights NGOs as subversives. Much of the Colombian NGO sector represents the interests and concerns of middle- and upper-income groups, though notable exceptions do occur. More often, however, when socioeconomically marginalized groups (such as displaced *campesinos,* shantytown residents, small miners, or villagers adversely affected by large-scale development) manage to organize and make claims on the political system, they become targets of paramilitary violence.

Illegal Armed Actors: Guerrillas, Drug Traffickers, and Paramilitaries

Three types of illegitimate actors challenge the Colombian political system: guerrillas, drug traffickers, and paramilitary groups. The guerrillas call for a redistribution of power and resources away from foreign interests and national "oligarchs" to the poor, the drug traffickers seek to produce and trade their illicit goods with impunity, and the paramilitaries claim to be defending society from guerrillas and from the opponents of economic progress. Though their goals and methods differ in important ways, these armed groups also have much in common, such as: employing violence to achieve their aims; assassinating government officials; extorting, kidnapping, murdering, and maiming civilians; recruiting pre-adolescent children; and offering excuses and rationalizations for harming innocents.

Other commonalities help explain why these groups persist. All three derive at least part of their financing from drug trafficking activities, earnings that amount to hundreds of millions of dollars per year (for each type of illegal armed actor). Moreover, all three draw their foot soldiers from the rural and urban poor. Finally, all three benefit from Colombia's unusually rugged terrain because impassable mountains, dense jungles, and vast plains favor clandestine and insurgent activities by impeding detection and eradication efforts.

Guerilla Groups

Two decades ago four main guerrilla groups were operating in Colombia: the Armed Forces of the Colombian Revolution (FARC), the Army of National Liberation (ELN), the Nineteenth of April Movement (M–19), and the Popular Army of Liberation (EPL). The latter two demobilized in 1990; the FARC and the ELN remain in combat today, sometimes collaborating. The FARC, the largest, most militant, best-armed, and best-trained guerrilla group, had roughly twenty thousand active combatants in 2003.

Since its origins in the self-defense forces of *campesino* villages during *la violencia*, the FARC has had close ties with the Communist Party, and remains dominated by Marxists today. FARC strongholds have tended to be frontier regions neglected by the national government and plagued by general lawlessness. The FARC has acted as a de facto state in such areas and also serves as a gendarme for squatters and peasants growing illicit crops. The FARC's ailing septuagenarian leader, Manuel Marulanda Vélez, also known as Tirofijo, is a former Liberal *campesino* who took up arms in the 1940s and has been fighting the government since.

During the 1990s popular support for the FARC all but vanished for several reasons. The fall of the Soviet Union brought an end to some of the FARC's financing, and made its Marxist ideology seem anachronistic. The FARC increasingly relied on protection rents from the cocaine and heroin sectors, and intensified its longstanding practices of kidnapping for ransom and extorting ranches and businesses. These tactics financed the guerrillas' military expansion, but did not win them new sympathizers. In addition, the FARC faced greater pressure from paramilitary groups and the increasingly U.S.-fortified Colombian military. In response, the guerrillas grew more inclined to engage in actions that harmed civilians, such as using landmines and the notoriously inaccurate gas-cylinder bombs, hijacking commercial jets, assassinating elected officials, murdering peace activists, and attacking an upscale family recreation center in the heart of Bogotá. Despite losing whatever positive image the FARC had with the general public, the group continued to gain territory and combatants throughout the decade.

At the end of the 1990s the Pastrana government granted the FARC a cease-fire zone of 42,000 square kilometers in an effort to jump-start peace talks. The FARC used the zone to its advantage and strengthened its forces, just as it had done during a truce with the government in the mid-1980s. Flexing greater muscle this time, the FARC resisted negotiations, enraging the military and much of the civilian elite, and raising alarm in Washington over the weak bargaining position of the Colombian government. Before leaving office Pastrana called off the cease-fire and the military invaded the zone. The Uribe government has not pursued negotiations with the FARC.

While it existed the M–19 was Colombia's second largest guerrilla group. Formed by middle- and upper-class young people in reaction to claims of fraud in the 1970 elections, the M–19 was viewed as more dynamic and less committed to Marxist-Leninist doctrine than the FARC, particularly in its early years. It gained instant notoriety for its theft of Bolivar's sword and for taking a group of foreign diplomats hostage. By the late 1980s the M–19 leadership was decimated by clashes with the army and police, and in 1989 the group signed an agreement with the Barco government whereby leader Carlos Pizarro and eight hundred militants turned over their arms and demobilized in exchange for reincorporation into civilian life. Leading a new political party called the AD-M19, Pizarro entered the 1990 presidential race in the wake of the assassination of the UP's presidential candidate. Pizarro became an articulate spokesman for peace, but was assassinated just forty-five days after having laid down his arms.

The small Maoist-oriented EPL was active in the Magdalena River valley and linked with a wing of the Communist Party. Numbering less than 1,500, it was known for strict discipline and its critique of the FARC's involvement in drug trafficking. The EPL financed its activities with kidnappings and assaults on landed elites. The EPL joined the FARC in accepting the 1984 cease-fire and demobilized in 1990, but reappeared later in the decade.

Inspired by the Cuban Revolution and supported by Havana, the ELN is another rural Marxist insurgency formed in the 1960s. It is the second largest guerrilla group in Colombia today but its membership has fallen since the late

1990s from 5,000 to about 3,500. The ELN is known for sabotaging the pipeline carrying most of Colombia's export petroleum. The hundreds of pipeline bombings the ELN has carried out have damaged the national economy, devastated local ecosystems, and incinerated at least one village.

Originally based in Santander, for many years the ELN controlled large tracts of oil-rich lands in the *llanos*. In the early 1980s the large sums that the ELN reportedly extorted from an oil pipeline construction operation allowed the guerrilla group, which had dwindled in size at that point, to re-arm and expand its ranks dramatically. The coal and oil sectors were lucrative targets for the ELN's kidnapping and extortion activities until the mid-1990s, when the ELN lost territory to challengers. Today, firms in the energy sector are more likely to pay protection money to security services with paramilitary links rather than be extorted by the ELN. Also, U.S. participation in the Colombian conflict has increasingly prioritized the energy sector, which further places the ELN on the defensive. On-and-off talks between the ELN and the Pastrana and Uribe governments have not produced results.

Drug Traffickers

Drug traffickers exercise considerable power in Colombian society, sometimes subtly, other times using brutal violence. In the 1980s and 1990s there were three competing groups of drug traffickers: the Medellín cartel, the Cali cartel, and the Atlantic Coast cartel. Today there are dozens of trafficking organizations. Abundant evidence exists documenting the investment of drug earnings into legitimate businesses in Colombia (including a professional soccer team), politics, the military, and the police forces. Drug traffickers have used bribes and intimidation to corrupt individual Colombians of every rank. The following excerpt from a 1988 warning, received by a judge who was contemplating bringing a known drug dealer to trial in connection with the assassination of a newspaper editor, illustrates a tactic used by the traffickers:

> The most serious thing is that . . . not even the slightest evidence exists against Mr. Escobar. We have also heard . . . you will be given a foreign diplomatic position. But we want to remind you that . . . you are making a big error that will blemish your life and will make it cursed until the end of your days. You know perfectly well that we are capable of executing you at any place on this planet. You should also know that in the meantime you will see the fall, one by one, of all of the members of your family. We advise you to rethink it, since later you will not have time to be sorry about it. Be absolutely certain that in calling Mr. Escobar to trial you will remain without forebears or descendants in your genealogical tree.[6]

Drug traffickers have murdered tens of thousands of Colombian judges, police officers, soldiers, journalists, public functionaries, and journalists. At times any Colombian who opposed the power of the traffickers, regardless of stature, was at risk. High-profile assassination victims include a justice minister, an attorney general, three presidential candidates, the publisher of one the nation's largest newspapers, and a beloved comedian.

In addition to their direct contribution to violence in Colombia, drug traffickers have played a key role in the rise of paramilitary violence. In the 1980s newly rich drug traffickers purchased extensive ranches, often in areas with a guerrilla presence. The drug lords equipped and trained private armies to guard their assets and deter kidnapping or extortion by the guerrillas. The traffickers shared with other large landowners a deep hatred of not only the crimes of the guerrillas, but also their goal of massive land reform. Drug traffickers thus joined other elites in creating paramilitary groups in certain regions. Before long, some of the trafficker-created paramilitary groups became directly involved in drug trafficking, grew autonomous, and amassed great wealth and power. While it is true that drug traffickers sporadically seek accommodation with guerrilla groups, more frequently the two groups clash over turf, the division of profits, and the size of the share to be paid to *campesino* growers.

In August 1989 drug traffickers assassinated Senator Luis Carlos Galán, a dynamic reformer who was leading in the preference polls for the 1990 presidential election. Galán was an articulate advocate of stronger action against the narcos. The day after Galán's murder, President Barco declared all-out war on the traffickers and received forceful U.S. backing. Key elements of the government offensive were to confiscate the property of suspected drug kingpins and extradite individuals under indictment in the United States. The drug dealers responded with a massive urban bombing campaign in Bogotá and Medellín. By the end of 1989 several mid-level narcos had been extradited and one of the leaders of the Medellín cartel, José Gonzalo Rodríguez Gacha, had been killed in a battle with government troops.

President Gaviria initiated a kind of plea-bargaining with traffickers that had little precedent in Colombia. Traffickers that surrendered and confessed to at least one crime received reduced sentences (the Constituent Assembly had prohibited extradition). Gaviria's policy brought the surrender of the three Ochoa brothers and Pablo Escobar of the Medellín group. The notorious Escobar, however, escaped after a little over a year in prison, and he evaded capture for fifteen months. When Escobar was killed by government troops in December 1993, it marked the end of the Medellín cartel—the most brazen, violent, and politically ambitious trafficking group. The leaders of the Cali cartel either surrendered or were captured during the Samper years.

The defeat of the Medellín and Cali cartels, however, did not end the drug trade. Because new leaders and smaller groups replaced the dismantled ones, drug exports did not decline, and global demand for illegal drugs continued to rise. The U.S. Drug Enforcement Agency commented that the lower-profile groups were even tougher to combat than their predecessors. Considering that drug trafficking has produced at least six Colombian billionaires and some 160 millionaires, there will always be a large pool of would-be traffickers no matter how many individuals the government captures or kills. One potential source of change—a transformation of the prohibitionist approach—is highly unlikely on the U.S. side, though Colombian elites openly debate decriminalization. Finally, while drug trafficking's direct contribution to violence in Colombia may have declined, its role in undermining the rule of law remains a crucial problem.

Paramilitary Groups

The third set of illegal armed actors is the paramilitary groups, also referred to as "self-defense groups," or "death squads."[7] The origins of these groups date back to colonial times when regional elites employed private militias to protect and advance their interests in areas where government forces were weak or absent. Coca Cola's employment of brutal private security contractors can arguably be seen as a recent manifestation of the pattern. A less controversial example would be when drug lords collaborated with other elites in the 1980s to create *Muerte a Secuestrados* (Death to Kidnappers, MAS), a group whose mission was to kill the kidnappers preying on rural elites. MAS operatives did not succeed in killing many kidnapper-guerrillas, but they did kill many left-leaning civilians, individuals accused of helping guerrillas, and people they declared socially undesirable, such as street children, muggers, prostitutes, and derelicts.

The other source of the paramilitary phenomena is the Colombian state. In 1964 a presidential decree legitimized the creation of armed civil self-defense units as a counterinsurgency policy. In 1989 these government-sponsored private militias were declared unconstitutional. Despite the change in the law, however, evidence periodically surfaces of ongoing collusion between paramilitary groups and specific military brigades. Nor has the government pursued counterparamilitary efforts with the same vigor that it fights guerrillas.

The government has also authorized new forms of paramilitary activity. In the early 1990s *convivires* were organized in urban neighborhoods with assistance from the national government. Though touted as neighborhood crime watches, abuses occurred. When the program was terminated under Pastrana, some *conviveres* had merged with paramilitary groups and some pre-existing paramilitary groups, posing as *convivires,* had used the program to obtain weapons and ammunition from the government. More recently, the current president, Alvaro Uribe, has implemented a program in which the military recruits civilians to gather intelligence on suspected insurgents and to work with the army to capture and kill guerrillas. The Uribe government also initiated negotiations with paramilitaries.

It was in the 1990s that paramilitary groups dramatically increased their size, range, and arsenal. They claim to have fifteen thousand combatants. Paramilitaries employ terror tactics such as arriving in a town with a list of names, torturing and murdering certain residents in the public square, then making ominous warnings before departing. Though many more murders of civilians are attributed to the paramilitaries than to the guerrillas, the paramilitaries have largely enjoyed impunity. Some government agencies document and prosecute paramilitary violence, but these offices possess limited resources and little power relative to the branches of government and the parts of society that view the paramilitaries as allies in the war against the guerrillas.

In 1997 hundreds of paramilitary groups from around the country became loosely affiliated under the United Self-Defense Groups of Colombia (AUC), an organization founded by Carlos Castaño. Castaño's leadership and media campaign helped the paramilitaries improve their public image. It is unclear how Castaño's presumed death will affect negotiations between the Uribe government and the AUC. It is clear, however, that the strength of paramilitary groups in Colombia underscores fundamental problems: The Colombian state does not monopolize the use of organized violence within the national territory, and the government has used private militias against its enemies at the cost of empowering brutal actors over whom it has limited control.

Since 2000 direct combat between paramilitary forces and guerrillas has increased just as U.S.-trained army battalions are engaging guerrilla forces in more frequent battles. The principal victims of the conflict, as always, are the rural Colombians caught in the crossfire. Like their predecessors in times past, millions have fled to urban shantytowns and neighboring countries. And in one of Colombia's longstanding and painful ironies, from the ranks of the children displaced by the violence, new belligerents will be recruited to fight on all sides.

Govenment Machinery

The Gaviria administration attempted to address the public order problem by convoking a Constituent Assembly to rewrite the venerable 1886 constitution. Seventy-four delegates, elected by proportional representation and including former guerrillas, indigenous representatives, and civil society activists, met in Bogotá in 1991, and the new constitution was proclaimed on July 4.

Table 9.1, comparing the old and new constitutions, shows that Colombia's national government remains very similar, at least in appearance, to the U.S. model of three branches of government with a separation of powers and checks and balances. Although the executive is still the most powerful branch of government, the constitution of 1991 gives more power to the Congress. The president was allowed only one term in office, with no reelection ever. The increased power of the Congress so far exists only on paper. The new constitution attempts to strengthen the judiciary through a National Prosecutor's Office and a new division of judicial powers between the Supreme Court and the Constitutional Court.

The new constitution also attempts to decentralize a system in which power had become increasingly centralized. Departments and municipalities now have weak powers of taxation, and the national government is obliged to share revenues from income and value-added taxes with local governments over the coming years. Meanwhile, democratization measures target all levels: The popular election of governors (previously appointed by the president) was instituted after the popular election of mayors that began in 1988. Further, there are provisions for the recall of elected officials, for citizen-initiated legislation, for class-action suits, and for the collective rights of indigenous communities. (In 1992 Congress passed the first law arising from a citizen's initiative, addressing the crime of kidnapping.) Measures were adopted to combat nepotism and place limits on official travel, and officials can be removed for failure to fulfill campaign promises.

President Uribe proposed that the 1991 constitution be amended to allow a sitting president to be reelected, and Congress passed the amendment in the 2003 and 2004 sessions. In 2005 the Constitutional Court ruled that the amendment had been adopted in a procedurally correct way. Given Uribe's high approval ratings among likely voters—70 percent in mid-2004—it is probable that Uribe will be the winner in the 2006 presidential elections.

The current electoral system is one of proportional representation for both houses of Congress, departmental assemblies, and municipal councils. The new constitution has an unusual feature: the hundred-member Senate is elected from a national constituency, and given proportional representation, any party that receives 1 percent of the national vote should receive one senator. This change was intended to give parties other than the dominant Liberals and Conservatives some representation.

In 2006 Colombia will use a new electoral system in the congressional elections. With the old system of proportional representation party lists were given a number of seats according to the proportion of the vote received. The candidates elected were then chosen by the order in which the party had

Table 9.1 A Comparison of "Democratic" Features of the Colombian
Constitutions of 1886 and 1991.

Feature	1886	1991
President		
Election	Plurality, every four years	Majority, every four years
Terms	Unlimited but not successive	One
Vice President	None, but with a "designate" elected by the Congress	Elected at same time as president; does not have to be from same party; can be elected president but not following term
Cabinet	Appointed and removed by president	Appointed and removed by president; can be censured by the Congress
Governors	Appointed by president	Elected
Congress	Each house by departmental constituency, proportional representation	House by departmental constituency, proportional representation; Senate by national constituency, proportional representation
Number of posts	Multiple candidacy possible Alternates for posts	One post only No alternates
New "democratic" features		Recall elections; initiative and referendum for legislation and constitutional amendments; limits on relatives holding posts; limits on travel; no regional funds from Congress; members of Congress lose post if miss more than six votes during session; any official can be removed if does not follow campaign promises
Judiciary	Traditional code-law system in which judges investigate as well as try cases	National Prosecutor's Office, separate from judiciary and charged with investigation of crimes and coordination of investigative bodies

placed them on the list. Under the new "preferential" system voters can choose any candidate on a party list for which they vote. After it is determined how many seats a party list has received, the votes for the individual candidates will be counted, and those receiving the most votes will be elected to the Congress.

In the past Colombians took pride in having a "mixed" economy—one in which certain industries, such as communications, electricity, and natural resources, were government-owned and run. Others, especially in the area of consumer goods, were financed purely by private capital, either Colombian or foreign. In still others the government was one of several stockholders. The end result was a society in which the government played a much larger part in the economy than it does in the United States, and government spending represents a larger percentage of the GNP.

Since the Barco and Gaviria governments Colombia has been implementing neoliberal policies typical of those adopted elsewhere in Latin America. Privatization in Colombia has been less extensive than in some nations, in part because fewer industries were state-owned in the first place. The most dramatic shift has been in the lowering of tariffs. The "economic opening" has created profound changes. As in the rest of the world, in Colombia there have been both winners (consumers with money to buy imported goods, globally competitive industries) and losers (workers in industries formerly protected and lower-income groups generally, because they lack the means to protect themselves from the effects of external shocks). Colombian political elites since Gaviria have remained committed to the *apertura*, but the greater vulnerability of the economy to global forces has elicited controversy. It is not certain that future presidents will be able to ignore the social costs of opening the economy.

One product of the traditional government role in the economy is a large bureaucracy. Before the National Front bureaucratic posts were one of the chief spoils of the political system, with the changing of the party in the presidency leading to a nearly complete turnover in the bureaucracy. This practice ended with the National Front, but the principle of spoils did not, and the bureaucracy grew rapidly. Bureaucratic posts are sought after because they provide a decent salary, the chance to avoid working with one's hands, and some prestige. However, the technical training of government bureaucrats has not been a strength. The bureaucracy has served more as a source of desirable jobs for distributing to well-connected young people than as an object of sustained efforts to develop bureaucratic expertise. Whether or not to establish a genuine career administration has long been the subject of lively debate.

In an attempt to minimize the spoils problem, decentralized institutes were set up to administer certain programs and government industries, and this form of bureaucracy has become predominant. In 1976, 36 percent of government employees fell into this category, as compared with 26 percent who were teachers and 8 percent who were in agencies directly under the cabinet ministries. In 1975 fully 59.5 percent of the national budget was spent by the decentralized institutes. It is not clear whether these decentralized institutes have been less vulnerable than the regular bureaucracy to the politics of spoils or whether they have encouraged the development of bureaucratic excellence.

Public Policy

In Colombia the public policy process is conditioned by the government machinery just described. Bureaucracies are not efficient in carrying out the laws proposed by the president and passed by the Congress, nor do the majority of *campesinos* and urban poor benefit from the product of national policymaking. The National Front system and its aftermath impeded strong, innovative policymaking because the president had to contend with half his cabinet, half of Congress, and half the governors and mayors being members of the other party. Shortly after taking office, a president became a kind of lame duck as political actors would begin looking around for the next president, someone who would not even be of the incumbent party. This pattern, along with the personalism and factionalism of the parties, made it difficult for presidents to obtain the majority needed for policy implementation. By the time of the first genuinely non-Front government of Virgilio Barco in 1986, the Liberals had no experience operating like members of a party in power, nor were the Conservatives familiar with how a loyal opposition party conducts itself.

This is not to say that all policy initiatives were a complete failure, as macroeconomic policymaking was clearly successful in maintaining steady growth and relatively low external debt, and real gains were achieved in education, health, and housing through the 1980s. Rather, it is the longstanding failure of government policies to improve the welfare of many Colombians living in squalor and marginality that indicts the policy process overall. In particular, the failure to implement meaningful agrarian reform or to integrate remote rural areas into the legitimate economy has had very grave consequences.

Back in the 1980s with his predecessor's failed negotiations with insurgents in mind, President Barco declared he would end "absolute poverty" by addressing the lack of government services in the countryside. Absolute poverty was defined as not having sufficient income for food or clothing, a designation that, in 1986, applied to 45 percent of the Colombian people. Little progress was made during Barco's term, and conditions for the poor have worsened since then. Leftist insurgents are stronger than ever. Land tenure conflicts continued to be contested violently, exacerbated by the number of drug traffickers buying large tracts of land and then persecuting squatters. In the urban sector demand for housing and public services outstripped supply as more of the rural population was displaced to the cities. Restoring public order increasingly consumed the attention of the executive branch, and fewer resources were assigned to other policy areas. Today Colombia's most glaring policy issue remains the security problem. Although estimates of the extent of their domains vary, there is no doubt that guerrilla groups, paramilitaries, and drug trafficking organizations operate in a substantial portion of Colombian territory. No Latin American government has faced wealthier or better-armed domestic adversaries.

Prospects

During the twentieth century the resilience of the Colombian political system was remarkable. The traditional parties remained dominant despite civil strife tearing the social fabric, an intractable leftist insurgency, and drug kingpins seeking to terrorize politicians into submission. The Colombian population doubled about every twenty-four years (this rate has now "slowed" to every thirty years), and millions of landless peasants filled the cities. The economy saw rapid modernization, steady growth, severe recession, and deep structural reform. Despite all these challenges, however, the Colombian political system remained essentially the same: elitist, patrimonial, civilian, modified two-party, and largely closed to the poor multitudes. Despite being one of the most liberal democratic polities in Latin America, Colombia did less for its poor citizens than many of its neighbors. This outcome was partly due to the security problem, but it is also because the political system, whether by design or accident, has favored nondecisions. Of course, not making a decision favors the status quo, which in turn has favored a small sector of the population. Consequently Colombians enjoy the right to vote every four years for unlimited numbers of candidates, but lack the "human rights" of *pan, techo, y tierra* (food, housing, and land) or physical safety.

Álvaro Uribe rejected the peace policies of his predecessor and strengthened the military, with growing assistance from the United States, and intensified the counter-guerrilla war. At the end of 2002 the Uribe government signed a cease-fire with AUC, the paramilitary organization. Although 2,624 paramilitary troops demobilized during 2004, much remained to be accomplished. Paramilitary operations continued in early 2005 in various parts of the country, including Córdoba and Antioquia. In Colombia and abroad many questioned whether the negotiations with the AUC would result in impunity for crimes committed by paramilitaries. The National Congress passed a "Law of Justice and Peace," on the issue. The problem for Colombian officials is how to balance the concern for justice with the reality that the paramilitaries are demobilizing without having been defeated militarily, and are loath to volunteer for prosecution.

Under Uribe the economy rebounded and some indices of violence were down. Tourism within the country became less dangerous and many Colombians were expressing a more positive attitude about their country. Nevertheless, in mid-2006 war with the FARC continued unabated and there was only slight progress in negotiations with the ELN. Over a million Colombians were war refugees in their own country. Colombia still supplied 90 percent of the cocaine consumed in the United States. And a paramilitary leader stated that at least 35 percent of the members of the national congress had been elected with paramilitary support.

It is likely that Colombia's near-term future promises more of the same. The country will probably continue with its flawed variant of liberal democracy, with modifications of the constitution of 1991 producing only subtle changes. Violence will still undermine the quality of life for the middle and upper classes and cause capital flight and brain drain, but by and large many individuals and firms will carry on as usual. The two-thirds of Colombians who are poor will most likely continue to live in dire circumstances, experience harrowing violence, and provide a pool of potential recruits for the armed groups destroying the nation. Opportunities for predatory and illicit economic gain will remain, and constitute powerful incentives for antisocial behavior. Political openings like that of the new constitution will be insufficient to persuade guerrilla groups to demobilize, especially given the fate of those who did so in the past. Drug traffickers will continue to have considerable influence in Colombia, and the power of paramilitary groups will probably keep growing.

There is little threat of an open seizure of power by drug traffickers or paramilitaries, but the insidious manipulation of the law by these groups is likely to persist. The prospects for the guerrillas to achieve military victory are extremely remote. At the same time it is also highly improbable that the guerrilla phenomenon will be completely eradicated by the Uribe government's military approach. Similarly, little chance exists that the government will be removed by a popular movement like those witnessed in Argentina and Bolivia.

A military coup is unlikely but remains a small possibility. During the 1980s it appeared that the traditional system would break down, causing the military to step in as it did in 1953. This did not happen, and in 1991 there was little military reaction when President Gaviria named the first civilian minister of war since the 1940s. Nor did the military assert itself during the scandal-paralyzed Samper presidency. Should the traditional order collapse, the chance of a coup would increase significantly. Such a collapse is unlikely, however, given the U.S. financial and military commitment to shoring up the present system.

A more hopeful but less likely scenario is that both significant reform and substantive peace will be achieved in Colombia under Uribe. There are indications that a more responsive democracy and greater judicial efficiency are developing as a result of the constitution of 1991, and that some political leaders aspire to genuinely change their country. The Colombian population has demonstrated a great capacity for resilience and innovation, and with new leadership in Bogotá and Washington, much is possible. Two formidable challenges will have to be addressed. First, political democracy and the rule of law will have to be strengthened enough so that homicide is no longer a major cause of death and an effective block to social change and justice. Second, economic rights and opportunities will have to be distributed more fairly so that Colombians who start off with nothing are not doomed to choose between grinding poverty and illegal enterprises.

Suggestions for Further Reading

Berquist, Charles, Ricardo Peñaranda, and Gonzalo Sánchez, eds. *Violence in Colombia: The Contemporary Crisis in Historical Perspective*. Wilmington, DE: Scholarly Resources, 1992.

Fals Borda, Orlando. *Peasant Society in the Colombian Andes: A Sociological Study of Saucío*. Gainesville: University of Florida Press, 1955.

Hartlyn, Jonathan. *The Politics of Coalition Rule in Colombia*. New York: Cambridge University Press, 1988.

Kirk, Robin. *More Terrible Than Death: Massacres, Drugs and America's War in Colombia*. New York: Public Affairs, 2003.

Kline, Harvey F. *Colombia: Democracy Under Assault*. Boulder, CO: Westview, 1995.

———. *State Building and Conflict Resolution in Colombia, 1986–1994*. Tuscaloosa: University of Alabama Press, 1999.

Leal Buitrago, Francisco. *Estado y política en Colombia*. Bogotá: Siglo Veintiuno, 1984.

Leal Buitrago, Francisco, and Andrés Dávila de Guevara. *Clientelismo: El sistema político y su expresión regional*. Bogotá: Tercer Mundo Editores, 1990.

Leal Buitrago, Francisco, and León Zamosc, eds. *Al filo del caos: Crisis política en la Colombia de los años 80*. Bogotá: Tercer Mundo Editores, 1990.

Martz, John D. *Colombia: A Contemporary Political Survey*. Chapel Hill: University of North Carolina Press, 1962.

———. *The Politics of Clientelism: Democracy and the State in Colombia*. New Brunswick, NJ: Transaction, 1997.

Molano, Alfredo. *The Dispossessed: Chronicles of the* Desterrados *of Colombia*. Chicago: Haymarket Books, 2005.

Oquist, Paul. *Violence, Conflict, and Politics in Colombia*. New York: Academic Press, 1980.

Urrutia, Miguel. *The Development of the Colombian Labor Movement*. New Haven, CT: Yale University Press, 1969.

Notes

1. *Cifras de violencia 1996–2002*, Vol. 0, No. 1 (Bogota: Dirección de Justicia y Seguridad, Departamento Nacional de Planeación, 2003), http://www.dnp.gov.co.

2. Eduardo Santa, *Sociología política de Colombia* (Bogotá: Ediciones Tercer Mundo, 1964), 37.

3. Harvey F. Kline, "The National Front: Historical Perspective and Overview," in *Politics of Compromise: Coalition Government in Colombia*, ed. R. Albert Berry, Ronald G. Hellman, and Mauricio Solaún (New Brunswick, NJ: Transaction Books, 1980), 59–83.

4. Harvey F. Kline, *State Building and Conflict Resolution in Colombia, 1986–1994* (Tuscaloosa: The University of Alabama Press, 1999), 184–191.

5. Quoted in John D. Martz, *Colombia: A Contemporary Political Survey* (Chapel Hill: University of North Carolina Press, 1962), 84.

6. *El Espectador* (Bogotá), July 31, 1988.

7. In an interview with one of the authors of this chapter, a government official stated that, to the Colombian military, a "self-defense group" was one that they had armed, whereas a "paramilitary group" was one armed by someone else. Confidential interview, member of the Office of the Presidency, Bogotá, July 21, 1991.

10

Peru

Authoritarian Traditions, Troubled Democracy

David Scott Palmer

E ven in a region known for its diversity, Peru stands out. Within its borders are more subclimates than in any other Latin American country. A coastal desert gives way inland to imposing peaks of the Andes, high plains, and intermountain valleys, which in turn fall off to the dense tropical rain forest of the Amazon Basin. The population of twenty-eight million is equally varied, from large clusters of highland Indo-Americans and scattered communities of jungle counterparts to descendants of the Spanish conquerors and colonists and Afro-American slaves; European, Middle Eastern, Chinese, Japanese, and Korean immigrants; as well as a majority of mixed-race *mestizos*. The economy includes a significant export sector based on the extraction of copper, gold, iron ore, zinc, and oil; fish and fish meal; and farm products from recently modernized, totally irrigated coastal agriculture. Illegal drug production in jungle areas, mostly coca leaf and cocaine paste, is rebounding after a sharp decline in the late 1990s. Politics may be characterized over Peru's more than 180 years of independence as alternating between one form of authoritarian rule or another, with occasional forays into formal democracy.

In recent years Peru has experienced the region's most reformist and state-expanding military rule (1968–1980) as well as one of its most open democracies (1980–1992). The country has also suffered the most virulent insurgency, led by Shining Path (1980–1995), and one of only two lasting unconstitutional breaks in Latin America following the restoration of democracy in most countries

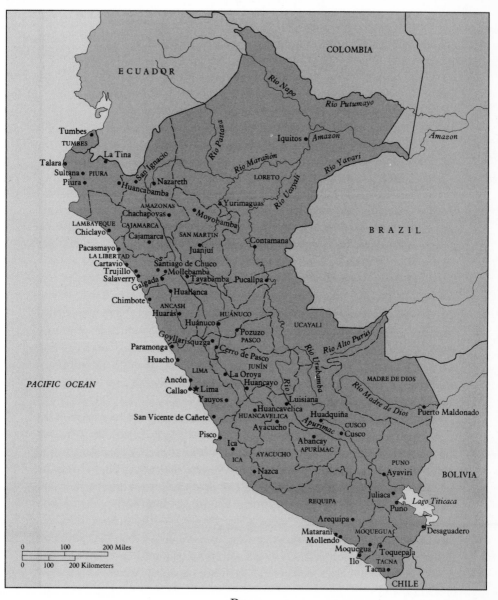

COLOMBIA

ECUADOR

Tumbes
TUMBES
La Tina
Talara
Sultana • PIURA
Piura
Huancabamba
Nazareth
San Ignacio
AMAZONAS
Chachapoyas
Moyobamba
LAMBAYEQUE
CAJAMARCA
Chiclayo
Cajamarca
SAN MARTIN
Pacasmayo
Juanjuí
LA LIBERTAD
Cartavio
Santiago de Chuco
Trujillo
Mollebamba
Salaverry
Tayabamba
Galgada
Huallanca
Chimbote
ANCASH
Huarás
HUÁNUCO
Huánuco
Goyllarisquizga
Pozuzo
Paramonga
PASCO
Huacho
Cerro de Pasco
LIMA
JUNÍN
Ancón
La Oroya
Callao
★ Lima
Huancayo
Yauyos
Luisiana
Huancavelica
Huadquiña
San Vicente de Cañete
HUANCAVELICA
Ayacucho
CUSCO
Pisco
Abancay
Cusco
Ica
APURÍMAC
ICA
AYACUCHO
PUNO
Nazca
Ayaviri
REQUIPA
Juliaca
BOLIVIA
Puno
Lago Titicaca
Arequipa
Matarani
MOQUEGUA
Desaguadero
Mollendo
Moquegua
Toquepala
Ilo
TACNA
Tacna
CHILE

Iquitos
Amazon
Amazon
Rio Napo
Rio Putumayo
Rio Pataza
Rio Marañón
LORETO
Yurimaguas
Rio Ucayali
Rio Yavari
Contamana
BRAZIL
Pucallpa
UCAYALI
Rio Uruhamba
Rio Alto Purús
MADRE DE DIOS
Rio Madre de Dios
Puerto Maldonado
Rio Apurímac

PACIFIC OCEAN

0   100   200 Miles
0   100   200 Kilometers

PERU

(1992–1993). Peru has also experienced the longest term in office by an elected head of state—eleven years—between 1990 and 2000. During the 1990s the country also moved abruptly from high levels of state economic control to become one of the most open economies in the hemisphere and developed one of Latin America's most successful programs of extreme poverty reduction. At the same time political leadership instituted an array of arbitrary controls that led many observers to characterize Peruvian politics of the late 1990s as a "democratic dictatorship." While the return to an open political process in 2000–2001 was welcomed by all, its practice fell far short of its promise, leaving Peru's democracy in a troubled state.

Political Culture

Key among the factors shaping the political culture and history of Peru is its almost three hundred years under Spanish colonial rule. The main elements of Spanish control were authoritarian political institutions and mercantilist economic structures, both of which gave colonialists little experience in handling their own affairs. The carryover into the postcolonial period was greater in Peru than in other Latin American countries, not only because control was imposed more consistently but also because of the nature of the independence movement itself. The belated struggle for independence was more of a conservative reaction to liberalizing forces in Spain and elsewhere than a genuine revolution, and it came largely from outside. As a result, despite the introduction of some liberal organizations and procedures, Peru did not break with the colonial past until after 1824.

Not surprisingly, therefore, authoritarian rule continued long after independence. No civilian president was elected until Manuel Pardo in 1872, although there were some enlightened military leaders such as Ramón Castilla (1845–1851, 1854–1862). Also continuing were neomercantilist economic policies as Great Britain replaced Spain as Peru's major trading partner and its source of most capital and investment. Of the few local entrepreneurs who emerged in this context, most acted as agents for British interests. Peru did experience its first economic boom during this period, based on the extraction for fertilizer of the rich deposits of guano (bird droppings) on islands off the coast. The economic benefits were short-lived, however, because of the outbreak of the War of the Pacific (1879–1883).

The war forced the political break with Peru's past that independence had not provided. Chile wrested from Peru the coastal department of Tarapacá, with its immense nitrate deposits, and occupied a large portion of the country, including Lima. Politically, this disaster demonstrated the weakness of existing institutions and contributed to the emergence of Peru's only sustained period of limited liberal democracy (1895–1919). Economically, the war bankrupted the country and the traditional elite. Because many of Peru's basic resources were mortgaged, Peru became even more dependent on British interests. This coincidence of sharply increased economic dependence and liberal democracy set the pattern for a limited state and private foreign enterprise that most Peruvian governments tried to follow until the 1968 military coup.

In addition, much of Peru's independent political life has been marked by a flamboyant leadership style that has tended to garner support on the basis of personal appeal rather than institutional loyalties and obligations. Many leaders have tended to place personal interests above obligation to any political party organization or even to the nation. As a result, most parties have been personalist vehicles, and most presidencies have involved tumultuous struggles among contending personalities, often ending in military coups. Furthermore, until very recently a large percentage of the national population was not integrated into national economic, political, or cultural life. The Indo-American population of Peru, although in numbers predominant until the 1970s, has participated in national society only in the most subordinate of roles, such as peon, day laborer, and maid. Historically, the only path for those in this population to escape repudiation by the dominant society was to abandon their own heritage and work their way into that of the Spanish. Among the most important changes in contemporary Peru is large-scale Indo-American immigration to towns and cities, where migrants feel they—or their children—can become a part of the dominant culture: Catholic, Hispanic, Spanish-speaking. In addition, the constitution of 1979 gave illiterates—predominantly native Americans—the right to vote for the first time in national and municipal elections.

As to the economy, Peru was much slower than most of Latin America in shifting from the liberal model of a limited state and an open economy to one marked by greater state intervention. This occurred in most of the region as the result of such events as the Mexican and the Russian revolutions, Italy's corporatist state under Mussolini, and the Great Depression. The liberal model endured for so long in Peru for several reasons. Domestic elites were willing to retain strong foreign economic control. The military was largely under elite dominance. Political leadership kept its personalistic and populist character. A noncommunist, mass-based political party absorbed most of the emerging social forces. The Indo-American cultural "barrier" slowed the flow of new elements into the national society. As a result, politics and the economy did not change in any basic way until 1968, when a military coup ushered in a period of unprecedented reform.

Historical Background

Peruvian political history may be divided into the following periods: consolidation (1824–1895), limited civilian democracy (1895–1919), populism and mass parties (1919–1968), reformist military rule (1968–1980), full civilian democracy (1980–1992), *autogolpe* (self-coup) and its aftermath (1992–1993), "direct democracy" (1993–2000), and the return to full, if turbulent, civilian democracy (2000–present).

Consolidation (1824–1895)

Peru took much longer than most Latin American countries to evolve a reasonably stable political and economic system. Because Peru had been the core part of a larger viceroyalty during the colonial period it took some time just to define the country's national territory. The boundaries were roughly hewn out between 1829 and 1841. Augustín Gamarra and José de la Mar failed to capture Ecuador for Peru in 1829. In the Battle of Yungay in 1839, Andrés Santa Cruz lost his post as protector of the Peru-Bolivia confederation when he was defeated by a Chilean army, causing the confederation's collapse. In 1841 in the Battle of Ingavi, Gamarra was killed in his attempt to annex Bolivia to Peru.

Once the boundaries were more or less settled, there remained the key problem of establishing reasonable procedures for attaining and succeeding to political office. Peru had at least fifteen constitutions in its first forty years as an independent country, but force remained the normal route to political power. Of the thirty-five presidents during this period, only four were elected according to constitutional procedures, and no civilians held power for more than a few months. Regional *caudillos* often attempted to impose themselves on the government, which by the 1840s had become an important source of revenue because of the income from guano.

Unlike much of Latin America during the nineteenth century, Peru was divided politically less by a conservative-liberal cleavage and more by the issue of military or civilian rule. By the 1860s partisans of civilian rule were beginning to organize themselves into a civilista movement. The War of the Pacific dramatically demonstrated the need for professionalization of the Peruvian military and helped provoke the formal establishment of the Civilista Party as well as a number of more personalistic contenders. The eventual result was Peru's first extended period of civilian rule starting in 1895.

The War of the Pacific also more firmly embedded the tendency to depend on foreign markets, foreign entrepreneurship, and foreign loans. War debts of more than $200 million were canceled by British interests in 1889 in exchange for Peru's railroads, the Lake Titicaca steamship line, a large tract of jungle land, free use of major ports, a Peruvian government subsidy, and large quantities of guano.

Limited Civilian Democracy (1895–1919)

Peru's longest period of civilian rule began in 1895. While the military reorganized itself under the guidance of a French mission, a coalition of forces among an emerging commercial elite gained control of the government. Embracing neopositivist ideals of renovation, modernization, and innovation, the civilians also advanced the classic liberal precept of a government that would serve to enhance the capacity of the private sector. Their main political objective was the very modest one of keeping civilians in power. This effort implied fostering a civilian state and a civilian society by increased government expenditures for communications, education, and health. These were financed by taxes on rapidly expanding exports, by revenues from new foreign investments (largely U.S.), and by new foreign loans after Peru's international credit was restored in 1907.

Civilian rule was somewhat tenuous even at its height. The Civilista Party, although reasonably well organized, suffered periodic severe internal divisions. Other parties, such as the Liberal, the Democratic, and the Conservative, were personalistic and rose and fell with the fortunes of their individual leaders.

The civilian democratic interlude, ensured when President Nicolás de Piérola (1895–1899) provided for the direct election of his successors, was undone by various factors. One was the severe domestic inflation precipitated by the international economic crisis accompanying World War I. Another was the growing unwillingness of elite-oriented parties to respond to a wide array of demands from new groups entering the political system as the result of expanded government services, especially education. To a certain degree the elites had problems in responding to the longer-term consequences of their own success. Also corrosive to civilian rule were the actions of some leaders themselves. In particular, Presidents Augusto B. Leguía (1908–1912, 1919–1930) and Guillermo Billinghurst (1912–1914) operated in self-serving and personalistic ways. Billinghurst, once elected, eschewed Civilista Party support to make populist appeals to the Lima "masses."

Although he was beholden to the commercial elite, Billinghurst did not try to work within the party or the economic elite to try to bring about some quiet accommodation that might have avoided a confrontation. Growing dismay among elite members gradually drew them to the military, which intervened in 1914 just long enough to remove Billinghurst from office. Leguía, after ruling constitutionally during his first presidency, ended once and for all the shaky civilian democracy in 1919. Rather than work out a behind-the-scenes accommodation with opposition elements in 1919 after he had won democratic election, he led a successful coup of his own and ruled without open elections until being ousted by the military in 1930.

Populism and Mass Parties (1919–1968)

The populism of this period took two forms: civilian, exemplified by Leguía, and military, best illustrated by General Manuel Odría (1948–1956). Both forms were characterized by efforts to stymie political organizations and to encourage loyalty to the person of the president through favored treatment for the elites and by the distribution of goods, jobs, and services to politically aware nonelites. Both forms were also marked by very favorable treatment for the foreign investor and lender; thus, they maintained long-standing external dependence relationships.

Both civilian and military populism had a number of important effects on the Peruvian political system. They permitted elites to retain control through their narrowly based interest group organizations (the National Agrarian Society, SNA; the National Mining Society, SNM; and the National Industrial Society, SNI) and their clubs (Nacional and La Unión). When confronted after 1930 with Peru's first mass-based political party, the American Popular Revolutionary Alliance (APRA), the elites were forced to rely on the military to carry out their political will because they had no comparable party to turn to. The military, in turn, found it could accomplish its own objectives by directly intervening in the political system rather than by working through organized intermediaries. Thus populism, by discouraging political parties, contributed significantly to continued political instability.

Between 1914 and 1984 the only elected civilian to complete a term as president, his first, was Manuel Prado (1939–1945, 1956–1962). Why he did so is instructive. He was of the elite and accepted by it. He did not try to upset the status quo. He gained the military's favor by supporting its material and budget requirements. He reached an implicit modus vivendi with APRA. He happened to be president during a period when foreign market prices for Peruvian primary-product exports were relatively high and stable.

Perhaps the most important political event in pre-1968 Peru was the organization of APRA. Although founded in Mexico by exiled student leader Víctor Raúl Haya de la Torre in 1924, APRA soon became a genuinely mass-based political party in Peru with a fully articulated—if not completely coherent—ideology. By most accounts APRA was strong enough to determine the outcome of all open elections held in Peru after 1931. For more than fifty years, however, the military ensured that the party would never rule directly.

Although APRA has had a strong populist appeal, the party's importance for Peruvian politics rests on its reformist ideology and its organizational capacity. With the exception of Lima, APRA absorbed most of the newly emerging social forces in the more integrated parts of the country between the 1920s and the 1950s, most particularly labor, students, and the more marginal middle sectors of the north coast. The party's appeal thus helped prevent the emergence of a more radical alternative. Furthermore, even though APRA was an outsider for most of the period from its founding to 1956, it never overthrew the system. At key junctures the party leadership searched for accommodation and compromise to gain entry even while continuing to resort to assassinations and abortive putsches in trying to impress political insiders with its power.

Between 1956 and 1982 APRA became a center-conservative party willing to make almost any compromise to gain greater formal political power. In 1956 APRA supported the conservative Manuel Prado in his successful bid for a second term as president and worked with him throughout his administration in what was called in Peru *La Convivencia* (living together). When APRA won open elections in 1962 but was just shy of the constitutionally required one-third, the party made a pact with its former archenemy Odría to govern together. At this point the military intervened and ran the country for a year before facilitating elections, won by its favored candidate, Popular Action's (AP) Fernando Belaúnde Terry. During the Belaúnde administration (1963–1968) APRA formed an alliance with Odría forces in congress to obtain a majority and block or water down many of AP's reforms. Although such actions discredited the party for many, APRA remained Peru's best-organized and most unified political force.

The AP, founded in 1956, brought reformist elements into the system just as APRA had done before. AP's appeal was greater in the sierra and south, where APRA was weak. Thus, the two parties complemented each other by region, and between them they channeled into the system virtually the entire next wave of newly mobilized popular forces.

In spite of APRA-Odría political obstructionism important reforms were carried out between 1963 and 1968 under AP, including establishment of various new agricultural programs; expansion of secondary and university education, cooperatives, and development corporations; and reinstitution of municipal elections. For all intents and purposes the extremist threat to Peruvian institutions was stillborn. However, the opposition in Congress often blunted initiatives or refused to fund them. In addition, the U.S. government, anxious to assist Standard Oil Company's settlement of the investment-expropriation dispute between its Peruvian subsidiary, the International Petroleum Company (IPC), and the Peruvian government, withheld for more than two years Alliance for Progress funds badly needed by the Belaúnde administration to help finance its reforms. Growing economic difficulties in 1967 and 1968 eroded public confidence, and a poorly handled IPC nationalization agreement sealed Belaúnde's fate. On October 3, 1968, with a bloodless coup, the armed forces began long-term, institutionalized military rule in Peru.

Reformist Military Rule (1968–1980)

"The time has come," stated the new military regime's first manifesto, "to dedicate our national energies to the transformation of the economic, social, and cultural structures of Peru." The underlying themes of the military's major statements during the *docenio* (twelve-year rule) included a commitment to change, national pride, social solidarity, the end of dependency, a worker-managed economy, and "a fully participatory social democracy which is neither capitalist nor communist but humanistic." Past governments had declared their intention to change Peru, but this one was prepared to act. What was surprising, given Peru's history of military intervention on behalf of the elites, was that a major reason the 1968 coup occurred was because the Belaúnde government had failed to deliver on promises of significant reform.

Why did the military become an instrument for reform in Peru? The answer lies mostly in developments related to the military itself occurring over a number of years. One was the officers' educational experience after the mid-1950s in the Center for Higher Military Studies (CAEM). Another was a small but intense antiguerrilla campaign in 1965. Third was the effect on military institutional development of continuous U.S. military training from the 1940s through the 1960s. Fourth was the U.S. government's decision in 1967 not to sell jet fighter planes to Peru, which crystallized nationalist sentiment. Last was a vigorous and successful army-led civic action program after 1959. These factors prompted most of the officer corps, at least within the army, to conclude that the best protection for national security was national development. In their view civilian politicians and political parties had failed to meet the development challenge in the 1960s. Many officers concluded that only the military, with its monopoly on legitimate force, was capable of leading Peru toward this goal.

Once in power, the military called itself revolutionary but practiced reform. Almost without exception, the 1968–1975 policy initiatives were based on the twin assumptions of continued economic growth with improved distribution of this growth, and the willingness of economic elites to accept incentives to redirect their wealth toward new productive activities. The military's policies were not based on redistributing the existing economic pie.

Significant changes occurred. One of the most important was the rapid expansion of state influence and control. New ministries, agencies, and banks were established; basic services were expropriated, as were some large foreign companies in mining, fishing, and agriculture, with compensation and reinvestment incentives; and state enterprises or cooperatives were established in their place. Important areas of heavy industry were reserved for the state, new investment laws placed various controls on the private sector, and government employment mushroomed. At the same time, Peru pursued the objective of enhancing development by diversifying its external relationships, thereby reducing the country's economic and political dependency.

Another significant initiative was a large-scale agrarian reform program, which effectively eliminated large private landholdings. About 360,000 farm families received land between 1969 and 1980, most as members of farm cooperatives. Commitment to cooperatives illustrated the regime's concern for popular participation at various levels. Neighborhood organizations, worker communities, and cooperatives of several types proliferated after 1970, as did various coordinating bodies. All of these changes represented substantial adjustments in past practices and for a time appeared likely to succeed.

By 1971 the military's model for the future political system of Peru had emerged in more or less coherent form: corporatism. This model perceived Peruvian social and political reality in terms of an organic whole, organized naturally by functional sectors and within each sector by a natural hierarchy. Government was to serve as the overarching body to initiate, coordinate, and resolve disputes within or among sectors. It was apparently assumed that the new model would eventually replace the old, political party-based one, because of the dramatic increase in the size and capacity of government and the incentives provided to popular sectors to relate to it rather than to parties and interest groups. This assumption proved false.

Four major factors led to the regime's undoing. First and most fundamental, the military's reform plans were much too ambitious. Leaders wanted to do too much in too many areas in too short a time. Second, success was premised on continued economic growth, which stopped after 1974 when economic difficulties multiplied rapidly. With locally generated resources not available as expected, the military government turned to foreign loans, often short-term ones, to keep up the momentum. This policy had produced a severe debt crisis by 1978, and partly explains Peru's recurring economic problems thereafter. Third, those in power failed to consult openly and as equals with the citizens, the presumed beneficiaries of the reforms. This neglect contributed to popular resentment and mistrust as well as to a number of inappropriate and counterproductive policies. Finally, the illness after 1973 of the head of state, General Juan Velasco Alvarado, contributed to a loss of the institutional unity of the armed forces themselves, which his dynamic and forceful leadership had helped to instill. The eventual result was a mixture of old and new programs in yet another overlay, increasingly ill-financed, confusing to the citizens, and ultimately unsuccessful.

An August 1975 coup, led by General Francisco Morales Bermúdez and supported by the military establishment, gently eased out the ill and increasingly erratic General Velasco and ushered in the consolidating phase of the *docenio*. With the exception of agrarian reform, initiatives were quietly abandoned or sharply curtailed. By 1977 mounting economic and political pressures prompted the military regime to initiate a gradual return to civilian rule.

The resulting Constituent Assembly elections in 1978 represented another political milestone because they included participation by an array of leftist parties, which garnered an unprecedented 36 percent of the vote although APRA won the most seats. The Assembly itself was led by Haya de la Torre, another first because the military for years had kept Haya, head of APRA, from power. These elections marked the beginning of significant involvement in the system by the Marxist left. The Assembly produced the constitution of 1979, which set up national elections every five years and municipal elections every three years, beginning in 1980. One irony of the elections was that they returned to the presidency the same person who had been so unceremoniously unseated in 1968.

Full Civilian Democracy (1980–1992)

This time Belaúnde's AP was able to forge a majority in Congress, in coalition with the small Popular Christian Party (PPC), and won the first plurality in the municipal elections as well. However, events conspired once again to make life difficult for the governing authorities.

Inflation continued to increase; at 60 percent in 1980, it exceeded 100 percent by 1984. The recession deepened so that in 1983 the GNP actually declined by over 10 percent, and real wages eroded during Belaúnde's second administration (1980–1985) by over 30 percent. World market prices for Peru's exports—copper, oil, sugar, fishmeal, and minerals—remained low or declined even further. Devastating weather accompanied the arrival in 1982 of the El Niño ocean current, and crops and communications networks in the northern half of Peru were destroyed because of rain and flood; in the south, crops withered as a result of drought.

Given the unfavorable economic developments the foreign debt burden became even more onerous, from $8.4 billion in 1980 to over $13 billion by 1985. International Monetary Fund (IMF) agreements provided new external resources and debt refinancing but also imposed restrictive domestic economic policies, which sparked a great deal of controversy. Belaúnde ultimately hedged on these requirements, thus provoking a breakdown in the IMF agreement and leaving a substantial burden for the next civilian administration, that of Alán García Pérez (1985–1990).

Another unanticipated problem for the civilian government was the growing violence associated with the guerrilla activities of Shining Path. Originally based in the isolated south-central sierra department of Ayacucho and headed by former professors and students from the local University of Huamanga, Shining Path advocated a peasant-based republic forged through revolution. The group's ideology was Marxist-Leninist, based on the principles of Mao and José Carlos Mariátegui, a leading Peruvian intellectual of the 1920s who founded what became the Communist Party of Peru. After some fifteen years of preparation—which included study groups, control of the University of Huamanga, leadership training in China, and work in the Native American peasant-dominated local countryside—Shining Path launched its people's war on the very eve of the May 1980 national election that ended the *docenio* of military rule.

The Belaúnde administration did not take the group seriously for almost three full years. Only in December 1982 did the government declare an emergency zone in the Ayacucho area and send in the military to deal with the problem. By the end of Belaúnde's term over six thousand had perished in the violence, most in 1983 (1,977) and 1984 (3,587); human rights violations had skyrocketed; and over $1 billion in property damage had occurred. A new guerrilla group had appeared as well in 1984, the Lima-originated Tupac Amarú Revolutionary Movement (MRTA), which contributed to popular concerns over the spreading political violence.

These economic and political difficulties substantially weakened popular support for Belaúnde and for the AP in the 1983 municipal elections. In the 1985 presidential vote, the AP candidate was routed, gaining only 6 percent of the total. The largely Marxist United Left party (IU) garnered 21 percent for its candidate, Alfonso Barrantes, and a rejuvenated APRA, with the youthful (thirty-six) Alán García as its standard-bearer, won with 46 percent.

The García victory was doubly historic: After a fifty-five-year struggle APRA had finally gained both the presidency and a majority in both houses of Congress, and for the first time in forty years an elected civilian president handed power over to an elected successor (only the second time since 1912). The 1986 municipal elections also saw substantial APRA gains, including, for the first time ever, the mayorship of Lima.

Alán García's forceful, nationalistic leadership put the international banking community on notice that Peru would be limiting repayments on its debt (now over $14 billion) to 10 percent of export earnings. Domestic initiatives, especially in agriculture, contributed to long-overdue economic growth at rates of 9 percent in 1985 and 7 percent in 1986. But the recovery ran out of steam in 1987. The economy never did recover from the surprise presidential announcement that year nationalizing domestic banks, even though this ill-considered attempt ultimately failed.

The second half of García's term was an unmitigated disaster. Peru suspended all foreign debt repayments, so international credit dried up. Inflation skyrocketed to 1,722 percent in 1988, 2,600 percent in 1989, and 7,650 percent in 1990. The economy declined by more than 20 percent during this period. Political violence, which had ebbed between 1985 and 1987, surged anew. By the end of the García government (1985–1990) casualties exceeded twenty thousand and direct and indirect damages exceeded $14 billion. Total foreign debt with arrearages was over $23 billion. Not surprisingly, García's popularity plummeted from an 80 percent favorable rating early in his term to single digits near the end.

Although rumors abounded of a possible coup, military spokespersons committed their institutions to uphold civilian rule. Parties across the political spectrum competed aggressively for support in the November 1989 municipal elections and the April 1990 presidential and congressional vote. In 1989 the IU divided badly, squandering a historic opportunity. From virtual oblivion Peru's right reemerged, centered on the capacity of the novelist Mario Vargas Llosa to galvanize popular concern over President García's failures. A new coalition, the Democratic Front (FREDEMO), was formed among conservative and centrist parties, including former President Belaúnde's AP, perennial conservative candidate Luis Bedoya Reyes's PPC, and Vargas Llosa's new Liberty Movement. To the surprise of many the Democratic Front captured a plurality of mayoralties in the 1989 municipal elections.

However, Shining Path also used the elections to step up its campaign of violence and terror by killing over a hundred candidates and local officials and intimidating scores of others into resigning. As a result, about 25 percent of Peru's eighteen hundred district and provincial councils could not carry out their elections at all, and the total valid vote cast in the rest was sharply reduced.

In the run-up to the April 1990 national elections, opinion polls made Vargas Llosa the heavy favorite. Many were stunned when another political newcomer, National Agrarian University President Alberto Fujimori, came from less than 3 percent in the polls a month before the vote to finish second with 25 percent (just behind Vargas Llosa, with 28 percent). In June Fujimori won easily in the runoff required of the top two contenders when no one got an absolute majority. His victory was explained as the electoral expression of popular frustration with politics-as-usual. There was also the sense that Vargas Llosa was too removed from the economic hardships suffered by most Peruvians and had become too identified with the politicians of the right.

Once in office President Fujimori launched almost immediately an economic shock program even more severe than that proposed by Vargas Llosa during the campaign. He argued that economic recovery could not be secured until Peru's economic mess had been straightened out and the country's international credit standing restored. In the short run, however, his drastic measures accelerated inflation to historic highs, further reduced domestic economic activity (28 percent in 1990), and pushed several million more Peruvians below the poverty line (to some twelve to fourteen million, or 60 to 70 percent of the population). Congress went along for the most part, even though Fujimori's party grouping, Cambio 90, held only about one quarter of the seats. Most Peruvians also went along as well: Fujimori's level of support in opinion polls remained consistently above 50 percent.

By early 1992 such drastic measures were beginning to produce the desired results. Inflation was sharply reduced (139 percent in 1991). International economic reinsertion was on the verge of being accomplished after monthly payments were resumed to the international financial institutions starting in late 1990 along with regular and extensive negotiations. Signs of economic recovery also began to appear. Beginning in October 1991 the United States increased bilateral economic assistance and initiated its first substantial military aid in over twenty years.

The Peruvian congress was becoming somewhat more restive and assertive, particularly with regard to human rights issues, but did authorize emergency executive-branch decree powers and approve most of the results. Public support had flagged somewhat, from over 70 percent to the mid-50s, still high by international standards. Although political violence continued to be a serious problem (3,745 deaths in 1990 and 3,044 in 1991), government forces had also had some successes against both Shining Path and the MRTA. Given this overall essentially positive panorama, few were prepared for President Fujimori's April 5, 1992, declaration "temporarily suspending" democracy in Peru.

The Autogolpe *and its Aftermath (1992–1993)*

This *autogolpe* (self-coup) drew immediate and almost universal international condemnation. With armed-forces support, Fujimori dissolved Congress, the judiciary, and the general accounting office and began to rule by decree. The United States immediately suspended all assistance save humanitarian and counternarcotics aid. It also used its influence to ensure postponement by the IFIs of Peru's economic reinstatement as well as of new aid by most of the dozen countries making up the Peru Support Group. The Organization of American States (OAS) deplored democracy's suspension, pressed vigorously for its reinstatement, and provided international monitors to oversee and validate new elections.

Fujimori, chastened by the intensity of the international response, agreed immediately to prompt electoral restoration. This was accomplished with national elections for a new, smaller, one-house congress-cum-constitutional-convention in November 1992 and municipal elections in January 1993. The result was a substantially different political dynamic: The traditional parties were largely marginalized, the political process was much more concentrated in the presidency, and Fujimori now had a congressional majority. Furthermore, former President García, Fujimori's bête noire, was forced into exile after the *autogolpe* and lost his leadership role in APRA.

The new constitution was narrowly approved (52–48 percent) by a referendum in October 1993. It recentralized government authority, set the bases for privatization and economic liberalization, provided the death penalty for terrorism, and allowed for the immediate reelection of the sitting president. As the *autogolpe* worked out, then, Fujimori was very much the winner.

However, the April 1992 suspension of democracy could easily have turned out to be a colossal disaster. Suspension of international economic assistance postponed economic recovery in Peru by at least a year. The populace lost access to the political system through its elected congressional representatives. Shining Path moved quickly to expand violent activities and recruitment and began openly predicting that revolutionary victory was imminent.

What saved Fujimori's authoritarian gamble was the careful police work of a small, specialized antiterrorist group in the Ministry of the Interior, formed under García, which paid off with the dramatic capture of Shining Path leader Abimael Guzmán and key lieutenants on September 12, 1992. Several hundred other guerrilla operatives were rounded up in the following weeks, thwarting what was to have been a massive Shining Path offensive to close out the year. To be sure, tougher antiterrorist decrees issued in the aftermath of the *autogolpe* permitted rapid trials in military courts and life terms without parole for some two hundred key figures. However, the sheer good fortune of capturing the bulk of the Shining Path leadership, more than any other development, legitimated the *autogolpe* and gave the Fujimori government the political space to pursue its ambitious national reconstruction agenda.

"Direct Democracy" (1993–2000)

President Fujimori remained in office longer than any elected civilian government in Latin America in recent times. Although his government was accused of multiple machinations to ensure his continuation in office, he also had a broad base of popular support. Such widespread approval came in part from his government's ability to restore economic and political stability to Peru. Inflation virtually ended (dropping from 57 percent in 1992 to 3 percent by 2000). Economic growth was restored (averaging over 7 percent from 1994 through 1997) with economic liberalization and Peru's reinsertion into the international financial community. Between 1993 and 1998 Peru received over $10 billion in new investment and $8 billion in new loans, and signed a Brady Plan with foreign creditors that reduced foreign debt by more than $5 billion (to just under $19 billion by 1997). A variety of innovative local development initiatives reduced poverty by about 20 percent between 1991 and 1997, and eliminated almost 50 percent of extreme poverty. Political violence was dramatically curtailed to levels by 1998 of less than 10 percent of early 1990s levels (or about 300 reported incidents and 150 deaths), a decline that continued to the end of Fujimori's presidency.

Under Fujimori's administrations there was a major revamping of the bureaucracy, which included the creation of multiple new agencies focused on development centered in the Ministry of the Presidency. Many of these agencies concentrated on poverty reduction programs, especially in the poorest districts of the country. Largely due to these activities extreme poverty declined from 31 percent to 15 percent between 1991 and 1998, and overall poverty declined from about half the population to two fifths. In addition, the infusion of modest new resources at the local community level (most projects were limited to a maximum total expenditure of $6,000 apiece) also contributed to the creation of many new local organizations to administer the projects.

Over the course of the Fujimori decade, political parties were further undermined by a combination of government initiatives and their own limitations. Independent groups, including the president's own, proliferated and dominated the 1995 national elections and the 1995 and 1998 municipal votes. No traditional party except for APRA received more than 5 percent of the vote in the 1995 national elections, a dramatic turnaround from the 1980s.

After an overwhelming mandate in 1995, with 64 percent of the valid vote and a majority in congress as well, President Fujimori called for "direct democracy without parties or intermediaries." His administration worked to make this happen by increasing expenditures for local development projects and by providing direct monthly stipends to municipal governments. His government also changed the political rules, often arbitrarily and unconstitutionally, to make it difficult to rebuild a robust political party system and to undermine the opposition's attempts to mount an effective electoral campaign.

The media and the opposition were also intimidated through wiretaps, physical assault, and character assassination campaigns that were orchestrated by the Peruvian National Intelligence System (SIN) and directed by Fujimori's closest ally and confidant, Vladimiro Montesinos. President Fujimori thwarted a national referendum in 1998 on the issue of a third term, for which

1.4 million signatures had been secured, by having his congressional majority vote not to accept its validity. Obviously direct democracy, as actually carried out, was being defined selectively to include programs that were perceived to benefit the Fujimori government and to exclude those that might pose a risk to its continued dominance. At the same time many of the programs carried out in its name served to lift Peru's poorest out of the most abject poverty.

Having set up the electoral machinery and procedures in his favor, President Fujimori surprised no one by deciding to run for a third, constitutionally dubious term in the national elections of 2000. Unlike what had occurred in 1995, however, he came close (with over 49 percent of the valid vote) but did not secure an absolute majority in the first round, nor did his supporters win a majority in Congress. He was forced into a runoff with second-place finisher Alejandro Toledo, a U.S.-educated economist from a humble indigenous background but without political experience. The best efforts of the international community, led by the OAS Election Observer Mission, to ensure a free and fair voting process for the runoff were not successful. Toledo withdrew in protest, international and domestic official observers declined to oversee the vote, and the incumbent won with 52 percent of the valid vote (about one-third of all ballots cast were spoiled in protest).

Events soon revealed the Pyrrhic quality of this 2000 electoral "victory." Inaugurated amidst massive protest and tear gas in July, Fujimori was gone by November. Precipitating his downfall was the videotaped revelation that his closest partner in the re-reelection project, SIN director Montesinos, was bribing elected representatives of the opposition to ensure a pro-Fujimori majority in congress. In spite of President Fujimori's desperate moves to maintain control—including firing and forcing Montesinos into exile and calling for early elections in which he would not be a candidate—popular indignation overwhelmed his maneuverings. By early November opposition parties and groupings had regained control of Congress. They refused to accept Fujimori's letter of resignation from Japan, where he had fled in ignominy, but declared the presidency vacant instead on grounds of "moral incapacity." A transitional government led by the next in line for chief of state, president of congress and long-time AP representative Valentín Paniagua, took the oath of office on November 22. Fujimori's "direct democracy," for all of its accomplishments, ended in disgrace.

Full-But-Troubled Democracy (2000–Present)

The Paniagua interim presidency (2000–2001), though only nine months in duration, was surprisingly effective in righting the ship of state and putting it back on course. Amidst multiple new revelations of official misdoing during the Fujimori years, scores of former high level civilian and military leaders were tracked down and arrested for corruption and abuse of position, including Montesinos himself from his refuge in Venezuela. A Truth and Reconciliation Commission was established to document the human rights abuses committed by police, military, and Shining Path alike during the "people's war." Attempts to bring Fujimori back from exile in Japan to face Peruvian justice were unsuccessful, however, as it turned out that he had Japanese citizenship and could not be extradited.

New elections in April 2001 were as free and fair as those of 2000 were tainted. A hard-fought first round between Lourdes Flores Nano of National Unity (UN) on the right, and Toledo of Peru Possible (PP) and APRA's García on the center-left saw Toledo (with 37 percent of the vote) and García (with 26 percent) edge out Flores (24 percent) for the runoff. Here, García's efforts to cast himself as a wiser and more experienced leader fell short. Toledo, who had led the opposition to Fujimori in the aftermath of the 2000 electoral debacle, won with 54 percent of the vote, though his PP party had only a minority in congress.

The Toledo presidency (2001–2006) stumbled politically from the start. Almost as soon as he took office in July, he faced a plethora of demands—ranging from opposition to privatization, to seeking a greater share of foreign corporate taxes, to ending coca eradication—from an array of local organizations in department capitals, which his government handled badly in almost every case. Amidst violence and property damage, promises were made and not kept, decisions reached and reversed, and new programs announced but not funded. The president's disorganization, his libertine personal life, his assertive if talented Belgian wife, and the controversial personal advisors and family members who surrounded him all contributed to growing popular disillusionment with his administration. Toledo's popularity declined to single digits for much of his five-year mandate, even in the context of renewed and sustained economic growth, and rumors were rife of an early resignation.

However tainted Toledo's presidency, there was never a perception that Peruvian democracy itself would collapse. Attention has turned to the 2006 elections, with leading candidates all well-known figures from the past: García and APRA, Flores and UN, Paniagua and AP, and even Fujimori himself. The military, still recovering from the scandals of the Fujimori era and still trying to regain a semblance of institutional unity and coherence, shows no signs of political restiveness. Imperfect and incomplete, democracy remains the only political show in Peru.

Social and Political Groups

Organized social and political groups have played less of a role in Peruvian affairs than in most other Latin American countries until quite recently. The reasons may be traced in part to the strong patterns of Spanish domination that inhibited growth long after the formal Spanish presence was removed. What emerged instead was a strong sense of individualism within the context of region and family for that small portion of the total population that was actually included within the nation's political system.

In the decades following independence governments were made and unmade by regional *caudillos* or officials whose power was based on control of arms, personal appeal, and family or regional ties. The best lands were increasingly controlled by non-Indo-Americans, who took advantage of post-independence decrees and constitutions that removed Indo-Americans and their preserves from state protection. The Church also lost some of its land-based financial strength, and *beneficencias* (private beneficent societies) took over the ownership and administration of many church properties. Thus, political and economic power was quite fragmented in nineteenth-century Peru. The disastrous War of the Pacific abruptly ended the beginnings of economic consolidation that had been based on the guano export boom.

With the establishment of limited civilian democracy between 1895 and 1919, some of what were to become the country's most important interest groups were founded, including the National Agrarian Society (SNA), the National Mining Society (SNM), and the National Industrial Society (SNI). However, for a long time the important decisions affecting the country were usually made in the Club Nacional, formed much earlier (1855) and the lone survivor of post-1968 reforms. Even the military operated between 1914 and 1962 largely as the "watchdog of the oligarchy." Thus, elites could determine policy outside the electoral arena when necessary and had limited incentives to operate within any party system.

The changes produced by the reform military governments of 1968 to 1980 overturned the old elites and gave rise to opportunities for new sets of social actors through the rapid expansion of various types of "local units of participation." These included various cooperative forms in agriculture, neighborhood associations in the squatter settlements, and worker self-management communities in industry and mining. At their peak in the late 1970s these entities incorporated as many as eight hundred thousand workers.

Such a proliferation of local-participation organizations gave the military government the advantage of providing an alternative for citizen participation at the level of workplace and residence at a time when normal participation by political parties at the national level was cut off. Although the benefits of membership in local-participation organizations were often significant, most members were by and large from the working-class elite. Because growth of these enterprises was predicated on profit generation, and because economic conditions in most years since 1975 have not favored such growth, these organizations never developed as expected.

Responsibility for organizing, coordinating, and controlling citizen participation was entrusted after 1971 to the National Social Mobilization Support System (SINAMOS), initially an "umbrella" agency incorporating several other government agencies, most of whose top leadership positions were held by military officers. As SINAMOS became operative, its regional offices became a focal point of opposition to government policies, and some offices were sacked and burned in 1973 and 1975. These disturbances showed the limits of popular support for the government. As a result of a conflict between the national police and the military large groups of citizens took to the streets of Lima and several provincial capitals and engaged in massive looting and burning sprees with antigovernment overtones. These events were a key precipitant of the August 1975 coup, and SINAMOS itself was phased out in 1978.

With the restoration of civilian rule in 1980 parties and unions regained their roles as transmitters of their members' concerns to government authorities, largely supplanting the structure so laboriously fashioned by the military regime. Vigorous political participation through a score of parties covering the entire ideological spectrum characterized the 1980s, with power alternating between center-right and center-left groups at the national executive level and substantial representation in congress by the Marxist left. In municipal elections all major political organizations won their share of cities and towns at different times, with pluralities shifting from AP to IU to APRA and back to IU. An unanticipated legacy of long-term reformist military rule, then, was to usher in a historically unprecedented level of partisan politics, institutionalized to a degree that few people foresaw and proceeding apace in spite of profound domestic economic difficulties and a substantial guerrilla movement.

However, with the breakup of IU in 1988–1989 and widespread popular disappointment with party politics as successive elected governments failed to respond to citizen needs, political independents came to dominate national and local elections in the 1990s, and union membership and influence declined. Fujimori's 1990 election and the widely supported 1992 *autogolpe* reflected the shift to "antiparty" politics in Peru. So, too, did the independent-dominated 1992 congressional/constitutional assembly elections and the 1993 local elections, which served together to restore formal democracy. One result, then, was the progressive deinstitutionalization of electoral politics in Peru and a return to more personalistic approaches at the center, as well as to a dramatic increase of popular organizations at the local level seeking to satisfy their needs and demands in the newly available political space.

These new social actors included neighborhood or community improvement groups, mothers' clubs, coca growers' associations, and school-parent organizations. Although they were usually focused on gaining official responses to immediate needs or perceived abuses, some also expressed concerns based on ethnic identification. With weakened parties and unions and new locally-directed government and nongovernmental organization programs, such newly mobilized groups filled an important role in articulating citizen demands to improve local conditions.

Over the course of Peruvian political history elections have tended to be intermittent and tentative, and electoral restrictions kept most Peruvians out of the national political arena. Property ownership requirements were not lifted until 1931, when the secret ballot was also introduced. Women were not enfranchised until 1956, and a literacy requirement remained in effect until the advent of universal suffrage in 1980.

The political party scene in Peru is quite fragmented. Furthermore, it is dominated by personalism across the entire ideological spectrum. AP split into pro- and anti-Belaúnde factions, although it came back together with the Belaúnde victory in 1980, only to divide again after 1985. APRA divided after the death of Haya de la Torre in 1979, but the progressive faction regained control after the election of Haya's protégé, Alán García, as party head in 1982 and president in 1985. The García government's problems after 1987 contributed to new divisions within APRA. A small but influential Christian Democratic party (DC) also divided into a tiny leftist faction allied with IU and a larger conservative group (PPC), which formed part of FREDEMO between 1988 and 1992 but reclaimed its independent status after that alliance collapsed.

The Marxist political movement founded by Mariátegui became the Communist Party of Peru (PCP), which retained its Moscow-oriented core while fragmenting almost endlessly into Maoist, Castroite, and Trotskyite splinters. All shared pieces of equally divided urban and rural union movements, although the PCP controlled the largest portion (about 75 percent). With economic crises and economic liberalization initiatives, union organizations have declined from about 30 percent of the formal workforce in the early 1980s to less than 10 percent two decades later.

The public prominence of Shining Path after 1980 and its recourse to guerrilla tactics evoked an almost universally negative response from Peru's Marxist left; most of the Communist movement was not inclined to pursue its goals through violence. When most of its members were joined (however loosely) in the IU during the 1980s, the Communists were the second largest political force in terms of electoral support (peaking in the 1986 municipal elections at 31 percent of the total vote). The rise of an organized left operating within rather than outside the political system was one of the positive legacies of the military *docenio*, but IU's breakup in 1989 sharply reduced the role of the left in national politics after 1990.

During the 1990s Peru's parties became even more divided and numerous. In part this was because those that exercised power in the 1980s did it badly, thus discrediting them in the view of most of the public. In part it was because party leadership continued to place personal over institutional concerns. It was also the result of the adroit manipulation of new political rules and procedures by Fujimori governments in which weak new political groups were encouraged over strong parties. In 1995 fourteen groups contended for the presidency and twenty for Congress, with traditional parties capturing less than 15 percent of the valid vote, a pattern repeated with twelve contenders in 2000. The 1998 municipal elections consisted largely of "flash" parties that functioned only for the vote itself, with eighty-nine of ninety-four Lima districts and department capitals won by candidates from these groups. The orientation of politics toward personalities rather than organizations favored the most visible political personality, President Fujimori himself.

Even with his departure, however, the party system has remained weak, particularly at the local election level, where flash parties continue to dominate. Although transitional president Paniagua demonstrated that traditional parties were capable of playing a positive role, his successor has presided over a new party group (PP) that epitomizes the personality-driven and weak organizational nature that has come to characterize most political organizations in Peru. Nevertheless, in the run-up to the 2006 elections there are signs of revival for the older and more established parties, perhaps in part a reaction to the chaotic Toledo/PP style of governance. Three of the leading contenders represent such organizations (APRA, AP, and UN—incorporating the old PPC). However, it is still not clear that a more stable party-dominated political system can be restored.

Government Machinery

The Peruvian government of most of the twentieth century may be characterized as small, centralized, and personalistic. Until the 1960s government employees constituted a very small proportion of the workforce and were usually selected on the basis of party affiliation, family ties, or friendship. Ministry bureaucracies were concentrated in Lima. Government presence in the provinces was limited to prefects and their staffs, military garrisons in border areas, small detachments of national police, schoolteachers, and a few judges, all appointed by authorities in Lima.

A government monopoly of the guano industry and of tobacco, matches, and salt marketing were among the few official ventures before 1960. Until the 1960s the central bank was privately controlled, and even government taxes were collected by private agencies. Within the government the executive branch predominated. During periods when congress was functioning, however, the executive's authority was subject to numerous checks, including congress's powers to interrogate and censure ministers and to appropriate funds.

The government's size and scope increased considerably during the first Belaúnde administration, especially in new government agencies: for example, provincial development corporations, a national housing agency, a domestic peace corps (Cooperación Popular), a national planning institute, a cooperative organization, and squatter settlement organizations. Total government employment increased from 179,000 in 1960 (6 percent of the workforce) to 270,000 in 1967 (7 percent of the workforce). The public sector's share of the gross domestic product grew from 8 percent to 11 percent during the same period.

However, the most dramatic changes in the size and scope of the state machinery occurred between 1968 and 1980. The military regime pursued a nationalistic ideology advancing the virtue of government involvement to accelerate development. Most existing ministries were reorganized, and numerous new ministries and autonomous agencies were created. By 1973 total government employment had increased by almost 50 percent over 1967 figures to 401,000 (9 percent of the workforce) and by 1975 to an estimated 450,000 (11 percent of the workforce). The public sector's share of the gross domestic product doubled between 1967 and 1975 to 22 percent.

Although a great deal of attention was given to the need to decentralize government to make it more accessible to a larger share of the population, in practice central government activities remained as concentrated in Lima as they had been historically. Budget increases tended to go toward construction, equipment, and white-collar employment in the capital rather than for activities in the provinces.

The political and financial crises of 1975 and the change of government brought to an end the dynamic phase of public sector reforms. Resource limitations, growing popular opposition, and the inability of the military regime to act effectively to implement its own decrees prevented full implementation of the corporatist model articulated between 1971 and 1975. However, the 1979 constitution, drawn up by an APRA-IU majority, retained the statist orientation of the Peruvian political system even as it set the basis for civilian rule.

With the return to democracy in 1980, President Belaúnde announced his intention to restore the dynamism of the private sector and to reduce the role of government. Continuing economic problems and substantial public resistance made these changes difficult to carry out. The García government moved quickly to implement long-standing APRA decentralization goals, including regional development corporations, expanded agricultural credit, and regional legislatures, while working simultaneously to win the confidence of domestic entrepreneurs. Initial successes were substantial. However, by the end of García's term they had been overwhelmed by an ill-advised nationalization of domestic banks and Peru's worst economic crisis in one hundred years. Central government employment expanded from six hundred thousand employees in 1985 to one million in 1990, but with half the budget.

The Fujimori administration, after implementing drastic shock measures to stop Peru's economic hemorrhaging, began to move the country toward economic liberalization. This process involved selling off state enterprises created or nationalized under the 1968–1980 military regimes, retiring tens of thousands of government employees and reorganizing ministries to be able to dismiss thousands more, and overhauling the legal framework to favor private property and investment. Tax collection was also overhauled, so that government began to be able to pay its own way again. Collections increased from less than 4 percent of GDP in 1989 to 14 percent by 1995. Over the course of the 1990s over one hundred former state agencies were privatized, generating around $8 billion in new foreign investment. The 1993 constitution incorporated these changes but also further concentrated power in the presidency and in central government rather than regional or local governments. New government agencies, several designed to emphasize microdevelopment projects in Peru's poorest districts, began to operate in the early 1990s. Overall, government did not become smaller during the Fujimori years of the 1990s; however, it was dramatically changed and reorganized.

The Toledo government ended some of the Fujimori regime's government agencies and reorganized others, but also reduced their efficiency through political patronage. It also embarked on a new decentralization initiative in 2003–2004, with elections of officials at the department level for the first time along with greater local taxing authority. While this new level of regional government authority may serve to deflect popular pressure away from central government, it remains to be seen whether or not this latest experiment in decentralization, unlike President García's initiative, can be effective.

Public Policy

Historically, public policy in Peru may be characterized as limited. Laissez-faire liberalism applied from the 1890s up to 1968 with few exceptions. Most services were privately owned and the government's role was normally that of facilitator or expediter for the private sector, including foreign enterprises.

Unlike many Latin American countries Peru did not respond to the challenge of the world depression after 1929 by sharp increases in public services and enterprise. This difference resulted from the simultaneous challenge to elites posed by APRA, with its advocacy of sharply expanded state control. By successfully keeping APRA from power in the 1930s elites also retained a limited state. By the time APRA finally entered the political arena as a legitimate force in 1956 its position on the role of the state was much more accommodating to elite interests.

The electoral campaigns of 1961–1962 and 1962–1963 raised more explicitly the need for a greater public sector role. The ultimate winners, AP and Belaúnde, worked actively between 1963 and 1968 to make the state a more dynamic force and to create a climate of increased popular expectations regarding what the state could and should do.

Between 1968 and 1980 the military government served as the major force for an unprecedented expansion of the state. Such rapid expansion posed challenges of its own, and in trying to do so much so quickly the government spread itself too thin. Although providing new job opportunities for the middle class, the rapidly expanding bureaucracy often had difficulty delivering promised goods and services, especially in outlying provinces. Official announcements and periodic flurries of activity raised expectations and often turned government offices into "lightning rods" for popular demands that could not be met. Growing economic resource limitations compounded the problems.

The 1968 expropriation of the International Petroleum Company put all on notice that the military government was serious about its reform objectives. This action served to unite the armed forces around the goal of establishing the legitimacy of the new regime with the citizenry. It also demonstrated to the U.S. government and foreign investors that Peru would no longer accept the degree of foreign influence that had prevailed in the country up to that point. Other expropriations of important foreign investments also took place, but with compensation. New outside investment was welcomed under stricter regulation and occurred principally in copper mining and oil exploration. Foreign loans were avidly sought and were acquired at record levels.

Thus, even while adopting a radical posture in foreign economic relations the military government recognized the necessity of continued foreign loans and investments to help accomplish national development goals. However, such heavy international borrowing after 1971, in part a result of the reluctance of the domestic private sector to invest in spite of generous incentives, came back to haunt the government. Prices for some Peruvian exports declined markedly, domestic production of others also declined, and optimistic forecasts concerning probable oil exports proved erroneous. A severe financial crisis resulted between 1975 and 1977. Consequently, many development objectives were compromised, and the very legitimacy of the regime came into question.

Subsequent civilian governments have had to face many of the same problems. Although no new nationalizations occurred under Belaúnde, efforts to sell some enterprises back into private hands and to encourage new foreign investment were largely thwarted by domestic depression, international recession, and large debt-repayment responsibilities. The García administration adopted a much more nationalistic and government-activist posture, with debt repayments tied to export earnings and some nationalizations, among other measures. However, over the last half of APRA rule the economic crisis overshadowed other policy priorities and discredited statist approaches to development.

Fujimori's government, coming to power at a time of unprecedented economic and political problems, succeeded in reversing the twenty-five-year trend toward larger government in Peru. Privatization and economic liberalization became the watchwords of the 1990s and contributed to the resumption of economic growth after 1993. Even though government did not become smaller in the 1990s, it was substantially reorganized, even "reinvented"; during these years the private sector also expanded markedly. Popular protest, however, has thwarted most efforts by the Toledo administration to continue the privatization process. Even so, it has not reversed changes already introduced.

The agrarian reform of 1969 was the most far-reaching of all the military government's policy initiatives. However, without enough arable land to go around, the majority of the needy farmers did not benefit. The better-off coastal farmers received most of the reform's redistributive benefits, and the central government's major effort in the more isolated sierra was too little and too late. Part of the continuing problem is the center's limited ability to affect the periphery, even with the best of intentions. As a result many cooperative enterprises in the sierra never operated effectively, which contributed to a move back to private ownership in the 1980s.

A byproduct of the reform was a serious decline in agricultural production, which was overcome only partially by the Belaúnde government's sharp reduction in food subsidies and the resulting increase in food prices after 1980. The García administration sharply expanded agricultural credit until 1988, thus helping to boost production. However, the same agrarian reform problems that led Belaúnde to reprivatize a large number of the agricultural cooperatives also contributed to the ability of Shining Path to expand its influence in the more marginal Indian highlands. From the elections of 1980 onward the sections of Peru with the highest levels of blank and spoiled votes and abstention rates were these very areas: Ayacucho, Apurímac, and Huancavelica in particular.

Although the threat posed by Shining Path has passed, the farmers of the Peruvian sierra in particular still lack access to credit and technical assistance to be able to modernize, a problem that neither Fujimori nor Toledo took steps to address. As a result of central government neglect in a part of the country that continues to have most of the farm population engaged in traditional, usually subsistence agriculture, the population remains predominantly poor and marginalized. The outward migration to the cities (over one hundred thousand per year), that has resulted from a combination of guerrilla violence in the 1980s and early 1990s and continuing limited economic possibilities, poses multiple challenges for a country endemically deficient in new employment opportunities.

Official combined unemployment and underemployment figures have ebbed and flowed between 50 and 80 percent of the economically active population. Overall real-wage statistics show a similarly variable pattern, with some improvement during the first half of the García administration, followed by precipitous erosion over the next five years. Without the dynamic informal sector, an array of economic activities outside official purview and measurement, the average Peruvian might be even worse off. Estimates suggest that about 60 percent of the nation's economy and two-thirds of the jobs are to be found in this sector. These figures do not include up to three hundred thousand peasant families who live off the coca and cocaine-paste industry, concentrated in the 1980s and early 1990s in the Huallaga valley 250 miles northeast of Lima. Peru was until the late 1990s the world's largest producer of coca leaf (60–65 percent), the raw material for cocaine. Recently supplanted by Colombia, Peru still produces about one-third of all coca leaf grown.

Inflation undermined the economic foundations of Peru during the five-year García presidency with a staggering 2,000,000 percent cumulative increase. By 1993 the annual inflation rate was down to 39 percent, the lowest since 1977. Inflation levels ever since have ceased to be a problem for Peru, averaging 3 percent or less since the late 1990s. Economic growth returned as well, averaging over 7 percent between 1994 and 1997, and after a late 1990s recession back to 3 to 6 percent growth between 2001 and 2005.

What the Fujimori government was able to do in the public policy arena over the decade of the 1990s, whatever its failings as a democracy, was to restore a viable state that was able to respond effectively to the unprecedented set of problems that faced Peru when Fujimori first took office. Most particularly, his administrations eliminated inflation, restored economic growth, reduced levels of political violence, and developed multiple small programs for the neediest sectors of the population. Although many challenges remained, Peru at the millennium once again had a government that worked. The Toledo administration inherited a reasonably well functioning state and, unlike his predecessor, has operated democratically. However, his government has by and large been unable to build on this base, largely because of ineffectual leadership at the highest levels.

Foreign Affairs

Historically, Peru's foreign relations have been conditioned by boundary disputes, diverse natural resources, domestic political and economic objectives, and the Humboldt Current. From independence on, boundaries were a matter of dispute and a prime motivator of Peruvian diplomacy. Wars and armed conflicts have occasionally broken out. In the south the loss of nitrate-rich Tarapacá and Arica to Chile in the War of the Pacific (1879–1883), ratified by the Tacna-Arica Treaty (1929), has conditioned relations with Bolivia and Chile for over a century and has given a certain defensive dimension to foreign policy. In the north Peru ceded Leticia to Colombia in 1932, an unpopular move, but successfully pursued a brief war with Ecuador in 1941 to assert its historic claim to substantial lands in the northeastern Amazon basin. Although Ecuador signed the Rio Protocol of 1942 accepting the new frontier, officials renounced it in 1960. Armed clashes have broken out periodically ever since and have required the good offices of the Rio Protocol guarantor powers (Argentina, Chile, Brazil, and the United States) to try to resolve them.

Peru's natural resources are numerous and diverse. They include sugar, cotton, rice, fish and fish products, and minerals such as copper, iron ore, natural gas, gold, silver, and oil. Such diversity has often served to protect Peru from the uncertainties of international markets and from being objects of foreign investments. Peru joined forces with Ecuador and Chile as early as 1952 to proclaim a two-hundred-mile territorial limit in ocean waters, a claim to the rich fishing of the Humboldt Current, that eventually worked its way into international law in the 1970s as a two-hundred-mile economic zone. The Peruvian government was also a driving force behind the Andean Pact, begun in 1969 to expand markets, diversify trade, and apply common foreign-investment criteria among the Andean countries. Economic nationalism joined political nationalism as a major component of Peruvian foreign policy for most of the period between 1968 and 1990. This resulted in expanded state control of previous foreign holdings in agriculture, mining, and fishing and closer regulation of remaining or new enterprises.

The military government's stated objective in international affairs from 1968 to 1980 was the elimination of dependency, a call also taken to heart by the APRA administration of Alán García from 1985 to 1990. This goal led to Peru's taking a number of steps to alter its international position to at least diversify—if not end—its dependence. These steps included new trade and diplomatic relationships with the socialist bloc and conscious diversification of Peru's trade, investment, and loan assistance so as not to rely on a just a few sources as in the past. These policies continued during the Belaúnde administration and may have helped for a time to keep the severe economic problems from becoming even worse. García pursued a more nationalistic strategy, which contributed to economic growth in 1986 and 1987 before developing into a new, more severe crisis between 1988 and 1993.

Beginning with the 1968 military takeover, Peru attempted to strengthen its developing-nation position. It took on an important leadership role among the Third World nonaligned countries. Unfortunately, Peru's struggle to diversify its dependence and to achieve a position of Third World leadership was seriously compromised by the country's growing economic difficulties after 1975. In 1978, 1982, and 1984 Peruvian governments were forced to accept stringent IMF conditions for the continuance of economic and loan assistance.

Beginning with Alán García's inaugural address in July 1985, however, Peru committed itself to an independent debt-repayment position. By the end of 1987 Peru was in arrears to governments, international agencies, and foreign private banks; by the end of 1988 economic nationalism had contributed to producing Peru's most severe domestic economic crisis in over a hundred years. The elected reformist APRA government found itself as constrained by international forces as its reformist military predecessor, in spite of equally strenuous efforts to break with past patterns and move Peru along a more independent course in the foreign affairs arena.

Domestic factors interfered with this goal as well. In June 1986 President García hosted the annual meeting of the Socialist International (SI) in a bid to reassert Peru's independent reformist credentials. However, a Shining Path assassination attempt on the Peruvian president during the meeting, followed almost immediately by a coordinated prison uprising of jailed guerrillas, brutally repressed with almost three hundred inmate deaths, thoroughly embarrassed the Peruvian head of state and dashed any hopes García held for SI leadership.

The combination of deep domestic economic crisis and changing international realities contributed to a dramatic shift in Peru's foreign economic policies in the 1990s. Privatization and economic liberalization opened the country once again to private investment. Economic nationalism receded rapidly as a cornerstone of Peru's foreign relations. Over the 1990s scores of public enterprises were privatized, tariffs slashed, foreign debt repayments resumed, and legal foundations for private investment restored. Foreign investment more than doubled, from about $4 billion in 1993 to over $9 billion in 1998. Peru led efforts to reconstitute the Andean Pact as the Andean Group on terms much more favorable to private sector activity. The international financial community became a major source of government development programs once again. Although foreign debt increased to over $30 billion by 1998, with scheduled repayments running at about half of export earnings, most specialists continued to see Peru as a good credit risk.

Perhaps Peru's most significant foreign policy success in recent decades was the successful negotiation with Ecuador of a definitive border settlement in 1998. The Peru-Ecuador boundary dispute had been the longest standing in Latin America, and had provoked almost two dozen armed clashes between the countries since the Rio Protocol signing and ratification in 1942. The most violent was the major confrontation between January and March 1995, costing over $1 billion and causing hundreds of casualties.

Negotiations could proceed under the Rio Protocol aegis, unlike some previous clashes, because Ecuador once again accepted its jurisdiction. However, the negotiations were arduous and slow. Only after three and a half years were the heads of states of both countries able to reach an agreement, and only with the arbitration of the guarantors. The final border became the one agreed to in 1942, but with Ecuador having access to and private ownership of a symbolic square kilometer of territory at Tiwinza, an area of fierce fighting in 1995. The agreement also included a separate treaty of navigation and commerce for Ecuador on the Amazon and its tributaries and a commitment by the Inter-American Development bank (IADB) and the World Bank (WB) to some $3 billion in border integration and development projects.

The role of U.S. public and private participation in Peru has always been quite complex. Private investment grew rapidly in the early twentieth century but was almost exclusively in isolated enclaves on the north coast (oil and sugar, later cotton and fish meal) and in the sierra (copper, other minerals, later iron). Successive governments encouraged such investment. Even during the military *docenio*, in spite of some expropriations and a conscious attempt to diversify sources of foreign investment, substantial new U.S. investment took place, particularly in copper (Southern Peru Copper Company) and oil exploration and production (Occidental Petroleum Company).

The Belaúnde government's policy toward private investment was more open but only partly successful owing to international and domestic economic problems. The García administration's nationalistic posture in a context of growing economic and political difficulties discouraged most new investment, domestic or foreign, between 1985 and 1990. Fujimori's shift to privatization and economic liberalization began slowly, given Peru's grave problems, but gathered momentum beginning in 1993 with several hundred million dollars in portfolio and direct investments. Between 1993 and 1998 over one hundred public enterprises were privatized and over $6 billion in new foreign investment generated. Spanish investment was the largest, with $2.4 of the $9.8 billion total as of 1998; U.S. second, with $1.6 billion; and British third, with $1.2 billion.

However one may debate the issue of foreign dependence, U.S. investment and loans in Peru before 1930 served to balance the country's extreme reliance on Great Britain. The enclave nature of this assistance had both positive and negative impacts: reduction of economic-ripple effects on the rest of the Peruvian economy, provision of islands of relative economic privilege for workers in which unions could become established, and creation of small areas of virtual foreign hegemony within Peru.

With growing economic nationalism in Peru in the 1960s the U.S. government collaborated closely with U.S. businesses to try to work out solutions satisfactory to U.S. interests. The IPC case between 1963 and 1968 illustrates this policy in the extreme. One basis for Peru's desire to expropriate IPC rested on well-founded claims that the concessions giving Standard Oil of New Jersey subsoil rights in La Brea y Parinas (near Talara) in 1921 and 1922 were illegal. The U.S. government supported Standard Oil's position, and when negotiations bogged down periodically, U.S. government foreign assistance and loans under the Alliance for Progress were interrupted. The Belaúnde government, under duress, finally struck a bargain with the company, but the controversial terms generated public debate and turmoil and provided the immediate precipitant for the 1968 coup.

Within a week after taking power the military nationalized IPC. This and subsequent periodic expropriations kept most new official U.S. aid suspended between 1968 and 1972, except for relief and rehabilitation assistance after a 1970 earthquake. Eventually, the military regime found itself obliged to resolve expropriations with financial settlements that companies considered fair, in part as a result of U.S. government pressure but also because the Peruvian government wanted and needed continued foreign private investment and loans.

Historically, the U.S. government presence in Peru was not a large one. Starting in 1938, however, because of U.S. security concerns with international fascism in the hemisphere, and after World War II with international communism, the U.S. government has been a major actor. Between 1945 and 1975 grants and loans to Peru totaled $1.107 billion, of which $194 million was military assistance. Aid funds during Belaúnde's first term, when available, went primarily for projects in marginal sectors the opposition-controlled Peruvian congress was unwilling to fund. A large-scale civic action program for the military in the 1960s helped shape officers' views on the national development mission of the Peruvian armed forces. The U.S. government's refusal to permit the sale of jet fighters to Peru in 1967 also shaped the armed forces' perspectives. This action helped Peruvian officers realize that their own welfare, as well as that of their country, would be enhanced by diversifying their sources of supply and, hence, their dependence as well.

Actions and reactions by both Peruvian and U.S. governments since 1968—including aid and loan cutoffs, the expulsion of most of the large U.S. military mission, and the end of the Peace Corps presence until its small-scale renewal in 2003—considerably lowered the official U.S. profile in the country. García's prickly relationship with the United States limited U.S. programs to modest economic aid and drug interdiction and eradication assistance. Between 1973 and 1990 Peru had a substantial military sales and assistance relationship with the Soviet Union, in excess of $1 billion. This included the training in Peru and in the Eastern bloc of several hundred army and air force personnel each year, and up to a hundred Soviet advisers in Peru.

In October 1991 U.S. government offers to increase economic and military assistance substantially after Fujimori's election as part of the counter-drug Andean Initiative began to be implemented. All but humanitarian and some counter-narcotics aid were suspended by the United States, however, after Fujimori's April 1992 *autogolpe*. Continuing concerns over human rights violations delayed aid restoration after democratic forms were reinstated in 1993. Gradually, however, U.S. aid to Peru increased over the decade to a level averaging over $100 million per year, mainly for programs in development, democracy, counter-narcotics, and food assistance.

The U.S. role in counter-drug programs in Peru since the mid-1990s has been controversial. Funds for eradication and alternative development have had an impact on cocaine production, but interdiction of planes that appeared to be transporting drugs was suspended after a U.S. missionary's plane was mistakenly shot down in 1999. During the latter years of the increasingly undemocratic Fujimori administration, U.S. policy favored counterdrug activity over pressure to maintain democratic practice. With the Toledo government, continuing counternarcotics activity has contributed to significant increases in organized resistance by coca growers, posing additional challenges for Peruvian authorities.

Conclusions

Peru as an independent nation has had great difficulty in overcoming its authoritarian legacy. About three-fourths of the time nondemocratic governments have ruled the country. The Spanish colonial heritage was an important factor impeding the evolution of liberal-democratic institutions in the nineteenth century. Additional considerations, including international market forces, the incorporation of more and more of the population into the national political and economic system, and political leadership perceptions and actions, prevented the emergence of a stable institutional structure in the twentieth century.

The reformist military governments of 1968 to 1980 tried but failed to construct a new participatory model of community-based politics and a new economic model based on a leading role for the state. Their failure was based on their inability to appreciate the boundaries within which reformers must operate to accomplish development objectives, in particular the degree to which political leaders in a country like Peru are hemmed in by forces largely beyond their control. The full electoral democracy established in 1980 began with great enthusiasm and promise, but soon fell prey to some of the same problems that had undermined its authoritarian predecessors. It also had to cope with Latin America's most radical and violent guerrilla organization, the Shining Path, and handled that challenge poorly as well. Once again, a combination of circumstances and political leadership predispositions led over time to the dismantling of democracy in 1992, with Fujimori's *autogolpe*.

President Fujimori succeeded where his civilian predecessors had failed by pursuing a new strategy to deal with Shining Path and by implementing a new economic liberalization model that ended hyperinflation and restored economic growth. These successes gave him the popular support necessary to set up a new political system under the constitution of 1993.

This system contained democratic forms and procedures, but numerous mechanisms as well that gave untoward control to the head of state. Although many new government agencies and programs worked to benefit the less privileged at the periphery, the quality of democracy and democratic discourse in the center was progressively eroded. Parties became little more than personalist vehicles. Most of the media were cowed. Opponents were often harassed and intimidated. Peru became a prime example in Latin America of a government that manipulates democratic procedures to ensure its own continuance in power. The result was democratic in form but authoritarian in substance, Peru's latest manifestation of its long authoritarian tradition.

President Toledo represents the restoration of open democracy in Peru, the product of a combination of growing hubris by Fujimori, Montesinos, and key cohorts within business, military, and police, and a remarkable outpouring of popular indignation. Nevertheless, democratic practice since 2001 has become increasingly chaotic and problematic, even in the midst of sustained economic growth. The 2006 elections will represent another opportunity for Peruvian political leaders to regain the faith of the citizenry by reconstituting the effectiveness of the state that came to characterize the Fujimori years, but within a fully democratic order. Only time will tell if they are up to the task.

Suggestions for Further Reading

Cameron, Maxwell A. and Philip Mauceri, eds. *The Peruvian Labyrinth: Polity, Society, Economy*. University Park: Pennsylvania State University Press, 1997.

Clayton, Lawrence A. *Peru and the United States: The Condor and the Eagle*. Athens: University of Georgia Press, 1999.

Dietz, Henry A. *Urban Poverty, Political Participation, and the State: Lima 1970–1990*. Pittsburgh: University of Pittsburgh Press, 1998.

Fumerton, Mario. *From Victims to Heroes: Peasant Counter-rebellion and Civil War in Ayacucho, Peru, 1980–2000*. Amsterdam: Thela Publishers, 2002.

Marcella, Gabriel, and Richard Downes, eds. *Security Cooperation in the Western Hemisphere: Resolving the Ecuador-Peru Conflict*. Miami, FL: North-South Center Press, University of Miami, 1999.

McClintock, Cynthia. *Revolutionary Movements in Latin America: El Salvador's FMLN and Peru's Shining Path*. Washington, D.C.: U.S. Institute of Peace Press, 1998.

——— and Fabian Vallas. *The United States and Peru: Cooperation—At a Cost*. New York: Routledge, 2003.

Palmer, David Scott, ed. *Shining Path of Peru*, 2d ed. New York: St. Martin's Press, 1994.

Rudolph, James D. *Peru: The Evolution of a Crisis*. New York: Praeger, 1992.

Stern, Steve J., ed. *Shining and Other Paths: War and Society in Peru, 1980–1995*. Durham, NC: Duke University Press, 1998.

11

Venezuela
Consolidating a Different Democracy

David J. Myers

I n the presidential election campaign of 1998, then-candidate Hugo
Chávez Frías promised that if elected he would create a "different democracy." He repeated this promise at his inauguration as president on February 2, 1999. After more than six years of the Chávez presidency, his different
democracy remains a work in progress. Supporters argue that the fiery populist is building a political regime that will broaden participation and purge
Venezuela of the savage neoliberalism that previous governments introduced
in the 1990s. Supporters also believe that only such policies can eliminate the
glaring inequalities between the impoverished majority and the small affluent
class that survived the downward economic spiral of the past two decades.
Opponents counter that presidential rhetoric promising increased participation and forced equality is little more than cover for a radical socialist agenda
that smacks of communism. Supporters and opponents agree, however, that
the political system that President Chávez and his "Bolivarian Revolutionaries" are crafting is indeed "different" from the liberal polity that characterized
Venezuela between 1958 and 1998.

Victory in the regional and local elections of October 31, 2004, proved an
important milestone in President Chávez's drive to consolidate a "different democracy." His allies captured twenty-one of the twenty-three regional governorships (and the prestigious and powerful "High Mayor" of Greater Caracas)
and 239 of the 335 mayoralties. Government candidates also scored a resounding triumph in the municipal council elections of August 7, 2005. The
opposition, bitter and dispirited, was not shocked by these defeats. President

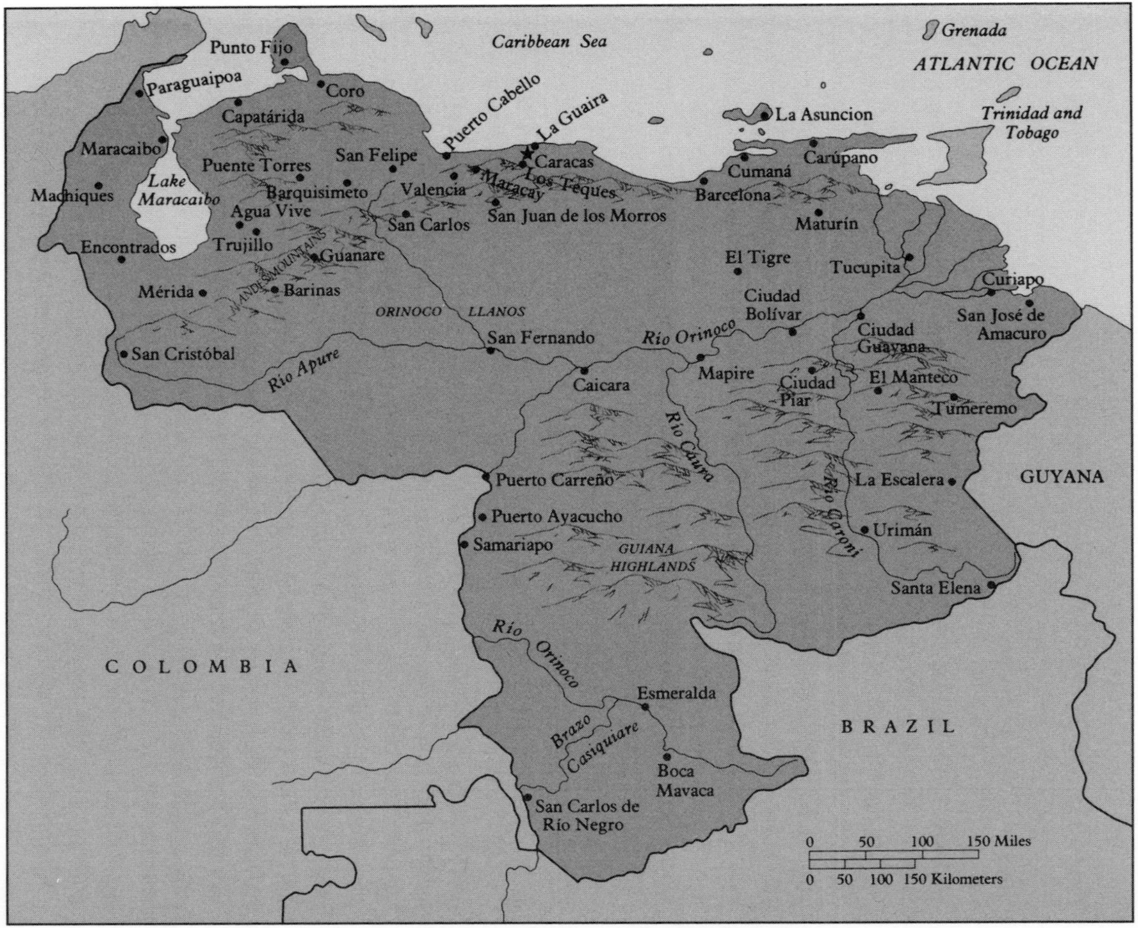
Caribbean Sea
Grenada
ATLANTIC OCEAN
Trinidad and Tobago
Punto Fijo
Paraguaipoa
Coro
Capatárida
Maracaibo
Lake Maracaibo
Machiques
Encontrados
Puente Torres
Barquisimeto
Agua Vive
Trujillo
Guanare
Mérida
Barinas
ANDES MOUNTAINS
San Felipe
Puerto Cabello
La Guaira
Caracas
Los Teques
Maracay
Valencia
San Carlos
San Juan de los Morros
La Asuncion
Carúpano
Cumaná
Barcelona
Maturín
El Tigre
Tucupita
Curiapo
San José de Amacuro
Ciudad Bolívar
Ciudad Guayana
ORINOCO LLANOS
San Fernando
Río Orinoco
San Cristóbal
Río Apure
Caicara
Mapire
Ciudad Piar
El Manteco
Tumeremo
Río Caura
Río Caroní
La Escalera
GUYANA
Puerto Carreño
Puerto Ayacucho
Samariapo
GUIANA HIGHLANDS
Urimán
Santa Elena
COLOMBIA
Río Orinoco
Esmeralda
Brazo Casiquiare
Boca Mavaca
San Carlos de Río Negro
BRAZIL
0 50 100 150 Miles
0 50 100 150 Kilometers

VENEZUELA

Chávez's victories in October 2004 and August 2005 flowed from his triumph in the revocatory referendum of August 15, 2004. In that election he beat back a two-year effort by the opposition to remove him from office by constitutional means. In a process lasting from November 2003 through May 2004 opponents of the government secured enough valid signatures to force a recall election. They were confident that voters would remove the president from office. In an unexpected turnabout President Chávez won by a decisive majority (59 percent–41 percent). These results flew in the face of public opinion polls that earlier in the year showed support for the president falling below 40 percent. Indeed, some exit polls on the afternoon of August 15 suggested that the President had lost. When the complete returns indicated otherwise opposition leaders reacted with shock and disbelief. Only after audits of the voting machines by international observers from the Organization of American States and the Carter Center failed to detect evidence of fraud did most of the opposition accept the results. Even then, however, a sizable minority continued to argue that the government had manipulated electoral results in favor of the president. Disillusionment and lingering doubts over the validity of the electoral process led many to abstain in the elections of October 2004 and August 2005.

The results of elections between August 15, 2004 and August 7, 2005 completed the marginalization of those who had ruled Venezuela between 1958 and 1998. Marginalization came six-and-a-half years after former paratrooper Hugo Chávez repeated the oath that made him Venezuela's ninth consecutively elected democratic president, on February 2, 1999. The inauguration took place one day short of the date seven years earlier when then-Lieutenant Colonel Chávez mounted the abortive military coup in which he almost toppled the government of President Carlos Andrés Pérez (1989–1993). Failure was followed by eighteen months in jail, a pardon by President Rafael Caldera (1994–1999), and several years in the political wilderness. Hugo Chávez then confounded his enemies by mounting a skillful campaign for the presidency and winning the national elections of December 5, 1998. He received 57 percent of the total popular vote. Confident in his triumph and contemptuous of his political opponents, the newly inaugurated president proclaimed the existing 1961 constitution to be "moribund," and promised a "New Democracy," one that would be honest, responsive, and worthy of the Venezuelan people.

In rapid succession President Chávez organized a referendum (on April 25, 1999) in which 85 percent of the voters authorized balloting for delegates to a Constituent Assembly that would draft the new constitution, then another election on July 25 that gave Chávez supporters 122 of the 131 seats in the Constituent Assembly. The Assembly submitted its draft constitution for approval in a national referendum on December 15, 1999. A yes vote by 72 percent of participants made this document the law of the land (it became Venezuela's twenty-sixth constitution). Thus ended Venezuela's four-decade-long experiment with *Punto Fijo* democracy,[1] a political regime that President John F. Kennedy once called Latin America's best hope for freedom.

For President Chávez the old democracy's defenders were "degenerates," "rancid oligarchs," and "squealing pigs"—"Hood Robins" all (in contrast to Robin Hood, Venezuelans describe a "Hood Robin" as one who steals from the people to increase personal wealth). The new president charged the leaders of Venezuela's long-dominant political parties, Democratic Action (*Acción Democrática*, AD) and the Social Christians (*el Partido Socialcristiano*, COPEI) with being the worst of the Hood Robins. He proclaimed that they robbed, lied, corrupted, and ultimately impoverished what should have been one of Latin America's wealthiest and most advanced countries.

The financial, physical, and economic milieu in which Venezuelans found themselves at the end of the twentieth century supported the Hood Robin metaphor. Between 1959 and 1999 hundreds of billions of dollars in revenue from the international sale of petroleum flowed into the country, but a myriad of public works projects remained half-finished or in a deteriorated state due to lack of maintenance, the social security system was bankrupt, and thousands of abandoned children lived in sewers and contributed to the increasing lawlessness in the cities. Venezuelan elites had demonstrated a lack of confidence in their own leadership by transferring more than $100 billion in capital to safe havens in Europe, the United States, and the Orient. Although the country seemed well on the way to developing a large skilled middle class in the 1970s and 1980s, as of 1999 more than 80 percent of the population lived below the poverty line. Outrage over the failure of democratically elected governments after 1983 even to maintain the quality of life enjoyed at that time by most Venezuelans permeated all aspects of national life.

Not only did Hugo Chávez Frias successfully identify himself with the rage of his countrymen at the two ruling political parties, he also promised that he would mobilize the armed forces to bring change. In the first years of his presidency Chávez staged appearances at which military units mingled with crowds when he appeared in public. Pageantry and rhetoric transmitted the new order's distaste for the old democratic politics that were castigated as the primary cause of Venezuela's economic decline. Over and over again the audience heard the armed forces praised as honorable, patriotic, and competent; an institution that the political parties had used badly for more than forty years. President Chávez also spoke approvingly of the New National Ideal, the modernization program of General Marcos Pérez Jiménez, the populist dictator who ruled Venezuela between 1951 and 1958. From his exile in Madrid the aging dictator expressed his approval.

Venezuela's unexpected flight from liberal democracy is not the only reason for interest in the country. Between 1945 and 1989 Venezuela changed from a rural to an urban society while appearing to avoid chaos and soften the pain of modernization. Literacy rates rose dramatically, indigenous heavy industry took shape, and for a brief moment Venezuelans enjoyed one of Latin America's highest standards of living. Prosperity ended in the 1980s when falling revenues from the international sale of petroleum undermined the economic and political institutions that since the late 1950s had allocated economic and political resources. Post-1958 democracy, the fruit of pacts among elites, allowed new actors to enter the ruling class, expanded the middle sectors, and improved living standards among the poor. The government's inability to honor and deepen these pacts in the 1980s led to constitutional crises in 1992 and 1993 and to Hugo Chávez's electoral success in 1998.

Venezuela is also important because of its activist foreign policy. Venezuelan democratic leaders supported the United States during the Cold War even though they grew anxious when Washington flashed military power in pursuit of its economic and security interests in the Caribbean Basin. Strains in U.S.-Venezuelan relations also surfaced in the 1970s, when President Carlos Andrés Pérez joined with other leaders of the "South" to seek more favorable economic treatment from the industrial "North." Here Venezuela's role in strengthening the Organization of Petroleum Exporting Countries (OPEC) and creating the Economic System for Latin America (*Sistema Económica para America Latina*) proved especially irritating to Washington. Irritation all but disappeared in the early 1990s when Venezuela's state oil company (*Petróleos de Venezuela*, PETROVEN) regularly exceeded OPEC production quotas. In 1999, however, President Chávez reduced output in tandem with other OPEC producers, and over the next six years the price of a barrel of crude oil rose from $9 to $63. Chávez viewed this striking improvement as confirming his suspicions that the United States had been exploiting Venezuela. As a counterweight to U.S. influence in Venezuela he cultivated close ties with Fidel Castro's Cuba. This angered the U.S. government, but the options available to President George W. Bush for dealing with Chávez were constrained given the popular support he enjoyed at home and the 1.5 million barrels of petroleum a day that Venezuela supplied to the United States.

Land and People

Geography and history have shaped contemporary Venezuelan politics. Nestled in the northeastern quadrant of South America between 1 and 13 degrees north of the equator, Venezuela is hot and tropical. Cool temperatures predominate only at altitudes above 3,280 feet (1,000 meters). The country's 25.8

million inhabitants live in an area of 352,150 square miles (912,050 square kilometers), roughly the size of Texas and Oklahoma combined. Stretching some 1,750 miles (2,816 kilometers) along the Caribbean Sea and the Atlantic Ocean, Venezuela extends south into continental South America. It encompasses snow-covered mountains rising to 16,427 feet (5,007 meters, Pico Bolívar) and reaches into the Orinoco and Amazon jungles. Some 3,000 miles (4,800 kilometers) of continental borders form frontiers with Colombia, Brazil, and Guyana. The Orinoco River, one of the largest and most navigable rivers in the world, drains four-fifths of the country. But the mountains, not the river or the plains, have historically been Venezuela's most influential geographical features. The dominant colonial settlements, agricultural estates, and urban centers are nestled in cool mountain valleys, and until 1925 when petroleum extraction became Venezuela's most important economic activity, these valleys formed the unchallenged economic, administrative, and social heartland.

Geographers divide Venezuela into five regions: the Guyana Highlands, the Orinoco Lowlands, the Northern Mountains, the Maracaibo Basin/Coastal Lowlands, and the numerous small islands along the Caribbean coast. These regions vary immensely in size, resources, climate, population, and historical input.

The Guyana Highlands, encompassing 45 percent of the national territory, is the largest region. Historically remote, poor, and sparsely populated, Guyana became a symbol during the Punto Fijo years of the government's drive to industrialize and reduce dependence on imported manufactures from the North Atlantic region. Guyana's industrial and mining centers remain oases of modern civilization surrounded by dense tropical forests. Ancient plateaus, some extending for 125 miles (200 kilometers), rise more than 3,280 feet (1,000 meters) above the jungle floor. From their heights tumble breathtaking waterfalls, including the planet's highest uninterrupted one, Angel Falls. On these plateaus flourish flora and fauna that exist nowhere else. Until the late 1950s Guyana exerted little influence on national affairs; however, subsequent government investment in the region has made Guyana's industrial infrastructure central to Venezuela's development aspirations.[2]

Lying between the southernmost part of Venezuela and the coastal mountains are the great grassland prairies (*llanos*) of the Orinoco Lowlands. They occupy 33 percent of the national territory and support roughly 20 percent of the population. For six months of the year this vast, featureless plain, 620 miles (1,000 kilometers) long and 400 miles (645 kilometers) wide, is subject to rainfall so heavy that much of it lies under water. As the ensuing dry season progresses, the mud turns to deep layers of dust, vegetation shrivels, the heat becomes intense, and streams dry up. Even the aboriginal Indians avoided this harsh area, and it remained for the Europeans and *mestizos* to settle and colonize it. Although the region is far from ideal for raising cattle, a type of culture based on that industry has grown there and continues to be managed by a rough, and for many years lawless, breed of man (*el llanero*) for whom cattle-raising is a way of life. President Hugo Chávez is a *llanero*.

The Northern Mountains constitute the third major geographical region. Although they encompass only 12 percent of Venezuela's land area, they support roughly two-thirds of the country's population. The principal mountain chain consists of the coastal range and the Sierra Nevada de Mérida. In the coastal range are found the capital city of Caracas, the Valencia-Maracay industrial center, large coffee holdings, sugar haciendas, and rich farmlands surrounding Lake Valencia. Because of its agricultural importance this region was for many years dominated by a rural oligarchy and large estates maintained by cheap peasant labor. Although coastal-range political leaders have played a central role in Venezuelan history, they have often lost to more aggressive rivals from less-favored regions.

The high and rugged Sierra Nevada de Mérida is a western spur of the Andes. With peaks rising to 16,400 feet (5,000 meters), its early inaccessibility discouraged great agricultural estates (*latifundios*); the Venezuelan Andes were characterized by medium-sized landholdings and populated by small clusters of people, both *mestizos* and Indians. Despite the presence of an influential university in the city of Mérida, Andean Venezuela remained isolated until the rise of coffee as a commercial crop. It is a region where religion and family ties are strong, as are the historic values of Hispanic culture. Thus, Andinos hold personalism, hierarchy, and military power in high regard, which partly explains why so many Venezuelan leaders—from Cipriano Castro to Carlos Andrés Pérez—have come from this region.

Ten percent of Venezuela's national territory consists of a narrow, partly arid, partly swampy belt of lowland lying between the steeply rising coastal mountains and the Caribbean Sea. This region comprises the Maracaibo basin and the Coastal Lowlands. Most of Venezuela's oil is found in the Maracaibo basin, and the region's drained swampland has been transformed into rich farms and cattle ranches. However, over 80 percent of the basin's inhabitants are classified as urban. Most reside in Greater Maracaibo, the country's second-largest metropolitan region. Beginning in the 1920s oil exploitation transformed the Maracaibo Basin into a thriving commercial, industrial, and educational center. In contrast, tourism is the most important economic activity of the eastern Coastal Lowlands. Here are located the best Caribbean beaches, and the climate is clear and dry. African influence is stronger in this region than anywhere else in Venezuela.

In addition to the mainland, there are seventy-two islands of varied size and description. The most important and best known is Margarita, in the state of Nueva Esparta. The site of some of the oldest Spanish settlements in Latin America, Margarita is a thriving free port and tourist center.

Most Venezuelans are an amalgam of Caucasian, Amerindian, and black. They have a common culture, predominantly Hispanic but with important Amerindian and African strands. Overwhelmingly Roman Catholic (85 percent) and Spanish-speaking, Venezuelans view themselves as members of a single ethnic mixture. The national census does not classify according to race or ethnicity (except for Amerindians in the Orinoco and Amazon jungles), so it is only possible to make educated guesses. Pure Caucasians make up between 10 and 15 percent of the total population. A small number belong to proud families who trace their ancestry to renowned Spanish names, but most of the pure Caucasians immigrated to Venezuela from southern Europe during the 1950s. Perhaps 10 percent of Venezuelans are black, less than 3 percent are pure Amerindian, and between 70 and 80 percent are of mixed ancestry. Ethnic mixing has occurred at all social levels, and ethnicity does not serve to distinguish either separate groups or classes. Large numbers of people with strong Amerindian and black ancestry have become leaders in politics, business, and culture. Nevertheless, Caucasian features are valued, and their predominance is greater among the higher social and economic strata.

Internal migration since World War II has transformed Venezuela from a rural society into one that is highly urbanized. First, peasants abandoned the countryside and rural villages for regional market towns. Second, townspeople subsequently moved to the large cities. Initially, Caracas received a disproportionate number of these migrants, mushrooming from a center of about five hundred thousand in 1945 to a diverse metropolis of just over five million in 2005. Four other cities—Maracaibo, Valencia, Barquisimeto, and Barcelona-Puerto La Cruz—boast populations of more than one million. In contrast, large areas of rural Venezuela are depopulated. Census estimates in 2000 placed the total urban population at just over 80 percent. In addition, the metropolitan areas have received most of the at least two million illegal immigrants from Colombia, Ecuador, and Trinidad. These *indocumentados* (literally, "undocumented" illegals) are concentrated in Maracaibo and Caracas, along the Colombian border, and in the eastern state of Sucre.

Historical and Political Economy

The history of Venezuela is one of progressive integration into the North Atlantic area. Integration began when Christopher Columbus landed in eastern Venezuela during his third voyage in 1498. The Venezuelan mainland was the first area of South America to be explored by Spain, but the region proved a disappointment, especially when contrasted with the riches discovered in Peru and Mexico. Disappointment led to neglect, and Venezuela remained a colonial backwater until the latter half of the eighteenth century. At that time Spain's Bourbon monarchs chose to update their imperial organization.

Consolidating Political Order and the
Transition to Liberal Democracy

The spatial pattern that crystallized between 1750 and 1800 has exerted a strong influence on the course of Venezuelan history. At that time Venezuela's "mature colonial society" revolved around Caracas, the regional capital city. The Spanish government's creation of a captaincy general located in Caracas brought together under unified administrative control the region's semi-independent provinces. Power based in Caracas became the most important symbol of the colony's new maturity, and it tied Venezuela's other regions into a single management bureaucracy. However, Venezuela had little time to enjoy its newfound maturity. Napoleon's invasion of the Iberian peninsula in 1807–1808 led to twenty years of civil strife in Latin America, and the fighting ended only after all of Spain's continental colonies had gained their independence.

The war for independence destroyed Venezuela's colonial bureaucracy in a clash of bandit armies that confiscated and reallocated property. Old methods of defining legitimacy and right were replaced by a new system based almost entirely on force and favor with those who controlled force. This modification of the colonial order came as a logical extension of political authority being militarized. Militarization also confirmed the primacy of Caracas. After Venezuela separated from Gran Colombia in 1830, control over Venezuela, more than ever, meant control of the capital city.

Between 1830 and 1920 Venezuela evolved into a commercial bureaucratic outpost of the industrializing North Atlantic. Beneath the confusion of civil strife, ideological conflict, and class warfare, Venezuela's mature colonial society was changing. Political and economic elites struggled to cope with the new demands placed on the old organization by the country's gradual integration into international commerce. As part of this commerce, which capitalists in Western Europe and the United States designed to nourish their domestic industries, Venezuela came to provide certain agricultural commodities in exchange for a mixed package of finished goods produced abroad. Control over this trade remained in the hands of entrepreneurs, financiers, and companies based in the North Atlantic; thus, Venezuelan elites had to adjust to the requirements of the new relationships.

The increasing stability of the commercial bureaucratic pattern led to the consolidation of political order during the late nineteenth and early twentieth centuries. Crucial in this process were the pacification and development programs initiated by General Antonio Guzmán Blanco (1870–1888) and consolidated by General Juan Vicente Gómez (1908–1935). Gómez took the essential relationships inherent in Guzmán Blanco's programs for exploiting Venezuela's niche in the international arena and—by applying ruthless logic aided by a monopoly of technology and communications—developed them to their conclusion. Along with the bureaucracy and repression of his regime Gómez fixed the bureaucratic commercial pattern in its final form before Venezuela succumbed to the overwhelming pressure of what historian John Lombardi has labeled the "petroleum-based technological imperium."[3]

Over the final decade of Gómez's rule (1925–1935) the "petroleum-based technological imperium" overpowered the commercial bureaucratic system. This arrangement was and is the product of opportunities and complexities endemic to petroleum exploitation. Transformation involved creating modern systems of transportation and communication and diffusing industrial technology into the oilfields. It also facilitated the intervention of foreign interest groups and ideologies into Venezuela's internal politics.

Caracas, measured by any set of variables, gained disproportionately from the new economic regime, although not until after Juan Vicente Gómez passed from the scene. The long-lived dictator disliked and distrusted Caraqueños, residents of Caracas, and he ruled from Maracay, a small settlement some sixty miles to the west of Caracas. Gómez's successors launched a major effort to bring standards of comfort in the capital up to those of urban North Atlantic countries. University education, art, culture, social services, architectural and urban grandeur—whatever the North Atlantic imitation, Caracas residents monopolized it to an ever-growing degree. Thus, Venezuela's capital acquired the trappings of modernity while the rest of country remained much the same. Caracas attracted the ambitious, the wealthy, and the young from other regions. The distance separating Caracas from the interior grew greater until no other center could compare with it.

The "petroleum-based technological imperium" was arguably the single most important factor shaping twentieth-century political development. It played a key role during Venezuela's journey (1935–1959) from primitive dictatorship through party-centered democracy to a more direct "New Democracy." This journey began in the late 1920s, even before the passing of General Juan Vicente Gómez. At that time the demands of managing the new extractive economy exceeded the capabilities of the nineteenth-century commercial bureaucratic structures to broker social, economic, and political conflict. This prompted the search for new institutions, and growing U.S. influence throughout the Caribbean led Gómez's successors to experiment with limited political democracy. The elitist tenor of this experiment proved its undoing.

In October 1945 junior military officers joined with working- and middle-class reformers from the interior to seize power in a short but bloody coup d'état. Democracy for the few gave way to democracy for the masses. The new system's dominant radicals used their leftist political party, Democratic Action (*Acción Democrática,* AD), to gain total control of the government and then to pass legislation that began to redistribute wealth, power, and cultural authority. The upper and middle classes panicked, turning to the military for protection. In November 1948 the armed forces overthrew the popularly elected government of Rómulo Gallegos, outlawed the dominant AD political party, and established a military junta to govern the country.

The new military regime portrayed its seizure of power as necessary to prevent Communists and their Soviet Union masters from derailing Venezuela's integration into post–World War II North Atlantic capitalism. Governments presided over by Colonel Carlos Delgado Chalbaud (1948–1950) and General Marcos Pérez Jiménez (1952–1958) favored importers and merchants at the expense of the industrialists. They took advantage of the strong global demand for petroleum to increase exports of crude oil by 7.4 percent and petroleum products by 14 percent per annum. For a brief period this reliance on the oil industry's growth to fund import-driven economic development appeared to be working. The increase in Venezuela's domestic product averaged an extraordinary 9.4 percent per year during the middle 1950s. National income also grew rapidly, with the country enjoying one of the highest rates of increase in the world: 5.7 percent when adjusted for population growth.

Economic and political circumstances deteriorated after 1956. The condition of having a dynamic enclave petroleum economy surrounded by inefficient agricultural production had long been a source of political stress. The basic problem lay in the contrast between the living standards (high and increasing versus low and stagnating) of those who enjoyed the fruits of the technologically based petroleum imperium and those on the outside. In addition, by late 1957 a host of grandiose public works projects stood incomplete, especially in Caracas. The dictatorship had financed them by using short-term treasury bills but escalating costs and stagnating petroleum income pushed public indebtedness beyond the government's ability to pay. The economic situation became critical in 1957, leading financial elites to criticize the military regime openly. General Pérez Jiménez sought to counter declining support with increased repression. This only stiffened the resolve of his enemies, who received support from the U.S. government. Early in the morning of January 23, 1958, after he lost control over Caracas, Marcos Pérez Jiménez fled the country.[4]

Fair and open elections took place at the end of 1958 and reform-minded Rómulo Betancourt (AD) won the presidency with almost 50 percent of the total vote. The AD also gained control of Congress, but the opportunistic

Democratic Republican Union (URD), the Social Christian party (COPEI), and the Venezuelan Communist Party (PCV) elected significant delegations. The three major political parties (AD, URD, and COPEI) agreed to share power in the previously noted Pact of Punto Fijo, which gave to militants from each important bureaucratic positions and a place in the leadership of each major interest group organization (e.g., the Labor Confederation, the Peasant Federation, and professional associations such as the Engineering Guild). In addition to sharing power, the leaders of AD, URD, and COPEI agreed to build support for economic pluralism before undertaking far-reaching wealth redistribution.[5] Agreement on this reformist agenda was a critical first step in securing legitimacy for post-1958 democracy.

Traditional elites and the leaders of the mass-based political parties opted for the Punto Fijo reconciliation system in 1958 because of their disastrous experience with military rule, and because they anticipated that distributive politics funded by ample resources would be the norm. They calculated that income from the foreign sales of petroleum, if not squandered (here the example of General Pérez Jiménez loomed large), would provide the resources with which they could successfully broker the demands of traditional elites and previously excluded political actors. Leaders of the Labor Confederation and Peasant Federation were to be incorporated into this expanded distributive process and empowered to service their clients. Punto Fijo democrats calculated that this system would avoid the widespread revolutionary violence that had convulsed Cuba and culminated in Fidel Castro's imposition of communism.

The Petroleum Roller Coaster and Institutional Stress

The flow of petroleum revenue to Venezuela's central government between 1958 and 1988 had sharp ups and downs, like the ride on a roller coaster. These ups and downs stressed the institutions of post-1958 democracy, which, as suggested above, assumed there would be a steady flow of ample resources from overseas sales. Throughout the 1960s energy prices inched upward, more or less fulfilling elite expectations. However, revenue from petroleum tripled in the middle 1970s. More than 80 percent of the total income that Venezuela received between 1945 and 1989 came during the administrations of Carlos Andrés Pérez (1974–1979), Luis Herrera Campíns (1979–1984) and Jaime Lusinchi (1984–1989).

Benefiting from international events over which Venezuela had no control, these three governments and their economic allies administered unprecedented wealth. The quadrupling of the market price of a barrel of petroleum in 1973 allowed the government of Carlos Andrés Pérez (CAP) to create a potpourri of state corporations and to initiate a multitude of infrastructural development projects. CAP also nationalized, with mutually agreed-upon compensation to foreign investors, the iron and petroleum industries. However, he invested in many projects whose payoff would be only in the long term, and he continued to spend massively on importing food. By the end of his term the state had yet to extend its economic largesse on an equitable basis to large numbers of people, and charges of corruption swirled about the government. Thus, despite general optimism and prosperity, voters entrusted the presidency in 1978 to the opposition COPEI Party.

President Luis Herrera presided over a volatile economy. At the time of his inauguration in February 1979 Venezuela appeared headed for a period of prolonged budgetary deficits. Before austerity programs could be implemented, new increases in the price of petroleum doubled the government's income. Unprepared for this favorable turn of events President Herrera was unable to take advantage of it. Improvised policies and corruption led to economic stagnation. Unprecedented borrowing tripled the country's international debt (public and private) to $35 billion. The conjunction of economic stagnation, debt repayment obligations, and declining petroleum revenue forced President Herrera to devalue the currency and implement an austerity program in February 1983. This allowed AD to recapture the presidency.

The administration of Jaime Lusinchi would be the last hurrah for traditional distributive politics. President Lusinchi made a fundamental mistake in economic policy when he opted to restructure only at the margins. After some initial successes Venezuela's economy resumed its decline. Reduced income from petroleum in the national election year of 1988 was not matched by decreases in spending. The government, determined to avoid an economic recession just prior to the presidential elections, ran a balance-of-payments deficit of $4 billion. In response the economy grew by 5 percent, and AD's Carlos Andrés Pérez won a second presidency. However, Lusinchi's refusal to come to grips with Venezuela's reduced circumstances restricted the options open to his successor. For decades the country had consumed more than it produced; inescapably, to restore balance, real incomes and consumption had to decline.

The New Departure and its Consequences

On February 2, 1989, President Pérez assumed office. Three weeks later Venezuelans were stunned when their new leader announced that foreign reserves were severely depleted; that in 1988 the country had run a fiscal deficit exceeding 9 percent of the GDP; that the current account of the balance of payments had its largest deficit in history; and that all prices in the economy, from interest rates and black beans to medicines and bus fares, were artificially low and impossible to maintain. President Pérez warned that only bitter medicine could cure these maladies, but when he administered the first dose three days of rioting and looting left more than three hundred dead and the country overwhelmed with panic, perplexity, and rage. It was the worst outbreak of violence since the early 1960s, when the then-struggling democratic government clashed with Castroite guerrillas. Fallout from the 1989 riots would weaken President Pérez, doom efforts by his successor to restore the regime's legitimacy, and bring to power its most intractable enemies.

In the immediate aftermath of the February 1989 rioting there was reason to hope that President Pérez might be able to right the foundering ship of post-1958 democracy. Venezuela settled into a deceptive calm. People appeared resigned to painful adjustments even though conditions screamed that the petroleum-fueled distribution network could no longer sustain existing institutions.[6] President Pérez used this calm to implement a neoliberal economic package, *El Gran Viraje*—the Great Turnaround. This radical departure from the past relied on four sets of policies: macroeconomic stabilization, trade liberalization, privatization, and deregulation. Macroeconomic stabilization encompassed measures such as establishment of a single, freely floating rate for foreign exchange; the removal of price controls on all private goods and services except those on a list of eighteen specific staple items; market-determined interest rates; reductions in real public spending; and significant increases in the prices of goods produced by the public sector as well as in the rates of public utilities.

Trade liberalization and privatization brought profound change. Government planners removed nontariff barriers covering 94 percent of local manufactures and eliminated special permits for exports, simultaneously restructuring the tariff system, thus bringing the country's average tariff level down from 35 percent in 1988 to around 10 percent in 1990. Entry into GATT consolidated the freest trade regime of the post-1958 era. In response the foreign commercial banks reduced and restructured $20 billion of Venezuela's public debt. Finally, a new foreign investment regime eliminated most restrictions on foreign investors and minimized bureaucratic interference in their financial, commercial, and technological transactions. Government prescreening or pre-approval on foreign investment projects was no longer required; all restrictions on profit remittances and capital repatriation were lifted; and, for the first time the stock market was opened to overseas investors.

The Pérez administration took concrete steps to privatize deficit-prone state enterprises. By the end of 1992 four commercial banks, the national airline, the telephone company, as well as the cellular telephone system, a shipyard, the ports, sugar mills, and several hotels had all been sold. Other activities slated for privatization included horse-racing tracks, a second airline, additional hotels, the Caracas water-supply system, regional electric distribution facilities, and the public television network. These changes, dramatic reversals for a president who had nationalized petroleum and led the Latin America Social Democratic Movement, confirmed the serious loss in capability that Venezuela's distributive network had experienced.

Deregulation, as suggested above, accompanied macroeconomic stabilization, trade liberalization, and privatization. It also marked changes made in the government's social programs. Slated for elimination were subsidies in which payments and other allocations were transferred to specific private firms producing basic staples to keep their prices low (e.g., corn, flour, milk, sugar, poultry, sardines, and so forth). The government began to replace them with a nutritional grant program that established a direct cash transfer to mothers of children enrolled in schools located in poor areas. President Pérez also launched a maternal health care program and a worker protection plan based on unemployment compensation payments for six months. However, the trauma of change, the rigidities of established bureaucracies, and a scarcity of funds slowed implementation of the new programs.

The repercussions of President Pérez's economic restructuring were felt throughout the 1990s. Early in the decade Venezuela's economy set world records. However, these records masked the deterioration of state institutions, which became less capable of acting on the basis of technical and professional criteria. Carried into policy areas such as health care, transportation, and agriculture, poor performance by the state further undermined the quality of life for most Venezuelans. Purchasing power also declined. Decay seemed pervasive, and this perception undercut the government's legitimacy even more.

The socioeconomic tensions that eroded societal support for the Pérez government also crystallized inside the armed forces. During the 1970s the highly professional military promotion system of the early democratic system was relaxed and politicized. This spurred a strong rivalry between factions inside the officer corps, creating significant incentives for aspiring officers and their protégés to block or even sabotage the career development and possibilities for promotion of their rivals. Until the fiscal crisis of the 1980s those who lost in this Byzantine competition normally received middle-level executive positions within the myriad of state enterprises. This became impossible as budgets tightened and the public sector contracted and increased the incentives for the losers to overturn the status quo.

Another consequence of the fiscal crisis for the armed forces was that the daily needs of enlisted soldiers and junior officers became grossly underfunded. This created strong resentment toward the senior ranks, which were viewed as increasingly remote and preoccupied with contracts to procure sophisticated military hardware, and with the politics of promotion. Tensions between junior and senior officers were exacerbated by the fact that the former had received extensive opportunities to complement their military training with professional education at home and abroad, thus differentiating their experience in the profession from that of older officers. These belonged to a generation that came of age in the war against leftist guerrillas during the 1960s. To summarize, reduced economic circumstances and distinct generational experiences conspired to create distrust between junior and senior officers, to erode discipline within the armed forces, and to undermine their cohesion. Given these conditions, the military as an institution ceased to be a bulwark of support for the political regime.

The crisis broke on February 4, 1992, when a group of junior military officers calling themselves the Bolivarian Military Movement attempted a coup that came perilously close to succeeding. Although much in the Bolivarian Military Movement's program was confused, its call for the affluent and dishonest to be tried for crimes against the nation struck a responsive cord among the majority who had suffered during a decade of economic hardship. Thus, although the coup failed, it emboldened the opponents of President Pérez, his austerity plan, and even long-forgotten enemies of post-1958 democracy.

The fifteen months that separated the February 1992 coup attempt from President Carlos Andrés Pérez's suspension from office in May 1993 proved remarkable for their turbulence and intensifying opposition to the government. Former President Rafael Caldera stopped just short of proclaiming that the Bolivarian Military Movement's cause was just, and President Isaías Medina's last minister of the interior, Arturo Uslar Pietri, suggested that forcing Pérez from office before the end of his term might make amends for the revolution of 1945. In late November 1992 the military (this time the navy, air force, and marines) mounted a second unsuccessful coup, and Venezuela's once-robust macroeconomic indicators faded. During May 1993 the attorney general, Ramón Escobar Salom, assembled persuasive evidence that President Pérez had misused government funds. The Supreme Court then found "merit" in these charges, and the Senate suspended the president from office to face trial before the Supreme Court.

The eight months that followed raised more questions than they answered. After AD and COPEI came to an agreement, their senators selected one of their own, Ramón J. Velásquez, to serve as interim president. Velásquez, a political intellectual, oversaw free and open elections in December 1993 for president, Congress, and the state legislatures. However, during his brief stewardship the economy failed to recover, privatization stalled, and bitterness over declining living standards intensified. The Velásquez legacy to his successor, Rafael Caldera (1994–1999), was perhaps an even chance of preserving Punto Fijo democracy.

The new government received high rates of approval from the public during its first eighteen months. President Caldera's expulsion from COPEI, the political party he founded and led for five decades, allowed him to capitalize on hostility toward the established political parties and their neoliberalism. For almost two years Rafael Caldera endeavored to set the clock back to a past that he viewed positively, the years of his first presidency (1969–1974). He blamed corruption and the neoliberal policies of Carlos Andrés Pérez for the country's ills. Soon after taking office President Caldera moved against CAP's backers in the financial community. The unintended consequence of that decision was the collapse of the entire banking system, a turn of events that severely damaged the government's capability to grow the economy.

In July 1996 President Caldera made a complete turnaround from his campaign rhetoric and earlier policies. He negotiated a structural-adjustment agreement with the International Monetary Fund that reinstated many of the neoliberal reforms (as a program called *Agenda Venezuela*) that he had previously criticized. The fruits of Caldera's earlier policies, despite their popularity when first announced, were an inflation rate of 103 percent (1996) and an increase in the foreign public debt to $26.5 billion. In addition, the government had not built mechanisms of participation likely to generate support for the return to a more market-oriented development strategy. When it came to implementing *Agenda Venezuela* President Caldera actually increased centralization. He and Luis Alfaro Ucero, the secretary general of AD, allied in the Congress to give the national executive new powers to amend the consumer protection law and intervene in the foreign exchange market. This cooperation unmasked AD as a silent partner in the government. After implementing *Agenda Venezuela* neither Caldera nor Ucero had much credibility.

The opportunity to make dramatic changes in the political system came with the national elections of 1998. Voters went to the polls to choose the president and members of congress. COPEI and AD nominated presidential candidates with fatal flaws, which underscored their isolation. Just prior to the presidential voting, AD and COPEI abandoned their nominees and threw their support behind the promising but ultimately unsuccessful candidacy of Enrique Salas Römer, the independent governor of Carabobo. The real story of the presidential election campaign, however, was the meteoric rise of Hugo Chávez. He personified opposition to post-1958 liberal democracy, and on December 6 voters elected him president by a decisive margin.

Chávez rewrote the rules of Venezuelan politics in 1999. At his February inauguration he vowed to replace the existing "moribund" and "unjust" order with a new and responsive democracy. As mentioned previously, he quickly organized a referendum in which 85 percent of the voters authorized elections that would select delegates to a Constituent Assembly whose charge was to draft the new constitution. In the elections of July 25 Chávez supporters won 122 of the 131 seats in the Constituent Assembly. Debate in the Assembly reflected simmering dissatisfaction with traditional elites, whose apprehensions triggered capital flight of over $4 billion. Thus, despite rising oil prices in 1999 the economy contracted by 5.5 percent. President Chávez and his allies, however, gave their highest priority to restructuring political institutions. On December 15, in a national referendum, approval by 72 percent of voters made their new constitution the law of the land.

Political Parties, Elections, and Interest Groups

Political Parties and Elections

Events between 1998 and 2005 transformed the political party system. Two political parties, the AD and COPEI, had been the core of post-1958 liberal democracy. Both had strong indigenous roots, although the former maintained ties to the European Social Democrats and the latter to the Christian Democrats. For many years AD and COPEI efficiently performed the functions most often associated with modern political parties: mobilizing supporters, recruiting individuals to fill government positions, mediating the demands of competing interests, and creating symbols that strengthened support for the political regime. However, at the beginning of 2005 identification with the AD had fallen to barely 5 percent, and COPEI teetered on the brink of extinction. They were shells of the organizations that had institutionalized and dominated Venezuela's competitive, centrist party system (see Table 11.1).

Other political parties played major roles in the Punto Fijo political regime,[7] but until the elections of 1993, only the nominees of AD and COPEI had captured the presidency. The URD, a personalistic party drawing support from the left and the center-right, helped to establish post-1958 democracy; however, internal conflicts led to its demise. Leaders of the People's Electoral Movement (*Movimiento Electoral del Pueblo*, MEP) split from AD in 1967, but five years later most of their supporters returned to AD. The Movement To Socialism (*Movimento al Socialismo*, MAS) began as a faction inside the PCV that opposed the 1968 Soviet invasion of Czechoslovakia. This faction's defection finished PCV as a competitive electoral force, and MAS became regime-supportive until the 1998 national elections. Between 1973 and 1993, MAS was the third political party of the democratic regime. Finally, another group of breakaways from the PCV formed Radical Cause (*CAUSA R*), a militant leftist

Table 11.1 National, Congressional, Regional, and Local Election Results (Venezuela: 1988–2005)

Year	Election Type	Winner/Party % Vote	%Punto Fijo Regime Ruling Parties	% anti-Punto Fijo Regime Parties	% Abstention
1988 Dec.	Presidential	Pérez AD 53	94	6	18
1988 Dec.	Legislative	AD 43	74	27	18
1989 Dec.	Regional/Local	AD 40	71	39	55
1992 Dec.	Regional/Local	COPEI 42	78	32	60
1993 Dec.	Congressional	AD 24	46	54	40
1993 Dec.	Presidential	Caldera CN/MAS 31	46	54	40
1995 Dec.	Regional/Local	AD 35	56	44	55
1998 Dec.	Presidential	Chávez MVR 56	11	91	36
1998 Nov.	Congressional	AD 25	37	63	46
2000 July	Presidential	Chávez MVR 59	0	100	44
*	National Assembly	MVR 46% of seats / 39% of seats	21% of seats	79% of seats	44
2000 Dec.	Municipal Councils	MVR	28% of seats	72% of seats	76
2004 Oct.	Governors,	21(of 23) MVR/allies	9% of seats	91 % of seats	55
	Mayors	238 (of 335) MVR/allies	29% of seats	71% of seats	
2005 Aug.	Municipal Councils **	MVR/allies 1911 (of 2389)	17% of seats ***	80% of seats	68

* Party alliances varied from electoral district to electoral district. Consequently, it is not possible to calculate the national percent of the National Assembly vote received by each political party.

** Does not include election results for neighborhood councils.

*** 3% of the seats won by local candidates whose ties to the government and opposition are unknown.

Source: author's calculations based on official statistics of the Consejo Supremo Electoral (1958–1998) and the Consejo Nacional Electoral (2000, 2005).

political party that enjoyed little success until the 1993 presidential elections. Soon afterward CAUSA R itself split in two.

The traditional political parties' loss of legitimacy allowed Hugo Chávez Frías to transform the political party system, beginning with the 1998 national election campaign. Chávez supporters organized the Fifth Republic Movement (*Movimiento Quinto República*, or MVR) in 1997 as an electoral vehicle for their leader's presidential candidacy. At that time Chávez was running a distant second in the public opinion polls to Irene Sáez, the former beauty queen who had been elected mayor of Chacao, an upscale municipality in eastern Caracas. Sáez's popularity began a prolonged decline in early 1998, with a dramatic plunge occurring at midyear when she accepted the presidential nomination of COPEI. In tandem with Irene's decline, support for Hugo Chávez increased. He assembled an anti-establishment coalition of thirteen political parties, the Patriotic Pole (*Polo Patriótico*), which included the Communists, URD, MEP, and other forgotten remnants of challengers that AD and COPEI had defeated and marginalized. Two other members of the Patriotic Pole retained important electoral followings: the MAS and the Fatherland for All (*Patria Para Todos*, PPT), the majority faction of what earlier was CAUSA R. In early April 1998 public opinion polls showed Hugo Chávez Frías pulling ahead of all other presidential contenders.

The traditional political elite mobilized to defeat Hugo Chávez Frías once they realized the magnitude of his appeal. Allied entrepreneurs and their international partners turned to Enrique Salas Römer, the Yale-educated governor of Venezuela's richest and most highly industrialized state, Carabobo, as the reformist alternative. Foreign consultants crafted a campaign that promised change and economic growth. For its part the once-dominant AD committed the greatest blunder in its history: party elders nominated septuagenarian Luis Alfaro Ucero, the AD secretary general, as its presidential candidate. Alfaro's campaign spent heavily, but his support never passed 10 percent in the public opinion polls. Hugo Chávez Frías won the December 6, 1998 presidential election with just under 57 percent of the popular vote.

Twenty months later on July 31, 2000 Venezuela held elections for the first time under the new 1999 constitution. In what electoral officials called a "mega-election," voters chose the president, all governors and mayors, and all members of the new unicameral National Assembly. AD and COPEI declined to contest the presidency. Chávez's only significant challenger was Lieutenant Colonel Francis Árias Cárdenas, his second in command during the unsuccessful military coup of February 4, 1992. Árias split with Chávez over the president's leftward drift and the Bolivarian revolution anticlericalism. Árias garnered one-third of the total presidential vote and Chávez captured 60 percent, slightly more than in 1998. The MVR and its allies secured

46 percent of the seats in the National Assembly, while AD and COPEI together held only 21 percent. The remaining third of the seats in the National Assembly were controlled either by allies of the MVR or regional political parties that had supported the candidacy of Árias Cárdenas. Most importantly, Hugo Chávez's supporters controlled the National Assembly, but they lacked the two-thirds majority necessary for changing the constitution.

Venezuela's party system remained in flux between the mega-elections of July 2000 and the regional and local elections of October 31, 2004. AD and COPEI continued to lose support in public opinion surveys. One new opposition party, *Primero Justicia* (Justice First) did develop a loyal following. However, support for *Primero Justicia* was concentrated in the upper-middle class neighborhoods of Eastern Caracas. AD, COPEI, and MAS, opposition parties that once boasted national support, could not shake perceptions that they offered little more than a return to discredited liberal democracy. The coalescing of the traditional political parties in 2001 as a loose umbrella organization, the *Coordinadora Democratica* reinforced this perception. The *Coordinadora Democratica* spearheaded efforts to remove the government, first through organizing strikes in 2002 and 2003 and then by mounting the unsuccessful revocatory referendum to remove the president in 2004. The fallout from these failures, as suggested earlier, paved the way for resounding electoral victories by President Chávez and his allies in the regional and local elections of October 2004 and August 2005. Public opinion polls in advance of the December 4, 2005, elections for the National Assembly indicated that the MVR and its allies would gain up to 80 percent of the seats. In other words, voting results in 2004 and 2005 placed President Chávez in an all but unassailable position as he prepared to run for reelection in 2006.

In a related matter the 1999 constitution establishes the electoral power as a separate branch of government. This development was a reaction against the Punto Fijo regime in which political parties dominated the Supreme Electoral Council and oversaw the tabulation of voting results. Party control of the Supreme Electoral Council played an important role in maintaining electoral domination by AD and COPEI. These two were the only political parties with organizations in every municipality, and evidence exists that they sometimes divided among themselves the votes of third political parties at polling places where smaller political parties had no observers. The worst excesses of this abuse were eliminated with the 1998 elections, when a reorganized electoral council mobilized a random sample of citizens as poll watchers, and the mega-elections of 2000 employed this system.

The independent electoral power envisioned in the 1999 constitution fell under the control of President Chávez and his supporters from the beginning. While the government named talented and capable individuals to the

National Electoral Council (*Consejo Nacional Electoral*-CNE), it never gained the trust of the opposition. Instead, from the time that opponents of the government began gathering signatures for the referendum to oust President Chávez the impartiality of CNE was a bone of contention.

Interest Groups

Bolivarian Venezuela is less supportive of demand-making by organized interests than was post-1958 liberal democracy. President Chávez sees organized interests as impediments to communicating directly with the people. His Bolivarian outlook holds a view of democracy that is more in the mode of Rousseau than of Locke. Nevertheless, many institutional and associational interest groups retain influence. The armed forces and the Church, both historically elitist, are the most important institutional interests. The business community and professionals, also elitist, operate in an associational mode, as do such mass-based interests as labor and peasants. These mass-based interest groups coalesced in the late 1930s and 1940s, organized as part of the strategy by reformist party leaders to wrest political power from the heirs of General Juan Vicente Gómez. Six decades later Hugo Chávez came to power vilifying political parties, and he has undercut the power of the mass-based groups that were allied with them. He has also undercut organizations that emerged within civil society in the 1980s for the purpose of making Punto Fijo democracy more open and participatory. Finally, the urban poor, always a force with anomic potential, never secured a place in the constellation of clients serviced by the traditional political parties. The urban poor voted overwhelmingly for Chávez in the 1998 presidential election. Once in office President Chávez oversaw a major organizational effort that transformed slum dwellers into the mainstay of his support.

The military, along with the church and the landed elite, dominated from independence until General Pérez Jiménez fled the country on January 23, 1958. The provisional junta that took power faced nationwide strikes supported by business, labor, and other groups demanding civilian political rule. Confused and dispirited, the army acquiesced to the election of its nemesis, Rómulo Betancourt, as president. The Betancourt government then had to fight an insurgency mounted by leftist guerrillas who sought to establish a Castroite regime in Venezuela. The counterinsurgency effort that defeated the guerrillas forged a bond between the armed forces and civilian leaders. Until the urban riots of February 1989 this bond remained a formidable obstacle to direct military intervention in politics.

After 1989 the armed forces could not be depended upon to make demands through constitutional channels. Instead, they became institutions that, under conditions judged favorable by the officer corps, might intervene directly in politics. There are several reasons for this transformation. First, simmering frustration with party-based governments' management of the economy made violent protests increasingly common, and the last two Punto Fijo governments asked the military to assist the police in preserving order on several occasions. Second, the armed forces faulted liberal democratic governments for not maintaining police capabilities, and this raised questions about how budgets had been spent.

Distress over corruption and institutional decay underlay other military concerns with post-1958 democracy. The experience of using force against protesting civilians led many in the military to question their support of an unpopular, party-centered regime dominated by autocratic gerontocracies that appeared unscrupulous and isolated. Finally, as suggested earlier, the opulent life styles of young politicians and businessmen during the 1990s, when contrasted with the economic difficulties experienced by junior officers, created resentments in the armed forces against the political and economic establishment. President Pérez sought to address these grievances after the unsuccessful coups of February and November 1992, and in early 1994 President Caldera made his own special overtures to the officer corps. Neither was able to return the armed forces to the regime-supportive stance that they maintained between 1960 and 1989.

In the first years of the Chávez government the military was divided into three factions. One supported the Bolivarian Revolution, another was vehemently opposed, and a third argued that the armed forces should remain apolitical and focus on professional enhancement. President Chávez, however, was determined to transform the armed forces into a pillar of support for his regime, for he viewed the military as special, an institution more honorable than any other. He also saw the bureaucracy as corrupt and incompetent. Correspondingly, he launched *Plan Bolívar 2000*, an improvised departure that funneled funds for infrastructure maintenance and development through regional military garrison commanders. Some officers opposed this policy, while others used the opportunities that accompany the construction of public works for personal enrichment. In general, Venezuela's physical infrastructure deteriorated under military stewardship.

In early 2002 factions in the military opposed to President Chávez viewed with increasing concern his leftward drift. On April 11, 2002, a march in Caracas by hundreds of thousands of government opponents ended in shootings that killed and wounded more than fifteen individuals. Opposition leaders and government security forces blamed each other. This incident became an excuse for military officers opposed to President Chávez to remove him from office. They replaced him with Pedro Carmona Estanga, president of the umbrella business confederation, FEDECAMARAS. However, the perpetrators of the coup could not agree on how to organize a government. Carmona, rather than promising to investigate the incident of April 11, appeared intent on establishing a dictatorship that would take vengeance on the Bolivarians. Disillusionment and confusion gave supporters of President Chávez the opportunity to regroup. In less than forty-eight hours factions loyal to the president took control and reinstalled President Chávez.

After the coup of April 11 President Chávez never again trusted the armed forces. Not only did he purge officers suspected of having sympathized with the coup, he also marginalized all who were not seen as active supporters of the Bolivarian Revolution. In addition, he organized militias of reserves among unemployed slum dwellers and changed official military doctrine to take advantage of these reserves. On January 29, 2005, the secretary of the National Defense Council (*Consejo de Defensa de la Nación*) announced that the new military doctrine gave priority for preparing for asymmetric warfare (*Guerra Asimétrica*). By this the secretary implied that Venezuela recognized that it could not resist a conventional invasion by the United States (now seen as Venezuela's most likely military opponent). However, once invaders had landed and occupied territory the newly formed militias would mount an insurgency that would turn the tide. This doctrine also gave the government a national security rationale for strengthening forces composed of individuals from strata most supportive of the president.

The ecclesiastical hierarchy made peace with AD, historically an anticlerical political party, during the administration of President Rómulo Betancourt. Subsequently, the bishops supported post-1958 liberal democracy.[8] Nevertheless, their enthusiasm was tempered by an acknowledgment of problems that included corruption, decay in the judiciary, unemployment, inequality, and moral deterioration. The *Centro Guimilla*, a Jesuit think tank, leveled especially biting criticism at AD and COPEI in the 1970s and 1980s. After the urban riots of February 1989 and two unsuccessful coups in 1992 the Episcopal Conference issued public statements intended to put distance between the church and the neoliberal policies of President Carlos Andrés Pérez. Church leaders gave strong backing to the second Caldera government and maneuvered behind the scenes to effect a reconciliation of the president and the COPEI political party.

The bishops viewed the rise of Hugo Chávez with alarm, especially his reliance on advice from militant leftists whose antagonism toward parochial education predated the revolution of October 1945. Still, the ecclesiastical hierarchy took no official position in the referendum that approved the 1999 constitution, although some influential clerics argued that ratification would be a first step in depriving the Church of its cultural influence. After the unsuccessful coup of April 11, 2002, relations between the ecclesiastical hierarchy and the government deteriorated. President Chávez suggested on more than one occasion that the church had supported the coup, while influential clerics condemned government policies for undermining democracy.

Private-sector interests in Venezuela are diverse, ranging from local agribusinesses to multinational manufacturers. During the *Trienio* (1945–1948), the democratic interlude between military dictatorships, businesspeople were united in their opposition to AD's reformist Marxism with its emphasis on regulation and state intervention in the economy; but like the military and the church, the business community accommodated to party-dominated democracy and prospered. Private-sector leaders anticipated developing similarly beneficial arrangements with the Chávez government. As the Bolivarians revealed their sympathy for socialism, however, government-business relations cooled. When the president of the most important private-sector organization, FEDECAMARAS, agreed to serve as provisional president in the short-lived provisional government of April 2002, already cool relations turned frigid.

Two hundred individual groups comprise FEDECAMARAS, but the institution is dominated by four pivotal interests: industry, trade, cattle-raising, and agriculture. Each possesses its own chamber: CONINDUSTRIA for industry, CONSECOMERCIO for commerce, FENAGAN for cattle-raising, and FEDEAGRO for agriculture. Because these key interests have different and sometimes conflicting priorities, the single-interest or intermediate chambers are as important as centers of political demands as FEDECAMARAS.

Multinational corporations have long been important players in domestic Venezuelan politics. After President Pérez implemented his "Great Turnaround" in 1989 a torrent of foreign capital flowed into the country. It left almost as rapidly following the unsuccessful coups in 1992, and returned in force in 1996, when the state petroleum company (*Petróleos de Venezuela*, PETROVEN) signaled a willingness to accept overseas assistance to implement plans that would double Venezuela's oil production capability. Private foreign investment again fled in 1999 when President Chávez voiced criticisms of capitalism and multinational corporations.

Organized labor and peasants, two associational interest groups, emerged in the late 1930s and 1940s. A third, professionals, traces its origins to the nineteenth century. Reformist party leaders developed labor and peasant organizations as part of their mobilization strategy to wrest political power from the entrenched Andean cabal.[9] Labor and peasant leaders, as well as professionals, were subject to party discipline throughout the Punto Fijo era. Failure to comply with instructions from one's political party risked sanctions and possibly expulsion. Expulsion from the party usually entailed loss of leadership positions within the tied interest group. Building on these connections, AD and

COPEI extended power sharing as defined in the Pact of Punto Fijo into worker, peasant, and professional organizations.

Following approval of the 1999 constitution the leading labor organization, *Confederación Venezolano de Trabajo* (Venezuelan Confederation of Workers, CTV) opened negotiations with the government, offering to eliminate the influence of AD and COPEI in their unions in return for recognition by the national government. This was not acceptable to President Chávez, who began to organize his own Bolivarian trade unions. Consequently, the CTV joined with FEDECAMARAS and other opponents of the government in a series of strikes that convulsed the country in 2002 and 2003. In March of 2003, after breaking the final and most virulent strike, President Chávez discharged 17,000 workers belonging to the Federation of Petroleum Workers (FEDEPETROL). Other contracts with CTV unions were simply ignored. The CTV carried on, but as a shadow of its former self; and government-funded Bolivarian trade unions grow stronger.

Until the mid-1980s Venezuela's urban poor were only weakly integrated into the Punto Fijo system. This was largely because the political parties having the greatest appeal to slum dwellers during the decade of regime consolidation (the 1960s) lost out to AD and COPEI, neither of which paid much attention to the slums. The demand-making structures that eventually crystallized among the slum dwellers were different from the party-dominated associations of workers, peasants, and professionals. Slum dwellers organized out of frustrations caused by the state's failure during the petroleum bonanza to use its ample revenues to improve their living conditions. Initially, the most important organization to represent the urban poor was the Center at the Service of Popular Action (CESAP). During the 1980s CESAP settled on the strategy of working within the existing regime. This choice undermined its legitimacy when the second Pérez and Caldera governments adopted neoliberalism, which convinced the urban poor that under conditions of scarcity Punto Fijo elites would take back the few benefits they had given.

The perception that they had been abandoned by AD and COPEI underpinned the massive support that slum dwellers give Hugo Chávez Frías in the presidential elections of 1998 and 2000. Soon after taking office in 1999 the President began organizing supporters in the slums into *Círculos Bolivarianos* (Bolivarian Circles). The Bolivarian Circles were diverse. On one hand, they taught young women to sew, manage small businesses, and provided needed child care. On the other, they assisted the government in identifying its supporters and opponents. There was much concern among opposition leaders that the Bolivarian Circles were precursors of institutions that would exercise dictatorial control over the urban poor.

Government Structures

Venezuelan state organization has been in flux since 2000, when the shift began to institutions envisioned by the constitution of 1999. The new constitution mandates a presidential system with five separate branches of government: the executive, the legislative, the judicial, the electoral, and the people's power. Twenty-three states and a capital district interact in a polity whose leaders have yet to agree on the balance of power among the central, regional, and local governments. Under the previous 1961 constitution the polity had grown more decentralized, and the 1999 constitution envisions a Federal Council of Government to oversee decentralization. Nevertheless, for reasons peculiar to the unitary, centralistic tensions in Hispanic and Roman Catholic constitutional development, Venezuela's subnational politics have remained closely connected with patterns set in Caracas.

The national executive of the 1999 constitution is more powerful than its predecessor, which was itself viewed as a strong presidency. A popularly elected president, eligible for reelection to a second consecutive six-year term, presides over the national government. The president is commander-in-chief of the armed forces and appoints a cabinet composed of twenty-five ministries. The president can freely remove members of the cabinet. The constellation of cabinet ministries reflects the Bolivarian preference for state control. They range from the powerful Ministry of Interior Relations and Justice to the recently created Ministry of Food. The president is also empowered to name and remove at will the vice president, who assumes the presidency if that office falls vacant.

A unique feature of the presidency under Hugo Chávez is the use of numerous "Missions" (*Misiones*) to allocate resources. As indicated earlier, because President Chávez viewed the bureaucracy he inherited as corrupt and tied to AD and COPEI, he used regional military commanders to allocate resources during the first years of his government. After the unsuccessful military coup of April 2002 procedures changed. President Chávez established a number of improvised institutions called Missiones. For example, the Ministry of Education was bypassed to establish special Bolivarian programs for literacy (*Misión Robinson*), accelerated high school degree programs (*Misión Ribas*), and revolutionary Bolivarian Universities (*Misión Sucre*). Other high profile *Misiones* include programs that provide services to the slums (*Misión Barrio Adentro*) and distribute food to the poor at subsidized prices in popular markets (*Misión Mercal*). In all, the official website of the Venezuelan government lists twelve such Misiones (as of September 2005). Funding for the *Misiones* passes through the president's office from the state petroleum company *Petróleos de Venezuela* (PDVSA) rather than from the Central Bank to allocating institutions, as was established practice. The *Misiones* budgets are closely guarded, although to fund them the president can draw freely on the more than $25 billion that the Venezuelan government is estimated to hold abroad.

The 1999 constitution substituted a unicameral National Assembly for the bicameral Congress that under the previous constitution was the font of central government lawmaking. This National Assembly has less autonomy and fewer prerogatives in relation to the national executive than its predecessor, which reflects the disrepute into which Congress had fallen during the Punto Fijo era. The 1999 constitution allows the president to dissolve a recalcitrant National Assembly and call for new elections. In addition, legislation can be introduced into the National Assembly from seven sources: the national executive, the Delegative Commission of the National Assembly, any three members (Deputies) of the National Assembly, the Supreme Tribunal, the Electoral Power, the Citizen's Power, and by petition bearing the signature of 0.1 percent of registered voters.

The first National Assembly was elected in the mega-elections of July 31, 2000, and as discussed earlier the MVR and its allies gained roughly 55 percent of the seats. The Assembly has 160 members, with each state, regardless of population, electing at least three deputies. In a departure from tradition the Amerindian community elects three deputies. Deputies are elected in a mixed system for terms of five years and are eligible for reelection to two additional consecutive terms. Sixty percent of each state's deputies are elected in single-member, winner-take-all districts and 40 percent on the basis of proportional representation, by party list. The 1999 constitution creates the office of National Assembly president and provides for two vice presidents. It also sets the number of permanent commissions at a maximum of fifteen. This limitation reflects the Bolivarian belief that the numerous permanent commissions in the previous Congress had evolved into privileged sinecures from which corrupt party leaders peddled their influence for personal gain.

The 1999 constitution places the Supreme Judicial Tribunal at the apex of the judicial power. The Supreme Judicial Tribunal meets in several kinds of sessions: plenary; political-administrative; electoral; and ones that deal with civil, penal, and social matters. Justices of the Supreme Tribunal are to be elected for terms of twelve years and cannot run for reelection. During their term in offices they are forbidden to engage in partisan political activity; indeed, the 1999 constitution goes to great length to shield the entire judiciary from the influence of political parties. For example, entry into the judicial career, and promotion, is by competitive examination only. Procedure for institutionalizing the judiciary awaits action by the first National Assembly. Finally, like its predecessor the constitution of 1999 establishes separate courts for the military. Going back to the Castillian tradition of the military *fuero* (right), this system protects members of the armed forces from being tried by civilian courts.

The Citizen Power, a new branch of government, was established in reaction to the widely held perception that during post-1958 democracy, government had become unresponsive, abusive, and corrupt. The Citizen Power is a kind of ombudsman and watchdog. The maximum authority of this branch of government is the Moral Republican Council, an institution composed of three individuals: the public prosecutor (*Fiscal*), the national comptroller (*Contralor General de la República*), and an official known as the People's Defender. The People's Defender "promotes, defends and watches out for" constitutional rights and guarantees. By a two-thirds vote, the National Assembly designates the People's Defender, who serves for a single period of seven years. Because Venezuela has little experience with this branch of government, the extent of its power and influence remains in flux.

Policymaking

Policymaking in Venezuela is conditioned by a number of previously discussed characteristics. Critical in the "New Democracy" is a growing tendency to assess all policies in terms of their ability to advance the Bolivarian Revolution as defined by President Chávez. Equally important has been the substantial per capita petroleum income available for distribution by the Venezuelan state, its dramatic expansion during the early 1970s and contraction in the late 1980s and 1990s, and dramatic recovery, beginning in 2003. Other influential characteristics include the Hispanic tradition of centralized and hierarchical authority, influence from the North Atlantic on domestic political evolution, and efforts to industrialize by expanding, privatizing and again expanding the role of the state in the economy. These characteristics shape policymaking in the four central policy arenas: service delivery, economic development, public order and safety, and foreign and national defense.

Service Delivery Policy

Service delivery immediately and directly affects quality of life, and its highly diverse components include housing, infrastructure development, health, sanitation, food, environment, social security, education, urban development, culture, and transportation. Until the revolution of 1945 only the upper class enjoyed access to quality services, and one of the most attractive dimensions of the AD's early program was its promise to use the state to extend high-quality services to all. Billions of dollars in petroleum revenue enabled AD and COPEI to accustom Venezuelans to the highest level of service delivery in Latin America, but declines in revenue quickly led to deterioration in the quality of public services. Efforts to privatize selected public services in the 1990s yielded mixed results, and President Chávez abandoned the policy.

The making and implementing of most service delivery policies are controlled directly by the national government. The Ministry of Health and Social Development provides health care and administers social security programs. Infrastructure, environment, education, housing, food, and culture each have their own ministries. Sanitation, on the other hand, is a municipal service, and rural electrification (Autonomous Corporation for Developing Electricity, CADAFE) lies with decentralized public administration entities. This was also true for telecommunications, which was transferred to the private sector during the administration of Rafael Caldera.

Economic Development Policy

Economic development revolves around activities that expand capacity to produce goods and commodities for internal consumption and for export. Its impact on quality of life, although just as important as service delivery, is less immediate and direct. Like service delivery policy, economic development policy's issue areas are highly diverse; they include mineral extraction, industry, commerce, finance, and planning. Venezuela's private sector has long played a pivotal role in all facets of economic development policy, and in the present era of reduced petroleum revenue, this role is growing. Thus, to a greater extent than in service delivery policy, government decisions affecting economic development are scrutinized by businesspeople for evidence that the "New Democracy's" leaders remain committed to economic pluralism.

Although mineral extraction has been almost exclusively a national government prerogative, the private sector remains important for industrial activity. Venezuelan mineral extraction, despite the importance of gold, iron, and bauxite, revolves around petroleum. Nationalization of the $5 billion oil industry, the product of a broad national consensus, occurred on January 1, 1976. To manage and coordinate the newly nationalized petroleum industry the government created *Petróleos de Venezuela* (PDVSA), a state corporation attached to what is now the Ministry of Energy and Petroleum.

With the decline of petroleum prices and the demands of debt servicing in 1982, the executive branch began to overrule PDVSA executives. Important benchmarks were President Herrera Campíns's decision to transfer $8 billion in PDVSA reserves to the Central Bank, Minister of Energy Hernández Grisanti's withholding of approval for the company's 1988 investment budget, and President Pérez's order in 1992 that PDVSA sell many of its European and North American refineries. One of President Chávez's first decisions was to replace the president of PDVSA with an individual from his inner circle. Income from sales of petroleum by PDVSA, as discussed earlier, fund President Chávez's *Misiones*.

Industrial policymaking involves the government continually setting boundaries between the public and private sectors. Many capital-intensive heavy industries—for example, steel (*Siderurgía del Orinoco*, SIDOR), aluminum (*Aluminio del Caroní* S.A., ALCASA), and petrochemicals (*Petroquímica de Venezuela*, PEQUIVEN)—are organized as state corporations. Public-sector regional development corporations exist for all major regions. Still, the private sector controls a broad range of other industries (e.g., automobile manufacturing, textiles, construction, and cement). The Ministry of Light Industries and Commerce is a source of capital for politically favored industrial activities.

Finance and commerce are issue areas that involve especially intensive public-sector/private-sector interaction. The Ministry of the Treasury and the Central Bank set the broad financial parameters within which economic development is pursued. During the Punto Fijo era the minister of the treasury normally came from the business community; the president of the Central Bank, in contrast, generally belonged to the government party's cadre of financial experts. The 1999 constitution gives the national executive increased authority to intervene in the Central Bank, and President Chávez has been highly interventionist.

Finally, the Ministry of Planning (CORDIPLAN) has responsibility for overseeing economic development and service delivery planning. CORDIPLAN receives plans from each of the government ministries, their ascribed institutes, and the state corporations; its role is to eliminate duplication and set overall priorities. Depending on the president's confidence in the minister directing CORDIPLAN this ministry may exercise strong influence or do little more than compile the plans it collects.

Public Order and Safety Policy

Public order and safety policy are comparatively homogeneous and revolves aroud the Ministry of Interior and Justice. This ministry serves as the president's right hand in exercising political control. It also oversees the National Identification Service, policing and the Office of Immigration. In the Bolivarian Republic, as during the Punto Fijo era, this ministry is given to one of the president's closest political confidants.

Responsibility for public order leads to the Interior Ministry's being entrusted with operation of a national police force, called the Directorate of Intelligence and Prevention Services (DISIP). The director of DISIP, although under the minister's direct supervision, has unhindered access to the president. Popularly referred to as the political police, DISIP is responsible for gathering political intelligence; safeguarding political order; supervising foreigners within the country; and, in coordination with the National Guard, narcotics control. The National Guard operates as a second national police force; in rural areas it is normally the most important agent for law enforcement and it patrols the borders and the coast. A third national police force, the Technical and Judicial Police (*Policia Técnica Judicial*, PTJ), is charged with protecting the rights and liberties of citizens. It resembles the U.S. Federal Bureau of Investigation in purpose, and has primary responsibility for criminal investigation and the arrest of suspects. The Ministry of Interior and Justice also oversees the penal system, allocates government subsidies to the Roman Catholic Church, and ratifies clerical appointments.

Foreign and National Defense Policy

Defense. Foreign and defense policymaking, a constitutionally mandated presidential responsibility, is centered in the ministries of Defense and Foreign Affairs, and in the institutes and state entities attached to them. The Ministry of Energy and Petroleum, because of Venezuela's heavy dependence on international petroleum markets, also plays an important role in foreign policy. Petroleum policy has been discussed earlier, so the focus here is on traditional national and foreign policy concerns: defense of the frontiers, control of the national territory, relations with foreign powers, and an array of nonpetroleum international economic issues.

Despite substantial overlap in the assigned tasks of the ministries of Defense and Foreign Affairs, coordination between them was minimal until the 1980s. The most important explanation for this shortcoming is that since independence the critical missions of the armed forces have been internal. Presidents Betancourt and Raúl Leoni (1963–1968) strengthened relations between AD and the military during their successful campaigns against leftist insurgents, and throughout the Punto Fijo period the primary mission of the military was to exercise control over the national territory in a manner that discouraged dissidents from attempting guerrilla warfare. Thus, the armed forces cultivated ties with those domestic groups that traditionally provide recruits for any insurgency—youth living in the slums and peasants. The National Guard, Venezuela's fourth armed service, was especially active in this area.

The Chief of Staff (*Estado Mayor General*) coordinated the military establishment until after the 1958 revolution. Early in the Punto Fijo period President Rómulo Betancourt replaced the centralized General Staff with a Joint Staff (*Estado Mayor Conjunto*), which became an advisory rather than a centralizing organ. Defense policies and budgets, rather than being managed centrally, became the prerogative of the individual services. Two factors inclined Betancourt to make this change. First, the post-1958 party regime was searching for ways to control the armed forces, and party leaders calculated that they would have greater leverage when making military policy if they dealt with multiple actors. The Joint Staff system institutionalized this leverage by allowing civilian politicians to play on interservice rivalries, especially resentments in the navy, air force, and National Guard over the army's use of the General Staff to dominate them. Second, as confirmed by the two unsuccessful coup attempts during 1992, when the armed forces are divided into four actors coordination from within the military institution for political purposes is difficult.

The 1999 constitution provides for the reunification of the armed forces under a single Chief of Staff. It also envisions a more active political role for the uniformed services and attempts to minimize the capability of civilian politicians to intrude into military affairs. President Chávez has selected many members of his cabinet from former comrades in arms; many regional governors elected under the banner of the government political party are retired military. As discussed earlier, since the military coup of April 11, 2002, President Chávez has purged the officer corps of individuals suspected of disloyalty. He ordered imposition of the doctrine of asymmetric warfare in large part to justify creation of popular militias as a counterweight to the regular armed forces.

Foreign Policy.   Foreign policymaking and implementation, also constitutionally mandated presidential responsibilities, center on the Ministry of Foreign Relations. During the Punto Fijo era presidents often selected prominent independents for the position of foreign minister as a way of building support among traditional interests. Over time AD and COPEI each formed a cadre of foreign policy experts. The professional foreign service was co-opted into these cadres, which also manages the Foreign Trade Institute (*Instituto de Comercio Exterior*, ICE). Established in the early 1970s, ICE oversees and stimulates Venezuela's nonpetroleum exports. President Chávez has appointed some of his most reliable collaborators to the position of Minister of Foreign Affairs. One of the most important charges given his appointees has been to purge the foreign service of diplomats with long-standing ties to AD and COPEI.

Until the middle of the twentieth century commerce with the North Atlantic countries was the only truly important dimension of Venezuela's international relations, and ties with Western Europe and North America remain central. Their primacy derives from, and is determined by, the composition of

Venezuelan exports and imports. Historically, Venezuela exchanged raw materials for manufactured goods from the North Atlantic, but beginning in the 1950s Venezuela used petroleum revenue to purchase industrial machinery and technology as well. Traditional suppliers on both sides of the North Atlantic stood ready to supply both.

Venezuelan diplomacy has long attempted to reduce the importance of relations with the North Atlantic countries, but here successes have been meager and fleeting. Cooperation within OPEC to set the price of petroleum acquired great importance during the 1960s, and in the 1980s coordination with other debtor countries in negotiating repayment terms with OECD country banks became a priority. Both issues presented opportunities for Caracas to resurrect rhetoric associated with such anti-European and anti-U.S. themes as Latin American unity, Bolivarian solidarity, and Hispanic cultural superiority. These themes have been taken to new heights by President Hugo Chávez. The Chávez government began early to voice unease with U.S. influence over Latin America in general and Venezuela in particular. President Chávez's clash with President George W. Bush at the April 2001 Quebec summit on free trade in the Americas opened a rift with the United States that is unprecedented. In the heady ambiance of an August 8, 2005 global student conference (in Caracas) President Chávez excoriated the Bush administration's Iraq policy and characterized the United States as "the most savage, cruel and murderous empire that has existed in the history of the world."[10]

Relations with other Latin American countries, although rocky early in the Punto Fijo period, improved after 1970. The policy of refusing to recognize governments that used force to gain power (the Betancourt Doctrine) isolated Venezuela from many of its neighbors during the 1960s. The first Caldera government's emphasis on international social justice provided a basis for interstate cooperation within Latin America that reduced Venezuelan isolation. Caldera also initiated a policy of countering Brazilian development in the Amazon basin with efforts to integrate Venezuela's own Amazonian periphery with coastal Caribbean population centers. Not only official Brazilian programs but also intrusions by itinerant Brazilian gold miners into the Venezuelan Amazon have caused concern in Caracas over the years. However, while Brazil's programs in the region far surpass those of Venezuela, the vastness of the Amazon basin makes the presence of both appear like drops in a bucket. Thus, this potentially explosive rivalry is unrealized, and President Chávez pursues closer ties with his southern neighbor as part of the strategy to counterbalance U.S. influence.

Three final concerns of Venezuelan foreign policy are integration into MERCOSUR and relations with Colombia and Cuba. Bolivarian strategists see MERCOSUR as a formidable barrier to plans by the U.S. government to create a hemispheric free-trade zone. President Chávez has expressed a strong preference for increasing commerce among South American countries and orienting the continent's trade toward Western Europe and Asia. In addition, hostility toward the United States led President Chávez to deepen his predecessor's opposition to Drug Enforcement Agency (DEA) overflights of Venezuela in pursuit of narco-traffickers. In August 2005 President Chávez broke relations with the Drug Enforcement Agency (DEA) after accusing the Bush administration of using DEA agents to spy on Venezuela. Nevertheless, Chávez has condemned the drug cartels and cooperated with Colombian President Alvaro Uribe to improve border security along the Venezuelan-Colombian frontier.

Finally, President Hugo Chávez's affinity and cooperation with Fidel Castro stands in sharp contrast to Punto Fijo-era policy. While presidents between 1958 and 1998 were also uneasy over U. S. influence in the Caribbean Basin, they condemned Fidel Castro's alliance with the Soviet Union, held a generally negative view of his communist regime, and in the 1990s applauded Cuba's move toward a more pluralist political system. Under Chávez, however, Venezuela has demonstrated an affinity for militant socialism and hostility toward liberal democracy. The millions of dollars in petroleum that Venezuela sends each month to Cuba in exchange for Cuban teachers and medical doctors has freed Fidel Castro from accommodating to pressures that his regime become more pluralistic as a condition for increased trade and investment from Western Europe and the United States.

Prospects

The most plausible shape of Venezuela's political regime in the years after President Chávez completes his first term in office is some variant of electoral democracy—a political regime that holds minimally acceptable elections but lacks some crucial dimensions of liberal democracy. These crucial dimensions include the failure to fully respect requirements that the rule of law be applied equally to all citizens, and curtailment of some basic freedoms of organization and expression, at least for some groups. Also, based on recent experience it is likely that the national executive will not respect the division of powers or provide horizontal accountability. On the other hand, from time to time the opposition likely will be allowed to win some surprising victories. One great unknown is the extent to which the Bolivarian Republic will respect basic liberties. There have been some violations of basic liberties to this point but they are the exception.

As in the past the international environment will play a major role in shaping Venezuelan politics. Moderate rises in petroleum prices allowed the Chávez government to compensate for capital flight in 1998 and 1999 and to invest modestly in 2000. Events between 2001 and 2005 have made it all but impossible for President Chávez to convince Venezuelan businessmen to repatriate funds that they transferred out of the country or to entice foreigners to bring in new capital. However, the spike in petroleum prices that began in 2003 provided more funds than the government could have hoped to obtain from capital repatriation or foreign investment. It also allowed the national executive to dominate all aspects of the economy to an extent not seen since the petrobonanza years of the 1970s. Abundant resources to expand the regime's distributive capability at that time gave liberal democracy a legitimacy that lasted for more than two decades. It is likely that the current favorable position of Venezuela in the international political economy will consolidate the Bolivarian Revolution's hold on power for some time to come.

Suggestions for Further Reading

Alexander, Robert J. *Rómulo Betancourt and the Transformation of Venezuela*. New Brunswick, NJ: Transaction Books, 1992.

Buxton, Julia. *The Failure of Political Reform in Venezuela*. Aldershot, United Kingdom: Ashgate, 2001.

Coronil, Fernando. *The Magical State: Nature, Money, and Modernity in Venezuela*. Chicago: The University of Chicago Press, 1997.

Crisp, Brian F. *Democratic Institutional Design: The Powers and Incentives of Venezuelan Politicians and Interest Groups*. Stanford, CA: Stanford University Press, 2000.

Ellner, Steve, and Daniel Hellinger. *Venezuelan Politics in the Chávez Era: Class, Polarization & Conflict*. Boulder, CO: Lynne Rienner, 2003.

Friedman, Elizabeth J. *Unfinished Transitions: Women and Gendered Development of Democracy in Venezuela, 1936–1996*. University Park: Penn State University Press, 2000.

Gil Yepes, José A. *The Challenge of Venezuelan Democracy*. New Brunswick, NJ: Transaction Books, 1981

Gónzalez, Nestor G. *Venezuelan Civil-Military Relations: Past, Present, and Future*. Carlisle Barracks, PA: Army War College, 1996.

Karl, Terry L. *The Paradox of Plenty: Oil Booms and Petro-States*. Berkeley and Los Angeles: University of California Press, 1997.

Lombardi, John V. *Venezuela: The Search for Order, The Dream of Progress*. New York: Oxford University Press, 1982.

Martz, John D., and David J. Myers. *Venezuela: The Democratic Experience*. Rev. ed. Westport, CT: Greenwood Press, 1986.

McCoy, Jennifer L., and David J. Myers. *The Unraveling of Representative Democracy in Venezuela*. Baltimore: Johns Hopkins University Press, 2004.

Molina, José E. "The Presidential and Parliamentary Election of the Bolivarian Revolution in Venezuela: Change and Continuity (1998–2000)". *Bulletin of Latin American Research* 21. 2002: 219–247.

Notes

1. Venezuela's post-1958 democracy was popularly known as *"Punto Fijo"* democracy, the designation derived from the name of the house (belonging to Rafael Caldera) where party leaders signed a political pact to share power in the wake of the overthrow of General Marcos Pérez Jiménez.

2. Iêda Siquiera Wiarda, "Venezuela: The Politics of Democratic Development," in *Latin American Politics and Development*, 2d ed., ed. Howard J. Wiarda and Harvey F. Kline (Boulder, CO: Westview, 1985), 293–296.

3. John V. Lombardi, "Patterns of Venezuela's Past," in *Venezuela: The Democratic Experience*, rev. ed., ed. John D. Martz and David J. Myers (Westport, CT: Praeger-Greenwood, 1986), 7–21.

4. Gustavo Escobar, "El Laberinto de la Economía," in *El caso Venezolano: Una Ilusión de armonía*, ed. Moisés Naim and Ramón Pinango (Caracas: Ediciones IESA, 1985), 74–80.

5. Judith Ewell, *Venezuela: A Century of Change* (Palo Alto, CA: Stanford University Press, 1984), 124–127.

6. Moisés Naim, "The Launching of Radical Policy Changes, 1989–1991," in *Venezuela in the Wake of Radical Reform*, ed. Joseph S. Tulchin (Boulder, CO: Lynne Rienner, 1992), Chapter 4.

7. The best overview of the evolution of Venezuela's system of political parties in English is José Molina, "The Unraveling of Venezuela's Party System," in Jennifer L. McCoy and David J. Myers, eds. *The Unraveling of Representative Democracy in Venezuela* (Baltimore: Johns Hopkins University Press, 2004), chapter 8.

8. A more comprehensive discussion appears in Daniel H. Levine, *Popular Voices in Latin American Catholicism* (Princeton, NJ: Princeton University Press, 1992), 65–91.

9. Two rival labor confederations, the Unified Center of Venezuelan Workers (CUTV, estimated membership eighty thousand) and the Confederation of Autonomous Unions (CODESA, estimated membership sixty thousand) provided alternatives to the CTV during post-1958 democracy. The CUTV coalesced during the guerrilla struggle of the 1960s after the CTV expelled Communists and members of the radical leftist Movement of the Revolutionary Left (MIR). CODESA is allied with COPEI. They have disappeared in the new democracy of Hugo Chávez.

10. CNN Website, posted 10 August 2005.

12

Uruguay
Balancing Growth and Democracy

Ronald H. McDonald and Martin Weinstein

U ruguay is the smallest of the South American republics, but the distinctiveness of its political experience and innovations far transcends its size.[1] It is perhaps best known today as a long-standing democracy that "failed," one now struggling to reaffirm and redefine its democratic traditions. However, it is also a country that in the nineteenth century created democracy out of chaos and translated its traditional corporatist values and realities into democratic institutions. It experienced a profound disillusionment with the modern premises of economic growth and stability, as well as a period of escalating political instability and incremental military intervention. In 1985 Uruguay reestablished democratic government and politics, and since then it has been preoccupied with defining the meaning of "normalcy" in the new context.

Uruguay often has been viewed as a historical exception to the general pattern of politics in Latin America, an isolated instance of enlightened pluralistic politics in a region of corporatist authoritarianism. Uruguayans, in fact, have shared the same corporatist values as most of their neighbors but, almost uniquely, have shaped them into distinctive democratic processes and traditions, borrowing selectively from the experiences of Europe and the United States and, as necessary, making innovations to suit their own environment. Today Uruguay has reestablished its democratic heritage and revitalized its historic values, and in the process has cautiously explored new forms of organization and reevaluated the failed premises that eroded its traditional democracy.

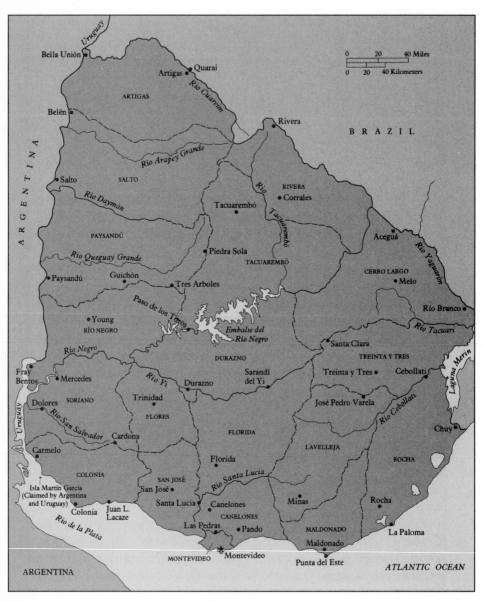

Bella Unión

Uruguay

Artigas • Quarai

ARTIGAS

Río Cuareim

Belén •

Rivera

BRAZIL

Río Arapey Grande

A R G E N T I N A

Salto • SALTO

Río Daymán

RIVERA

Corrales

Tacuarembó

PAYSANDÚ

Río Queguay Grande

Piedra Sola

Río Tacuarembó

TACUAREMBÓ

Aceguá

CERRO LARGO

Río Yaguarón

Paysandú • Guichón • Tres Arboles

Melo

Río Branco •

Paso de los Toros

Embalse del
Río Negro

Río Tacuari

Young •

RÍO NEGRO

Río Negro

DURAZNO

Santa Clara

TREINTA Y TRES

Fray
Bentos

Mercedes •

Río Yí

Durazno

Sarandí
del Yí

Treinta y Tres •

Cebollatí

Laguna Merín

Dolores •

SORIANO

Trinidad

José Pedro Varela

Río Cebollatí

Río San Salvador

Cardona

FLORES

FLORIDA

Chuy •

Carmelo •

COLONIA

SAN JOSÉ

San José •

Florida

LAVALLEJA

ROCHA

Isla Martín García
(Claimed by Argentina
and Uruguay)

Colonia • Juan L.
Lacaze

Santa Lucía •

Río Santa Lucía

Minas

Rocha •

Río de la Plata

Las Pedras
• Pando

Canelones

CANELONES

MALDONADO

La Paloma

ARGENTINA

MONTEVIDEO Montevideo

Maldonado

Punta del Este

ATLANTIC OCEAN

0   20   40 Miles
0   20   40 Kilometers

URUGUAY

The unique qualities of Uruguayan democracy have been little known, let alone understood, outside the country. Outwardly the country seems to have many similarities with other democracies, including regular and meaningful elections, a rule of law that respects and protects individual liberties and freedoms, and a policy-making process that is responsive to public opinion and scrutiny. Yet these qualities exist within a distinctively Latin American context, which recognizes and incorporates corporatist assumptions in the democratic processes, utilizing such familiar devices as co-optation, parity, coparticipation, and charismatic leadership. Many of the premises, the logic of the country's traditional democracy, proved unreliable, and in the mid-twentieth century Uruguay went through a period of sustained political and economic decay, violence, and ultimately authoritarian military rule.

The establishment of Uruguayan democracy originally was the result of an armistice between contentious landowners and provincial *caudillos* who came to recognize the potential for significant profits from increased exports. The politicians also saw democracy as a way to create political stability and gain political support from a rapidly expanding urban middle class committed to consumerism, consumption, and the benefits of state-provided services and welfare. Uruguayan democracy was based on an important economic assumption: Economic growth was inevitable, irreversible, and largely a spontaneous process that could subsidize the expanding and increasingly costly demands of a democratic society, an assumption common to other liberal democracies, including the United States.

The political ideas that underlay Uruguayan democracy were forcefully and explicitly articulated by its most influential statesman, José Batlle y Ordóñez. These included the belief that political stability was essential for prosperity and growth; that it would be achieved only by allowing free but balanced access to political power under a rule of law; that it could be sustained only by responding to the needs and demands of the masses; and that it must be protected from the pernicious influences of ambitious executives, politicians, and international opportunists while guaranteeing a strong role for the state. Batlle was strongly anticlerical; he believed that the church and Catholicism were an organized threat to secular control and progress, and that the church and state should be totally separated.

What is important about the Uruguayan experience is its relevance to other democracies whose processes, welfare, and stability are based on similar assumptions. The reexamination in Uruguay of fundamental democratic premises and values, particularly within a context of economic stress, was not an easy task, nor were the questions of blame and retribution for individuals and institutions that were culpable for the collapse of the democratic system. The concerns ultimately raised the issue of how normalcy would be defined within the new and reevaluated contemporary context. It is still unclear how much the result will borrow from the past, from neighboring societies in Latin America, or from new premises and new values. Uruguay has dealt with crises and dilemmas that would test any democracy, and for that reason its experience, both the universal and the parochial dimensions, merits careful evaluation.

Economic History and Social Context

Uruguayan economic history is particularly important for understanding the country's politics and government. Early in the twentieth century Uruguay became a largely middle-class country with one of the highest standards of living in Latin America, but it subsequently experienced a protracted economic decline that challenged and eventually helped destroy its democratic politics. Uruguayan exports failed to remain viable and competitive internationally; its domestic economy became heavily dependent upon services rather than agricultural and industrial activities; its dependency on imports, particularly for energy, created massive financial problems; and its commitment to consumption rather than productivity distorted national priorities and created an escalating international debt and uncontrolled inflation. Uruguay's economic success and its subsequent decay were both influenced by international economic realities, most of them beyond the country's control.

Uruguay's wealth was generated by the export of traditional commodities, principally wool, mutton, lamb, cattle, and grains. The economy was too small to industrialize rationally or efficiently, and the effort to do so encouraged import-substitution-industrialization (ISI) and protectionist trade policies, which in turn created inefficient monopolies, both foreign and domestic, along with equally inefficient state-owned enterprises. The domestic economic situation was complicated by high production costs and profit expectations resulting from high-risk industrial ventures. It was also complicated by modern but unrealistic economic expectations of workers, who effectively organized and created politically influential labor unions.

By the end of the nineteenth century the worldwide demand for Uruguayan exports had grown dramatically; traditional fibers like wool had not yet been challenged by synthetic ones, and by the mid-1870s the technology of refrigerated ships had made the export of fresh meat possible. The rural sector provided the capital on which the nation's development and wealth were based, subsidizing the industrial, commercial, and financial interests of the capital city, Montevideo. Export revenues allowed the importation of consumer goods demanded by the urban dwellers and helped supply the capital for Montevideo's own inefficient industrialization. Because the small-scale industrialization was inefficient, expensive, and monopolistic, industrial products could not compete in export markets or domestically in quality or price with imports. However, the workers who the industries employed, concentrated in and around the capital city, grew in number and became more highly organized and politically active than their rural counterparts; for them the process of industrialization was popular. There emerged an inevitable conflict between the rural and urban interests in the country, one in which the capital city eventually prevailed by virtue of its greater population. The situation was a corrosive and dangerous one in which the affluence, growth, and consumption of the urban area were being subsidized by the rural areas, whose economy was slowly deteriorating.

By the end of World War II the demand for Uruguayan exports had begun to decline. Other supplies of fresh meat were available in international markets, particularly for Uruguay's largest trading partner, Great Britain, and wool fibers were being replaced by synthetic ones. Rather than responding to these changes, the traditional rural economy continued producing the same export commodities, and so export revenues decreased within a context of shrinking demand.[2] Uruguay's failure to renovate its export economy and to recognize and respond to major shifts in international demand and new technologies set in motion a slow process of economic decay, which went largely unnoticed by the public until after decades its cumulative effects were clearly visible. The eventual political implications were disastrous.

At the end of World War II neighboring Argentina and Brazil, not to mention Mexico, were effectively industrializing at rapid rates, but industrial growth in Uruguay had slowed dramatically. The worsening imbalance between export revenues and import costs, an imbalance seriously aggravated by the sharp rise in the cost of imported energy in the 1970s, severely strained the country's financial solvency and encouraged two further and ultimately disastrous economic decisions. To sustain economic growth and financial liquidity the civilian governments expanded the money supply, inducing rapid and at times rampant inflation, and the country increasingly borrowed money from international sources to subsidize its worsening trade deficit.

The first policy eroded the confidence of Uruguayan investors and encouraged an accelerating capital flight and decline in investment. It also destroyed the ability of the urban middle and working classes to save or to maintain (not to mention to improve) their living standards, which eventually alienated a substantial portion of the electorate and eroded confidence in the economic system. The second policy created a massive international debt, which by the mid-1980s was equal to about half the annual national per capita income. In the decade from 1977 to 1986 the level of international debt in Uruguay increased by more than 400 percent, one of the highest rates of increase in the hemisphere, and that was largely under a military government committed to economic austerity and willing to endure the response to unpopular policies.

Economic decay was not an unpredictable, catastrophic experience that instantly devastated living standards and economic activity. It was slow, incremental, and entirely predictable, but the difficult political decisions required to reverse it were not or could not be made, even by a military government. As economic conditions deteriorated following World War II and a brief boom brought on by the Korean War, increasing demands were imposed on the government to provide compensatory services and subsidization, which in turn created more public spending and inflation, further discouraged domestic and foreign investment, and ultimately reinforced the general pattern of economic decline and the political problems associated with it. Although the country had achieved one of the highest standards of living in Latin America, Uruguay began to face apparently unsolvable economic problems, which continue to frustrate the nation's politics and politicians today.

The country's economic performance in the 1990s was strong by historical standards, thanks for the most part to the creation of the Southern Common Market with its significant increase in intraregional trade. Gross domestic product grew by 7.9 percent in 1992, 3.0 percent in 1993, and 6.3 percent in 1994; slid to a negative 1.8 percent in 1995; and moved back nicely with a 5.3 percent increase in 1996, 5.1 percent in 1997, and 5.3 percent in 1998. Brazil's currency crisis put Uruguay in recession in 1999. The big news on the economic front is that Uruguay's decades-old battle with inflation is finally close to victory. Inflation was only 4.5 percent for the first six months of 1998, making that year the first in memory with single-digit inflation. The inflation rate has trended downward since 1998.

The government deficit was reduced to 1.4 percent of the GDP in 1997, with a reduction to 1.2 percent for 1998, but an increase in 1999 due to the recession. Net public foreign debt as a percent of GDP declined from a high of 44 percent during the debt crisis of the 1980s to a manageable 13 percent of GDP in 1996. Private investment in machinery and equipment more than quadrupled (admittedly from very low levels) from 1986 to 1996. However, Uruguay continues to have a poor investment and savings rate and a not very stellar record of attracting foreign investment.

Imports and exports grew at about 13 percent in 1996 and 1997, again reflecting increased trade with Argentina and Brazil. Only 7 percent of Uruguay's exports are destined for the United States, which only supplies 12 percent of its imports. On the other hand, Argentina and Brazil together accounted for 46 percent of exports in 1996, and some 43 percent of imports, with Brazil alone the destination of over one-third of Uruguay's exports.

Unemployment in this security-conscious country remains stubbornly high, at about 11 percent of the workforce. Unemployment rose significantly in 1996 but strong economic growth in 1996–1997 reduced it to the average of recent years. Nevertheless, this relatively high unemployment rate has helped the left in terms of its credibility and criticism of the government.

When all is said and done the tiny Uruguayan economy, coupled with the state's historic commitment to welfare policies, allows a homogeneous population of some 3.2 million people to maintain the highest Physical Quality of Life Index (PQLI) in Latin America, according to the United Nations.

The Uruguayan people are themselves a distinctive mixture. During the colonial period the country had virtually no indigenous population. Most immigrants were from Spain and Italy, the latter primarily in the late nineteenth and early twentieth centuries. These were largely middle- and working-class people from urban areas, attracted to the prosperous and expanding Uruguayan economy, who remained in the capital city of Montevideo. They brought with them European political attitudes and economic expectations, which were absorbed into the country's party politics. Today about half the national population resides in the capital city. Rural life, perhaps because of its historic economic importance, spawned a mythology of its own centered about the gaucho, but the reality of rural life has little in common with the myths. During the period of economic decay following World War II and the Korean War there was a substantial migration of urban Uruguayans out of the country, many of them to Argentina and Brazil, a process reinforced by the turbulent political conditions of the 1960s and the subsequent military dictatorship.

Uruguay was one of the first nations in Latin America to make a major commitment to public education, with the result that a high level of literacy was achieved at a relatively early time. With literacy came high levels of political awareness and participation along with modern socioeconomic expectations.

Political Organization in Uruguay

Uruguay is a highly organized society, with clearly defined interest groups and complex political parties, but the society is organized in organic rather than pluralistic ways. The framework for this organization was devised by José Batlle to achieve political stability out of the chaotic experience of civil wars, international intervention, and party-organized conflict.

The nineteenth century produced two political parties: the Colorado Party and the National Party, more commonly known as the Blanco Party (the parties originally were identified by the color of the brassards their adherents wore during armed confrontations). After generations of fighting for national hegemony, often with international provocation from Brazil, Argentina, and Great Britain, the possibility of economic prosperity, which came in the 1870s with the potential for a rapid expansion of exports, dramatized the advantages of cooperation rather than armed conflict for advancing the economic interests of both sides. The resolution of the civil conflict was promoted and eventually achieved by José Batlle.

Batlle was a descendant of a politically prominent and influential Uruguayan family that has produced many important political leaders. He was elected president twice, in 1903 and 1911, and established the framework for modern Uruguayan politics and government. After defeating the Blancos in the last of the civil wars he established a political compromise with them based on the concepts of parity and coparticipation. Parity recognized the "legitimate" interests of the Blancos in the rural departments where they were strong, and Batlle all but ceded these departments to their control. He also accepted their participation in the national government, proportional to their share of the national vote, and allowed them a share of government patronage and revenues. The Blanco Party won only three subsequent national elections—in 1958, 1962, and 1989—and became virtually a permanent minority. Batlle's Colorado Party consistently attracted more voters nationally than the Blancos, but it was willing to share with the Blancos the exercise and benefits of power. The 1952 constitution went so far as to formalize coparticipation by awarding two of five positions on the boards of all state enterprises to the minority party.

Batlle designed an electoral system that incorporates parity and coparticipation both within and between the nation's political parties.[3] The Uruguayan electoral system regulates parties, elections, and the distribution of legislative seats, establishing *lemas* and *sublemas*, which are equivalent to parties and party factions. Lemas are made up of sublemas, factions that are the supporters or political machines of individual leaders. Anyone can form a sublema, acquire formal identification within a lema, and in effect create a personal political organization with a separate identity. The electoral strength of a sublema and its leader adds to the total vote of a lema, which in turn determines both lema and sublema legislative representation. Ambitious political leaders are thereby permitted into the political system and can exercise political influence proportional to their ability to attract votes. Their organizations are integrated into the larger lema, or party coalition, and they have a vested interest in the success of other sublemas, which they nonetheless campaign against because their representation is determined by their share of the cumulative vote for the lema. Presidential elections used to have the effect of combining a primary election with a general election.

Sublemas in Uruguay form the nucleus of political organization and encourage a clientele relationship between the party leaders and the voters. Constituents with problems can request help from sublema leaders and their organizations, and in Montevideo sublemas maintain neighborhood clubs and organize campaigning. Through cross-endorsement, cross-listing, and a sharing of candidates, they form additional coalitions among themselves within the lemas, coalitions that constantly shift from one election to another.

The lema system is formalized by proportional representation, which allocates legislative representation according to the size of the popular vote. Campaign costs are also subsidized for sublemas according to the size of their vote. For the voter the system encourages a general identification with a lema and a personal identification with a sublema. The general electoral system also reinforces the Colorado and Blanco parties, which benefit principally from it, and restrains the growth and success of new or smaller parties.

José Batlle built the Colorado Party into the majority political organization by mobilizing the urban classes of Montevideo and appealing to their interests. He proposed—and while president implemented—vast public programs of education, culture, welfare, and social security. He encouraged industrialization and resisted foreign penetration of the country's economy. Batlle advocated abolishing the presidency as an institution and replacing it with a rotating collegial executive, an idea he borrowed from Switzerland. His reasoning was that the dictatorships that were so common in Latin America were the result of an inevitable greed for power, and because one could not change human nature, the only way to prevent dictatorships was to abolish the presidency and replace it with an institution that dispersed power. Batlle was by profession a journalist (he founded El Día, the largest daily newspaper in Montevideo), and he used his journalistic interest to further his political objectives, a process that continues today in Uruguay. Opposition to his leadership arose within the Colorado Party, and anti-Batllista factions (sublemas) were formed.

Batlle's ideas were visionary for their time: He initiated a modern welfare state in Uruguay long before it had been tried elsewhere. He was a consummate politician, but his political pragmatism was tempered by his idealism. Batlle believed he could eliminate instability and turmoil by expanding and organizing the political base of the country and by responding to the basic needs of the Uruguayan people.

In spite of his influence and success Batlle's ideas were based on two vulnerable assumptions, both of which proved to be erroneous and eventually contributed to the decay of Uruguayan democracy. The first was the assumption of continued economic growth and prosperity, a common perspective among industrializing nations during the nineteenth century. This assumption was drawn from the experiences of large nations, specifically Great Britain, France, Germany, and the United States, and proved inappropriate for Uruguay. The second was the assumption that a collegial executive could prevent authoritarian governments. Uruguay did not experiment with a pure form of collegial executive until the 1950s, perhaps the worst possible moment because the economy was in the process of decline and strong leadership was desperately needed. Ironically, for eight of the twelve collegial executive years the government was controlled by the Blanco Party, the first time in the twentieth century it had prevailed in national elections. The experiment with a collegial executive, combined with the economic dilemmas for which no answers could be found, contributed to the political paralysis that encouraged a revolutionary group known as the Tupamaros and, ultimately, military intervention. The Tupamaros did not succeed in taking power, but they did provoke the military to do so.

There have always been minor political parties in Uruguay. One of the oldest was the Civic Union (UC), a conservative Catholic organization that provided an alternative to the prevailing tradition of anticlericalism that Batlle sponsored. By the 1960s several small parties combined with a dissident liberal sublema of the Colorado Party to form an electoral coalition, originally known as the Leftist Front of Freedom (FIDEL) and ultimately as the Broad Front (*Frente Amplio*). Included in the Broad Front were the Communist Party of Uruguay, the Christian Democratic Party, the Socialist Party, and List 99 of the Colorado Party, established by Zelmar Michelini. By combining the strengths of small parties in the 1971, 1984, and 1989 elections, the coalition posed a serious threat to the two traditional lemas, which in many ways are themselves political coalitions. Civic Union disappeared following redemocratization, replaced by *Nuevo Espacio* (New Space), an organization of radical Catholics and social democrats, some of whom had supported the Broad Front.

Like the political parties, economic interests have been well organized in Uruguay. The organizations include national associations of ranchers, business enterprises, and labor. Labor organizations emerged very early in Uruguay and were modeled after their European counterparts. The largest labor organization, the National Confederation of Workers (CNT), is Marxist, but its strength has not necessarily been translated into votes for Marxist parties. Organized workers were a principal target for Batlle's policies, and a large proportion have been Colorado Party supporters in spite of their union's orientation. The CNT was outlawed under the dictatorship, but a new organization, the *Plenario Intersindical de Trabajadores* (PIT), formed in the early 1980s and subsequently merged with the CNT after the reestablishment of democracy.

The political scenario that eventually produced a military dictatorship is a long and complex one. Military intervention occurred gradually, although by mid-1973 the military was fully in control of the government. The Tupamaro revolutionary movement, specializing in urban terrorism in the capital city, became a highly destabilizing influence during the 1960s. The government retaliated with a state of siege, massive arrests, torture, suppression of political leaders and groups, and censorship, but these actions were ineffective and even counterproductive. The military gradually assumed responsibility for the Tupamaro threat and brought the civilian institution under its control.

The military regime had both successes and failures in managing the economy, but the experience proved unpopular with Uruguayans and divisive for the military. No single military leader was able to consolidate his control, although one (Gregorio Álvarez) tried. The military response to the Tupamaros was brutal and, for Uruguay, unprecedented. The movement was crushed, but at exceptionally high costs to Uruguayan legal and political values. In fact, the guerrillas were crushed before the military took control of the government in June 1973. The military ruled until 1985.

By the early 1980s the military leaders had begun to recognize the inevitability of restoring civilian rule and began looking for a way to maximize their continuing influence and minimize any retribution against them—individually and institutionally—after leaving power. They looked for inspiration to Brazil, whose officers were methodically and gradually returning that country's government to civilian control, and they were aware of the chaotic experience occurring in Argentina, where the military was leaving power in disgrace and facing civilian retribution.

The military regime decided to hold a referendum in 1980 on a new constitution that would protect the military's political influence, a referendum held under conditions of tight controls and censorship. Not only was the measure defeated, it was so decisively defeated that the regime had no choice but to acknowledge its failure. At that point military officers began negotiating with civilian political leaders, at least those they were willing to talk with, about conditions for a return to civilian rule. This change was formally achieved in March 1985 after elections the preceding November in which two of the major presidential contenders, Wilson Ferreira Aldunate of the Blanco Party and Liber Seregni of the Broad Front, were prohibited from being candidates.

The victor in 1985 was a Colorado Party candidate, Julio María Sanguinetti. Party voting and the resulting legislative representation were very similar to what they had been in 1971—the last election before the total military takeover. The Colorado regime encountered difficulties and controversies in its quest for normalization, and in the 1989 elections the Blanco party, for only the third time in history, prevailed, winning a plurality in the two legislative chambers and electing a president, the moderate Blanco leader Luis Alberto Lacalle. In 1994 the Colorados again won the presidency, but only barely, with the Blancos and the Broad Front close behind. National politics seemed to have been transformed by that election, perhaps permanently, to a three-party system.

Government Structure and Policies

Uruguay has a centralized government and is divided into nineteen departments, including the capital city of Montevideo. Virtually all decisions in the country are made at the national level. The 1966 constitution allows departments to elect local legislatures comprising thirty-one members and an intendente, the departmental administrative officer.

The president is popularly elected for a five-year term, and all elections in the country are held simultaneously. The legislature is bicameral, with ninety-nine representatives in the Chamber of Deputies, elected from districts, and thirty-one in the Senate, with the nation as a single district. All are elected by proportional representation. The current constitution was adopted in 1966 in the aftermath of the twelve-year experiment with a collegial executive. The legislature has considerable power and is organized through a system of committees.

In December 1996, after years of discussion, a reform was narrowly approved by the voters in a constitutional plebiscite. Under the new system each party can run only one presidential candidate, who will be chosen by primaries conducted in each party and ratified at a party convention. To be elected president the successful candidate must receive at least 50 percent of the total vote or face a runoff (ballotage) against his nearest competitor. Given the 1994 electoral results such a runoff appeared all but a certainty for 1999, which in fact turned out to be the case, as discussed below.

This constitutional reform, which passed by the barest margin (50.3 percent) in a national referendum, represents a revolutionary change in the electoral system. In brief, the most significant features are as follows:

1. Although elections will continue to take place every five years, unlike the old system each party can now have only one presidential candidate.
2. A primary system was established to determine each party's candidate. The successful candidate must obtain at least 40 percent of the primary vote, with a 10 percent difference between the winner and the nearest competitor. If not, a party convention will choose the candidate.
3. To win the presidency the successful candidate must obtain an absolute majority of the votes. If not, a second round (ballotage) will take place between the top finalists. The first round will take place the last Sunday in October. If a second round is required, it will take place the last Sunday in November.
4. Local elections are now separated from national elections. Elections for *intendentes* of the nineteen departments and their local legislative bodies will take place in May of the year following the presidential and congressional elections.

There are several major implications of these reforms. First, the elected president will be able to claim majority support, a result unheard of under the old system. Second, voters may have to choose from candidates not of their party, or even of their liking, in the second round. Third, the primary system may help produce a real party leader as opposed to the historical norm of leaders of party factions. Finally, local governments will be elected at a different time from the national government, allowing ticket-splitting for the first time in history. This may help generate more power at the local level and, with it, more demands on the central government.

The Uruguayan economy is a distinctive mixture of private and public enterprises. Most of the economy is privately owned and managed, but about 20 percent of the gross domestic product (GDP) comes from state-owned companies. The largest of the state-owned monopolies is the *Asociación Nacional de Combustibles, Alcohol y Portland* (ANCAP), which refines petroleum and manufactures alcohol and cement. That agency alone accounts for 4 percent of the GDP. In the 1970s there was an effort to encourage international banking in Uruguay to provide "offshore" benefits to foreign banks and investors and stimulate economic development by encouraging new investments in the country. The policy was partially successful and was supported by the military regimes and the subsequent civilian governments.

What has historically given Uruguay the appearance of a welfare state has been not so much the direct participation of the government in the economy but the benefits provided by the government. Nowhere is this situation more apparent than in the social security system, which partially supports over 350,000 retired Uruguayans, a number equal to almost one-third of the active workforce. Low population growth means Uruguay has the highest proportion of retired persons of any Latin American nation, and this fact, combined with state-provided retirement benefits, creates an enormous financial burden on the people who are economically active.

The economic problems facing the Sanguinetti government in 1985 were formidable. The rural economy needed revitalization, both for export objectives and for food production; Uruguay had one of the highest per capita international debts in the region; national investment and economic growth were low; and the foreign trade situation was critical, with exports failing to provide sufficient revenues to pay for the energy, resources, and manufactured goods the country needed to import as well as to service its international debt. The only course the government had available was economic austerity, not a policy designed to cushion the return to civilian, democratic government. Besides these economic problems the erosion of public services and programs and a decline in real income and savings during the twelve years of military control had stimulated new demands, which were difficult for political leaders to ignore in the restored democratic environment, but even more difficult for them to meet. Economic performance during the Colorado administration of President Julio Sanguinetti was better than most expected, based on a policy of economic liberalism.

The next president, Blanco leader Luis Alberto Lacalle, continued that policy, significantly reducing the foreign debt, renegotiating debt payments, attracting new investment, and repatriating fugitive capital. Efforts to privatize state corporations, however, met considerable opposition, resulting in another plebiscite in 1993 that overturned with 72 percent of the vote a legislative decision to sell the state telephone monopoly (ANTEL). Plans to privatize the state natural gas monopoly, the state fishing corporation, and the state electric utility seemed at least temporarily moribund. After the vote president Lacalle sarcastically observed, "Uruguay is a country that has been very happy for a very long time, and prefers a little with security rather than a lot with risk." Normalcy in Uruguay apparently meant public enterprises and service as usual, but Lacalle did cut Uruguay's high tariffs and joined the regional Southern Common Market, consisting of Argentina, Brazil, Paraguay, and Uruguay.

The Uruguayan military is professional by Latin American standards and, except for the recent dictatorship, it stayed out of politics for most of the twentieth century. During the dictatorship the size of the military grew at least 400 percent, and defense expenditures rose appreciably to a percentage of the GDP far exceeding that of Brazil, Argentina, or Mexico.

One of the principal objectives of normalization following redemocratization was to bring the military under the control of civilians, and the major issue was how to deal with military leaders who were responsible for human rights violations during the dictatorship. The issue plagued the Sanguinetti government, which was otherwise preoccupied with economic problems, and impeded the normalization of national politics. In late 1987 the legislature passed an amnesty bill that prevented prosecution of military and police personnel for human rights violations during the dictatorship. The legislation was very unpopular and provoked a petition campaign to hold a referendum on the legislation and the question of immunity. Public opinion polls showed that a majority of Uruguayans believed that military personnel did commit human rights violations during the dictatorship and that those who did should be punished. The petition campaign forced a referendum, which was held in April 1989, but the effort to overturn the immunity legislation failed by a negative vote of 53 percent. The majority of voters in Montevideo, however, voted in favor of the referendum. The fate of the disappeared continues to be an issue in Uruguayan politics.

The Uruguayan military never engaged in the mass killings their Argentine and Chilean comrades are so infamous for. However, they did arrest thousands and subject them to torture while also imposing a draconian rule on Uruguay's citizens from 1973 to 1985. The number of disappeared in Uruguay totaled a few dozen, with some 140 Uruguayans sharing the same fate in Argentina. The whereabouts of these individuals has never been clarified by the Uruguayan military. Children born to captive and subsequently disappeared Uruguayans are being sought by their relatives in much the same manner as the mothers and grandmothers of the Plaza de Mayo in Argentina. President Batlle was directly involved in this issue and planned to convene a commission to investigate and issue a report on the matter.

Many government leaders had felt that it was necessary to end the bitter recriminations and focus on the task of economic development. They also wanted to finesse an issue that might create a confrontation with military leaders and raise the possibility of another military intervention. Their efforts seem to have had the desired effects. Former Tupamaros have been largely reintegrated into national politics through the Broad Front. Their former leader, Raúl Sendic, ironically died in Paris shortly before the plebiscite. The military has remained out of politics and under civilian control, but it is unclear whether its political influence has been permanently contained.

The first truly open national elections since the end of the military dictatorship were held on November 26, 1989. The Blanco Party won a plurality of the vote with 38 percent, and one of its leaders, Luis Alberto Lacalle, was elected president. Colorado candidates received less than one-third of the vote, and the Broad Front about one-fifth. The latter did, however, receive a plurality (34 percent) in the municipal elections for the city of Montevideo, electing a Socialist mayor, Dr. Tabaré Vásquez, and a majority of the municipal council. The failure of the Colorados to mobilize their traditional support in Montevideo was critical to their loss, but the results were ambiguous on the question of electoral realignment. They seemed to imply at the least a three-way party competition in the future.

National elections held in November 1994 confirmed that implication. Former President Julio Sanguinetti (1985–1989) barely won the election as the Colorado Party presidential candidate, and his party received only about 32 percent of the vote. The Blanco Party received somewhat more than 31 percent and the Broad Front, in a coalition known as the Progressive Front, only slightly less. The election signaled the end of the traditional two-party dominance of Uruguayan politics and a new balance between the three political forces. The Broad Front won the majority of Montevideo for the second consecutive time. After his inauguration in March 1995, President Sanguinetti stressed the need to reform the burdensome social security system in the country, in which there is now one retired person for every two workers, and which consumes almost 40 percent of the national budget.

The 1999 party primaries proved no contest for the left, where Tabaré Vásquez easily won the nomination, and for the Blancos, whose former president, Luis Lacalle, also won handily but found himself with a bitterly divided party. The Colorado primary was hard fought, but in the end perennial candidate Jorge Batlle, son of one president and grandnephew of another, won the nomination.

In the first round of the elections the left, in a historic breakthrough, finished first with some 39 percent of the vote. The Colorado candidate finished second with 32 percent, and the Blancos finished a dismal third with only 22 percent. The Frente Amplio thus emerged as the single largest political force in the country, with high hopes of capturing the presidency in a runoff election with the Colorados. The Blanco leadership threw its support to Batlle, but no one could be sure that the rank and file would follow suit. Up until ten days before the second round all the polls showed Vásquez with a slight lead, but the final poll results showed that Batlle had pulled into a statistical dead heat. Uruguayans were both apprehensive and excited as election day approached. The undecided voters broke heavily for Batlle, who prevailed by 52 to 45 percent.

Uruguay began the new century with a wake-up call to its traditional parties. The voters indicated that although a majority still favors the rule of Colorados and Blancos, they wanted more creative solutions to the country's endemic problems of high unemployment and mediocre growth. They also wanted politicians who do not feel they are entitled to their power and get too comfortable sharing its spoils with friends and family.

Even before the events of September 11, 2001 was a difficult year for Uruguay. President Batlle's first full calendar year in office confronted him with a worsening of Uruguay's economic situation exacerbated by an outbreak of Foot-and-Mouth disease (*Aftosa*) that seriously disrupted Uruguay's meat exports. The government had hoped that 2001 would bring modest economic growth after two years of recession. Unfortunately, the continued devaluation of the Brazilian currency—the *Real*—and the deepening economic and political crisis in Argentina had adverse effects on both Uruguayan exports and tourism. With these internal and external conditions unemployment skyrocketed to some 16 percent and the GDP was a negative 1.1 percent for the first half of the year. The only good news on the economic front was the continued low inflation rate of 4 to 5 percent.

Unfortunately, 2002 was a year of worsening economic crisis for Uruguay.[4] The financial meltdown in Argentina and the political and economic instability in Brazil caused by the election of the leftist candidate Luis Inacio Lula da Silva (Lula) led to a deepening recession in Uruguay.

The most negative effect on the Uruguayan economy was produced by the freeze on deposits in Argentina caused by the collapse of the Argentine peso when that government abandoned its convertibility plan, which pegged its currency at one-to-one with the U.S. dollar. This forced many Argentines to withdraw dollars from their bank accounts in the traditionally safe haven of

Montevideo. The subsequent collapse of two banks in Uruguay had many Uruguayans fearing for the safety of their banking system, leading them also to withdraw funds. The result was that in the first seven months of the year Uruguay lost 81 percent of its foreign reserves. The country's sovereign debt abruptly declined from investment grade to junk status during the same period. The Gross Domestic Product fell 7.8 percent in the first half of the year and was expected to contract some 10 or 11 percent for the year as a whole. Uruguay's GDP has declined some 20 percent since the recession started in 1999. Unemployment climbed to a record 17 percent. Inflation, which was a mere 3.59 percent in 2001, hit 24 percent by September and was expected to go slightly higher by the end of the year.

President Jorge Batlle of the ruling Colorado Party tried to contain the damage but was obliged to accept the resignation of his Minister of the Economy, Albert Bensión, and replace him with the more highly respected Alejandro Atchugarry. The good will Batlle enjoyed in Washington helped him obtain a $1.5 billion bridge loan from the United States to keep the banking system solvent until over $3 billion in funds could arrive from the IMF, the World Bank, and the Inter-American Development Bank (IADB). Politically, the left appeared to be gaining strength as a result of the economic crisis. By October, polls showed that the leader of the leftist coalition, Dr. Tabaré Vásquez, would receive some 50 percent of the vote.

The following year proved no less difficult for the Uruguayan economy, but not as disastrous as the previous one. (After a fall in Gross Domestic Product of over 10 percent in 2002 and a further decline of 6 percent in the first half of 2003, data for the second half pointed to enough economic strengthening to lead to the expectation that Uruguay would record no growth or a modest decline for the year as a whole. In May Uruguay successfully renegotiated its private debt with an innovative bond exchange that stretched out the repayment schedule, thus giving some breathing room for the last two years of the Batlle Administration and the first year of the next government. The banking system remained deeply depressed with nonperforming loans running at 25 percent at private banks and a staggering 50 percent at such key public institutions as the Banco de la República and the Mortgage Bank (Banco Hipotecario). The later institution lost $1.1 billion in 2002.

The year 2004 was an exciting and pivotal time in Uruguay. After nearly four years of sharply negative growth the economy—aided by recovery in Argentina, strong growth in Brazil, and excellent commodity prices—grew by a robust 13.6 percent in the first half of the year. Unfortunately for the ruling Colorado Party, little of this positive macroeconomic performance filtered down to Uruguay's poor or to the middle class. Unemployment remained above 13 percent, and more than one-third of Uruguayans lived in poverty.

In this context the presidential and congressional elections that took place on October 31 marked a sea change in Uruguayan politics. Throughout the year the polls showed that the leftist coalition known as the Broad Front-Progressive Encounter was the largest party in the country. The question that remained was whether it would secure the 50 percent plus one vote it needed in order to avoid a runoff with one of the traditional parties, the Blanco Party (PN) or the Colorados. In the last two weeks before the election all of Uruguay's polls agreed that the socialists had reached the magical number needed to avoid a second round and that Tabaré Vásquez would be president. Dr. Tabaré Vásquez (known as Tabaré) is a sixty-four-year-old oncologist who has been the political leader of the Frente Amplio leftist coalition since he was their presidential candidate in 1994. Tabaré had been elected mayor *(intendente)* of Montevideo in 1989 in what was a breakthrough election for the left. A Socialist Party militant, Tabaré is photogenic and charismatic and has carefully juggled his coalition that includes social democrats, democratic socialists, socialists, communists, and ex-Tupamaros.

In the election itself, the left received 50.4 percent of the vote, followed by the Blancos (34 percent) and the Colorados (10 percent). Vásquez was to assume office on March 1, 2005. The historic victory by Vásquez and the left was seen by many to further strengthen the hand of Brazilian President Luiz Inácio Lula da Silva as he sought to turn MERCOSUR into the major voice for Latin American economic integration and the chief interlocutor with both the European Union and the United States in trade negotiations. Vásquez's victory was the latest example in South America of a move to the left and center-left.

Globalization, the Challenges for Economic Growth, and the Consolidation of Democracy

Democracy has been very successfully consolidated in Uruguay. There have been five democratic national elections since the restoration of democracy at the end of 1984, and all three major parties have now won at least one of these elections. Elections in Uruguay are remarkably clean with full civil liberties, freedom of the press, and electronic media a given. The recent victory by the left is taken by most as a sign of democratic maturity rather than a harbinger of future political conflict.

Globalization and regionalization under MERCOSUR has shown mixed results for Uruguay. The neoliberal model adopted by Blanco president Luis Lacalle (1989–1994) and Colorado president Julio Sanguinetti (1994–1999) brought decent growth and an explosion of consumer credit in the mid- and late 1990s along with a boost in tourism and trade with its two large neighbors. Unfortunately, Jorge Batlle, Colorado President from 2000 to 2004, presided over the worst financial crises since the depression after the 1999 Brazilian devaluation led to a financial meltdown in Argentina that, not suprisingly, spread to Uruguay. The economic crisis in the first three years of the new millennium was a key factor in the left's electoral victory.

China and India may have an increasingly important role to play in Uruguay's future. Already, the Indian software giant, Ta-Ta Consultancy, is guaranteeing a job to all computer science graduates in Uruguay. China's huge demand for food and raw materials is already benefiting the Southern Cone and Uruguay should get a piece of this export boom.

If the left can ride and manage this positive economic scenario, its election could prove to be more than a one-term phenomenon .

Suggestions for Further Reading

Campiglia, Nestor. *Los Grupos de Presión y el Proceso Político*. Montevideo: Arca, 1969.

Garce, Adolfo, and Jaffe, Jaime. *La era progresista*. Montevideo: Editorial Fin de Siglo, 2004.

Gillespie, Charles G. "Activists and Floating Voters: The Unheeded Lessons of Uruguay's 1982 Primaries." In *Elections and Democratization in Latin America, 1980–1985*, ed. P. W. Drake and E. Silva. San Diego, CA: Center for Iberian and Latin American Studies, Center for U.S.-Mexican Studies, Institute of the Americas, 1986.

Gonzales, Luis E. *Political Structures and Democracy in Uruguay*. Notre Dame, IN: University of Notre Dame Press, 1991.

Handelman, Howard. "Prelude to Elections: The Military's Legitimacy Crisis and the 1980 Constitutional Plebiscite in Uruguay." In *Elections and Democratization in Latin America, 1980–1985*, ed. P. W. Drake and E. Silva. San Diego, CA: Center for Iberian and Latin American Studies, Center for U.S.-Mexican Studies, Institute of the Americas, 1986.

———. "Uruguay." *In Military Government and the Movement toward Democracy in South America*, ed. H. Handelman and T. G. Sanders. Bloomington: Indiana University Press, 1981.

Kaufman, Eli. *Uruguay in Transition*. New Brunswick, NJ: Transaction Books, 1978.

McDonald, Ronald H. "Legislative Politics in Uruguay: A Preliminary Analysis." In *Latin American Legislatures: Their Role and Influence*, ed. W. H. Agor. New York: Praeger, 1971.

———. "Redemocratization in Uruguay." In *Liberalization and Redemocratization in Latin America*, ed. G. Lopez and M. Stohl. Westport, CT: Greenwood, 1987.

————. "The Rise of Military Politics in Uruguay." *Inter-American Economic Affairs* 28 (1975): 25–43.

————. "Uruguay." In *Political Parties and Elections in Latin America*, ed. Ronald H. McDonald and J. Mark Ruhl. Boulder, CO: Westview Press, 1989.

Rial, Juan. "The Uruguayan Elections of 1984: A Triumph of the Center." In *Elections and Democratization in Latin America, 1980–1985*, ed. P.W. Drake and E. Silva, San Diego, CA: Center for Iberian and Latin American Studies, Center for U.S.-Mexican Studies, Institute of the Americas, 1986.

Taylor, Philip B. "The Electoral System in Uruguay." *Journal of Politics* 17 (1955): 19–42.

————. "Interests and Institutional Dysfunction in Uruguay." *American Political Science Review* 58 (1963): 62–74.

Weinstein, Martin. *Uruguay: The Politics of Failure*. Westport, CT: Greenwood, 1975.

————. *Uruguay: Democracy at the Crossroads*. Boulder, CO: Westview Press, 1988.

Notes

1. The bulk of this chapter was co-authored with Ronald H. MacDonald. The material from 2001 on is my [Martin Weinstein's] sole responsibility.

2. By comparison, Argentina has been reasonably successful in adjusting its rural exports—balancing cattle and grain exports—as international demand and prices have changed.

3. The discussion in the next several paragraphs is adopted from my [Martin Weinstein's] entries on Uruguay in the 2002–2004 editions of the *Britannica Book of the Year*.

4. For a more extensive discussion see Ronald H. McDonald and J. Mark Ruhl, *Political Parties and Elections in Latin America* (Boulder, CO: Westview Press, 1989), 91–110.

13

Paraguay
Democracy Challenged

Paul C. Sondrol

Sixteen years since the 1989 coup d'état ending General Alfredo Stroessner's thirty-five-year autocracy, Paraguay's crawl toward democracy shows both substantive and symbolic progress, while lingering authoritarian/praetorian impulses, corruption, and impunity systematically prevail over justice and the rule of law. In 2005 Paraguayan politics is a hybrid political system lying somewhere between a less-than-democratic and less-than-truly authoritarian regime.

Semitropical Paraguay is bordered by Argentina to the south and west, Bolivia to the north, and Brazil to the east. The country's name comes from the river dividing the fertile grasslands of the east from the drier Chaco region of the north and west. Slightly smaller than California (157,047 square miles) and located in the heart of South America, Paraguay, with fewer than six million people, is one of the least densely populated countries on earth.

Paraguay, like Uruguay, is a buffer state, historically ensnared between the combined and conflicting ambitions of Argentina and Brazil. The history of Paraguayan foreign relations is one of attempts to maintain sovereignty by counterbalancing the covetous influences of its powerful neighbors. Like Bolivia, Paraguay is landlocked, and this status and remoteness, and the problems that are a direct consequence of this isolation, continue to impact foreign policy.

Paraguay's political experience is largely a monotonous history of dictators, coups, and bloody wars. This authoritarian, militarist heritage has produced a nation that today remains comparatively poor, parochial, and underdeveloped. Paraguay's experience of periodic military invasions from Argentina, Bolivia, and Brazil has exaggerated the nation's insecurity, accented its authoritarian politics, and solidified an ultranationalist mentality.

Paraguayans are the most racially and culturally homogeneous peoples in Latin America (95 percent of the population is *mestizo*), thus avoiding the racial/class cleavages found in other Hispanic countries. Seventeen indigenous peoples constitute 3 percent of the population and remain the most marginalized sector of Paraguayan society. Paraguay is one of the few bilingual countries in the Western Hemisphere and the only one where an aboriginal language, Guaraní, is spoken more widely than a European tongue. Government and most business is conducted in Spanish, but 90 percent of the population speaks Guaraní. The extremely arid Chaco region, bordering Bolivia, contains about 60 percent of Paraguay's territory but only 3 to 4 percent of the population. Most Paraguayans live east of the Paraguay river on isolated farms or in small villages or towns in the lush arcadia.

History and Political Culture

Both Portuguese and Spaniards explored Paraguay, fruitlessly looking for gold, in the early sixteenth century. Asunción, the oldest city in the Rio de la Plata basin, was founded by the Spanish in 1537 after hostile Indians forced them to abandon fortifications near present-day Buenos Aires. Asunción became the administrative center of Spanish colonial power over southern South America between 1537 and 1617, but the lack of precious metals and its remoteness soon relegated the town to little more than a fortified trading post and bulwark against the Portuguese in Brazil.

Spaniards in Paraguay quickly found that survival in such a poor, isolated place required independence; they developed their own ways and resented interference by neglectful Spanish authorities. Overwhelmingly dependent on a subsistence agrarian economy lacking easy access to markets, the colony lapsed into a stagnant backwater. With the transfer of colonial government to Buenos Aires in 1617, Spanish interest in Paraguay virtually ceased.

Spanish settlers in Paraguay developed a cordial relationship with the native Guaraní and formed alliances against more ferocious tribes, as well as for food, labor, and concubines. Within a generation Spaniards were incorporated into the Indian lineage system on a kinship basis. The extensive polygamy influenced subsequent cultural developments in colonial Paraguay and produced a different social order than those elsewhere in South America. Acculturation, intermarriage, and racial miscegenation resulted in a few generations in a unique racial culture amalgamated from Spanish and indigenous influences, with few socio-cultural distinctions separating rulers from the ruled. Paraguay

BOLIVIA

• Fortín Ingavi

Fortín Madrejón •

• Villazón

BRAZIL

Fuerte Olimpo •
Puerto Guaraní •

GRAN CHACO

Puerto Sastre •

Bella Vista

Mariscal • Minas-cué •
Estigarribia
• La Esmeralda   Filadelfia •   Puerto Casado •

Pedro Juan Caballero •

Rio Pilcomayo

Rio Verde

Horqueta •
Concepción •
• Puerto Ybapobó

Rio Paraguay

• San Pedro

Rio Bermejo

• Rosario
San Estanislao

Rio Pilcomayo

Villa
Hayes

ARGENTINA

Asunción ★

• Coacupé
Coronel Oviedo •

Itaipu •
• Hernandarias

Paraguarí •
Villarrica •

Puerto
Presidente
Stroessner •

Foz do
Iguaçu

• Caazapá
Boquerón •

Corpus •

Rio Alto Paraná

• Pilar
San Juan
Bautista •
Desmochados •

Capitán Meza •

Yacireta •

Encarnación •

Rio Paraná

0   25   50   100 Miles

0 25 50   100 Kilometers

PARAGUAY

evolved into a homogeneous, egalitarian *mestizo* society whose citizens claimed a higher degree of internal cultural unity than most other Latin American nations. This early sense of collective identity was a point of strength in Paraguay's bid for independence and early nation-building.

In 1776 Paraguay was placed under the larger jurisdiction of the newly created Viceroyalty of the Rio de la Plata, seated in Buenos Aires. Independent Paraguayans refused in 1810 to give allegiance to Argentine leaders who were declaring independence from Spain. Paraguayans subsequently beat back invading Argentine armies in two decisive battles in early 1811, ending both Spanish and Argentine control over Paraguay.

Nineteenth-Century Politics

Paraguay's first national government was a junta of militia officers unprepared for self-government, resulting in near-anarchy between 1811 and 1813. Independence leaders ultimately turned to one of the few university-educated Paraguayans with administrative experience, Dr. José Gaspar Rodríguez de Francia. Ascetic and mystical, Francia was named Supreme Dictator in 1814. Francia set Paraguay's finances on a sound basis, ruthlessly quelled internal disorder, and accelerated the construction of an army and national defenses.

El Supremo, as Francia was called, succeeded in preserving Paraguayan independence by fending off domination from Argentina and Brazil. The former refused to recognize Paraguay's independence and blockaded its foreign trade; the latter engaged in repeated military clashes along the disputed northern frontier. Francia responded to these foreign threats with a policy of isolation and autonomous development, sealing Paraguay's borders and restricting foreign contact, forcing self-reliance. Francia created a socialist state a century before the Bolsheviks from lands expropriated from his hated Spanish and *criollo* enemies. He built state farms and factories for armaments, ironworks, and ships, while income from the land expropriations and state monopolies on tobacco and yerba maté provided a consistent profit.

The Franciata further eroded the Spanish social base by banning marriages between whites, thus accelerating the *mestizaje*, or ethnic-mixing and homogenization of the population. Following the discovery of an assassination plot in 1821, in a whirlwind of mass arrests, torture, and executions, the Spanish were obliterated as an identifiable ruling caste in Paraguay. Francia managed to maintain Paraguay in peace and stability while other South American states were paralyzed by civil wars and political chaos in the early postindependence period. But the scope of Francia's police state control was far more pervasive and penetrative than that of brutal but bumbling *caudillos* elsewhere. The long-standing Franciata was a fateful precedent for Paraguay in its formative years of national development.

The personalist tradition continued following Francia's death in 1840 when Carlos Antonio López, a *mestizo* lawyer, emerged from a junta as president in 1844. *El Excelentisimo* ruled as national dictator of Paraguay for another eighteen years. López built the rudiments of political institutions in this era (a court system, a bureaucracy), but government in mid-nineteenth-century Paraguay remained a despotic, nepotistic affair in which the López family owned and operated Paraguay as a private fiefdom until 1869. Opposition to López was suicidal, and state regulations applied to all aspects of society, but the dictator ended Francia's surreal solitude and reopened Paraguay to international trade and commerce. López established diplomatic relations with numerous countries including the United States, built the first railroad in South America, and modernized the Paraguayan military. By the time López died in 1862 Paraguay was a regional power in southern South America.

Carlos Antonio's son, Francisco Solano López, was named president in 1862. Vainglorious, cultured, and cruel, *El Mariscal* fancied himself a Latin Napoleon and soon aimed to forge an alliance with Uruguay to counter the might of Argentina and Brazil in the Plata basin. Paraguay's meddling in the realm of these giants plunged the nation into the most savage and brutal war in the history of Latin America.

The War of the Triple Alliance (1865–1870) combined the armies of Argentina, Brazil, and Uruguay against Paraguay, which lost over half its population and surrendered 25 percent of its national territory. After five years of slaughter, including the sacking of Asunción and Solano López's death in battle, Paraguay's complete defeat ended the first chapter of its national history. The nationalist era of autocratic, state-directed development was over.

The years between 1870 and 1932 witnessed political confusion, economic collapse, and foreign domination. A new, alien, liberal constitution, limiting the power of the state and expanding individual rights, was established by the occupying Brazilians, as was a provisional government representing neither the history nor spirit of Paraguayan political culture. Novel notions of citizen participation and self-government lacked resonance in a nation unfamiliar with democracy and reeling from the demise of half its population and most of its male leadership. The chronic political instability of the postwar years in Paraguay reflected the jarring impact of one of the greatest military disasters in modern history.

After 1870 a dozen years of anarchy and violence involving various military chieftains precluded any real recovery from the war's devastation. In a climate of assassinations and intrigue the political agenda of Paraguayan leaders who survived the war was a rather basic affair: rebuild a shattered economy, settle boundary disputes and indemnification questions, get foreign troops off Paraguayan soil, and control the national government. Paraguay's party system began to take shape in 1887, when the political elite divided into two groupings. The Colorados, officially the National Republican Association (*Asociación Nacional Republicana*, ANR), dominated government between 1876 and 1904 and claimed lineage to the Franciata and López dictatorships. The Liberals proclaimed themselves the vanguard of limited government and civil liberties, but have always suffered an antipatriotic stigma via their collaboration with the occupying Brazilians.

Paraguay's traditional multiclass, two-party system is one of the oldest in the world. Yet despite the institutionalized nature of the traditional parties and their extreme partisanship, Colorados and Liberals are both weakly organized, mass-based, nonideological, personality-driven patronage machines of political bosses and supporters. For over a century these parties have played an often violent game over national power and control, not ideology. Control of the national government means control of the few sources of wealth in an impoverished state like Paraguay. As a result, the Colorado and Liberal parties have long remained venal and repressive toward one another, fanning partisan hatreds over generations.

As neither Colorados nor Liberals had much regard for democratic ideals, the net result after 1870 was a cycle of repression and revolt over decades of instability. Following thirty years of Colorado rule dominated by party founder General Bernardino Caballero, the Liberal "revolution" of 1904 wrested power, ruling for the next three decades in the most unstable era in Paraguayan history. Between 1870 and 1938 Paraguay had thirty-four presidents, two of whom were assassinated and three overthrown.

After 1870 Argentine, Brazilian, and British speculators were the main beneficiaries of Paraguay's bankrupt economy. Foreign capital bought up vast tracts of land sold by Paraguayan governments at low prices as revenue for the destitute nation. The old state-owned lands of the Franciata and vast tracts owned by the López family were parceled out in the Land Law sales of 1883 and 1885. By the time sales were curtailed in 1915 ninety thousand square miles of land in Paraguay, comprising fully 35 percent of the area of the country, had been sold to foreigners. Prosperity was nurtured by the land sales, and by 1900 Paraguay finally began to recover from the devastation of the Triple Alliance War, regaining its prewar population of around five hundred thousand people living mainly in rural areas. At the beginning of the twentieth century, however, Paraguay remained a crude, insular, backward economy and polity.

The Twentieth Century

Although prosperity and trade increased in Paraguay after 1900, endemic political instability, notably civil wars in 1904, 1922, and, most seriously, in 1947, hindered sustained economic and political development. By the mid-1920s Paraguay was again threatened from without, this time from the north. Bolivia, deprived of its Pacific coastline from its defeat in the War of the Pacific against Chile (1879–1883), now looked east to find an alternate outlet to the sea. Bolivia capitalized upon Paraguay's political instability in the early 1900s to build a series of forts in the disputed territory of the Chaco desert, beginning a relentless thrust southward toward the Paraná river, running south through Argentina to the Atlantic. When war came in 1932 Bolivia's German-trained army held every statistical advantage. But Bolivia sent an army of largely highland Indians into the mud, swamp, and tropical heat of the Chaco lowlands, where they were annihilated in battle against a highly mobilized Paraguayan military, fighting on its own terrain against a foreign aggressor. Over the next two years the Paraguayans won a string of bloody confrontations and were at the steppes of the Andes when a truce was signed in 1935.

The Gran Chaco War heightened social mobilization in Paraguay, generating demands by various classes and economic sectors that the existing Liberal regime could not meet. Standards of living in Paraguay in the mid-1930s were woefully low. Working conditions, especially in the *yerbales* (yerba maté plantations) were atrocious and Paraguay's educational system was the poorest in South America. In the 1930s Asunción remained a somnolent boondock, largely lacking paved roads, running water, or even electricity in other than a handful of homes and government buildings. On February 17, 1936, a military coup led by war hero Colonel Rafael Franco removed Liberal President Eusebio Ayala. The "Febreristas" were a motley crew of Fascists, Social Democrats, and Marxists who revivified the old images of the Franciata and López dictatorships, advocated an authoritarian, corporatist, one-party state modeled on Mussolini's Italy, and explicitly rejected nineteenth-century liberalism.

With the Febrerista coup of 1936 civilian supremacy in Paraguayan politics ended for the next sixty years. Another military uprising toppled the Febreristas in August 1937. Chaco War veteran General José F. Estigarribia seized power in 1940 and formally scrapped the 1870 Liberal constitution, replacing it with a new document enshrining presidential dictatorship and a powerful, regulatory state. When Estigarribia died in an airplane crash months after taking power his successor, General Higinio Morínigo became military dictator.

Morínigo's regime (1940–1948) was far more repressive than its predecessors. Morínigo outlawed the Liberal Party in 1942 and ruled over an openly pro-Nazi regime as Paraguay became a nest of Fascist intrigue during World War II. The war brought prosperity to Paraguay in response to world demand for agricultural exports, but the defeat of the Axis powers and pressure from the United States prompted Morínigo to liberalize his dictatorship in 1946. When Morínigo tried to reintroduce authoritarian controls in 1947 a military rebellion plunged Paraguay into a bloody, five-month-long civil war. Although 80 percent of the officer corps went over to the rebel side, Morínigo's outgunned forces nevertheless won. It was a pyrrhic victory; Morínigo was deposed by the now-ascendant Colorado Party in early 1948. Now civil service positions in the bureaucracy and promotion within the armed forces were contingent upon Colorado Party affiliation. Meanwhile, the military, divided by factions loyal to various officers jockeying for power, revolted and seized control in 1948, three times in 1949, and finally in 1954, when General Alfredo Stroessner carried out his *golpe*.

The Stroessner Regime

Stroessner consolidated his dictatorship, becoming by 1989 the longest-ruling leader in Paraguayan history. Stroessner built his tyranny on the Colorado Party and the military, with Stroessner as *caudillo* over both institutions. Unlike the more faceless military juntas surrounding Paraguay, Stroessner secured a popular base for his dictatorship, bringing the Colorado Party (the primary instrument of patronage) under his formal control and penetrating society via a national network of party branches and block wards. The Colorados acquired "official" status, sponsoring Stroessner's eight successive presidential candidacies, building a personality cult for the dictator, and providing a mass base to counterbalance the military. By 1967 Stroessner's purges had left the Colorados Stronista, monolithic, and with immense grassroots support and representing one of Latin America's most powerful political movements. To the preexisting ultranationalism of the Colorado Party Stronismo added a demagogic, populist tone as well as a newer, maniacal, anticommunist national security doctrine.

Along with the Colorados, the armed forces were the other key pillar—and ultimate guarantor—of the regime. Loyalty to Stroessner by the officer corps formed the basis of *caudillismo:* personalist rule supported by loyal retainers, rewarded with wealth and power. A notorious web of corruption developed in the officer corps, now solidly Colorado. Stroessner also adroitly appealed to their corporate interests by reorienting their role and mission to one of guaranteeing the regime against "Communist" insurgency. High military spending and public acclaim by Stroessner added luster to the armed forces. Unlike neighboring military regimes, Stroessner also shielded his military from controversy, leaving most repression and human rights abuses to the secret police. The "Stronato" continually utilized the shopworn menace of "Communist subversion" to move against any sign of independence or militancy among peasants, students, workers, or the church before these challenged the regime. The 1992 discovery of detailed documentation from the regime's intelligence agencies reveals the pervasiveness with which the dictatorship's lidless eye cast a penetrative gaze over almost all social institutions, belying stereotypes that Stroessner's was simply an old-fashioned, poorly organized autocracy.

By 1988 when Stroessner won his eighth reelection, the aging dictator's detachment from day-to-day decision-making, a growing succession crisis, and a worsening economic situation all served to rot the regime. Paraguayans themselves had also changed. They were a more mobilized, expectant population, no longer overwhelmingly rural and atomized. White-collar professionals outside the regime chafed at the ongoing centralization of power and corruption. The international context was also different as Paraguay was now surrounded by new democracies in Argentina, Brazil, and Uruguay. Divisions emerged in the once monolithic Colorado Party, threatening its symbiotic axis with the military. A "militant" faction remained fanatically devoted to Stroessner as president-for-life and ultimately to his son, Colonel Gustavo Stroessner. The "traditionalist" Colorados argued for a nonpersonalist transition after Stroessner to ensure continued Colorado Party hegemony. A violent coup d'état in early 1989, led by military rebels loyal to traditionalist General Andrés Rodríguez, deposed Stroessner, sending him into exile in Brazil.

Paraguay in Transition

General Rodríguez quickly consolidated power, purging the Colorados and armed forces of high-ranking militants. Rodríguez initiated something of a Paraguayan glasnost, releasing political prisoners, relaxing press restrictions, and allowing Paraguayan exiles to return. Snap elections in May 1989, three months following the coup, were won by Rodríguez and the Colorado juggernaut with a lopsided 74 percent of the vote. Rodríguez was inaugurated on May 15, 1989, for a four-year term.

Over the course of Rodríguez's presidency Paraguay experienced significant political and economic reforms and took remarkable steps toward rejoining the international community after decades of ostracism and isolation. The façade of Colorado unity cracked when Dr. Carlos Filizzola, an independent candidate, won Asunción's mayoral race in 1991. The establishment of a new constitution in 1992 prohibited party membership for new military officers (but not those already serving), and Rodríguez's technocratic economists privatized

some money-losing state enterprises, reduced government spending, simpli-
fied the tax code, and eliminated controls on interest rates and foreign exchange transactions. Corruption, integral to Stroessner's kleptocracy and
deeply engrained in Paraguayan culture, skyrocketed after 1993, when the
country entered a deep recession. Paraguay's enormous black market represents the country's most dynamic economic sector, and ranking military officers hold lucrative side interests in narcotics, contraband, prostitution, and
money-laundering. Rodríguez himself was reportedly involved during his entire career in parasitic rake-offs, graft, and cronyism, and was not about to address the issue.

Colorado divisions continued into 1993 over the party's presidential candidacy. Conservative construction magnate Juan Carlos Wasmosy ultimately prevailed, representing the continuing alliance between the military, dominant
economic groups, and Colorado politicians that formed the triad of the Stronato. Intimidation against opposition parties and open intervention by the military preceding national elections in May 1993 showed that party/military elites
would only accept a Colorado victory. Reflecting this mood, army commander
General Lino Oviedo stated that the Colorados, together with the military,
would continue to rule Paraguay forever, whether anyone liked it or not.

Wasmosy won the presidential election on May 9, 1993, with 40 percent
of the vote, beating Domingo Laíno of the *Partido Liberal Radical Auténtico*
(PLRA, 32 percent) and Guillermo Caballero Vargas of the new independent
movement *Encuentro Nacional* (PEN, 23 percent). The failure of both opposition candidates to unite, unseat the ruling Colorados, and initiate a practice
of party coparticipation was a historic opportunity lost.

With strong remnants of the military/Colorado alliance remaining, movement from authoritarianism to some form of democracy was problematic in
Paraguay. Citizen participation, in the form of strikes and protest marches by
peasants, workers, and government employees, became more visible; social
groups began to network and organize. Yet regime elites, most of whom had
supported Stroessner for decades, paid only lip service and remained uncom-
mitted beyond expediency to democracy.

Political crisis erupted in April 1996 when President Wasmosy dismissed
army strongman General Oviedo, who refused to step down. With Oviedo in
revolt and threatening to kill the president, Wasmosy was temporarily forced to
take refuge in the U.S. embassy. Crucial to ending the crisis without bloodshed
was the massive show of support Wasmosy received from the Clinton administration, the Organization of American States, and the Southern Common
Market (MERCOSUR) governments of Argentina, Brazil, and Uruguay. The
renegade Oviedo was finally forced to resign. Paraguay's shaky electoral system

triumphed, but Oviedo's barracks revolt was a dark reminder that ingrained praetorian tendencies do not suddenly disappear with regime change.

Tension again mounted in September 1997 when the Colorados nominated Oviedo as their party candidate for the presidential elections in 1998, despite internal party opposition and negative reactions in Washington. When Wasmosy ordered Oviedo's arrest on charges of "insulting" the president, the general went into hiding and campaigned as a fugitive for forty-one days. As Paraguay continued its madcap course to the May 1998 national elections, Oviedo surrendered and campaigned from jail. The MERCOSUR giants Argentina and Brazil again arbitrated Paraguayan politics by threatening the country's membership in the free trade bloc if Oviedo were elected. Business elites and economists, alarmed over the political instability and its impact on the economy, estimated that in 1995 there were over a half-million under- and unemployed in a nation of some five-and-a-half million. The Paraguayan economy grew only 1.3 percent in 1996 and 2.6 percent in 1997. Foreign investors, skittish about the political bedlam, withheld badly needed currency.

By the 1998 elections politics was so helter-skelter in Paraguay that after General Oviedo was sentenced to ten years in prison (for his 1996 coup attempt), he continued to run for president and led in the polls until the Supreme Court nullified his candidacy. Oviedo's running mate, civilian engineer Raul Cubas, then became the Colorado Party presidential candidate, and Cubas's archenemy, Luis María Argaña, an old stronista, became the vice-presidential nominee. Colorado upheaval was still not enough to help opposition Democratic Alliance (Liberal Party) candidate Domingo Laíno, who lost the May 1998 election, with 46 percent to Cubas's 52 percent of the vote. With their motto, "Cubas in government, Oviedo in power," the Colorado Party extended its control over national government past the half-century mark.

Experts predicted that Cubas's most urgent task would be to revive Paraguay's economy, now in recession. With most of the economy underground (a government watchdog agency estimated more than $6 billion was pilfered in 1997 and 1998), Paraguay's was also one of the last old-fashioned economies in which the state controlled telecommunications, energy, ports, and other important industries, whose workers were largely Colorados. But by February 1999, when Paraguay had reached a milestone decade since Stroessner, President Cubas was locked in a power struggle with his own vice president and faced impeachment for defying the Supreme Court and freeing General Oviedo from prison as his first act in office.

On March 23, 1999, Vice President Luis Maria Argaña was machine-gunned in downtown Asunción. With Argaña's assassination Paraguayan politics had crossed the Rubicon from vicious rhetoric to violence. Argaña's faction of Colorados immediately blamed Cubas and his master, Oviedo. Cubas was impeached by Congress a week later, after Asunción's central square became a bloody battleground in response to Argaña's murder, with rooftop snipers killing six and wounding hundreds in battling rival blocs. Coup rumors swirled in the capital and prodemocracy demonstrations flooded the streets. The ambassadors of Brazil, the United States, and the Vatican met with Cubas and negotiated his resignation in the face of mounting street demonstrations, and a new Colorado-dominant coalition government, headed by former-Senate President and Colorado, Luis González Macchi, took power. Oviedo fled the country.

August 2000 vice-presidential elections (to cover the vacancy of assassinated Vice-President Argaña) resulted in a narrow, but astounding, victory for the Liberal (PLRA) party; this was the first time a Liberal was elected to Paraguay's executive since 1939 and the first time any opposition candidate had won an executive position via election since before the Colorado party came to power in 1947. González Macchi's "national unity" administration soon fell apart when the PLRA withdrew from the government, but the ruling Colorados remained split between *argañistas* and *oviedistas*.

The economic picture was equally murky. The government drastically downgraded Paraguay's growth estimates for 2001 from the original 3.5 percent to only 1.5 percent, and the country's fiscal deficit was a record $257 million. The social deficit was worse. Proclaiming that Paraguay's economic and social crisis had reached extreme limits, the Catholic Church denounced the government's insensitivity and ineffectualness in addressing poverty. Waves of protest marches and highway blockings by peasant associations and trade unions were launched in March against the administration, increasingly seen as incompetent in the face of mounting land invasions by *campesinos,* a prolonged banking crisis/scandal, a police abduction/torture scandal, privatization (of state monopolies) fiascos and concomitant pressure from the International Monetary Fund, escalating crime (especially kidnappings), and pervasive corruption and cronyism at all levels of government.

In September 2002 the nongovernmental organization Transparency International rated Paraguay as the most corrupt country in Latin America and the third most corrupt in the world. This was no surprise to Paraguayans, 23 percent of whom in an opinion survey responded that the country was being run by the mafia. A 2001 UN study had already underlined "the absence of a culture of legality" in Paraguay. Responding to the charge, Colorado plutocrats were outraged . . . outraged! With masterful irony, party bigwigs helped organize rallies demanding "action" against corruption.

In February 2003 President González Macchi survived his second impeachment attempt and prepared to skulk out his unremarkable term, ending in

August. The winner of the April 27 presidential election was no surprise: Nicanor Duarte of the ruling Colorado party, 14 percent ahead of the PLRA candidate. The Colorado party also took the mayoralty of Asunción. The Colorados, in power uninterruptedly since 1947, seemed impervious by the collapse of the Stroessner dictatorship in 1989.

Political Groups

The Colorado Party supported Stroessner for thirty-four years, only splintering in 1989 over the succession issue, not over any notions of democracy. After Stroessner's fall the Colorados' vaunted granite-like unity imploded, with infighting among various factions clustering around political bosses. A notable bloc is the *Unión Nacional de Ciudadanos Éticos* (UNACE), led by exiled former general Lino Oviedo. In the April 2003 elections UNACE attracted a surprising 13 percent of the vote for Oviedo's toady, Guillermo Sánchez. As the party in power for almost sixty years the Colorados hold vast financial and organizational advantages over all other parties.

The Liberal Party, out of power since the end of the Chaco War, was illegal from 1942 to 1967. Despite claimed "democratic" ideals, during their years in power (1904–1936) the Liberals showed themselves to be the same elitist, exclusionary group as the Colorados. In exchange for recognition the Liberal Party provided token opposition during the dictatorship. Best known for its charismatic leader, Domingo Laíno, the PLRA (Authentic Liberal Radical Party) was promised the vice presidency in the new coalition government of President González Macchi. This promise was broken and elections for the post were delayed until late 2000. By then the PLRA withdrew from Macchi's national unity government.

A seemingly important challenge to the traditional two political parties in Paraguay was Carlos Filizzola's 1991 election as mayor of Asunción under his Asunción For All movement (*Asunción Para Todos*, APT). The Colorados recaptured that office in 2001. The National Encounter party (*Encuentro Nacional*, PEN), inspired by Filizzola's APT victory and headed by prominent businessman Guillermo Caballero Vargas, emerged as another challenger, contesting the presidential elections in 1993 and 1998. A social-democratic movement, the PEN had important support among intellectuals, youth, and other Paraguayans disenchanted with the Colorado or Liberal parties. But the April 2003 elections illustrated the extent to which PEN, since 1993 Paraguay's third largest party, had shrunk; receiving only 0.05 percent of the national vote.

The Catholic Church and Church-related groups constituted a moral challenge to the Stroessner dictatorship in the face of unbending repression, calling attention to human rights abuses, corruption, and the extreme concentration of landholdings in the hands of regime elites. Following the 1989 coup something of a modus vivendi developed between the government and the Church, with the latter remaining a persistent voice for social justice in the "new" Paraguay. The clergy also remained traditional defenders of church prerogatives concerning abortion, education policy, and religious orthodoxy.

During the Great Depression Paraguayan governments never initiated import-substitution-industrialization (ISI), instead depending on the country's agricultural exports—mainly cotton, soybeans, tobacco, and yerba—for national income. Moreover, Stroessner reasoned that limited industrialization obviated the rise of an industrial working class and unions capable of threatening the regime. Therefore an urban working class, with class consciousness, never developed. Most economic enterprises, located in and around Asunción, are family-owned firms where personal, not professional, patron-client relations prevail. The Stroessner regime curtailed both the size and potential influence of the labor movement by co-optation, repression, and thorough Colorado Party penetration of Paraguayan industry, as well as policies discouraging large enterprises. Fewer than twenty thousand of Paraguay's 1.5 million wage earners are organized, and the small size of the domestic market does not spark the demand to support a consequential industrialization program.

Despite massive general strikes over falling wages by labor confederations in 1994 that paralyzed Asunción and prompted the army to deploy tanks in the streets, the Wasmosy government took no discernible action to address problems such as wage increases or land reform. The banal populism of the Colorados already incorporates the leftist rhetoric of labor, and the emotional loyalty of at least a million Paraguayans to the party saps labor of impetus and clarity.

Paraguay's peasant organizations, key actors in a still predominantly rural country, via their umbrella *Mesa Coordinadora Nacional de Organizaciones Campesinas* (MCNOC), pressures the government to improve access to credit, land reform, and an end to official harassment of peasant activists. Heretofore, aside from current President Duarte's platitudes of "development with a human face," the Colorado regime has not implemented policies to alleviate the chronic suffering of the two million Paraguayans in poverty.

Public Policy

Paraguay's progress in political liberalization contrasts sharply with the absence of significant public policy to reduce inequality or poverty, reflecting the very limited view of "democracy" by Colorado elites. The rise of newer social movements and a free press publicizing group concerns illustrates both the changes and continuities in Paraguay. For example, given the durability of an authoritarian and patriarchal political culture, public policies designed to combat gender inequality and discrimination (domestic violence, reproductive rights) were nonexistent until 1992. A notable increase in political participation by women and expansion of legal rights via reform of the civil code is obviated by negligible women's power in real political decision making. The women's movement in Paraguay remains a largely urban, middle-class affair.

The inequality of land ownership and pressures for landholdings by landless peasants (Paraguay's largest social group) remains another problem area of public policy. Peasants, believing that Stroessner's fall entitled them to land, began an upsurge in land invasions after 1989. The Paraguayan government, siding with landholding elites, responded with sometimes violent repression and has thus far rejected demands for policies of redistribution and the amelioration of rural poverty. Increasing social inequality and heightening polarization may well increase social conflict. Still, the Colorados, with strong links to the landowners' association, the Rural Association of Paraguay (ARP), together effectively block substantive agrarian reform.

Paraguay's Colorado government also faces growing demands to respond to the social deficit in health, public housing, and education. Pressures now come from newly elected municipal governments and governors. The invigoration of local government and the concomitant greater opportunities for political participation from regions other than the central zone around Asunción stand among the most significant achievements of post-Stroessner Paraguay.

An extremely poor nation like Paraguay pays a high price for the rampant corruption, sloppy organization, endemic patronage, and stifling inefficiency of its public sector that absorbs scarce resources, wastes opportunities, and distorts market prices. Paraguay's membership in the Southern Common Market of two hundred million people is increasingly viewed, as was the giant Itaipú hydroelectric project a generation ago, as a panacea to generate economic growth that has yet to materialize.

The International Arena

The ability of a country to carry on a dynamic foreign policy and to deal forcefully with other nations in pursuit of its national interests is largely determined by its domestic capabilities and resources. In international affairs Paraguay negotiates from a weak position. Paraguay's landlocked isolation in the interior of the continent deprives it of strategic importance. Its small population is largely poor, rural, and uneducated. The economy is underdeveloped and bereft of important mineral resources. Paraguay possesses little in the way of vital financial, social, and natural attributes needed to give it some heft in international affairs.

Paraguay's history of violent conflict with threatening neighbor-states imbues her foreign policy with a determination to now maintain friendly relations with them, especially Argentina and Brazil. Paraguay was overwhelmingly dependent on Argentina until the 1970s. As late as 1969 all of Paraguay's road, rail, and river links with the outside world passed through Argentine territory.

Beginning in the 1950s, however, the Stroessner regime began to approach Brazil for developmental assistance and to counteract Argentine influences. Brazil built a bridge between the two countries over the Paraná river at the border town of Ciudad del Este that offered an alternative export route with a free trade port at Paranaguá, and built a highway from Paraguay to the Brazilian coast. The giant Itaipú project, a joint Brazilian-Paraguayan venture (with Brazil providing 90 percent of the financing) solidified the changed regional axis of power; by 1982 Argentina's share of Paraguayan exports fell to less than half, while Brazil's share rose from nothing to 58 percent.

By the early 1980s increased Brazilian economic penetration into Paraguay began to alarm the nation, as well as Argentina—Brazil's archrival—of the possibility of Paraguay becoming an economic satellite of Brazil. Paraguayans began to complain about Brazilian capital taking over Paraguayan firms, and Brazilian food, goods, and even music replacing Paraguayan products. Increasing immigration by Brazilian peasants into eastern Paraguay and Brazilian speculators driving up land prices only added to Paraguayan anxiety and resentment.

Still, regional trade diversification gave Paraguay increased leverage in its international political and economic contacts. By the early 1990s the Rodríguez government initiated a rapprochement with Argentina, holding several summits and signing significant trade agreements, suggesting that traditional "pendulum" politics remains the basis of Paraguayan foreign policy toward its larger neighbors.

Paraguay's deepening integration into the new global economy is seen most clearly at the regional level in its membership in the Southern Common Market (Mercado Común del Sur-MERCOSUR). Formed by Argentina, Brazil, Paraguay, and Uruguay in 1991, MERCOSUR eliminated tariffs on all trade except automobiles and sugar and agreed to and partially implemented a common external tariff (CET). Significantly, MERCOSUR incorporates a democratic clause that was used to pressure Paraguay during General Oviedo's 1996 barracks revolt. Paraguay was again threatened with expulsion from MERCOSUR in 1999 during the political crisis following the assassination of Vice President Argaña that spawned street violence and coup rumors.

Since World War II foreign relations between the United States and Paraguay have been conditioned by mutual interests involving national security, trade, and investment. After using economic and military aid to buy the

Morínigo regime's alignment against the Nazis in 1944 the United States continued to use leverage over Paraguay during the Cold War. In return for generous amounts of economic and military aid and political legitimacy General Stroessner became a staunch defender of U.S. foreign policy. For the United States at the apogee of the Cold War, anticommunist dictators of Stroessner's ilk were not unwelcome. Stroessner broke diplomatic relations with Castro's Cuba and supported the U.S.-engineered expulsion of Cuba from the Organization of American States. Paraguay outlawed the Communist Party, refused to establish relations with communist countries, and voted slavishly with the United States in the OAS and the United Nations.

Paraguayan-U.S. relations during the Stronato were cordial and reliable during the 1950s and 1960s, becoming more troubled over democracy and human rights issues from 1976 to the end of the regime in 1989. Bilateral relations deteriorated rapidly during the Carter administration, which announced that it would no longer ignore human rights violations in Paraguay. With Ronald Reagan's election in 1980 expected improvement in bilateral relations did not materialize, as human rights policy had become an essential component of U.S. foreign policy.

Rodríguez's political liberalization considerably improved U.S.-Paraguayan relations after 1989. High-level U.S. governmental and military officials visited Asunción, praising the positive changes in government and increasing U.S. economic and technical assistance. The first Bush administration pressured Paraguay to create an antidrug agency in Asunción, but Paraguay's fight against drug trafficking deteriorated as General Lino Oviedo's power increased and Paraguay verged on near-anarchy. In 1998 the United States gave Paraguay its second failing grade in recent years during the annual drug certification process. The U.S. government was equally concerned with Oviedo's militarism and his reported links to the influx of Arab-dominated Mafiosi at the triple border where Paraguay, Argentina, and Brazil meet. A legacy of the Stroessner dictatorship, the culture of corruption in Paraguay heightens U.S. fears of the "Colombianization" of Paraguay as a rising gangster state.

Paraguay's relations with Europe continue to expand. Contacts with France, Germany, Great Britain, Italy, and Spain focus on trade, technical assistance, and cultural exchange. After Argentina, Brazil, and the United States, Western European nations are the largest importers of Paraguayan goods, such as tobacco and tannin. Paraguay imports more goods from Germany than from any other European nation. Germans are undoubtedly the most important non-Spanish-speaking European immigrant group in Paraguay in terms of business enterprises and agricultural colonies.

Paraguayan contacts with Asia are also growing. Relations with Japan are long-standing. Thousands of Japanese have settled in Paraguay since the 1930s and today Japanese capital, technical aid, and industrial investment surpasses the rest of Asia together. During the Cold War Paraguay maintained strong diplomatic relations with anticommunist regimes in South Korea and the Republic of China (Taiwan), but today Paraguay is expanding links with the People's Republic of China.

Paraguay-African relations are minimal except for South Africa and Egypt. Because of their shared pariah status, Stroessner's Paraguay and Apartheid South Africa developed strong bilateral relations beginning in the 1970s. With regard to the Middle East, Israel's outcast status was understood in Paraguay and during the Stroessner regime the Mossad intelligence agency helped train Paraguay's dreaded secret police, the fanatical DT, or Technical Division for the Repression of Communism. Aside from Egypt, Paraguay has little contact with the rest of the Arab world.

Regarding international organizations, by virtue of her last-minute declaration of war against the Axis in World War II Paraguay was entitled to sign the Declaration of the United Nations, becoming a charter member. But Paraguay's small size and relative unimportance in international affairs works against much influence in the UN. In the Organization of American States Paraguay's status as a lesser developed country has obtained it special trade/aid concessions but, in all, Paraguay plays a minor role in hemispheric politics.

Prospects

In 2004 President Nicanor Duarte's attempt to cast himself as a determined reformer and anticorruption campaigner took some knocks; from symbolic attempts to purge and modernize the national police to old-style closed-door pettifoggery in apportioning Supreme Court seats, Duarte and the ruling Colorados demonstrated essential semi-authoritarian behavior—to wit, that things have to change a little if they are to remain basically the same. An occasional criminal investigation and prosecution of some corrupt officials focuses mass attention away from fundamental questions regarding the state and regime and toward a few "bad apples" who are "the cause" of the slow pace of reform.

Undoubtedly, civil and political rights are extensive today in Paraguay, considerably beyond anything existing during the Stroessner dictatorship. But opposition can exist and even severely criticize the system without fundamental challenge to it. Entrenched Colorado elites, many of whom are old stronistas, continue the time-tested personalist politics and back-room chicanery to exclude or limit interests in the full exercise of rights viewed as antagonistic to Colorado hegemony. Colorado domination over the course of the transition has stifled reform in land ownership, resisted breaking ties with the politicized military, opposed income distribution questions, and stalled on fiscal and electoral transparency. There have been no widespread investigations of human rights abuses that occurred during the long twilight years of the Stronato.

Widespread rural poverty, the lack of any substantive agrarian reform, the dearth of governmental response to the social deficit in housing, public health, and education all reflect the lack of sufficient clout and representation of Paraguayan civil society vis-à-vis the government, as well as the power and vested interests within the Colorado party and its continued alliance with the military and conservative economic elites.

The new Duarte administration surely faces heightened expectations and growing demands to respond to Paraguay's social crisis. Colorado governments since 1989 have fomented limited political liberalization but failed to address chronic economic and social concerns—especially corruption—displaying little difference in this regard from the Stroessner regime. The distribution of land in Paraguay, among the most skewed in Latin America, might well result in Paraguay's version of Mexico's Chiapas insurgency. Continuing Stroessner's model, Colorado presidents, despite populist blandishments, support the interests of large landowners, the business class, and the military in their dealings with peasants, workers, and civil society.

It may well be that in 2005 Paraguay represents less an imperfect democracy and more a successful semi-authoritarian regime. The hegemonic Colorado party today resembles that of the Mexican Institutional Revolutionary Party (PRI) during its long (until 2000) domination over Mexican state and society. Individual leaders like Stroessner are no longer eternal, but the Colorado party is. If the Colorados have their way, the system will never change.

Suggestions for Further Reading

Kelly, Phillip, and Thomas Wigham. "Democracy in Bolivia and Paraguay." In *Assessing Democracy in Latin America*, ed. Philip Kelly. Boulder, CO: Westview Press, 1998.

Lambert, Peter. "A Decade of Electoral Democracy: Continuity, Change and Crisis in Paraguay." *Bulletin of Latin American Research* 19 (2000): 379–396.

Lambert, Peter, and Andrew Nickson, eds. *The Transition to Democracy in Paraguay*. New York: St. Martin's Press, 1997.

Lewis, Paul H. *Political Parties and Generations in Paraguay's Liberal Era, 1869–1940*. Chapel Hill: University of North Carolina Press, 1993.

Mora, Frank O. "From Dictatorship to Democracy: The U.S. and Regime Change in Paraguay, 1954–1994." *Bulletin of Latin American Research* 17, no. 1 (1997): 59–79.

Roett, Riordan, and Richard Sacks. *Paraguay: The Personalist Legacy.* Boulder, CO: Westview Press, 1991.

Turner, Brian. *Community Politics and Peasant-State Relations in Paraguay.* Lanham, MD: University Press of America, 1993.

Valenzuela, Arturo. "Paraguay: The Coup That Didn't Happen." *Journal of Democracy* 8 (1997): 43–55.

Zagorski, Paul W. "Democratic Breakdown in Paraguay and Venezuela: The Shape of Things to Come for Latin America?" *Armed Forces and Society* 30, no. 1 (2003): 87–116.

14

Bolivia

The Construction of a
Multiethnic Democracy

Donna Lee Van Cott

B olivia has had one of the most tempestuous, unstable, and chaotic histories in all of Latin America. It is also one of the most divided ethnically, a fact that has been alternatively denied, suppressed, or manipulated by most of its leaders. But in 1994 Bolivians undertook a comprehensive reform of the political constitution imposed by military populist René Barrientos in 1967, which is still in effect. For the first time the political regime formally recognized the "multiethnic and pluricultural" nature of Bolivian society and the endurance of forms of political organization outside of the state. After more than a century of striving to reduce cultural differences to economic class and to impose a uniform, universal set of government institutions, today Bolivian law recognizes the public and official nature of indigenous languages, legal systems, and forms of organization with roots in pre-conquest Andean societies.

This revolutionary change represents a fundamentally different approach to addressing the country's extreme poverty and weak political institutions and to reversing a legacy of extreme political instability marked by more than 190 attempted coups since independence. Bolivia is the first of Latin America's most ethnically diverse countries to take this step.

Geograhy and Social Groups

At the time of independence in 1825 Bolivia was the most predominantly Indian (73 percent) of the new American republics and its social and ethnic

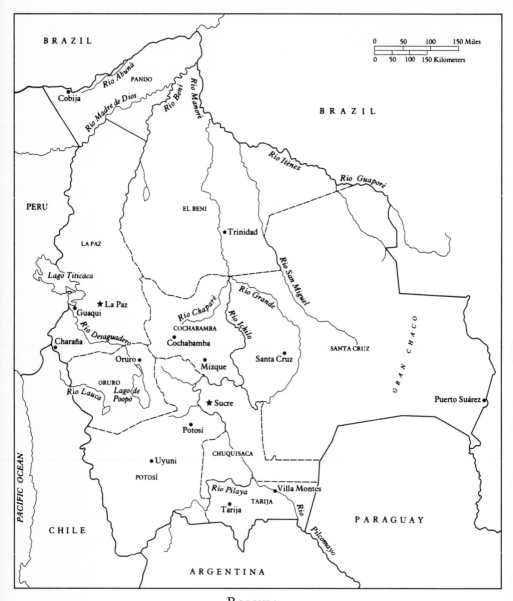

BRAZIL

Rio Abuná

PANDO

• Cobija

Rio Madre de Dios

Rio Beni

Rio Mamoré

BRAZIL

Rio Iténez

Rio Guaporé

PERU

EL BENI

• Trinidad

LA PAZ

Rio San Miguel

Lago Titicaca

★ La Paz

• Guaqui

Rio Desaguadero

Rio Chaparé

COCHABAMBA

Rio Grande

Rio Ichilo

• Charaña

Rio Lauca

Oruro •

• Cochabamba

SANTA CRUZ

GRAN CHACO

• Mizque

Santa Cruz •

ORURO

Lago de Poopó

★ Sucre

Puerto Suárez •

PACIFIC OCEAN

• Potosí

CHUQUISACA

• Uyuni

POTOSÍ

Rio Pilaya

• Villa Montes

TARIJA

Rio

• Tarija

PARAGUAY

CHILE

Pilcomayo

ARGENTINA

BOLIVIA

stratification among the most rigid. Bolivian society was really two societies: one Spanish and one indigenous. The predominance of the native population and its separation from Europeanized Bolivia was made possible in part by the country's geographic fragmentation and extreme climates. Bolivia's nine departments span the Andes mountain ranges in the west, which surpass 12,000 feet (3,657 meters) in some places; Amazon rainforest in the east; and a dry, sparsely populated, lowland Chaco region in the south. The lack of navigable rivers and the difficulty and expense of building highways and railroads across dramatic changes in elevation have impeded the economic and political integration of the country and generated sharp interregional rivalries and hostilities. Bolivia's forbidding geography and climatic extremes presented barriers to European settlement, resulting in a small population for such an extensive geographical territory, the sixth largest country in South America. Approximately nine million Bolivians are spread throughout a territory of 424,000 square miles (1,098,580 square kilometers). Bolivia is one of Latin America's most rural countries; more than a third live in communities of 250 people or less. At the other extreme more than half of Bolivians are crowded into one of four cities—La Paz, El Alto, Cochabamba, and Santa Cruz.

After independence, landed elites abolished the Crown's protections of indigenous communal land rights. By the end of the nineteenth century they had seized the majority of arable land, forcing landless Indians to barter their labor to the growing hacienda class in exchange for the right of subsistence agriculture on hacienda lands. In the mid-nineteenth century only about 20 percent of the population could speak Spanish as a first or second language. The only way for Indians to enter national life was to migrate to the cities, learn Spanish, and take up an urban trade. The minority that did so created a new caste of mixed-race *cholos*.

Today indigenous people comprise 66 percent of Bolivia's total population, the largest proportion in South America. Approximately 35 percent of Bolivians are of Quechua descent, another 25 percent are Aymará. There are dozens of distinct, less numerous indigenous groups in the eastern lowlands. There are also approximately 30,000 Afro-Bolivians. Bolivia's extreme ethnic diversity has impeded the construction of a common national identity. The close association of ethnicity with economic opportunities created a rigid race-based class structure that has trapped the majority in extreme rural poverty and impeded efforts to modernize and industrialize the economy. Bolivians are also divided by regional identities, particularly between predominantly white residents of the eastern department of Santa Cruz, who call themselves "*Cambas,*" and highland-dwelling "*Kollas,*" who bear more visible traces of indigenous ancestry.

Interest Groups

Until the 1980s two traditional corporate actors dominated Bolivian politics—the armed forces and organized labor. As their influence declined in the 1980s three new corporate actors confronted the state directly. The first to have an influence was the Bolivian Confederation of Private Entrepreneurs (CEPB). The business sector led the movement to oust the brutal and corrupt Luís García Meza regime in 1981. Another important new actor that represents the entrepreneurial elite is the departmental civic committees, which emerged in the 1970s. They express elite interests in the departmental capitals, typically demanding improved public services in urban areas and greater political and administrative autonomy for the departments. In 2004 civic committees in the eastern, lowland departments launched a drive for political and administrative autonomy that opened a new era of interregional political conflict. In the wealthy Department of Santa Cruz, the movement for regional autonomy has taken on ethnonational overtones as elites seek to defend the sovereignty of the "Camba Nation" from Kolla political dominance.

The *campesino* (indigenous peasant) movement also became an autonomous political force in the 1980s. Taking advantage of the new democratic political environment, it expanded upon the base of an independent network of *campesino* organizations that gained independence from the state during the 1970s. Politically independent indigenous leaders emerged within the *campesino* unions in the late 1960s, spurred by dramatic gains in literacy and access to formal education. Between 1973 and 1979 Aymará students, intellectuals, clergy, and *campesino* leaders forged the ideological foundation for an indigenous movement based on the then-novel combination of the idea of cultural oppression propagated by indigenous intellectuals with the existing leftist discourse of economic and political oppression. They established a dense network of hierarchically arranged *campesino* organizations and invoked the memory of Tupaj Katari, an eighteenth century indigenous rebel. The *"kataristas"* transformed the labor movement in Bolivia by supplanting the waning influence of the miners and contributing a distinctive cultural analysis to the class-based rhetoric of the labor movement. A number of *katarista* political parties were founded in the late 1970s, but these were plagued by internal factionalism as well as immense barriers to electoral success erected by the political elite.

The *campesino* movement projected a coherent political voice in the 1980s and 1990s through the Bolivian Coordinator of Syndical Unions and *Campesino* Workers (CSUTCB), formed in 1979. The CSUTCB placed the idea of "pluriculturality" on the political agenda and introduced the concept of "unity in diversity" into a wide range of political tendencies, including the

Left, the emerging populist parties, and even traditional parties, which were increasingly trying to attract the ethnically diverse urban migrant population of La Paz. After 2000 ideological differences and personal rivalries among the top leadership group weakened the peasant movement. During the 1990s the impetus for indigenous mobilization shifted to the lowlands, where distinct indigenous ethnic communities had begun to form their own organizations to defend their territories and natural resources against increasing incursions by the expanding economic elite. Following a series of preliminary encounters, in 1982 Amazonian Indians formed CIDOB (the Indigenous Confederation of the East and Amazon of Bolivia).

Political Parties and Elections

Once Bolivia's once-plentiful silver resources were exhausted, the country plunged into economic stagnation and international isolation. Constant battles over territory with Bolivia's neighbors created the need for a strong military, which dominated politics until its humiliating defeat by Chile in the War of the Pacific (1879–1883). The loss of its Pacific coast provinces and rich copper and nitrate deposits furthered the isolation of the now-landlocked country. The silver mining elite replaced the discredited military at the helm of government and established a bipartisan system that monopolized politics until the 1930s. In contrast to other Latin American states, where the political role and privileges of the Catholic Church were a major source of conflict between Liberal and Conservative parties in the late nineteenth and early twentieth centuries, Bolivian politics has never been much influenced by religious issues and the Catholic Church has been relatively apolitical and weak. In 1898 Liberals defeated Conservatives in a civil war and established a centralized, unitary, presidential political system based in La Paz. Bolivian political parties' contemporary fragmentation, electoralism, and personalism are deeply rooted in this period of constant violent conflict among multiple forces characterized by strong leadership and factionalism. During periods of relative calm the two parties established the chief raison d'être of the system: the circulation of political patronage, jobs, and influence among a tiny middle-class elite.

The discovery of tin at the end of the nineteenth century facilitated the reintegration of the country into international markets and the establishment of a new highland-based, tin-mining elite. The tin boom ushered in an era of relative political stability and prosperity and witnessed the generation of unprecedented unity within the oligarchy, now made up of the landed and urban economic elite. The growth of the left in the 1920s inspired the formation of an alliance among the traditional parties in defense of the interests of the economic elite. The threat from the left increased as disaffected veterans sought to punish the government for its poor management of the Chaco War (1932–1935), in which Bolivia lost significant territory to Paraguay. The reduction of property and literacy requirements injected class-based confrontation into a party system that remained essentially an arena for personalistic disputes among the oligarchy and a tiny middle class dependent upon public-sector employment. Since most jobs were controlled by the executive, control of the presidency became crucial to economic survival.

Seeking to expand its base beyond the middle class by incorporating newly enfranchised workers, the National Revolutionary Movement (MNR), founded in 1940, allied with the Bolivian Workers' Central (COB) and took on the cause of the mineworkers, who had founded the country's largest union in 1944. The MNR began to appeal directly to Quechua and Aymará Indians for support. The party harnessed the disaffection engendered by the disastrous Chaco War and the Great Depression behind a program of nationalism and populism that challenged the dominance of the tin mining-based oligarchy, which had been gravely weakened by the decline of tin prices in the 1930s.

During the military government of 1946–1952, the increasing militancy of organized labor destabilized the political order. In 1951 the military prevented the MNR from assuming power following its landslide electoral victory. In April 1952 the MNR armed Indians and workers and overthrew the military government. The reforms the MNR enacted following the revolution swept away a political order based on the alliance between the tin barons and landed elite and the restriction of political representation to the oligarchy and middle class. The destruction of the oligarchy was accomplished by eliminating its economic base: the mines and the haciendas. The MNR nationalized the tin mines and established the state mining company (COMIBOL) and supported *campesinos* in their struggle to recuperate ancestral communal lands. These moves launched a state-centered development model that endured until the mid-1980s.

Taking as its model the corporatist structure of Mexico's durable postrevolutionary governing party, the Party of the Institutional Revolution (PRI), MNR leaders sought to channel and moderate the popular social forces unleashed by the revolution. They rewarded *campesinos* for their support against the military by enfranchising the illiterate and abolishing coercive labor relations. The MNR propagated a dense network of unions to co-opt and control the *campesino* vote—in some areas, building on the structures of the Andean *ayllus* (traditional native communities with discontinuous territories). Under MNR leadership Bolivia embarked on an unprecedented twelve years of relative political stability. Increasing tensions within the MNR coalition and the growing militancy and autonomy of the COB, however, prompted president Victor Paz Estenssoro to rely increasingly on the military to maintain power. The more populist, redistributive economic platform of organized labor hindered the goal of middle-class politicians to revive economic growth by establishing a capitalist, outward-oriented economic model. The government's efforts to restructure the mining industry angered the militant miners' union, depriving the MNR of its most stalwart shock troops when, in 1964, a military junta led by General René Barrientos overthrew the Paz Estenssoro government.

Barrientos inherited the allegiance of the peasantry by co-opting its leadership and maintaining support for agrarian reform. After Barrientos's death in 1969 a series of military coups installed a succession of populist and leftist military governments. Labor's brief reprieve ended in 1971 when General Hugo Banzer installed himself in a bloody coup and commenced a repressive regime that would last eight years. Banzer reduced the importance of *campesinos* in national politics and repressed their autonomous organizations. The *military-campesino* pact began to unravel. Banzer lost the support of the middle classes as a result of his economic mismanagement, the corruption of his military regime, and the unsustainable level of foreign debt he took on. In 1977 a hunger strike led by miners' wives solidified opposition to the regime and forced Banzer to step down and renounce plans to run for reelection.

Bolivians began a tortuous transition to civilian rule. Three presidential elections were held in four years in an attempt to yield a clear winner whom the military would tolerate. The military leadership canceled the July 1978 elections once they realized that the left was likely to win. Elections held one year later failed to produce the required absolute majority. To avoid a nasty fight in the Congress the congressional leadership opted to hold a new election the following year, naming the president of the Senate as interim president. In November the military overthrew the interim president. Following intense popular opposition the military capitulated and appointed as president congressional deputy Lydia Gueiler Tejada, who served long enough to preside over new elections in June 1980. Hernán Siles Zuazo won a plurality victory but before he could take office, on July 17, 1980, General Luis García Meza overthrew Gueiler. García Meza presided over one of the most brutal regimes in Bolivian history, earning international condemnation and galvanizing the democratic opposition. He was forced to step down in August 1981 after losing control of the military. His 1982 failed coup attempt led to the appointment of a military leader to oversee new elections.

The democratic era finally dawned in Bolivia in 1982 when the reconvened 1980 Congress selected as president Hernán Siles Zuazo, leader of the leftist Democratic Popular Unity (UDP) coalition. The demands of the UDP's constituency for increased state spending on the poor were unrealistic in light of the urgent need for fiscal austerity. Due to the mismanagement of the Banzer regime, the massive foreign debt it contracted, and the massive corruption of the military, the economy collapsed. When Siles took office, debt service totaled 50 percent of export earnings. Declining agricultural and mineral production, combined with Siles's poor management and political skills, aggravated the situation. As annual inflation reached 20,000 percent, Siles was forced to resign and hold early elections.

An alliance between the MNR and Banzer's center-right Democratic Action Party (ADN) governed Bolivia between 1985 and 1989, led by Víctor Paz Estenssoro—his fourth and last stint as president of Bolivia. Banzer had won a plurality with 28.5 percent of the vote, just ahead of the MNR's 26.4 percent. The third major party on the scene was the Leftist Revolutionary Movement (MIR), the only significant leftist party to survive the UDP coalition. Slowly, a more coherent multiparty system was beginning to emerge out of the nearly seventy parties that had competed in 1978. Banzer and Paz Estenssoro signed a "Pact for Democracy" on October 17, 1985, committing their parties to work in Congress to pass necessary economic reforms while using the executive's control of force to suppress the capacity of a weakened labor movement to obstruct reform. The government's New Economic Policy reduced inflation to 11 percent in one year and reduced a massive fiscal deficit through a shock program that devalued the currency and drastically cut state spending. The Paz Estenssoro government also liberalized the economy in order to restore international capital flows and took steps to shift the engine of economic growth from the bloated and inefficient state to the private sector.

The success of the structural adjustment earned the country the generous support of international financial institutions and support of the United States, which initiated a number of debt-relief packages and poured development assistance into the impoverished country. The country's spiral into hyperinflation and fiscal crisis had ended, but it would take much longer to reactivate the stagnant economy and tackle the hemisphere's second-highest poverty rate. Throughout most of the 1990s Bolivia registered social welfare indicators that are more common to Sub-Saharan Africa than to Latin America, despite the establishment of a Social Emergency Fund to alleviate the suffering of the most vulnerable. The MNR-ADN government executed its plan over the fierce opposition of labor, imposing three states of siege and banishing hundreds of labor leaders to prevent the COB from sabotaging the austerity package. An estimated 40 to 45 percent of state miners and factory workers were fired between 1985 and 1987, reducing the size of the most politicized sectors of the labor movement accordingly.

The MNR-ADN alliance broke down as Banzer and the MNR's rising star, Planning Minister Gonzalo Sánchez de Lozada, vied for position before the 1989 presidential elections. A secret addendum to the Pact for Democracy had committed the MNR to supporting Banzer in 1989's presidential elections.

Believing he could win an outright majority, Sánchez de Lozada reneged on this promise. The outcome of the 1989 elections shook the weak foundations of the fragile party system. The bitterness of the electoral battle prevented Banzer, who finished second with 22.7 percent of the vote, from supporting the plurality winner, Sánchez de Lozada with 23.07 percent, in the presidency. After three months of intense interparty wrangling, at Banzer's insistence, in August 1989 the ADN congressional delegation voted for the MIR's Jaime Paz Zamora. The ADN and MIR, together with two minor parties, established a "Patriotic Accord" government, an alliance that pitted the left and right against the center of the political spectrum. Although he had finished third with 20 percent of the vote, Paz Zamora assumed the presidency.

By 1989 five parties had come to dominate elections. Between them they would consistently take two-thirds of the vote until 2002. These were the ADN, MIR, MNR, and two new populist parties that emerged in 1989. The first, Conscience of the Fatherland (CONDEPA), was led by media mogul Carlos Palenque, who built on the popularity of his television and radio programs among the lower-class Aymará migrants in La Paz and in El Alto, the massive slum city perched above it. The second, the Civic Solidarity Union (UCS), was led by Santa Cruz-based Max Fernández, owner of the country's largest brewery. Two additional key players in the 1990s were the leftist Free Bolivia Movement (MBL), with a limited base consisting of highland, middle-class intellectuals, and the largest of the *katarista* parties, the Tupaj Katari Revolutionary Movement of Liberation (MRTKL).

In an effort to recapture the indigenous vote for the MNR, in his second run for the presidency Sánchez de Lozada chose as his vice presidential running-mate Víctor Hugo Cárdenas, an Aymará linguist who represented the MRTKL in Congress between 1985 and 1989. The controversial choice capitalized on the popularity of indigenous themes in the early 1990s. In the June 1993 elections Sánchez de Lozada and Cárdenas won 35.6 percent of valid votes with the widest victory margin (14 percent) of any candidate since the military annulled the 1980 elections. Many analysts attributed to Cárdenas the ticket's win in the majority Aymará department of La Paz, which the MNR had not carried since the democratic transition. To ensure passage of his legislative agenda Sánchez de Lozada invited the UCS and MBL to join the government.

Despite strong economic growth and relative political stability during Sánchez de Lozada's term, the MNR came in second with 18.2 percent of the vote in the 1997 national elections, behind Banzer's ADN, which won 20 percent. The political ascent of the lowland-based ADN reflects the shift in the political center of gravity away from the highland mining elite, where it had resided for over a century. The MIR, UCS, and CONDEPA each earned between 16 and 18 percent of the valid vote. The populist parties' strong showing was surprising because the charismatic leaders of both parties died before the 1997 elections. Both political vehicles were inherited by family members.

In 1997 a new actor joined the national political party system. The increasingly militant coca growers and their allies in the indigenous and peasant movements formed the Assembly of the Sovereignty of the Peoples to compete in 1995's first-ever municipal elections. Coca leaf is grown legally in Bolivia for domestic consumption in tea and other nonnarcotic products in a limited territory in the Yungas region of La Paz; the coca growers of the Chapare region of Cochabamba are seeking to expand that area to include crops currently deemed illegal under Bolivian law. The party swept municipalities in the Chapare region and won a total of ten mayoralties and forty-nine councilors in Cochabamba and five councilors in other highland departments. The four congressional seats they won in 1997 provided a national platform for their anti-eradication agenda. The party split in two in 1999, a result of increasing fragmentation of the national peasant movement. Unable to surmount high barriers to legal registration, both parties have appeared on the ballot by borrowing the name of a number of defunct leftist parties. The sector led by coca growers' leader Evo Morales now competes as the Movement Toward Socialism (MAS).

The MNR and MBL were shut out of the government when Banzer formed a "megacoalition" with MIR, UCS, and CONDEPA, which together controlled 80 percent of the seats in Congress. Nevertheless, Banzer faced serious challenges. His "win" actually placed second to the level of abstention (28.82 percent) in a country where voting is obligatory, and maintaining a large, programmatically incoherent coalition proved to be impossible. Banzer also had to combat his legacy as an authoritarian dictator in the 1970s, both at home and abroad. Banzer refused to continue pro-indigenous programs, such as land titling, and responded to protests with repression. Relations with organized groups worsened as economic conditions declined. Banzer's eradication of 80 to 90 percent of the coca crop pleased the United States government, but deprived rural growers of approximately $500 million in income. In comparison, only $80 million was distributed to provide agricultural alternatives. The Banzer-Quiroga government's unpopular policies, explained below, caused many former supporters of the traditional parties to seek alternatives in 2002.

Popular frustration exploded into massive civil unrest in April and September 2000 and continued until the 2002 elections. The government's decision, under pressure from the World Bank to privatize water services in Cochabamba, launched this era. The American company that bought the water concession (Bechtel) raised prices 35 percent, which most people could not afford. Cochabambinos declared a "Water War" with the national government that persisted for months. The government responded with a state of siege and the detention, injury, and killing of protestors. The Cochabambinos stood their ground and won, expelling Bechtel. This victory fueled a wave of parallel, independent protests by the coca growers and highland peasants, who repeatedly blocked national highways in 2000 and 2001. Banzer stepped down in August 2001 after being diagnosed with cancer. Vice President Jorge "Tuto" Quiroga assumed the presidency and continued Banzer's repressive policy, particularly with respect to the opposition to coca eradication in the Chapare region of Cochabamba.

The poor response of traditional parties to the demands raised by a broad array of disaffected social groups led many voters to seek an alternative in the 2002 elections. The 2000–2001 protests increased the national presence and popularity of their leaders, particularly coca growers leader and national deputy Evo Morales and Felipe Quispe, a radical Aymará ethnonationalist who leads a sector of the *campesino* organization CSUTCB. The mobilizations made Morales and Quispe, both of whom ran for president in 2002 at the head of recently established indigenous peoples-based political parties, into national symbols of defiance of the Bolivian government and the United States. Statements made by the U.S. ambassador the week prior to the elections—essentially threatening the Bolivian people that a win for Evo Morales would result in economic sanctions by the United States—probably gave him the extra support needed to finish second behind Gonzalo Sánchez de Lozada.

Evo Morales's political party MAS won 20.94 percent of the vote, finishing less than two percentage points behind the winning MNR (22.46 percent). Although he lost the presidency, Morales won his district and returned to Congress. Quispe's party, the Pachakutik Indigenous Movement (MIP), won 6.09 percent of votes, placing the new party ahead of established parties like UCS, ADN, and Condepa. The total for both indigenous parties together—27.03 percent—is truly a revolutionary milestone in the representation of indigenous peoples and far exceeds the votes by the winning MNR. The 2002 elections marked the end of the equilibrated five-party system in effect since 1989. The combined vote for the five major elite-led parties dropped to 48 percent, with the main three winning only 42.2 percent. The ADN, CONDEPA, and UCS virtually disappeared. These results indicate that the Bolivian party system, like many in South America in the late 1990s and early 2000s, has experienced dealignment.

The second Sánchez de Lozada administration quickly ran into trouble with disaffected social movements. A violent revolt against an IMF-mandated income tax increase in February 2003 was followed in September and October by a broad popular movement to unseat the president. The original trigger for these protests was a skirmish in a town near Lake Titicaca in late September between the police and Felipe Quispe's followers, who had killed two suspected cattle rustlers. After police arrested one of those involved, Quispe organized roadblocks in protest. The violence escalated after several protesters and police were killed when the government tried to rescue tourists and others being held hostage. Quispe added the President's proposal to sell natural gas to multinational corporations through a port in Chile to the reasons for the roadblocks, which included seventy-two issues that had been negotiated with the government following protests in 2001, but on which the government had not fulfilled its promises. Opposition to the gas plan resonated with most Bolivians, who regard Chile as the country's bitter enemy, since the country lost its coastline to Chile during the late-nineteenth-century War of the Pacific. Violent confrontations between protesters and the police and military left an estimated eighty-two people dead and hundreds injured.

On October 17, 2003, President Gonzalo Sánchez de Lozada fled the country following five days of violent conflict between government security forces and a broad array of civil society groups in the capital and its outskirts. Sánchez de Lozada's use of excessive military force against mostly unarmed indigenous protesters cost him the support of the *mestizo* (mixed-race) middle class, coalition partners, his vice president, and, ultimately, the U.S. Embassy.

Constitutional order was preserved when Vice President Carlos Mesa, a well-regarded journalist and historian, assumed the presidency and promised to swiftly address the principal demand of the opposition: constitutional changes that would allow a popular referendum on the unpopular gas plan and the convocation of a constituent assembly. The referendum on the gas issue took place on July 18 and a constituent assembly was scheduled for late 2005.

Mesa's auspicious start belied the trouble to come. Lacking political skills and institutional support, the president grew weaker. The vague wording of the referendum left congressional leaders with little guidance and the draft hydrocarbon law languished as investors waited for news of the new legal environment and investment declined. In late 2004 a diverse set of highly mobilized social movements besieged the president, who was unable to negotiate or impose a resolution to conflicting demands. In 2005 the country was convulsed by conflict between lowland elites seeking greater political and economic autonomy from the national government, and the rest of the country, which demanded the immediate convocation of the constituent assembly that had been promised. Lowland elites sought to impose their vision of autonomy on the new constitution, an effort widely rejected by the rest of the country. The issue fractured political parties and paralyzed a Congress already divided between lowland and highland delegations and between the traditional parties and the new indigenous electoral vehicles. In addition, after Congress finally produced a new law regulating the production and sale of oil and natural gas, leftist and popular social movements launched multiple marches, protests, and blockades that, by May 2005, threatened to provoke another unconstitutional transfer of political power. Mesa already had threatened to resign twice, an option rejected by most political actors up until this point given the absence of an attractive constitutional alternative. While leftist groups demanded nationalization of hydrocarbon resources, others demanded a greater share of royalties for the Bolivian people. Meanwhile many business groups and international investors rejected the law, arguing that it violates existing contracts and would make foreign investment unprofitable.

Transforming the State

A main thrust of the MNR-ADN alliance had been the transformation of Bolivia's highly state-centered economy into a market-based economy. This required reducing the number of people dependent upon the state for jobs. This has been the most difficult task of the economic and political reforms that followed the democratic transition because of the strong hold on the political decision-making apparatus by professionals and bureaucrats dependent upon the state for their livelihoods. The Patriotic Accord government that followed made slow progress toward reducing the economic role of the state. Paz Zamora opened investment in mining and hydrocarbons to foreigners and passed a privatization law that focused on smaller government enterprises. But critics charged that these reforms were merely tinkering around the edges and that transformation of the state-led model had not progressed significantly relative to progress in neighboring countries. In 1989 the state remained the largest source of investment and major industries remained in state hands.

In the second half of its term the Patriotic Accord government addressed political and institutional reforms that awaited the resolution of the economic crisis. Political reform became urgent in 1989 due to the drain on government legitimacy caused by the ascension to the presidency of the third-place candidate and the resulting inability of the government to address an accumulation of problems since the turbulent transition. These included rapid urban migration, the depopulation and economic marginalization of rural areas, and the absence of state services and authority in the majority of the territory. Paz Zamora's slim mandate and indecisiveness stalled reform until an independent drive by Sánchez de Lozada was implemented to lead a constitutional reform that would improve his chances of taking office should 1989's electoral outcome be repeated in 1993. Sánchez de Lozada, Paz Zamora, and Banzer finally approved a set of political reforms in 1993. Realizing that there was not enough time prior to the end of the legislative term to launch a comprehensive constitutional reform, the three decided to proceed only where substantial consensus existed and to defer action on controversial issues. In the end four issues were chosen: judicial reform, required to end an institutional conflict between the MNR-controlled Supreme Court and the ADN-MIR controlled Congress; the reform of Article 90, which now required that Congress choose from among the top two presidential candidates in the event of a plurality victory; the reform of Article 60 to elect half the seats in the lower house through single-member districts; and administrative decentralization.

Unexpected time remained prior to the end of the legislative session, enabling the party chiefs to work on a few other issues, including the rights of the indigenous population. Sánchez de Lozada's policy institute had prepared constitutional modifications with respect to this theme. Their work coincided with an awakening among the political elite to the importance of addressing the indigenous movement's constitutional claims. That awakening commenced on August 15, 1990, when the Indigenous Confederation of the Beni (CPIB), a member organization of CIDOB, initiated a three-hundred-thirty-mile, thirty-five-day March for Territory and Dignity from Trinidad to La Paz. The principal goal of the march was state recognition of the territorial rights of the indigenous peoples. But the march would take on a greater importance: It dramatically raised awareness among the political class of the indigenous problems; it presented the indigenous territory issue as a political rather than an agrarian issue; and it provided the impetus for increased organizing within the indigenous movement and for coordination between the Amazonian and *campesino* movements.

By the time of 1993's constitutional reform effort mainstream intellectuals and the political elite were receptive to cultural approaches to political reform. The 1990 march brought to public consciousness an agenda of cultural identity and territory that was distinct from the *campesino* demands of the past and that laid the basis for the recognition of the pluricultural nature of Bolivian society in the 1993 Law of Constitutional Reform. Sánchez de Lozada's decisive electoral victory enabled him to avoid negotiating with opposition parties, which had frustrated prior comprehensive reform efforts. Civil society organizations representing popular sectors were in a state of severe crisis owing to the neoliberal reforms of the previous governments, as well as internal contradictions within their leadership, structure, and mission. They proved unable to block the state-led reform or to articulate a viable alternative. The labor sector had lost support from its base, owing to the rise of representational alternatives, such as traditional *ayllu* authorities and populist political parties.

Sánchez de Lozada reactivated the market-oriented reform agenda that had stagnated during the Patriotic Accord government and designed and forced through Congress a set of statutory laws that garnered him financial support from international financial institutions and foreign governments. Under the 1994 Law of Popular Participation (LPP) newly constituted municipalities received ownership of and responsibility for the administration of health, education, sanitation, and transportation infrastructure, as well as for the establishment of sports and cultural programs and economic development projects. To carry out their new responsibilities, municipalities receive 20 percent of government revenues, have the authority to collect some local taxes, and are eligible under certain conditions to receive additional resources from national development funds.

Taken together, the LPP and the constitutional reform represent an attempt to integrate a Western-Liberal state composed of uniform structures and norms with culturally and socially diverse civil society organizations, most of which are organized according to non-Western, communitarian norms. This is achieved by recognizing the legitimate representative function of existing *campesino,* indigenous, and urban neighborhood organizations and incorporating them into municipal government and development planning. Their representatives—selected according to community custom—serve on newly created oversight committees, which have the authority to obtain access to all information regarding the receipt and expenditure of municipal coparticipation funds. In the event of suspected mismanagement or corruption the oversight committee may begin a process of higher-government review that may lead to the suspension of resources by the Senate. In addition to their oversight function the committees transmit community development priorities to the municipal governments through a process called participatory municipal planning. The committees have yet to fulfill their promise due to their domination by political parties and insufficient resources and technical support provided for civil society organizations.

The centerpiece of Sánchez de Lozada's effort to reduce the public sector and modernize the relationship between state and economy was the 1995 Capitalization Law, which enabled private, international investment funds to "capitalize" half of the stock of key public enterprises. The law was supported by extensive reforms of the judicial system and statutory laws affecting hydrocarbons, mining, forestry, and telecommunications. Funds generated by the sale of half the stock in these enterprises were used to create a pension fund for Bolivians born at the time of the sale, distributed for the first time in 1997. Opposition to the capitalization law may have cost the MNR the 1997 elections.

The Banzer-Quiroga government placed its own mark on state institutions. In order to counter the centrifugal tendency of the megacoalition, key policy

decisions were centralized within the ADN. The government reconceptual-
ized the popular participation scheme as a tool for the alleviation of poverty
and shifted the emphasis of decentralization from the municipal to the departmental level. Greater resources and responsibilities were shifted to this level of
government to enhance the ADN's future electoral chances and to facilitate
the proportional distribution of patronage jobs among coalition partners.
Multicultural symbolism was deleted from the government's discourse, in
marked contrast to the ethnic authorities, languages, and ceremonial objects
incorporated during the Sánchez de Lozada-Cárdenas administration.

During the Banzer-Quiroga government some progress was made with
respect to implementing judicial reforms codified in the 1995 constitutional reform. That reform created a Judiciary Council to professionalize and regulate
judges, a Constitutional Tribunal to handle constitutional questions, and a
People's Defender to protect citizens from abuses by public officials. A host of
reforms to the criminal, civil, and administrative codes followed. Among the
most important of these was the creation of a new Code of Criminal Procedure, which went into effect on May 31, 2001. It shifted Bolivia from a written, inquisitorial, and mostly secret model to one that is adversarial, more
transparent, and allows for oral proceedings—an important change in a country with high illiteracy. The new code requires that translators or interpreters
be made available to non-Spanish speakers and that defense attorneys be provided to the indigent without charge. However, public defenders are poorly
trained, underpaid, and stretched too thin, leaving legal assistants—who lack
the legal standing to protect defendants and intervene in official proceedings—
to substitute for them. Still, the code makes legal proceedings more efficient.

Final approval and implementation of judicial reforms continued during
the second Sánchez de Lozada administration. However, their realization was
continually delayed by the lack of professionalism and training among the
country's judiciary and the resistance of political party leaders, who want to
maintain control over judicial appointments for patronage purposes. In addition, the military has resisted efforts to submit its personnel to civilian justice.
The new code also implemented indigenous people's constitutional rights to
use their customary forms of dispute resolution. Progress also was made during the Sánchez de Lozada-Mesa administration in establishing structures to
eliminate corruption and promote greater government transparency and accountability. Upon taking office Carlos Mesa successfully instituted a number
of constitutional changes that indigenous peoples and civil society organizations had been demanding for several years. On February 20, 2004, Mesa promulgated a law to reform the constitution, which Congress had approved with
uncharacteristic speed. Among the reforms included was the legalization of
binding or consultative referenda and legislative initiatives; the legalization

of a constituent assembly, an option barred by the 1967 Barrientos constitution; and a measure allowing "citizens' groupings" and indigenous peoples to stand for election. Indigenous groups and others had been demanding these changes for 10 years.

Public Policy and International Dependence

Bolivia is heavily dependent on foreign assistance, particularly from the United States. International experts and foreign-run policy institutes permeate government agencies, which rely on their technical expertise. This dependency places enormous pressure on Bolivian executives to adopt policies supported by the U.S. government in areas of its greatest interest, particularly with respect to stopping the flow of cocaine into the United States.

By the mid-1980s Bolivia had become the world's second-most important source of coca leaf and the third largest producer of cocaine hydrochloride. The United States has prioritized action on the drug issue ahead of issues of much greater concern to Bolivians, such as reactivating the stagnant economy and reducing poverty. Since cocaine is Bolivia's chief source of income, bringing more than half a billion dollars into the economy annually, drug interdiction tends to conflict with economic aspirations. The counternarcotics issue is sensitive also because of the imposing presence of the U.S. drug enforcement complex in Bolivia and the legitimacy problems this has caused for Bolivian governments since 1985, all of whom have been heavily dependent on U.S. economic assistance that is tied to U.S. drug-interdiction targets. The suppression of coca growing is complicated by the traditional consumption and spiritual use of coca leaf within indigenous cultures, which enables coca growers to defend their production of coca leaf in export-growing zones like the Chapare as a cultural right. The coca growers, many of whom are former miners dislocated by the economic adjustment, have launched several disruptive national demonstrations, taking advantage of growing public support for indigenous rights.

Meeting U.S. coca eradication targets was among President Banzer's highest priorities. Relying on force and battling an increasingly militant coca growers' movement with considerable domestic and international public support, the Banzer-Quiroga government eradicated 80 to 90 percent of the coca crop. As a result, the Chapare-based coca movement was somewhat weakened. Nevertheless, by building a grassroots political base through the political party MAS, coca growers leader Evo Morales won the 2006 presidential election. The coca growers' party has broadened its base since 2002 and won the highest percentage of the vote in the December 2004 municipal elections.

Conclusion

Although the results of the recent wave of political reform remain to be seen, the transformation of political life generated by the incorporation of ethnic issues into mainstream politics, and of political parties representing the long-excluded indigenous majority into the political system, constitutes a second Bolivian Revolution. As was the case after the 1952 Revolution, it will take some time for Bolivians to adjust to this new political and social reality. Already weak democratic institutions have been further weakened by the constant state of political upheaval since 2000. New judicial institutions are too fragile to resolve political and constitutional impasses; Congress is divided by regional, ethnic, class, and ideological differences; and the executive is increasingly isolated. The political party system that for years had moderated political conflict by equitably distributing state resources among the elite has been radically transformed by the incorporation of "anti-systemic parties" led by social movement leaders who are unwilling to play by the old political rules.

When elections are next held (probably in 2007) new political parties will compete alongside dozens of citizens' groups and indigenous peoples' organizations, further fragmenting the political scene. The income gap between the impoverished indigenous majority and a tiny, wealthy elite based in the booming lowland export economy is increasing, making the transparent and democratic design and implementation of economic and social policies with broad-based support virtually impossible. These problems are exacerbated by the rise of the lowland autonomy movements in the departments of Santa Cruz and Tarija, where valuable natural resources are located. The challenges that lie ahead are daunting and the stakes are high.

Suggestions for Further Reading

Albó, Xavier. "And from Kataristas to MNRistas? The Surprising and Bold Alliance between Aymarás and Neoliberals in Bolivia." In *Indigenous Peoples and Democracy in Latin America*. Ed. Donna Lee Van Cott, 55–82. New York: St. Martin's Press, 1994.

Crabtree, John, and Laurence Whitehead. *Towards Democratic Viability: The Bolivian Experience*. New York: Palgrave, 2001.

Gamarra, Eduardo A. "Facing the Twenty-First Century: Bolivia in the 1990s." In *Deepening Democracy in Latin America*. Ed. Kurt von Mettenheim and James Malloy. Pittsburgh: University of Pittsburgh Press, 1998.

Gamarra, Eduardo A., and James M. Malloy. "The Patrimonial Dynamics of Party Politics in Bolivia." In *Building Democratic Institutions: Party Systems in*

Latin America. Ed. Scott Mainwaring and Timothy Scully, 399–433. Stanford, CA: Stanford University Press, 1995.

Klein, Herbert. *Bolivia: The Evolution of a Multi-Ethnic Society.* 2nd ed. Oxford: Oxford University Press, 1992.

Ticona, Esteban, Rojas O. Gonzalo y Xavier Albó. *Votos y Wiphalas. Campesinos y pueblos originarios en Democracia.* Centro de Investigación 43. La Paz: Fundación Milenio/CIPCA, 1995.

Van Cott, Donna Lee. "From Exclusion to Inclusion: Bolivia's 2002 Elections." *Journal of Latin American Studies* 35, 4 (2003): 751–76.

————. *The Friendly Liquidation of the Past. The Politics of Diversity in Latin America.* Pittsburgh: University of Pittsburgh Press, 2000.

15

Ecuador

The Fragility of Dependent Democracy

David W. Dent

Ecuador's fragile democracy continues to creak under the strain of presidents—six of them since 1996—who have failed to serve out their term of office. On April 20, 2005, Lucio Gutiérrez (known by his detractors as *Sucio Lucio* or Dirty Lucio), a former army colonel who had taken part in the military coup in 2000 and was elected to the presidency in 2002 with promises to end Ecuador's dependency on international oil companies and the World Bank and its austerity punishments, was removed from office by Congress and large street protests. Within a few days Alfredo Palacio, Gutiérrez's elected vice president, was appointed by Congress to replace the former president, who took refuge in the Brazilian embassy after an arrest warrant was issued against him. Within a few days the battle for political power was over; however, legitimate authority remained elusive as ever as thousands of indigenous women gathered outside the presidential palace chanting *"Fuera todos! Fuera todos!"* (Everyone out). Ecuador's democracy remains deeply discredited, unable to escape the endemic corruption, abuse of political authority, constant turmoil, and economic dependence on World Bank program loans and U.S. Treasury Department officials that are rapidly contributing to the creation of an ungovernable petro-state. Moreover, the Democratic Charter of the Organization of American States (OAS) proved to be a weak instrument for preventing the "people's coup" that removed President Gutiérrez from office after months of undemocratic rule.

The fate of Lucio Gutiérrez reveals a consistent pattern in Ecuadorian politics where presidents are unable to fulfill campaign promises to root out corruption, reform the economy, and meet the demands of fiscal reform from

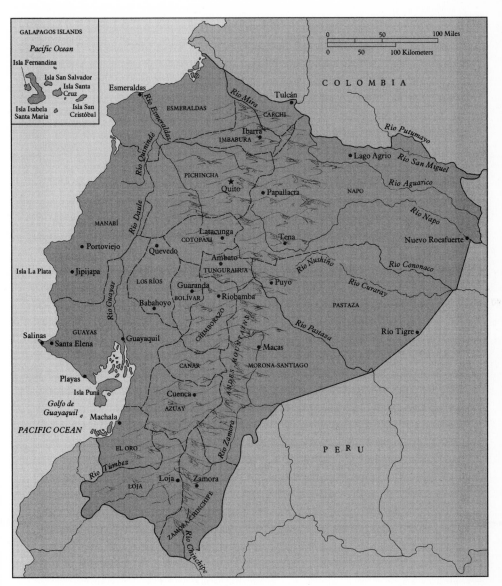

0   50   100 Miles

0   50   100 Kilometers

COLOMBIA

Esmeraldas

Río Mira   Tulcán

Río Esmeraldas   ESMERALDAS   CARCHI

Río Putumayo

Ibarra
IMBABURA

Lago Agrio   *Río San Miguel*

Río Quinindé

PICHINCHA

Río Aguarico

★
Quito   Papallacta   NAPO

Río Napo

Río Daule

MANABÍ

Latacunga
COTOPAXI
Tena

Nuevo Rocafuerte

Portoviejo

Quevedo

Ambato
TUNGURAHUA

Río Nushiño

Río Cononaco

Isla La Plata   Jipijapa

LOS RÍOS

Guaranda
BOLÍVAR

Puyo

Río Curaray

Río Guayas

Babahoyo

Riobamba

PASTAZA

Río Pastaza

Río Tigre

Salinas   GUAYAS
Santa Elena

Guayaquil

ANDES MOUNTAINS

CHIMBORAZO

Macas

Playas

CAÑAR

MORONA-SANTIAGO

Isla Puná

*Golfo de
Guayaquil*

Cuenca
AZUAY

PACIFIC OCEAN   Machala

Río Zamora

EL ORO

PERU

Río Tumbez

Loja   Zamora

LOJA

ZAMORA-CHINCHIPE

Río Chinchipe

ECUADOR

international lending agencies. After becoming Ecuador's sixth president in seven years in 2003, Gutiérrez alienated large segments of the population with his austere fiscal reforms and misuse of government funds drawn from oil revenues. After narrowly escaping impeachment measures carried out by Congress he decided to remove twenty-seven of the thirty-one Supreme Court justices, claiming they supported the impeachment attempts and were sympathetic to the opposition political parties. Several months later the new (and improved, according to the president) Supreme Court overturned corruption charges against exiled former president Abdalá Bucaram, which allowed him to return from Panama. This heavy-handed act of political manipulation and authoritarianism brought tens of thousands of angry Ecuadorians to the streets demanding Gutiérrez leave the presidency because of misguided policies, corruption, and subservience to economic programs orchestrated by the IMF and World Bank that led to higher taxes and fuel prices and fewer restraints on firing workers. It now appears that constitutional checks on power no longer have the ability to restrain presidents if they feel that democracy impedes their ability to reward friends, punish political enemies, and satisfy foreign investors for their own personal gain.

Since 1979 Ecuador has tried to consolidate its democratic system; presidents with different political ideologies—populists, conservatives, democratic socialists, or Christian democrats—and programs struggled to legitimize their authority, particularly after they carried out severe austerity measures in violation of their populist campaign promises. Effective presidential rule was hampered by the difficulty of building coalitions with small and fractious legislative parties that were in constant flux as representatives changed their party identification and refused to endorse executive branch policies. Elections were judged to be relatively free and competitive, but Ecuador's democratic institutions remained extremely fragile, and what often took place in the public realm was mired in rampant corruption and bureaucratic ineptitude.

Ironically, despite substantial oil reserves (oil reserves are estimated at 4.4 billion barrels), a diversity of agricultural exports (bananas, coffee, cacao, cut flowers, fish), and a high potential for eco-tourism, Ecuador remains one of the poorest—and weakest—Latin American countries. With natural disasters and sharp declines in world petroleum prices in the late 1990s, Ecuador's economy declined, the banking system collapsed, and the government defaulted on its external debt. After the national currency depreciated by 70 percent in 1999 the Jamil Mahuad administration decided to dollarize the economy. Dollarization occurs when a country officially adopts the U.S. dollar as its only legal tender instead of applying a flexible exchange rate.

Between 1997 and 2005 Ecuador's six presidents were charged with either corruption or abuse of authority, a combustible mixture that angered opposition members in Congress and brought millions of protesters into the streets. The current political morass is magnified by the growing authoritarianism in Venezuela and Peru and escalating guerrilla insurgencies and political violence in Colombia, which is showing signs of having a contagious effect on Ecuador. With the prospects for more indigenous protests and greater support for military takeovers to "save" the *patria* if national security is threatened, consolidating a set of democratic rules will be even more difficult in the years to come.

A History of Culture of Traditionalism

Located between Colombia and Peru, Ecuador is the second smallest nation in South America. Geographical and ethnic diversity has posed formidable obstacles to its economic and political development. Four distinct regions— highlands *(sierra)*, coast *(costa)*, East or Amazon Basin *(oriente)*, and the Galápagos Islands—constitute present-day Ecuador. Its national territory has been nibbled away since independence in 1830. For example, Ecuador was originally twice its present size, but Brazil, Colombia, and Peru have each taken large portions of Amazonia where their borders converge. In 1941 Peru invaded and grabbed almost half of Ecuador's territory.

Long accustomed to strong paternalistic leadership, Ecuadorians have never fully overcome the regional fragmentation between the highlands and the coast, epitomized by the intense rivalry between Quito, the highland capital, and the port city of Guayaquil. The population of fourteen million is roughly 40 percent Indian, 45 percent *mestizo*, 10 percent Caucasian, and 5 percent black. The population is divided almost equally between the highlands, where the *serranos* are predominantly Indian or *mestizo*, and the coast, where the population contains Afro-Indians, Europeans, and *mestizo* elements. There is a sizable African component in the northern Pacific region, descendants of people brought to work in the sugarcane plantations. Ethnicity in Ecuador is somewhat malleable, meaning that Indians can become "white" by leaving behind their traditional dress, culture, and language. These ethnic differences also suggest a political and cultural disunity, and even today such disunity continues to be an obstacle to the development of a true sense of national identity.

This quality of fragmentation can be traced back virtually to the founding of Quito and Guayaquil, in 1534 and 1537, respectively. Long before the enfeeblement of the Spanish monarchy and the independence struggle of the early nineteenth century, the traditions of authoritarianism and personalism had become deeply entrenched. This legacy helped to create a political environment that encourages corruption and abuse of authority in government. By drafting and approving new constitutions—twenty different ones have been written since gaining independence from Spain—Ecuador's state builders have tried to compensate for the lack of democratic consolidation and the disorganization of the party system. The regional and class divisions and conflicts have marked Ecuadorian society for centuries.

Military victory by independence forces at the Battle of Pinchincha on the slopes above Quito on May 24, 1822, assured the ouster of the royalists; and the breakup of independent Gran Colombia (present-day Ecuador, Colombia, Panama, and Venezuela) in 1830 brought the Venezuelan-born general Juan José Flores to Ecuador's presidency. A dominant figure for fifteen years, he was later followed by other authoritarian leaders, most notably Gabriel García Moreno for the Conservatives and the Liberals' Eloy Alfaro.

García Moreno came to power in 1861 as the apotheosis of Conservative rule. A religious zealot who assigned the Jesuits responsibility for national education and officially dedicated Ecuador to the Sacred Heart of Jesus in 1873, García Moreno also stimulated a concerted drive to diversify the economy, provide an economic infrastructure, and organize efficiently the functions of the state. Assassinated on the steps of the government palace in 1875, he nonetheless had erected a vigorous theocratic system that survived another twenty years. Only in 1895 did the Liberals seize power under Alfaro, and their rule endured for the next half century. While Alfaro occupied the presidency from 1895 to 1901 and 1906 to 1911, the power of the church was curbed, foreign investment was encouraged, and further public works were undertaken. Unwilling to relinquish power, Alfaro was killed by a once-adoring Quito mob in January 1912, but the Liberal hegemony continued for a full half century.

By this time the ineffable José María Velasco Ibarra had emerged on the political scene. A charismatic figure who combined demagogic oratory with moralistic austerity, Velasco overshadowed Ecuador's national politics for nearly fifty years. He ultimately reached the presidency five times (first in 1934 to 1935 and for the last time in 1968 to 1972), but only once did he serve out his constitutional term. Whether exercising power or planning his return from exile, Velasco remained a force until his death in 1979 at the age of eighty-four. A gifted personalistic leader but disastrously unskilled as an executive and administrator, he effectively assured a high degree of systemic instability while retarding the institutionalization of political parties, which he loathed because of their antipersonal focus.

Ecuador experienced twenty-one different governments between 1925 and 1948. After an unusual interim of three successful constitutional periods (1948–1960), there was a return to more familiar patterns. From 1960 to 1979 there were eight different governments, including the last two of Velasco; 1970 to 1979 was a dictatorial decade under first a civilian regime, then two consecutive military ones. The death of Velasco put an end to the decades of populist-military confrontations that characterized the pre-1979 period. Since 1979 there have been eleven presidents and nine presidential elections, each with a different solution to the central task of economic and political reform.

The democratic restoration that took place with the 1979 inauguration of Jaime Roldós put Ecuador at the forefront of Latin American returns to democracy. Along with the election of Roldós and his running mate, Osvaldo Hurtado (both in their thirties), came a new generation of political leaders to replace the remnants of *velasquismo* and former presidents who had retired from the political scene. The political party system was still far from institutionalized, but it did number several new entries and enjoyed an organizational structure and programmatic orientation absent before 1979.

The early Roldós-Hurtado years provided a sense of optimism that effective democracy could be established and their campaign promises of economic progress and social reform would be carried out. However, another border conflict with Peru in early 1981 followed by the death of Roldós in a plane crash in the same year dashed hopes of confronting the forces opposed to progressive reform. Vice President Hurtado was allowed to complete the remainder of Roldós's term.

The two presidents that followed, León Febres Cordero (1984–1988) and Rodrigo Borja (1988–1992), tried different developmental paths and foreign policies, but neither was successful with his policy prescriptions. Febres followed strict free-market policies, mimicked the Reagan administration's Latin American policies, angered the military, and was outright scornful of the rights of the opposition. Borja came from the democratic left, with a socialist ideology similar to European political thought. However, social-democratic government was frustrated by a large foreign debt, an ailing economy, opposition from Washington, and the unpleasant task of having to embrace austerity measures to satisfy international lenders. Ecuador struggled through the rest of the decade, with elections in 1992 (Sixto Durám Ballén), 1996 (Abdalá Bucaram), and 1998 (Jamil Mahuad), each offering a different brand of Ecuadorian party ideology and public policy prescriptions.

After seeking the post for years, the former mayor of Guayaquil, Abdalá Bucaram, won the presidency in July 1996 using blistering attacks on the Ecuadorian "oligarchy" (of which he was a part) and offering the masses a government for the poor. To attract women voters he chose as his running mate Rosalía Arteaga, who became the first female vice president of Ecuador. A flamboyant campaigner, Bucaram (nicknamed *El Loco*, the madman) epitomized the tradition of populist politics in Ecuador with his personalistic style and volatile campaign rhetoric. After becoming president Bucaram retreated from his populist campaign promises and adopted economic measures to reduce the protective role of the state. Within weeks of his inauguration opponents had tagged the president and his inner circle "Ali Abdalá and the 40 thieves." His revised economic policies produced painful increases in the cost of telephone service, cooking gas, gasoline, and electricity that were made worse by rampant corruption and favoritism. The public might have put up with the corruption—Bucaram's stock-in-trade—but his austerity measures resulted in a general strike and days of angry protest that led the Congress to remove the president on flimsy charges of "mental incompetence" in February 1997. With burlap bags full of cash (estimated to contain tens of millions of dollars), Bucaram left for exile in Panama, where he had fled before after running into political trouble in his homeland. The head of the legislature, Fabián Alarcón, was appointed by Congress to serve as president until elections could be held in 1998.

During the week-long crisis Ecuador had three declared presidents—the ousted Bucaram, Fabián Alarcón, and Rosalía Arteaga (vice president)—but no one in charge. With a forceful military determined to avoid a power vacuum, Congress at first picked Bucaram's vice president as interim president, but after a few days changed course and allowed Alarcón to serve until a new election could be held in 1998. Arteaga claimed at the time that she was replaced because of machismo and fears among the military and some members of Congress that as a woman she could not be an effective president. Although the chaotic episode that removed Bucaram seemed like comic opera in its response to a constitutional crisis and massive demonstrations against the regime, the outcome did not require either military intervention from the United States or a coup led by Ecuador's armed forces. The head of the military, General Paco Moncayo, said at the time that the military would remain neutral, occupying itself with other more important matters.

The fate of Jamil Mahuad in early 2000 was different. Unable to solve Ecuador's economic problems, he resorted to a plan to replace the *sucre*, the national currency that had lost 70 percent of its value against the U.S. dollar in 1999. In so doing, Mahuad hoped to curb inflation, bring down interest rates, and attract foreign investment. It was clearly a last-ditch effort that exacerbated the growing crisis—many believed that dollarization would devastate *sucre*-based savings—and led to the military coup that drove him from power. Ecuador continues to rely on dollarization although it is not universally recognized as the solution to the country's economic and political difficulties.

Parties, Elections, and Domestic Political Forces

For the past fifty years Ecuador has experienced shifting alliances between Liberals and Conservatives and a variety of small parties and factions that

formed after 1962 and continue to operate in a more unpredictable—and often chaotic—party system. By the 1970s Ecuador's historical Conservative
Party (*Partido Conservador*, PC) and Radical Liberal Party (*Partido Liberal
Radical*, PLR) had faded into the background, and the oft-resuscitated *ve-
lasquista* movement faded away after the collapse of Velasco's fifth and final
administration in 1972.

The eras in which the Conservative and Liberal parties enjoyed periods of
complete domination are long gone. What gradually emerged were new, more
programmatically oriented organizations, accompanied by modernizing movements consistent with well-established populist traditions. The elections of
1971 and 1979 reflected the political changes then in progress. Traditionalistic
forces were fragmented, and the Democratic Left (*Izquierda Democrática*,
ID)—originally formed by dissident Liberal reformers—was joined by the
Christian Democratic Popular Democracy (*Democracia Popular*, DP) as a representative of distinguishable doctrinal beliefs. The Marxist left was marked
by several splinter groups, but it also shared in the emergence of a new generation of leaders. Ecuadorian populism was epitomized by the Concentration of
Popular Forces (*Concertación de Fuerzas Populares*, CFP), a Guayaquil-based
party long controlled by Assad Bucaram, a charismatic if controversial figure
who rose from an impoverished background to become the nation's single
most popular mass leader since the venerable Velasco.

The outgoing military, fearful of the Bucaram temperament as well as his
antiestablishment rhetoric, succeeded in annulling his candidacy, after which
the CFP named the youthful Roldós, whose wife was a niece of Bucaram. Alliance with DP produced the Roldós-Hurtado ticket, which unexpectedly led
the field in a six-candidate race. Defying traditionalist efforts to annul or otherwise bar them from office, Roldós and Hurtado won a subsequent runoff
between the two leading slates when, on April 28, 1979, the reformists steam-
rolled the conservative candidacy of Sixto Durán Ballén with 68.5 percent of
the vote. Also elected was a solid CFP congressional majority under the iron-
fisted control of Bucaram. From the very outset, however, the struggle for
power between Roldós and Bucaram (who regarded the electoral victory
as his) weakened the government and underlined the fragility of the nascent
democracy.

The regionally based populism personified by Bucaram and his CFP later
reemerged with his nephew Abdalá Bucaram, who ran a strong race in the
1988 presidential contest as part of the Ecuadorian Roldist Party (*Partido Rol-
dosista Ecuatoriano*, PRE). The organizational remnants of the CFP by then
were being contested by two of Assad's sons, and his widow attempted to mediate. It was with Abdalá Bucaram and the PRE, however, that the nondoctri-
nal, opportunistic, and mass-based populism of Guayaquil and the coast was

finding expression by the close of the 1980s. In the meantime more structured and self-consciously programmatic politics were being exemplified by the ID and the DP. ID was notable in that it created a nationwide party organization, although it lacked popular strength with the Guayaquil masses. Rodrigo Borja guided the party while also developing the Ecuadorian version of social democracy. The DP (Christian Democrats) remained smaller and not as well organized, although building toward the future while their founder occupied the presidency.

The adolescence of the party system was underlined when seventeen organizations contested the January 1984 elections. Among nine presidential candidates Rodrigo Borja presented the reformist option against León Febres Cordero, standard-bearer of the traditional alliance, National Reconstruction Front (*Frente de Reconstrucción Nacional*, FRN). With illiterates voting for the first time—a major shift in electoral custom—a record high of 2.5 million citizens participated. Borja won narrowly, with 28.4 percent to Febres's 27.5 percent, only to be upset in the second-round runoff on May 6, 1984, by 46.6 to 43.8 percent. The combative Febres had run a vigorous personal campaign, scattering promises in the best tradition of Ecuadorian populism. When he entered office, however, he did so with an economic approach frankly derived from the Chicago school theories of free-market capitalism. A reformist bloc known as the Progressive Front (*Frente Progresista*) controlled the unicameral Congress.

During Febres's tumultuous term in office the party system continued to be stretched and twisted by the enduring conflict between traditionalist and reformist sectors. By 1988 the unpopularity of the Febres administration had left the conservative parties weaker than ever. In contrast, ID was prepared to lead the reformist drive, seconded at least indirectly by the Christian Democrats. Populism also retained its place in party politics under the aegis of Abdalá Bucaram and the PRE. In the January 1988 contest Borja and ID led; with some 20.8 percent Borja headed a field in which Bucaram surprised observers with his 15.6 percent second-place finish. Sixto Durán, as the conservative candidate, could not overcome Febres's unpopularity, finished third, and thus failed to reach the May 8 runoff. On that date, after a campaign marked by Bucaram's remarkably colorful, often scatological rhetoric, Borja on his third attempt won the presidency with a margin of some 47 to 40 percent. He also entered office with a congressional majority; twenty-nine members of the ID plus DP and other sympathizers initially provided at least forty votes in the seventy-one member body.

The party-based strength of the new Borja administration did not contradict the relative fragility of the democratic system. For the decade of the 1990s it appeared that the ID and DP would continue to be moderate options for reform; the ever-fragmented left would offer varied forms of more radical change; personalism would be most evident in the populism of an Abdalá Bucaram; and traditional forces, although powerful and well-financed, would have difficulty mounting and maintaining a significant party organization. The undeniable success of the national party system in recent years was tempered by the frequent outbursts that still rocked the body politic, particularly after the election of Bucaram in 1996.

Many of the outbursts came from domestic interest groups, especially labor, students, business, and ethnicized peasant groups. The first two have the potential for temporary interruptions or for some adjustment of public policy; the third still enjoys sweeping influence on the broad direction of public policy; and the fourth represents a new power contender able to mobilize the indigenous population in opposition to neoliberal economic policies that are perceived as detrimental to their interests.

Organized labor has historically been weak and poorly organized, a condition that has been slow to change. Three self-styled "national" confederations have been increasing their collective action as the Workers' United Front (*Frente Unitario de Trabajadores*, FUT). The first effective twenty-four-hour general strike was called by the FUT in October 1985, and the tempo of similar antigovernment protests mounted throughout the remainder of the Febres government. The domination of the Communist Party of the Confederation of Ecuadorian Workers (*Confederación de Trabajadores del Ecuador*, CTE), the oldest and most important FUT member, combined with the decline in workers' wages and worsening living conditions throughout the 1980s to augment labor's impact.

Recent efforts to reform Ecuador's battered economy by imposing radical austerity measures to please international lenders have had to confront organized protests from thousands of indigenous citizens, who make up between one-quarter and one-third of the population. To gain greater leverage over the political system Indian groups determined to preserve their environment and culture have created political parties (*Movimiento Nuevo País*–Pachakutik) and interest groups (Confederation of Indian Nations of Ecuador) with progressive reform policies. For the past ten years the indigenous population has established itself as a significant force in Ecuadorian politics, capable of mounting street protests and electing indigenous representatives in Congress.

Students' and women's groups also play important parts in the political process. The highly politicized students respond swiftly and angrily to arbitrary government, viewing themselves as the major defenders of the poor and the oppressed. Their leadership is often fragmented by bitter internal rivalries and ideological strife; nonetheless, the students constitute an interest group that is an important political participant. In the past decade dozens of organizations have developed to deal with women's issues. Ironically, despite the fact that Ecuador was the first South American country to give women the right to vote, progress toward sexual equality in politics, the workplace, and at home has been painfully slow.

The array of business groups and chambers of commerce that formalize the interests of Ecuadorian industrialists, entrepreneurs, and agriculturalists exercises far greater and more constant authority in the setting of national policy. Although far from monolithic, the private sector constitutes a power force, which generally sees the task of government as being the protection of its own interests rather than representing all socioeconomic sectors. In this orientation the nation's business leadership is joined by the ranking hierarchy of the Church, although internal debate occasionally dilutes the inherent conservatism of the religious leaders in Ecuador.

Government Institutions and The Role of the State

Formally, Ecuador has a presidential government with a unicameral legislature, which in 2005 consisted of nine political parties with representation. Ecuador is faced with numerous parties in which no one party stands a chance of gaining power alone. This means that parties must work with each other in an effort to form coalition governments. The multiparty system also means that in the vote for president a runoff election is often needed to produce a clear winner. For example, in 2002, in the first round Lucio Gutiérrez (*Partido Sociedad Patriotica 21 de Enero*, (PSP)/*Movimiento de Unidad Plurinacional Pachakutik-Nuevo Pais* (MUPP-NP) won 20.2 percent of the vote against 17.4 percent for his closest competitor, Alvaro Noboa (*Partido Renovador Institucional Acción* [PRIAN]); in the second round he won 54.3 percent against Noboa's 45.7 percent. Defections by party members of the National Congress are commonplace, resulting in frequent changes in the number of seats held by the various political parties.

The operating style of government in Ecuador has been authoritarian, whether the regime is civilian or military. Flamboyant and charismatic figures rather than political platforms have been a mainstay of Ecuadorian politics. Constraints on executive power depend more on political dynamics than on formal government structures. A president relies far more on individual prestige, oligarchic approval, and military support than on Congress or the courts. The judicial system in particular has been subject to manipulation by the executive, as happened in December 2004 when President Gutiérrez removed 90 percent of the justices of the Supreme Court, claiming the judges were behind an impeachment attempt the previous month and were sympathetic to the major opposition parties, particularly the Social Christians. The same lack of judicial independence is true of the Supreme Electoral Tribunal and even the Tribunal of Guarantees, which is assigned responsibility for guarding the constitutionality of government actions and regulations. In contrast, the legislative branch has gradually been expanding its role and impact since the 1979 restoration of elected government.

The 1978 constitution gave Ecuador a unicameral system, as embodied in the *Cámara Nacional de Representantes* (CNR). This body has sometimes been irresponsible and destructive as others were in earlier times; in the early 1980s there was still occasional reliance on sidearms, and galleries were often packed by either pro- or antigovernment mobs. Even so, the enlarging vistas of democratic government have contributed to greater congressional authority. If presidents have tilted angrily with the CNR, they have also sought to deal with it as a legitimate arm of constitutional government. Whatever the contributions of the CNR to the Ecuadorian body politic, as a national legislative institution it remains erratic in substance and in policy impact. Presidents who find it difficult to work with Congress have tried to get their way through the use of favoritism and referenda.

Even though the executive remains the dominant branch of the national government, the president's power has been declining and the authority of the state is relatively weak overall. Presidents who arrive in power through democratic means must try to operate in an environment where effective authority is undermined by many factors that characterize Ecuador's fragile political system: the lack of state revenue (compounded by tax evasion, natural disasters such as earthquakes and floods, and world market fluctuations for its major exports); competition and dissension, with decentralized pockets of authority in rural areas combined with the significant power and autonomy that resides in the mayor of Guayaquil; rampant corruption, nepotism, and a swollen and inefficient bureaucracy; a fragmented and weak party system, sometimes with many parties competing for seats in the unicameral legislature; a chronic and destabilizing disconnection between the presidency and Congress, making policymaking difficult while tempting leaders to rule in an authoritarian fashion; a fundamental dependency on external actors (the United States, World Bank, International Monetary Fund), which often means catering to the United States and not opposing Washington's Latin American policy; and a military establishment that retains a high degree of autonomy, access to substantial amounts of petroleum revenue, and opposition to subordination to civilian leadership. The success of some form of democratic rule is threatened further by the fact that Ecuadorians express one of the lowest levels of satisfaction with democracy in Latin America. Clearly, Ecuador must overcome a political system that is hampered by serious residual elements of an authoritarian political culture if it wants to do more than muddle through with a fragile and dependent "democracy" in a constant state of economic and political crisis.

Although less professionalized than the armed forces of neighboring states, the Ecuadorian military has undertaken serious efforts at modernization in recent years, particularly during the military governments (1972–1979). Even as the armed forces were planning their withdrawal from power, it was with the conscious intention of maintaining and deepening the military's institutional advances as well as being significant levers of power. Linkages with civilian elites have been forged by the growing practice of retired officers entering into business at high management levels. All of this residual power means that the armed forces, in contrast to civilian authority, wield considerable power over the direction of domestic and foreign policy.

Military loyalty to constitutional procedures was tested when Jaime Roldós was killed, but after a few hours of uncertainty the decision to support Osvaldo Hurtado was reached. Institutional patience was more severely tested during the next administration as President Febres, constantly attacked by the political opposition on grounds of high-handed rule, also followed a capricious path with the military. Scornful of institutional autonomy, Febres frequently overrode existing procedures and practices while indulging in favoritism toward certain officers. There were numerous incidents, the most serious of which nearly provoked his ouster.

Controversy over charges of high-level corruption on the part of General Frank Vargas Pazzos, chief of the Joint Command, led to his arrest in March 1986 and, shortly thereafter, a brief armed rebellion at Quito's air base. Months of complicated maneuvering, bargaining, and broken promises led to Febres's seizure by pro-Vargas paratroopers on January 16, 1987. The release of the president after a few hours was followed by a new exchange of charges in which military loyalty was again severely tested. Vargas, a distinguished pilot and military figure, subsequently launched a presidential bid, finishing fourth in the 1988 contest. The question of military loyalty to constitutionality was also raised when Abdalá Bucaram, an outspokenly hostile critic of the military, reached the presidential runoff.

In systemic terms these events merely underline the fragility of Ecuadorean democracy and the immaturity of civil-military relations. In a 1991 survey conducted in Quito and Guayaquil, nearly 80 percent of respondents rated the armed forces and the Church as the most trustworthy institutions in the country. In sharp contrast, more than three-quarters lacked confidence in the political parties and the three branches of government. The almost complete absence of a democratic political culture was made evident by the 7 percent of respondents who agreed that the armed forces should take over the government if national security was threatened.

The rise and fall of Lucio Gutiérrez (2003–2005) can be attributed to the Ecuadorian military. He ran for president in 2002 as a candidate of the January 21 Patriotic Society Party (PSP), named for the date of the 2000 coup against Jamil Mahuad, and this helped legitimize his campaign two years later. After weeks of political unrest, in April 2005 Ecuador's military announced publicly that they were withdrawing their support for Gutiérrez and he was quickly removed from power.

The Politics of Development

The functioning of government structures has helped only marginally to alter the essentially elitist and discriminatory distribution of national wealth. Traditional attitudes of dominant social groups, mediated through authoritarian patterns, have militated against the realization of reforms in such major policy areas as health, housing, and education. Furthermore, the loosely redistributionist inclinations of several past governments proved only modestly different in impact from the distinctive free market approach of León Febres Cordero and his collaborators. The latter approach involved a concerted effort to reduce government regulation, promote private enterprise, encourage foreign investment, reschedule the foreign debt, and employ petroleum earnings as the base on which to build economic growth. As the government's official plan stated, it was committed to stabilizing the economy and restoring its capacity for growth through control of inflation while simultaneously strengthening output growth, income, employment, savings, exports, and domestic and foreign investment; regulating imports; and rationalizing the distribution of vital products.

Febres enjoyed early success in seeking more favorable terms for debt servicing. Eased investment regulations were adopted and a new series of oil exploration contracts also brought an infusion of fresh funds. Nontraditional exports (Panama hats, shrimp, fresh-cut flowers, textiles, petroleum) increased, and there was some progress in housing and generally with public works, although there was marked regional favoritism toward Guayaquil and the coast. At the same time, by the close of Febres's term there had been a deterioration in the areas of manufacturing and industry. Perhaps the single policy area of greatest effectiveness was preventative medicine and health, thanks in some part to the efforts of the president's wife on behalf of a national program of free infant medicine.

On balance, however, the decidedly mixed record of the administration said less about the capacities of the free market system and more about government ineffectiveness in the face of unanticipated economic calamity. Until 1987 Febres's policy relied substantially on an overproduction of oil. Consistently exceeding the quotas established by OPEC, Ecuador was nonetheless a slave to world prices. In this respect, its experience was consistent with that of earlier governments. All of these factors testify to the endemic obstacles to productive policymaking that governments of very different economic and doctrinal outlooks must share.

The International Arena

To govern Ecuador successfully also means getting along with major actors in the international arena, particularly the United States and international financial institutions such as the IMF and the World Bank. The impact of globalization and the necessity of following demands for neoliberal reforms and economic restructuring has placed severe strains on small countries like Ecuador. Presidents who attempt economic reforms by imposing austerity measures on the population—privatizing public companies, reducing government subsidies, and reducing the size of the bureaucracy—can usually please international financial analysts and the U.S. ambassador, but at the price of social upheaval, violent protests, massive labor strikes, and declining support among major segments of the population.

The involvement of the United States in Ecuador has fluctuated over time, but in most cases it has been associated with trade and commerce, border disputes, tuna-fishing rights, perceived security needs related to the nearby Panama Canal, corruption, terrorism, and drug trafficking in the Andes region. A close friendship with the United States is less a foreign policy principle than the inherent dependency of a small (and weak) state with limited resources. There have been times in the history of U.S.-Ecuadorian relations when even dictators could be tolerated if they expressed friendship and did not interfere with the goals of U.S. foreign policy. At the same time Ecuadorian politicians—both dictators and democrats—have been masters of the art of manipulating U.S. policy for the purpose of obtaining loans, more investment, and economic assistance. During the decade of the 1990s the IMF and the World Bank had a marked impact on Ecuador due to its foreign debt problems, the most severe in Latin America.

Since the 1970s Washington has pressured Ecuador to hold national elections when the military was in power, worked behind the scenes to support constitutionality at the time of Jaime Roldós's death, made evident its desire that the Febres administration serve out its term of office during the Reagan years, and criticized the government for the dramatic rise in corruption during the short reign of President Bucaram in 1996 to 1997. The Clinton administration, through the U.S. ambassador, pressured the military to relinquish power during the weekend coup in January 2000 by telling the junta that it would face severe international financial sanctions and declining support if it did not return to civilian rule.

Ecuadorian presidents who kowtow to Washington can create hardships for themselves in governing at home. For example, Febres's overt pro-U.S. posture triggered acrimonious debate in 1987 with his acceptance of some six thousand U.S. troops (rotated in contingents of six hundred on a biweekly basis from May through October) to help postearthquake reconstruction efforts in the Amazon basin. Operation Blazing Trails involved the use of unarmed troops to repair bridges and roads in the devastated province of Napo, at a cost of some U.S. $7 million. Both Marxist and centrist leaders denounced the action as endangering national sovereignty, and there were frequent charges that Washington was in fact seeking a new military training base. After Ecuador's Congress passed a resolution calling for an immediate troop withdrawal, U.S. troops prepared to depart. When the departure finally took place in October 1987, very little road-building had been accomplished, and anti-U.S. attitudes had been fanned by the debate.

Ecuador's small size is largely the result of border conflicts with Colombia, Peru, and Brazil. Since the 1830s Ecuador has lost 61 percent of its total land area, mostly to Peru in a costly and lopsided battle in 1941. From 1941 to 1995 war erupted three times in territory disputed by Ecuador and Peru. Peruvian troops invaded Ecuador in 1995, and sporadic fighting continued for weeks before an emergency meeting of the OAS arranged for mutual negotiations that helped resolve the differences. It was several months before troops were withdrawn from the contested area. The 1995 war was a costly affair in terms of casualties (three hundred on both sides) and expenditures (U.S. $500 million), and it took more than three years for Presidents Jamil Mahuad and Alberto Fujimori to finalize a peace agreement in which Peru retained sovereignty over the disputed territory while giving ownership to Ecuador.

With the help of Argentina, Brazil, Chile, and the United States, both nations signed a peace treaty in October 1998 because they realized that trade, economic growth, and environmental preservation are more important than nationalistic politics and war. By dividing sovereignty and ownership of the land, the dignity and honor of both countries was preserved, a negotiation strategy developed by the Project on Negotiation at Harvard Law School. Nevertheless, the high cost and intensity of the war surprised Washington and raised questions in the Clinton administration about its democracy promotion rhetoric, particularly the popular theory that "democracies do not go to war against each other."

Despite the loss of an outlet to the Amazon River after the 1941 war with Peru, Ecuador attempted to extend its territorial rights to include sole control over the natural resources and territorial sea within two hundred miles of its coastline. On the basis of this claim a lengthy political and legal battle started with the United States and other maritime powers over territorial claims and fishing rights, particularly the lucrative tuna catch. During the 1950s and 1960s the United States and Ecuador engaged in what became known as the "tuna wars," in which the U.S. tuna fleet was captured and fined, leading to retaliation by Washington. The tuna wars passed into history after the United States accepted the two-hundred-mile economic zone approved by the United Nations Conference on the Law of the Sea.

Multilateral ties through international organizations concerned with economic commodities, trade, and integration are less valuable to Ecuador now than they were at the time the various agreements were signed. For example, the Andean Pact (now known as the Andean Community) has not lived up to the country's initial expectations and its provisions are often viewed as taking too little account of Ecuador's economic conditions. Ecuador joined OPEC in 1973 when its oil bonanza looked promising, but withdrew in 1992, protesting the high annual membership fee of U.S. $2 million and the inability to gain approval for increasing its production quota. However, Ecuador decided to continue its linkage to OPEC as a nonvoting association member like Mexico and other countries.

The rise of drug trafficking in the Andes and of regional terrorism have also influenced Ecuador's relations with its Andean neighbors and the United States. This policy concern became an important one for the Febres administration and has continued with the presidency of Lucio Gutiérrez. The magnitude of the drug industry, especially in light of conditions in Colombia, virtually guarantees that Ecuador cannot avoid having its territory used for transshipment, growing illicit crops, and arms smuggling. In addition, the rebel war in Colombia is now spreading to Ecuador, where Colombian guerrillas (mainly the Revolutionary Armed Forces of Colombia, *Fuerzas Armadas Revolucionarias de Colombia*, FARC) have used Ecuadorian territory as a base of operations for drug trafficking, smuggling of arms, and mass kidnappings.

Ecuador's fragile political system is highly vulnerable to the influence of narco-trafficking, but its politicians have been most willing to follow U.S. antidrug strategy—control, repression, and militarization—designed by the State Department and controlled by U.S. government agencies. It is a strategy that has been criticized for its harmful effects on Andean societies, including the diversion of needed resources to the military, human rights abuses, and negative reactions directed at the United States and its antidrug policies. In April 1999 the U.S. military signed a short-term agreement with Ecuador for the use of airfields (now called Forward Operating Locations) in Manta to conduct antidrug flights over the Andes.

Ecuador has not experienced the level of narco-terrorism and guerrilla violence found in Colombia and Peru. However, during the 1980s two groups— *Alfaro Vive, Carajo!* (AVC) and the *Montoneros Patria Libre* (MPL)—became active, taking responsibility for a chain of robberies and kidnappings until they agreed to lay down their arms and participate in a "national dialogue" with the ID government of President Borja. The AVC group was absorbed into ID in 1991, although sporadic acts of violence have continued through the 1990s under a variety of different names. Ecuador, traditionally one of South America's tranquil states, was thus moving toward the destabilizing conditions that were so prevalent in the two closest neighboring republics. Popular dissatisfaction with democracy and a poverty rate exceeding 60 percent has contributed to sharp increases in Ecuadorian emigration to the United States.

The narrow election victory of Jamil Mahuad in 1998 set in motion a number of policies that aggravated an existing fiscal crisis that in turn triggered massive protests and violence, human rights violations, and a showdown between the IMF and Congress over how to meet its foreign-debt obligations and carry out needed reforms. To satisfy the economic elites of Guayaquil, the new Mahuad administration eliminated income taxes and replaced them with a 1 percent tax on financial transactions. As the economic crisis worsened during the first two years of the Mahuad administration, the IMF stepped into the fray by demanding the reintroduction of the income tax to increase government revenue and reduce the fiscal deficit, criticized the corruption tied to Mahuad's bank bailouts, and reversed itself after insisting on cuts in public spending after years of reductions. Although the pact with the IMF may satisfy some private investors and the United States, Ecuador's Congress is resistant to the mandated reforms that include tax reform and the elimination of many tax exemptions. Moreover, by spending scarce public resources on the police and military to handle social disorder and pushing a questionable currency-modification proposal, President Mahuad exacerbated the economic meltdown that contributed to his removal from office after only seventeen months. The economic crisis of the late 1990s helped bring Lucio Gutiérrez (2003–2005) to power with promises of fighting corruption and introducing populist economic reforms. Ecuador benefited from higher petroleum prices after 2003, but fiscal irresponsibility and excess spending on social sector programs floundered the economy and Ecuador's Congress voted to remove him from office in April 2005.

Conclusion

Ecuador's democratic system remains fragile and strongly dependent on international economic forces, powerful foreign influences, and even acts of nature over which there can be no control. Ecuador is located in one of South America's most conflicted regions and presents a number of challenges for U.S. foreign policy. Washington would like to see Ecuador democratic, prosperous, and a positive force in curbing the spread of narco-terrorism and political violence in the northern Andes. However, many of the central features of Ecuadorian politics are antithetical to the creation of a stable and efficient system.

The last series of democratically-elected presidents has done little to reverse the growing dissatisfaction with the present economic and political system. The signs of political change in the Andes—where presidents have restricted civil liberties to maintain order; combat corruption, drug trafficking, and terrorism; and improve economic management—worry many in the international community, and the adoption of a nationwide version of this "solution" to these dilemmas should not be ruled out in the next decade, especially when voters praise these authoritarian measures. It is hard to imagine how current neoliberal policy guidelines favored by international financial organizations and the United States can help Ecuador deal with its fragile democracy and improve its weak and antiquated economic system.

Suggestions for Further Reading

Biles, Robert E. "Democracy for the Few: Ecuador's Crisis-Prone Democracy." In *Assessing Democracy in Latin America*. Ed. Philip Kelly. Boulder, CO: Westview Press, 1998.

Conaghan, Catherine M., and James M. Malloy. *Unsettling Statecraft: Democracy and Neoliberalism in the Central Andes*. Pittsburgh: University of Pittsburg Press, 1994.

Dent, David W. *The Legacy of the Monroe Doctrine: A Reference Guide to U.S. Involvement in Latin America and the Caribbean*. Westport, CT: Greenwood, 1999.

Gerlach, Allen. *Indians, Oil, and Politics: A Recent History of Ecuador*. Wilmington, DE: SR Books, 2003.

Hey, Jeanne A. K. *Theories of Dependent Foreign Policy and the Case of Ecuador in the 1980s*. Athens: Ohio University Center for International Studies, 1995.

Isaacs, Anita. *Military Rule and Transition in Ecuador, 1972–92*. Pittsburgh: University of Pittsburgh Press, 1993.

Martz, John D. *The Military in Ecuador: The Policy and Politics of Authoritarian Rule*. Albuquerque, NM: Latin American Institute, University of New Mexico, 1988.

———. *Politics and Petroleum in Ecuador*. New Brunswick, NJ: Transaction Books, 1987.

Sawyer, Suzana. *Crude Chronicles: Indigenous Politics, Multinational Oil, and Neoliberalism in Ecuador*. Durham, NC: Duke University Press, 2004.

Schodt, David W. *Ecuador: An Andean Enigma*. Boulder, CO: Westview Press, 1987.

Selverston-Scher, Melina. *Ethnopolitics in Ecuador: Indigenous Rights and the Strengthening of Democracy*. Miami: University of Miami, North/South Center Press, 2001.

Warren, Kay B., and Jean E. Jackson, eds. *Indigenous Movements, Self-Representation, and the State in Latin America*. Austin: University of Texas Press, 2002.

PART III

The Political Systems of
Central and Middle
America and the Caribbean

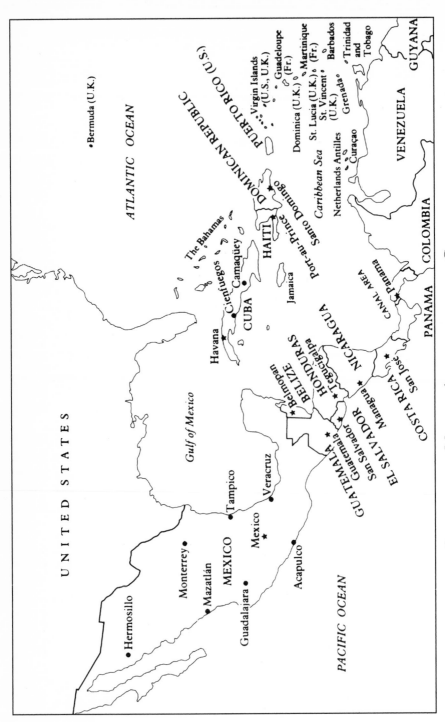

CENTRAL AND MIDDLE AMERICA AND THE CARIBBEAN

16

Mexico
The Emergence of a Messianic Reformer

George W. Grayson

M exico is a country of 106 million people that shares a two-thousand-mile-long frontier with the United States, stands as one of its northern neighbor's biggest trading partners, is its second largest supplier of oil, has proven a magnet for American investors, and is witnessing surging integration of its economy with that of the United States through the North American Free Trade Agreement (NAFTA).

On a negative note, each year hundreds of thousands of illegal workers pour into the United States from Mexico; powerful Mexican and Colombian drug cartels ship huge quantities of cocaine, heroin, and marijuana across the Rio Grande to American consumers; and violent bands—including the dreaded Mara Salvatruchas—operate along the U.S.-Mexican border. As a result of mutual interests Washington has assigned thirty-five U.S. agencies to the American embassy in Mexico City, more than to any other country in the world.

Arrogant observers used to scoff that "Democracy existed 364 days a year in Mexico; it was only missing on Election Day!" Then came the political reforms promoted by President Ernesto Zedillo (1994–2000): a new electoral registry; counterfeit-proof voter cards; the organization, supervision, and counting of ballots by the civilian-controlled Federal Electoral Institute (IFE); and the creation of a federal electoral tribunal as the final arbiter of political disputes. After the election woes in Florida in 2000 many analysts concluded that—in federal contests, at least—balloting was more transparent and credible in Mexico than in certain U.S. states.

MEXICO

In 2000 Vicente Fox, a member of the center-right National Action Party (PAN) won the presidency, breaking the seventy-one-year grip of the Revolutionary Institutional Party (PRI) on the executive branch. Late–2005 public-opinion surveys indicated that Fox, who leaves office on December 1, 2006, may be succeeded by Andrés Manuel López Obrador, Mexico City's former mayor, and nominee of the nationalist-leftist Democratic Revolutionary Party (PRD).

Corporatist Political Culture

If elected, the messianic López Obrador may introduce his own variant of corporatism, a sociopolitical system that provides representation via professional and occupational groupings rather than through individuals representing geographic constituencies. Although corporatism could function democratically, it tends to be top-down, authoritarian, and statist, a mechanism for regulating change and maintaining discipline over interest groups and their members. It is antiliberal, antipluralist, and antifree-enterprise. Virtually absent in U.S. political discourse and traditions, corporatism exhibits deep roots in Mexico. Its presence will blind observers (who rely on nominal written and rhetorical expressions of the country's politics) to the underlying distribution of power.

Although a yawning gulf continues to separate the U.S. and Mexican polities on a de facto basis, differences have narrowed because of the liberalization epitomized by NAFTA, other external economic influences, and the modernization of Mexico's electoral procedures.

Indeed, a medley of factors—NAFTA, the privatization of hundreds of state firms, Mexico's links with the global economy, and IFE, nominating primaries, and other political reforms—have enhanced electoral democracy and pluralism at the expense of corporatism, at least in the northern and central parts of the country. The politics of the impoverished South remain remarkably traditional, hierarchical, and beset by old-style bosses known as "dinosaurs." Bosses and reformers continue to cross swords in Mexico City, where the PRD has replaced the PRI as the dominant force.

Recent political and economic reforms have won international praise. However, the erosion of corporatism diminishes the controls exerted when the PRI dominated the political landscape. As a consequence, Mexicans suffer ubiquitous police corruption, an unprofessional judiciary, an ineffective Congress, quasi-monopolies in key economic sectors, and the rise of new political actors, such as nongovernmental organizations (NGOs) pursuing human rights and narco-traffickers seeking riches. Of 146 countries that Transparency International surveyed for its 2004 Corruption Perception Index, Mexico tied with Ghana and Thailand as the sixty-fourth most corrupt country.

Formal and Real Power

In Mexico the organization of real power bears little resemblance to the formalities of its 1917 constitution. That document envisions a political arrangement that, superficially at least, mirrors that of the United States: legal separation of powers; establishment of checks and balances; and dispersal of authority among legislative, executive, and judicial branches with distinct and specified duties, complete with a presidential veto. Just as does the occupant of the White House, Mexico's chief executive commands the armed forces, can mobilize state militias, and takes the lead in treaty-making and other foreign-policy initiatives. Moreover, the country's official name, "The United States of Mexico," implies a federal system of government. Mexico's thirty-one states also approximate their neighbors to the north in terms of formal organization, institutions, and rights vis-à-vis the national government. In addition, Mexico's capital, known as the *Distrito Federal*, or D.F., exists as a quasi-independent enclave and seat of national power, like the District of Columbia.

Behind such apparent similarities lies a paradox. The current system was designed for a powerful executive, who—during most of the PRI's reign—handpicked his successor through a process known as the *dedazo* or "big finger," removed governors and other officials at will, rewarded allies with generous public contracts, manipulated PRI officials and party decision-making, and spent millions of dollars in discretionary funds as he saw fit. No wonder that pre-Zedillo chief executives were said to combine the attributes of the British monarch, U.S. president, and pope. Although periodic crises afflicted the regime, it generally functioned effectively—if corruptly—under a powerful executive. Under the last years of Zedillo and during the Fox presidency the Congress has become a competing power center. Rather than acting constructively, the legislators have used their newly acquired influence to frustrate fiscal, labor, and energy reforms. Such deadlock and drift has exacerbated public disapproval of Mexico's political actors and institutions.

Independence, La Reforma, and Porfirio Díaz

Notions of strong leaders and authoritarian artifices arrived in Mexico with the Spaniards, who began to infuse a corporatist outlook in what they called "New Spain." Although the organization and mission of the Roman Catholic Church typified basic corporatist practices, institutions such as *audiencias reales*—or "royal courts"—represented the authority of the crown itself in New Spain. In addition, corporatist influences also manifested themselves through the crystallization of four well-recognized classes. *Peninsulares*, or European-born individuals, occupied a higher social stratum than *criollos* or Europeans born in the New World. *Mestizos* arose from mixed marriages between Spaniards and Indians—with the latter eking out a living at the base of a distended social pyramid. Currently, *mestizos* constitute about three-fourths of the population, followed by Indians with 15 percent, and whites with 9 percent.

History would not preserve Mexican colonial society in amber. Over time, successive waves of revolution, nationalism, and industrialization reshaped the world and, with it, Mexico's socioeconomic and ideological contours. Yet the Iberian pattern of Mexico's corporatist order not only survived but remained paramount until the late twentieth century. After attaining freedom from Spain in 1821 Mexico adopted representative and democratic forms of government on paper. In fact, the nascent regime retained the centralized, elitist, and corporatist heritage bequeathed by Iberia. Only Mexico's first president, Guadalupe Victoria, a naive devotee of republicanism, managed to struggle through his term (1824–1829). During the half-century after independence, some forty-eight regimes rose and fell in kaleidoscopic fashion as thirty different men occupied the National Palace where viceroys formerly resided. These processor leaders included two emperors—one indigenous, Agustín I (1822–1823); the other French-imposed Hapsburg Archduke Maximilian (1863–1867)—both of whom were executed. The same conditions that nurtured the unscrupulous, authoritarian Santa Anna, who succeeded Victoria in the presidency, also produced Benito Juárez, a Zapotec Indian born to misery. He and his Liberal followers attacked the now-discredited institutions of Spanish origin so inextricably bound to authoritarianism, Roman Catholicism, and corporatism. These reformers promulgated the 1857 constitution, which stressed individual rights and laissez-faire economics over corporatism, separated church and state, called for secular schools, and fortified the legislative branch at the expense of the executive.

These changes sparked a bloody, three-year "War of Reform" that ended with a Liberal victory in 1861. Taking advantage of America's preoccupation with its Civil War, Napoleon III responded to the pleas of local conservatives and imposed Maximilian of Austria as emperor of Mexico. The ouster of French troops—catalyzed by General Porfirio Díaz's resounding triumph in Puebla in April 1867—resulted in Maximilian's death at the hands of a firing squad.

In 1876 Díaz assumed the presidency under the banner of "no reelection," a mordantly ironic slogan betrayed by his three-and-one-half decades of ruthless primacy. The "hero of Puebla" stressed economic growth over political development. He and his technocratic advisers known as *científicos* (scientists) concentrated on attracting foreign capital, opening mines, clearing farm lands, building a national infrastructure, and spurring development. As a former general, Díaz realized the danger that military chiefs posed to any Mexican head of state.

Rather than waving sticks at his foes, he preferred to seduce them with carrots, in the form of choice assignment, civilian posts, lucrative business concessions, and outright bribery. "A dog with a bone in its mouth cannot bite," he reasoned.

His policies yielded a cornucopia of riches for Díaz, his cohorts, and the ranchers, businessmen, and foreign entrepreneurs who basked in his favor. Meanwhile, the majority of the population endured economic, social, and political privations. Just after the turn of the century, peasant leaders Emiliano Zapata and Francisco "Pancho" Villa, labor chiefs, and political idealist Francisco I. Madero mounted resolute challenges to Díaz's autocratic rule.

Díaz's crude stealing of the 1910 election enkindled a Madero-led uprising that toppled the dictatorship and vaulted Madero into the presidency. A right-wing coup cut short Madero's term in 1913, plunging the country into a revolution that consumed one million lives—nearly 5 percent of the population—over a three-year period. Ultimately, a newly emergent Constitutionalist movement in the North, headed by "First Chief" Venustiano Carranza, gathered an army composed of defecting federal troops and Madero loyalists. This force vanquished elements of the old order before turning its guns on agrarian supporters of Villa and Zapata. In the course of events liberal reformers lost control to radicals, who dominated the writing of the nation's new fundamental law.

The 1917 Constitution: Groundwork for "Revolutionary Nationalism"

On first reading, the 1917 constitution appears to be a liberal charter antithetical to historic corporatist doctrine and tradition. Indeed, the drafters of the document lifted two-thirds of its contents whole from the 1857 compact. In addition, radical officers from the North whose work enjoyed the blessing of Álvaro Obregón, the revolution's outstanding military figure, overshadowed the "Renovators" or gradualists linked to interim President Carranza. Although forced to hammer out some compromises, the northern Jacobins stamped their indelible mark on the charter's provisions. Among other steps, they:

1. provided that the state offer free, universal, secular education (Article 3);
2. stipulated that the oil, natural gas, and other subsoil minerals belonged to the state, which could restrict private ownership of these resources (Article 27);
3. authorized the division of large estates into small holdings (Article 27);
4. required protection of workers, including maximum workdays, equal salaries for men and women, and the right of workers to form unions and to strike (Article 123);

5. empowered legislatures to limit the number of priests in their states and denied the Roman Catholic Church the right either to hold property and or involve itself in politics (Article 130); and
6. endorsed a plethora of approaches—private, public, cooperative, communal—to economic development.

The document abounded with contradictions. The provision vouchsafing the sanctity of contract, for example, clashed with sweeping official discretion on the proper use of surface and subsoil holdings. In addition, the ambitiousness of the constitution exceeded the resources available in Mexico's war-ravaged economy. Finally, Carranza ignored socioeconomic innovations sponsored by progressive governors, provoking the First Chief's overthrow by Obregón.

Obregón (1920–1924) and his successor, Plutarco Elías Calles (1924–1928), blessed the burgeoning trade unions, peasant leagues, and political parties as instruments to gather and express the concerns of their members or, at least, of their leaders. They also perceived such organizations—especially labor centrals—as part and parcel of a revolutionary state that could form a counterpoise to foreign corporations and renegade military units.

Obregón and Calles began a risky process of balancing organized interests that continues to the present. They turned to the constitution for legitimacy, bending its articles around corporatist precepts to mollify competing power brokers. The 1917 compact, for example, enshrined the concept of collective farms, *ejidos*, so admired by revolutionary agrarians. At the same time, old-line conservatives, a force long identified with military might, viewed communal peasant landholdings as anathema. The constitution had laid out a preliminary blueprint for the rational management of a modern corporatist state, but not a democracy. In the years to follow, Mexican leaders would forge the best-articulated, single-party corporatist matrix in Latin America, a model that lasted more than seventy years.

Calles, the 1928 Crisis, and the Birth of a Revolutionary Party

In 1924 Calles, a steadfast supporter of Obregón during the civil war, succeeded his comrade-in-arms as president. During his term Calles took advantage of a recovering economy to implement some of the populist policies initiated by his predecessor. In August 1928, at the height of the Catholic-led Cristero Rebellion, a deranged artist assassinated Obregón, who again had won the presidency but had yet to be inaugurated for a second term. What action could Calles take to prevent a violent struggle by dozens of power hungry regional and local leaders?

His answer took the form of a "revolutionary party"—a precursor to today's PRI—composed of military strongmen, regional strongmen, chiefs of small parties, and some agrarian and labor bosses. From the beginning, these men of action downplayed ideology in favor of channeling popular support into an effective power apparatus that would maximize their freedom of action in their own bailiwicks. Federal employees were required to join the new national organization and contribute dues equivalent to a week's pay, thus funding a professional staff and forging links to the bureaucracy that would become a hallmark of the official party. Through innovative governance and forceful guidance Calles had provided a brilliant entrée for his successor and Mexico's first modern president, General Lázaro Cárdenas.

Cárdenas Transforms a Confederal Party Into a Corporatist Machine

Calles recruited Cárdenas on the premise that he would be a puppet attractive to left-wingers committed to the constitution's social precepts. The young, attractive general from Michoacán surprised his benefactor by establishing an independent power base. In 1938 Lázaro Cárdenas transformed the forerunner of the PRI, which had sprung to life nine years earlier, into a durable party edifice, constructed on four major pillars. As it evolved, this corporatist structure comprised the peasant, labor, popular/middle class, and military sectors. Each collectivity, with the exception of the military sector that was disbanded, exerted influence through mass-membership organizations with smaller constituent parts. These included the National Peasant Confederation (CNC); the Mexican Workers' Confederation (CTM); and in 1943 the National Confederation of Popular Organizations (CNOP) for teachers, bureaucrats, shopkeepers, professionals, and other middle-class citizens. Only the National Executive Committee (CEN)—the party's central apparatus—linked these occupationally oriented entities. Cárdenas's radical recasting of the revolutionary party displayed corporatist tenets, but in a manner that would divide social groups and fortify presidential authority. Although the president regarded Mexico's workers and peasants—long reviled by elites as faceless masses—as the most important components of society, he assigned them to separate sectors. Moreover, he separated government employees—concentrated in the Federation of State Workers' Unions (FSTSE)—from their blue-collar CTM brethren. FSTSE leaders were required to adhere to the no-reelection mandate, but no such restriction applied to secretaries-general of unions in the labor sector. As a result, the redoubtable Fidel "Don Fidel" Velázquez held sway over the CTM for a half-century before his death in 1997.

Cárdenas gave impulse to the unionization of workers, higher wages, and improved working conditions. In addition, he bestowed on peasants land titles to more than twenty million hectares, nearly twice the total granted by his six predecessors. This land reform benefited not only individual property owners but also residents of collective farms, known as *ejidos*. Above all, Cárdenas expanded the authority of the chief executive in Mexican society.

Import-Substitution-Industrialism (ISI) and Corporatism

In the aftermath of World War II President Miguel Alemán Valdés (1946–1952) and his successors threw up a protectionist wall around Mexico's economy to attract domestic and foreign manufacturers to a country long dependent on oil and agricultural exports. Other incentives in the import-substitution (ISI) model included an undervalued currency, tax concessions, low-interest loans, inexpensive energy, a malleable union movement, and the construction of ports, roads, and rail spurs to assist the so-called "infant industries." In the early 1960s new ISI provisions included the establishment of twin-plant *maquiladora* plants—with capital-intensive work performed above the Rio Grande, labor-focused tasks carried out in Mexico, and preferential tariffs applied to goods shipped back to the United States.

These government-directed policies sparked an "economic miracle," demonstrated by a growth rate that averaged 6 percent between 1955 and 1971, before opportunities for domestic production waned. The myriad of permits, tariffs, rules, and regulations required to implement ISI spawned an army of bureaucrats, many of whom owed their jobs to the PRI. Thanks to nationalizations, the number of public firms mushroomed, and the state eventually accounted for one-third of national economic activity. In the early 1980s the federal government employed more than three million people.

Many of the spry, eager, new industrialists eventually grew fat, lethargic, whiny, and inefficient. Sheltered from competition at home, hundreds of their firms could not hold their own in international markets. Flagging growth exacerbated the underlying political stress that burst forth in 1968 as several thousand unarmed students, housewives, doctors, teachers, and other middle class elements demonstrated for higher salaries and political liberties. Tensions boiled over on October 2, 1968, when army and police units fired on demonstrators in downtown Mexico City. The "Tlatelolco Massacre" represented a watershed in modern Mexican history. Its victims were not the usual target of repression—peasants, trade unionists, and shantytown dwellers—but members of the middle class. Within a few hours Mexico's image shifted from that of a potential democracy to a heavy-handed authoritarian regime.

The discovery of Mideast-sized oil deposits in the Isthmus of Tehuantepec rekindled growth, and the economy expanded an average rate of 8.4 percent between 1978 and 1981. This was a temporary reprieve, for the economy became overheated by oil revenues. Evidence of this situation appeared in an overvalued currency; mounting dependence on external credits to import food, capital equipment, and luxury goods; a moribund agricultural sector; and—above all— outsized budget deficits fed by prodigious spending by a rapidly expanding bureaucracy. Moreover, the locating, lifting, and selling of black gold nurtured the most egregious corruption ever witnessed in a country infamous for ill-gotten gains. "It doesn't matter if they steal a bit," a taxi driver used to forking over *mordidas* (bribes) told a *New York Times* reporter, "but they shouldn't steal so much." In the spring of 1981 an international oil glut turned a seller's market into one that favored buyers. While a traumatized President José López Portillo tried to blame the owners of the nationalized banks for the debacle, an exodus of capital forced Mexico to sharply tighten its belt in accord with a rigorous plan devised by the International Monetary Fund (IMF).

From ISI to Neoliberalism

Aided by Budget and Planning Secretary Carlos Salinas de Gortari, President Miguel de la Madrid (1982–1988) began to dismantle the formidable cocoon sheltering the nation's debt-ridden economy. Mexico began to advance its own version of *perestroika*: phasing out subsidies; selling off state companies; curbing bureaucratic growth; joining the General Agreement on Tariffs and Trade, now the World Trade Organization (WTO); and negotiating a trade and investment understanding with the United States. Upon succeeding de la Madrid, President Salinas initiated conversations with his American and Canadian counterparts over the formation of a continent-wide free-trade accord. NAFTA took effect on January 1, 1994. Although Salinas played a pivotal role in opening his nation's economy, he allowed credit to expand rapidly during his last year in office. As a result Ernesto Zedillo (1994–2000), Salinas's personal choice for the presidency, inherited a grossly overvalued peso. The poorly handled devaluation in late December 1994 incited soaring interest rates, wiped out the savings of many middle-class families, and swelled the ranks of the unemployed. To his credit, Zedillo, a Yale-trained economist, worked closely with the administration of President Bill Clinton, the IMF, and European nations to combat his nation's worst downturn since the Great Depression. Just as Zedillo was beginning to address the crisis Raúl Salinas—Carlos's older brother—was imprisoned for allegedly masterminding the death of his ex-brother-in-law and for stealing millions of dollars from the state food company in which he had worked.

Opposition Wins in 1997 and 2000

The combination of economic crisis and political corruption encouraged Mexican voters to punish the PRI in 1997 when they went to the polls to elect members of Congress and the mayor of Mexico City. For the first time since its founding the PRI lost its majority in the House of Delegates, while the PRD's Cuauhtémoc Cárdenas, son of the former president, captured the D.F.'s city hall. Zedillo's astute leadership put the economy back on track by 2000, but Mexicans were ready for change. As a result, they gave Fox (42.5 percent) a victory over the PRI's Francisco Labastida (36.1 percent), and the PRD's Cárdenas (16.6 percent).

Known as the "Marlboro Man" because of his six-foot-five-inch height and craggy good looks, Fox excoriated the PRI throughout the campaign. He continually lambasted the party for venality, mismanagement, poverty, unemployment, poor schools, inadequate health-care facilities, pollution, and a multitude of other problems. In contrast, he promised to spur a 7 percent growth rate, create one million new jobs annually, boost oil production, clean up corruption, reform the judiciary, eradicate poverty, clean the environment, improve the quality of social services, negotiate a sweeping immigration reform with the United States, and end the conflict in Chiapas where the Zapatista Army of National Liberation (EZLN) had sparked an uprising in early 1994. Headlines hailed Fox's triumph as signaling a "New Era in Mexico."

By the 2003 congressional elections Fox was not just a lame duck but a dead duck. While a superb vote getter, he turned out to abhor politics and politicians. After his victory he believed that a "democratic bonus" derived from defeating the odious PRI would propel his formidable agenda through Congress. As a result, he showed scant interest in involving the PRI, the PAN, the PRD, and other power contenders in revising the roles of the political and economic game to reflect the system's surging pluralism. A wiser man would have pursued a variant of the Moncloa Accords hammered out in Spain after the 1975 death of dictator Francisco Franco. In this pact the once-antagonistic left and right negotiated an ambitious covenant that propelled the country from authoritarianism to democracy. Needless to say, Spain in the 1970s differed from Mexico in 2000. Unlike Franco, who passed away, the PRI—while suffering shock—lived on. Despite losing the presidency, the PRI remained the country's best-organized party and dominant office-holder. It continued to boast remnants of its deteriorating corporatist structure, particularly among bureaucrats and peasants.

Forging a Moncloa-type compact would have posed a Herculean challenge: PRI kingpins, who believed the presidency to be their birthright, resented Fox's vilification of their record; the PRD blanched at his fondness for free enterprise over state economic intrusiveness; and, worst of all, the new chief executive seemed oblivious to the imperative of reaching a mutual understanding on national priorities and relations between and among the several branches of government.

Even as Fox turned a blind eye to alliance-building he drove a wedge between the presidency and his own party. The Marlboro Man passed over astute PAN politicians when forming his cabinet, relying instead on loyalists from his home state of Guanajuato and recruits from head-hunting firms. He also ignored the Mexican Green Party, his coalition partner in the campaign, and made no effort to amalgamate the PAN and the *Amigos de Fox*, a parallel structure that he had formed to raise money and augment turnout during his campaign. Many PAN senators and deputies also bristled at Fox's welcoming the Zapatistas to Mexico City in 2001. The legislators pointed out that the rebels had never run for office, much less win an election. Furthermore, their support for "autonomy" for Indian municipalities enhanced the clout of conservative village patriarchs at the expense of competitive elections and women's rights.

Taking a page from the guerrillas' media-grabbing techniques, machete-waving activists denounced the placement of a new Mexico City airport just outside the capital. Fox had termed this badly needed project a major objective of his government. Yet the president abandoned the venture when his clumsy representatives failed to strike an accord with the rabble rousers, who enjoyed the backing of López Obrador. This episode illuminated the anemic political know-how within his entourage, whom pundits began to deride as the "Montessori Cabinet" in light of its members' fondness of self-expression over teamwork.

Instead of marshalling the formidable resources at his disposal to pursue one or two vital concerns, Fox flitted from one "priority" to another. This "flavor of the month" approach found him ricocheting from tax reform to immigration initiatives, from UN gambits to small-business promotion, from crime-fighting to López Obrador-bashing, to budget matters, and so forth. Much to the chagrin of PAN stalwarts, he encouraged the political flirtations of his peripatetic wife, Marta Sahagún, who hinted loudly that she would like to succeed her husband in *Los Pinos* presidential residence.

In 2004 President Fox called for Mexicans not to be disillusioned with democracy during the transition from authoritarian rule. While he promised that "the best is yet to come," thousands of demonstrators virtually closed down much of Mexico City. In September 2005, five years into his term, in his annual speech to the Congress the president boasted that he had not tried to rule in an authoritarian way like previous presidents, but had respected the rule of Congress. He had made the government more transparent and stabilized the economy, laying the cornerstones for democracy.

Bilateral Relations

His problems at home aside, Fox believed that the United States would lend a helping hand. After all, he cooperated with Washington in combating drug flows; he warmly endorsed Citicorp's tax-free $12.5 billion purchase of Mexico's second-largest financial institution, Banamex; he introduced greater transparency in government; and he crafted prudent monetary and fiscal policies. At first George W. Bush appeared eager to back schemes for more guest workers, additional visas, and the legalization of the four million "undocumented" Mexicans residing in the United States. Then Fox, who was slow to align himself with the White House after the September 11, 2001 tragedy, vociferously opposed sending American troops to Iraq. As the U.S. chief executive began to concentrate on the "War on Terrorism," the Middle East, and Asia, Mexico slipped to the margin of his radar screen.

The 2006 Presidential Showdown

As Fox prepares to complete his term he leaves behind a fragmented, dispirited PAN. In the run-up to the party's nominating convention Santiago Creel competed with former Energy Secretary Felipe Calderón and former Environmental Secretary Alberto Cárdenas. Should Creel become the candidate he will be a long shot inasmuch as he is saddled with Fox's unimpressive record as well as his own disappointing performance as government secretary. Outgoing party president Roberto Madrazo is vying for the PRI nomination with former Mexico State Governor Arturo Montiel. PRI elites resonate to Montiel on the grounds that he is more "electable" than a wheeler-dealer like the wealthy Madrazo who leaves a trail of broken promises and is linked to corrupt, unsavory characters. Yet Madrazo, who has an iron grip on the party's machinery, appears poised to capture the nomination, even if it means high-level defections by his detractors within the party. PRI strategists believe their party can win if turnout is low, it maximizes its rural or "green" vote, and its candidate exposes the inconsistencies in López Obrador's fifty-plank platform. The stakes are high, for another six years out of power would ensure their party's fragmentation.

Those who bolt the PRI may cast their lot with López Obrador. While Fox raised citizens' ambitions in 2000, few expected much from Mexico City's new executive who took office five days after the presidential inauguration. The capital has a reputation for "devouring" mayors because of the ubiquitous street crime, gridlock, pollution, corruption, unemployment, and "come-back tomorrow" bureaucracy.

In contrast to the floundering Fox, López Obrador attacked waste like a fundamentalist preacher reviling sin. As part of his zeal for "republican austerity" he exposed the excesses of his predecessors, cut his own salary and that of other top officials, and curbed bureaucrats' access to cell phones, computers, credit cards, air travel, and city vehicles. The belt-tightening, he claimed, enabled him to confer $60 per month each on senior citizens, the disabled, and single mothers who head households. He also lavished scholarships on poor students, procured low-interest loans for small businesses, and opened the University of Mexico City, which admits students based on a lottery rather than entrance exams. In addition, he courted the middle class by constructing new bridges and access roads, as well as building second tiers on key arteries to speed traffic flows.

Furthermore, he convinced billionaire Carlos Slim, Mexico City's Cardinal Archbishop, and the Fox administration to join the D.F. in restoring the Historic Center, where crumbling colonial buildings had become venues for prostitutes, drug dealers, sleazy night clubs, and criminal gangs. He rechristened the capital "the City of Hope." He trumpeted his successes in predawn news conferences, known as *mananeros* after the practice of early-morning love-making by peasants too exhausted for night-time intimacy. These well-attended sessions often allowed the mayor to set the agenda for the day's first news cycle, while responses to his controversial statements often dominated the afternoon cycle.

Above all, the meet-the-press sessions permitted him to distinguish himself from other public figures. While they slept, he was on the job. While they rode in fancy automobiles, he arrived at city hall in a beat-up Nissan. While they decorated their speeches with flowery phrases, he spoke the idiom of the common man. While they made excuses for the infighting that paralyzed Congress, he announced new programs for needy and working-class families. The upshot was that López Obrador projected the image of a "poor Christ" who renounces material comforts to pursue his vocation of service.

López Obrador exhibits messianic tendencies. Upon completing his university studies he worked side-by-side with Chontal Indians in his native Tabasco state. Later, as president of the local PRI, he attempted to force old-guard mayors to follow through on campaign promises to uplift the poor in their communities. Upon bolting the PRI he turned Tabasco's PRD into a virtual parallel government, which provided housing, legal assistance, medical care, and free books to the downtrodden. His slogan during the 2000 mayoral campaign was "For the Good of Everyone, Above All the Poor."

If López Obrador
Captures the Presidency

He complements his zeal to help the "have nots" with a disdain for legislative initiatives, a readiness to play the victimization card when scandals erupt in his administration, vagueness in policy pronouncements, and a penchant for secrecy. If his goals are noble and his motives pure, he reasons, why should anyone question his expenditures on stipends to the elderly and highway projects? On a national level this zealous approach could involve mobilizing the masses to pressure PRI and PAN members of Congress into ratifying his agenda.

López Obrador's supporters argue that, in fact, he is a political pragmatist, as evinced by his assurance to respect NAFTA and continue Fox's prudent anti-inflation program. If a "President López Obrador" downplayed his self-righteous authoritarianism in favor of coalition-building in Congress, he could benefit the downtrodden whom Mexico's pampered elite has long ignored. But part of any successful strategy must involve moves that he has adamantly opposed; namely, welcoming private capital into Pemex, the sprawling national oil monopoly, privatizing some or all of the acutely inefficient state-owned electricity sector, and raising taxes in a country where collections equal only 12 percent of the Gross Domestic Product—one-third of the figure for Brazil. On the other hand, if he harnesses mass appeal to run roughshod over institutions, the result could be legislative paralysis, widespread social conflict, increased drug trafficking, and the conversion of the current flood of northbound illegals migrants into a tidal wave.

Suggestions for Further Reading

Bruhn, Kathleen. *Taking on Goliath: The Emergence of a New Left Party and the Struggle for Democracy in Mexico*. University Park: Pennsylvania State University Press, 1997.

Camp, Roderic Ai. *Politics in Mexico: The Decline of Authoritarianism*. 3d ed. New York: Oxford University Press, 1999.

Centeno, Miguel Angel. *Democracy within Reasons: Technocratic Revolution in Mexico*. University Park: Pennsylvania State University Press, 1994.

Crandall, Russell, Guadalupe Paz, and Riordan Roett, eds. *Mexico's Democracy at Work: Political and Economic Dynamics*. Boulder, CO: Lynne Rienner, 2005.

Grayson, George W. "Running After a Fallen Fox." *Harvard International Review* (Spring 2005): 22–26.

Grayson, George W. "Mexico's Favorite Son." *ForeignPolicy.com* (August 9, 2005).

López Obrador, Andrés Manuel. *Un proyecto alternativo de nación*. Mexico City: Grijalbo, 2004.

Peschard-Sverdrup, Armand B., and Sara R. Rioff, eds. *Mexican Governance: From Single-Party Rule to Divided Government.* Washington, DC: CSIS Press, 2005.

Wiarda, Howard J. "Dismantling Corporatism: The Problem of Latin America." *World Affairs* 156 (Spring 1994): 199–203.

17

Cuba

Development, Revolution, and Decay

Juan M. del Aguila

A s the only nation in the Western Hemisphere that has adopted revolutionary Communism for its model of political development, Cuba stands separate from other Latin American nations. The revolution of 1959 and its subsequent radicalization have attracted the interest of students of politics as well as that of policymakers, journalists, intellectuals, and ordinary people, many of whom have been inspired by "the Cuban example." In addition, the central role played by President Fidel Castro from the beginning of the revolution is key to understanding developments in Cuba in the years since he and his followers came to power, partly because under his leadership Cuba has become an influential actor in regional politics and has engaged in an unusual degree of revolutionary activism abroad. Like other *caudillos* (political strongmen) of his generation President Castro personifies his country to observers the world over, but as will be made clear in this chapter, his own transformation from an impetuous young revolutionary to an aging dictator parallels the course of the revolution itself.

The politics of revolutionary development have moved Cuba through periods of radical transformation in the economy and the social system, through phases when pragmatism and moderation shaped domestic priorities and affected social attitudes, and finally to the stable totalitarianism of the 1980s characterized by growing difficulties at home and partial retrenchment abroad. In effect, the revolution and its consequences can be understood as an ongoing experiment in the process of achieving mature nationhood, but as with any experiment Cuba's has been characterized by fits and starts, abrupt

CUBA

policy reversals, intense criticism of the real nature of socialism and revolution, and evident exhaustion.

Cuba's limited participation in Latin America, its diminished role in the Third World, and its defunct membership in the former Communist world impose major constraints on its participation in international affairs. Unable to inspire others to carry out revolutions, Cuba sees its influence considerably reduced and is left without powerful friends or allies. Without strategic protection or vital economic support—that is, lacking the resources that facilitated high-profile activism abroad—Cuba's internationalist ventures are a thing of the past. Fewer resources and reduced influence have turned Cuba into a marginal actor in regional and international affairs in the post-Cold War system.

Cuba's economy and social system must now get by without the $5–7 billion in resources from former Communist countries. Because no new sources of wealth are being developed that will fill the gap, living standards are plummeting and social discontent is rising. Growing numbers of Cubans are demoralized and have little hope for the future. President Castro believed that unresolved difficulties placed "the Nation, the Revolution and Socialism" in great peril and that the 1990s was "the most difficult decade in History."

History, Political Culture, and Early Development

Cuba, the largest of the Greater Antilles, is located at the entrance of the Gulf of Mexico some 112 nautical miles (208 kilometers) from the United States. Its 44,218 square miles (114,525 square kilometers) of total surface stretch over a varied topography that includes mountain ranges, rolling hills, plains, and hundreds of rivers and streams. The principal mountain ranges lie in the eastern, central, and western provinces, and the highest mountain, Pico Turquino, rises to some 6,500 feet (1,981 meters) in the Sierra Maestra range.

The country's coastline is indented with several deep harbors and ports: Mariel and Havana in the west; Nuevitas, Nipe, and Santiago de Cuba in the east; and others along the southern coastline. From the colonial period to the present Cuba has relied heavily on foreign commerce for its prosperity, so a sound maritime infrastructure is critical for its trade. After 1959 Cuba shifted its structure of foreign trade away from the United States and toward the Soviet bloc. The Cuban merchant marine has also expanded dramatically since 1959.

Unlike many other developing countries, Cuba has not experienced a dramatic rise in population, and its demographic growth rates remain stable. Population growth averages around 1 percent, which alleviates the burden on employment and services that plagues many countries in the Third World. Of the country's eleven million inhabitants 69 percent reside in urban areas and the rest live in small towns and in the less densely populated rural areas. Most Cubans have lived in large cities and towns since the 1930s, and by the late 1980s over 20 percent of the population lived in the capital city of Havana or its environs. Part of the infrastructure of some of Cuba's larger cities is deteriorating owing to neglect, scarce resources, and the sheer passage of time: Havana was founded by Spanish settlers in 1514, Santiago de Cuba in 1515.

Caucasians, mulattoes, and blacks are practically the only ethnic groups in the country. Whites make up 66 percent of the population, mulattoes nearly 22 percent, and blacks approximately 12 percent. Whites were the dominant ethnic group during the twentieth century and many are descendants of the creole elite of colonial Cuba. Intraregional and seasonal migration is a fact of life in Caribbean societies, but although migration to Cuba from other Caribbean and Latin American countries has been low, small numbers of migrants from some Caribbean islands settled in Cuba earlier in the twentieth century. No Indian subcultures exist because for all practical purposes the mostly primitive Indian communities that inhabited the island in precolonial times disappeared early in the colonial period.

Although racial differences were evident in prerevolutionary Cuba, no deep racial cleavages existed between whites and nonwhites; occupation and income levels established social differences among the races, but they also affected status for blacks, whites, and mulattoes as individuals of a particular race. Racial prejudices were found among many whites and between blacks and mulattoes. Subtle forms of segregation were a manifestation of these basic attitudes, but overt racial conflict rarely erupted. Snobbery and elitism often characterized the behavior of the white upper classes, but more than racism shaped such behavior. Changes in the social system and class structure, which have reduced racial and class differences, have further dampened friction among the races but have not eliminated the psycho-social dimensions of racism.

Some scholars, such as Carlos Moore, maintain that "in social, cultural and psychological terms, race pervades the everyday life of every Cuban, white or black," and that "Cuban society was racist prior to 1959 and is steadfastly so today." Moore and others believe that racism is part of a complex cultural legacy rooted in slavery, subsequently exacerbated by social indifference and political neglect, and that revolutionary intolerance has created new racial barriers. He contends that "revolutionary Cuba is a more intolerant and inhospitable environment for the expression of black distinctiveness than was pre-revolutionary Cuba,"[1] mostly as a consequence of ideological intolerance. On the other hand, the Cuban government considers race and racism to be extremely delicate issues and maintains that the latter is no longer a major social problem. It is evident that the issue of race—rooted in Cuba's history and memory—has not disappeared under socialism, partly because racial harmony cannot be achieved by simply declaring that racism has been abolished.

Columbus discovered Cuba during his first trip to the New World in 1492, but because the island lacked substantial mineral wealth and had not developed an advanced indigenous civilization it remained sparsely populated well into the eighteenth century. The fifty thousand or so native Indians at the time of the discovery were gradually subdued by Spanish settlers under the *encomienda* system. They were forced to search for precious minerals, work in agriculture, fish, and also engage in primitive forms of trade. Brutal treatment, disease, poor nutrition, and the harmful effects of servitude itself decimated the Indian population, and little trace of their social system remains. Efforts to Christianize the Indians were not entirely successful, and often the Spanish settlers used violence to instill the "proper" attitudes among the Indians. Catholic missions were established and charged with propagating and maintaining the faith, so that friars and priests played important roles in the early life of the colony. The Catholic Church subsequently grew in numbers, wealth, and influence, and its notions of order, faith, spirituality, and salvation pervaded Cuba's cultural foundation.

The Spanish settlers of Cuba were a heterogeneous lot. Many came from Andalucía and other southern regions of Spain, and as was the case elsewhere in Latin America, the lure of gold, a sense of adventure, and the opportunity to escape the Spanish caste system brought thousands of settlers to Cuba and the New World. But the Cuban colony remained poor and the prospects of growing fabulously wealthy were greater on the mainland. The colonial regime at this time was weak and ineffective, and Spain itself had little interest in Cuba's development. Franklin Knight writes that "throughout the sixteenth century, the colony [Cuba] virtually stagnated, challenged by pirates, ravaged by hurricanes, plagued by diseases, and depopulated by the magnetic pull of Mexico and Peru."[2] In short, the foundations of Cuba as a colony stemmed from a social system dominated by *peninsulares* and supported by the Catholic Church. The native population failed to resist the impact of a stronger culture and quickly disappeared.

Black slaves were brought to Cuba by the thousands from the 1700s to the middle of the nineteenth century, replacing Indians as laborers on sugarcane plantations, as servants in the larger towns and cities, and as manual laborers in service occupations. A census taken in 1791 showed that out of a total population of 273,000, 56 percent were white and that slaves made up the largest proportion of the black population; a century later another census showed that over the entire colonial period, nearly 375,000 black slaves had been brought to Cuba. It is a fact that the slave trade contributed to the wealth of many planters and traders.

Cuba's economy originally revolved around tobacco and, subsequently, cof-fee cultivation, but it gradually became a plantation economy geared to sugar cultivation, production, and export. The island's geographical location offers the right temperatures as well as the necessary rainfall for sugar production, and the terrain of the lowlands is suitable for harvesting cane. Indeed, econo-mists and historians maintain that the island's comparative advantage in sugar production was soon realized and that earnings from sugar exports fi-nanced the imports of foodstuffs, textiles, machinery, and other capital goods.

The combination of sugar, slavery, and the plantation economy shaped the colonial social structure and laid the foundation for an economy geared to for-eign commerce, but it did not produce a society of small landowners and rural proprietors. Differences among *peninsulares, criollos,* slaves, and *libertos* (slaves who had obtained their freedom) were evidence of a hierarchical system un-mindful of any notion of social equality. As depicted by popular novels, books, and documents of the time, colonial Cuba remained unaffected by changes taking place elsewhere and therefore stayed under the tight control of Spain. On the other hand the benefits of free trade were strongly felt during the En-glish occupation of Havana in 1762–1763, as new markets were found and the economy was further integrated into regional and international commercial networks. Geopolitical rivalries with Great Britain and the United States in time forced Spain to modify the mercantilist regime, and it gradually gave way to a more open trading system. Spain sought to reestablish political control over its colonial domains, including Cuba, in the early nineteenth century, but the impact of liberal ideas, added to the introduction of capital and new tech-nology, stimulated new thinking.

An influential group of thinkers and wealthy oligarchs like Francisco Arango and Ignacio Montalvo believed in the promise of positivism and in-dividual will, and educators like José de la Luz y Caballero and the priest Félix Varela engendered an early commitment to political independence and nationhood. Although education was restricted to the creole elite and to the people who could afford it and was influenced by Catholic beliefs, its benefits were felt by a growing number of progressive *criollos*. A rift between the people who were committed to the preservation of the colonial regime and those who believed in Cuba's gradual emancipation and eventual indepen-dence shaped the politics of the period and forced a reassessment of relations between Cuba and Spain. Racial considerations affected each outlook, and Knight maintains that

the slave society during the nineteenth century was equally one of ferment and strife. Its strengths created its inherent weaknesses. A divided society was also a divisive society. Tensions existed within the white groups as well as between white and nonwhite. In Cuba, the most enduring of the Caribbean slave societies, the white groups split basically between *peninsulares* and *criollos*.[3]

In summary, the colonial system was marked by inequality and hierarchy, and its economic foundation rested on a plantation economy and slavery. Early advocates of Cuba's struggle for independence faced ideological divisions and clashing interests, which allowed Spain to maintain control over the colony. Lacking clear pro-independence leadership, often fearing the consequences of a social revolution, and without political cohesion or class consciousness, the creole plantocracy accepted its politically subordinate status.

Struggles for Independence, 1868–1901

The emergence of new political currents in the 1860s stemmed from the need to challenge Spanish domination and to improve Cuba's economic position. On the one hand a nationalistic and clearly separatist movement advocated confrontation and war against Spain if those were the only means of achieving independence. More moderate elements, represented by the Reformist party founded in 1862, advocated representation for Cuba in the Spanish Cortes, administrative reforms, and liberal trade policies. The issue of slavery often divided the creoles, as did class and economic differences between the eastern and western planters. The latter feared a social revolution and tended to be more conservative. Still, Spain's refusal to grant meaningful concessions to the Cubans and its failure to satisfy legitimate political demands led to rebellion in 1868 and a decade of bloody and destructive warfare.

The rebels were led by Carlos Manuel de Céspedes, a patriot and moderately wealthy planter from Oriente province. Other political and military leaders like Generals Antonio Maceo and Máximo Gómez fought bravely during the protracted struggle, but latent political divisions among the rebels weakened their effort. Nationalism fed the rebel cause, as did the commitment to emancipate Cuba from colonial domination. Spain poured thousands of troops into Cuba and sent one of its best generals, Arsenio Martínez Campos, to lead the Spanish forces. Yet the failure to truly carry the war to the western provinces; the deaths of Céspedes, Ignacio Agramonte, and other leaders; the absence of external help; and the lack of support on the part of many Cubans doomed the rebel cause.

Nearly 250,000 people on both sides lost their lives in the struggle, and Cuba's infrastructure was devastated. The war cost Spain approximately $300 million and was both a cause and a consequence of political quarrels among its own elites. Yet Spain and the rebels signed an armistice in 1878 that led to a tenuous peace and a period of self-criticism and questioning on the part of those Cubans who still advocated independence. On the other hand the Cubans' ability to wage a protracted struggle, endure enormous sacrifices, and exhibit national aspirations demonstrated that a new political consciousness was emerging and that emancipation was achievable. Differences over slavery, regional tensions, and the balance between civilian leaders and military *caudillos* would have to be resolved before a new war would start, or else Cuba would remain a colony.

Cuba's political economy changed in the last decades of the nineteenth century, partly because the restoration of political stability created economic opportunities for domestic and foreign capital. New technology transformed the sugar industry so that production revolved around foreign-owned industrial complexes, which limited opportunities for local management and participation. A growing worldwide demand for sugar allowed producers to plan with economies of scale in mind, and the industry benefited from new markets, principally in the United States. Spain introduced fees and taxes on Cuba's exports in the early 1890s that adversely affected domestic producers, partly because it feared growing U.S. penetration of Cuba, but these measures did not really isolate Cuba from the United States.

A growing dependence on the U.S. market for trade, investment, technology, and industrial inputs characterized U.S.-Cuban relations in the 1880s and 1890s, even while Spain maintained political control. In 1896 U.S. investments in Cuba were estimated at $50 million, concentrated in mining and sugar holdings. Trade between the two countries was valued at $27 million in 1897, and the composition of that trade showed that the United States exported to Cuba manufactured and industrial goods and imported sugar, molasses, tobacco, and a few nonmanufactured products. United States Consul William Elliot Gonzalez publicly recognized that "the Island practically depends completely on the U.S. market for its sugar exports" and that associated industries like the railroads, warehouses, port facilities, and their financial and labor support structures depended directly on the U.S. market.

There is little doubt that this growing penetration of a weak economy dominated by sugar and its derivative production by a growing capitalist, industrial power meant that the colonial regime was subjected to internal and external pressures. Once again, pro-independence forces gathered to challenge Spanish authority and assert claims for independence and sovereignty and to do so with a new and more compelling sense of unity and national purpose. New leaders, principally José Martí, had forged a more mature vision of political emancipation and nationalism, and the issue of slavery had been laid to rest since its abolition in the 1880s. In short, ideologically and organizationally, the separatists were in a stronger position than in the 1860s, whereas Spain vacillated between granting meaningful reforms and reimposing absolutist government.

As the founder of the Cuban Revolutionary Party (PRC) in exile and as the intellectual force and principal civilian organizer of the war effort, José Martí represented a younger generation of Cubans committed to the total liberation of the country. Martí believed that war was brutal but necessary, "a political process that would definitively resolve a situation in which fear of war is a paralyzing element," and held that "patriotism is a sacred obligation when one struggles to create conditions in the motherland that would improve the lives of one's countrymen."

In the *Manifiesto de Montecristi,* a critical document issued in 1895, the civilian-military leadership spoke for two generations of Cubans and stated that after the war "the nation would be constituted from its roots, with its own viable institutions, so that a government would be unable to lead it into tyranny." The manifesto asserted that the nation returned to war "with an enlightened and democratic people, cognizant of its own and others' rights" and sure of "its republican education." It is thus quite clear that the people struggling for independence advocated representative government and democratic institutions and were influenced by nationalism, liberalism, and self-determination rather than by absolutism, Marxism, or notions of class struggle.

The war raged back and forth for three years, with the rebels fighting a guerrilla struggle and Spain following a more conventional strategy. Rebel columns moved westward across the countryside, burning and sacking properties and cane fields, attacking small towns, and disrupting the economy. Spain's hated policy of "reconcentration" forced hundreds of thousands of Cubans into fortified towns and military compounds, and hunger, desolation, and brutality decimated the population. Thousands died, including Martí and Maceo, and property losses were valued in the millions of dollars.

A military stalemate between rebel and Spanish forces and sensationalist accounts of the fighting published in the United States led to U.S. military intervention in 1898. The Cuban question had become an important issue in U.S. domestic politics, and Spain as well as the rebels had attempted to influence U.S. public opinion. There is solid evidence that the McKinley administration preferred a negotiated settlement that would bring independence to Cuba and that it urged Spain to give up its control. Spain rejected diplomatic entreaties and offers of mediation from European powers and obstinately refused to accept either military or political defeat. In April 1898 the U.S. Congress passed a resolution granting President McKinley's request for authority to end hostilities in Cuba, but it also disavowed any interest in exercising sovereignty, jurisdiction, or control over Cuba once Spain had been driven out.

The U.S. occupation of Cuba lasted until 1902, and many students of Cuban politics believe that it created a legacy of resentment and frustration because, in part, U.S. intervention prevented the Cubans from achieving a complete victory over Spain. United States military authorities partly rebuilt the nation's infrastructure and brought about significant improvements in public health, education, public administration, and finance, but Cuban nationalists and many intellectuals felt a sense of political impotence and frustration. Subsequently, the inclusion of the Platt Amendment, passed in 1901 by the U.S. Congress, in the Cuban constitution meant that Cuba became a U.S. protectorate rather than a sovereign nation because the amendment granted territorial concessions to the United States, placed financial restrictions on the Cuban government, and allowed the United States to intervene in Cuba's internal affairs.

Cuba's foreign economic relations were subsequently shaped by a Reciprocity Treaty (1903), which granted preferential treatment to Cuban sugar in the U.S. market and reduced tariffs on U.S. exports to Cuba. U.S. investments in Cuba's sugar industry, cattle industry, public services, utilities, and other properties had reached $200 million by 1909, nearly 50 percent of all foreign investment in Cuba. The Platt Amendment and the Reciprocity Treaty facilitated a growing U.S. influence in Cuba and were often perceived as neocolonialist measures aimed at protecting U.S. interests in the island. Many politicians, businesspeople, owners of sugar estates, and some conservative intellectuals felt that the U.S. "tutelage" was not necessarily detrimental. The U.S. presence thus created a significant political cleavage, separating those people who felt it to be beneficial and necessary for Cuba's early development from nationalists who saw it as a direct infringement of genuine self-determination. The views of Ramón Ruiz illustrate a scholarly consensus on these matters, namely, that the Platt Amendment limited Cuba's first experience in self-government and "offered the Cubans a facile way out of domestic difficulties. Reliance on the United States eventually engendered among Cubans a loss of faith in their Republic and in their own nationality."[4]

The Political Development
of Prerevolutionary Cuba

Political competition during the early republican period existed predominantly between the Liberal and Conservative parties. These parties—and others—were essentially controlled by the political *caudillos* José Miguel Gómez and Mario García Menocal, respectively, and did not articulate clear political philosophies or programs. The political system was based on client arrangements and patronage networks, so partisan loyalties were often exchanged for political favors. Electoral fraud and administrative corruption were common, and elections were often cynically viewed as attempts by manipulative politicians to preserve or expand personal power. Public office was held in disrepute, politics was used as a means of self-enrichment, and the democratic ideals that had motivated Martí and other revolutionary leaders remained little more than abstractions.

On the other hand respected intellectuals like Fernando Ortiz and Enrique José Varona formed part of an emerging democratic intelligentsia that rejected politics as a means to private gain and advocated civic-mindedness, cultural emancipation, and, above all, honest and democratic government. Varona asserted that "to govern is to watch over compliance with laws, and provide the means for that compliance," and he pointed out that "our public ills are the work of all of us." Ortiz, in turn, criticized the poor conditions found in most of the rural areas, where peasants, seasonal workers, and unskilled laborers toiled under difficult conditions and lived at barely subsistence levels. He attacked the evils of monoculture and the subordination of the economy to foreign capital, and he suggested that the revolutionary generation had betrayed principles articulated earlier. Reformist groups founded the opinion journal known as *Revista de Avance,* and other people joined the Cuban Council of Civic Renovation. Through writing, public speaking, and political organization a cultural revival encouraged debate, much of it focused on the need to cleanse the political culture and establish viable institutions. Finally, many critics framed their charges against the postcolonial regime according to anti-imperialist principles, appealing to students, intellectuals, labor leaders, and others to unite to bring about political change.

Gerardo Machado was elected as a popular president in 1924, but he became a virtual dictator following his contrived reelection in 1928 and his violation of constitutional norms. From that point on politics took on a violent character. Government and opposition alike engaged in terrorism, shootings, and political assassinations, indicating that institutions were unable to resolve political conflicts and that force was seen as a legitimate arbiter of political disputes.

The Great Depression had a devastating effect on the economy. Plummeting sugar prices affected the livelihood of hundreds of thousands of families, and unemployment, social misery, and rural banditry reflected a deeper structural crisis. The government sought to alleviate the problems by acquiring new loans from U.S. bankers, but the country's creditworthiness was shaky and it had previously accumulated substantial debts. Cuba's economic and financial dependence on the United States meant that the impact of the Depression was felt in business, finance, public administration, and government itself, so that the options were limited. Breaking the economic bonds with the

United States would wreak havoc and plunge the country into instability and chaos. Managing the crisis through technical approaches and financial legerdemain would only postpone the day of reckoning. Robert Smith describes the complexity of the situation and its interrelatedness:

> During the closing months of 1930 the situation in Cuba degenerated rapidly. The economic picture had been deteriorating for several years and the world-wide depression added problems to an already serious situation. This helped stimulate opposition to Machado, and the threats of disorder mounted.[5]

Student protesters challenged the police in the streets, but resistance to Machado also involved professionals, middle-class elements, labor leaders, and the Communist Party. One of the leading anti-Machado organizations was the University Students Directorate, through which a new generation of activists and revolutionaries advocated a complete and definitive change of regime. The Communist Party attacked Machado from orthodox Marxist positions, depicting him as the instrument of foreign interests and as the enemy of the working class. The party called for popular mobilization, strikes, and urban confrontations, but its calls failed to spark a popular revolution and often led to internecine struggles with other groups. Finally, the ABC, a secret, cellular organization made up of middle-sector individuals, intellectuals, and students dissatisfied with the politics of the University Students' Directorate, played a prominent role in the struggle against the dictator. The ABC stood for liberty and social justice, and its programs called for economic and political reforms. ABC cells engaged in clandestine activities and were often involved in violent incidents; the organization's strategy at one point aimed at Machado's assassination. In short, the opposition was unified in its commitment to driving Machado from power and ending the dictatorship, but it was also tactically and ideologically divided. The political agenda of the noncommunist groups called for democratization, socioeconomic change, and a challenge to U.S. interests in Cuba, but their failure to rally mass support against the dictatorship proved to be one of their major weaknesses.

The army proved to be a critical contender because its support was essential for either keeping Machado in power or shifting the balance to his adversaries. The army was structured on parochial loyalties rather than merit, and its military competence was questionable. It remained the pillar of order and stability but it also felt the violent political fragmentation that ultimately ousted Machado. Some lower-rank members, many of whom came from humble backgrounds and viewed the army as a vehicle for self-improvement and social mobility, demanded higher pay and an end to the politicization of promotions.

Such internal pressure, at a time when a crisis of political authority affected the government's freedom of action and paralyzed decision-making, opened the way for an internal revolt led by then-sergeant Fulgencio E. Batista y Zaldívar. Under his leadership the army sought to contain revolutionary outbursts and directly influence the selection of presidents. It would play a central role during the following decades.

Finally, as had been the case since 1898, the United States played the role of ultimate power broker. In 1933 the new Roosevelt Administration, through Sumner Welles as its special ambassador, shaped a resolution to Cuba's political crisis that preserved U.S. interests and restored stability. Welles succeeded in his mediation efforts, partly because the ABC and other groups accepted his presence and partly because the army failed to support Machado at a critical moment. Through Welles's efforts a weak government under Carlos Manuel de Céspedes succeeded Machado, but that regime was quickly overthrown. A five-member executive committee headed by Ramón Grau San Martín, a physician and university professor, took power briefly, but it too gave way to a more revolutionary government, still led by Grau. Jaime Suchlicki maintains that these events constitute a "turning point in Cuba's history," marking the "army's entrance as an organized force into the running of government and Batista's emergence as the self-appointed chief of the armed forces and the arbiter of Cuba's destiny for years to come."[6]

The revolutionary government ruled amid great agitation and was opposed by the U.S. embassy, powerful business interests, conservatives fearful of administrative anarchy, and the ABC. Its support came from the University Students' Directorate, liberal elements in the press, and, for part of its tenure, Batista and the army. Principally because of the efforts of Antonio Guiteras as minister of government (*secretario de gobernación*), the government established an eight-hour day for workers, required that at least 50 percent of all employees in industry and commerce be Cuban, proclaimed university autonomy, and granted peasants rights to the land they occupied. In addition, the government dissolved all political parties that had collaborated with Machado, reduced rates on utilities, and granted women the right to vote. Guiteras believed in the need for a radical revolution that would uproot the framework of "economic imperialism" affecting Cuba's economic and political development, but neither he nor Grau could effectively centralize power to carry basic reforms forward.

From exile after the revolutionary government's demise and its replacement by a pro-U.S. conservative regime, Guiteras recognized that the "work of a revolutionary government cannot be improvised lightly once in power. It presupposes a preparatory work that [the revolutionary government] could not have had," partly "because it lacked an organized political force able to support it."

One cannot overestimate the impact of the truncated revolution of 1933 on the succeeding generation's psychological makeup, its social agenda, or the political determination of its most able leaders. The incomplete business of 1933 left a sense of frustration among the protagonists of reform and revolution, but in time the goals were rechristened. The failure to democratize politics, achieve economic sovereignty, and cohesively assert a national will shaped the ethos of future reformers and revolutionaries, for whom "the lessons of 1933" laid the foundation for new departures.

Social Democracy and Authoritarianism in the 1940s and 1950s

After the brief revolutionary interlude in 1933 national politics in Cuba went through a period of realignment and moderate authoritarianism characterized by the conservative domination of weak and undemocratic regimes supported by Batista and the army. Taking advantage of improved economic conditions and secure from military threats or revolutionary outbursts, the regimes governed by partially satisfying political demands and reintroduced client arrangements. On the other hand electoral irregularities, corruption, episodic repression, and the subordination of civil authority to military pressures retarded the development of viable governing institutions, so the system remained personalist and moderately authoritarian.

In his excellent study *Revolution and Reaction in Cuba,* Samuel Farber suggests that "the contrast between the civilian-democratic and the militarist-authoritarian traditions" formed the key political cleavage and that neither the democratic left in exile nor the Communist Party effectively challenged this order. Farber points to relative improvements in civil liberties and a new toleration for moderate domestic opposition groups as evidence of an implicit bargain between the conservative sectors and their opponents, characterized by economic populism and the maintenance of dependent capitalism.[7]

Economic dependence on the United States meant that domestic capital played an increasingly important role, and Cuban interests gradually acquired a growing share of ownership in the sugar industry. Measures like the Reciprocity Treaty and the Jones-Costigan Act, in addition to the policies of the Export-Import Bank, stabilized Cuba's economy and gave confidence to domestic producers, who always looked to the U.S. market as the preferred outlet for Cuban products. U.S.-mandated quotas for sugar guaranteed that Cuba's principal export would enter the United States under a preferential tariff and led to the expansion of acreage and production. The United States supplied 54 percent of Cuba's imports in 1933, a figure that increased to nearly 65 percent at the end of the decade and some 81 percent by 1950. What Cuba bought was purchased in the United States, and although having a dynamic market close by proved to be convenient, it also retarded Cuba's industrial development.

A major threshold in the process of political development was reached in 1940 following the enactment of a democratic and progressive constitution, itself the result of political compromises among the democratic left, conservatives, and Communists. This constitution established universal suffrage and freedom of political organization, recognized Western-style civil rights, and abolished the death penalty. Women, children, and workers received social protection, and racial and sexual discrimination was outlawed. Public education was mandated, and the needs of rural children in particular were identified. Private property was legitimated in a broad social context and the state was charged with "orienting the national economy." Industrial development, agrarian reform, and greater rural-urban integration were set as national priorities, and the state was granted greater powers in national development, public administration, and fiscal and monetary policies.

The constitution reflected a complex bargain between the rising middle sectors and traditional interests, and in explicitly framing a tutelary role for the state in economic and social affairs it incorporated then-current ideas and political philosophies. If properly observed and enforced, the constitution potentially could have served as the legal and ideological foundation of a lasting democratic order, one that rejected radical approaches but permitted vigorous reformism. Consciously or otherwise, its framers believed that the proper balance between order and liberty had been set and that dependent capitalism could be made to serve broad social interests, not just those of influential elites. Unfortunately, the failure of Cuba's democratic regimes in general and educational institutions in particular to instill the values that a fragile democracy requires if it is to survive a legacy of authoritarianism, corruption, and strongman rule undermined constitutional principles, and violence and gangsterism soon reappeared.

The Auténtico (Authentic) administrations of Ramón Grau (1944–1948) and his successor Carlos Prío (1948–1952) initiated reforms in agriculture, fiscal management, labor, and education and also maintained respect for civil liberties. National elections were competitive and clean, and Conservative, Liberal, Social-Democratic, and Communist parties received electoral support. Public subsidies, bureaucratic employment, and the creation of new state agencies led to gains among middle-class and professional groups, but agricultural development lagged and the power of foreign interests was not directly confronted. Worst of all, political violence and urban-based gangsterism threatened the integrity of the democratic regimes, and neither Grau nor Prío was able to stem the violence. Corruption was spawned by a vast system of patronage, payoffs, and bribes, and Grau's minister of education turned his office into a powerful political machine and an illegal financial network. Student activists turned the University of Havana into a haven for gun-toting thugs and criminal factions and often paralyzed the institution through intimidation and brutality. According to Suchlicki,

> An entire system of nepotism, favoritism and gangsterism predominated. Despite numerous accomplishments, the Auténticos failed to provide the country with honest government or to diversify Cuba's one-crop economy. The reformist zeal evident during Grau's first administration had diminished considerably in the intervening decade, and Grau himself seemed softened after years of exile and frustration. When confronted with the reality of Cuban politics, the early idealism and reformism of [student leaders and others] gave way to materialism and opportunism.[8]

The political aspirations and national expectations that had been generated were only partially fulfilled by the two Social-Democratic administrations: Modernization through reformism did not curb the power of vested interests or foreign capital, and central authority proved weak and incapable of eradicating violence and corruption. To the unfinished agenda of 1933 were added the unrealized promises of the democratic reformers, and scandals and internecine quarrels in Cuba's leadership class eroded public trust in government. The state, supported by neither a dominant class nor a traditional oligarchy, failed to convert diffuse support into legitimately accepted rule, and the nation simply drifted.

Batista's bloodless but effective coup in March 1952 ended the constitutional regime and restored order superficially through political authoritarianism. Cuba's political development was cut short by the coup, and the system proved vulnerable to force. Proclaiming that worry about the lack of guarantees for life and property had led him to accept "the imperious mandate" and usurp power, Batista and his supporters found little resistance to their actions. Prominent national figures, business organizations, labor leaders, a few church officials, and the leadership of the Popular Socialist Party (PSP, the Communist Party) either endorsed the coup or rejoiced at the Auténticos's demise. The Veterans' Association and the Bankers' Association gave their approval and the Cuban Workers' Confederation pledged to cooperate with the new government. Except for scattered protests by students, denunciations by Catholic lay leaders, and isolated instances of civil resistance, the coup provoked neither massive popular repudiation nor legal-institutional opposition.

During his time in office Batista was unable to legitimate his regime either through elections, good relations with the United States, or negotiations with his opponents. Opposition to Batista included moderate, democratic elements sympathetic to the Auténticos but willing to entertain confrontational approaches; traditional politicians (like those in the Society for Friends of the Republic) who believed that Batista would "come around" if a safe way out of the political stalemate was found; and revolutionaries unwilling to accept halfway solutions or electoral shenanigans. Feeling politically secure, Batista refused calls for new elections and thus spurned a reasonable approach that might have prevented the radicalization of many of his opponents. As a result, insurrection and "armed struggle" became attractive and even justifiable because there was no viable political center on which a national compromise could be achieved.

Several revolutionary groups, including Fidel Castro's Twenty-sixth of July Movement, participated in the struggle against the dictatorship. Among these, the Revolutionary Directorate (DR) stood out because of its uncompromising ferocity and violent strategy aimed at assassinating Batista himself. Led by the charismatic student leader José Antonio Echeverría, the DR was not the vanguard of a social revolution but an organization committed to ending the dictatorship. Ramón Bonachea and Marta San Martín contend that the DR's "immediate task was to overthrow the dictator, establish a democratic form of government, and then carry out a revolutionary program to solve the problems of landless peasants, exploited workers and young people condemned to economic oblivion."[9]

As one of the founders of the Twenty-sixth of July Movement and as its undisputed leader, Fidel Castro played a central role in the insurrection against Batista's dictatorship. A group led by Castro attacked a military garrison in the city of Santiago in 1953, but the attack failed and many of Castro's followers were either killed or subsequently arrested and shot. He was captured and tried for subversion, but as a trained lawyer with oratorical skills Castro used the trial to issue an indictment of the government. Portraying his cause as just and inspired by patriotism and Martí's ideals, Castro called for a return to constitutional government, agrarian reform, profit-sharing arrangements between owners and workers, and social improvements in rural Cuba. He was convicted and sentenced to fifteen years in prison but was subsequently released in 1954 under an amnesty program.

Castro's political beliefs and true intentions before he came to power have been the focus of considerable debate. Some people argue that his commitment to armed struggle reflected the compelling facts that no compromise was possible with Batista and that rebellion itself is justified by lofty principles of Western political theory. Others maintain that Castro harbored Marxist beliefs during his days at the university but that he kept the Communists away from his movement so that it could appeal to the Cuban middle class. Some of his former close associates, like Carlos Franqui, say that Castro's *caudillo* temperament and his egomaniacal pursuit of personal power raised unresolved questions among his followers regarding what path a Castro-led government would take, but that they realized confronting Castro would not be easy. Finally, moderates such as Mario Llerena collaborated with Castro's movement because they sincerely believed in its democratic nature and could not conceive of Castro either as a Communist or as a future dictator.

Fidel Castro himself has given many contradictory accounts of his thinking at the time, describing himself in 1961 as "a Marxist-Leninist until the day that I die," as "a utopian communist captivated by the incontestable truths of Marxist literature," as a "humanist" who believed in "bread and freedom," and as an anti-imperialist revolutionary. Speaking to the Brazilian Frei Betto in 1985 Castro stated that "before I was a utopian communist or a Marxist, I was a follower of Martí [*martiano*] and a profound admirer of our people's heroic struggles." In the same interview Castro stated, "I had conceived of a revolutionary strategy that would lead to a profound social revolution, but through phases . . . the masses needed to be taken to the revolution through phases" because their consciousness could not be developed overnight. Finally, Castro reveals that he saw the Communists as "isolated, but as potential allies," and that he had good relations with Communist leaders during his student days.[10] And yet at other times Castro praised representative democracy, free elections, and political and economic rights. He purposely understated his most radical beliefs to portray himself as a moderate to the Cuban people and to not frighten the United States. Subsequently, it became clear that he saw himself as the undisputed leader of a radical revolution that would emancipate Cuba and also as the champion of a protracted struggle against the United States.

It is thus unequivocally clear that before he came to power Castro was neither a member of the Communist Party nor a doctrinal Marxist. Rather, he was committed to a radical revolution whose final outcome could not have been foreseen but that placed him in the center of power. In addition, one of his top lieutenants, the Argentine revolutionary Ernesto (Ché) Guevara, was a committed Marxist, as was Fidel's younger brother Raúl Castro. Indeed, the Twenty-sixth of July Movement itself was divided between moderates who rejected communism as well as traditional Latin American authoritarianism, and radicals like Guevara who believed that the solution to the world's problems lay behind the Iron Curtain. Finally, one of the key documents of the movement, *Nuestra Razón* (*Our Purpose*), defined the revolution's goals as establishing a free and sovereign country, a democratic republic, an independent economy, and a distinct national culture.

A popular view is thus completely discredited, namely, that U.S. policy failures drove Castro and his regime to communism and forced them into the Soviet bloc. For tactical reasons the rebel leadership did not speak candidly with its own people and uttered deceptive and self-serving statements. At a minimum, *Nuestra Razón* committed the revolutionaries to constitutional government, political pluralism, and respect for civil and property rights. A radical minority led by Castro saw themselves as the self-anointed vanguard of an epic political struggle against capitalism, the Cuban middle class, and U.S. influence in Cuba, and they launched a mass movement that created an unstoppable momentum.

The guerrilla phase of the insurrection ended successfully for the rebels in December 1958. Domestic isolation, rebel victories in eastern Cuba, and loss of support from Washington convinced Batista that his regime could survive only if the guerrillas were defeated. However, the army was poorly led, partly because some of its top generals were corrupt and frightened, and a forty-thousand-man army disintegrated when it faced several popular uprisings, demonstrating a profound loss of morale and an alarming unwillingness to fight a few hundred guerrillas. Cornered and without options, Batista and many of his closest allies fled at dawn on January 1, 1959, paving the way for a total victory by the guerrilla forces.

The breakdown of the authoritarian regime stemmed from its inherent illegitimacy, its refusal to accept an authentic electoral solution during a time of crisis, and its unfounded belief in the use of force and repression. The progressive alienation from the regime of the Cuban middle class reduced the probability that it would become a moderating force and lead a democratic restoration. In a situation in which traditional political forces were discredited and no dependable class base existed, popular support moved toward the revolutionaries. Deeply felt commitments to fundamental change emerged in the midst of an unprecedented vacuum, caused by the collapse of institutions and shifts in the locus of authority over brief spans of time. The guerrillas were able to assume power without direct consent but with massive social approval, and national euphoria was the order of the day.

The Cuban Revolution

Neither the insurrection against Batista nor the social revolution that the new regime began to carry out stemmed from deep-seated popular dissatisfaction with the development pattern of Cuba's dependent capitalism. The evidence shows that Cuba had reached a moderate degree of modernization by the late 1950s. Indicators such as literacy rate (75 percent), proportion of the population living in urban areas (around 57 percent), life expectancy (approximately sixty years), and the size of the middle class (between 25 and 30 percent of the population) suggest that Cuba's level of development was comparable to that of other, more advanced Latin American nations.

On the other hand urban-rural contrasts were marked and the quality of life for the average *guajiro* (peasant) family was well below that of the average urbanite. Health services and educational opportunities were much better in Havana and other larger cities than in the small provincial towns or isolated rural communities, and the best jobs and occupations were not available in rural Cuba. Seasonal unemployment also affected the rural areas disproportionately, and a rural proletariat dependent on the mills for employment saw its economic situation deteriorate once the sugar harvest ended.

In effect, neither the model of Cuba as a chronically underdeveloped society, as depicted by the Cuban government, nor that of an idyllic island characterized by social harmony, a sound economy, and a bustling population fits reality. At the time of the revolution the nation was developing slowly as a dependent capitalist country, in which wealth was not evenly distributed but in which middle sectors and a substantial portion of the working class had made social gains. Although Cuba's political autonomy had remained subject to foreign pressures, the imperatives of capitalist modernization had not obliterated Cuba's cultural integrity, social structure, or economic system.

The success of the revolution can be better explained by political factors than by socioeconomic criteria. The failure of prerevolution governments to develop and nourish viable ruling institutions or to sustain a national ethos of civic-mindedness left those regimes vulnerable to force and strongman rule and to subversion from within. Legal and constitutional norms were not fully developed, and too many people viewed politics and public office as ways to obtain private, selfish gains. No idea of the public good had taken root, and the political culture revolved around traditional notions of order, loyalty, patrimony, and authority.

The new regime was originally divided among advocates of liberal democracy and a mixed economy and the more radical sectors around Castro and Guevara that called for a social revolution. The radicals believed that the basic capitalist system needed to be abolished and the social system uprooted so that the power of vested economic interests, some of them foreign based, could be reduced. To eradicate economic evils associated with a dependent capitalist system, statist practices and antimarket doctrines shaped policy-making, and the revolutionary elite was fully aware that to increase state power meant to increase its own. The agrarian reform of 1959 satisfied long-standing claims of peasants and rural workers, and it also made sense politically. The urban reform of 1960, which socialized Cuban-owned businesses and privately owned real estate, adversely affected the private sector's strength. By 1961 banking, wholesale trade, and foreign trade had been fully collectivized, as had 85 percent of industry and 80 percent of the construction business. This collectivization produced a massive transfer of power and resources from the private economy into the public sector, which was precisely the purpose and intended effect.

Structural changes combined with populist, redistributive measures signaled a willingness to incur domestic costs and foreign anger to accelerate the process of radicalizing the revolution. The revolutionary elite believed that to slow down was to court disaster, that momentum itself was proof that the masses supported the regime and enthusiastically joined the assault on capitalism and the private sector. Huge rallies commanded the attention of the populace, and during marathon speeches Castro often mesmerized crowds. The regime realized that social mobilization could serve as a form of explicit consent, and it established mass organizations like the Committees for the Defense of the Revolution, the Federation of Cuban Women, and the Union of Communist Youth to reach the grass roots.

Once it became evident that a radical social revolution committed to socialism was in the making—led by individuals seeking total power—an opposition emerged that attempted to restrain or defeat the revolutionary elite. As often happens in revolutionary situations, a decisive struggle between radicals and moderates ensued, between people committed to some form of democracy and those who would settle for radical socialism and nothing else. Both sides knew that only one would prevail, that no compromise was possible, and that personal risks were involved. The opposition included Catholic organizations, disaffected cadres from Castro's own ranks, respected democratic figures, and other anticommunist elements.

The Communist Party neither carried the Castroites to victory nor became the vehicle on which the revolutionary coalition moved against the private sector and the middle class. Leading Communists like Blas Roca and Aníbal Escalante perceived Castro as an ideological neophyte, unschooled in Marxist verities and unwilling to subordinate his own authority or the power of his movement to orthodox frameworks. The party had criticized the Castroites in the 1950s as "bourgeois adventurers," and its opposition to Batista had been measured, not confrontational. Ideologically, the party still believed in the revolutionary potential of the Cuban working class, and its political work had focused on the labor movement. Needless to say, the party was in no position to assume a leadership role, and its belief that when the revolution came it would become its vanguard was quickly shattered.

In essence, Castro's relationship with the Communist Party stemmed from his desire to limit the damage inflicted on his regime by the defection of noncommunist revolutionaries as well as from the need to enlist Soviet support. The party shrewdly provided organization when Castro's own was being shaken up, and it offered a dialectical explanation for the society's troubles. Andrés Suárez believes that "the Communists played no role, neither in the political leadership of the country nor in the leadership of the students or of the trade unions," but that the party's discipline, support of "national unity," and foreign connections facilitated understandings with Castro.[11]

By the mid-1960s revolutionary changes restructuring class, property, political, and foreign policy relationships had eliminated a dependent capitalist order replete with U.S. influence and moved the country toward radical socialism. The state took over the basic means of production as well as domestic and foreign commerce, industry, transportation, and utilities. Agriculture was reorganized into collective and state farms, but peasants could produce some goods on small, privately owned plots. The mass media were under state control, as was the national system of telecommunications. Party cadres supervised the information network, and Marxism-Leninism shaped the content of public discussion. Dissident intellectuals, nonconformists, and political opponents of the regime were arbitrarily imprisoned, scorned, or forced to leave the country. Nearly five hundred thousand Cubans had left by the mid-1960s, and this number had grown to over 1.5 million by the 1990s.

The regime proscribed dissent and political opposition and forced explicit definitions of loyalty to the system. No opposition parties existed, nor could groups or sectors legally defy the revolutionary state. The legal system came under state control. The court system applied "revolutionary justice" to political offenses, and revolutionary tribunals enforced order and discipline with little evidence of due process. Summary trials of alleged counterrevolutionaries took place, long sentences were imposed on the revolution's opponents, and hundreds were executed. This was a time of social confrontation, characterized by a "we-versus-they" mentality that divided families and intimidated individuals and groups. Thousands of political prisoners served time during the following decades, and many suffered brutal treatment at the hands of guards and prison officials.

The educational system was radically reorganized and centralized, and education was treated as a key to the process of political socialization. National literacy campaigns pushed literacy rates to the mid-90th percentile, but the quality of instruction left much to be desired. Much of Cuba's history was revised and rewritten, and patriotism and national virtues were highlighted. U.S. influence over Cuba's destiny was made the root of many ills. The number of primary schools went from 7,567 in 1958 to 14,807 in 1968, and enrollment doubled during the same period. Thousands of new teachers were trained, rural education in particular was emphasized and supported, and women enjoyed new educational opportunities. Nelson Valdés has noted that students were "required to devote school time to three types of work: educational, productive and socially useful,"[12] so pupils worked in agriculture and volunteer campaigns while they studied.

Considerable resources were devoted to public health. Most of the basic medical services were provided free under a government-run health system that included preventive care, specialized services, and even advanced treatment for common or rare diseases. Over the years hundreds of clinics, hospitals, and specialized-care facilities were built and staffed by thousands of graduates in medicine, nursing, and health-related fields. As a result, life expectancy in the 1990s was about seventy-six years of age, and Cuba's infant mortality rate of approximately ten in one thousand ranks among the best for developing countries. However, adverse economic conditions affect the quality of care. Critical shortages of technologies, medicines, and essential supplies delay treatment and affect the service provided. Without many critical medical imports from the former Communist nations, the system is stressed; unfortunately, this comes precisely when the demand for medical services is increasing because of economic difficulties. In some instances nutritional deficiencies stemming from food shortages have led to the outbreak of optical neuritis and other diseases that result from low caloric intake. Thus, one of the more notable social achievements of the revolution is increasingly compromised.

The revolutionary development strategy of the 1960s was affected by controversy over economic policy. On the one hand socialist ideologues led by Ché Guevara argued that a strong moral foundation must be prepared if socialism was to succeed and that egalitarianism, altruism, and collectivism must be its core values. A cultural transformation must accompany structural changes and instill new values and attitudes among the masses. Arguing that the development of revolutionary consciousness was as important as satisfying material expectations, Guevara articulated a utopian view of "the new man" that radical socialism would create. In his famous essay "Man and Socialism," Guevara's thinking is apparent:

> In these countries [including Cuba] there is no form of education for worthwhile social labor, and wealth remains distant from the masses. Underdevelopment and the habitual flow of capital toward "civilized" countries make it impossible to change rapidly without sacrifice. There remains a long road to be traversed in order to construct a solid economic base; and the temptation to follow the paths of material interest, used as a stimulus for accelerated development, is very great.[13]

On the opposite side stood the more pragmatic policymakers and people schooled in "scientific socialism" rather than in Guevara's utopianism. They knew that Cuba was a poor agricultural country without a large industrial base and with little technological innovation on which to launch grandiose development schemes. Consequently, they held that encouraging production and discipline through material incentives and tangible rewards was probably more effective than abstract appeals to altruism and selflessness.

In the end the final arbiter of all disputes, Castro himself, settled the issue and approved Guevara's approach, reversing industrialization policies, accepting moral stimuli, and launching the nation on an all-out campaign against underdevelopment that promised to produce ten million tons (nine million metric tons) of sugar. At its conclusion in 1970 the economy was completely unbalanced, growth rates had plummeted, and scarcity and shortfalls were evident in every sector. Only 8.5 million tons (7.7 million metric tons) of sugar had been produced and, according to Castro, the results constituted a moral defeat. Economists like Carmelo Mesa-Lago, Sergio Roca, and others have demonstrated that long-lasting damage was done to the infrastructure by such a colossally wrongheaded approach to development. Although chastened by the losses in production and national morale, the regime and its leader (who offered to resign but stayed on because the crowds still hailed him) survived their first systemic crisis.

In conclusion, regime consolidation came about through sustained mobilization, direct exhortation, and a top-to-bottom direction of an ongoing revolutionary agenda rather than through elections. Rewards and sanctions were utilized to elicit compliance with revolutionary policies, but care was exercised not to alienate key sectors of the working class, peasantry, and urban proletariat. These sectors formed the class basis for the new regime once the middle class had been destroyed and the upper strata had either left the country or accepted a dramatic loss in privilege and status. Daily life became intensely political.

Society and Government in the 1980s and 1990s

Needing to regularize the political process and to establish national ruling institutions through which stability could be preserved, the revolutionary elite succeeded in reorganizing the state and the Communist Party and created ruling councils at the local level. Fundamental changes in government became evident, especially in the manner in which central authority is exercised, in President Castro's role as chief decision-maker, in the critical role of the Cuban Communist Party (PCC), and in the organization of social forces. A new socialist constitution was enacted in 1976, defining the PCC "as the leading force in the state and in society," but also outlining the powers of national, provincial, and local organs. Party congresses in 1975, 1980, 1986, and 1991 strengthened the party's hegemonic role, provided forums for discussion of national problems, and set broad strategies for future development.

A new economic model, the System of Direction and Economic Planning (SPDE), framed policies in the late 1970s and early 1980s, taking into consideration criteria such as efficiency, rationality, prices, and other "economic mechanisms." This framework accepted the validity of material incentives and market processes and introduced wage differentials, production norms, monetary controls, and taxes. Carmelo Mesa-Lago writes that "SPDE takes into account the law of supply and demand and the need of monetary and mercantile relations in the transitional state"—presumably prior to reaching socialism—but that it does not abolish central planning.[14]

The adoption of the SPDE reflected a consensus among planners and technocrats regarding the need for limited market reforms to increase economic efficiency and expand output. At the time other Communist countries were experimenting with "market socialism," and some were suggesting that Cuba enact policies that would bring its system more into line with that of its major trading partners in the (now defunct) Council of Mutual Economic Assistance (CMEA). Under the SPDE the emphasis would shift from building "socialist consciousness" through voluntarism and ideological appeals to the satisfaction of consumer demands through market mechanisms.

A central question faced by the Cuban regime is the degree to which the satisfaction of consumer demands is essential for regime legitimacy and stability. The economic crisis of the 1990s brings this into focus because the lack of resources and the adoption of ill-advised policies deepen austerity. Promises that socialism would produce abundance and prosperity have never been fulfilled, and in fact what the regime calls "a special period in peacetime" is really an admission of economic failure. Much evidence indicates that the standard of living has declined by nearly 50 percent since 1990 and is unlikely to improve in the next few years. Such a dramatic deterioration in economic conditions inevitably produces resentment and political disaffection; in short, the social contract between the regime and the masses may be irreparably frayed.

The regime believes, however, that limited economic reform may prevent economic collapse. The new development strategy sanctions capitalist principles without renouncing socialism, but ideology matters less than the compelling need for economic recovery. For instance, the rules governing foreign investment have been liberalized and tourist hotels and other facilities have been built with foreign capital. Joint ventures in specific sectors are now legal and it is likely that some industrial, commercial, and agricultural enterprises will be privatized. Holding dollars is no longer illegal, and in fact special stores where only dollar purchases can be made are now in business. Some forms of private employment are once again permitted, and material incentives are recognized as important factors in making workers more productive. Finally, the government is changing its policy regarding the Cuban community in exile, welcoming those who return as tourists and no longer labeling them "traitors" or "worms."

In all probability these reforms will not produce a sustainable economic recovery. In the end the system's ability to satisfy basic needs and maintain a safety net is severely undermined by a lack of resources; this drives down social consumption and the standard of living itself. There is little doubt that economic pain is widespread, that indices of social poverty are rising, and that grim economic conditions will last for several years. More than passing difficulties brought about by the loss of economic and technical assistance once available from the Communist world, the systemic crisis of the 1990s could lead to economic collapse.[15]

At the same time the Cuban regime faces neither ethnic unrest nor expressions of regional supremacy, and this is due to the absence of genuinely oppressed ethnic minorities and because regionalism is simply not a potent political force. In fact, Cuba has achieved a remarkable degree of political stability and continuity, either as a result of genuine national unity or because its ruling elite and the Communist Party itself are not completely discredited. Socialism appears to have engendered widespread political passivity—albeit laced with discouragement and sullenness—in the present generation, and nationalism is indeed a galvanizing force. Cubans are constantly told by their government that unity is the supreme value, that social divisions weaken the polity and create opportunities for "the enemy," that vigilance on all fronts is essential, and that "imperialism never sleeps." Although many of these claims are patently fraudulent and little more than shopworn slogans, their impact is considerable. In the absence of contrary information or any real debate on the merits of continuity or change, the status quo is preferred.

The Governmental Framework

Cuba's highest-ranking executive organ is the Council of Ministers (CM), composed of the head of state and government, several vice presidents, the head of the Central Planning Agency, and "others determined by law." Fidel Castro is its president, and he is also head of state and government, first secretary of the Communist Party, and commander-in-chief. In fact, all lines of authority converge on President Castro so that, as Jorge Domínguez and others point out, the "maximum leader's" central role has been formalized. His brother Raúl is the CM's first vice president as well as minister of defense and second secretary of the Communist Party. The Castro brothers thus maintain executive control over the central administrative organs and their personal power is nearly absolute.

The CM has the power to conduct foreign relations and foreign trade, maintain internal security, and draft bills for the National Assembly. It has an executive committee whose members control and coordinate the work of ministries and other central organizations. All of its members belong to the Communist Party, and some—like Minister of Culture Armando Hart and Armed Forces Vice Minister General Abelardo Colomé—also belong to the party's Political Bureau.

The Council of State (CS) functions as the executive committee of the National Assembly between legislative sessions, and it is modeled on the Presidium of the former Soviet Union's Supreme Soviet. The CS issues decrees, exercises legislative initiative, can order general mobilization, and can replace ministers. It has some thirty-one members, including several of the twenty-five members of the Political Bureau elected at the Fourth Congress of the Cuban Communist Party in 1991. In addition to the Castro brothers the CS includes influential policymakers such as Carlos Lage, the "economic czar"; José R. Machado, an orthodox Communist who oversees the party's organization; Jorge Lezcano, a Communist Party secretary with some administrative experience; and Roberto Robaina, a former leader of the Union of Young Communists and foreign minister.

The National Assembly of People's Power (NA) is the national legislature. Deputies are elected for five-year terms, but the Assembly holds only two brief sessions per year. In the 1991–1996 *quinquenio* (five-year term) each of its 589 deputies stood for roughly twenty thousand inhabitants. Deputies are directly elected by the people. Among the NA's formal powers, it can decide on constitutional reforms, discuss and approve (but not disapprove) the national budget, plan for economic and social development, and elect judges. In practice, legislative initiative is not exercised, the NA cannot challenge the political leadership, and it is, in fact, a rubber-stamp body. In his study on "the nature of Cuban democracy," Archibald Ritter notes that what partly explains the Assembly's impotence is "insufficient time, support staff, and financial resources to permit individual members to scrutinize problem areas, pieces of legislation, and reports independently and carefully."[16] Some of its work takes place in specialized commissions, such as Child Care and Women's Rights, Defense and Internal Order, and Complaints and Suggestions. Seventeen percent of its members are either educators, health workers, or scientists; 15 percent are presidents of People's Councils; 13 percent work in production and services; and 12 percent are officials from local and provincial Organs of People's Power (OPP). Other deputies are trade union leaders; members of the armed forces and the Ministry of the Interior; high officials in government and the Communist Party; and a few students, athletes, journalists, and religious leaders. Of its 589 members, 506 were elected for the first time in 1993; the average age for all deputies is forty-three.

The underrepresentation of workers, peasants, and women suggests that these groups have yet to transform enhanced status into political influence. For now the typical deputy is a fairly well-educated, probably white, male who is either a full-time party bureaucrat or a white-collar employee. The real center of legislative power and initiative lies in the Council of State, and Ritter's conclusion is that "at the level of the National Assembly, a large proportion of the process of leadership selection and policy formulation is carried out by the party within the shell or framework of the National Assembly."[17]

The Organs of People's Power

Cuba's 14 provinces are subdivided into 169 municipalities, each governed by an Assembly of Delegates of People's Power. Their members serve terms of two-and-a-half years, and they are directly elected at the grassroots. The nominating process is carefully monitored by the party and by nominating commissions so that a candidate's political attitudes must be acceptable. Democratic-style campaigning is not permitted, and candidates cannot reach their supporters via independently controlled media. Claims that these assemblies constitute "socialist democracy in action" stretch one's understanding of what democracy really means and of what constitutes effective political competition in a one-party state in which basic liberties and freedom of speech are severely restricted.

In 1992, 13,432 delegates were elected to these assemblies, 13 percent of them women. A substantial number of these delegates are either Communist Party members or leaders in mass organizations like the Federation of Cuban Women or the Committees for Defense of the Revolution. Membership in the party or any of the mass organizations facilitates political mobility and confers higher status. The assemblies provide a local forum for popular grievances and deal with various problems such as repairing dilapidated housing, monitoring conditions in day-care centers, distributing health information, and cleaning up local sites. The assemblies' work may either overlap that of mass organizations or take advantage of proximity at the grassroots level. The assemblies depend on national organs for resources, thus often curtailing local initiatives.

The Cuban Communist Party

The PCC has undergone significant transformations since the 1960s, when Castroites took effective control of its organization and eliminated political adversaries. The party atrophied in the 1960s and by 1969 membership was only fifty-five thousand. Lip service was paid to its leading role but, in fact, the rambunctious politics of the period and the ad hoc manner in which policies were framed forced the party to the sidelines. The "microfaction affair" in 1968, in which orthodox, former PSP cadres led by Aníbal Escalante attempted to sow division in the ranks and provoke Castro's downfall, led to a bitter internal struggle and the subsequent arrest of some thirty-five members of the microfaction. Purges followed and the guilty party members were sent to jail. This affair severely undermined the party's credibility but it demonstrated that challenges to Castro could be politically fatal. Scholars often speculate that there are divisions among members of the party's top organs, such as the Central Committee, but if so, these divisions have not erupted in a serious challenge to President Castro.

Scheduled congresses were canceled, and the First Congress did not take place until 1975. Party membership went from 202,807 members and candidates in 1975 to some 481,000 in 1981 and 600,000 in the 1990s. The proportions of workers (43 percent) and women (22 percent) are higher than in the past, and the party is making efforts to recruit quality candidates. Its presence at all levels of government and society and in the armed forces suggests that its vertical and horizontal integration has been effective, as are its penetrative capabilities.

On the other hand substantive questions emerged in the 1980s regarding the ideological rigor of the cadres, their discipline, and their willingness to lead through example and sacrifice. The regime is aware that it must reinvigorate the party at the grassroots and struggle against atrophy and indolence. President Castro frequently reminds party members of their solemn obligations, of their historical mission on behalf of socialism and the revolution itself, and of the high personal standards expected of both the leaders as well as the rank and file. Instances of corruption in the party were common in the late 1980s. It suffered from scandals, poor leadership, careless management, lack of discipline, and other deficiencies. Many (perhaps thousands) of party leaders, members, and militants were purged in the late 1980s and early 1990s when the quality of their work was found wanting and when abuses of authority and cases of personal corruption were discovered. In short, the party was severely shaken up prior to its Fourth Congress, and there is reason to believe that the purges involved cadres that advocated major economic and political reforms.

Some of the "negative tendencies" found in the party's performance stemmed from its failure to monitor the illegal activities of high officials—many of whom were party members—in the Ministry of the Interior, the armed forces, and elsewhere. In addition, party members were embroiled in the arrest, trial, and execution of Division General Arnaldo Ochoa and three other officers in

1989. General Ochoa, a decorated veteran of the Angolan war and a "Hero of the Revolution," was found guilty of corruption and involvement in drug trafficking. Colonel Antonio de la Guardia, a ranking officer in the Ministry of the Interior and one of President Castro's favorite spies, was found guilty of involvement in drug trafficking, money laundering, and other illegalities. Several officers received long sentences; others, such as the powerful minister of the interior, General José Abrantes, were subsequently removed from their positions.

It is almost certain that the Castro brothers knew about some of the activities of their subordinates, especially those related to the use of Cuban air space and sea lanes by drug traffickers. Given the regime's highly centralized decision-making structure and the sensitive nature of the group's work, it is most unlikely that top political leaders did not know what was happening. Colonel de la Guardia and his twin brother, General Patricio de la Guardia, serving a thirty-year sentence, were loyal Castroites and friends of President Castro and other leaders. The defendants did not have effective legal representation, nor was due process observed during what became a grotesque "show trial." Abject confessions and instances of self-degradation characterized the defendants' demeanor. President Castro himself instigated the prosecution and asked for the death penalty for Ochoa, de la Guardia, and two others. The quick resolution of the crisis indicates that it was viewed by the leadership as a major political threat, making a summary verdict a foregone conclusion. In the end the Castros succeeded in shifting responsibility for the scandal to their subordinates, meanwhile avoiding any culpability for what they themselves had approved.

Changes made at the Fourth Congress indicate that, although continuity at the top is important, promoting new members to the Political Bureau alleviates some generational pressures and makes way for leaders of important functional groups or sectors. For example, fourteen of the twenty-five members are new, and only six members remain of those elected at the First Congress in 1965. Party secretaries Alfredo Hondal and Jorge Lezcano are new members, as are the division generals Leopoldo Cintra and Julio Casas. Three of the twenty-five members are women, but the well-known president of the Federation of Cuban Women, Vilma Espín, is no longer among them. Some promotions are clearly idiosyncratic; others stem from the fact that President Castro often rewards his favorites with high-level appointments. Major decisions in domestic and foreign policy are made at this level, and members comprise "the elite of the elite." It can be assumed that decisions are reached by consensus after some discussion, but it is extremely unlikely that, individually or as a group, members can effectively oppose President Castro. New members in particular are unlikely to assert themselves in the rarefied atmosphere of the group, so bringing in new blood is not necessarily indicative of new policy directions. Within this elite the lines of accountability run *from* not *toward* President Castro, so personnel changes seldom affect the elite in general and certainly not the president's absolute power. The leadership is aware that institutional elitism breeds privilege and inequality, undermines the egalitarian rhetoric of socialism, and leads to the formation of what many people regard as "a new class," but these contradictions are generic to socialism itself.

The Lost Decades

The collapse of orthodox communism in the former Soviet Union and Eastern Europe prompted the Cuban leadership to declare a "Special Period in Peacetime" in the early 1990s. A strategy of economic survival took shape under conditions of severe austerity and hardship, largely because the $5–6 billion annual subsidy from former Communist allies was no longer available. During the "special period" consumption dropped dramatically, services and subsidies provided by the state were eliminated or reduced, and the standard of living for the average individual or household fell precipitously.

Economic hardships multiplied under this strategy. The state bureaucracy was downsized, factories and industries shut down, subsidies either reduced or eliminated in transportation, agriculture, construction, housing, and other sectors. Draconian measures to conserve energy were imposed, causing total or partial blackouts on a regular basis. Unemployment and partial unemployment rose as workers saw their jobs disappear and their schedules severely disrupted, all of which adversely affect the standard of living for millions of individuals and households. In sum, for the great majority of Cubans, conditions under the "special period" were similar to those in wartime without the violence and were nothing less than disastrous, an altogether shattering and traumatizing experience harking back to the days of colonial rule.

President Castro summarily declared that the Special Period was over in 2004, even though the economic contraction that led to it had not abated. Growth rates have been quite erratic in this decade and Cuba's unproductive and uncompetitive economy is simply unable to generate the material or financial resources needed to sustain its eleven million people. In his major study, *The Cuban Economy Today: Salvation or Damnation?* (2005), Professor Mesa-Lago shows that the annual growth rate for 1990–2000 was 1.2 percent, the worst in Latin America. A very modest rebound started with 3.0 percent growth in 2001, 1.5 percent in 2002, 2.6 percent in 2003 and roughly 2.0–2.5 percent in 2004. Castro's predictions for stronger improvement in 2005–2006 should not be taken seriously given documented manipulation of statistics by the government, unresolved structural problems aggravated by the end of economic reforms, and Castro's documented record of outlandish and unrealized predictions. Overall, studies show that the economy has not recovered from the losses of the last fifteen years and that the standard of living is significantly worse than in the late 1980s. Rather than progress, developmental regression characterizes the 1991–2005 period, or two lost decades.

One of the reasons for the economy's abysmal performance is the catastrophic collapse of the sugar industry. Once the crown jewel of Cuba's political economy, the industry is in ruins and no longer the dominant sector of the command system. Total output in the 1990s hovered around four million metric tons per harvest, regularly falling short of planned targets and not generating adequate levels of hard currency. Precipitous declines forced the government to import sugar to meet export commitments and domestic demand when output went from 3.5 million metric tons in 2001 to 2.2 million in 2003 and 1.3 million in 2004–2005. The last harvest was the smallest in a century.

The government closed down about half of the sugar mills in 2002 in order to reduce costs and presumably increase the efficiency of the rest, so that only fifty-six of the country's seventy-five mills were active during the 2004–2005 harvest. Interruptions in production causing costly delays that drive yields down are frequent, bringing unexpected costs for repairs. Thousands of technicians, laborers, administrative personnel, and farm hands who lost jobs due to the closing of the mills received some compensation and were urged to train for other jobs, without much success. Unemployment rose in communities affected by the shutdown of the mills, driving an already low standard of living into further decline. The ruins of abandoned sugar mills vividly stand as social metaphors for what was once a world-class industry.

Explanations for the collapse of the Cuban sugar industry include obsolete technology that became too costly to repair, recurring problems with inputs delaying the planting and harvesting cycle, managerial and administrative incompetence at different levels of production, and sporadic labor-related difficulties. President Castro appointed General Ulises Rosales as Minister of Sugar in 1997 to restore morale and impose discipline on an inefficient industry. General Rosales was a career military officer completely untrained for the job, so it is not surprising that his own and the industry's performance were stunning failures. To make matters worse, international competition from Australia, Brazil, the Dominican Republic, and other strong exporters keeps worldwide sugar prices low. That significantly reduces total earnings from sugar exports for Cuba, compared to more than $1 billion dollars earned in the late 1980s.

Cuba's failure to reinsert itself into the evolving global economic system is reflected in its foreign debt, which has escalated dramatically despite the moratorium on that debt declared in 1986. As of 2004 Cuba's total hard currency debt stood at $13.3 billion and its debt in transferable rubles stands at an estimated $22 billion. Most of the debt in dollars is owed to Japan ($2.3 billion), Argentina ($2.0 billion), Spain ($1.7 billion) and France ($1.3 billion). Due to its staggering hard currency debt, the moratorium, and its chronic and unproductive command system, Cuba finds it extremely difficult to raise fresh loans and credits. Its international credit ranking is one of the lowest in the world, dramatically illustrating the high risks of either lending to Cuba or doing business with its government.

The Venezuelan Connection

On the other hand a new and deepening relationship between Cuba and the government of Hugo Chávez in Venezuela is paying off handsomely for Cuba. Cuba and Venezuela are increasingly bound together politically and ideologically, with Fidel Castro and Hugo Chávez becoming strong personal friends and political allies. Several bilateral agreements signed on very favorable terms for Cuba since 2001 are in effect in areas such as health, education, transportation, and energy. Venezuela's oil exports to Cuba constitute the island's new economic lifeline.

A mutually dependent and complex relationship is taking shape without the vast asymmetries of Cuba's relationship with the former Communist bloc, but rather with a clear strategic purpose. It is reasonable to maintain that Castro's brain, experience, and audacity lie behind some of Chavez's risky foreign policy initiatives such as strengthening relations with Iran and other radical and rogue states, warming up to the People's Republic of China, or financing radical indigenous leaders like Evo Morales in Bolivia. Flush with petrodollars and energized by delusions of revolutionary greatness and his own toxic rhetoric, Chávez believes in the Bolivarian vision of a united Latin America under *his* (and Venezuelan) leadership.

Some one hundred thousand barrels per day are provided to Cuba on very generous terms. *The New York Times* reports that "Venezuela has been supplying cut-price oil to Mr. Castro in a deal that helps ease Cuba's energy and transport problems." That lengthy blackouts and interruptions in electrical service ordered by the state are part of daily life indicates that purchases of oil from Venezuela have not resolved Cuba's energy crisis. Imports from Venezuela run well below Cuba's needs and are a fraction of the six million barrels the former Soviet Union supplied in the 1980s and 1990s, but imports cushion chronic shortages in supply. Second, there is evidence that Cuba resells some of the oil in order to take advantage of high prices, at the expense of domestic consumption and with the approval of the Chávez government. The market value of subsidized Venezuelan oil imported by Cuba in 2004 was $940 million and it is expected to grow to $1.1 billion in 2005. The total impact on the Cuban economy of subsidized oil and exports of goods and services in 2004 was estimated at $1.5 billion, which comprises a significant proportion of total Gross Domestic Product. In the next few years more imports and fresh financing will surely turn Venezuela into Cuba's top creditor.

Under the (previously mentioned) agreements an estimated twenty-five to thirty thousand Cuban doctors, medical specialists, health care personnel, and experts in education, sports, and other social fields work in Venezuela, earning Cuba approximately $288 million in 2003–2004. Supplying human capital for an important ally in Latin America replicates the policy of "internationalism" carried out by Cuba in the 1970s and 1980s, then (and still) focused on the developing world. The policy generates revenue for Cuba as well as symbolic and emotional capital for Chávez and Castro in the region.

Though the policies are sold by each leader as "providing services to the poor and oppressed," an unintended consequence is that growing needs in areas of the Cuban health care system go unmet because thousands of providers work in Venezuela. And numerous press reports indicate that prestigious Venezuelan professional medical associations energetically protest the presence of Cuban personnel in their country and question their ideology, training, and professionalism.

Fidel Castro anointed Chávez as his "designated revolutionary heir," that is, as the leader willing and able to promote "a Bolivarian revolution" in Latin America. If Castro and Chávez stick to the plan, then the region faces rising tensions and political instability. It remains to be seen if the region's democratic governments embrace "the Bolivarian vision" or, rather, conclude that Chávez is a danger to liberty and to electoral, representative democracy in the region.

Chávez holds Castro in high esteem as an experienced, successful and ruthless *caudillo* who has survived U.S. attempts to undermine the revolution since the Eisenhower administration. A bombastic and populist demagogue committed to defying the United States and spreading his influence in the region, Chávez maintains that Cuba and Venezuela "swim in a sea of happiness." Strong oil prices bring billions of petrodollars into Chávez's treasury, but much of the money is squandered in pursuit of the Bolivarian dream.

El Chavismo repackages nationalism, anti-imperialism, and revolution for conditions in the postcommunist world. In fact, it is a turgid doctrine with a heavy dose of reckless populism at its core. One can dismiss as lunacy Chávez's advocacy of "socialism for the twenty-first century," but it constitutes a serious political threat aimed at destroying Venezuela's middle and upper sectors and what is left of its democratic institutions, private economy, and independent media. Promoting class warfare at home and destabilization in his neighborhood leave no doubt that Chávez aims for *Venezuela hoy y Latino América mañana.*

To sum up, Venezuela's (and the region's) unresolved grievances fuel a visceral anti-American, anticapitalist, antiglobalization, illiberal mentality that generates political capital for protomessianic leaders promising to vanquish hunger, disease, illiteracy and chronic poverty. Venezuela's neighbors would be well-advised to muster the political will to resist anachronistic messianic messages or cynical offers of economic and social assistance. With Hugo and Fidel consulting regularly on many domestic and foreign policy issues and holding public mutual admiration fests every time they meet, Venezuela and Cuba form an emerging axis of power in the region.

Tourism, Dollarization, and De-dollarization

A second source of revenue for Cuba is tourism. The industry is moderately rebounding and generating badly needed hard currency. Some two million tourists reportedly visited Cuba in 2004, with net earnings estimated to be in the $300–500 million range. Expanding tourist facilities is a top economic priority, requiring that long-held ideological prejudices against "contamination from capitalism" be overlooked. The government aggressively looks for ways that would bring more tourists to the island and it purchases flashy advertising in Europe and Latin America portraying the natural wonders of the landscape and Cuba's legendary cultural sensuality.

The same factors that lure tourists to other islands in the region bring them to Cuba: lots of sun, white sand beaches stretching for miles, the prospect of "a romantic getaway," cheap sex, and the certainty that a great time will be had at a nominal cost. Numerous reports in the international media link the rise of prostitution in Cuba to the tourist trade, and it is quite evident that young, single males from Europe and Latin America arrive in droves expecting a fabulous time. Most tourists arrive from Canada, Spain, Germany, Italy, and several Latin American countries, with international airlines providing regular service to Havana or charter bookings directly to Varadero beach and other destinations.

Foreign-owned hotel chains own property along the northern coastline, dotted by world-class beaches and new facilities designed to please visitors. Professor Mesa-Lago reports that gross revenue from tourism went from $1.9 billion in 1999 to $2.2 billion in 2004, a modest increase at a time when terrorism affected international travel. Still, tourism is a volatile political issue for a government that for strictly ideological reasons failed to take advantage of tourism as part of its development strategy for thirty years. Second, competition in the region cuts into Cuba's earnings from tourism once the novelty of "going to the last socialist outpost" wears off. Expansion, in short, is a must. Third, Mesa-Lago points out that "until Cuba is capable of providing its needed inputs domestically the multiplying effect of the tourist industry will not take place." And finally, as a dollar-based enclave surrounded by a command economy subject to the vagaries of economic conditions in source countries, tourism does not constitute the foundation upon which a sound development strategy can be sustained.

Of particular significance is the fact that the government selects those employees that work in the industry, and then pays their salaries in pesos while it receives dollars from their employers. Placing loyalists, supporters, and even members of the Communist Party with foreign firms rewards these persons with a measure of job security and access to goods and services unavailable in the regular domestic economy. A new type of "socialist clientelism" developing under the auspices of foreign capital serves state interests as well as those of individuals who are "politically safe" and see their militancy rewarded. Workers in the tourist industry form part of a privileged sector in the labor force, that is, of workers that see their standard of living improve because they work in the most dynamic sector of the economy from which they draw creature comforts unavailable elsewhere.

Since there is no free labor contract in Cuba defining the relations between a worker and a foreign employer, the state in fact exacts "surplus labor" from workers who automatically see their salaries reduced when they receive pesos that are worth around 20 to $1. Access to tourist venues is highly restricted to outsiders for political reasons, a blatant form of discrimination against citizens in their own country. The marked contrast between the hardship and sacrifice of daily life for ordinary citizens and the luxury, comfort, and pleasure of life found in tourist venues illustrates why promoting tourism exacerbates tensions between tourists who enjoy privileges, and ordinary citizens who can only dream of "the good capitalist life."

Spanish, Canadian, and other foreign firms operating in Cuba's tourist industry in joint ventures with the state remain silent about what is an extraordinarily exploitative practice, preferring to stay in the government's good graces rather than raise issues that would upset the authorities. But Cuba has not become the pot of gold that foreign investors expected ten years ago. In fact, as the process of adaptation to external market forces pushes the government into partnerships with foreign firms, attracting foreign capital to the tourist as well as other industries is running into major problems. For example, in the 1990s reportedly some 383 joint ventures were signed between the state and foreign capital in areas such as mining, transportation, and other sectors. At the time foreign investors expected that a permanent opening up of the economy to foreign capital would be state policy.

In this decade Castro's perennial anticapitalist rantings, his decision to freeze the reform process, and poor earnings by foreign firms increase the risks for foreign investors. In addition, mind-boggling bureaucratic and administrative barriers, the absence of a legal system for the resolution of disputes, and opportunities elsewhere have slowed the entry of foreign capital into Cuba. Of the 313 joint ventures still active in 2003, only 133 remained in early 2005 and another 67 were expected to close.

Another source of hard currency is Cuban exiles, who presumably send anywhere from $300 to $600 million (estimates vary greatly and some analysts put the total figure at around $1 billion) annually in remittances to their relatives. A significant tightening of U.S. policy toward Cuba under the Bush administration makes this more difficult, because the new restrictions limit visits to Cuba from Cuban Americans to one every three years and remittances to immediate family only. With a few exceptions restrictions were tightened over conventional travel by U.S. citizens as well. The Cuban government denounced what it correctly perceived as an effort to cut into the dollars flowing into the economy and it shamelessly lamented the fact that Cuban families would suffer as consequence. In fact, the Cuban government's response aimed to divide the Cuban American community on a very emotional and controversial issue and create problems for the Bush administration from some its strongest political supporters.

The harsh climate surrounding visits by émigrés pits the enduring strength of familial bonds against Communist ideology. Thousands of anti-Castro, anticommunist Cuban Americans return to visit their homeland, spending dollars as well as distributing consumer goods unavailable in the domestic market. A growing minority of Cuban Americans living in the United States are unhappy with the Bush administration's restrictions, particularly many of those coming to the United States since the Mariel boatlift (when Castro emptied his jails and insane asylums and sent thousands of undesirables to the United States) in 1980. The Cuban government skillfully exploits the desire for families on both sides of the Florida Straits to see each other at least once every three years, blaming the United States for keeping families divided. The U.S. firm Western Union offers direct wire transfers to Cuba under licenses issued by the U.S. government, but other (legal and illegal) means of transferring money are used as well by Cuban Americans concerned about their relatives' economic plight.

At the nadir of the economic crisis in 1993 the government legalized the practice of holding dollars, making the U.S. currency the most coveted means of exchange. Millions of ordinary Cubans, such as professionals moonlighting as taxi drivers, young women selling themselves as prostitutes, or academics "invited" by American universities, lust after dollars in order to dramatically increase their purchasing power in a country where average salaries run to

$10–15 per month. At the time dollarization was seen as a desperate effort at economic survival and, in fact, the policy alleviated some disturbing macroeconomic tendencies.

Dollarization was abruptly ended in 2004 when the Central Bank declared that purchases in dollars as well as the holding of dollars by ordinary citizens would be illegal. A new currency, the convertible peso, appeared with a fixed exchange rate, and those holding dollars were urged to change them into convertible pesos. A 10 percent tax was imposed on exchanges from dollars to convertible pesos, affecting Cubans, tourists, banks, hotels, and dollar-only shops. Additional restrictions imposed on state enterprises engaged in trading in dollars and on other economic actors force enterprises to obtain approval for any dollar-based transaction.

Mesa-Lago maintains (and I concur) that such a dramatic reversal of policy stems from "the severe and growing scarcity of hard currency, due to the failure of Cuba's economic policies" and its burdensome external debt. A second explanation is that radical egalitarianism could not be sustained in a dollarized economy driven by forces antithetical to the official ideology. Where "the good life" is reserved for the privileged military and political and administrative elites with access to dollars, the government's call for "revolutionary sacrifice" is farcical. State priorities trump social or individual consumption because the state needs to increase revenues in hard currency from households as well as from all financial and commercial sources. Through de-dollarization, the state willfully imposed severe costs on individuals and families holding dollars, sacrificing the general welfare in the hope of ameliorating short- and medium-term financial stresses.

With cradle-to-grave protections from the state a thing of the past, a kind of savage, unregulated, and primitive capitalism is making inroads into what is still an unreformed command economy. Chasing dollars subverts the social order, undermines the official discourse on the "revolution's social achievements" (*logros de la revolución*), and definitively eviscerates the memory of Cuban socialism. The transformation of the state into the largest cashier in an economy where the "currency of the empire holds sway"—even after de-dollarization—indicates as no other fact would that forty-five years of radical socialism have ruined the economy, caused widespread impoverishment, and subjected the population to frustration and hopelessness.

With convertible or regular pesos essentially worthless, finding dollars is *the* national obsession. A popular refrain once held that "sin azúcar no hay país" (there is no country without sugar), but one's epitaph would be that "los dólares acabaron con la revolución" (the dollars ended the revolution), and also exposed a decayed society and an economic wasteland.

While the need for major structural and macroeconomic reforms is evident, the political leadership (see table 17.1) refuses to approve the necessary changes

Table 17.1   Members of the Political Bureau of the Cuban Communist Party (PCC)

(2004–05)

Member	Office(s) Held
Fidel Castro	President, Council of State
	President, Council of Ministers
	Commander in Chief, Revolutionary Armed Forces
	First Secretary, PCC
Raúl Castro	First Vice-President, Council of State
	First Vice-President, Council of Ministers
	Minister, Revolutionary Armed Forces
	Second Secretary, PCC
Juan Almeida	Vice-President, Council of State
Concepción Campa	Director, Finlay General Institute
Julio Casas	Division General
	Vice-Minister, Armed Forces
José R. Machado	Vice-President, Council of State
Abelardo Colomé	Corps General
	Minister of Interior
	Vice-President, Council of State
Ricardo Alarcón	President, National Assembly
	Member, Council of State
Carlos Lage	Vice-President, Council of State
	Executive Secretary, Council of Ministers
Felipe Pérez	Member, Council of State
	Minister of Foreign Relations
Esteban Lazo	Vice-President, Council of State
Ulises Rosales	Division General
	First Vice-Minister, Armed Forces
	Minister of Sugar Industry
	Member, Council of State
Pedro Ross	General Secretary, Cuban Workers' Confederation
Abel Prieto	Minister of Culture
Alfredo Jordán	Minister of Agriculture
Leopoldo Cintra	Division General
	Chief, Western Army
Ramón Espinosa	Division General
	Chief, Eastern Army
Yadira García	Member, President Castro's staff
	Minister of Basic Industry (2004)
Pedro Saez	PCC First Secretary, Havana
Juan C. Robinson	PCC First Secretary, Santiago de Cuba
Jorge L. Sierra	PCC First Secretary, Holguín
Misael Enamorado	PCC First Secretary, Las Tunas
Miguel Díaz Canel	PCC First Secretary, Villa Clara

Source: Table compiled by author from several sources.

for purely political and quite cynical reasons. The government fears the emergence of independent, private economic activity and remains committed to a pervasive system of social controls. Thus, discouraging individual initiative, limiting self-employment, and controlling the distribution of resources in order to perpetuate a dependent relationship between households and the state remain state policy. Stagnation through central control is preferable to sustained growth generated by market forces, so the latter are suppressed.

During the Fifth (and last) Congress of the Communist Party, held in 1997, President Castro rejected reforms that would expand market forces and gradually reduce the role of the state in management, production, and resource allocation on the grounds that no return to capitalism should be expected. Introducing private enterprise on a large scale is anathema to a regime captive to failed economic doctrines, illustrating once again that economic rationality is subordinated to the goal of maximum political control. Indeed, Castro categorically stated that: "We will do what's necessary without renouncing our principles. We don't like capitalism and we will not abandon our socialist system."

To sum up, the uneven performance of the Cuban economy in the last decades, characterized by low growth rates, unending energy shortages, declines in consumption, and continued state control over broad sectors of the economy is attributable in part to the collapse of preferential relationships with former Communist countries. A second explanation stems from the failed doctrines and wrong-headed policies rooted in a command system. But what really trumps all empirical or even ideological explanations are Castro's stunning subordination of the national interest to his undiminished totalitarian vocation, and the loyal elites' pathological obsession with the maintenance of political control at the expense of the general welfare. At the dawn of a new millennium and after nearly half a century of communism, the leader's own demons and his government's unwillingness to embark on a path of renewal leaves broad sectors of the population impoverished, disengaged, and with a grim future.

The International Arena

The key factors framing Cuba's role in the world are revolutionary messianism, an anti-U.S. and anti-imperialistic stance, a legacy of defiance, and Marxist-Leninist ideology. President Castro's revolutionary convictions as well as his shrewdness and episodic demagogic outbursts—often in the midst of crisis and bipolar confrontations—make Cuba an influential actor in regional politics and in parts of the Third World. Still, the country's foreign relations, intended to maximize its international standing and degree of influence abroad, are subject to domestic pressures and external constraints.

In the 1960s Cuba's revolutionary messianism led it to support guerrilla movements in Venezuela, Bolivia, Guatemala, and Nicaragua. Subsequently, Cuba assisted groups like the M–19 in Colombia, the MIR in Chile, the Tupamaros in Uruguay, the Montoneros in Argentina, and the Farabundo Martí National Liberation Front in El Salvador. Cuban support has varied according to political circumstances and the country's own capabilities, but in practically all cases it has involved either training guerrillas in Cuba and sending them out or supplying weapons and logistical assistance to such groups. At times Cuba has provided sanctuary for revolutionaries from various countries, and Sandinista leaders like Tomás Borge and others have spent some time in Cuba. President Castro has repeatedly stated that as a revolutionary country Cuba is obliged to offer moral as well as material support to revolutionaries fighting their own wars of liberation, and the constitution of 1976 includes this principle.

Through a vigorous assertion of proletarian internationalism Cuba once maintained thousands of cadres abroad on various missions. The regime's view has been that through proletarian internationalism Cubans fulfilled their self-imposed revolutionary duties and advanced the cause of socialism and Marxism-Leninism, but the policy has had explicit geopolitical aims. In the late 1980s approximately eighty-five thousand Cubans were stationed abroad either as combat troops (in Angola and Ethiopia) or as technical and economic advisers (in Nicaragua). Contingents included doctors, nurses, and health care personnel as well as construction workers, teachers, agronomists, and other professionals. Intelligence people, political operatives, and security personnel served abroad—often disguised as *internacionalistas* (internationalist workers)—and supplemented the work of intelligence agencies. In some cases Cuba earned hard currency as a result of these missions because countries like Libya and Angola paid Cuba in dollars for its services while the Cuban government paid its people's salaries in pesos.

On occasion fulfillment of these international duties has led to war or confrontation with status quo powers (such as South Africa) or, as was the case in Grenada in 1983, direct clashes with U.S. forces. In Angola Cuba supported a corrupt Marxist dictatorship and in Ethiopia it backed a brutal Marxist regime. The Angolan war started in the wake of the Portuguese collapse in southwestern Africa in the mid-1970s, and Cuban forces helped turn the tide for Angola's Popular Movement for the Liberation of Angola (MPLA). Cuban troops were stationed in Angola until 1991 and fought against South African regulars and guerrillas connected with the Union for the Total Independence of Angola (UNITA). Official Cuban government casualty sources listed twenty-three hundred dead, including several hundred from diseases and accidents. (Additional hundreds were wounded.) In all likelihood this figure underestimates the total number of casualties because not all the bodies were recovered from the battlefields. In December 1988 agreements signed among Cuba, South Africa, and Angola formalized an end to Cuba's participation in the Angolan war and established a schedule for South African troops to leave Namibia and Cuban troops to leave Angola. All fifty thousand Cuban combat troops had left by the end of May 1991; the government and UNITA signed a peace agreement that promised democracy. There is little doubt that improvements in East-West relations, escalating costs at home, and the failure to achieve a military victory forced Cuba (as well as Angola and South Africa) to negotiate seriously.[18]

In the 1980s Cuba resumed diplomatic relations with influential Latin American states like Argentina, Brazil, and Peru. It appeared that Havana preferred normalization of state-to-state relations to active support for some guerrilla movements, and key Latin American governments were seeking ways to bring Cuba back into the Latin American community. A process of reciprocity is under way that allows Cuba to expand critical ties in exchange for pragmatic recognition on its part that democratic processes in Latin America are legitimate. Suspicions regarding Cuba's ties to revolutionary networks and its intrusive behavior moderate Latin America's willingness to renew relations, but sectors of the left sympathize with Cuba and often pressure governments to recognize Havana.

Cuba's relations with Russia are markedly different from its friendly relations with the former Soviet Union. The defeat of hard-line Communists by Boris Yeltsin and the reformers eliminated the prospect that Communists will return to power in Moscow. Second, the values shaping the reform process in Russia (pluralism, free elections, accountability, entrepreneurship) are the opposite of those still dominant in Cuba, and therefore the cultural and ideological framework defining a new bilateral relationship is radically different from what prevailed under Leonid Brezhnev and Mikhail Gorbachev. Third, the reformers know that President Castro supported the August 1991 coup that aimed to restore Communist rule in Russia; consequently, they feel no kinship or solidarity with Cuba or Castro. Simply put, Cuba and Castro were outcasts in the eyes of Yeltsin and the reformers in Russia and in Eastern Europe, many of whom view Cuba as an economic basket case and an outdated police state.

Russia, Poland, the Czech and Slovak Republics, Hungary, and others deal with Cuba pragmatically and in a very businesslike manner. Gone are the days when Cuba received preferential economic treatment and strong political support. These nations have adopted Western-style democracy and market economics, while Cuba refuses to liberalize its economy or tolerate political opposition and pluralism. In fact, Cuba's former allies have denounced its abuses of human rights at the United Nations Commission on Human Rights and have called for an end to repression and political persecution. Because

Cuba's internal practices are under international scrutiny it can no longer count on the protection and "solidarity" of its former allies.

Finally, although U.S.-Cuban relations fluctuate between hostility and tolerance, neither country is prepared to make the crucial political concessions that would lead to a genuine rapprochement. Formal diplomatic relations were broken in 1961, but "interest sections" opened in Washington and Havana in 1977. Issues raised by the United States have included Cuba's strategic relationship with the Soviet Union, its revolutionary activism in Africa and Latin America, and problems in the area of human rights. Historical grievances, nationalism, the U.S. economic embargo, and Cuba's insistence on sovereignty and on earning its powerful neighbor's respect have shaped that country's outlook. The two governments collaborate on matters related to emigration and family reunification, and in 1985 signed an agreement allowing thousands of Cubans to emigrate to the United States. Restoring relations with Cuba was not a high priority for the Clinton Administration, and Cuban officials repeatedly state that they are prepared to wait for a change of official attitude in Washington.

Prospects for Breakdown and Regime Change

Predictions about the demise of Cuban socialism, or about the major transformations that were necessary for the system to survive, have neither been realized nor are likely to be met in the foreseeable future. Contrary to what many experts, social scientists (including this writer), and regime opponents have held, the system has proved to be more resilient than anticipated. Limited economic reforms introduced in the 1990s placed a bottom under what could have been an economic cataclysm, blunting the edge of social pressures that could have exploded into political disorder.

Broadly speaking, that resiliency is rooted in nationalism, not quite yet a spent force. President Castro's commitment to rule until the very day he dies gives the system inordinate strength as well, notwithstanding the high costs stemming from his absolutist vocation and single-minded intransigence. The loyalty and relative cohesion of strategic elites such as the party apparatus; the armed forces; and younger, proven cadres involved in administration and management limit the probability that a reformist faction would shake up the system.

Finally, repression and fear sustain what a Catholic Church document identified as "induced defenselessness" in the population—namely a widespread sense of fatalism and hopelessness. A credible alternative to Castro's leadership and Communist rule has not emerged, although rising levels of political disaffection and outright dissent and opposition are increasingly evident on a national scale.

Assuming that economic crisis and social decay would force the revolutionary leadership to either abandon socialism or approve major structural reforms that would transform it was a mistake. A survival strategy of adaptation introduced in the early 1990s, combining major ideological reversals with limited macroeconomic changes and a partial opening for foreign capital, generated sufficient resources to maintain social stability and elite cohesion, one of the crucial determinants of the regime's survival.

Although downsized, the armed forces as an institution remain loyal to the revolution and its historic leaders, occupying a larger presence in Communist Party organs following the 1997 Party Congress. At the same time high-ranking active and retired officers close to Second Secretary Raúl Castro expanded their economic presence, creating a web of relationships with foreign capital that led to the emergence of a new class of entrepreneurs well-positioned to take advantage of economic opportunities.

There are signs of political and economic change sprouting beneath the surface of a highly authoritarian one-party state. Democratic ideas are slowly reemerging. Political dissidence, for instance, is rapidly growing, and dozens of human rights organizations use what political space is available to call for free elections, democracy, and the rule of law. Elizardo Sánchez, Gustavo Arcos, and other prominent dissidents are well known abroad and receive support from influential Latin American and European governments. Finally, the long-silent hierarchy of the Catholic Church is publicly calling for change and reconciliation through a national dialogue between the regime and its opponents in Cuba and in the exile community. In a powerful pastoral letter in 1993 the Church points to "instances of uncertainty and hopelessness in the people" and speaks of a "deterioration in the moral climate that lead to violent incidents in the cities and towns." In short, the Church is slowly taking sides against the regime. Its concerted moral and ethical appeal resonates among Catholics and nonbelievers alike and indicates that the Church is preparing for a post-Communist Cuba.

Some believe that a peaceful transition to a democratic system is possible—that, given reason and goodwill between the regime and its opponents, through negotiation and dialogue a social catastrophe can be avoided. Others maintain that a "hard" and resilient Communist dictatorship led by a messianic leader like Fidel Castro is unshakable and therefore negotiations are unlikely to bring about a change in regime. The prospect of the Castros' engineering their own departure from power seems remote because they have the specter of bloody reprisals against the old leadership in eastern Europe before them. Nor is it likely that they can survive by riding out the worst effects of the economic crisis.

Conclusion

Cuba's political development following its independence was characterized by clientelism, strongman rule, and military intervention in politics, and the legitimacy of the early regimes seldom rested on popular consent. In the 1940s and 1950s democratic reformism failed to develop viable ruling institutions, and corrupt governments undermined public support for political democracy. Authoritarian regimes alienated the rising middle sectors and relied on coercion rather than on consent, seldom ruling with popular support. Economic dependency made national development difficult and resulted in a social system without cohesion.

Radical structural transformation uprooted capitalism and reordered the political system through mobilization and charismatic rule because the revolutionary elite believed that development could be achieved only through political and economic centralization. Egalitarianism, unity, and social militancy became the supreme values of the new Marxist order, and pluralism, representative democracy, and a mixed economy were consciously rejected. Private education was abolished, and the state reshaped the entire educational system, expanding health services as well. State control of industry, commerce, telecommunications, agriculture, and even small-scale production created a large bureaucracy, which led to a new technocracy composed of administrators, planners, managers, and "producers of culture and information." A new class with its own vested interests thus appeared.

The economic crisis has sped up the process of cultural decay and definitively demonstrated that revolutionary socialism will never produce prosperity or freedom. Neither an expanded tourist industry nor new developments in microbiology, liberalized rules for foreign investment, and the partial "dollarization" of the economy will reverse the economic debacle. In fact, these "concessions to capitalism" indicate just how desperate the regime is for any economic respite. Unanticipated social and psychological effects are already evident, as are confrontations between regime supporters and opponents.

Finally, the minimal satisfaction of some material needs is jeopardized by incompetence and corruption in the management of an economy that is spinning out of control. Its political impact is evident in increasing disaffection; the flight of thousands to the United States in perilous journeys; and the defection of hundreds of erstwhile regime supporters and members of the professional, military, cultural, technocratic, and sports elites. Losses of human capital aggravate the economic crisis and are a clear sign that millions of Cubans have reached the end of the line and see no way out of a national calamity. And so it goes for the last Utopia.

Suggestions for Further Reading

Alfonso, Pablo. *Los Fieles de Castro.* Miami: Ediciones Cambio, 1991.

Azicri, Max. *Cuba: Politics, Economics, and Society.* London: Pinter, 1988.

Baloyra, Enrique, and James Morris, eds. *Conflict and Change in Cuba.* Albuquerque: University of New Mexico Press, 1993.

Brundenius, Claes. *Revolutionary Cuba: Economic Growth, Income Distribution, and Basic Needs.* Boulder, CO: Westview Press, 1983.

Del Aguila, Juan M. *Cuba: Dilemmas of a Revolution.* 3rd ed. Boulder, CO: Westview Press, 1994.

Díaz-Briquets, Sergio, ed. *Cuban Internationalism in Sub-Saharan Africa.* Pittsburgh: Duquesne University Press, 1989.

Domínguez, Jorge I. *Cuba: Order and Revolution.* Cambridge, MA: Belknap Press of Harvard University Press, 1978.

Erisman, H. Michael, and John Kirk, eds. *Cuban Foreign Policy Confronts a New International Order.* Boulder, CO: Lynne Rienner, 1991.

Halebsky, Sandor, and John Kirk, eds. *Cuba in Transition.* Boulder, CO: Westview Press, 1992.

Horowitz, Irving L., ed. *Cuban Communism.* 7th ed. New Brunswick, NJ: Transaction Books, 1989.

Llovio Menéndez, José L. *Insider: My Hidden Life as a Revolutionary in Cuba.* New York: Bantam, 1988.

Mazarr, Michael J. *Semper Fidel: America and Cuba, 1776–1988.* Baltimore: Nautical and Aviation Publishing Company of America, 1988.

Mesa-Lago, Carmelo. *The Economy of Socialist Cuba.* Albuquerque: University of New Mexico Press, 1981.

Oppenheimer, Andrés. *Castro's Final Hour.* New York: Simon & Schuster, 1992.

Pérez, Louis A. *Cuba: Between Reform and Revolution.* New York: Oxford University Press, 1988.

Rabkin, Rhoda P. *Cuban Politics.* New York: Praeger, 1991.

Smith, Wayne S. *The Closest of Enemies: A Personal and Diplomatic Account of U.S.-Cuban Relations Since 1957.* New York: W. W. Norton, 1987.

Stone, Elizabeth, ed. *Women and the Cuban Revolution.* New York: Pathfinder, 1981.

Notes

1. Carlos Moore, "Race Relations in Socialist Cuba," in *Socialist Cuba: Past Interpretations and Future Challenges,* ed. Sergio Roca (Boulder, CO: Westview Press, 1988), 175–206.

2. Franklin Knight, *The Caribbean* (New York: Oxford University Press, 1978), 32.

3. Ibid., 119.

4. Ramón Ruiz, *Cuba: The Making of a Revolution* (New York: W. W. Norton, 1968), 31.

5. Robert F. Smith, *The United States and Cuba* (New Haven, CT: College and University Press, 1960), 127.

6. Jaime Suchlicki, *Cuba: From Columbus to Castro,* 2nd ed., rev. (Washington, DC: Pergamon-Brassey's, 1986), 109.

7. Samuel Farber, *Revolution and Reaction in Cuba, 1933–1960* (Middletown, CT: Wesleyan University Press, 1976).

8. Suchlicki, *Cuba: From Columbus to Castro,* 125.

9. Ramón L. Bonachea and Marta San Martín, *The Cuban Insurrection, 1952–1959* (New Brunswick, NJ: Transaction Books, 1974).

10. All of the quotes appear in *Fidel y la Religión* (Santo Domingo: Editora Alfa y Omega, 1985).

11. Andrés Suárez, *Cuba: Castroism and Communism 1959–1966* (Cambridge, MA: MIT Press, 1967).

12. Nelson P. Valdés, "Radical Transformation of Cuban Education," in *Cuba in Revolution,* ed. Rolando E. Bonachea and Nelson P. Valdés (Garden City, NY: Anchor, 1972), 433.

13. Quoted from Donald C. Hodges, *The Legacy of Che Guevara: A Documentary Study* (London: Thames and Hudson), 96.

14. Carmelo Mesa-Lago, *The Economy of Socialist Cuba* (Albuquerque: University of New Mexico Press, 1981), 29.

15. On economic conditions see Eliana Cardoso and Ann Helwege, *Cuba After Communism* (Cambridge, MA: MIT Press, 1992); Carmelo Mesa-Lago, ed., *Cuba After the Cold War* (Pittsburgh: University of Pittsburgh Press, 1993); and Andrew Zimbalist, "Teetering on the Brink: Cuba's Current Economic and Political Crisis," *Journal of Latin American Studies* 24, no. 2 (1992): 407–418. For a thoughtful analysis of the health system see Julie Feinsilver, *Healing the Masses* (Berkeley: University of California Press, 1993).

16. Archibald Ritter, "The Organs of People's Power and the Communist Party: The Patterns of Cuban Democracy," in *Cuba: Twenty-Five Years of Revolution, 1959–1984,* ed. Sandor Halebsky and John M. Kirk (New York: Praeger, 1985), 286.

17. Ibid., 289.

18. "Cuba: Fourth Congress of the Cuban Communist Party," *Foreign Broadcast Information Service—Latin America* (Washington, DC, October 1991).

18

Costa Rica

Mitchell A. Seligson

Virtually all the studies comparing Central American nations contain the phrase, "with the exception of Costa Rica"; travelogues, and even many academic studies, refer to Costa Rica as the "Switzerland of Central America." The propagation of the notion of Costa Rican exceptionalism has become so widespread that the first-time tourist is likely to be surprised to find a Central American nation, not an alpine one. Yet, as with most stereotypes, there is more than a grain of truth in this one: Costa Rica is different from its neighbors in three very fundamental ways.

First, levels of social and economic development are far higher in Costa Rica than elsewhere in Central America.[1] Life expectancy at birth for Costa Ricans was seventy-eight years in 2001, exceeding by one year that of the United States and higher than any other country in Latin America. The under-five infant mortality, a universally used measure for comparing development, stood at eleven per one thousand live births in 2001, compared with forty-three in Nicaragua and thirty-eight in Honduras. In terms of the proportion of college-age students attending an institution of higher education, by 1989 Costa Rica surpassed even Switzerland, with 27 percent enrolled versus 26 percent in Switzerland. Costa Rica's rate also surpassed the United Kingdom (24 percent) and was nearly twice as high as that for El Salvador (17 percent), its closest competitor in Central America in the area of college enrollments.

Second, Costa Rica has the longest and deepest tradition of democratic governance of any nation in Central America. Indeed, experts rated Costa Rica as the most democratic country in all of Latin America for many years.[2] Civil liberties, including freedom of press, speech, and assembly, are widely respected and protected. Free and open elections have become the hallmark of Costa Rica's style of politics, with observers throughout the world seeking to

COSTA RICA

copy elements of an electoral system that faithfully guarantees against voting fraud and corruption. Human rights, so often brutally abused in other Central American nations, are carefully respected, and one rarely hears of even allegations of their violation.[3]

Third, Costa Rica is a peaceful island in a violent region. It abolished its army over forty years ago and is constitutionally prohibited from forming another one. Although there have been minor incursions and incidents over the years along Costa Rica's northern and southern borders, border guards and paramilitary units have been adequate to cope with these international conflicts. Costa Rica would be incapable of mounting a credible defense against a determined aggressor, but Costa Rica's friends in Latin America have often made it clear that they would use their military forces to deter thoughts of any such move. Indeed, on at least one occasion, Venezuela has gone so far as to land some of its air force planes in Costa Rica as a symbol of its readiness to assist. Strikes and protests are rarely violent, and negotiation is the most common mechanism for resolving disputes. Although Costa Rica has not been immune to terrorist attacks, their number and severity have been quite limited.

Costa Rica, then, stands out from its neighbors as being more advanced socially, economically, and politically and as more democratic and peaceful. There have been many attempts to determine why Costa Rica diverges from the regional pattern. Some studies have focused on historical accidents as an explanation, others on the mixture of resources (especially land and labor), and yet others on questions of ethnic homogeneity. To date, no comprehensive explanation has been established, yet partial explanations incorporating each of the mentioned features seem plausible. In this short introduction to Costa Rica these elements will be articulated as factors that seem to explain Costa Rican distinctiveness.

History and Political Culture

Costa Rica, the southernmost country in the group of five colonies that united into a loose federation shortly after gaining independence from Spain in the early 1820s, developed in isolation from its neighbors to the north. This isolation was partially a result of historical factors, since politics pivoted around Guatemala, the colonial seat of power. It was also partially the result of a geographic factor, namely, that the bulk of Costa Rica's population resided in San José, Cartago, and Heredia, towns located on the *meseta central* (central plateau), and thus was largely cut off from both the Pacific Ocean and the Caribbean Sea as well as from Nicaragua to the north and from Panama to the south.

Although Costa Rica can boast that it is more than twice the size of El Salvador, its 19,650 square miles (50,900 square kilometers) make it less than half the size of Guatemala and Honduras and only slightly more than one-third the size of Nicaragua. In U.S. terms, it is tiny—about the size of West Virginia. The usable territory is further reduced by the presence of a mountain chain that cuts through the center of the country, running from north to south. The mountain chain is studded with active volcanoes, and the most recent eruption of one in 1963 caused widespread damage to crops. The net effect of the mountains, volcanoes, and other natural formations is a reduction of arable land to an estimated 53 percent of the total land area.

Costa Rica was further weakened by the absence of large Indian populations widely found elsewhere in Central America. In Guatemala, for example, the conquering Spaniards were able to rely upon a large supply of Indians to undertake heavy labor in the mines and in the fields. Although there is evidence that prior to the conquest there were perhaps as many as four hundred thousand Indians living in the territory that was to become Costa Rica, by the end of the sixteenth century there were fewer than twenty thousand—and according to some estimates, as few as forty-five hundred by 1581.[4]

Isolation, mountains, volcanoes, and the absence of a sizable indigenous workforce do not seem to add up to a very promising base for the impressive developments that Costa Rica eventually achieved. Paradoxically, however, what seemed like disadvantages turned out to be significant advantages for Costa Rica. Isolation proved a blessing by removing the country from the civil wars and violence that so rapidly came to characterize postindependence Central America. Later, the dictatorial rule and foreign invasions that plagued the region had little direct impact on Costa Rica. Hence, in contrast to its neighbors to both the north and the south (Nicaragua and Panama), Costa Rica has never experienced an invasion of U.S. Marines. The mountains provided altitude and the volcanoes rich soil, both of which were required for what was to prove to be a highly successful coffee industry. Finally, the absence of a large indigenous population meant that the repressive labor systems (especially the encomienda system) that predominated in much of the rest of Latin America could not prosper in Costa Rica.

The colonial period in Costa Rica was one of widespread poverty. Early explorers found little of the gold and silver that so strongly stimulated Spanish migration to the New World. Had they discovered major mines, no doubt they would have found ways of importing a labor force to work them. But the mines were never found, the labor was not imported, and the flood of colonizers who settled elsewhere was only a trickle in Costa Rica. There are reports that as late as 1675 there were only five hundred to seven hundred Spanish settlers in Costa Rica, and by 1720 the number had barely exceeded three thousand. It was not until the mid-1850s that the total population of the country exceeded one hundred thousand.

The small population, both indigenous and immigrant, together with the absence of major gold and silver mines, meant that agriculture became the principal source of economic activity throughout the colonial period. Although the soil was rich and a wide variety of crops grew well, farming was directed toward subsistence agriculture. As a result, Costa Rica had little to trade in exchange for needed goods that were not available locally. The initial poverty reinforced itself by placing beyond the reach of the settlers the farm tools and other implements and artifacts needed for a more productive economy and a more comfortable lifestyle.

Throughout the colonial period efforts were made to add vitality to the fragile local economy. Attention was focused on export agriculture, especially cacao and tobacco. Both crops grew well and fetched high prices on the international market, but both eventually failed in Costa Rica. In the case of cacao, which was grown in the tropical lowlands bordering on the Caribbean Sea, marauding Indians from Nicaragua, in league with British pirates, systematically raided the plantations and stole the crop. Tobacco grew in the highlands and therefore was protected against such raids, but Spain declared a monopoly on tobacco exports and drove down profit margins for producers to the point that the cultivation of tobacco no longer proved worth the effort. By the end of the colonial period Costa Rica had not been able to find a way out of its poverty.

Independence was delivered as a gift to Costa Rica in 1821 when the isthmus, under the leadership of Guatemala, became independent from Spain. Although there was a brief period in which Costa Rica was joined with the other nations of Central America into a federation, shortly afterward independent political rule was established in the nation. Very early on in the postcolonial period the fledgling government took critical steps to help develop a stronger economic base for the country. One of these was the granting of land to all people who were willing to plant coffee on it. As a result, coffee cultivation increased dramatically in the first half of the nineteenth century, and by the 1840s direct exports of Costa Rican coffee to the markets in Europe had begun. The product was well received by the buyers and quickly achieved recognition for its high quality.

Coffee exports soon became the principal engine of economic growth for Costa Rica. The income from these exports made it possible for coffee producers to import new tools and building materials and the state was also able to invest funds in critical infrastructure projects, especially roads and ports to facilitate the production and export of coffee. One major project that grew out of the effort to facilitate coffee exports was the construction of a railroad to the Caribbean port of Limón. Until the completion of this project virtually all coffee exports had been shipped to Europe via the Pacific coast port of Puntarenas, around the tip of South America, and then to Europe. The shipping costs of the lengthy voyage were very high and reduced profits for the producers.

The railroad to the Caribbean served to cut those costs. Its construction was financed by a series of foreign loans, which Costa Rica found itself unable to repay even before the railroad was completed. As a result, the U.S.-owned firm that had contracted to build the railroad began to plant bananas to subsidize its construction. From this small start the United Fruit Company developed, and it became the major economic influence in the Caribbean tropical lowlands of Costa Rica up through the 1930s, after which time the company moved its operations to the Pacific coastal lowlands. Banana cultivation provided employment for the railroad workers who had migrated to Costa Rica from Jamaica and later for job seekers from Costa Rica's highlands. The Jamaican blacks came to be the only demographically significant ethnic minority in the country, although today they account for less than 2 percent of the population.

Coffee and bananas proved to be the mainstays of the economy through the middle of the twentieth century. Over the years coffee fields were expanded to cover a wide area along the chain of mountains that runs through the country, an expansion caused by coffee farmers in search of new land on which to grow their crop. As the territory suitable for coffee-growing shrank, settlers moved to other areas where they planted basic grains; in the higher mountain regions, they grew vegetables or raised dairy cattle. In the province of Guanacaste the broad flatlands proved suitable for cattle raising, and a major export industry of fresh beef developed between Costa Rica and the United States. When the United Fruit Company left the Caribbean lowlands because of the onset of debilitating banana diseases there, those banana fields lay abandoned until the 1950s, when the discovery of new, resistant varieties allowed other companies to reinitiate the banana industry in that area. The economy of the 1980s, then, rested upon the export of coffee, bananas, and beef. The recent introduction of so-called nontraditional crops, such as flowers, melons, tropical fruits, and vegetables, has also begun to produce significant export earnings. Costa Rica's natural beauty, accompanied by a wise policy of establishing a large network of national parks, has produced a major source of income through the establishment of a rapidly growing eco-tourism industry. Tourists come from all over the world to visit Costa Rica's rain forests and enjoy its incomparable beaches. Today tourism is second only to bananas and coffee as an earner of foreign exchange. The most recent expansion of the economy has been in the area of high technology, especially the manufacture of computer components for such giants as Intel, as well as in the export of software.

Although agriculture has been the traditional base of the economy, Costa Rica's joining the Central American Common Market in the early 1960s led to significant industrialization. By 1990 agriculture was producing only one-sixth of the gross domestic product, and industry and manufacturing nearly one-half. The growth of industry has paralleled the growth of urbanization, and today over half of the population is urban.

Politics and Parties[5]

Poverty and the absence of a wealthy ruling class that derived its power from a slave or Indian population proved to be factors that favored the development of democracy in Costa Rica. Local government had its origins in colonial Costa Rica when local *cabildos* (city councils) were established in 1812. When independence was announced a procedure was established that involved the popular election of delegates to a constitutional convention, and indirect, representative democracy was established in the first constitutional arrangements. A weak presidency was created, with the term of office limited to only three months, within a rotating directorate.

But all was not favorable for democratic rule. The system was weakened by regional rivalries between the two major population centers, San José and Cartago, and civil wars punctuated the first twenty years of independence, as did coups, assassinations, and invasions. In 1844 a new constitution was drafted and approved, and it divided the government into three separate branches: legislative, executive, and judicial. Voting rights were established, but restrictions were many: To be eligible to vote, one had to be married, male, a property owner, and at least twenty-five years of age. Less than 3 percent of the population voted in the first elections under this new constitution. But even this limited form of democracy was extinguished by a coup within two years.

Additional efforts at constitution making, more coups, and countercoups occurred until 1890. In that year a period of political stability and democratic rule was initiated that lasted, virtually unbroken, until 1948. Direct elections were instituted in 1913, and a new constitution drafted in 1917 granted numerous social guarantees to the working population. Although this document was to be replaced in 1919, in the years that followed Costa Ricans made continual improvements in the election laws and procedures. In 1925 the secret ballot was instituted, and in 1927 the Civil Registry, which made a verifiable voter-registration system possible, was established.

Political parties were first organized in the nineteenth century, but they were little more than loose, personalist coalitions built around the leading economic interests until 1940. In that year the coffee oligarchy elected Rafael Angel Calderón Guardia to power and was surprised when he quickly moved in a populist direction. Calderón, a physician who had developed a large following among the urban poor, embarked upon a major program to introduce social legislation. In 1942 he began a social security program and approved a minimum wage law. He also established an eight-hour workday and legalized unions. In 1943, after the Nazi invasion of the Soviet Union, he formed an electoral alliance with the Costa Rican Communist party, known as the Popular Vanguard party. This party, organized in 1929, had attempted to run candidates for local office in the 1932 elections, but after it was barred from doing so, it became increasingly involved in labor protests that took place during the Great Depression, especially among banana workers.

The alliance between Calderón and the Communists caused great concern and division within Costa Rica, but in the 1944 elections the alliance forces won, supporting a candidate of Calderón's choosing. With World War II over and the Cold War beginning the wartime alliance of convenience with the Communists became the target of increasingly strong protests within Costa Rica, and in 1948 a coalition of the traditional coffee oligarchy in league with young reformist social democrats defeated Calderón, who was once again running for the presidency. The legislature, however, had the responsibility of declaring the results of the election, and with Calderón's supporters in the majority, it annulled the election.

The reaction to the maneuver was swift and violent. An armed group led by José (Pepe) Figueres Ferrer organized in the mountains to the south of the capital and, aided by unionized banana workers, began a series of skirmishes with the government forces. After a brief but bloody civil war, Figueres triumphed. He took over the government and ran it for a year and a half, during which time a new constitution was drafted and approved. Although it was a modern constitution, guaranteeing a wide range of rights, it outlawed parties that were perceived as threatening to democratic rule, such as the Communist Party.

Four major consequences of the civil war of 1948 have served to shape Costa Rican politics ever since. First, the new constitution abolished the army and replaced it with a paramilitary force of civil guards. Without an army, it is far more difficult for dissenting forces to engineer a coup, and indeed, there have been no successful attempts to dislodge civilian rule since 1948. Second, Figueres did what no other successful leader of a coup in Latin America has ever done: He voluntarily turned the control of the government over to the victor of the annulled election. By doing so, he firmly established a respect for elections that had been growing in Costa Rica since the turn of the century. Third, the civil war largely delegitimized the Communist Party, and since that time, even after the elimination of the constitutional prohibition on Communist candidates' running for office, the voting strength of the Communist party has not exceeded three percent of the total presidential vote. Fourth, Figueres ushered in with him a group of social reformers who in many ways merely expanded upon programs begun by Calderón, yet also sought to spur economic development and social progress without resorting to outright socialist schemes.

Once Figueres relinquished power he began to build a new party, called the National Liberation party (PLN), to compete in the 1953 elections, which he won handily. From the moment of that election through 1998 the presidency has oscillated between control by the PLN and control by a coalition of opposition forces.

Since 1998, however, party politics in Costa Rica have been shifting. New political parties, often forming coalitions with other minor parties, have entered the electoral arena in force. At the same time, electoral abstention has been increasing substantially. The result has been that the PLN has lost much of its firm grip on the presidency. In 2002 for the first time ever, elections went into a second round because of a strong run by a third party. At the local level, that of the *cantón,* voting for third parties has become even stronger. There has also been a rapidly growing increase in the number of females in politics, first at the local level and more recently, after the approval of a quota law, at the level of the national legislature.

Governmental Structure

Since 1949 Costa Rica has operated under the constitution that grew out of the 1948 civil war. Power is shared among the president, a unicameral legislature, and the courts. Members of the legislature and the president are elected every four years. Presidents cannot be reelected, and victorious deputies cannot run for reelection in the next election but must wait a full four years. Candidates for the legislature, representing each of the seven provinces of the country, are selected by party conventions. The ability of a sitting president to implement programs has always depended upon the strength of congressional support.

In order to implement the wide range of social and economic development programs envisioned by the leaders of the PLN, numerous autonomous and semiautonomous agencies have been created. Hence, one agency handles electric and telephone services, another water supply, and yet another automobile and home insurance. These agencies have been a positive force for development and have spawned many creative ideas. For example, the automobile and home insurance agency also runs the fire department, which guarantees that it is in the insurance agency's interest to have an efficient fire-fighting service. The autonomy of these agencies has helped to isolate them from partisan political pressure. Yet, along with their autonomy has come the problem of an excessive decentralization of control. As a result, central planning and budgetary control have become extremely difficult as agencies and their functions have proliferated over the years.

Policymaking

The modern state that Costa Rica has evolved into can be largely credited with the achievements that were noted at the beginning of this chapter. The high standard of living that has been attained, however, has been built on an economy that remains largely agrarian-based. Most industrialization is of the assembly type, and as much as 90 cents of each dollar of output is made up of imported materials. The continuously growing government and parastatal (part private, part state-run) bureaucracies further increased costs without adding to production.

By the mid-1970s it was beginning to become clear that the growth model of the post–civil war period was running out of steam and that the economy could no longer support the expense of a widespread social welfare net and a bloated public sector. Yet little was done to correct the system under successive PLN presidents. Then, beginning in 1980, under the leadership of an opposition president, the system began to come apart. In order to shore up local production and consumption, and taking advantage of cheap loans being offered by foreign banks that were awash in petrodollars as a result of the dramatic rise in world petroleum prices, Costa Rica began to borrow wildly. Over a very short span of time the country's foreign debt grew to the point at which it exceeded the equivalent of the total annual national production, and by 1982 Costa Rica had one of the highest per capita foreign debts in the world. The local currency was devalued again and again, inflation and unemployment rose, and the system seemed headed for a crash.

By late 1981 the future seemed grim indeed. Yet, while similar circumstances have led to coups in other Latin American countries, Costa Ricans waited patiently for the elections of 1982, and once again voted in the PLN. A dramatic plan for recovery was put in place by the victorious president, and the plan proved successful in stabilizing the economic picture. Inflation dropped, employment rose, the currency was revalued, and an effort was made to rationalize the foreign debt. These actions restored confidence in the system, but they did not return to the citizens the benefits of the growth that had been lost during the 1980–1982 period. Belts had to be tightened, taxes were increased, and prices rose. Economic growth picked up a bit, but there was no dramatic recovery.

Throughout the 1980s Costa Rica followed a slow path to economic recovery. Under the leadership of the Central Bank's president, Eduardo Lizano, the PLN conducted a strenuous and ultimately successful effort to renegotiate important components of the foreign debt. The recovery would have been stronger if it had not been for the precipitous decline in coffee prices brought on by the collapse of the International Coffee Organization's system of quotas and prices. Throughout the period, and on into the 1990s when the opposition again took office as a result of the 1990 election, Costa Rica operated under a strict International Monetary Fund (IMF) mandate to cut public expenditures and hold down inflation. Although the IMF goals have not always been met, by 1993 the economy had essentially recovered to its pre-1980 levels, and has enjoyed modest growth ever since.

The International Arena

In 1986 the PLN broke the pattern of electoral victory that had normally oscillated between the opposition party and itself by winning the election. It did so under the leadership of Oscar Arias Sánchez, and Arias took power in an increasingly threatening international environment brought on by the crisis in Nicaragua.

When the Sandinista revolutionaries were fighting to overthrow the Somoza dictatorship in the late 1970s, they found extensive support in their neighbor to the south. Although Costa Rica remained officially neutral in that conflict, there was a long-standing antipathy for Somoza and the harsh dictatorial regime that he represented. Public support for a Sandinista victory was overwhelming, and there is much evidence that the government of Costa Rica did what it could to help.[6]

Once the Sandinistas took power, however, relations between Costa Rica and the new regime rapidly deteriorated. Costa Ricans perceived the revolution as having a Marxist-Leninist orientation, and as such, it presented two threats to Costa Rica. First, it was a threat because of the fear that Communist "expansionism" would mean Nicaragua would eventually attempt to take over Costa Rica. Second, it presented a threat to internal stability because it was feared that disgruntled Costa Ricans, especially among the university youth, would turn to revolutionary activity. In fact, in a small way the second expectation was realized. Terrorism, which had been almost unknown in Costa Rica, erupted with a number of ugly incidents in which lives were lost, and several clandestine "people's prisons" were discovered that were apparently designed to be used to hide victims of political kidnappings. With the Reagan administration in the White House, yet a third fear gripped Costa Ricans. This was the fear that the United States would invade Nicaragua, possibly using Costa Rican territory as a base of operations. Such an event would thrust Costa Rica into an international military conflict for which it was not prepared and that it did not want. Indeed, as the Iran-Contra hearings were later to demonstrate, a clandestine airstrip was built in Costa Rica to help ferry arms to the contra rebels, and a plan was developed for a so-called Southern strategy, also involving Costa Rican territory.

On top of all of these concerns was the growing problem of Nicaraguan refugees. As the contra war grew in ferocity and the Nicaraguan economy deteriorated, waves of refugees joined those already in Costa Rica who had fled the initial takeover of the Sandinistas. If the contras or a direct U.S. invasion were able to overthrow the Sandinistas, it was feared there would be yet another, far larger wave of immigrants made up of the defeated Sandinistas, who, it was not doubted, would begin planning for a new invasion. In short, Costa Ricans mortally feared being caught up in an impossible international conflict that could only result in deep harm being done to their country's national economy, society, and moral fiber.

Upon assuming office Oscar Arias dedicated himself to bringing peace to the region. Bringing peace was not only appropriate for a country that had long been noted for its internal peace and lack of an army but it was also urgently needed if Costa Rica hoped to avoid the problems noted above. Arias managed to draw together the leaders of all of the Central American countries and develop a peace plan that was not only to involve Nicaragua but would also serve to end the civil war in El Salvador and the guerrilla war in Guatemala. For his efforts Arias was awarded the Nobel Peace Prize.

In recent years there has been an effort to focus on trade relations with the U.S. While Costa Rica has always remained skeptical of joining with its neighbors in the region, in 2005 the Central American Free Trade Agreement (CAFTA) was approved by the U.S. government. If all nations in the region ratify it, Costa Rica will form part of a growing trade bloc.

Conclusions

In the 1990 elections the PLN lost the presidency to an opposition coalition led by the son of Calderón Guardia. Within a few months of this loss the Sandinistas in Nicaragua were defeated in an upset election. These two elections saw the new decade emerging with new leadership in these two Central American neighbors. The dominant parties of the decade of the 1980s, the PLN in Costa Rica and the Sandinista National Liberation Front in Nicaragua, were being asked by the voters to take a backseat and allow fresh faces to try their hand at economic development, democratization, and peace. The dramatic changes in the Soviet Union and Eastern Europe did not go unnoticed in Central America, as capitalism and democracy rapidly began to replace socialism and dictatorship. In this context, peaceful, democratic Costa Rica faces new opportunities for regional leadership as the one country in Central America with a long tradition of democracy. On the domestic scene the ability of coffee, banana, and beef exports to cover the costs of financing growth is clearly limited. Nontraditional exports and tourism are helping, however. Costa Rica's open, democratic style of governance seems to enable the country to withstand crises that would cause others to wilt. If the past is any guide to the future, Costa Rica will rise to the test and overcome its problems.

New challenges faced Costa Rica as the century drew to a close. Democratic rights were being expanded as a result of the creation of the "Sala IV," a constitutional court, which has been augmenting individual liberties at a rapid pace. Yet, many Costa Ricans wonder if this movement has gone too far, and there are signs of growing discontent. In the new century Costa Rica has had incidents of mass protest that it had not experienced before. As already noted, voting abstention, historically never very high, has increased markedly, a sign for some of growing disenchantment with the political system.[7] Political leaders have been sensitive to this shift in voter sentiment and have begun a new process of institutional reform that promises to maintain Costa Rican politics on an even keel, but many feel that the old parties are not capable of real democratization. Corruption scandals have become more widespread and have reached higher than ever before, implicating several former presidents. If past is any guide to the future, however, Costa Ricans will find a way to retain their democratic and peaceful traditions.

Suggestions for Further Reading

Bell, John Patrick. *Crisis in Costa Rica.* Austin: University of Texas Press, 1971.

Biesanz, Richard, Karen Zubris Biesanz, and Mavis Hiltunen Biesanz. *The Costa Ricans.* Englewood Cliffs, NJ: Prentice-Hall, 1982.

Booth, John A. *Costa Rica: Quest for Democracy.* Boulder, CO: Westview Press, 1998.

Edelman, Marc, and Joanne Kenan, eds. *The Costa Rica Reader.* New York: Grove Weidenfeld, 1989.

Gudmundson, Lowell. *Costa Rica Before Coffee: Society and Economy on the Eve of the Export Boom.* Baton Rouge: Louisiana State University Press, 1986.

Hall, Carolyn. *Costa Rica: A Geographical Interpretation in Historical Perspective.* Boulder, CO: Westview Press, 1985.

Hall, Carolyn, and Héctor Pérez Brignoli. *Historical Atlas of Central America.* Norman: University of Oklahoma Press, 2003.

Seligson, Mitchell A. *Peasants of Costa Rica and the Development of Agrarian Capitalism.* Madison: University of Wisconsin Press, 1980.

———. "Ordinary Elections in Extraordinary Times: The Political Economy of Voting in Costa Rica." In *Elections and Democracy in Central America,* ed. John A. Booth and Mitchell A. Seligson, 158–184. Chapel Hill: University of North Carolina Press, 1989.

Seligson, Mitchell A., and Edward N. Muller. "Democratic Stability and Economic Crisis: Costa Rica, 1978–1983." *International Studies Quarterly* 31 (September 1987): 301–326.

Vargas-Cullell, Jorge, Luis Rosero-Bixby, and Mitchell A. Seligson. *La Cultura política de la democracia en Costa Rica, 2004.* San José, Costa Rica: Centro Centroamericano de Población (CCP), 2005.

Winson, Anthony. *Coffee and Democracy in Modern Costa Rica.* New York: St. Martin's Press, 1989.

Yashar, Deborah J. *Demanding Democracy: Reform and Reaction in Costa Rica and Guatemala, 1870s–1950s* (Stanford, CA: Stanford University Press, 1997).

Notes

1. The data in this paragraph are drawn from the World Bank, *World Development Report, 2003* (New York: Oxford University Press, 2003) and The United Nations Development Program, *Human Development Report, 2003* (New York: Oxford University Press, 2003).

2. See the various years of the Freedom House index.

3. The Latin American Studies Association reports that the National Reconciliation Commission established as part of the Central American peace accord of 1987 found that "no one in Costa Rica claimed that there were systematic violations of human rights or denial of freedom of expression in the country" (Latin American Studies Association, "Final Report of the LASA Commission on Compliance with the Central America Peace Accord" [Pittsburgh: LASA, March 15, 1988], 8).

4. Hall reports 17,166 in 1569 (Ibid., 72), whereas another source reports the lower figure (Mitchell A. Seligson, *Peasants of Costa Rica and the Development of Agrarian Capitalism.* Madison: University of Wisconsin Press, 1980, 4).

5. This section draws on Mitchell A. Seligson, "Costa Rica and Jamaica," in *Competitive Elections in Developing Countries,* ed. Myron Weiner and Ergun Ozbudun (Durham, NC: Duke University Press, 1987).

6. See Mitchell A. Seligson and William Carroll, "The Costa Rican Role in the Sandinista Victory," in *Nicaragua in Revolution,* ed. Thomas W. Walker (New York: Praeger, 1982), 331–344.

7. Seligson, Mitchell A. "Trouble in Paradise: The Impact of the Erosion of System Support in Costa Rica, 1978–1999." *Latin America Research Review* 37, no. 1 (2002): 160–185.

19

Nicaragua
The Politics of Frustration

Richard L. Millett

Nicaragua, largest in area of the Central American Republics, has a history marked by unfulfilled promises, frustrated hopes, and violent internal conflicts and external interventions. The Sandinista revolution of 1979–1990 now seems to be yet another episode in this dreary history. Obsessed with the past and dominated by conflicting personal ambitions, Nicaragua's political system offers few solutions to the nation's overwhelming social and economic problems.

Despite—or perhaps because of—this history, Nicaragua has enjoyed disproportionate attention from U.S. scholars and political activists. Ruled briefly in the nineteenth century by an American filibuster, William Walker; occupied twice by the U.S. Marines in the first third of the twentieth century; and the scene of a nearly decade-long conflict between a Marxist regime and U.S.-sponsored counterrevolutionary insurgents in the 1980s, the nation has frequently been the subject of fierce policy debates within the United States. The United States and other nations have also been interested in Nicaragua's potential as an interoceanic canal route. In addition, the Sandinista revolution in 1979 seemed to present an opportunity to test both the potential for social revolution in Central America and the possibility of creating a less dogmatic socialist state. Such hopes, like Nicaragua's aspirations to be the site of a canal, would remain unfulfilled.

History

From the colonial period until the present Nicaragua has been the scene of international rivalries. Its indigenous population was decimated, in part, to

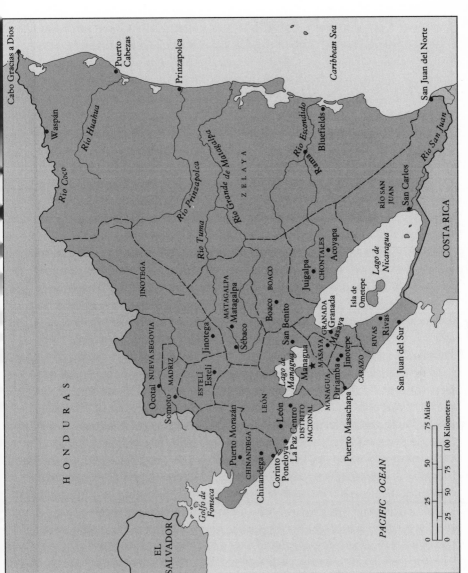

NICARAGUA

HONDURAS

EL SALVADOR

Cabo Gracias a Dios

Waspán

Río Coco

Río Huahua

Puerto Cabezas

Prinzapolca

Río Prinzapolca

Río Grande de Matagalpa

ZELAYA

Río Tuma

JINOTEGA

Río Escondido

Rama

Bluefields

Caribbean Sea

San Juan del Norte

Río San Juan

RÍO SAN JUAN

San Carlos

San Juan del Sur

COSTA RICA

Lago de Nicaragua

Isla de Ometepe

Juigalpa

CHONTALES

Acoyapa

BOACO

Boaco

San Benito

MATAGALPA

Matagalpa

Sébaco

Jinotega

Jinotega

Ocotal

NUEVA SEGOVIA

Somoto

MADRIZ

ESTELÍ

Estelí

LEÓN

León

Poneloya

Corinto

Chinandega

CHINANDEGA

Golfo de Fonseca

Puerto Morazán

La Paz Centro

DISTRITO NACIONAL

Lago de Managua

Managua

MANAGUA

Dirimba

Jinotepe

CARAZO

MASAYA

Masaya

GRANADA

Granada

RIVAS

Rivas

Puerto Masachapa

PACIFIC OCEAN

0   25   50   75 Miles
0 25 50 75 100 Kilometers

provide labor for the mines of Peru. The British waged a prolonged conflict over the rule of the Caribbean Coast and competed with the United States for control over the potential transisthmian canal route. The nineteenth-century filibustering expedition of William Walker reflected both rivalries over control of the isthmian transit route and plans to annex lands for the expansion of slavery. It also was a product of the interminable civil conflicts between the Liberal and Conservative parties, both of which at times preferred foreign intervention to defeat at the hands of their domestic opponents. Ultimately, fear of reviving the slavery issue led the Pierce Administration to cut off supplies and reinforcements to Walker, thwarting his ambition to rule Central America and underscoring the U.S. tendency to determine regional polices based on domestic political issues. Washington's decision to build a canal through Panama rather than Nicaragua damaged relations and led to the 1912 Marine intervention. Fearing that Nicaragua's Liberals might grant a canal concession to some other nation, the United States entered into a de facto alliance with the Conservatives, with the presence of a small Marine unit ensuring Conservative rule until the mid-1920s.

The United States then attempted to withdraw the Marines and promote honest elections and a professional military, but these efforts only contributed to another civil conflict and a much larger intervention in 1927. Washington imposed a peace settlement on Nicaragua's warring factions, providing for general disarmament, U.S. supervision of the next two presidential elections, and the creation of a U.S.-officered and -trained constabulary force to be known as the National Guard.

One Liberal general, Augusto César Sandino, rejected the terms and launched a guerrilla war against the Marines and the National Guard. Although never able to seriously threaten the government, Sandino's resistance endured until the last Marines departed at the start of 1933. Sandino then negotiated peace terms but, a year later, was murdered by the National Guard.

That force's commander, General Anastasio Somoza García, used the Guard to propel himself into the presidency in 1936, inaugurating over forty-two years of Somoza family rule. The Somozas used three basic instruments—control of the National Guard, manipulation of the Liberal Party, and the image of a close alliance with the United States—to perpetuate themselves in power. In the process they amassed vast personal wealth and established a network of corruption. The dynasty's founder was assassinated in 1956, but his sons Luís and Anastasio Somoza Debayle managed to hold on to power. They provided the United States with the launching pad for the abortive 1961 Bay of Pigs invasion of Cuba and, in turn, Fidel Castro supported the creation of an anti-Somoza insurgency. When the Somozas used the devastating 1971 earthquake that leveled Managua to further enrich themselves and their cronies, popular discontent increased dramatically. A Marxist guerrilla movement, the Sandinista Liberation Front (FSLN), had been in existence since the early 1960s, but now it began to attract support from wider elements of society. When opposition newspaper editor and political leader Pedro Joaquín Chamorro was murdered in early 1978 popular discontent exploded. Political and economic pressures exerted by business leaders, with some support from the Carter administration, failed to oust President Anastasio Somoza Debayle, and national and international support increasingly coalesced around the Sandinistas. After a prolonged and bloody struggle, the Sandinistas forced Somoza into exile and occupied the capital in July 1979.

Sandinista leaders initially convinced non-FSLN politicians and business leaders to cooperate with the FSLN in forming a broad-based government. However, it soon became clear that real power lay with the nine-member Sandinista National Directorate, which was intent on creating a controlled economy, supporting other Central American insurgency movements, and establishing close ties with Cuba and the Soviet Union. Internal political conflict increased, and with the inauguration of the Reagan administration in 1981 the United States began to support armed resistance to Sandinista rule. Known as contras, these forces inflicted significant economic damage, but were never able to seriously challenge Sandinista power. Elections were held in 1984 but, protesting conditions that they claimed made effective participation impossible, major elements of the internal political opposition boycotted the process. The FSLN used these elections to consolidate control, installing party leader Daniel Ortega as president and adopting a new constitution that incorporated the aims and principles of a Socialist revolution. However, a combination of the costs of the ongoing contra war, the impact of a U.S. economic boycott, and the FSLN's own economic mismanagement ultimately devastated the economy and undermined FSLN efforts to consolidate their control.

A combination of mediation by Central America's presidents and a decision by the Bush administration to pursue negotiated solutions to Central America's conflicts led to internationally supervised elections in 1990. To the surprise of the FSLN, these were won decisively by a fourteen-party coalition headed by Violetta Barios de Chamorro, widow of Pedro Joaquín. The FSLN, however, remained the largest bloc in the legislature. To govern effectively, the Chamorro administration made working agreements with the FSLN, including leaving General Humberto Ortega, brother of ex-president Daniel Ortega, in command of the military. This, however, broke up Chamorro's own coalition and created new problems with the U.S. Congress.

Under the Chamorro administration, Nicaragua experienced six years of political turmoil, economic crisis, and citizen insecurity. Determined to "govern from below," the FSLN promoted strikes, obstructed legislation, and resisted military reforms. Conservative elements ultimately gained control of the legislature and engaged in a fierce battle with the administration over constitutional amendments. Jobless and landless, former members of both the contra and Sandinista forces again took up arms, returning some rural areas to a virtual state of war. Despite all this, some progress was made. Annual inflation, which under FSLN rule had passed 30,000 percent, fell to under 20 percent. The strength of the military was greatly reduced, the police brought under government control, and the draft ended. Most contras disarmed and some refugees returned. Humberto Ortega was eventually replaced as military commander, demonstrating a loss of FSLN control over the armed forces.

After a bitter fight the constitution was amended to reduce executive powers, protect private property, depoliticize the military, and bar the reelection of the president or of any close relative. Finally, the Chamorro administration conducted reasonably fair—if far from perfect—elections in 1996 and peacefully transferred power to another party. The 1996 elections produced over twenty candidates, but quickly became a race between Daniel Ortega of the FSLN and an alliance of Nicaragua's fractionated Liberals, headed by Managua Mayor Jose Arnaldo Alemán. Alemán was elected president with 51 percent of the vote to 37.7 percent for Ortega. The Alemán administration managed to improve relations with the United States, but the economy remained a disaster and charges of corruption threatened to engulf the regime. In addition, the devastation of Hurricane Mitch in 1998 further undermined efforts at economic recovery. By the end of his term Alemán was seeking means to ensure his immunity from future prosecution. Constitutional amendments, approved by the legislature at the start of 2000, reduced the role of smaller parties, undercut the independence of the Comptroller General's office, and made it more difficult to convict a president.

A combination of the changes in the electoral system, fears of a Sandinista return to power, and pressures from the United States insured the victory in the 2001 elections of Alemán's hand-picked candidate, his Vice President Enrique Bolaños Geyer. But once in office President Bolaños turned on his predecessor, actively seeking his prosecution for massive corruption. He succeeded in getting Alemán convicted and imprisoned, but it cost him the support of the Liberal Party, leaving him with only a small minority support in Congress and producing efforts by the Liberals to form an alliance with the FSLN and force him from office. Alemán continued to control the party even while under house arrest and, often in alliance with the FSLN, gained control of the legislature and used it against Bolaños. Nicaragua entered into a prolonged period of political paralysis as various factions maneuvered to gain an advantage in the scheduled 2006 elections.

Social Structure

Nicaragua, at the beginning of the twenty-first century, had a population of approximately 4.5 million. Most Nicaraguans are *mestizos*. Some Indians along the Caribbean coast remain ethnically distinct. There is also a strong Afro-Caribbean influence on the Atlantic coast, where much of the population emigrated from the British Caribbean. Because of its ethnic makeup and its isolation from the rest of the nation, the Caribbean coast was granted a measure of political and cultural autonomy in 1987.

The majority of Nicaraguans are Roman Catholic, but Protestant groups have made major inroads, and the nation today is perhaps 15 percent Evangelical. An evangelical political party finished third in the 1996 elections.

Nicaragua is the largest Central American nation in area and its economy is heavily dependent on agriculture. Nevertheless, it is also the region's most urbanized nation. Flows of refugees from conflict in the countryside exacerbated this situation in the 1980s and 1990s, and today the nation is over 60 percent urban. Unemployment and underemployment often run above 50 percent in urban areas. Nicaragua has the hemisphere's second-lowest GNP per capita and Central America's highest infant mortality rate.

Both business and labor are relatively well organized in Nicaragua. Many of the largest labor and peasant organizations are controlled by the FSLN. The major business group, the Superior Council of Private Enterprise (COSEP), was a center of anti-Sandinista opposition. Its former president, Enrique Bolaños, is Nicaragua's current president.

In contrast to most of the hemisphere, the military has never been a truly autonomous actor in Nicaraguan politics. It was first the tool of traditional parties, then the instrument of a foreign intervention, then the guardians of a prolonged family dynasty, and finally the bulwark of support for a revolutionary political project. Today, its ties to the FSLN have considerably weakened, and it is becoming more like a traditional Central American military. Several regular changes of command have taken place, fears that it would intervene in the political process have largely evaporated, and its size has been greatly reduced. It even sent a contingent to Iraq. Today the greatest remaining issue is disposal of its aging surface-to-air missiles, which Washington fears might find their way into terrorist hands.

Nicaragua's mass media have always been highly politicized. Under the Somozas, and again under the Sandinistas the newspaper *La Prensa*, controlled by the Chamorro family, became a symbol of resistance to the regime in power. Over the last forty years radio has become even more important than print media in efforts to boost support for or mobilize opposition to a particular regime. Television, too, has steadily increased its influence. By the mid-1990s there were nearly a quarter of a million television sets. Television was largely government controlled until the 1990s, but today both national channels and widely available foreign programming reflect a wide variety of views.

Political Institutions and Parties

Nicaragua is governed under the Sandinista-authored constitution of 1987, but this was significantly altered by a series of amendments adopted in 1995. In many ways the government structure follows traditional Central American patterns, with a unicameral legislature, a prohibition on immediate presidential reelection, an independent electoral authority, a Supreme Court, and numerous autonomous agencies. Local government consists of two levels—departmental and municipal. There are fifteen departments plus the two semi-autonomous regions along the Caribbean coast. Outside of these coastal regions, departments are generally dominated by the central government, but municipal governments have had a growing degree of autonomy.

Beginning in 1990 Nicaraguans elected municipal officials directly. The powers of municipal government were strengthened, and mayors became the most important local political figures, as illustrated by Alemán's use of that post in Managua to rise to national prominence. At least fifteen Nicaraguan cities have populations over fifty thousand, and metropolitan Managua's population is about two million.

Under the rule of the Somoza family the executive branch was totally dominant, and the legislature and courts generally rubber-stamped whatever the president wanted. The FSLN's 1987 constitution strengthened executive authority even further. In both cases there was an extra-constitutional power that controlled the government. Under the Somozas this was the Somoza family and the National Guard. Under the Sandinistas it was the FSLN's nine-member national directorate. Today, political power is largely in the hands of elected officials. The president and vice president are elected for five-year terms and, along with close family members, are barred from immediate reelection. Presidential powers have been broad, including the right to propose a budget, appoint cabinet members and other high officials, and, prior to 1995, to rule by decree. These powers were significantly reduced by the 1995 amendments, but the president still retained considerable independent authority, especially if a state of national emergency is declared. In 2005 the National Assembly adopted a series of changes designed to further curb presidential powers. President Bolaños denounced these as illegal and was supported by the other Central American nations and the United States, but the legislature claims they are in effect, further contributing to the political deadlock.

Nicaragua's unicameral legislature has ninety-three members. Complex constitutional provisions provide that twenty seats be elected from national party lists and seventy be elected departmentally, under a system of proportionate representation. In addition, defeated presidential candidates who win a bit over 1 percent of the vote are also given a seat. This encouraged a proliferation of parties, with eleven actually winning one or more seats in 1996. But in 2001 only the Liberal Alliance, the FSLN and the Conservatives (who won just one seat) gained seats in the legislature. Electoral law reforms in 2000 had changed the system, curbing the proliferation of smaller parties but also concentrating power in the hands of the two dominant parties. The revised constitution gives the Legislative Assembly broad powers, including the ability to enact laws, override presidential vetoes with a simple majority vote, and amend the constitution with a 60 percent majority. Under present circumstances this is virtually impossible unless the Liberals and the FSLN agree.

As in much of Latin America, a weak judicial system presents a significant obstacle to efforts at democratic consolidation. Nicaragua has little tradition of an independent judiciary, and partisan efforts to manipulate the Supreme Court are constant. As a result the Court, at times, is unable to function. Lower courts are poorly staffed and overwhelmed by the rising crime rate. Conviction rates in criminal cases have run under 5 percent. One result is that prisoners often spend prolonged periods of incarceration before coming to trial. Prisons are badly overcrowded and conditions fall well below minimal international standards.

A fourth power is the Supreme Electoral Council (CSE), which not only runs elections and certifies the results but also controls the Civil Register and issues citizens their identity cards (*cédulas*). In January 2000 an agreement between the Liberals and the FSLN reformed the electoral law, eliminating provisions requiring broad representation of political parties in the administration of local polling stations and giving the CSE virtual carte blanche in the appointment of these officials. The seven members of the CSE would be appointed by the Legislative Assembly and would need the approval of 60 percent of those voting. This ensured that the FSLN and the Liberals would have to agree on members and that smaller parties would have no effective voice in the process. To gain a place on the ballot any party that failed to win 3 percent of the vote in the previous general election must obtain the signatures of 3 percent of eligible voters. Only the Liberal Alliance, the FSLN, and the Nicaraguan Christian Way (CCN) qualified for exemption from this provision. Nicaragua's Conservative Party managed to gain a spot on the 2001 ballot but its presidential candidate only garnered 1.4 percent of the vote. Municipal elections in 2004 gave control of most of Nicaragua's cities to the

FSLN. Elections for president, vice president, and assembly members are set for late 2006. Suffrage is universal for those sixteen and older. In presidential elections there will be a second round of voting between the two leading candidates if the leading candidate does not obtain 40 percent of the vote or 35 percent or more with a margin of 5 percent over the second place candidate. The CSE will set the date for this election, but it must be within forty-five days of the general election.

Among the most important of the autonomous governmental institutions are the Central Bank and the Office of the Comptroller. The Central Bank controls the currency, disburses government funds, and exercises some control over private banks. The Comptroller oversees the disbursement of government funds and audits government accounts. Both have been the scene of bitter partisan fights. In 1990 the Central Bank disbursed over $24 million of government funds to individual Sandinista leaders in the last weeks of Sandinista rule.

Nicaragua has dozens of political parties, many of which exist only to promote individual ambitions and have no national structure. Only three currently have the right to a place on the ballot. The political scene is dominated by the Liberal Alliance and the FSLN. The Liberal Alliance is headed by President Alemán and merges three elements of Nicaragua's traditional Liberal Party. Because this party was long the vehicle of the Somoza dynasty it is frequently accused of having ties with elements of that regime. The party has strong support among Nicaragua's upper and middle classes. It is probusiness, generally supportive of the United States in international affairs, and has traditionally been strongly anti-Sandinista. Today it seems equally preoccupied with opposing President Bolaños and has forged a pact with the FSLN to oppose Bolaños and inhibit efforts of other parties and/or political alliances to gain legal status. It suffered major defeats in the 2004 municipal elections.

The FSLN has modified its Marxist rhetoric and now portrays itself as more of a social democratic party. It has strong support within the labor movement and in other mass popular organizations. It advocates increased government control over the economy, expanded social welfare policies, and an independent foreign policy. Its support has been damaged by a reputation for corruption derived from the massive looting of state resources at the end of its period in power; by deep internal divisions that resulted in the defection of some of the leadership before the 1996 elections; and by personal scandals revolving around the Party's leader, former-president Daniel Ortega. In 2004 Managua mayor Herty Lewites tried to challenge Ortega for the FSLN's presidential nomination. Despite polls showing him a clear popular favorite his efforts were blocked and he was expelled from the party. Despite its internal divisions the party significantly increased its strength in the 2004 municipal elections.

Nicaragua's other parties account for less than one-fifth of the electorate. President Bolaños has tried to unify parts of the Liberal and Conservative Parties along with the Social Christian Party into a new Alliance for the Republic (APRE) but this won only 12 percent of the vote in the 2004 municipal elections. The CCN, which won just over 4 percent of the vote in 1996, represents an effort to convert the growing community of Nicaraguan evangelicals into a political force. However, this community is itself deeply divided, the party lacks experienced leaders and grassroots organization, and its future is far from assured.

Nicaragua's traditional Conservative Party is divided into several factions, and many of its supporters voted for Alemán in 1996 to ensure a Sandinista defeat. It gained a spot on the 2001 ballot, but pressures to support Bolaños in order to avert a possible Ortega victory and a lack of funds contributed to its winning only 1.4 percent of the vote. The Christian Democrats are smaller and even more divided, and their future is more problematical. Other political factions, including the Sandinista Renewal Movement (MRS), led by former vice president Sergio Ramírez, will have an even more difficult time gaining the legal status necessary to participate in future elections. This will both encourage new alliances and work to reduce significantly the number of political parties. In August 2005 the tiny Alternative Christian Party announced its support for Lewites for president in 2006 and it was widely expected that other parties such as the MRS would try to join with it in a new electoral alliance.

Public Policy

Nicaragua's public policies at the start of the twenty-first century are a strange mixture of the revolutionary heritage of the Sandinistas and the conservative policies of the current administration. Ratification of a free trade agreement with the United States is a major issue. Efforts to keep inflation under control have been undermined by persistent budget deficits. In addition, the decline in coffee prices has badly hurt export earnings. The prevailing climate of corruption has jeopardized many international aid sources and held up agreements with the International Monetary Fund. Industry has lagged behind other sectors in the limited economic recovery that has occurred, further exacerbating the high rate of urban unemployment. Economic growth in 2004 was the best in many years, but rising petroleum prices and domestic political turmoil threaten future prospects.

The Bolaños administration has made some efforts to deal with the crisis in social welfare, health, and education, but its lack of support in the Assembly has crippled its efforts. Privatization efforts are well advanced, but the combined effects of a lack of investor confidence, continued concerns over

Sandinista influence, and high-level corruption have produced disappointing results.

Nicaragua's external debt totals over $6 billion. Prospects for debt forgiveness by foreign governments and international financial organizations seemed significantly enhanced in the wake of Hurricane Mitch. Nicaragua was included in the World Bank's "Highly Indebted Poor Countries" program, making it eligible for the forgiveness of up to 80 percent of its debt, but this has been limited by the ongoing political crisis. The nation consistently runs a high deficit in its current accounts and depends on external aid to cover this. It even depends on foreign assistance for such basic programs as conducting elections.

Nicaragua has little in the way of a regular civil service. Most government positions, at both the national and local level, are seen as rewards for political support. The bureaucracy has been reduced from the massive levels it reached in the 1980s, but is still inefficient and widely viewed as corrupt. Disputes over political patronage are a constant theme because apportioning positions is both a major motivation for and a constant source of tension in the formation and maintenance of political alliances.

Foreign Policy

Nicaragua's foreign policy revolves around three principal foci. These are the maintenance of good relations with the United States; the constant search for foreign assistance and debt relief; and relations with other Central American nations, notably territorial issues with Honduras and Costa Rica.

Initiatives in these areas are, at times, openly contradictory. The Bolaños administration has been a strong supporter of free trade arrangements with the United States (CAFTA) but has been unable to secure ratification in the Assembly. Other Central American governments have tried to support the administration in its struggles with the Assembly, but have had little apparent impact. Foreign policy is further hampered by the tendency to make major appointments on the basis of domestic political considerations rather than competency, by the deteriorating international image of both major parties, and by persistent property disputes dating back to the 1979 revolution.

Despite open U.S. efforts to topple the Sandinista regime, formal diplomatic relations were never broken off. The inauguration of President Chamorro ended these tensions, but other issues soon arose. Conservative circles in the United States, often centered around Senator Jesse Helms (R-NC), opposed the Chamorro administration's working arrangements with the FSLN and made a constant issue of property claims against the government advanced by Nicaraguans living in the United States. Aid and loans were held up, contacts with the Nicaraguan military were blocked, and investment discouraged. Relations improved somewhat under the Alemán administration. Progress was made in resolving the property issue and some military-to-military contacts were established. Fears that the United States might force the return of thousands of Nicaraguans who had fled north in the 1980s were eased by executive actions that granted most an indefinite stay. This was of crucial importance for Nicaragua, not only because their return would have exacerbated unemployment but because remittances from Nicaraguans in the United States and elsewhere were a major source of hard currency. The Bolaños administration attempted to improve relations with the United States, but its efforts were handicapped by domestic political turmoil and by the emerging issue of disposal of the surface-to-air missiles. Nicaraguan governments over the past decade have had generally good relations with Europe and with some of the international financial institutions. The Scandinavian nations were especially forthcoming with assistance. Spain and other members of the European Union also provided vital assistance. Hurricane Mitch did produce a new outpouring of assistance, but increased evidence of corruption, the failure of the government to undertake needed economic reforms, and the constant political conflict caused nations such as Denmark and Sweden to slow aid disbursements and begin to seek greater conditionality.

Relations with other Central American states were very tense during the Sandinista years. Nicaragua's support for regional revolutionary movements created constant problems with El Salvador. The contras' use of Honduras and Costa Rica as bases for actions against the Sandinistas and the presence of large numbers of Nicaraguan refugees in both nations not only produced political problems but also led to a series of bitter clashes which, in the Honduran case, frequently spilled over the border. For a time fears of a regional war were quite real. Ultimately, however, a regional initiative, led by Costa Rican President Oscar Arias, helped resolve the tensions and end the contra war.

Relations under the Chamorro administration were largely quiet. Many of the refugees returned home, and the emphasis was on rebuilding regional cooperation rather than preparing for armed conflict. The continued presence of large numbers of Nicaraguans in Costa Rica was a source of some concern, but never approached the point of crisis. A Central American parliament was created; regional presidents met frequently; and fears of regional war vanished.

Under the Alemán administration a series of border disputes with both Costa Rica and Honduras, combined with Nicaraguan anger over Honduran recognition of Colombia's claim to disputed areas in the Caribbean, produced renewed tensions, and the Bolaños administration has been unable to resolve these issues. In addition, Nicaragua's continued economic crisis has provided a major obstacle to regional growth and development.

An Uncertain Future

Nicaragua's future, as the 2006 elections loom, is uncertain at best. Although there seems little danger of a return to the open violence of previous decades, armed bands still roam remote areas and both common and organized criminal activity is at near-record levels. Politics remain mired in bitter conflicts, reflecting both personal rivalries and past disputes. The population seems increasingly cynical about the entire process, seeing little hope offered by any party and believing that corruption and extreme partisanship will continue to be the norm. Should the Liberals and the FSLN work together to deny Lewites a place on the 2006 ballot these attitudes will undoubtedly deepen. The nation's reservoir of international sympathy and goodwill, generated by the events of the 1970s and 1980s and reinforced by the impact of Hurricane Mitch, seems increasingly exhausted. Social conditions are terrible, poverty is endemic, much of the infrastructure is inadequate and worn out, and both human and financial capital tend to seek foreign prospects.

Nicaragua is not without important assets. Rural areas are generally not overpopulated, and the nation has some of the best soils in the hemisphere. Its geographic position offers several advantages, especially if a project to improve traffic to the Atlantic via the San Juan River reaches fruition. International contacts forged in the past two decades, along with the considerable resources of the Nicaraguan Diaspora, notably those in Miami, are significant potential assets.

The situation is far from hopeless, but the key will be developing a credible, competent political leadership concerned more with national well-being than with personal aggrandizement. Unfortunately, the nation has little tradition of such leadership, and the most likely prospect seems to be continued suffering and turmoil for the bulk of the population.

Suggestions for Further Reading

Literature on Nicaragua is extensive, but much of that produced in recent decades is highly partisan and of limited value. Other works are narrowly specialized. The following are recommended as starting points for a fuller understanding of Nicaragua's past and present.

Booth, John A. *The End and the Beginning: The Nicaraguan Revolution*. Boulder, CO: Westview Press, 1985.
Christian, Shirley. *Revolution in the Family*. New York: Vintage, 1986.
Close, David. *Nicaragua: The Chamorro Years*. Boulder, CO: Lynne Rienner, 1999.

Colburn, Forrest D. *Post-Revolutionary Nicaragua*. Berkeley and Los Angeles: University of California Press, 1986.

Gilbert, Dennis. *Sandinistas: The Party and the Revolution*. Malden, MA: Basil Blackwell, 1988.

Gutman, Roy. *Banana Diplomacy: The Making of American Policy in Nicaragua*. New York: Simon & Schuster, 1988.

Kirk, John M. *Politics and the Catholic Church in Nicaragua*. Gainesville: University Press of Florida, 1992.

Macaulay, Neill. *The Sandino Affair*. Durham, NC: Duke University Press, 1985.

Merrill, Tim L., ed. *Nicaragua: A Country Study*. Washington, DC: Government Printing Office, 1994.

Millett, Richard. *Guardians of the Dynasty*. New York: Orbis, 1977.

Pastor, Robert. *Condemned to Repetition: The United States and Nicaragua*. Princeton, NJ: Princeton University Press, 1987.

Seligson, Mitchell, and John Booth, eds. *Elections and Democracy in Central America Revisited*. Pittsburgh: University of Pittsburgh Press, 1995.

Spalding, Rose. *Capitalists and Revolution in Nicaragua: Opposition and Accommodation, 1979–1993*. Chapel Hill: University of North Carolina Press, 1995.

Walter, Knut. *The Regime of Anastasio Somoza, 1936–1956*. Chapel Hill: University of North Carolina Press, 1993.

20

El Salvador

Tommie Sue Montgomery and Christine J. Wade

"El Salvador is such a beautiful country," Catholic lay missioner Jean Donovan wrote home not long before she and three nuns were murdered by the Salvadoran National Guard in December 1980. "Where else would you see roses in December?"

This paradox—the extraordinary beauty of volcanoes, lakes, and Pacific coastline on one hand, and the intentional violence of a political system whose leaders were more committed to maintaining themselves in power than to addressing the profound socioeconomic needs of the population on the other—has characterized much of El Salvador's history since Spaniards first arrived in 1522. Still, the decade of the 1990s witnessed unprecedented efforts, following eleven years of civil war, to upend the second half of this paradox: to establish a competitive and honest electoral system, a functioning judiciary, an apolitical military, a civilian police force—in short, an open, democratic political system.

For these reasons El Salvador offers a model of how to move from war to peace, how to create (however imperfect) democratic processes, and how to change the political culture of a country in less than a decade.

Background

Geography

El Salvador is the only country in Central America without an "Atlantic coast"—or, more accurately, a Caribbean coast. About the size of Massachusetts (21,040 square kilometers) and lying east to west, it is bordered by Honduras on the north, Guatemala on the west, and the Gulf of Fonseca (on the

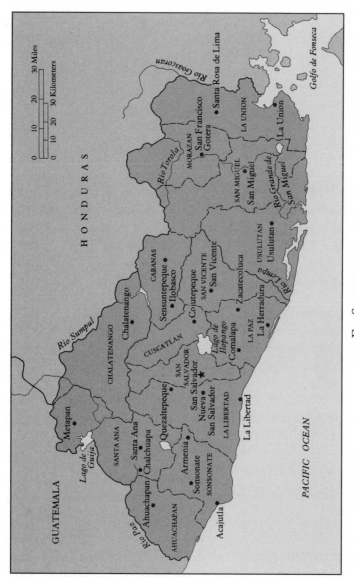

El Salvador

other side of which lies Nicaragua) on the east. From the black volcanic sand of the flat Pacific coast, to the necklace of volcanoes that dot the landscape from west to east and the volcanic lakes in between, to the mountains in the north, El Salvador is a country of dramatic contrasts. Its tropical climate, only ten degrees north of the equator, means that it enjoys two seasons: wet (May–October) and dry (November–April). In the rainy season the country is a lush green; the rest of the year it is brown and arid. These conditions have been exacerbated over the last half century by increasing deforestation, which has contributed to appalling erosion and a decline in arable land. In 2000 only 5 percent of El Salvador's territory remained forests and woodland; 29 percent were permanent pastures, 8 percent were permanent crops (mostly coffee and sugar cane), and 27 percent arable land.

History[1]

Until the end of the twentieth century the history of El Salvador could be understood in terms of an interlocking and interacting series of phenomena that took shape during the three hundred years after the Spanish conquest in the 1520s and continued beyond independence in the early 1800s. These phenomena may be summarized as:

1. an economic cycle of "booms" and depressions that replayed itself as variations on a theme several times between the sixteenth and nineteenth centuries;
2. dependence on a monocrop economy as the "key to wealth,"[2] leading to dependence on outside markets;
3. exploitation of the labor supply, first the Indians and later the peasants;
4. concentration of the land in the hands of an ever-decreasing number of proprietors;
5. extreme concentration of wealth in a few hands by the late nineteenth century, coupled with the utter deprivation of the overwhelming majority of the population;
6. a laissez-faire economic philosophy and an absolute belief in the sanctity of private property;
7. a classical liberal notion of the purpose of government—to maintain order; and,
8. periodic rebellion by exploited segments of the population against perceived injustices.

These phenomena produced two persistent patterns. First, the distribution of resources was unequal from the beginning and the effects were cumulative as population pressures exacerbated inequities in the extreme. Second, there was always conflict between communal lands and private property, with the latter regularly gaining at the expense of the former.

The earliest colonists in Cuzcatlán, like their countrymen elsewhere in Spanish America, were driven by a desire for instant wealth that could be sent back to Spain as a nest egg (after giving the crown its share) to await the master's return. But, because the land called *Cuzcatlán* by its indigenous inhabitants had few natural resources—unlike Bolivia and Mexico with their rich silver and gold mines—the search for a "key to wealth" began soon after the first Spanish settlement in Villa San Salvador. This search was the first step in a cycle that would repeat itself three times before 1900 and was characterized by

1. discovery of a new crop;
2. rapid development of the crop;
3. a period of great prosperity from the export of the crop;
4. dramatic decline or stagnation;
5. an economic depression during which a frantic search for a replacement crop ensued; and,
6. discovery of a new crop and the beginning of another cycle.

Cacao, which was being cultivated by the Indians when the Spanish arrived—and was usurped and converted into an export crop by the conquerors—was followed by indigo in the eighteenth century and coffee in the nineteenth. Not until the mid-twentieth century would there be any significant effort at crop diversification. As each cycle unfolded more and more communal land, which was the indigenous pattern of land tenure throughout Latin America, was taken over by the Europeans and turned into private property. The development of a monocrop economy, in which the cycles of development and decline were similar and only the crop changed, had significant consequences for El Salvador's later history.

The decline of cacao in the late seventeenth century and the extended economic depression that followed created a need for the colonials to find a means of survival. This led to development of the *hacienda* system, which was not unlike plantations in the antebellum South in that they were largely self-sufficient. The development of *haciendas* led, in turn, to the creation of new relationships between landowners and indigenous folk or peasants that could be characterized, for the most part, as feudal. These new relationships were established primarily through debt peonage, a means of permanently binding the Indians to a *hacienda*, usually by tricking them into a debt they could not repay. Another dependent relationship was sharecropping, in which the peasants either gave part of the harvest from their small plots or worked several days a week for the *patrono*.

The expansion of *haciendas* in the eighteenth century, which grew in number with each succeeding depression, had the added effect of concentrating land in a decreasing number of hands, primarily through usurpation of communal lands without compensation to the former owners. Meanwhile, the *hacendados* (land owners) exercised increasingly firm control over the political life of the colony by the late eighteenth century, establishing a pattern of economic and political control that would continue for 150 years.

This pattern of land concentration and crop choice had other effects. Particularly during the indigo and coffee cycles, which were labor-intensive for only three months, a vast workforce remained under- or unemployed the rest of the year. This, in turn, had profound social consequences. Men migrated around the country, even throughout Central America, looking for work and would be gone for extended periods. Women tended to stay put, and the rate of births outside marriage became the highest in the region. By the early 1920s, 59 percent of births in El Salvador were "natural children,"[3] as compared with 49 percent in Guatemala and 24 percent in Costa Rica. Other social costs included a literacy rate of only 30 percent in 1900, high levels of malnutrition, and rampant alcoholism; in 1918 liquor consumption produced 25 percent of public revenue.

Further, the emphasis on a monocrop economy produced, from the 1500s onward, a need to import foodstuffs, including basic grains. While the landowners and small middle class could afford to pay for the imported goods, the peasantry could not. As a result, sorghum, which was used as fodder in Guatemala, was a principal food grain in El Salvador.

Finally, the usurpation of land led, during the colonial period, to periodic indigenous revolts that grew in size and number after independence. A major revolt occurred in 1832 in central El Salvador and lasted a year until its indigenous leader, Anastacio Aquino, was captured, shot, decapitated, and had his head publicly displayed as a warning to other would-be rebels. The unrest in the countryside required the creation of local, then state "security forces," which were, from the beginning, in the pay of the landowners and always at their beck and call.

The struggle for independence in El Salvador coincided with movements elsewhere in Central America during the second decade of the nineteenth century. Growing popular demonstrations in support of independence were joined by political leaders; in 1814 one demonstration was led by San Salvador's mayor, who organized and armed his people with what, by 1980, would be called "popular arms"—rocks, machetes, and the like. In the 1820s a newly independent Mexico, looking to assert its hegemony over the region, twice invaded El Salvador and twice was driven out. In July 1823 the Federal Republic of Central America was created by the five former Central American colonies and a year later Manuel José Arce, a Salvadoran, was elected its first president. This experiment lasted for fifteen years, then broke apart in the wake of a liberal-conservative struggle[4] that was exacerbated by regional economic woes—the beginning of the end of the indigo cycle. The desire for some sort of Central American union, however, survived as part of the regional political culture and would reemerge in the late twentieth century in the forms of the Central American Common Market and the Central American Parliament.

Political Culture

The principles on which the republic was founded were those of classical liberalism—namely, that the role of the state was to maintain order, and economic policy was strictly laissez-faire with the sanctity of private property its guiding principle. There were differences in emphasis between those who stressed economic themes of the liberal creed and others who stressed political themes like free speech. All agreed, however, on the basic policies that would shape the Salvadoran nation: encouragement of coffee production (which replaced indigo), construction of railroads to the ports, elimination of communal lands, laws against vagrancy that permitted the state to force peasants to work for *hacendados* at low wages, and repression of rural unrest. From the latter part of the nineteenth century into the early twentieth century most Salvadoran presidents were both generals and major coffee growers; they shared this ideology and brooked no resistance to it.

The 1886 constitution guaranteed that the liberals' policies would be pursued without obstacle; it established a secular state, decentralized state authority by allowing for the popular election of municipal authorities, and confirmed the inviolability of private property. The notion that the state has some responsibility for the health, education, and general well-being of the people it governs was not a part of Salvadoran political culture. For example, the idea of collecting taxes to pay for roads, sewers, and schools was not on the radar screen of the Salvadoran elite—even into the late twentieth century. These notions, as we shall see, continue to struggle for legitimacy in the political discourse of the country.

The problem of dealing with irksome peasants who periodically rebelled against their *patronos* was solved by employing private armies for which the *patronos* paid. Elements of these armies would become the Rural Police and the Mounted Police, created by decrees in 1884 and 1889, respectively, in the western coffee growing departments. An 1895 decree extended these two forces over the entire country and the Rural Police eventually became the National Police. In 1912 the National Guard was created and trained by officers from Spain. Designed for the countryside, it was intended to eliminate the *hacendados'* private armies and their excesses. Within a few years, however, the Guard gained a reputation for being the "most cruel, most barbaric" security force.[5] A third security force, the Treasury Police (*Policía de Hacienda*), was created in 1936.

A national army was created in the late 1850s because El Salvador was living in fear of invasion from Guatemala. The army's attention was directed to defense of the national territory, while the task of maintaining order was left to the three "security forces." Not until the last quarter of the twentieth century would the army be used to control the people—a role that only ended with the 1991 peace accords.

By the late 1920s coffee was central to the economic life of the country. Production of *el grano de oro* (the gold grain) expanded rapidly while other crops and industries stagnated. This, coupled with growing business acumen and sophistication, moved the national economy from depression to boom. Coffee averaged between 75 and 80 percent of all exports between 1900 and 1922, then soared to 92 percent during the remainder of the 1920s. Similarly, land use increased dramatically. In 1919, 70,000 hectares were planted in coffee; by 1932 the figure had increased 34 percent to 106,000 hectares.[6]

Meanwhile, the average Salvadoran's living conditions deteriorated further. In a biting commentary El Salvador's most eloquent social critic, Alberto Masferrer, declared:

> . . . The coffee industry . . . has already occupied the high lands and is now descending to the valleys, displacing corn, rice, and beans. It is extended like the *conquistador*, spreading hunger and misery, reducing the former proprietors to the worst conditions. . . . Although it is possible to prove mathematically that these changes make the country richer, in fact they mean death. It is true that the costs of importing corn are small in relation to the benefits of the export of coffee, but do they give the imported grain to the poor? Or do they make them pay for it? Is the income of the *campesino* who has lost his land, adequate to provide corn, rice, beans, clothes, medicine, doctors, etc.? So, what good does it do to make money from the sale of coffee when it leaves so many people in misery?[7]

The *hacendados* were recalcitrant; in a letter to *Patria*, a newspaper that Masferrer edited, one wrote: "Why must one be bothered with planting corn . . . when one can plant coffee with little effort or risk? The idle lands around the volcanoes must be utilized. If the owners of these lands do not want to make use of them, they must sell them to those who would make them productive."[8] Many insisted that the peasants were being treated fairly—but Masferrer warned that "as long as justice is not the same for everyone, none of us is safe."[9] A more prescient observation came from James Hill, an immigrant *hacendado*: "The working people have meetings on Sundays and become excited. They say: 'We dig the holes for the trees, clean out the weeds, pick the trees, harvest the coffee. Who, then, earns the money? We earn it!' ... Yes, there will be problems one of these days."[10]

Those "problems" erupted five years later—the result of the socioeconomic conditions described above; an increasingly militant labor union movement, which had begun as World War I ended; and a flirtation with authentic electoral democracy at the beginning of the 1930s that ended in a coup d'état, stolen local elections, a disastrous peasant uprising that left thirty thousand dead, and a political division of labor: the army assumed control of the state for the next sixty years while the oligarchy continued to control the economy.[11]

Ethnicity, Social and Class Structure, and Interest Groups

Ethnic Patterns

As land ownership became increasingly concentrated in fewer hands during the eighteenth and nineteenth centuries, the ethnic composition of the country also changed. At the beginning of the seventeenth century the country was about 85 percent indigenous, 10 percent *mestizo* and 5 percent white. To this were added four to five thousand African slaves who were imported to work the cacao plantations as the indigenous population died out. That the country was well on its way to becoming a *mestizo* nation was evident by 1780 and that it had become one was clear thirty years later. By the twentieth century the slaves, who were freed in 1823, had been assimilated and officially ceased to exist as a separate racial group.[12] At the beginning of the twenty-first century, El Salvador's six million inhabitants were 94 percent *mestizo*, 5 percent indigenous, and 1 percent white.

Social and Class Structure

El Salvador has produced great wealth since the conquest, yet 48 percent of its people live below the poverty line, with 31 percent of those surviving on $1 per day. Poverty in rural areas is more acute, where close to 80 percent live below the poverty line. A "poor family" is defined by the Salvadoran Ministry of the Economy as one whose income is below the level that would finance the purchase of the "expanded food basket" (housing, food, education, health, and miscellaneous). An "extremely poor family" does not have sufficient income to purchase the "basic food basket," $129 per month in urban areas and $96 per month in rural areas.[13] In 2003 urban wages covered approximately 70 percent of the basic food basket while rural wages covered only 51.4 percent.[14]

With a per capita income in 2003 of $2,258, El Salvador ranked fifth lowest in the hemisphere. At the beginning of the century for every one thousand live births, thirty-two infants died and the death rate for children under five was thirty-nine children per thousand live births. Fewer than 50 percent of the population completes six years of school, 33 percent complete the ninth grade, and 20 percent finish high school. The literacy rate, at 80 percent nationwide and 75 percent in the countryside, is the one of the lowest in Latin America.

Like poverty, inequality has persisted in El Salvador despite overall growth during the past decade. In 2000 the richest 10 percent of the population consumed 40.6 percent of national income while the poorest 10 percent consumed a mere 0.9 percent.[15] El Salvador's GINI Index score was 53.2.[16]

Remittances

The income information that is not reflected in these data are the remittances, which are sent home by Salvadorans living and working abroad. In 2005 more than 1.5 million Salvadorans lived in the United States, and nearly 250,000 of them were under Temporary Protected Status (TPS), a special program that allowed individuals from specified countries to register to work legally in the U.S. In 1991, $790 million was sent to families in El Salvador; by 2004 that figure had increased to $2.5 billion, or 17 percent of El Salvador's GDP. Remittances are commonly used for housing and consumer goods, such as vehicles, televisions, and VCRs, as well as food and clothing. They have also kept the lid on a social pressure cooker; a war was fought in the 1980s in part because of severe economic deprivation. As we will see below, government policy since the end of the war has done little to address the imbalances. It can be argued that, without remittances, unhappiness with government inaction could have led to major social unrest. Remittances, then, not only increase the purchasing power of many Salvadorans, they also contribute to social stability.

The Churches and Social Change

The Second Vatican Council (1962) and the 1968 bishops' conference at Medellín, Colombia, precipitated profound changes in the Latin American Catholic Church. Vatican II defined the Church as a "community of equals" while Medellín called on the Church to denounce injustice, defend the oppressed, and establish a "preferential option for the poor"—providing what many viewed as the basis for liberation theology. The development of Christian Base Communities (*Comunidades Eclesiales de Base*, CEB) in the late 1960s and 1970s throughout the region was a reflection of and a means of teaching these tenets to people for whom the Church had been little more than a place for receiving the sacraments. In El Salvador the message of social justice offered through CEBs was labeled "Communist" and "subversive" by the right. Between 1972 and 1989 eighteen Catholic priests, one seminary student, one Lutheran minister, and three nuns and a layworker from the United States were murdered or disappeared for their work in defense of the poor and human rights.

Although he was selected in 1977 by the Vatican for the post of Archbishop because he was thought to be conservative, San Salvador's new archbishop, Oscar Arnulfo Romero, soon became a champion of social justice and called for an end to the violence that was consuming the country. His assassination while delivering mass on March 24, 1980, served as a catalyst for many to join the guerrillas. The murder of three Maryknoll nuns and a layworker in December reiterated the danger faced by religious workers. After Romero's death, dozens more priests and nuns were driven into exile, while a handful continued their ministries in guerrilla-controlled areas. Despite the violence the Catholic Church, along with the Anglicans and Lutherans, pushed for a negotiated end to the war throughout the 1980s. Ironically, it was this targeted violence against the Church that ultimately helped to end the war. On November 16, 1989, the U.S.-trained Atlacatl Batallion entered the grounds of the Jesuit *Universidad Centroamericana "José Simeón Cañas"* and killed six Jesuit professors, including the rector, their housekeeper, and her daughter. The murders forced the United States to suspend military aid and El Salvador's new president, Alfredo Cristiani, was forced to the negotiating table.

Many of the CEBs disbanded by the violence have yet to recover and a change in archbishops has hindered their regrowth. The 1994 appointment of Fernando Sáenz Lacalle, a member of Opus Dei, following the death of Romero's successor, Archbishop Arturo Rivera Damas, was seen as a blow to human rights and social justice. Sáenz LaCalle's contention that, like Marx, liberation theology was dead, signaled a return of the church to a pre-Vatican II sacramentalist role.

Political Parties and Elections[17]

Political parties did not emerge in El Salvador until the 1920s; until that time the presidency was passed around among members of the oligarchy. The first modern party was the Communist Party (*Partido Comunista de El Salvador*,

PCS), which was founded during a period of political liberalization in the late 1920s by Augustín Farabundo Martí, the educated son of a *mestizo* landowner. The party focused its organizing in southwestern El Salvador and participated in the January 1932 municipal and Assembly elections. The government's unwillingness to recognize PCS gains at the local level contributed directly to the uprising later that month. Another left-leaning party, the Salvadoran Labor Party, had won the 1931 presidential election but its candidate, Arturo Araujo, a progressive oligarch, was toppled in a coup d'état a month before the local elections. The coup and the uprising brought Araujo's vice president, General Maximiliano Hernández Martínez to power. The PCS was banned after the uprising, and for the next thirteen years the *Pro-Patria* (Pro-Fatherland) National Party, a personalist party created by Martínez, became the official—and only—political party allowed. Martínez's excesses led to his overthrow in 1944, the first of five coups that would be attempted by dissident elements in the army over the next thirty-five years. The official party changed names several times, finally becoming the National Conciliation Party (*Partido de Conciliacion Nacional*, PCN) in 1961. Regardless of name, the official party dominated elections until 1982, insuring that its candidate, always an army colonel or general, was elected president.

Meanwhile, a political opening in the early 1960s—promoted by the Alliance for Progress and an aggressive, strongly prodemocratic U.S. Ambassador, Murat Williams—led to the creation of several opposition parties, most notably the Christian Democrats (*Partido Demócrata Christiano*, PDC), a social democratic party, the Revolutionary National Movement (MNR), and the Nationalist Democratic Union (UDN), which was the PCS's legal front. The Christian Democrats won increasing numbers of seats in the Assembly during the 1960s, then the mayoralty of the three largest cities, including San Salvador, in 1968. These gains, together with smaller gains by other opposition parties, presented a growing challenge to the PCN; however, as Stephen Webre observed in his study of the PDC, the logical flaw in this opening of political space was that it "encouraged an active opposition but, by definition, forbade that opposition to come to power."[18] This reality was borne out by the 1972 presidential elections, in which a civilian coalition comprised of the PDC, MNR, and UDN was denied electoral victory by the army.

This event led many Salvadorans to conclude that electoral politics would get them nowhere and they opted for a revolutionary alternative that included political (mass, grassroots organizing) and military (armed struggle) dimensions. During the 1970s five revolutionary organizations, which had their roots in peasant uprisings of the previous century, in labor organizations of the 1920s, and in the PCS, began working among urban laborers and peasants. Divided over ideology and strategy for a decade, the five came together in the

Farabundo Martí National Liberation Front (*Frente Farabundo Martí para la Liberación Nacional*, FMLN) in October 1980. In January 1981 the FMLN initiated military operations that would plunge El Salvador into eleven years of civil war.

The last coup d'état of the twentieth century occurred in October 1979. Its goal was to remove military conservatives, derail the revolutionary movement, and institute long-overdue socioeconomic reforms. A number of prominent civilians who had been leaders of opposition parties and were forced into exile after 1972 returned to participate in the new government. It soon became clear, however, that a group of extremely conservative officers had displaced the progressive coup leaders and, two months after the coup, most of the civilians resigned. The United States encouraged the Christian Democrats to join the military in a new government; this however, split the party as some leaders—notably José Napoleón Duarte, the former mayor and exiled presidential candidate—accepted the military's offer while others left the party and created the Popular Social Christian Movement (MPSC), which allied itself with other center-left opposition parties, labor unions, and nongovernmental organizations (NGOs) to create the Democratic Revolutionary Front (FDR) in the spring of 1980. The FDR formed a political alliance with the FMLN and served as its international political voice for much of the next decade.

The United States, fearing another revolution in Central America, increased its involvement via a two-track policy. Politically, reforms and elections were emphasized; militarily, the Salvadoran armed forces were trained in counterinsurgency. Meanwhile, in May 1979 the generals informed their old allies in the oligarchy that they had to begin taking care of themselves.[19] This had two effects. One was the creation of paramilitary death squads, funded by wealthy members of the oligarchy in collaboration with sympathetic elements in the armed forces. The second was the creation in 1981 by some these same oligarchs of their own political party, the Nationalist Republican Alliance (*Alianza Nacionalista Republicana*, ARENA).

Following Ronald Reagan's assumption of the presidency in 1981 elections were identified as the means of putting El Salvador on the road to democracy and robbing the revolutionary movement of any remaining raison d'être. Elections for a Constituent Assembly that would write a new constitution were held in 1982 and, to everyone's shock, ARENA won a plurality of the seats and effective control of the Assembly. Only intervention by the U.S. Ambassador prevented ARENA from electing its founder, Roberto D'Aubuisson—a man closely tied to the death squads and identified ten years later by the United Nations' Truth Commission as the intellectual author of Archbishop Oscar Romero's assassination in March 1980—as interim president of the country. He had to settle for president of the Assembly.

In the 1984 presidential elections the man who had been denied in 1972, José Napoleón Duarte, defeated D'Aubuisson. This and subsequent elections in the next decade, for the Legislative Assembly in 1985, 1988, and 1991 and for president in 1989, provided a "democratic government" that rarely exhibited the conditions of a functioning democracy: freedom of speech, the media, and party organization; freedom for interest groups; the absence of state-sponsored terror; the absence of fear and coercion among the population; and subordination of the military to civilian rule. Indeed, the armed forces, formally removed from power, continued to wield effective political control of the country. Duarte, elected on a platform of economic reform and peace negotiations with the FMLN, delivered neither while presiding over one of the most corrupt governments in Salvadoran history. The PDC, rent by internal squabbles, split again in 1988—and lost the 1989 presidential election to a center-right ARENA candidate, Alfredo Cristiani, who successfully negotiated an end to the civil war.

The electoral process, nevertheless, had unintended and unanticipated consequences: it opened political space that had been closed by state repression in the early 1980s. New political parties emerged, split, and faded; NGOs and existing labor unions began to organize and demand better wages, working conditions, economic reforms, and peace. ARENA and the PDC tried to co-opt or organize parts of this movement; those who resisted were labeled "FMLN fronts" and suffered renewed repression. MPSC and MNR leaders returned from exile to begin testing the political waters. One of the earliest among these was Dr. Héctor Silva, who in 1997 and again in 2000 would be elected mayor of San Salvador in a coalition led by the FMLN.

At the presidential level El Salvador experienced two elections between the end of the war and the end of the century. The 1994 elections, hyperbolically dubbed the "elections of the century" because they were the first to occur after the war's end, because the FMLN was participating for the first time as a legal party, and because a president (who serves for five years), Assembly deputies, and mayors (who serve three year terms), were being elected. The results gave lie to the "common wisdom" of the previous decade that the FMLN had no popular support. Its candidate, Rubén Zamora, forced a run-off with ARENA's candidate, Armando Calderon Sol, who ultimately won. Meanwhile, the FMLN won twenty-one seats in the Legislative Assembly and thirteen mayoralties.

By the time of the next local elections in 1997, growing unhappiness across the country with ARENA's policies, particularly in the economic area, was reflected at the ballot box. The number of ARENA deputies dropped from 39 to 28 and the number of municipalities it controlled declined from 207 to 162. The FMLN, meanwhile, increased its Assembly seats to twenty-seven and its mayoralties to forty-eight. These results led the former rebels as well as many political pundits to predict that, with a strong candidate in 1999, the FMLN had a real chance of winning the presidency. It was not to be, however. The FMLN irretrievably damaged itself in a bitter internecine fight over who would be its presidential candidate. The August 1998 party nominating convention began in a spirit of unity but deteriorated into chaos as a relatively small group of radicals without credentials invaded the convention and drowned out the speech of the moderates' candidate, San Salvador mayor Héctor Silva. A month later the FMLN nominated a former guerrilla, Facundo Guardado, as its candidate. But the election was already lost. In March 1999 U.S.-educated Francisco Flores was elected president on the ARENA ticket in a landslide.

The widespread assumption following the 1999 election was that the FMLN was too deeply divided to put itself back together, that its days as a significant political party were numbered. That assessment, however, did not take into account the continuing and growing disenchantment with ARENA, which had been in power for a decade. To almost everyone's surprise, the FMLN came roaring back in the 2000 local elections, virtually matching ARENA's popular vote, winning for the first time more seats in the Assembly than its political nemesis (thirty-one to twenty-nine), and increasing by thirty the number of municipalities it would control for the next three years to seventy-eight. ARENA's hold on municipalities continued to decline, dropping to 124.[20] This pattern continued in the 2003 legislative and municipal elections, with the FMLN maintaining its thirty-one seats in the Assembly while ARENA lost two. The number of municipalities under ARENA governance fell to 113, and the FMLN experienced minimal losses although it managed to retain the capital. Other parties benefited from ARENA's decline. The PCN gained two Assembly seats and increased its municipalities from thirty-three to fifty while the center-left *Centro Democrático Unido* (CDU) also enjoyed small gains.

Many believed that the FMLN was on its way to winning the 2004 presidential election. Always a bridesmaid, the FMLN was again unable to duplicate its electoral successes of the previous four years. Having fallen out with former San Salvador mayor Héctor Silva who had attempted to mediate a health workers' strike against the party's wishes, the FMLN nominated former Communist Party leader Shafik Handal as its candidate for president after another turbulent nomination process. Silva ran on a coalition ticket with the CDU and PDC. ARENA's Antonio (Tony) Elías Saca, a thirty-eight-year-old businessman and former sportscaster, purportedly represented the new face of ARENA. ARENA's campaign war chest dwarfed that of the other parties as they outspent the FMLN by more than three to one. The campaign was fierce as ARENA reverted to Cold War rhetoric, labeled Handal a Communist who would turn El Salvador into "another Cuba" and further alleged that he supported terrorism. Worse, ARENA claimed, a Handal victory would severely damage relations with the United States and endanger the influx of remittances. The U.S. State Department intervened openly by sending the Assistant Secretary for Latin America to El Salvador to make it clear that his government preferred an ARENA victory, then allowing a White House aide to conduct a telephone interview with the Salvadoran press gathered for the occasion at ARENA's headquarters. It was, in essence, a campaign of fear. Saca soundly defeated Handal in the first round of voting.

After the election long-simmering internal tensions within the FMLN became full-blown arguments over the lessons of their second successive electoral debacle. Handal and his faction—called the "orthodox"—succeeded in maintaining control of the party apparatus at a November 2004 party congress, despite widespread sentiment for their removal. By June 2005 some of the party's most able and prominent "reformers" left the FMLN and created a new party, whose name they took from their history: the *Frente Democrático Revolucionario* (Democratic Revolutionary Front, FDR).

Government and Public Policy

The FMLN's conversion from revolutionary organization to legal political party was the result of peace negotiations that occurred between 1989 and the end of 1991. Leading a country that was demonstrably fatigued by war, President Cristiani pledged in his June 1989 inaugural to pursue peace negotiations with the FMLN. The flaw was that ARENA and the U.S. government, now headed by President George H. W. Bush, who wanted to extract the United States from Central America as expeditiously as possible, assumed that the only thing to negotiate with the FMLN was its surrender. The government's failure to negotiate in good faith and several assassinations of leftist political leaders in the fall of 1989 convinced the FMLN that it had to demonstrate its power. The most significant offensive since 1981, launched on November 11, brought the war to San Salvador for the first time. It revealed both the FMLN's inability to provoke a general uprising and the army's incompetence. It also exposed the bankruptcy of U.S. policy: despite nine years of training and over $2 billion in U.S. military aid, the army could not rout the FMLN from the capital. The army's murder of the Jesuits had an impact at least as great as the offensive itself. Together they marked the beginning of the end of the war.

In early 1990 the United Nations, at the request of both the government and the FMLN, initiated several months of shuttle diplomacy that resulted, by April, in an agreement to negotiate an end to the war. In July the first significant agreement, on human rights, was reached. This would lead, exactly one year later, to the establishment of the United Nations Observation and Verification Mission (ONUSAL), which opened with a human rights observation team that operated throughout the country—six months before the end of the war. Government balking in late 1990 led to another, smaller FMLN offensive and thereafter the negotiations proceeded to a successful conclusion on December 31, 1991.

The Chapultepec accords, so named for the castle in Mexico City where they were signed, sought to deal with the fundamental causes of the war by ending the armed conflict as quickly as possible by promoting democratization, guaranteeing absolute respect for human rights, and reunifying Salvadoran society. These objectives were unprecedented; no previous civil war had ended with an agreement not simply to stop shooting but to restructure society. The accords established a precise calendar for implementation during the cease-fire period that was to end October 15. They mandated demilitarization, including halving the size of the Armed Forces, eliminating the state security forces and the FMLN's guerrilla army; legalizing the FMLN as a political party; amending the constitution; reforming the electoral and judicial systems; settling the land distribution issue, one of the root causes of the war; and establishing independent commissions to identify those responsible for major human rights abuses and to purge the army of its most serious human rights violators.

To the credit of both sides the cease-fire was never broken. Despite difficulties, some of which threatened to derail the peace process at times, ONUSAL, with occasional help from several friendly embassies (Spain, Mexico, Venezuela, Colombia, and the United States), was able to keep the process moving forward. By 1993 a new police force, the National Civilian Police (*Policía Nacional Civil*, PNC) had replaced the old security forces; a new governmental institution, the National Council for Human Rights (*Procuraduría de Derechos Humanos*, PDH), was created where citizens could bring their complaints about governmental abuses; the army was reduced in size and in its barracks with all its special units disbanded and its officer corps purged; the virtually nonfunctioning judicial system was experiencing the first steps toward reform; the FMLN was a legal political party; and perhaps most significantly, there was a sea change in El Salvador's political culture: it was no longer acceptable to kill people for political reasons.

All these positive developments, however, took place in a context of effective political authoritarianism (albeit authoritarianism under continual assault by the peace accords themselves and the new actors on the political stage) and, during the Calderon Sol administration, weak presidential leadership.

Calderon was a model of indecision whose failure to follow through on policies he originally embraced caused frustration across the political spectrum. For example, Calderon promised to implement a system of property taxes, a much more progressive tax than the IVA (ad valorem)—which, at 13 percent on all purchases, hit the poor and working class much harder than the upper classes. Nothing happened. More significantly—because this was tied to compliance with the Peace Accords—he promised electoral reform, a dire need in view of the incompetence and partisanship that characterized the work of the Supreme Electoral Tribunal (TSE) in preparation for the 1994 elections. Calderon appointed a presidential commission that produced a series of recommendations that he publicly embraced and submitted to the Assembly. There they were buried by his own party.

The election of Francisco Flores, a young, U.S.-educated ARENA Assembly deputy, brought hope of greater competence and flexibility in the presidential palace. At the end of his first six months in office, however, the Central American University's (Universidad Centroamericana, UCA) year-end analysis noted that Flores had "promised to change the ways of doing politics and said he was the friend of dialogue and citizen participation. . . . But the new president was not everything he said he was. . . . [He] was hard and intransigent, even more than his predecessor. Far from infusing change between politics and society, he exacerbated lamentable and dangerous attitudes: negative toward dialogue with social sectors and civic participation, and lost to the value of *concertación* (collaboration and agreement) in policy making."[21]

Nowhere was this more apparent than Flores's response to a strike by the Social Security Institute Union (STISSS) in November 1999. Objecting to government plans to privatize the entire health system and the firing of 221 workers (in a grossly understaffed and inefficient system), physicians, technicians, and hospital workers shut down hospitals and clinics, literally occupying them in the style of traditional Latin American strikes. President Flores refused to negotiate and threatened to order the PNC to remove the strikers by force. The union refused to budge on its demands, San Salvador mayor Silva's effort to mediate failed, and the strike continued until thirty-six hours before the March 2000 elections when a marathon session resulted in an agreement to return to work. The government had already changed its privatization plan to awarding concessions (contracts) for service and the strikers agreed to let the Supreme Court of Justice decide the fate of the 221 dismissed workers. The eleventh hour resolution was intended to reflect positively on the government and ARENA, and negatively on the FMLN, which had supported the workers' demands. As a strategy, it failed. A second major healthcare strike erupted in October 2002 over the privatization of services. The strike ended nine months later following government assurances that the healthcare system would not be privatized. Whether this is the end of the healthcare privatization battle remains to be seen.

Flores's commitment to the neoliberal model was unwavering, despite significant public opposition to the policies. In January 2001 Flores's Law of Monetary Integration, which dollarized the economy, was passed by the legislature. Several public opinion surveys indicated that a majority of Salvadorans opposed dollarization and believed it had a negative effect on their pocketbook. The policy has had a disproportionate impact on the standard of living of the poor, where "rounding up" prices from the conversion became a common practice among vendors in the informal sector.[22] Thus, inflation for the poor was higher than for the general population.

In addition to the increasing unrest in the public sector the Flores government was also confronted with growing public insecurity. In 1999 El Salvador's murder rate was 127 per 100,000—the highest in the hemisphere. Flores cited the influx of criminal street gangs from the United States, such as *Mara Salvatrucha* and MS–18, as the reason for El Salvador's insecurity. Flores' *mano dura* legislation targeted gang activity, but did little to address the growing problem of social violence.

ARENA's fourth consecutive president, Antonio Elías Saca, promised to promote social and economic security. Shortly after taking office, Saca imposed *supra mano dura* in a further effort to crackdown on gang violence. While *mano dura* and its successor have been very popular with the public, they had little effect on stemming the violence.[23] Indeed, the judicial system refused to cooperate with Saca's policy of arresting and jailing young men who sport the identifying tattoos of gang members, arguing that individuals must be arrested for *doing something*, not for how they look. By July 2005—more than a year after *supra mano dura* went into effect—El Salvador's murder rate climbed to twelve per day, nearly double that of the previous year. The government continued to blame gangs for a majority of the homicides, but the level of impunity in the country made any statistics dubious.

Saca inherited a deteriorating economy from Flores. His solution for the country's economic malaise relied heavily on El Salvador's relationship with the United States. Saca's first priority was to guarantee the renewal of TPS status for Salvadorans in the United States to ensure the continued flow of remittances. The renewal of TPS was, in part, secured by El Salvador's troop commitment to the U.S.-led war in Iraq.[24] Additionally, by El Salvador's commitment to the Central American Free Trade Agreement (CAFTA) he hoped to bolster El Salvador's growing *maquila* industry that was fast becoming the centerpiece of the economy. In addition to this outward oriented economic policy Saca also announced the creation of a multipoint poverty reduction program. Part of the program entailed a plan to reduce extreme poverty by one-half, targeting some of El Salvador's poorest communities by providing nutrition, education, and healthcare. The proposed plan would target twenty thousand families its first year, growing to one hundred thousand families within the following four years. If the program comes to fruition, it will be the first comprehensive antipoverty program launched by the government.

Local Government

El Salvador has a highly centralized political system. Departmental governors are appointed by the president. Mayors are elected and have significant responsibility for delivery of services like electricity and water, but historically they have been dependent on funds allocated by the central government. Calderon promised the mayors (and the U.S. Agency for International Development, AID) that he would support proportional representation (PR) in elections for mayors and municipal councils. (A municipality is similar to a U.S. county; currently, whichever party wins the mayoralty also wins all the council seats.) He was effectively silenced by his own ARENA party with the argument that such power-sharing would create "chaos" and that it would take twenty years for municipalities to be ready for PR.[25]

There was cause for concern about municipal government; there are a few illiterate mayors. Other municipalities are so poor they are unviable. Still others are technically illegal because they have less than ten thousand inhabitants but continue to exist because no one has been willing to pay the political price of consolidation. Still, there are municipalities across the country where mayors and their councils are models for the remainder of the country. Municipal Development Committees in each village are elected on a nonpartisan basis and then work with the municipal government to define local needs and priorities. These mayors improved local tax collection—and maintained their popularity while doing so. In Nejapa, San Salvador, Rene Canjura (a former FMLN guerrilla) with extensive citizen input created a ten-year development plan and by 2004 had significant achievements to show for it. Whereas in 1996, when one was likely to see garbage all along the unpaved streets, in 2004 the main streets were paved and clean, the municipal market had been painted, and the central square was filled with trees and flowering plants. Potable water had been extended from 25 percent to 90 percent of the population. There were new soccer fields, a library that offers art and computer classes, and programs directed to women's development. In Sonsonate, one of El Salvador's smaller departmental capitals, Abraham López DeLeón (ARENA), successfully encouraged both town meetings and open council meetings as a means of promoting participation. These experiences provided the most vital form of democracy being practiced in El Salvador at the end of the twentieth century.

Women

Women's participation in public life grew from near zero in the 1970s to an increasing number of women in government a decade later. During the Cristiani administration, two of his most competent ministers, Planning and Education, were women. Two women were members of the FMLN's negotiating team at the peace talks. In 1999 the FMLN's vice presidential nominee was a woman and in 2004 the vice presidential nominees of ARENA and the CDU-PDC coalition tickets were women. The ARENA victory in 2004 gave El Salvador its first female vice president. After the 2003 elections, seventeen of 262 mayors were women, down from twenty-nine after 2000. All but six belonged to ARENA, four FMLN, and two PCN. In the Legislative Assembly ten of eighty-four deputies were women, an increase of one from 2000: seven FMLN and three ARENA.

In preparation for the 1994 elections a broad coalition of women's organizations hammered out an agenda called *Mujeres '94* (Women '94), which it asked every party to adopt as part of its platform. Only the FMLN agreed, thanks to the pressure of its women members. The FMLN also adopted a rule that one-third of all its candidates for office be women. This was a compromise; the women had pushed for 50 percent. By the mid-1990s women's organizations had formulated legislative bills to guarantee workers' rights in the *maquiladoras*; to make rape a public crime; to no longer requires a witness (other than the victim) to the rape in order to press charges; to require men to prove they are NOT the father of a child; and to insure inclusion of articles that protect women in the new penal code. None of these issues were on the national agenda five years earlier. A new education law guaranteed equal access for girls, barred discrimination based on gender, and proscribed sexist stereotypes in textbooks. Another issue absent from the national agenda at the end of the war was violence against women. Before the end of the decade the issue was receiving attention in the major newspapers—although too often accompanied by gratuitously exploitative photographs.

It's the Economy, Stupid

During the 1990s significant disagreement emerged among the economic elite over economic policy, as well as between important parts of the elite and the government.[26] El Salvador's once monolithic oligarchy disappeared. A generation earlier the monolith had two parts: the traditional agricultural sector whose wealth was exclusively in the land—coffee, cotton, and/or sugar cane—and the landowners who had diversified into finance and industry. By the middle of the decade there were four clearly identifiable sectors: financial, commercial, industrial, and agricultural. Agriculture, which dominated the Salvadoran economy into the 1980s—contributing 43 percent of the GDP in 1978, for example—became relatively insignificant in economic terms, commanding only 11 percent of the GDP in 2003—far behind remittances. By 2004 once-dominant coffee was only 7 percent of export earnings. In each of the first three sectors there was a small subsector that controlled the overwhelming majority of the capital within that sector. The result was not only intersector conflicts but intrasectional disputes, as smaller players battled to stay in the game.

Making matters worse, the Calderon government substituted sloganeering about "modernization of the state" and "privatization" for a coherent economic plan that could generate confidence for industrial investors—El Salvador's only hope for a stable economic future. After floundering for two years, in January 1995 Treasury Minister Manuel Enrique Hinds produced what became known as the "Hinds Plan," a five-point scheme that brought down on the government the wrath of the commercial and industrial sectors. The plan's components were: (1) reducing import taxes to zero; (2) establishing a fixed and convertible exchange rate; (3) "modernization" understood as (a) deregulation, (b) decentralization, (c) privatization of all goods and services administered by the state where possible and socially acceptable, and (d) administrative and financial restructuring; (4) increasing progressively public expenditures for social programs such as education and health up to 50 percent of the national budget in 1999; and (5) increasing the value added tax (IVA) from 10 to 14 percent. Eliminating import taxes meant El Salvador would be flooded with cheap imports against which local producers could not compete. Raising the IVA was viewed by parts of the private sector and the political opposition as having a profoundly negative—and regressive—impact on consumers.

The firestorm forced the government to back down for a time and completely scrap the first two points. Between 1995 and 1997, however, other parts of this plan were implemented piecemeal. Several of the bills requiring parliamentary approval were rammed through the Legislative Assembly by ARENA, often without following the Assembly's own procedures for hearings and debate. In practice, however, "decentralization" of power from the central government to the municipalities in practice meant "deconcentration"—the opening of central government offices in selected municipalities. "Privatization" meant selling off national utilities at prices well below their real value. And the increase in the IVA—to 13 percent, a compromise—outraged voters. Indeed, support for this measure by ARENA and the Democratic Party (PD—a splinter of the FMLN) cost both parties votes in the March 1997 elections. The pieces, however, were less than the sum of their parts and did not a coherent economic policy make.

The sale of the state-owned telephone and electric companies did not bring the much-touted efficiencies and reduced cost. On the contrary, as the UCA's weekly news analysis, *Proceso*, noted at the end of 1999, "many of the irregularities that existed when the state administered the telephone and electricity services were repeated point by point in the private providers. . . ." Free of state regulation, *Proceso* commented, these companies arbitrarily fixed prices and treated customers dismissively. This view was supported by a September 1999 survey; 95 percent of the respondents said that privatization of the phone company had not translated into lower prices; 77 percent said the quality of service had not improved, and 80 percent complained about access to installation. Even higher levels of unhappiness were found in relation to the delivery of electricity.[27] Still, the Flores government remained committed to privatizing the public sector.

Growth vs. Development

By 2000, after eleven years of neoliberal policies and World Bank and Inter-American Development Bank-mandated restructuring, El Salvador's economy was in deep trouble. From 1990 to 1995 GDP growth averaged 5 percent, but slowed the second half of the decade. By the turn of the century the economy showed no signs of recovery (GDP growth was 3.4 percent in 1999, 2.2 percent in 2002, and 1.8 percent in 2003). Equally significant, that growth was concentrated in very few hands—mostly in the financial sector—and "redistributive policies" was a dirty word in government circles. In its year-end review and analysis *Proceso* noted that neither the Calderon nor Flores governments had "developed policies to achieve an effective modernization of the economy, which implies diversification of production and agricultural exports, as well as a process of industrial reconversion that permits improvement in the competitiveness of that sector."[28] Indeed, industrialization after the war was largely confined to the creation of (mostly Asian-owned) *maquiladoras*, which, it might be argued, have become the latest "crop" in the economic cycles described earlier.[29]

Inflation complicated the picture for much of the 1990s. Running as high as 19.9 percent in 1992, by 1998 the cumulative inflation rate was 186 percent. By the turn of the century the government had inflation under control, although it continued to exceed growth. In 2003 the annual rate of inflation was 2.5 percent with less than 2 percent growth. Inflation doubled in 2004 while growth lagged at a mere 1.5 percent. The damage was done. Between December 1991 and August 1999 minimum daily salaries declined from 28.18 to 27.37 Colones.[30] In another measure, the GDP per inhabitant grew dramatically over the decade: from $1,002 in 1991 to $2,258 in 2003. Most of that increase, however, was lost to inflation. Further, some price increases disproportionally affected the poor. In late 1996, for example, bus fares increased 50 *centavos*—about 11 cents. Not much—until one realizes that many people have to take two buses to get to work (no "transfers") and that the increase applied to children attending school as well as to their parents. That 11-cent increase could approach $1.00 per day for a family whose monthly income may be only $200 to $250.

Conclusion

In 1992 El Salvador experienced one of the region's most profound political and social transformations. Years of war and violent oppression gave way to peace and democracy in one of the United Nations' most successful peace-keeping endeavors. But it was the political will of the actors in El Salvador that paved the road to peace. Philosophical changes in the ruling class and FMLN leadership, submission of the military to civilian rule, and respect for human rights were vital prerequisites for the transition to democracy. In 1994 El Salvador held the first truly democratic elections in its history, bringing the FMLN into the electoral fold. The 2000 and 2003 elections for mayors and members of the Legislative Assembly brought significant gains for the FMLN and losses for ARENA. The seventy-four FMLN-controlled municipalities—including seven of fourteen departmental (provincial) capitals—meant that at the local level the former rebels governed well over 50 percent of the Salvadoran population. Still, the FMLN was unable to woo voters in the 2004 presidential election and ARENA continued to dominate Salvadoran presidential politics. Further, the FMLN's internal woes raised concerns about whether it would be able to hold on to its Assembly seats and town halls.

Despite the problems described above, El Salvador's prospects for stable democratic governance continued to be positive; however, the socioeconomic horizon was cloudy. Despite significant growth in the early 1990s the gap between rich and poor was still vast and government rhetoric on the issue was not matched by a coherent policy to address it. The government's neoliberal agenda caused increasing public dissatisfaction and there appeared to be few alternative ideas on how to reactivate the slumping economy. The country's immense dependency upon remittances was increasingly apparent as people replaced coffee as El Salvador's most profitable export. Social violence replaced political violence as the number one social problem, and in 2005 the PNC was still ill-equipped and insufficiently trained to control it. Growing dissatisfaction with ARENA's policies was increasingly reflected at the ballot box in local and Assembly elections; unfortunately, the center-left's continuing inability to build a political party, together with the FMLN's factionalism meant that no viable alternative to ARENA was on the horizon in the middle of the new millennium's first decade. Thus, while El Salvador continued to present a façade of reform and progress, the oppressive realities of daily life for several million Salvadorans differed little from what they had been before war and peace came to their country.

Notes

1. This section and the next on political culture is drawn from *Revolution in El Salvador: From Civil Strife to Civil Peace* (Boulder, CO: Westview Press, 1995), Chap. 1, 25–28, 30–32.

2. Murdo J. MacLeod, *Spanish Central America: A Socioeconomic History 1520–1720* (Berkeley: University of California Press, 1973), 49. The concept of a repeating economic cycle, discussed below, is drawn from MacLeod.

3. The concept of illegitimacy does not exist in the Spanish language; one speaks of "*niños naturales*," never "*niños ilegitimos.*"

4. Latin American conservatives and liberals bear little resemblance to liberals and conservatives in the Anglo-American political tradition. Conservatives were aristocrats and monarchists who wished to keep church and state tied closely together and who were dedicated to preserving the church's wealth and privileges. Liberals were anticlerical and often antireligious. They were inclined to support free trade while conservatives preferred to erect tariff barriers to protect local textile production. Within El Salvador the differences were less than in other countries because the church did not have much wealth that could be confiscated. The liberals succeeded in abolishing monastic orders, establishing civil marriage, and taking some initial steps toward removing education from control by the clergy and creating a state education system.

5. Robert Varney Elam, "Appeal to Arms: The Army and Politics in El Salvador 1931–1964" (Ph.D. dissertation, University of New Mexico, 1968), 9.

6. Max P. Brannon, *El Salvador: Esquema estadística de la vida nacional* [Statistical outline of national life] (San Salvador: n.p., 1936), 22–24. By 1950 there were 115,429 hectares, or 75 percent of the total land under cultivation; in 1961, 139,000 hectares, or 87 percent of the total. Eduardo Colindres, *Fundamentos económicos de la burguesía salvadoreña* [Economic Fundamentals of the Salvadoran Bourgeoisie]. (San Salvador: UCA Editores, 1978), 72.

7. "La crisis del maíz" [The corn crisis], *Patria*, January 18, 1929.

8. *Patria*, January 4, 1929.

9. "Como anda la justicia en esta San Salvador" [How justice operates in San Salvador], *Patria*, November 30, 1928.

10. Arthur Ruhl, *The Central Americans* (New York: C. Scribner, 1928), 206.

11. How did El Salvador escape becoming another "banana republic" like Guatemala and Honduras? According to Dr. David Reyes-Guerra who, as a young engineer employed by the United Fruit Company in Guatemala in the early 1950s, read exchanges of letters from the 1930s between UFCo and Salvadoran president General Martinez, Martinez refused to give UFCo entrée. Said Dr. Reyes-Guerra, "That's why there are no bananas in El Salvador!" Conversation with David Reyes-Guerra, 21 July 2005, San Salvador.

12. Blacks were officially barred from living in El Salvador for many years, although this broke down in the 1980s as African American diplomats and military trainers were posted to the U.S. Embassy and U.S. Military Group, respectively. Other blacks came as journalists, human rights workers, and staff members of nongovernmental organizations and the United Nations. Still, racism is an ugly fact, particularly among the white (European) elite. In the early 1990s, for example, a very senior Salvadoran political official informed a senior official of the UN peacemaking mission (ONUSAL) that one of his aides, a Jamaican political officer (and a woman) was not welcome at their meetings.

The African heritage of many Salvadorans is apparent in a stroll down any street, especially in the capital. There seems to be no societal discrimination because of this. Rather, discrimination stems more from class than ethnic background.

13. "The Purchasing Power and the Basic Food Basket," *Proceso*, no. 1083, January 28, 2004.

14. Ibid.

15. United Nations Development Program, Human Development Report 2004, Table 14. Accessed at http://hdr.undp.org/reports/global/2004/pdf/

16. The GINI Index measures inequality of income distribution on a scale of 1 (perfect equality) to 100 (perfect inequality).

17. Portions of this section are drawn from Tommie Sue Montgomery, "El Salvador," in Charles Ameringer, *Political Parties of the Americas 1980s to 1990s* (Westport, CT: Greenwood Press, 1992), 281–301.

18. Stephen Webre, *José Napoleón Duarte and the Christian Democratic Party in Salvadoran Politics 1960–1972* (Baton Rouge: Louisiana State University Press, 1979), 181.

19. Laurie Becklund, "Death Squads: Deadly 'Other War,'" *Los Angeles Times*, December 18, 1983.

20. Throughout this period the Christian Democrats continued to fracture, becoming less of a viable party with each split. In 2000 the PDC won only five seats in the Assembly and eighteen municipalities.

21. "Balance Social," *Proceso*, no. 884, December 30, 1999. http://www.uca.edu.sv/publica//proceso/proc884.html

22. "The Socioeconomic Implications of Dollarization in El Salvador," *Latin American Politics and Society*, 46:3.

23. According to one University Public Opinion Institute poll, 88 percent agreed with *mano dura*. See "2003: The Supremacy of Politics," *Proceso*, no. 1079, December 24, 2003.

24. By 2005 El Salvador was the only Latin American country with troops still in Iraq.

25. This view was expressed by Assembly Deputy Juan Duch in an interview, December 1996.

26. This section is adapted from Tommie Sue Montgomery, "Constructing Democracy in El Salvador," *Current History*, February 1997, 62–63.

27. "Balance Social." *Proceso*, no. 884, December 30, 1999.

28. "Balance económico," *Proceso*, no. 884. December 30, 1999. http://www .uca.edu.sv/publica//proceso/proc844.html

29. Like coffee, the *maquilas* offer cheap labour ($4.00 per day) and poor working conditions. Unlike coffee, however, the workforce is largely female and the *maquilas* are mostly foreign-owned.

30. Ibid. In the late 1990s the Colon was stable at 8.8 to the dollar.

21

Guatemala

A Second Decade of Spring?

Dwight Wilson

G uatemala lived a democratic "Decade of Spring" between the 1944 uprising that sent dictator Jorge Ubico packing and the 1954 coup that
turned out the popularly elected administration of Jacobo Arbenz. The next
four decades would be an unhappy parade of military coups, countercoups,
and civilian governments, each trying to overcome the grinding underdevelopment and political violence that plagued this most populous Central
American republic. The thirty-six-year-long civil war that killed and dislocated hundreds of thousands of people finally came to a formal close in 1996.

With the end of armed conflict and the relaunching of electoral democracy, Guatemalans were hopeful that another decade of spring had dawned.
So far, it has not been a fully happy one, though, and many of the problems
that contributed to the turbulence of most of Guatemala's history have not
been solved by the recent peace accords or elections. What will follow in the
next decade—democratic deepening, return to organized violence, or something in between—is an open question.

History

Pedro de Alvarado, Hernando Cortés's standout lieutenant in the conquest of
Mexico, arrived in the western highlands of Guatemala ("land of trees" in local parlance) in 1524 leading an expedition of a few hundred Spaniards and
an auxiliary army of recently defeated Aztecs. Mayan civilization had flourished in the mountainous region from AD 300–600, after which time it lost

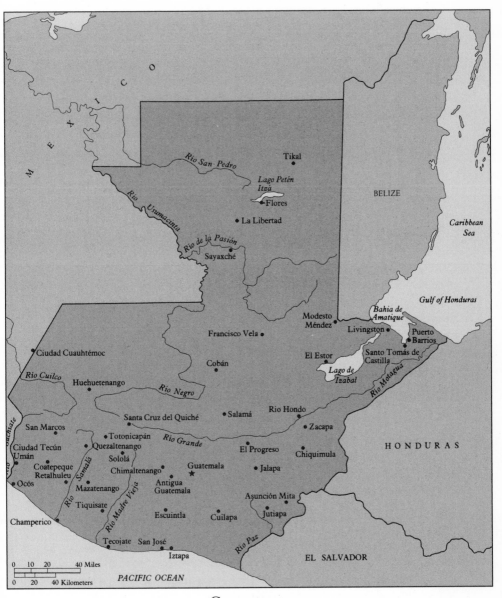

MEXICO

Río San Pedro

Tikal

Lago Petén
Itzá

BELIZE

• Flores

• La Libertad

Río Usumacinta

Río de la Pasión

• Sayaxché

*Caribbean
Sea*

Gulf of Honduras

Modesto
Méndez

*Bahía de
Amatique*

Francisco Vela •

Livingston •

Puerto
Barrios

• Ciudad Cuauhtémoc

El Estor •

Santo Tomás de
Castilla

Cobán •

*Lago de
Izabal*

Río Cuilco

Río Motagua

Huehuetenango •

Río Negro

Santa Cruz del Quiché •

• Salamá

Rio Hondo

San Marcos •

• Totonicapán

Río Grande

• Zacapa

Ciudad Tecún
Umán •

Quezaltenango •

El Progreso •

Chiquimula •

HONDURAS

Sololá •

Coatepeque
Retalhuleu •

Chimaltenango •

Guatemala
★

• Jalapa

Ocós •

Mazatenango •

Antigua
Guatemala

Río Samalá

Tiquisate •

Asunción Mita •

Río Madre Vieja

Champerico •

Escuintla •

Cuilapa •

Jutiapa •

Tecojate •

San José •

Río Paz

EL SALVADOR

Iztapa •

| 0 | 10 | 20 | | 40 Miles |

| 0 | 20 | 40 Kilometers |

PACIFIC OCEAN

GUATEMALA

much of its vigor and population. The Mayan center of gravity later moved north to the Yucatán where for several centuries many of its best known achievements in mathematics, astronomy, and architecture took place. Its star had again dimmed by the time of the Spanish arrival. Whereas the Aztecs in Mexico were united under Tenochtitlán, the Mayans lived in independent and squabbling city-states. Alvarado walked in on a war between the Quiché and Cakchiquel Indians that divided the cities into competing alliances. Alvarado allegedly killed with his own sword the legendary Tecúm Umán, the last Quiché king and Guatemalan national hero. The conquest required separate attention for each of the decentralized cities; Indians in the northern forests of Petén beat back the invading Spanish until the 1690s. Eventually, Hispanization proceeded by conversion to Catholicism, the priestly hierarchy and rituals of which mirrored indigenous religion. Uniquely in Central America, though, the majority Indian population stayed largely autonomous and unassimilated, a fact only beginning to change in recent generations.

The Kingdom of Guatemala developed into a new Captaincy-General, the seat of colonial government for all of Central America, which stretched from Chiapas to Costa Rica. It was the spiritual, cultural, and economic heart of the isthmus as well, but next to Mexico and Peru, the colonial jewels in the royal crown, Guatemala was a backwater. The precious metals prized by Spain dried up early there and the colony languished in relative obscurity, supplying the monarchy with mahogany, cacao, and dyes. Eighteenth-century revolutions in Europe—political and intellectual—could not escape notice even in the furthest corners of the empire, however.

Independence and Liberal Dictatorship

The independence movements agitating for separation from Spain in Mexico and South America were greeted in Central America with confusion and indecision, many municipalities acting separately from the central government in Guatemala. Most Central Americans resolved in favor of separation from Spain, but the question remained whether to form a separate country or append to Mexico. In the end Mexico itself decided in favor of the second alternative, swallowing the kingdom as a part of the short-lived Empire of Augustín Iturbide. After he was deposed Central Americans went their own way and declared their sovereignty (minus Chiapas, which stuck with Mexico).

Initially the kingdom stayed together, proclaiming itself the United Provinces of Central America in 1823. Under Liberal leadership the government set out to erase the Hispanic past and fashion the new nation according Enlightenment ideals. Hopes ran high that its location and prospects for an interoceanic canal would propel the federation into the ranks of the wealthiest nations on earth.

In fact, the factional strife—between anticlerical, progressive Liberals, and Conservatives pushing religion and tradition—that burned across the continent doomed the arrangement from the outset. The federation was pulled apart by dissension, jealousies, and rebellions, and was a dead letter by 1837.

As the federation crumbled in civil war a popular backlash against the Liberal assault on tradition filled the vacuum. In Guatemala a rustic and illiterate conservative *caudillo*, José Rafael Carrera, swept into power in 1840 at the head of a ragged army of devout Catholic Indians with the approval of the Church and landowning elite. Ruling until his death in 1865 Carrera dismantled the Liberal reforms, reinstituted the paternalistic fusion of church and state from the colonial regime, and oversaw the hegemony of Conservatism in Central America.

A Liberal counteroffensive across the isthmus closely followed Carrera's death. Another strongman came to rule Guatemala as an autocrat, this time in the name of democracy and constitutionalism rather than religion. Justo Rufino Barrios led the revolt that turned out the floundering Conservative regime and ruled with a stern hand beginning in 1873. He persistently denounced the tyranny of lifetime presidency while ruling until his death in 1885. Barrios believed firmly in order and progress and, following the ascendant Liberal program, did what he could to thrust Guatemala into the modern world of science and capitalism. He sponsored Liberal dictators in neighboring republics who nevertheless resisted his unilateral decree reuniting the federation; he was killed in action in El Salvador attempting to enforce his decision.

Liberal presidents reigned supreme following the Barrios years. Many were elected; most served their country until they died or were forcibly ejected. Executives enjoyed wide latitude, and constitutional niceties were easily amended to extend presidential terms and powers, making the presidency essentially an elective dictatorship. The Liberal reforms rotated the membership of the rulers—the Church was the big loser—but did not drastically change living conditions for the multitudes of Guatemalans.

The orthodoxy of the Liberal era dictated that the government hand stay out of the free exchange of goods and services except to ensure an attractive environment for commerce and investment. Agricultural export (mainly coffee) was encouraged as being the road to development, and Indian communal lands were put on the market to encourage production. Land-holding planters held unchallenged dominion over peasants. Landowners and the state frowned upon (and severely punished) labor organization, which was practically unknown. Continuing the *encomienda* tradition, labor laws ensured a continuing source of forced work for export agriculture.

The last of the long-term Liberal dictatorships was that of General Jorge Ubico y Castañeda. Beginning in 1931 he oversaw the modernization of national infrastructure, professionalized the military, encouraged commerce, and expanded the bureaucracy, and in so doing let loose a new and implacable political force: a frustrated and politically-minded middle class. During his third term in office Ubico managed to alienate much of the citizenry, whose dissatisfaction was made worse by the deplorable economic conditions of the Depression. Student protests in June of 1944 sparked a chain reaction of popular unrest that led to the general's resignation the same month and an uprising in October that ousted the military from the government altogether.

The Revolutionary Decade

The revolution that inaugurated the Decade of Spring was a modern movement in which the mobilized middle classes cast out the outdated nineteenth-century-style despotism. The budding popular sectors demanded an opening of the political sphere and participation in the affairs of state, a new development in Guatemala. Until now the multitudes had been unorganized and pliant, requiring periodic, forceful correction. The revolution opened unprecedented avenues for aggregation and communication to the excluded classes. Pluralism and liberal democracy could not so painlessly penetrate traditional Guatemala, however. The revolutionary period polarized Guatemalan society over progressive reforms, and all the while the threat of violence, a familiar political tool, loomed darkly.

Juan José Arévalo, a "spiritual socialist" known as the philosopher of the revolution, headed the first administration from 1945 to 1951. His moderately progressive government created channels of participation for the previously disenfranchised, a kind of New Deal for Guatemala. A new constitution at last gave popular organizations freedom to organize and strike, ended forced labor in the countryside, encouraged the assimilation of the Indians into national life (fiercely resisted by some Indians), and established a social security system. The relatively mild changes upset the traditional balance of interests, but Arévalo carefully sidestepped any radical impulses—like serious agrarian reform— that could have sent conservative forces over the edge. He failed, however, to establish a coherent party that would secure the revolution after his tenure, and the following administration did not imitate his tact.

Jacobo Arbenz Guzmán, a colonel who took part in the revolution, was elected in 1950 after his chief opponent, another revolutionary leader, met an untimely end at the hands of assassins. The Arbenz regime sought to further level the playing field for Indian peasants and urban laborers, funneled state resources to education and health, and broached the taboo subject of redistributing the highly concentrated land. Arbenz in this way collected many enemies among conservative forces in the military, business, and the Catholic Church.

An increasingly radical Arbenz regime also alarmed the Eisenhower administration on the lookout for Communist infiltration in the West. Arbenz stepped up fiery nationalist rhetoric toward the United States, looked benignly upon the participation of Communists in the government and labor unions, expropriated land owned by the United Fruit Company (the largest landholder in the country), and imported weapons from Czechoslovakia—the arms merchant of the Soviet bloc—to arm peasant and labor groups. Convinced Arbenz was intent on bolting to the Soviets, Eisenhower could swallow no more and threw his lot in with the armed opposition. The CIA lent financial and material support to disaffected members of the military, led by Colonel Carlos Castillo Armas, plotting to overthrow Arbenz.

The coup came on June 18, 1954. After ten days and a feckless defense Arbenz flew to exile. The covert assistance of the CIA has been hailed as a smashing success against creeping international Communism in some quarters, and in others remembered bitterly as the imperialist overthrow of a popularly elected reformer. The wild swinging of the political pendulum of the next years did begin in 1954, but in Guatemala social divisions and oppression had planted the seeds of discord long before the Cold War.

The Counterinsurgency

The post-1954 military government was confronted with a disintegrating society. Officers viewed the military as the last bastion of order, compelled to take extraordinary measures to defend against chaos and Communism. In order to restore a semblance of order the Armas and succeeding regimes set out to forcibly quell the activity of popular organizations let loose during the revolution. Economic indicators were upbeat in the 1960s and 1970s, contributing to middle- and upper-class satisfaction, but also feeding the restiveness of peasant and labor sectors anxious for the right to organize and share the wealth. Military governors allied with civilian technocrats attempted to manage economic and social diversification while guarding security as a revolutionary crisis gripped all of Central America.

A variety of leftist insurgents, including Communists and Indian peasant groups, took up arms around the country beginning in the early 1960s. The fighting waxed and waned with the strength of the guerrillas, who were twice nearly crushed—in the late 1960s and again in the early 1980s—only to regroup later and continue their campaign of attrition. Four of the principal groups banded together in 1982 to form the Guatemalan National Revolutionary Unity (URNG). The state nearly ceded control of the use of violence as guerrillas staged kidnappings and sabotaged infrastructure while the military blinked at private militias assassinating suspected subversives. The country had descended into intense polarization and civil war.

The dirty war reached its low in the early 1980s during the rule of General Efraín Ríos Montt, a Protestant evangelical with a penchant for messianic imagery. During Ríos Montt's eighteen-month dictatorship, he implemented his vision for securing peace and development, a plan of *frijoles y fusiles* (beans and guns) that combined populist redistributive measures with a merciless counterinsurgency campaign. The toll of the internecine war fell most heavily on the Indian population, provoking charges of a systematic campaign of genocide that invited international attention and sparked political fires in the United States and Europe.

Transition to Democracy

An elongated process of democratic transition began with the promulgation of a new constitution in 1984. Elections in 1985 ushered in a new Christian Democratic president, Vinicio Cerezo Arévalo, the first civilian government since 1969. Unpopular with the right and left, he was subject to coup attempts and denunciation as an agent of the military, but pursued a framework for a general peace in Central America. The government and URNG signed peace accords only in December of 1996, ending the shooting after thirty-six years, and transforming the rebels into electoral campaigners. During the war the military fended off rebellion and social conflict with systematic repression. Now elected civilians try to maintain the integrity of the same fractious nation as disillusionment and discontent seethe. The frustrations of governing pro-voked President Jorge Serrano Elías to attempt a Fujimori-style *autogolpe* in 1993 by illegally suspending the constitution and dismissing the legislature and Supreme Court, a maneuver that cost him the presidency. The fragile de-mocracy seems to lurch from one crisis to the next, but has since lived to see successive elections and orderly administrative turnover.

Society and Political Culture

Around thirteen million Guatemalans live in a land of renowned natural splendor that has promised—and delivered—easy riches, but only to a select few colonists, adventurers, and investors. Sixty percent of the population is Indian, situated primarily in the western highlands, speaking twenty-four dif-ferent languages (mostly Mayan), many of them ignorant of Spanish. Most people (approximately 80 percent) live in poverty, and the majority of those are Indians. Nearly three million inhabitants crowd the only major urban center, Guatemala City. It is a young country; over 40 percent of its people are younger than fifteen. Hopes that the youth will inherit an established constitutional democracy might hinge on the creation of a society more equitable than that of their parents.

The hierarchical system of exploitative labor familiar to most of Latin America characterizes centuries of Guatemalan political and social history. The Spanish adventurers of the sixteenth century coming to the new world on a civilizing and Christianizing crusade (one that might also prove quite profitable financially) established the core of a feudal society of landowners and state authorities squeezing labor out of Indians and poor *ladinos* in the hinterland, entrenching a strict observance of race and class that persists even now. A corporatist pyramid sent orders down and services up, first to the monarch and then to a president. Participation by the masses, when it occurred at all, was usually limited to rubber-stamping preselected candidates in safely mediated elections.

The mixture of blood between Europeans and Indians did not create understanding through living together. Liberal, Conservative, and military regimes varied in their policy approaches toward Indians, but all shared a haughty disdain for the indigenous peoples. Conquerors crusaded to civilize the savage, usually limited to promising to Christianize their subjects while impressing them into semislavery. Europeanized ladino elites have also viewed Indians with contempt, but mixed with an enthusiasm for assimilation into Guatemalan national society. Curiously, this can be accomplished within a single generation; racial identity is supplied through language and dress rather than genetics. An Indian who picks up Spanish and moves to the city becomes a ladino. Mayan communities have nonetheless demonstrated remarkable resilience in maintaining distinctive cultural patterns, less like Mexico and her sister republics where Hispanic hegemony was more complete. Though their cultures are unavoidably modified through synthesis, Indians have stayed outside the national structure, identifying with their parochial communities over an abstract Guatemala.

The culture of the conquest has been particularly strong in the old colonial capital. Strong currents of personalism, patrimonialism, militarism, and traditional Catholicism ran deep here and radiated outward to the rest of Central America. Recently though, currents have shifted, perhaps foreshadowing a striking shift in social and political relationships: democratic procedure has operated since the 1980s; Indians have continued a trend from the war years of greater organization and participation in national politics; the military has receded from outright domination of the political process; and Catholicism has watched half the churchgoing population embrace Protestantism.

Try as they might to reinforce elite rule and subservience of the lower strata, traditionalists failed to hold the clock still in the twentieth century. As the country diversified and modernized and the economy and government expanded to serve new demands, new groups impatient for their rights were thrown into the political mix. The middle class, the engine of democratization, exploded during the Ubico era, and the 1944 October Revolution changed the social and political terrain for good, but could not disenfranchise the old powers. Hierarchical, bossist patterns of behavior thus operate side by side with elements of participatory, constitutional democracy.

In spite of radical changes in the last century, and maybe unsurprisingly in this divided country with no history of limited government, liberal democracy has not met with stellar success. Some commitment to the rule of law manifested itself during Serrano's *autogolpe* when massive civil condemnation and even military disapproval forced his resignation. Nevertheless, support for democracy as a regime among the public has dropped consistently since then and in 2004 limped in at a dismal 35 percent, the lowest number in Latin America; satisfaction with the democratic government of Guatemala is even lower—at 21 percent.[1]

Clouding the issue further is the uncertainty that democracy in the Guatemalan idiom means much more than electing leaders—leaders who might then rule with an authoritarian free hand. A transition to procedural democracy has taken place, but commitment to liberal democracy as valuable in itself and the best regime—essential to the long-term survival of democracy—remains tenuous. Instead, presidents may simply fill the role of an elected national *patrón* at the head of an elaborate patronage network. While crime and corruption gnaw at the patience of the Guatemalan citizenry, the legitimacy of liberal democracy is far from a foregone conclusion.

Political Parties and Interest Groups

Iberian organic corporatism (reinforced by group-centered Indian traditions) has sharply conditioned state-society relations in Guatemala. Accordingly, the Guatemalan state has always kept a watchful eye on social segments, maintaining special laws for the formation and oversight of political parties and interest groups. Independent political opposition and civil society are only solidifying themselves since the rather recent transition to civilian government.

Political parties, usually considered the driving force in political competition, are weakly institutionalized in Guatemala. Without the political space to breathe in an elite-directed despotism, ideological parties offering alternative platforms to voters were scarcely known. The Liberal and Conservative parties that battled for total political domination in the nineteenth century engaged in machine politics, dispensing patronage in return for loyalty. Family and social ties normally determined party membership, and the factions took turns ruthlessly punishing each other when in power. Modern parties are fluid, a group of erratic coalitions and constantly shifting alliances often fashioned to serve the personal ambitions of political bosses or military factions, only to fizzle with the death or irrelevance of their leaders.

In the closed political atmosphere of the post-1954 era parties were subject to severe restrictions that allowed only officially tolerated parties to operate while the military acted as the power behind the throne. Only candidates representing vying military factions contested the first elections following the coup. Reformist military leaders in 1963 opened the door to a structured multiparty system, allowing a carefully managed pluralism. An official military party, the National Liberation Movement (MLN), competed with an assortment of other right-wing parties and sanctioned reformist parties, one of which, the Revolutionary Party (PR), won a surprise victory in the comparatively honest election of 1966.

Since the latest constitution (referred to as the *Carta Magna*) took effect a multitude of new parties and coalitions across the political spectrum has crowded the ballot, including the former armed guerrillas. Most of the main players in the old party system have reorganized or splintered into obscurity. In current elections voters choose from around twenty parties, many of which will not survive until the next election.

Oscar Berger of the Grand National Alliance (GANA), a makeshift coalition of three center-right parties, won the presidential election of 2003, beating out the candidate of the incumbent Guatemalan Republican Front (FRG), the personalist party of military strongman Ríos Montt. In the 2003 elections the largest number of seats in the Congress were won by GANA (forty-seven) and the FRG (forty-three). The National Unity of Hope (UNE) has emerged in recent years as the leader among left-leaning parties, earning thirty-two seats in 2003. The 2004 administrative transition was the fifth time a civilian government handed power over to another civilian government, a hopeful sign for democrats.

Given the underdeveloped state of most parties, organized interest groups have offered the most energetic representation for social sectors. Established interest groups are older, better organized, and more stable than most parties. The term "interest group" can be extended to embrace a wide range of sectors, including the old feudalistic corporate bodies as well as newer power contenders such as business, urban labor, and human rights groups. Lobbying in the halls of government is frequent, but since politics was a closed affair among tightly-knit elites for so long, many groups, particularly among the popular sectors, have been pushed into confrontational tactics. Rather than orderly, consensus-driven bargaining, competition often assumes a zero-sum character. Groups often resort to direct action over official channels, each threatening to use its own trump card—strikes, lockouts, demonstrations, or coups. Claimants to power might use whatever means at their disposal; the guerrillas, for instance, remade themselves from armed insurgents to legal political party.

Among prominent interest groups the Coordinating Committee of Agricultural, Commercial, Industrial, and Financial Associations (CACIF) gives voice to the economic elite that all governments hear; the National Coordination of Peasants' Organizations (CNOC) initiates seizures of uncultivated land; the General Coordination of Guatemalan Workers (CGTG) clashes with employers over pay and working conditions; the Group for Mutual Support (GAM) publicizes human rights concerns internationally. The dizzying array of competing groups appears chaotic and unmanageable, each group working at cross-purposes to some other. Insular groups and low social trust contribute to intergroup hostility and the occasional outburst of violence. Pluralism is a brute fact of social life in Guatemala, but not a public culture.

The State and Government Institutions

Historically reliant on simple force, the state has suffered from low legitimacy, and a lack of resources contributes to low effectiveness. A modern, centralized state structure began to emerge in the Liberal reform period, but many of the significant powers of the state authorities remained outside the definitions provided in the constitution and laws. Strong presidents and military dictators found it easy to give legal sanction to this or that preferred policy option through parliamentary fig leaves, decrees, and constitutional amendments or suspensions. State power hardly projected itself outside the capital, so large planters and political bosses acted with impunity in their rural domains. The fact of power has thus traditionally beaten out the rule of law.

Guatemala's constitutions have separated powers in the tripartite U.S. model, but in practice servile legislatures and judiciaries have respected the Hispanic tradition of strong executives. In addition to the three branches modern constitutions have established an independent Supreme Electoral Tribunal (TSE) to monitor elections.

The unicameral Congress consists of 158 members elected for four-year terms, one-quarter of them chosen by proportional representation, the rest with the first-past-the-post system—as in the United States. Parties that cannot muster 4 percent of the vote lose their registration and cannot compete in the next election. The president and vice president are also elected to four-year terms without the possibility of reelection.[2]

A Supreme Court of Justice sits at the top of the judicial branch, to which thirteen justices are elected by the Congress for five-year terms. The constitution guarantees the independence of the judiciary, and a special panel acting as a constitutional court exercises judicial review of legislative acts. The courts are weak, though, and criticized for the appearance of openness to political manipulation and threats.

Few radical changes are evident in the new fundamental law, but there is evidence that democratic practices are becoming more fully institutionalized. Perhaps most dramatically, the military appears satisfied that it has completed its stated historical mission of making Guatemala safe for democracy (the defense minister, a general, negotiated an end to the standoff during Serrano's *autogolpe*) and has accepted deep cuts in its budget and subordinated itself to civilian command. These are positive signs no doubt, but it bears remembering that legal prohibitions have always proved parchment barriers to political participation by the military.

Public Policy Issues

A number of social segments have gained grudging access to the political arena, but most people are still mired in problems of tragic dimensions. To the poverty and underdevelopment that has preoccupied all governments is added the burden of accountability for elected officials tackling entrenched social ills that defy easy solutions.

Government officials—civilian and military—have engaged in corruption at all levels as a matter of course. The transition to democracy has done little to alter perceptions of graft within the public sector. In 2000 President Alfonso Portillo Cabrera solemnly vowed to root out the massive corruption responsible for public contempt for officials. Four years later Portillo dodged corruption charges by absconding to Mexico.

Availability of guns and human desperation fuel an epidemic of violent street crime in both the cities and the country. Armed gangs target foreign tourists for highway holdups and kidnappings. Police have proven unproductive in dealing with the crisis and are often charged with complicity in organized crime. The new social plague of *Maras*—street gangs exported from Los Angeles to El Salvador to Guatemala—stretches the already thin resources of law enforcement in Guatemala City. The government declared war on the gangs responsible for hundreds of grotesque murders, a war it is ill-equipped to wage. Invitations for the military to help have raised concerns of backdoor remilitarization.

Politically motivated attacks, thousands of murdered women, and remobilization of death squads offer grim reminders that human rights violations do not vanish when the military retires from the presidential palace. In 1998 assassins bludgeoned and killed human rights activist Bishop Juan Gerardi Conedera in retaliation for a report blaming the military and its allies for almost all of the murders, disappearances, and rapes committed during the civil conflict and criticizing the impunity of those involved. A foot-dragging investigation ended with the conviction of three military officers and another priest. Rights promoters lament that the Gerardi case is an exceptional one profiting from international attention, and that most political killings go unpunished.

Implementation of the 1996 peace accords drags after ten years. Provisions for agrarian reforms and official recognition of Indian rights stir controversy. A package of constitutional amendments that would have given legal status to twenty-four Indian languages and guaranteed respect for their culture and traditions failed in a public referendum in 1999, a defeat for the full realization of the accords. Many thousands still suffer the direct effects of the armed conflict. A quarter of a million internal refugees, mostly Indians, scattered from their homes when the military destroyed more than four hundred villages; many of them have not been restored to their land as dictated by the peace agreements, and Indians continue to complain of mistreatment and discrimination by the state.

International Relations
and Globalization

As a colony Guatemala was kept isolated from the world around it, lest exotic ideologies infect a safely Iberian colony. After independence its foreign relations were limited mainly to securing foreign investment and disputing boundaries with neighbors Mexico and Belize.[3] Just as the old feudal order crumbled away under the forces of economic and social modernization and complexity, Guatemala in the twenty-first century is ineluctably drawn further into a global web of trade, communication, and migration. Further, an international ethos celebrating democracy means that Guatemala must contend with constant scrutiny by foreign governments and international human rights organizations as well as domestic civil and political groups.

Guatemala's primary international concerns are with regional economic integration, drug trafficking, and grave environmental degradation. A glimmer of the old dream of a united Central America shines through in efforts to confront these issues through cooperative regional organizations like the Organization of Central American States (ODECA), the System of Central American Integration (SICA), and the Central American Parliament (PARLACEN). Concrete steps toward integration are modest, though, and skeptics see PARLACEN in particular as a costly talk-shop and harbor for corrupt ex-presidents fleeing justice.[4]

Guatemala has always been deeply sensitive to conditions in the United States, which has at least partly determined the fates of a number of political leaders besides Arbenz. The Guatemalan economy is heavily dependent on aid from the United States, primarily provided through USAID. Assistance is tied to achievement of political and economic reforms aimed at democratic institutionalization and transparent government. Remittances from migrant Guatemalan workers in the United States funnel perhaps $3 billion yearly into Guatemalan homes (accurate figures are hard to come by), a desperately needed lifeline in a nation of dire unemployment and poverty.

As have most Latin American governments, successive administrations have pursued economic liberalization and diversification. Free trade agreements govern commerce with the Central American states and Mexico, and Guatemala joined the WTO in 1995. Political and business leaders hope the new U.S.–Central American Free Trade Agreement (CAFTA) will reinforce commercial growth, while detractors fear that it will only compound already gross inequalities.

Improvements in transportation, underresourced authorities, and a central location combine to make Guatemala prime real estate for international drug smugglers on their way to the United States. The government has put signatures on international counternarcotics and money laundering conventions to combat the trade, but performance in these areas has been underwhelming, earning a rebuke from the U.S. government in 2003. Greater attention to the area in recent years has produced some results, but the flood of drugs from abroad shows few signs of drying up.

Conclusion

Deep cleavages still criss-cross the Guatemalan social terrain: ladino and Indian; rich and poor; urban and rural; Catholic and Protestant. The old feudalistic order, stable for four centuries, crumbled under the weight of profound social-structural change and popular mobilization, degenerating into a protracted armed struggle. A liberal democratic scaffolding has been erected in its place, but the structure is still reconstituting itself.

Certainly a more open and participatory political atmosphere has replaced the counterinsurgency state's blanket of oppression, and the military has been (for now) defanged. Nonetheless, antidemocratic demagoguery or military intervention could offer a plausible alternative to ineffectual politicking in the event of an economic downturn, a population explosion, or unmitigated social violence. For now we cannot say whether there has occurred a deep shift in the relations between the individual and the state or only a modification on the surface while an authoritarian core persists below. The reality probably sits somewhere in between. At the close of a second decade of spring democratic consolidation in Guatemala still hangs in a delicate balance.

Suggestions for Further Reading

Immerman, Richard H. *The CIA in Guatemala: The Foreign Policy of Intervention.* Austin: University of Texas Press, 1982.

Jones, Chester Lloyd. *Guatemala, Past and Present.* Minneapolis: University of Minnesota Press, 1940.

Schneider, Ronald M. *Communism in Guatemala, 1944–1954.* NY: Praeger, 1958.

Smith, Carol A., ed. *Guatemalan Indians and the State: 1540–1988.* Austin: University of Texas Press, 1990.

Trudeau, Robert H. *Guatemalan Politics: The Popular Struggle for Democracy.* Boulder, CO: Lynne Rienner, 1993.

Woodward, Ralph Lee, Jr. *Central America: A Nation Divided*, 3rd edition. New York: Oxford University Press, 1999.

Yashar, Deborah. *Demanding Democracy: Reform and Reaction in Costa Rica and Guatemala.* Stanford, CA: Stanford University Press, 1997.

Notes

1. Figures are from the Latinobarómetro 2004 public opinion survey. Available on the web at www.latinobarometro.org.

2. Amendments changed the original length of terms served by elected officials.

3. The British colony was considered a violation of Spanish and Guatemalan sovereignty. President Serrano surprised—and angered—many when he unilaterally recognized Belize in 1991.

4. Presidents Portillo of Guatemala, Arnoldo Alemán of Nicaragua, and Mireya Moscoso of Panama have all claimed immunity from prosecution as deputies to PARLACEN.

22

Honduras
Problems of Democratic Consolidation

J. Mark Ruhl

H onduras would appear to be an unlikely candidate for democracy. It is one of the four poorest, least developed countries in the Americas. Throughout most of its history it has been ruled by a succession of dictatorial political bosses and military strongmen. In spite of the end of formal military rule in the early 1980s this authoritarian tradition persisted for many years. Behind a democratic facade the armed forces continued to exercise political control in an anticommunist alliance with the United States. Nevertheless, post–Cold War U.S. policy turned against the military during the 1990s, and an emboldened civil society pressured elected Honduran politicians to challenge the armed forces. As the power of the military receded, Honduras evolved into a more genuine democracy.

But can democracy endure over the long term in Honduras? Scholars assert that the consolidation of democracy requires that both political elites and the mass public accept the democratic process as legitimate and as "the only game in town."

Although Honduran civilian and military elites gradually have learned to abide by democratic rules, most ordinary Hondurans have found democratic governance to be a major disappointment. Neoliberal economic reforms required by international financial institutions have yet to reduce poverty or inequality in a country where three-quarters of the population still live below the poverty line. Moreover, widespread corruption has discredited one democratically chosen government after another. Elected leaders also have failed to stem an explosion in street crime and youth gang violence that has placed all

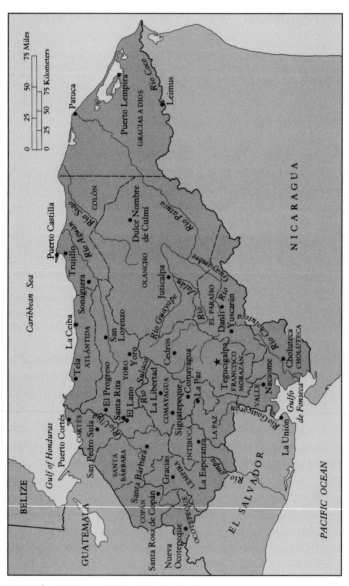

HONDURAS

Hondurans at risk. Because of these failures the Honduran democratic system has yet to earn the broad, unconditional support necessary to guarantee its long term survival.

History and Political Culture

Honduras is a mountainous, Pennsylvania-sized country of 6.5 million people. Its capital Tegucigalpa (851,000 population) is located high in the southern mountains, but its economic center is the commercial-industrial city of San Pedro Sula (489,000) on the tropical north coast. The majority of Hondurans live in rural areas where illiteracy is common (27 percent of Honduran adults are illiterate). Nearly 90 percent of the population is *mestizo*, but there are significant African-Honduran concentrations on the north coast and Bay Islands, as well as some remaining indigenous communities. Most Hondurans are Roman Catholics, although evangelical Protestants have made important gains during the last half-century. With a per capita GDP of $2,600 at purchasing power parity, Honduras is one of Latin America's poorest countries. Its economy depends on the export of bananas, coffee, and simple manufactured goods assembled in *maquiladora* factories as well as on remittances from Hondurans working in the United States.

Honduras has been ruled by authoritarian governments for most of its history. However, Honduran rulers and political elites were less repressive of popular sector groups and more willing to institute moderate reforms than their more violent counterparts in neighboring El Salvador, Guatemala, and Nicaragua. One of the reasons for this less confrontational style of elite-mass relations may lie in the fact that no coffee oligarchy ever gained dominance over land and politics in Honduras. While many powerful families in other Central American countries made their fortunes in coffee, Honduran elites of the late nineteenth and early twentieth centuries focused instead on small-scale cattle ranching, silver mining ventures, or small banana export enterprises.[1] None of these activities posed a threat to the peasantry in an underpopulated country where land was widely available well into the 1930s. Later, when coffee finally did become important in Honduras, it was grown primarily on small- and medium-sized farms. Although there was little friction between Honduran peasants and large landowners, constant battles for power among rival landed *caudillos* rendered the nation chronically unstable. These warring political bosses fought over the spoils of office rather than public policy. They promoted a clientelistic political tradition in which constitutional or electoral rules regularly were violated.

At the beginning of the twentieth century the United Fruit Company and other American banana enterprises established large plantations on the sparsely populated north coast. Hondurans who went to work for the banana giants eventually formed the strongest trade union movement in Central America. Although the banana companies exercised considerable leverage over Honduran governments, they could not always rely on public officials to repress striking workers. Stabilizing dictator Tiburcio Carías Andino (1932–1949) of the National Party was a loyal ally of United Fruit in this respect; however, leaders of the weaker Liberal Party were closer to labor. Juan Manuel Gálvez (1949–1954), Carías's moderate National Party successor, also negotiated a reasonably equitable settlement to the pivotal banana workers' strike of 1954. In addition, a new commercial-industrial elite with an important Arab-Honduran ("*Turco*") element formed on the north coast that generally backed the banana workers.[2] This cross-class, reformist coalition provided critical support to social democrat Ramón Villeda Morales, a physician who revitalized the Liberal Party in the 1950s.

The Honduran military also played a reformist role at times. Created with U.S. assistance in the 1940s, the armed forces soon became an important political actor independent of the feuding Liberal and National parties. The Honduran military first intervened in politics in 1956 to depose an unpopular provisional president. A military junta organized constituent assembly elections that produced a landslide victory for the long repressed Liberal opposition. But before returning to the barracks the military demanded that the new 1957 constitution guarantee its political autonomy. Future civilian presidents lost the power to select or dismiss the chief of the armed forces or to give orders directly to the military.

Liberal president Villeda Morales (1957–1963) met popular sector demands by introducing an urban social security system, a progressive labor code, and a small agrarian reform, but his actions upset new agricultural export elites (cotton, beef, and sugar) as well as traditional rural political bosses. Moreover, his creation of a Liberal-led Civil Guard to counterbalance the military incensed the armed forces leadership. When the Liberals' candidate to succeed Villeda threatened to end the military's political autonomy, the armed forces formed an alliance with the National Party and staged a preemptive coup in 1963.

Armed forces commander General Oswaldo López Arellano ruled Honduras for almost the entire period from 1963 to 1975. During the López era peasants organized to demand land reform in response to a land scarcity problem caused by rapid twentieth century population growth and the post–World War II expansion of commercial agriculture. Although López initially repressed these groups, he later permitted some land invasions. He also evicted about eighty thousand Salvadoran peasants living in Honduras in order to make more land available. During the 1969 war with El Salvador that followed, Honduran peasants, trade unionists, and the north coast business community rallied around the armed forces despite their previous differences with General López. Shortly thereafter the air force general broke with the National Party to form a progressive political alliance with these groups. After briefly allowing a bipartisan civilian government to take office in 1971 López returned to power via military coup in late 1972. His new government was populist in orientation, redistributing land to about one-fifth of the landless and land-poor population. General López also created a wide range of new government agencies that increased the role of the state in the economy and provided urban middle- and lower-class employment opportunities.

López was forced to resign the presidency in 1975 after being accused of taking a bribe from United Brands (formerly United Fruit) in exchange for reducing the export tax on bananas. His more conservative successors, Colonel Juan Melgar Castro (1975–1978) and General Policarpo Paz García (1978–1982), re-allied with the National Party and large landowners. Nonetheless, some land distribution continued, and trade unions remained important political players. The Honduran military's more accommodative stance encouraged popular sector organizations to continue to press their demands within established political channels. While highly repressive, intransigent governments in El Salvador, Nicaragua, and Guatemala drifted into civil war with radicalized popular sector oppositions, Honduras remained stable.

Democratic Elections and Military Dominance in the 1980s

With strong encouragement from the United States the Honduran armed forces allowed an elected civilian, Liberal Roberto Suazo Córdova to assume the presidency in 1982. Nonetheless, the military remained the dominant political actor with its political autonomy reaffirmed in a new 1982 constitution. In spite of the democratic veneer the armed forces grew larger and more powerful than ever as the United States raised military aid to unprecedented levels in return for permission to base anti-Sandinista Nicaraguan guerrillas in Honduras. President Suazo became the junior partner in an unsavory political alliance with Argentine-trained armed forces chief General Gustavo Alvárez Martínez.

A fervent anticommunist, General Alvárez conducted a small but brutal "dirty war" of torture and assassination against suspected revolutionaries. He also used the army and police to infiltrate unions, student organizations, and peasant groups presumed to have radical leanings. His violent antisubversive campaign was a sharp break with Honduran traditions. Fortunately, Alvárez's arrogance and drive for total control within the armed forces led to his ouster in an internal military coup in 1984. After his fall the military's antisubversive activities declined in intensity. Nevertheless, the military continued to maintain its supremacy over civilian authorities throughout the rest of the 1980s. During this period corruption within the armed forces reached new extremes. Honduras had by then become an important transshipment point in the international narcotics trade, and some senior officers became rich by protecting drug shipments.

Civilian president Suazo (1982–1986) also proved to be a threat to democratization. Like most other Honduran politicians the former country doctor had embarked on a political career not to pursue policy convictions but to acquire *chamba* (patronage) for his followers as well as wealth and power for himself. Not surprisingly, corruption was widespread in his administration, and short-term personal power calculations determined policy. Moreover, as his term drew to a close, Suazo used a variety of illegal means to try to continue in power beyond the single presidential term allowed by law. His machinations divided both traditional parties and precipitated a constitutional clash with the National Congress. Most of civil society mobilized against Suazo, but the crisis was not resolved until mediation by military officers produced a compromise electoral solution.

A Suazo opponent, Liberal José Azcona del Hoyo (1986–1990), emerged victorious from the 1985 presidential contest. Although the new president respected the constitutional limits of his office, his policy achievements were few. He lacked both a coherent plan of action and a secure base of support in the National Congress. Decisions about internal or external security policies remained mostly matters for negotiations between the United States embassy and the Honduran military.[3]

The Decline of the Military

The democratic electoral process Suazo had undermined was strengthened in 1990 when Liberal president Azcona passed the sash of office to his freely elected National Party successor Rafael Callejas. This ceremony marked the first democratic turnover of power between competing Honduran political parties in nearly sixty years. During the rest of the decade the electoral process became institutionalized with regular presidential and legislative elections every four years. Never before in its history had Honduras experienced such an extended period of peaceful electoral politics and regular executive succession. Yet, in spite of its free elections and expanded civil and political liberties Honduras could not be considered a real democracy as long as the military remained the strongest political actor.

With the end of the Cold War and the Central American civil wars the United States no longer needed the Honduran military as an ally against communism.[4] Instead, U.S. policy makers began to see the military as an unnecessary obstacle to democratization. By 1993 American military aid had been cut to almost nothing, and the U.S. embassy had become a strident critic of the armed forces. Encouraged by this dramatic reversal in U.S. policy, Honduran human rights organizations, student groups, unions, the Catholic Church, and even many business groups joined forces in an attack on the military's power and prerogatives. The unusual strength and breadth of this antimilitary movement persuaded Honduran party leaders to challenge the military on a range of issues. Mounting internal and external pressures forced Conservative President Rafael Callejas (1990–1994) to take action despite his long friendship with the armed forces. In 1992 he appointed the nation's first human rights commissioner, who soon issued a report implicating the armed forces in the disappearances of the 1980s dirty war. Callejas also appointed an Ad Hoc Commission for Institutional Reform in 1993 headed by Archbishop Oscar Andrés Rodríguez to look into charges of corruption and abuse of power within the military's national police branch. The Ad Hoc Commission recommended that the controversial investigative arm of the police be replaced by a civilian alternative under the control of a newly created Attorney General's office. These developments as well as an avalanche of press revelations about military corruption and other criminal activity placed the once unassailable armed forces on the defensive.

The political decline of the military accelerated under Callejas's Liberal successors Carlos Roberto Reina (1994–1998) and Carlos Flores Facussé (1998–2002). A former president of the Inter-American Court of Human Rights, Reina immediately instituted the Ad Hoc Commission's recommendations and later passed constitutional reforms that ended obligatory military service and stripped the armed forces of control of the entire National Police force. He also trimmed the military budget and removed the Honduran telecommunications system and other sources of illicit funding from armed forces management. With only low wages to offer, the military eventually shrank to less than one-third its former size. Although members of the military high command protested Reina's actions, they were forced to accept these reforms because the armed forces could no longer credibly threaten to destabilize or oust the civilian government. Military leaders recognized that a coup would instantly provoke a hostile reaction from the United States, the OAS, and Honduran civil society.

In early 1999 President Carlos Flores passed a constitutional reform that ended the military's formal political autonomy, placing the armed forces under a civilian defense minister for the first time since 1957. The formerly independent post of armed forces chief and the Superior Council of the Armed Forces, the military's collegial decision-making body, were abolished. In mid-1999 the Liberal president demonstrated his new authority by dismissing the armed forces chief of staff and several other high ranking officers and re-placing them with officers more inclined to accept civilian control without complaint. By the time National Party leader Ricardo Maduro assumed the presidency in 2002 the political subordination of the armed forces to civilian control was an accomplished fact. With this achievement Honduras finally completed the transition to procedural democracy that it had begun in the early 1980s. Unfortunately, Honduras's brand of democracy still leaves much to be desired.

Political Parties and Elections

Few Hondurans enter politics in order to serve the public interest. The tradi-tional Liberal (PLH) and National (PNH) parties are both nonprogrammatic, patron-client political machines primarily organized to compete for state jobs and resources. Each party is divided into several personalist factions. Com-peting faction leaders are key national actors who wield great influence over candidate selection and patronage distribution. Both parties choose their pres-idential candidate by means of a national primary election that pits factional contenders against one another. Both the Nationals and the Liberals are cen-trist, multiclass parties that benefit from widespread, although declining, hereditary party affiliation. The party identification balance traditionally fa-vored the Liberals, whose voter support was strongest in urban areas such as San Pedro Sula and in the more developed north coast departments, but in the nation's most recent elections in 2001 the National Party defeated the Liberals in all the main north coast departments and in both of the country's largest cities. Two minor reformist political parties, the Innovation and Unity Party (PINU) and the Christian Democrats (PDCH), as well as the newer, more leftist Democratic Unification Party (PUD), also participate in Honduran elections. None of these parties, however, have been able to garner substantial popular support. In 2001 the three minor parties together won only 3.5 per-cent of the presidential vote and 12.9 percent of the legislative vote.

The Honduran president is elected by plurality for a single four-year term. The unicameral National Congress is selected at the same time by propor-tional representation. Until split-ticket voting became possible in 1997, Hon-durans simply cast one party ballot for all national offices. Honduran elections are supervised by the Supreme Electoral Tribunal (TSE), whose three magis-trates (one PNH, one PLH, one PDCH in 2004) each required a two-thirds congressional majority for election. Since the 1980 Constituent Assembly elections restored electoral politics Honduras has held six consecutive general elections. With the exception of the 1985 electoral process that was marred by President Roberto Suazo's illegal interference, all of these contests have taken place without significant irregularities. The National Party won control of the presidency and the National Congress in the 1989 elections while the Liberal Party won in both 1993 and 1997. In 2001 the Nationals again captured the presidency but captured only a plurality of seats in the National Congress.

The 2001 presidential election pitted Stanford-educated economist and former central bank chief Ricardo Maduro of the National Party against National Congress president and former elementary school teacher Rafael Piñeda Ponce of the Liberal Party. Although the two candidates differed little on national issues, the much younger (age fifty-five) and more dynamic Maduro won the presidency by a wide margin, taking nearly 52 percent of the vote to Piñeda's (age seventy-two) 44 percent. The Nationals failed to garner a majority in the National Congress, winning 61 of the 128 seats contested to the Liberals' 55 seats; however, the Christian Democrats (four seats) later allied with the Nationals giving the larger party congressional control. The other two minor parties divided the remaining legislative seats (five PUD, three PINU). In a context of increasing public disillusionment with the performance of the democratic political system, about two-thirds of eligible Hondurans turned out to vote in 2001. This level of voter turnout represented a major decline from the over 80 percent turnout levels of the 1980s.

The most recent electoral cycle began with primary election campaigns in 2005 that involved eight Liberal Party presidential candidates and four National Party candidates. The party primaries produced easy victories for National Congress president Porfirio "Pepe" Lobo Sosa of the National Party, an anticrime hardliner who stressed the need to restore the death penalty, and Liberal rancher and congressman Manuel "Mel" Zelaya, who emphasized his rural roots. The two would face one another in the November 2005 presidential election.

Major Interest Groups

The military was the most powerful actor in Honduran politics from the 1960s until the middle 1990s, but its political influence has declined precipitously. Although General Oswaldo López Arellano championed land reform during the 1970s and General Gustavo Alvárez Martínez launched an anticommunist crusade in the 1980s, most Honduran military officers have been motivated by simple greed and lust for power. The armed forces have long been factionalized by personal and generational divisions. The military's loss of resources in the 1990s exacerbated these splits. President Flores's dismissal of a number of top officers in 1999 was intended not only to strengthen civilian control over the institution but also to reduce internal factional squabbling among *promociones* (military academy graduating classes). Although it no longer enjoys great political power, the military still operates the nation's only intelligence agency and often plays a key internal security role in assisting the police to patrol Honduras's crime-ridden cities.

The interest of the U.S. government in Honduras declined dramatically after the end of the Central American civil wars. Nevertheless, the U.S. embassy has remained a major political actor. American Ambassador Cresencio Arcos played a critical role in promoting the rise of the antimilitary movement in the early 1990s. In addition, U.S. economic leverage has helped international financial institutions force Honduran presidents to sustain unpopular neoliberal economic programs. The U.S. government continues to be an important source of resources, and contributed heavily to the international rebuilding effort after Hurricane Mitch destroyed much of the country's infrastructure in 1998.

The highly fragmented Honduran private business sector traditionally has been considered the weakest in Central America. Several competing investment groups contribute to political campaigns and vie for influence over government economic decisions. The business community is also split by region (San Pedro Sula-based versus Tegucigalpa-based enterprises), ethnicity (Arab-Honduran owned companies versus others), and the economic sector. The principal umbrella organizations for the private sector are the Honduran Private Enterprise Council (COHEP) and the Honduran Chamber of Commerce. Foreign investors in the *maquiladoras*, the banana industry, and elsewhere also naturally seek to influence Honduran government policy.

Honduras traditionally has had the strongest independent labor movement in Central America, although its unions have suffered from ideological divisions and internal leadership conflicts. The moderate, AFL-CIO–linked Honduran Workers' Confederation (CTH), which includes most banana workers, is the country's most important labor federation. The other major national labor organizations are the social-Christian General Confederation of Workers (CGT) and the smaller, leftist United Federation of Honduran Workers (FUTH). Some organizations within the fragmented peasant movement are affiliated with these three labor confederations while others exist independently. Labor unions that organize public sector employees—particularly teachers and health care workers—have been successful in using strikes to win important economic concessions from the government in recent years despite external demands for fiscal austerity.

Honduran civil society has strengthened of late as many new types of interest groups have become active. Antiglobalization groups like the National Grassroots Resistance (CNRP) have joined existing human rights proponents such as the Committee for the Defense of Human Rights in Honduras (CODEH) and traditional actors like the Roman Catholic Church to pressure government officials on a range of issues. In addition, student groups and women's organizations as well as newly organized urban slum dwellers and indigenous communities have become more active in the last two decades. Since the late 1990s unions, peasant organizations, slum dwellers, and indigenous groups have increasingly resorted to direct action (road blockages, marches on the capital) to press their demands for governmental assistance.

Government Institutions and Public Policymaking

The Honduran governmental system is highly centralized with power concentrated in the presidency. The president introduces most legislation and directs the activities of executive branch agencies. If the president heads a majority coalition of party factions in the National Congress his policy initiatives usually become law, often with little modification. However, public policymaking is often not the president's highest priority. The chief executive spends much of his time protecting his personal power base by distributing patronage and other material payoffs to supporters in his own and allied party factions and by countering the political moves of his enemies. The National Congress historically has not played a significant policy-making role; congressional seats generally have been viewed as rewards for factional loyalty rather than opportunities for public service. However, in recent years the National Congress has become more important in policymaking and executive oversight. This has been true especially when the National Congress has been controlled by party factions not affiliated with the president or when the president of the National Congress has harbored ambitions to become chief executive. Factions in the minority party become most influential in the National Congress when the president proposes constitutional reforms, which require a two-thirds majority in two consecutive legislative sessions.

At the beginning of every four-year presidential term the National Congress appoints the fifteen justices of the Honduran Supreme Court from a group of forty-five candidates approved by a nominating committee composed of civil society representatives. The Supreme Court justices then appoint the judges of the lower courts. The Honduran judiciary is highly politicized, and judicial corruption and incompetence are widespread. Few high-ranking civilian or military officials accused of corruption or abuse of power have ever been prosecuted successfully.

Effective policymaking is difficult in Honduras. Resources are scarce, the state bureaucracy is notoriously inefficient, and the political class is driven by spoils rather than policy goals. A few Honduran presidents, such as Liberal reformer Carlos Reina, have come into office with clear policy objectives;

however, the enactment of public policies to address national problems usually is driven by external pressure or by an acute internal crisis. The fundamental changes in Honduran economic policy that led to the adoption of neoliberalism in the 1990s, for example, were forced by an international credit boycott orchestrated by international financial institutions and the U.S. government.

Rafael Callejas began the process of orthodox structural economic reform in 1990. He cut the size of the nation's chronically high fiscal deficit by shrinking the bureaucracy and by increasing taxes.[5] He also liberalized trade, devalued the currency, and persuaded foreign investors to establish new *maquiladora* factories. These IMF-mandated policies reduced inflation and restored external financial support. Unfortunately, during his final year in office the National Party leader undermined the reform program by raising public capital spending by 50 percent and by granting large wage increases to public employees. These actions sent the fiscal deficit back up to unmanageable levels and rekindled inflation. Many believe that increased capital spending enabled Callejas and other corrupt officials to collect hefty kickbacks from contractors.

After some initial difficulties, the Reina administration capably implemented the nation's economic reform program. Although Reina made more concessions to organized labor than the IMF recommended, the Liberal government restored fiscal discipline and eventually met most IMF targets. Aided by rising coffee prices, booming *maquiladora* exports, and cheap oil imports, the Honduran economy was growing at about a 5 percent yearly rate when Reina left office in early 1998. During the first months of his term Liberal Carlos Flores maintained fiscal austerity and initiated the country's first privatization program, but his economic planning was completely disrupted by Hurricane Mitch in late 1998. The worst natural disaster to strike Honduras in the century forced a suspension of banana exports and destroyed the majority of the country's roads and bridges. Total damage to the Honduran economy was estimated at $5 billion.

President Flores personally supervised the rebuilding of the Honduran economy during the rest of his term and saw it resume a nearly 5 percent GDP growth rate by the year 2000 before falling coffee prices and a recession in the United States slowed growth the following year. The popular Flores, however, left his successor an overly large fiscal deficit (6 percent of the GDP), in part because he agreed to too generous a settlement to end a national teachers strike. President Maduro maintained neoliberal policies as the Honduran economy continued its modest recovery aided by a coffee price rebound and soaring remittances from Hondurans living in the United States (reaching nearly one billion dollars by 2004). The nation's fiscal deficit, however, remained too high under Maduro, and rising oil import costs weakened overall economic performance.

Although presidents Reina, Flores, and Maduro generally won praise from international financial institutions for their efforts to reform and expand the economy, most Hondurans saw little improvement in their miserable living conditions. Half of the population continues to subsist on the equivalent of less than one dollar a day. Tax reforms to reduce tax evasion by the well-to-do minority might have helped to better fund social programs to reduce deep inequalities, but few of those with influence in Honduran politics are interested in paying more taxes. Recent governments have also failed to revive the agrarian reform program that came to a halt during the Callejas administration, or addressed the still-rapid 2.5 percent Honduran population growth rate.

It is not difficult to understand why most Hondurans have been critical of the economic and social policies of their elected democratic leaders. Hondurans have also been deeply disillusioned by the high level of government corruption. In 2004 Transparency International rated Honduras as one of the six most corrupt countries in Latin America.[6] But for many the greatest disappointment has been their democratic rulers' inability to control the crime wave that has enveloped the country in the last decade. Bank robberies, homicides, car thefts, and muggings have soared, and new criminal organizations have proliferated. President Ricardo Maduro, whose own son had been killed by kidnappers, made attacking crime his number one priority, but his heavy-handed zero-tolerance policies directed against the Mara Salvatrucha, Calle 18, and related youth gangs were not especially successful. Although many gang members were imprisoned, more than one hundred thousand remained at large. Drug trafficking through Honduras also appears to have increased during Maduro's presidency. The small, underfunded, and poorly equipped national police force is inadequate to meet these challenges.

Few Hondurans base their opinions about government performance on foreign policy, although this is an area of major concern to the Honduran president and his advisors. Honduran foreign policy officials commonly devote more attention to their relations with the United States than to their ties with the rest of the world combined. Their principal goal is to secure economic resources, trade preferences, and favorable immigration policies from the United States. While the Central American civil wars raged in the 1980s Honduras had considerable leverage with U.S. officials who wished to use the country as a platform for counterrevolutionary activities in Nicaragua and El Salvador. After the end of these wars, however, Honduras lost its importance for the United States, and U.S. foreign aid declined sharply. Honduran foreign policy makers, nonetheless, continue to encourage greater Central American regional economic and security cooperation with the United States. Honduras has been a strong supporter of the Central American Free Trade Agreement (CAFTA) and briefly contributed a military unit to the U.S.-led coalition in Iraq in 2003.

Future Prospects

Honduras has made impressive democratic strides since the early 1990s. Three turnover elections (1989, 1993, 2001) demonstrate that the electoral system has become firmly institutionalized. The long dominant military also has been subordinated to civilian control. Most Honduran civilian politicians and active duty military officers accept the democratic system today, and fears of U.S. reprisals help keep the few who have not in check. Consequently, the chances of a reversion to authoritarian politics in the short term are minimal. However, Honduras is hardly a model democracy. The performance of elected democratic governments has fallen far short of public expectations. Most public officials have concentrated on capturing the legal and illegal spoils of office for themselves and their political networks rather than on addressing the needs of one of the poorest populations in the Americas. Neoliberal economic reforms have yet to improve the lives of the underprivileged majority. Street crime and gang violence continue to rage out of control.

The mass public's unhappiness with the quality of democratic governance in Honduras was indicated clearly in a recent cross-national *Latinobarómetro* survey of Latin Americans in which only 30 percent of Hondurans expressed satisfaction with the functioning of democracy in their country. Although 46 percent still preferred democracy to any other political system, fully 70 percent of Hondurans admitted that they would not mind the imposition of a non-democratic government if it would solve the nation's economic problems.[7] Among all Latin Americans, only Paraguayans showed greater interest in such an authoritarian alternative. For democracy to consolidate for the long term the Honduran mass public must develop a much stronger sense of allegiance to democracy. However, this can only happen if elected officials start to behave in a manner more worthy of public respect and begin to implement more governmental policies that tangibly improve the lives of ordinary people.

Suggestions for Further Reading

Euraque, Darío A. *Reinterpreting the Banana Republic: Region and State in Honduras, 1870–1972*. Chapel Hill: University of North Carolina Press, 1996.
Mahoney, James. *The Legacies of Liberalism: Path Dependence and Political Regimes in Central America*. Baltimore: Johns Hopkins University Press, 2001.

Merrill, Tim L., ed., *Honduras: A Country Study.* Washington, DC: U.S. Government Printing Office, 1995.

Morris, James A. *Honduras: Caudillo Politics and Military Rulers.* Boulder, CO: Westview Press, 1984.

Salomón, Leticia. *Democratización y sociedad civil en Honduras.* Tegucigalpa: Centro de Documentación de Honduras, 1994.

Schulz, Donald E., and Deborah S. Schulz. *The United States, Honduras, and the Crisis in Central America.* Boulder, CO: Westview Press, 1994.

Notes

1. The historical section of this chapter draws extensively on J. Mark Ruhl, "Honduras: Militarism and Democratization in Troubled Seas," in Thomas Walker and Ariel Armony, eds., *Repression, Resistence, and Democratic Transition in Central America* (Wilmington, DE: Scholarly Resources, 2000).

2. Darío A. Euraque, *Reinterpreting the Banana Republic: Region and State in Honduras, 1870–1972* (Chapel Hill: University of North Carolina Press, 1996), 96–97.

3. Mark B. Rosenberg, "Narcos and Políticos: The Politics of Drug Trafficking in Honduras," *Journal of Interamerican Studies and World Affairs* 30, no. 2–3 (1988): 152–153.

4. This analysis draws from J. Mark Ruhl, "Redefining Civil-Military Relations in Honduras," *Journal of Interamerican Studies and World Affairs* 38, no. 1 (1996): 41–53.

5. The analysis of economic policy draws on J. Mark Ruhl, "Doubting Democracy in Honduras," *Current History* 96 (1997): 84–85.

6. Transparency International Corruption Perceptions Index, 2004. www.transparency.org.

7. "Democracy's Low-Level Equilibrium," *The Economist* (August 13, 2004): 35–36.

23

The Dominican Republic

A Winding Road to
Democracy and Development

Esther M. Skelley

The Dominican Republic shares the Caribbean island of Hispaniola with the failed state of Haiti. In stark contrast to their chaotic neighbor, Dominicans have integrated into the globalized world, experienced record economic growth, and become a key trading partner with the United States. They have recently passed through a storm of economic crises with democratic institutions intact, perhaps even strengthened.

That said, this little country of about nine million people and forty-nine thousand square miles continues along a winding road toward democracy and development. The Dominican Republic long followed Latin American tradition with a triumvirate of power (oligarchy, church, and military). That is no longer so. After two American interventions and many decades of dictatorship and authoritarian "democracy," the Dominican Republic is maturing into a unique democratic state. Economic diversification has diminished the once dominant agriculture sector to less than 15 percent of the national gross domestic product. The land-holding oligarchs have gone into business and maintained a position at the top of society—albeit a somewhat diminished one. Meanwhile, the church and military have declined in power, but continue to act as arbiter and counterbalance to the state, respectively.

Although much has changed, Dominicans continue to live in a society characterized by family connections, patronage, and strict class divisions based on race and socioeconomic status. Despite great leaps in economic growth, a

DOMINICAN REPUBLIC

severe income gap remains, as a very large segment of the population still does not have access to even the most basic necessities of life.

The 2004 election brought Leonel Fernández to power on promises of economic stabilization and institutional reform aimed at strengthening government accountability and increasing transparency. With a track record of success in his first administration Fernández is likely to make good on his promises the second time around. The economy is already stabilizing. The confidence of foreign investors is being restored and the Dominican Republic-Central America-United States Free Trade Agreement (CAFTA-DR) has been passed. Several beginning steps have also been taken toward greater transparency and accountability. However, patronage is the grease that oils the institutions of the Dominican Republic, and it remains to be seen whether a society that has long preferred public handouts to public service is ready for such drastic change.

Background

Hispaniola was discovered by Columbus in 1492. The Spanish soon established Santo Domingo (now the Dominican capital) as their first capital in the New World. As agriculture and mining took off, Spain built churches, schools and hospitals. Through disease as well as arms the Spanish quickly eliminated most natives on the island and imported slaves from Africa. Over the next fifty years the colony received an influx of Spaniards and built a racially-based, two-class authoritarian system.

The early years of a state-run extraction economy quickly depleted the colony's mineral supply. The next two hundred years were marked by economic decline and social/political disarray as the Spanish, French, British, and pirates from the Netherlands competed for control of the island. The Spanish ceded the western third of the island to the French in 1697.

At the outset of the nineteenth century Santo Domingo's economy lagged far behind that of its western neighbor, Saint-Dominique (now Haiti), then the largest sugar producer in the world. The French colony's large slave population began to revolt in 1793. Soon thereafter former slaves from Saint-Dominique invaded Santo Domingo. In response, Spain sent forces in 1809 to occupy Santo Domingo and prevent a slave revolt there. After several years of weak Spanish rule the colony declared independence in 1821. No sooner did the Dominican Republic break free than the newly independent Haiti invaded and seized control. The Haitians began to modernize the sugar industry and freed the slaves. They also redistributed the land and drove out the Spanish elites. These moves greatly upset the Catholic Church, which owned most of the former colony's land, and led Santo Domingo to declare independence from Haiti in 1844.

The first two decades of Dominican independence were marked by repeated coups and Haitian invasions. Then, in 1861 the Spanish re-annexed their former colony. The Dominican Republic declared independence again in 1865 and power shifted between parties until Ulises Heureaux's dictatorship in 1882 provided stability and modernization. This modernization put the country into great debt.

After Heureaux's assassination in 1899 the United States feared an European intervention aimed at collecting debts. Consequently, the United States took control of Dominican customs receipts in 1905 and began economic restructuring in 1915. One year later U.S. Marines invaded to quell increasing political instability and depose the anti-American faction in power. Until their 1924 departure the marines built infrastructure, trained a Dominican army, and established the procedures for democratic government. The U.S. troops brought great advances in many areas, from health and sanitation to roads and education. They left behind a nation obsessed with baseball, one that in time produced major league greats such as Pedro Martinez, Manny Ramírez, and Sammy Soza. They also left behind a fledgling electoral democracy and a well trained army under General Rafael Trujillo.

In 1930, soon after the United States withdrew, Trujillo wrested power from the weak democratic government of President Horacio Vázquez. Trujillo immediately established a semifascist, totalitarian dictatorship that is widely regarded as the most repressive in Latin American history. He wielded a heavy and often brutal hand in all aspects of Dominican society for thirty years. He controlled the food supply and was responsible for sordid crimes ranging from forced prostitution to murder. In 1937 he ordered the massacre of thousands of Haitians along the Dominican border. This massacre marked the beginning of an anti-African and antianimist nationalist ideology, which the leading intellectuals of the day, Joaquín Balaguer and Manuel Arturo Peña Battle, contended was essential for the maintenance of independence and protection of the Haitian border. These same intellectuals helped Trujillo construct a corporatist system in which the government created state-sponsored, -regulated, and -controlled business, labor, and other groups to help regiment the citizenry.

The 1959 Castro Revolution in Cuba sparked fear in the United States that rising opposition against Trujillo would culminate in another socialist revolution in the Dominican Republic. With U.S. support a group of assassins killed Trujillo in 1961. However, there was no contingency plan in place and the political system spun into crisis.

Trujillo's puppet president, Joaquín Balaguer, assumed control of the state following the dictator's assassination, but was replaced by elected leftist Juan Bosch in 1962. A military coup removed Bosch from power and quickly led to civil war. The United States' fear that a socialist government would emerge victorious prompted another U.S. invasion of the Dominican Republic in 1965. Leading scholars contend that this fear was unfounded given that the rebels leading the revolt supported both democracy and the United States.[1] After a year of fighting, the U.S. peacekeepers and the Dominican factions reached an agreement that called for elections. This imposed reconciliation between Dominicans led to U.S. withdrawal.

Balaguer, a conservative, was elected in a 1966 violence-ridden election. He brought stability to the country. The United States contributed millions of dollars to his administration while turning a blind eye to his practices of clientelism and political repression. The 1978 election replaced Balaguer's corrupt government with the candidate favored by the Carter Administration, Antonio Guzmán. Four years later Jorge Blanco won on an anticorruption message, but did not follow through. He also failed to make good on his promise to never accept an IMF package. In 1984 he reached an agreement with the IMF that brought on mass riots and subsequent police brutality.

Balaguer was consequently returned to power in the 1986 election. He won the next two elections amid accusations of electoral fraud. This time his still authoritarian regime governed with less violence. He closed the economy despite the trend of liberalization spreading throughout Latin America. He invested in infrastructure and espoused an anti-Haitian nationalist ideology characterized by consistent police harassment of Haitian workers. Despite his authoritarian rule and election fraud Balaguer was considered by many to be a strong leader and father figure. Not only did he establish stability and promote modernization, he was known to garner support in the countryside by handing out money to passersby. In the end, the 1994 election irregularities aroused so much domestic and international opposition that a constitutional amendment was passed to prevent the president from seeking reelection. Nonagenarian Balaguer was consequently forced to serve only two years of his term.

The 1996 election that followed brought Leonel Fernández to power. Already on the upward path, the Dominican economy took off under the Fernández administration through diversification. The undeveloped and traditional sugar-dependent economy gave way to a sustained average growth rate of over 7 percent. It even surpassed the growth rates of the newly industrialized countries of East Asia. The constitution prevented Fernández from seeking reelection for a second term in 2000. Despite the candidacy of an aging Balaguer power was yielded to the opposition party of Hipólito Mejía. Growth was sustained for two years under the new administration, although at a lower rate of 3 to 4 percent.

By 2002 the economic and political outlook was very promising. With national gross domestic product up to $21.3 billion (more than double that of the early eighties), literacy up to 84 percent, and a rural population of less than one-third, the Dominican Republic was well on its way to modernization.[2] To top it all off, a peaceful exchange of power through the last three elections has placed Dominicans in the company of maturing democracies.

A devastating banking crisis brought this positive trend to a halt in 2003. It was discovered that the country's largest banks were engaged in rampant fraudulent activity that involved government officials and members of competing political parties alike. The Mejía administration's failure to prosecute those involved evoked widespread public protest. A government bailout of the banks that diverted a huge share of the national budget began a sharp economic decline. Inflation soared, business confidence dropped, and capital flight began. The cost of living increased exponentially as salaries decreased. Public unrest ensued. In response, Mejía took control of several media outlets. He also doubled the size of the military, reinstated and increased the pensions of retired officers and issued large numbers of motorcycles, helicopters, and cars to the military.

Despite Mejía's apparent attempts to buy off the armed forces and limit negative press as he campaigned for re-election, he conceded defeat in the 2004 election and transferred power peacefully. Leonel Fernández was elected to a second, nonconsecutive term on promises to increase government transparency and restore the prosperity of the 1990s. At printing he appears to be well on his way to doing just that.

Here we have a case of a country since independence in 1844 of weak institutions, great instability, and only a few years of effective government. If we consider Trujillo's assassination in 1961 and the subsequent political opening as the beginning of the Dominican Republic's transition to democracy, then that transition has been a very long one—forty-five years so far—and it is still incomplete and nonconsolidated. The Dominican Republic case shows that transitions to democracy in countries based on clan rivalries, patronage politics, and weak civil society and institutions can be very long indeed.

State-Society Relations

State-society relations in the Dominican Republic are characterized by class divisions, personality politics, and clientelism. The primary interest groups include extended family groups, the military, the Catholic Church, economic elites, the middle class, students, and organized labor. In addition to these domestic groups the United States has tremendous influence on public policy.[3]

Class relations are based not only on socioeconomic status but also on race. The upper class is comprised primarily of Dominicans of white or European descent. Mulattos form the middle class. The lowest class includes black

Dominicans descended from African slaves as well as Haitian immigrants. Those of European descent have historically dominated society, politics, and the economy. However, some black Dominicans have been able to work their way up, primarily through the military.

While the lowest 20 percent of the population earns only 5 percent of the nation's income, the highest 20 percent earns over 50 percent. This income gap translates into a deep divide between the political interests of the upper class and those of the lower classes. The interests of the upper class include trade, relations with the United States, the tourism industry, and social connections. In stark contrast and despite the significant improvements of the 1990s, the lower class is interested primarily in basic quality of life improvements. Although the urban poor are more likely to participate in the political process, it is the rural poor who are much worse off, with significantly lower literacy rates, life expectancies, and income.

It is important to also note the emerging middle and upper-middle class, which has grown to over 35 percent of the population since the economic boom of the 1990s. This group is politically divided. The upper-middle class is made up of businessmen and high-ranking military officers who tend to be politically conservative. The mid-middle class includes professionals, military officers, university students, and government midlevel managers, who also tend to be conservative, albeit less so. The lower-middle class is comprised of workers whose political leanings fluctuate between conservative and reformist politics, depending on the economic climate of the day.

Another defining characteristic of state-society relations is the centrality of extended family groups in politics and economics. Old family rivalries and clientelistic exchange of favors shape even the most far-reaching national policies. This is facilitated by the reality that those in power are usually interrelated on one level or another. From political parties to civil-military relations, family ties play an even greater role than policy issues and political ideology.

The oligarch-church-military triumvirate no longer holds the reins of power as it did in times past. The power of the Dominican military has decreased drastically in recent decades. It does, however, continue to ensure that its interests are served by the civilians in power. Given the Dominican history of military occupation, those civilians are always conscious of the military's ability to take the reins of power by force. Contrary to that of Western armed forces, the role of the Dominican military is not one of national defense. Instead, it serves as a political apparatus for its own self-preservation, self-enrichment, and the maintenance of social order. Once active in the foreground, its political machinations now take place primarily in the background. As recently as 2002 President Mejía provided financial incentives and resources to the military in an effort to secure its support. Further, the military's support of democracy is highly dependent on their satisfaction with salaries and perks. To this day rumors of impending coups are common and officers are known to facilitate drug trafficking through the Haitian border.

The Dominican Catholic Church has also traditionally been a power broker in Dominican politics. For many years the Church supported the brutal Trujillo regime and told parishioners how to vote. But a lack of resources and personnel has diminished the Church's current influence on voting and public policy. Although the Church's strength has declined significantly in recent decades, the Dominican Republic is still a Catholic country and the Church still plays a significant role in education and society. Successful Church mediation of election irregularities in recent years is but one example.

Just as the military and Church have declined in power, so too has the oligarchic pillar of the power triumvirate. The small landed oligarchy that once governed the Dominican Republic does so no more. The oligarchs did, however, go into business and, consequently, continue to have significant influence on the affairs of state. It was the business groups they formed that played a central role in the 1963 overthrow of Bosch's democratic government. Their influence has only grown since then as they have organized into a chamber of commerce and various business associations. Not only are they well connected and wealthy but the well-being of the Dominican economy depends on their success.

Organized labor seeks to influence public policy but is far less influential than it was in days past. The labor movement was long kept at bay under the authoritarian dictatorship of Trujillo. Following his assassination it became an important player in Dominican politics. Another period of suppression followed the revolution, but the booming economy of the 1990s reestablished the opportunity for organized labor to become a significant political player. The effectiveness of the eight confederations that comprise the labor movement is now diminished not from external forces but through internal division and competition.

The once prominent political role played by students has likewise lessened in recent years. After contributing significantly to the political transformation of the 1960s and the establishment of a more competitive democracy in the late 1970s, students have become decreasingly involved in politics and more oriented toward moving up the social/economic ladder. The major universities still serve as a platform for debate; however, students are now far more focused on economic advancement than they were in the long-gone 1970s when they incited political violence in protest against the repressive Balaguer regime.

As the political influence of the above groups has decreased over time, that of civil society has risen. Despite a conflict-ridden lead-up to the 1998 and 2000 elections, as well as the economic crisis that preceded the 2004 election, all went off without major incident. This victory for free and fair elections is due in part to the legitimizing effects of a large international observation presence. However, it is also the result of a civil society that has recently begun to thrive. In recent decades Dominican nongovernmental organizations have secured the attention and responsiveness of the country's leadership and they have done so in a very creative way. Although the Dominican Republic is progressing toward democratic maturity, it still runs largely on patronage and clientelism. Consequently, Dominican civil society stimulates grassroots activism, then when either local or national institutions serve as impediments to change it employs the old patronage practices to secure its aims. Although this may be criticized as only partial democracy, it works. New social groups now have more of a say because they have found the way to secure the ear of the leadership first through mobilization, then through patronage.[4]

Finally, the United States plays a major role in domestic Dominican policymaking. Although some anti-American sentiment followed the long military occupations, many Dominicans view the United States as a protector and benefactor. The who's who of Dominican society frequent American embassy parties and the United States ambassador has tremendous access to and influence over Dominican policymakers. It must also be noted, however, that the Dominican Republic has likewise learned how to secure its interests from the United States. This small Caribbean state is the third largest market for U.S. products in the Western Hemisphere (behind Mexico and Canada).[5] There are also hundreds of thousands of Dominican citizens who live in the United States and send a total of over $2 billion in remittances home each year. In addition, a large American citizen population resides in the Dominican Republic and is active in banking, business, religious groups, and educational institutions. These three factors significantly empower the Dominican lobby in Washington, D.C.

In sum, power still rests in the hands of the few. The economic elites, the military, well-connected civil society groups, and the United States have the greatest influence. The church, university students, and organized labor play a significant, albeit lesser, role. Unfortunately, the impoverished masses are still excluded from the equation. Perhaps the emerging civil society will take on the plight of and make a difference for the least fortunate bottom rung of Dominican society. A couple of organizations have attempted to do so in recent years in the education and health care arenas. However, secondary school enrollment remains far below 50 percent and infant mortality rates average approximately thirty deaths per one thousand births (as compared to deaths in the low single digits in Western Europe and North America). There is still much to be done.

Political Parties, Elections, and the Current State of Democracy

The political parties of the Dominican Republic contrast sharply with those of the developed nations. Many have arisen over the years, but three main parties have withstood the test of time. Each was formed in the *caudillo* tradition around the personality of one dynamic individual, as opposed to a particular political ideology. Despite the recent passing of all three founding fathers, election campaigns continue to extol the legacies of their deceased leaders and pay minimal attention to policy platforms. Social democrat Juan Bosch established the Dominican Revolutionary Party (PRD) in exile in the 1930s in support of social justice for the poor. It was not until Trujillo's 1961 assassination that the PRD became a significant player in Dominican politics, with close ties to the left wing of the U.S. Democratic Party and socialist parties in Europe and Latin America. Bosch was elected president in 1962 but was thrown out of office by a military coup after only seven months in office. Following the U.S. intervention in 1965 he lost the 1966 election to Balaguer.

The party suffered repression under the Balaguer administration and boycotted the elections of 1970 and 1974. Soon thereafter Bosch left the PRD to form the Party of Dominican Liberation. The party he left behind successfully united under Antonio Guzmán to become a formidable contender in the elections of 1978, 1982, and 2000. Guzmán won the 1978 election and another PRD candidate, Salvador Jorge Blanco, won the 1982 election. Both administrations were rife with corruption but allowed far more freedom than did earlier repressive regimes. PRD candidate Hipólito Mejía won the election in 2000. He then amended the constitution to allow his own reelection to an immediate second term. But his 2004 reelection campaign struggled to a defeat that resulted in yet another party split.

The Party of Dominican Liberation (PLD) was formed by Juan Bosch following his split from the PRD in 1973. He contended that both U.S. policy and democratization had failed. On this basis he sought a "dictatorship with popular support" in the likeness of the populist revolutionary regime in Peru. The PLD did not win popularity until discontent mounted with Balaguer's corrupt regime in the late 1980s. Bosch lost the fraudulent election of 1990. He then lost again in 1994, with young and charismatic running mate Leonel Fernández. Upon Bosch's retirement Fernández redirected the party to advocate economic liberalization and foreign investment. This move appealed to the middle class and business interests while his dynamic personality appealed to young voters. His victory in the 1996 election drew an end to the Balaguer era. Following Balaguer's steps toward modernization Fernández oversaw a period of record economic growth. Despite his success the constitution forbade him from seeking a second term. Further, corruption charges led to waning support for the party and a loss in the 2000 election. It was not until the economic crisis of 2003 that the PLD regained its footing. Once again, the charismatic Fernández won the election in 2004, this time with promises to restore economic stability and progress.

The center-right Reformist Party (PR) was established by Balaguer upon his return to the Dominican Republic in 1965. From 1966 through 1978 the PR served as his personal political apparatus. It mobilized voters, doled out favors, secured support, and repressed his opposition. Always savvy to an evolving political climate, Balaguer was quick to recognize that the PR in that form would no longer be acceptable to an increasingly democratic society. He therefore merged his party with the Social Christian Party to form the Social Christian Reform Party (PRSC) that still exists today. This was a smart move, as the PRSC won all three elections from 1986 through 1994, albeit amidst allegations of electoral fraud in 1990 and 1994. After the constitutional amendment was passed to prohibit Balaguer from seeking reelection, PRSC support declined. It garnered only 15 percent of the vote in 1996. Balaguer was allowed to run again in 2000, but he lost to the PRD. In a surprising move he waived his right to participate in a second round of voting against Mejía. The 2004 PRSC ticket was led by Eduardo Estrella in an attempt to honor the legacy of Balaguer. However, Estrella did not fare well and the future of the party now appears bleak.

Dominican elections have been rife with allegations of electoral fraud. As recently as 2000 the federal election board (Junta Central Electoral) was accused of political bias as thousands of voters were disenfranchised by inaccurate voter registration lists. Charged with ensuring a free, fair, and smooth election process, this politically appointed board went to great lengths in the 2004 election to shed its controversial past. More than ever before, domestic civil society groups such as *Participación Ciudadana* (PC) kept careful watch over 2004 election preparation activities. These groups monitored everything from the preparation of voter registration lists, *cedulas*, to ballot box delivery. In addition, large contingents of international election observation teams were sent by groups such as the Organization of American States and the Carter Center. A welcome presence, these election observers once again provided a legitimizing scrutiny of the electoral results.

Despite irregularities the last three elections were widely considered fair, honest, and open. None was contested by a major candidate. This indicates that the Dominican Republic has officially institutionalized the democratic process. At the same time it would be foolish to ignore the political corruption, patronage practices, and restricted media coverage that accompanied even the most recent election. Also worrisome is the continued threat of the use of violence as a campaign tactic. Not only did the incumbent double the size and increase the pay of the military prior to the 2004 election, but other candidates implied that they would send their supporters out into the streets if the balloting produced the "wrong" results. It can therefore be concluded that the Dominican transition toward democracy is not yet complete. But it is well on its way. Its political institutions withstood the 2003 economic crisis while civil society became more engaged. Democracy is taking a uniquely Dominican form (more centralized, executive centered, patronage as well as program oriented) and while there have been many bumps in the road, it is maturing nonetheless.[6]

Government Institutions

Dominican government institutions were built in the three-branch likeness of the U.S system. However, the executive, legislative, and judiciary branches have yet to function together as the system of checks and balances they were intended to be. The first two decades following the second (1965) U.S. intervention were characterized by a very weak and patronage-based legislature, judicial system, and bureaucracy, dominated by the authoritarian Balaguer regime. This was briefly interrupted by the Guzmán and Blanco administrations of the late 1970s and early 1980s, both of which were significantly less authoritarian. Their regimes allowed a significant degree of conflict and debate between parties as well as branches. But this small step toward greater independence of the other branches of government, as well as greater accountability, was reversed with the return of the Balaguer regime. From 1986 to 1996 Balaguer resumed authoritarian rule that bypassed the legislature and judiciary. He also used the government purse to pay for allegiance and secure favors. The 1996 election of Leonel Fernández ushered in a new era as he formed coalitions with competing factions and negotiated with the legislature. Congress successfully impeded much of Fernández's legislation proposals, especially those related to privatization and administrative reform.

The judiciary also has more power now than in earlier years, but is plagued with corruption. The Mejía administration did little to prosecute those in the government and private sector who held responsibility for the banking scandal. Despite advocacy by groups such as the Foundation of Institutionality and Justice (*Fundación Institucionalidad y Justicia*) as well as efforts by the second Fernández administration to implement reforms that increase judicial independence, the system is still deeply flawed. Its inability to decrease police violence (especially toward Haitians and the poorest Dominicans) is but one example.

The military has also played a central role in the affairs of the state. However, its role has decreased over time as democracy has advanced and military repression has become less the norm. Military force has not been used against political opponents or social protestors for quite a few years. Current military targets include the poor and drug traffickers along the Haitian border.

Finally, family ties and clientelist governance are so entrenched in the Dominican system that they combine to form an institution of their own. Every administration has worked this institution to its advantage. So too has much of the Dominican public. Unfortunately, patronage politics is responsible, at least in part, for the mismanagement of public funds and has consequently done little to alleviate the plight of the poor. Although there is continual discussion of the need to reduce corruption and decrease patronage practices in order to secure international confidence, real change in this area is highly unlikely. Institutional patronage is practically synonymous with the very essence of Dominican politics. As noted earlier, even civil society groups have figured out how to work within this framework in order to achieve their goals.

Main Public Policy Issue Areas

The top of the current Dominican public policy agenda is occupied by the pursuit of economic growth and stability. Record growth of 7 to 8 percent GDP in the 1990s declined to 3 to 4 percent in 2001 to 2002 and gave way to economic crisis in 2003. Since the 2004 presidential election the Fernández administration has sought to make good on campaign promises to restore economic confidence, alleviate poverty, and improve the Dominican quality of life. Central to these pursuits are efforts to combat inflation, restore consumer confidence in banks, increase government transparency, fight corruption, liberalize trade, and restore the confidence of foreign investors. Unfortunately, an ongoing energy crisis, PLD minority status in Congress, and a long-standing culture of clientelism all stand in the way of this reform agenda.

The electricity sector has collapsed in recent years due to financial mismanagement and the depreciation of the peso. Soaring oil prices have only compounded the situation. The result has been rolling blackouts that disrupt industry and leave consumers in the dark. In response to the energy crisis the government has subsidized nearly 90 percent of consumers' power supply and has taken measures to improve the financial administration of the electricity sector (by improving bill collection, reducing operating costs, etc.).

Although the legislative branch has historically failed to serve as an effective check-and-balance to the executive, this is decreasingly so due to the current administration's minority status in Congress. This trend is indicative of progress toward democratic consolidation, but is also proving a challenge to good faith efforts by the executive to restore economic stability and investor confidence. In addition, public administration is still highly centralized with few institutions in place to increase expenditure transparency. As a consequence, the public continues to expect and prefer favors above services. While several initiatives by the Fernández administration have been aimed at decreasing the patronage culture of government, political survival still depends on the practice of clientelism.

Despite these stumbling blocks great strides have been taken toward current policy goals. IMF loans and the reforms they require have strengthened the banking system and decreased public expenditures. The Dominican Republic-Central America-United States Free Trade Agreement (CAFTA-DR) has been passed, giving the Dominican Republic greater access to U.S. markets.

Also on the public policy agenda are social issues such as drug trafficking and immigration across the Haitian border as well as a deficient education system and high levels of youth unemployment. As a result of continued challenges in these areas crime rates are on the rise and race-based human rights violations continue.

The International Arena

The Dominican Republic is an active participant in the world system, albeit a primarily dependent one. The evolution from an agricultural export economy to a diversified economy has decreased Dominican dependence on some levels. However, the export of goods and services still accounts for nearly half the country's gross domestic product. Reliance on IMF loans, financing assurances from the Paris Club of rich countries, and foreign direct investment make dependence a continuing state of affairs. There is even a large international presence to monitor domestic elections. The electoral process continues to be overseen at the invitation of the Dominican government by multiple observation groups, such as those sent by the Carter Center and the Organization of American States.

The Dominican Republic has much at stake in its relations with the United States. To that end, Dominicans continually seek American favor. Recent examples of engagement with the United States include the Mejía Administration's contribution of troops to Operation Iraqi Freedom (although Mejía was forced by political outrage to withdraw all troops when injuries mounted). As is evidenced by his frequent trips to the United States, President Fernández is especially focused on relations with the giant to the north. His presence in policy conferences and his support for the priorities of the Bush Administration are unprecedented. This is partly due to his upbringing in Queens, New York. It is also due to a deep understanding of all the Dominican Republic can gain from the maintenance of good relations with the United States. Most recently, Fernández's ardent support for and commitment to successful negotiations on

CAFTA-DR have helped secure its adoption. He believes that the agreement will stimulate trade, encourage foreign investment, and create jobs.

Finally, the forces of globalization are apparent in many aspects of Dominican life, albeit with great discrepancies between classes. Cable television, the internet, and SUVs are common only among the upper classes. From the tourist industry that recovered from the negative effects of September 11, 2001, to fast food and shopping malls, affluent Dominicans have kept step with the globalization trend while the poor lag far behind. But even they are affected by the economic dynamism that globalization stimulates, even while it marginalizes some socioeconomic groups.

Conclusion

Dominican politics and development have taken many twists and turns, but this small Caribbean nation appears to be slowly progressing toward democratic consolidation, economic development, modernization, and global integration. Despite two American interventions, the brutal thirty-year Trujillo dictatorship, frequent election irregularities, and multiple administrations under an authoritarian Balaguer, the Dominicans have built a democracy that is well on its way toward maturity. Following the modernization efforts of Balaguer and the diversification of its economy, the unprecedented economic growth of the 1990s ushered in a new era for the Dominican people. But full consolidation of democracy is still a distant goal.

A severe income gap remains and a majority of the population is still stuck in the lower class, isolated from the benefits of globalization. The banking fiasco of 2003 and a continuing energy crisis dealt severe blows to the economy. However, with international support and the leadership of Leonel Fernández both the Dominican economy and democracy appear to have emerged triumphant. Corruption and patronage still characterize the Dominican political system, but civil society is emerging as a force to be reckoned with. Additionally, the government appears to be taking steps toward greater transparency and accountability. These changes are likely to proceed in a characteristically inconsistent—sometimes chaotic—and particularly Dominican way, but at present the political and economic future of the Dominican Republic looms very brightly on the horizon.

Suggestions for Further Reading

Atkins, G. Pope, and Larman C. Wilson. *The Dominican Republic and the United States: From Imperialism to Transnationalism.* Athens: The University of Georgia Press, 1998.

Choup, Anne Marie. "Limits to Democratic Development in Civil Society and the State: The Case of Santo Domingo." *Development and Change* 34, no. 1 (2003): 25–44.

Hartlyn, Jonathan. *The Struggle for Democratic Politics in the Dominican Republic.* Chapel Hill: University of North Carolina Press, 1998.

Kryzanek, Michael J. *U.S.-Latin American Relations.* Westport, CT: Praeger, 1996.

Moya Pons, Frank. *The Dominican Republic: A National History.* New Rochelle, NY: Hispaniola Books, 1995.

Oostindie, Gert, ed. *Ethnicity in the Caribbean.* London: Macmillan Caribbean, 1996.

Pomeroy, Carlton, and Steve Jacob. "From Mangos to Manufacturing: Uneven Development and its Impact on Social Well-Being in the Dominican Republic." *Social Indicators Research* 65 (2004): 73–107.

Soderland, Walter C. *Mass Media and Foreign Policy: Post-Cold War Crises in the Caribbean.* Westport, CT: Praeger, 2003.

Vargas-Lundius, Rosemary. *Peasants in Distress: Poverty and Unemployment in the Dominican Republic.* Boulder, CO: Westview Press, 1991.

Wiarda, Howard J., and Michael J. Kryzanek. *The Dominican Republic: A Caribbean Crucible*, 2nd ed. Boulder, CO: Westview Press, 1992.

Wiarda, Howard J., and Esther Skelley. *The 2004 Dominican Republic Elections: Post-Election Report.* Washington, DC: Center for Strategic and International Studies, 2004.

Notes

1. See Michael J. Kryzanek, *U.S.-Latin American Relations* (Westport: Praeger, 1996).

2. The World Bank, *World Development Indicators 2004* (Washington: The World Bank Group, 2004).

3. See Howard J. Wiarda and Michael J. Kryzanek. *The Dominican Republic: A Caribbean Crucible*, 2d ed. (Boulder: Westview, 1992).

4. See Anne Marie Choup, "Limits to Democratic Development in Civil Society and the State: The Case of Santo Domingo," *Development and Change*, vol. 34, no.1, 2003, pp. 25–44.

5. USDA Foreign Agricultural Service, *Dominican Republic Exporter Guide Annual.* 2004.

6. See Howard J. Wiarda and Esther Skelley, *The 2004 Dominican Republic Elections: Post-Election Report* (Washington: Center for Strategic and International Studies, 2004).

24

Panama
New Politics for a New Millennium?

Steve C. Ropp

O n September 1, 2004, the son of Panama's best-known military politician was sworn into office as president of his small country. Martín Torrijos was born into the family of the authoritarian populist General Omar Torrijos. Founder of the now-governing Democratic Revolutionary Party (PRD), Omar Torrijos is both famous and infamous for first leading a military coup (1968) and later for negotiating a new Panama Canal Treaty with U.S. President Jimmy Carter (1977). As the son of such a well-known and controversial political figure, Martín Torrijos brings a wealth of diverse experiences and perspectives to the job of president. For example, as a young man he not only served with the leftist Sandinista guerrillas in Nicaragua but also worked during his college years in the United States at a McDonald's restaurant in the heart of capitalist Chicago.

The president whom Martín Torrijos replaced in 2004 was also closely associated with a populist political figure, but one who had historically been treated as anathema by General Omar Torrijos and the military. Outgoing President Mireya Moscoso had grown up poor as the daughter of a schoolteacher in rural Panama. At a very young age she joined the Panamenista Party (PP) that was led by her future husband, Dr. Arnulfo Arias. Dr. Arias, who was elected president in 1940, 1949, and 1968, espoused a brand of incendiary nationalist and racially exclusionary populism that won him no friends either in Panama's racially mixed military or in the United States. As a consequence, he was never allowed to complete a full term in office. Following his death in 1988 his widow Mireya took up the mantle of leadership of his party and was elected President of the country in 1999.

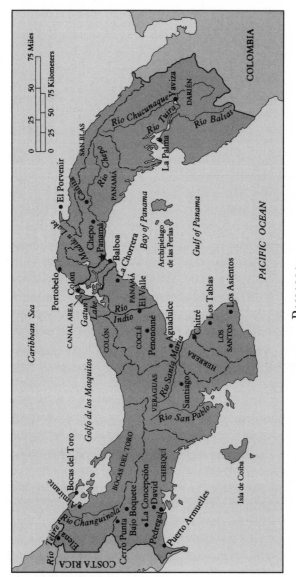

PANAMA

Populism is simply the direct and unmediated personal relationship that a charismatic leader establishes with his or her "people." As a result of its long and tortured history of authoritarian populist politics Panama's contemporary democratic political scene resembles nothing more than a landscape dominated by two extinct volcanoes. The first of these populist volcanoes erupted long ago in the 1930s when the followers of Dr. Arias rebelled against a rising tide of uncontrolled immigration and against an elitist urban commercial class that was perceived as too closely aligned with the United States. The second erupted in the late 1960s when officers within Panama's emerging military institution rebelled against the inept antimilitary populism of Dr. Arias and the continued presence on Panamanian soil (in the Panama Canal Zone) of the United States. Although these two populist volcanoes have lain dormant since their main vents were capped following the U.S. military invasion of 1989, they sometimes still show a few signs of life in this postpopulist age of liberal representative democracy and market economy.

President Martín Torrijos currently leads a country that has experienced more than fifteen years of liberal democratic governance—following closely upon the heels of two decades of uninterrupted populist military rule.[1] Military rule came to an abrupt end in December 1989 when President George H. W. Bush sent U.S. troops into Panama to destroy the Panamanian Defense Forces (PDF) and to capture its commander, General Manuel Antonio Noriega.[2] During the ensuing years democratic government was reestablished and three general elections were held (1994, 1999, and 2004). From the standpoint of assessing the current quality of Panama's new democracy it is also important to note that the two major political parties have demonstrated a willingness to relinquish the reins of power when defeated in open and fair elections.

However, any meaningful assessment of Panama's current political conditions and continuing prospects for democracy must rest on an understanding of the deeper forces that lie just below the country's political surface. Most fundamentally, Panama's two extinct populist volcanoes rest upon rigid underlying social and economic "tectonic plates" that have historically kept Panama's rich very rich and poor very poor. While the end of military government in 1989 and three successive democratic elections have created the impression that the country's political system has matured and that democracy has been consolidated, the underlying social and economic realities suggest that serious problems still remain. Can Panama's new political leaders and their parties successfully deal with the challenges presented by lingering class and racial differences in an age of rapid globalization? Will they prove willing and able to modernize the Panama Canal? And will they be able to shape a new role for their country in a changing twenty-first-century world? A closer look at

Panama's history and political culture may allow us to make a few preliminary judgments regarding these matters.

History and Political Culture

The Republic of Panama is a small, narrow country that joins Central America to South America. Shaped like a giant S and some 420 miles (675 kilometers) long, it winds from the border of Costa Rica in the west to Colombia in the east. In total area Panama encompasses some 29,209 square miles (75,651 square kilometers), making it slightly larger than the state of West Virginia. The population of about three million is largely composed of *mestizos* and mulattos together with black West Indians brought to Panama in the late nineteenth century to help construct the canal. Small numbers of native Indians occupy some of the interior provinces as well as the San Blas islands along the northern coast.

Panama is as much a location as it is a country. Its lack of significant size and its position between the Atlantic and Pacific oceans make Panama a vital strategic bridge. Although geography is not always destiny, the enduring legacy of the country's location has been to constantly reinforce a particular kind of laissez-faire economic thought and open economic practices.

Faith in the benefits of an open economy developed during colonial times when the isthmus served as a major transit point linking Spain to its most important colonial possessions along the west coast of South America. Legal trade with the Spanish colonies was supplemented by contraband trade in slaves and other "commodities." These illicit activities, particularly critical to the isthmian economy in hard times, served as a precursor to the more recent traffic under both military and civilian rule in merchandise such as arms and cocaine.

The result of Panama's early role as a strategic bridge was to concentrate economic resources in the hands of a small white urban commercial elite. The politicians who assumed leadership positions in Panama following independence in 1903 did not have ties to the traditional agricultural sector. Panama had never developed an *encomienda* system due to its lack of a large indigenous population, and unlike its Central American neighbors, Panama never experienced a nineteenth-century coffee boom.[3]

Throughout the twentieth century Panamanian politics was dominated by a struggle for power between the largely white urban commercial class and largely nonwhite (*mestizo* and black) groups that felt themselves excluded from the full benefits of nationhood. During the period of French and U.S. canal construction (1878–1914) large numbers of black workers were imported from Caribbean islands such as Jamaica and Barbados. These workers spoke English and were physically incorporated as an underclass into the

U.S.-controlled Canal Zone. Although their wages were low compared to those for white workers from the United States, they constituted an urban labor elite when compared with Panama's *mestizo* and black Spanish-speaking population.

During the 1920s and 1930s the Panamanian economy deteriorated owing to the termination of canal construction activities and, later, the Great Depression. Resentment began to grow, particularly among *mestizos* from the interior provinces, against West Indian blacks and against members of the urban commercial elite, who were viewed as natural allies of the United States. This resentment crystallized in 1923 with the formation of Community Action, a movement whose intent was to gain access for *mestizo* professionals and urban day laborers to the more lucrative jobs associated with the canal.

In the 1930s Dr. Arnulfo Arias emerged as the leader of this highly nationalistic popular movement. Elected president in 1940, he quickly promulgated a new constitution that contained discriminatory provisions against West Indians and Chinese. The political crisis precipitated by this constitutional change was resolved when the United States, upset with Arias's apparent sympathy with Italian Fascism, helped remove him from office. Although the political crisis associated with the rise of Community Action became more attenuated with the passage of time, Arnulfo Arias remained a major fixture in Panamanian politics until his death in 1988.

From the 1940s on, the struggle for political power between urban elites and populists such as Dr. Arias was increasingly influenced by the reemergence of the Panamanian military as a political force. The army was disbanded for the first time (the second time was in 1989) shortly after independence in 1903 because it was viewed as a threat to both the political hegemony of the commercial elite and to the United States. However, through a slow evolutionary process the army was reconstituted out of the small police force that had taken its place.[4] By the early 1950s the national police had been turned into a national guard and a colonel had been elected president with military backing.

After a turbulent period of civilian elitist democracy during the late 1950s and early 1960s a military coup against Arnulfo Arias brought Omar Torrijos to power. Torrijos then built a populist political base among marginal groups in both Panama City and the countryside. Farm collectives were formed, labor unions organized, and the government expanded dramatically to accommodate popular needs. In this regard, the Panamanian military government looked much like the one that emerged in Peru at the same time, and for much the same reasons.

When General Omar Torrijos and the military first seized power from President Arias in 1968 they did so as agents of social and economic change. Traditionally, Panama had been governed by an urban commercial elite that controlled the vast majority of the country's economic resources. Although some significant changes were made in this traditional structure of power during the earliest years of military rule, the military's social reform agenda slowly fell by the wayside as top officers became increasingly concerned with their own well-being. This in turn led them to become involved in a variety of illicit activities such as arms trafficking and drug smuggling.

The military's increasingly repressive and corrupt behavior following the 1968 overthrow of Dr. Arias finally created a significant domestic and international backlash in the mid-1980s. The precipitating event was the death of General Torrijos in 1981 and his eventual replacement by General Manuel Antonio Noriega. As head of the intelligence branch within the PDF Noriega was in a position not only to spy on his fellow officers but also to control the most lucrative of the military's illicit activities. The rapidly growing Medellín drug cartel (headquartered in neighboring Colombia) found his services useful for the laundering of their cocaine profits, and by the mid-1980s the PDF had become a drug trafficking mafia masquerading as a formal military institution.

Panama's crisis of military rule became so intense that it eventually drew the attention of the Reagan administration in the United States. For a variety of complex reasons having to do with General Noriega's stance on regional issues, his corruption, and increasing repression of domestic dissent, the Reagan administration applied economic sanctions in 1988. At the same time, it supported the domestic political opposition that was now to be found not only within Arnulfo Arias's Panamenista Party but also among portions of the urban commercial class that had previously supported the military government.

Beneath its surface complexities we can thus see the workings of the underlying "tectonic plates" in Panamanian politics. Historically, they produced a consistent tension that pitted urban elites against poverty-stricken groups excluded from the full benefits of Panama's strategic location. The result was cycles of elitist democracy and authoritarian populism that occurred in slightly different forms at various points in time, depending on the strength of various domestic political forces, the state of the global economy, and the level of involvement of the United States.

During the 1930s and 1940s Arias led a civilian popular movement aimed at increasing the political voice of rural *mestizos* and urban day laborers; in the 1970s the military spearheaded attempts to include additional marginalized rural and urban groups. Both of these authoritarian populist movements were eventually challenged and displaced by traditional urban forces acting in collaboration with the United States. Thus, the successful effort to restore civilian democratic rule in Panama, which resulted from the U.S. military invasion in 1989, was not particularly unique but rather reflective of a long-standing cyclical historical process.

Political Parties and Interest Groups

Panama's pattern of elitist democracy followed by periods of populist authoritarian rule influenced development of the country's party system. During periods of civilian elitist rule political parties reflected divisions within the urban commercial class based on personality clashes between individual leaders. There was a general lack of real differences in the policy agendas of these parties, extreme fragmentation reflected in their relatively large numbers, and an absence of party structures that survived any given election.

Although Panama's political party system has historically been fragmented and elitist, the sporadic emergence of both civilian (Arias) and military (Torrijos) populist movements has on occasion led to efforts by populist leaders to create dominant parties through outright elimination or manipulation of the competition. The urban commercial elite's "power resources" have been primarily its private sector financial assets, whereas those of the populists have been their control of the government apparatus itself. Thus, when populist leaders such as Arnulfo Arias and Omar Torrijos came to power they attempted to create dominant political parties largely based on their supporters in the various government bureaucracies.

During the period of elitist democracy that immediately preceded the military coup of 1968, approximately twenty small political parties vied for power. These parties were banned when General Torrijos assumed dictatorial control in the name of popular reform. However, deteriorating economic conditions in the mid-1970s led Torrijos to reassess the costs and benefits of direct military rule, and in 1978 he formed the PRD to incorporate various groups that supported his military regime.

Although the military, in response to internal and external pressures, allowed the holding of multiparty elections after 1976, the political system was clearly dominated by the PRD and its allies. Formation of the PRD suggested that the military wished to give permanent institutional form to its reformist ideals through the establishment of a new political party that would regularly win elections with military backing. When presidential elections were held in 1984 and 1989 the military had to resort to fraud to ensure a victory for the PRD candidate.

Following the U.S. military invasion the restoration of democracy led to a return of highly fragmented and personalistic party politics. The coalition of political parties that attempted to govern Panama in the wake of Noriega's removal quickly collapsed when leaders found that they had little in common beyond opposition to the military government. Although the elections of 1994, 1999, and 2004 were generally democratic, they also took place within the context of a multiparty system that remained unstable and highly polarized. In sum, the historical tendency to find extreme party fragmentation associated with elitist and/or externally imposed democratic structures has persisted into the new millennium.

However, twenty years of military rule did lead to some important changes in the relative importance and strength of various Panamanian interest groups and social movements. General Torrijos encouraged the formation of new labor unions to strengthen his popular base, and labor was legally empowered through the passage of a new labor code in 1972. Other groups that experienced changes after 1968 were business organizations and the Catholic Church. The business sector diversified and expanded to the point that there was less direct correspondence between its interests and those of most traditional political parties. Similarly, the Catholic Church, a historically docile institution in Panama, became increasingly involved in politics.

Although Panamanian politics retains many of the features it exhibited prior to twenty years of military rule, there have been a number of significant changes. One of the most important of these has been the growing gap between the traditional parties and newly emerging sectors, social movements, and interest groups. The party leadership is aging and increasingly out of touch with the realities of a new generation of Panamanians, whose aspirations the party leaders have not been able fully to ascertain. Continued movement of rural dwellers to Panama City has created a new electorate that is largely detached from the patterns of self-interest and coercion that assured its vote for the traditional parties in the past. In an effort to deal with the growing gap between political parties and the electorate both the PRD and the Panamenistas selected candidates in recent elections that would appeal to younger voters and to women.

Formal Government Structures

Panama's formal government structures are delineated in the country's four constitutions—those of 1904, 1941, 1946, and 1972. All of these constitutions assigned a predominant role to the president within a centralized unitary form of government that included executive, legislative, and judicial branches. Thus, Panama's formal government structures have historically been very much within the Iberian tradition, with the executive branch intended to dominate the other two. The president appointed provincial governors so his power extended directly down to the regional level; although local municipalities theoretically possessed some autonomy, this idea was not much honored in practice.

Although all four of these constitutions created governments in which the president was the dominant figure, Panama's populist governments assigned greater powers to the executive branch than did ones dominated by the urban commercial elite. The constitution of 1941, promulgated during the presidency of Arnulfo Arias, and the 1972 constitution, promulgated under military rule, are more expansive in terms of the president's prerogatives than those of 1904 or 1946.

When the Panamanian military seized power in 1968 it considerably altered traditional formal government structures. The National Assembly, which had come to be viewed by the military as an elite-dominated institution, was replaced with a much larger legislature whose members were elected from the country's 505 municipal subdistricts. The traditional political parties were banned from electoral participation, and short legislative sessions ensured that there would be no time to mount meaningful challenges to military executive authority.

The 1972 constitution, which created this new "popular legislature" also recognized the central role within the executive branch of General Torrijos and the defense forces. Although there was still a civilian president, real power was given to Torrijos as "maximum leader" of the Panamanian Revolution. The impotency of the president within this new constitutional structure was best expressed by the fact that he could neither appoint nor remove military personnel. The military legally became a fourth branch of government and the other three branches were constitutionally required to act in "harmonic collaboration" with the military.

As this military government gradually began to move toward the restoration of civilian democratic rule in the late 1970s, it allowed the 1972 constitution to be amended in such a way as to restrict the powers of the executive branch and expand those of the legislature. However, none of these changes transformed the military's original authoritarian constitution into a fully democratic one. Particularly lacking were provisions that allowed for full protection of human rights and freedom of expression.

Panama's current constitutional situation is quite different from that which followed President Arnulfo Arias's period of populist rule in the 1940s. This is because his attempt to expand presidential powers through constitutional change in 1941 was reversed by urban commercial elites in 1946 through promulgation of a new constitution. However, when civilian democrats replaced populist authoritarians in 1989 following the U.S. invasion, they continued to govern according to the provisions of the military's partially amended authoritarian constitution. This has created a difficult situation in which the fact that democratically elected governments have ruled using the military's old constitution, undermining their political legitimacy. It has also complicated the country's legislative picture because restoration of the National Assembly did not lead to abolition of the military's "popular legislature."[5]

Under the terms of the 1972 constitution political power continues to be concentrated in the executive branch and, more specifically, in the office of the president. President Martín Torrijos governs with the help of a Cabinet Council comprising the various ministers of state. The Legislative Assembly is limited in its general powers and has little control over the national budget. Although a Supreme Court does exist, it has historically demonstrated minimal independence from the executive branch, and various presidents have attempted to pack it with their followers. Perhaps the most significant change in formal government structures during the 1990s was provision for the independent election of mayors. Because Panama City and Colon are major metropolitan areas, this change from appointment to election created important new centers of political power.

Government Policies

As in most countries government policies in Panama have varied depending on the administration in power. The primary factor determining the general content of policy has been whether any particular administration fundamentally represented the interests of the urban commercial class or those of urban and rural middle- and lower-class groups.

When populist leaders have controlled the government there has been a tendency to alter the constitution in such a way as to allow for a broader role of government in public policy formation and implementation. For example, Arnulfo Arias's 1941 constitution mentioned the "social function" of private property for the first time, and the government was granted the right to intervene in conflicts between business and labor. New government agencies were also created to pursue expanded goals and objectives.

During the 1950s and 1960s presidential administrations dominated by the urban commercial class pursued social and economic policies that relied somewhat less on the central government. Their policies were reformist within the context of the U.S.-sponsored Alliance for Progress. Economic growth strategies were aimed at simultaneously expanding the dynamic, outwardly oriented service sector and encouraging continued growth of the domestically oriented industrial sector.

The military coup of 1968 initiated another wave of populist policymaking. Observers of politics under military rule noted a curious blend of populist development policies mixed with more conventional ones. Populist policies that were intended to redistribute goods to the popular sectors were the natural result of the military's disdain for the urban commercial class. The simultaneous pursuit of more conventional developmental policies, emphasizing continued growth of the more dynamic areas of the private sector, reflected the permanent historical reality of Panama's open service economy.

Major components of the military's populist policies included the implementation of land reform, enactment of a progressive labor code, and efforts to gain national control of the Panama Canal. The military's broadest popular constituency consisted of those Panamanians who wished to see the canal brought under national control. General Torrijos worked hard during the early 1970s to create an international support group that would help speed negotiations with the United States for a new treaty. Through such international coalition building, as well as support for changes in the treaty arrangements on the part of several U.S. presidential administrations, Torrijos was able to achieve his goal. In 1978 a treaty was ratified that returned the Canal Zone to Panama and stipulated that Panama would gain full control of the canal in the year 2000.

When Panama's thoroughly corrupt but populist military regime was overthrown in 1989, government policy underwent a radical reorientation. This reorientation was partly due to the fact that the commercial elite once again exercised considerable influence with those who controlled the levers of state power. But it also resulted from a sea change in global thinking concerning strategies of economic growth. In the post–Cold War world a new economic model emerged that stressed reduction of the size of the public sector through privatization of state corporations and a shift from the traditional economic growth strategy of import-substitution-industrialization to one of export-oriented industrialization.

Since 1989 successive Panamanian governments have attempted to restore the country's credibility with international financial institutions, foreign governments, and private investors. President Guillermo Endara (1989–1994) made some progress in reorienting Panama toward an export-oriented growth strategy. Tariffs were reduced on industrial goods to make the industrial sector more internationally competitive, and tax legislation was passed to encourage more foreign investment in export-oriented activities. However, the most significant changes in this regard came during the administration of Pérez Balladares (1994–1999). More strenuous efforts were made to attract foreign investment by selling off both state-run companies as well as reverted properties in the former Canal Zone, curbing the power of organized labor, and seeking membership in important world trade organizations.

President Moscoso's economic policies were largely aimed at mitigating some of the negative side effects of these various neoliberal economic reforms, particularly as they impacted her core political constituencies within the agricultural sector and government bureaucracy. However, President Torrijos has returned to policies that place more stress on fiscal responsibility and concern about the negative economic impact of government corruption. The economy has been growing well in recent years, but Panama continues to have a highly regressive tax system that Torrijos is determined to change. The hope is that such changes, coupled with anticipated reform of the country's social security system, reduction in the size of the bureaucracy, and aggressive efforts to end corruption, will not only restore the country's economic health by the end of his term in 2009 but also ensure it in the future through a change in Panama's world image.

Panama in a Twenty-first Century World

During the twentieth century Panama's place in the world was largely defined by its relationship with a single Great Power—the United States. This key bilateral relationship long determined the overall nature of Panama's global involvement because U.S. diplomats made sure during World War II and the subsequent Cold War years that relationships with adversarial Great Powers either were not allowed to develop in the first place or were subsequently minimized.

Panama's international contacts did multiply rapidly during the 1970s and 1980s due to a number of factors, including the progressive ideological stance of the country's military regime, its growing importance as a global service center, and the conflict in Central America. However, despite these developments Panama's pattern of global involvement during those decades can still largely be seen as resulting from the continued dominance of the United States. Efforts to expand international contacts were a reaction to such dominance and part of a national strategy designed to gain diplomatic leverage in the battle to negotiate new canal treaties.

During the Cold War years (1947–1989), the United States treated Panama as a "constant" in a relatively simple global security equation. With troops on the ground and planes in the air, the Panama Canal Zone could be used as a platform from which known quantities of U.S. power could be projected to deal with various global/regional security and humanitarian contingencies. Even during the years of the populist military rule (1968–1989) the United States was able to treat Panama as a "constant" in dealing with the civil wars that were then raging in Central America. When Panama itself became a problem during the Noriega years, the same simple calculus applied.

Now, all of that has changed. Following the departure of U.S. troops and planes from the isthmus and the transfer of the canal, Panama has become more of an "unknown" in a vastly more complex global security equation. This equation has become more complex in part because of the reemergence of a multipolar international system following the end of the Cold War. For example, one does not have to be an alarmist to note that the influence of the Asian Great Powers of Japan and China has grown significantly in Panama in recent years. Asian shipping firms control three of the country's four major ports and a significant proportion of foreign investment comes from that region. The Panamanian case is not unique in this regard, reflecting the broader pattern of Asian global and regional influence in the wake of economic globalization.[6]

Panama's future position in the world will also be affected by the political and economic strains in neighboring South American countries. Most important, Colombia is engaged in a civil war that pits several guerrilla groups that control large swaths of the nation's territory against the central government. This civil war has been spilling over into Panama in the form of heightened tensions in the border area associated with illicit flows of drugs, arms, people, and money. In addition, Colombians from all economic classes are playing an increasingly important role in Panama's development following the transfer of the canal.[7]

Equally important for assessing Panama's place in the world today is recognition of the growing regional influence of President Hugo Chávez in neighboring Venezuela. Chávez, a former army colonel who attempted to stage a coup in 1992, came to power in 1998 through democratic elections as a result of the frustration of ordinary Venezuelans with the corrupt nature of their country's political class. As president he moved quickly to render impotent Venezuela's formal democratic institutions. Together with other emerging populist leaders in Latin America who feed on frustration with neoliberal economic reforms, he provides an example to any aspiring populist politician in Panama who might want to follow his example.

Finally, Panama's future role will continue to be shaped by the presence on its territory of one of the most important transportation arteries in the world. As a result of the Panama Canal Treaties the United States assumed a formal commitment to help defend the canal against all external threats. However, when these treaties were negotiated thirty years ago few observers anticipated that the major threat would come from global terrorists rather than from hostile nation states. A sign that the United States has taken this threat particularly seriously since September 11, 2001, is the fact that the first Latin American president to visit with George W. Bush in 2005 at the beginning of his second term was Panama's new president, Martin Torrijos.[8]

Conclusions

The inauguration of President Martín Torrijos on September 1, 2004, reflects elements of both change and continuity in Panamanian politics since the U.S. military invasion of 1989. Change is reflected in the fact that Torrijos came to power as the result of a third successive democratic election (1994, 1999, and 2004), and as the first Panamanian president ever to be inaugurated when his country controlled the Panama Canal. Continuity can be seen in the fact that the new president represents a political party created by the military whose roots can be traced back to the longings of popular classes for radical economic and cultural change. Such continuity can also be seen in the fact that both Torrijos and his presidential predecessor represented such populist parties, although ones that were often at odds with each other.

Today, the legacy of previous populist attempts to liberate "the people" from the oppressive domination of the urban commercial elite can be seen in the overwhelming influence of the PRD and the Panamenistas in this new age of liberal representative democracy. And yet the leaders of these two parties, which have won every election since 1989, have not governed as authoritarian populists. For this reason Panama's contemporary political landscape appears to be dominated by two extinct volcanoes (populist political parties) whose past eruptions and the nationalist conflagrations they set off are now no more than a distant memory.

As relatively tranquil as the contemporary political scene may appear to be, it is somewhat deceptive. This is because Panama's two extinct volcanoes rest on rigid underlying tectonic plates that continue grinding away at each other. The fundamental fact to remember about Panama is that the gap between rich and poor remains one of the largest in the world.[9] As long as this remains the case we may hear new rumblings from new volcanoes in the not-too-distant future.

Notes

1. This was one of the longest periods of military rule in the modern-day history of Latin America. See Steve C. Ropp, "Explaining the Long-Term Maintenance of a Military Regime: Panama before the U.S. Invasion," *World Politics* 44 no. 2 (January 1992).

2. General Noriega was subsequently tried in the United States and sentenced to forty years in prison.

3. For an overview of Panama's early economic development and its implications for the distribution of political power, see Andrew Zimbalist and John Weeks, *Panama at the Crossroads: Economic Development and Political Change in the Twentieth Century* (Berkeley: University of California Press, 1991), pp. 1–19.

4. Thomas L. Pearcy, *We Answer Only to God: Politics and the Military in Panama 1903–1937* (Albuquerque: University of New Mexico Press, 1998).

5. Indeed, throughout Central America there are many constitutional remnants of authoritarian and corporate practice that have endured during this new

post–Cold War "age of democracy." For a description of the various corporatist aspects of present-day Central American constitutions, see Steve C. Ropp, "What About Corporatism in Central America?" in Howard J. Wiarda, ed., *Authoritarianism and Corporatism in Latin America—Revisited* (Gainesville: University Press of Florida, 2004).

6. Growing Asian influence in Central America and, more broadly, throughout the region has been noted for some time and by many observers. For example, trade between China and Latin America increased five-fold between 1999 and 2004. Richard Lapper, "Run for Investment Bulls as China Shops," *Financial Times*, April 13, 2005.

7. Steve C. Ropp, "Beyond U.S. Hegemony: Colombia's Persistent Role in the Shaping and Reshaping of Panama," *The Journal of Caribbean History* (forthcoming).

8. Although full details concerning the topics discussed at this April 2005 meeting are not available, they probably included the defense and future expansion of the canal, future cooperation with regard to transnational criminal activities such as drug trafficking, and the status of regional bi-lateral and multilateral free trade agreements.

9. Out of 99 countries for which there was an index of inequality available for the year 2004, Panama ranked 22nd. The fact that populist tendencies remain pronounced throughout Latin America in an age of liberal representative democracy can be attributed to very high levels of such inequality throughout the region. Eleven of the top twenty countries where the distribution of income is the most unequal are to be found in Latin America. *2004 CIA World Factbook.*

25

Haiti

The Failures of Governance

Georges A. Fauriol

H aiti, the second-oldest independent nation in the Western Hemi-sphere, celebrated its bicentennial in 2004 and had little to show for it. Discovered by Columbus in 1492 during his first voyage to the Americas, the nation has since then experienced all shades of development—except that of effective modern political and economic management. This dysfunctional character of Haitian political dynamics, an absence of conscious economic policymaking, and decayed social institutions has also triggered an unhappy and at times tragic record of interaction with the external world. Most recently this has played itself out in several episodes, first as a result of the collapse of the Duvalier dynasty in 1986, then in the context of U.S. military intervention to return President Jean-Bertrand Aristide to power, and again in 2004 to manage a messy transition in the wake of an abrupt conclusion to Aristide's second presidential term.

Born out of the economic excesses of slavery and the political violence of the French Revolution, Haiti emerged in 1804 as an independent nation. Its economy in ruins and its population exhausted, it began its career as a modern nation without any foreign friends. In fact, its early status as an outcast among the community of nations further increased its vulnerability to both internal and external threats. At the beginning of the twentieth century this overlap of threats ultimately generated direct U.S. political and military administration (1915–1934). Since 1986 the difficulties experienced by Haiti's development process has introduced into the life of the nation an almost continuous engagement from the international community, notably the Organization of

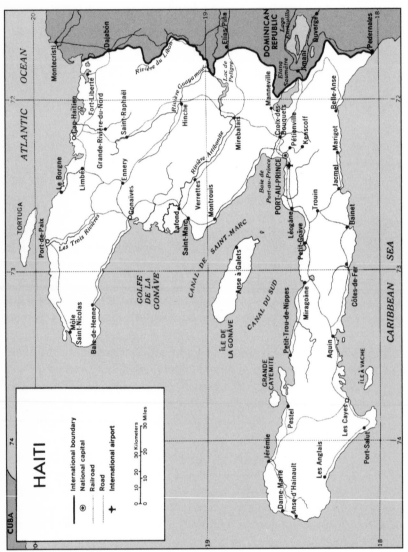

HAITI

American States, the United Nations, key governments (the United States, France, and Canada), and an extensive NGO and humanitarian community.

Despite these misfortunes Haiti has not lost the basic features of its national character. Its roots lie in a hybrid of French eighteenth-century colonialism, African culture, a marginal brand of Catholicism, and the aftereffects of the United States' strategic sweep in the Caribbean region. Indeed, the African cultural and spiritual features have remained almost unaltered for a majority of the population since they were first imported in the seventeenth century. The vitality of this primarily rural environment has survived in the face of economic adversity and the unusual lack of interest of the political leadership in the process of national development.

Roughly the size of the state of Maryland, Haiti occupies the western third of the island of Hispaniola, which it shares with the Dominican Republic. It lies at a crossroads of trading passages and strategic interests—Cuba lies to the immediate west across the Windward Passage, the open waters of the Atlantic Ocean bound Haiti on the north, and the Caribbean Sea lies to the south. Haiti remains ethnically and culturally distinct, being 95 percent black and the only independent French-speaking nation in the Western Hemisphere.

With an estimated average per capita gross national product (GNP) income of about $250, Haiti is also the poorest country in the region. In fact, a 52 percent literacy rate and a life expectancy of fifty-five years rank Haiti near the bottom on a global basis. A mountainous topography coupled with a failing agricultural program and land-management neglect have not only concentrated the country's estimated nine million people into the nominally fertile 28 percent of the country but also in recent years accentuated the flows of out-migration. Revenues from a few odd agricultural and mineral exports and collapsed offshore manufacturing and tourism sectors have limited economic impact, leaving much of the workforce on the margins of economic life. Haiti's surplus talent keeps leaving for other shores—including the United States, where the current population of Haitian origin is estimated to be about 1.2 million. An indeterminate portion of the economy is dependent on contraband and drug trafficking.

Study of the Haitian experience is frustrating. The most charitable characterization of Haiti's public administration is that the government has been at its relative best when pursuing a policy of benign neglect—leaving most of Haiti's peasants to their own autonomous devices. A very small and generally urbanized political and economic elite has for the most part directed priorities at maintaining its own fragile status quo and in sustaining a limited enclave of export-oriented commercial activity. Some writers speak of a "kleptocracy," or "predatory state," and of the "politics of squalor." Some allude to the "colonial" or "self-colonized" character of the Haitian society. Others borrow from development literature and assess Haiti in the context of a "transitional society."

The arrival on the political scene in the late 1980s of a radical populist political priest, Jean-Bertrand Aristide, gave currency to new notions of governance, in this case "deliberative" democracy. This implied a political leadership inclined to override institutional intermediaries found in mainstream western democracies, such as parliaments and political parties. Instead, more recent characterizations of Haiti imply disappointment and speak of a "failed state."[1] What, in fact, is a viable characterization of Haiti's politics and development process?

The Decay of the State

The Caribbean entered the historical record of the European world in 1492, the year Columbus discovered Haiti. Some three hundred years later Haiti fought its way to independence from France in 1804. In between there flourished a plantation colony characterized by extraordinary wealth and deep social and racial divisions. Few factors have had a more dramatic impact on today's Caribbean polities than their transformation some three hundred years ago from small colonies of settlement into economic dependencies of European powers.

The environment of sugar and slaves came crashing down in Haiti in the late eighteenth century. Saint-Dominique, as Haiti was then known, was the crown jewel of France's overseas empire. But the importation of over eight hundred thousand African slaves created an untenable socioeconomic milieu. Open racial and color conflict was set in motion with the violent explosions of the French Revolution after 1789, and what followed was the Haitian Revolution of 1789–1804, which ravaged the country to the core. In the bloody confusion blacks, lighter-skinned mulattoes, and whites built complex alliances and were helped along by the intervention of British, Spanish, and, naturally, French forces.

After independence in 1804 the early Haitian leaders faced the traditional patterns of nineteenth-century power politics. As a smaller state Haiti was treated as an object of policy, if dealt with at all. A spiritual heir to the French Revolution, it also provided a serious challenge as the first non-European postcolonial state in the modern world. According to diplomatic historian Rayford Logan's characterization, Haiti started out as a "power and enigma," turned into an "anomaly," became a "threat," and ultimately was an "outcast" among the nations of the earth.[2]

Lacking any viable institutions, Haiti initially evolved a remarkable collection of powerful personalities who shaped the nation's style of governance—

authoritarian, personalist, anchored in coercive power: Jean-Jacques Dessalines (1804–1806), Haiti's first emperor and efficient exterminator of the whites in Haiti; Henri Christophe (1807–1820), Haiti's first crowned king; Alexandre Pétion (1807–1818), Haiti's first president for life; and Jean-Pierre Boyer (1818–1843), who ruled over an increasingly crippled nation. At mid-century another extraordinary figure appeared—Faustin Soulouque (1847–1859), later Emperor Faustin I. He ordered a general massacre of the mulattoes, led the country in several abortive campaigns into the neighboring Dominican Republic, and further precipitated Haiti's deterioration.

By the dawn of the twentieth century Haiti was in debt to French, German, and U.S. financial interests. France had underwritten all external loans between 1825 and 1896 and owned the National Bank. The Germans held the trading sector. Most imports came from the United States, and after 1900 U.S. influence expanded into banking.

The 1915 U.S. intervention in Haiti was the result of severe disarray in that country's politics—suffice it to say that the degeneration of Haitian politics had indeed attained a new plateau. Of the twenty-two presidents who served between 1843 and 1915, one finished his term in office, three died a natural death while in office, one was blown up with the presidential palace, another one was probably poisoned, one was hacked to pieces, and one resigned. The fourteen others were overthrown. The sorry state of Haitian finances was also perceived by Washington as a Trojan horse for European intervention in the Caribbean. The object of the U.S. action was not to expose Haiti to U.S. exploitation but to promote Haitian political stability, financial rehabilitation, and economic development.

Yet Haiti remains one of the United States' least successful interventions. True, a minimum of financial order was established, debt was reduced, and the administration infrastructure was improved, but U.S. presence did not lead to democratic virtues or greater management capabilities among the Haitian elite. Violent anti-U.S. feelings triggered a review of U.S. policy in 1930. Faced with similar problems in Nicaragua, President Hoover and his successor, Franklin D. Roosevelt, were determined that the United States would exit from Haiti's tropical imbroglio as quickly as possible. Following the 1915–1934 U.S. period were twenty years during which Haitian governance slowly decayed under the weight of presidential excesses. This period came to an uninspired end with the 1957 elections that brought François Duvalier to power. What ensued was a harsh family rule that was to last until his son's downfall in 1986.

This has in turn been followed by a succession of failed attempts at democratic governance, at considerable cost to Haiti and the international apparatus supporting the efforts. This frames what might now be termed the

Aristide Presidencies: this begins with his election in late 1990, his ouster in September 1991 and the international isolation (1991–1994) of the ensuing military regime, a UN-mandated and U.S.-led military intervention (September 1994) leading to Aristide's return to office in October 1994, the election of his designated successor in late 1995 and the subsequent political paralysis (1997–2000), the reelection of Aristide in late 2000, and his departure in late February 2004, replaced by an interim regime operating under a UN mandate and a commitment for new elections by the end of 2005. This is obviously unfinished business.

The Character of Society

More than in any other country in the Western Hemisphere, the structure of Haitian politics underscores the isolated and traditional character of the country's society. Formal ideology is not a particularly useful component in explaining the course of Haitian developments. The character of the polity is therefore best assessed by a review of the following factors: religion, the nation's rural-urban bifurcation, cultural values, and the Haitian society's worldview.

Religious institutions are numerically and culturally important in the Caribbean, but in Haiti established churches have been to a degree displaced or absorbed by indigenous cults and practices derived from tradition and folklore. Although marginal in much of the region (the Rastafarians in Jamaica, for example), Voodoo in Haiti has been enriched by both Christianity and ancestral African rites for over three centuries to provide Haitians with a great emotional outlet.

Basic to Voodoo is the ancestral past and its impact on the present. There is a fatalism in its cosmos that does not leave much room for shaping the present or the future. Nature and humans contend with each other in a process forwarded by appeals to the many spirits who control all forces. An individual struggles to survive within an essentially static hierarchy.

This defensive character of Haitian religious culture has intermixed with the country's unique historical experience. The product of slavery and of harsh colonial conditions, the very origins of modern Haiti were fixed in a rejection of the white race, if not entirely of the culture that it represented. That viewpoint took its toll on the Haitian psyche. Although French and modernizing sociopolitical influences engaged the minute portion of the nation represented by the elite, the vast majority of the population remained tied to the slave experience and its eradication with the revolution of 1804. More African and Creole than French, more illiterate than literate, and historically more isolated than any other country in the Caribbean, Haitian culture has to a degree generated an enduring demoralized attitude regarding the nation's potential.

This fact has been made more acute by the exploitative preferences of the two sectors of Haitian society that might have taken the country out of its long dead-end run: the mulatto (lighter-skinned) minority, historically associated with the country's commercial activity, and the black elite, representing a politically governing class. The ensuing geographical separation of the elite from the masses and of the urban population from the rural one has had significant political and social implications. Accounting for perhaps 70 percent of the population, the peasantry has been excluded from national decision-making. The fact that national debates take place partly in French, a language that the vast majority of the population does not speak or read, underlines the fissures in Haitian political dynamics.

The heart of Haiti is its inner country—rural, poor, and dedicated to basic agricultural production. Long periods of isolation have made this part of Haiti a conservator of African traditions, and the traditional milieu is still the dominant environment of Haiti today. Roughly 80 percent of the population is made up of peasants who speak Creole and no French, are essentially illiterate, and live in social conditions reminiscent of past centuries; Voodoo is a spiritual influence despite the strong presence of Catholic and Protestant churches.

What has made life bearable for the average Haitian is the fact that government has historically not intruded into their lives. After 1957 the Duvalier regimes modernized notions of "government" by introducing a more formal and occasionally brutal local security presence. Disbanded in the 1990s, neither law enforcement nor much of a local administrative presence has reasserted itself. The growth of a corrupting drug trafficking economy has further eroded the capacity of local government to address economic, social, and security needs.

The other world of Haiti is built primarily around the capital and a few secondary towns. It is not only urban but also coastal in character. If the nation has developed any capital wealth since independence, this is where it is to be found. An urbanized and somewhat cosmopolitan elite has dedicated itself to trading as opposed to developing a national economy. This community includes the mulatto economic elite in a historically uneasy association with the black political classes

Institutional Patterns

The absence of a viable political development process has stunted the growth of socioeconomic and political interest groups normally found in a modernizing society. Likewise, the weakness of Haitian institutions has for the most part made it very difficult for the process of change to be channeled toward productive ends.

Government administration has constituted a center of influence, if for no other reason than that it has represented the source of jobs, money, gifts, and public favors—if not outright access to the national treasury. The urbanized sector for the most part consists of a docile, lower-middle class of Haitian society. Unionization, paralyzed under the Duvaliers, has not been a factor despite the limited rebirth of a trade-union movement in recent years. At its most senior echelon the public sector has included the lucky few who have had access to corrupt government patronage emanating from the presidential palace.

The Catholic Church's influence has rivaled that of the government. After the 1860s the church fulfilled an important educational mission and provided isolated communities with the rudiments of continuity and linkage to the outside world. Not surprisingly, the spiritual and political worlds have occasionally overlapped. As recently as the 1960s François Duvalier pushed through a "Haitianization" of the clergy, also reviving age-old frictions regarding appointments of the church hierarchy in Haiti. As elsewhere in the region, the clergy is split between conservative and liberal contingents.

The Catholic Church played a decisive role in the 1986 ouster of Jean-Claude Duvalier. Under pressure from the Vatican, the Church pulled back from a formal political role, but its engagement continued to be the conduit through which human rights and other sociopolitical concerns were exposed. The grassroots or "Ti Legliz" movement in the 1980s that was the basis for Aristide's arrival to power in 1990 created splits within the Church hierarchy and more generally within Haitian society. More recently the expanding grassroots involvement of evangelical Protestant denominations has translated into political movements at the national level and might affect a landscape historically dominated by the Roman Catholic Church.

Born out of revolutionary violence, Haiti never succeeded in constructing the structures of a civilian society capable of minimizing the rule of force. As a result, consolidation of political power in the hands of strongmen made the armed forces the institutional pillar of society. Part of Haiti's history is the story of competing mercenary bands (*cacos*) and peasant groups (*piquets*) fighting a ragtag government military. The trend was partially reversed after 1915 during the U.S. occupation led by U.S. Marines. Ironically, the most visible product of this period turned out to be the Garde d'Haiti—later transformed into Haiti's armed forces. They remained by default the only organization with a national political reach and a semblance of institutional cohesion.

With the Duvalier regime's collapse in 1986 the military inherited political control and promptly made an even bigger mess of things. The army was ultimately disbanded by Aristide in late 1994, and in a return to the past replaced by a national police. The rapid politicization of the police in the late 1990s failed in removing the use of force from the Haitian political scene.

This is what had happened after the first U.S. intervention in 1915. Worse yet, the intersection of a politicized police and the impact of drug trafficking created new pressures of their own. By most accounts the collapse of the Aristide government in 2004 was due to the increasing power and autonomy of renegade police and former military elements and the infiltration of these into the higher echelons of Haiti's government leadership.

Haiti's low level of political participation has generated few alternative institutions. Not only has the economic poverty of the nation centralized national authority into a minute urban constituency, but the cumulative ravages of crises since the 1980s have also undermined the reservoir of political leadership. The political party structure, anchored more by personalities than viable agendas, is weak and not likely to change quickly in a society used to authoritarian rule.

Likewise, modern social or political pressure groups typical of democratic environments (for example, human rights organizations, local community interests, women's groups, students, labor unions, the media) have found limited space to prosper. The small modern business community has remained cautious or sometimes co-opted by changing political winds. Yet in the growing vacuum created by a decade of crisis and paralysis civil society in general and portions of the private sector in particular have increased their political profile. This became evident in the lead-in to the collapse of the second Aristide presidency in 2004. Another pressure group with a potential role is Haiti's large exile community, limited for now to being a source of political money as well as economic investment through remittances.

From Duvalier to Aristide

The Duvalier era began in 1957 (Papa Doc became president for life in 1964) during a period of political confusion that included the collapse of the previous government (Paul Magloire), violence, and fraudulent elections. François Duvalier was the product of a movement toward a return to black culture and of a political resurgence that took hold during the U.S. occupation (1915–1934). In the 1920s a Haitian intellectual class had begun to evolve a potent political racialism derived from a reevaluation of the country's African tradition. This racialism initially evolved into a conception associated with the French-African negritude movement, which entailed a belief in the distinctive character of an African environmental heritage and a rejection of the superiority of European culture. As a form of "cultural decolonization," it was later elaborated by Haitians, including François Duvalier, into a rationale of black political power, which through the early 1970s constituted the framework of government control.

Who was François Duvalier? The person who held such a spell over Haitian affairs after 1957 was a soft-spoken physician and part-time ethnologist.

A black, or *noir*, by Haitian standards, Duvalier had four children, including one son, Jean-Claude (later to be known as Baby Doc). Unlike many of his colleagues in Haitian history François Duvalier was never a military man and, as a result of his writings, he was perceived as something of an intellectual. These characteristics confounded most observers and political opponents and initially misled the United States.

In practice, the Duvalier years were characterized by brutal political control, corruption, income inequalities, illiteracy, and environmental degradation, and compounded by brain drain. A shrewd autocrat, he ruthlessly suppressed opponents that were or appeared to challenge his authority. The influence of the mulatto elite was eroded, the political power of the Roman Catholic Church was reduced by allowing the government to have a say in the nomination of the Haitian church's leadership (which until then had been essentially French), and the army was purged and brought into line. A powerful paramilitary organization (*Volontaires de la Securité Nationale*, VSN)—the famed *Tonton Macoutes* (TTMs)—was established to protect the regime and enforce its directives.

Confounding most predictions, Jean-Claude Duvalier (Baby Doc) did initially show some durability after taking over in April 1971 following his father's death. An unknown quantity when he assumed office at age nineteen, his contact with the outside was limited by a closed environment of presidential advisers, family members, and security guards, and most notably his dynamic and controversial wife, Michèle Bennett, daughter of a mulatto business family. What was ultimately termed an "economic revolution" operationally implied greater solicitation of economic assistance from major donor countries (United States, France, Canada) and a consortium of international and private lending agencies. Yet the authoritarian and often aimless nature of Haitian governance ultimately led to Duvalier's downfall in 1986.

Duvalier faced Catholic Church militancy and declining support from Washington. The ensuing mobilization of the population was sanctioned during a visit by Pope John Paul II in 1983. The pope's references to "injustices" and the need for a more equitable society were seen as an indication of the Church's intent to champion change and take on an active political role. U.S. policy also shifted gradually, beginning with the Carter administration's emphasis on human rights followed by a broader global theme of freedom and democracy under the Ronald Reagan presidency. Likewise, Haiti became a matter of interest in the halls of the U.S. Congress. This was driven by public awareness resulting from the drama of Haitian refugee flows in the early 1980s as well as the political mobilization of segments of the African American political community on behalf of Haiti's struggles.

The collapse of the Duvalier regime began in November 1985 with a series of spontaneous riots in Gonaives that turned into a major antigovernment protest. The regime's ineptitude, coupled with the army's understandable reluctance to confront these street demonstrations with deadly force, led to the government's collapse and Duvalier's departure on board a U.S. military transport plane for exile in France on February 6, 1986. What followed was not, however, what either the Haitians or the international community had expected.

Governmental authority passed to the military-led Council of National Government for a transition period of unspecified length, led initially by General Henri Namphy. The ensuing near-anarchy subdued only when it finally appeared that the interim regime was planning for elections. U.S. foreign aid flows increased, as did support from other donors. Some progress was even achieved in stabilizing the economy. But the foundations upon which this stability was constructed were dangerously weak. International policy designs for a democratic society were projected into the future without attention to the near-term process on the ground in Haiti.

The first casualty was the bloody elections of late 1987, halted in the first hour of balloting by armed thugs linked to the army and Duvalierist allies. A truncated election was scheduled for January 1988, in which Leslie Manigat won the presidency. This unstable situation received little international support, and Manigat was overthrown in June. The political situation unraveled further as Namphy returned as head of the government, but in September he himself was pushed aside by General Prosper Avril. Avril governed from a position of declining authority; the balance of power within the military was upset (with a coup that nearly succeeded in April 1989), and the patience of the international donor community had begun to wear thin. Avril's reluctance to move toward elections led to the regime's collapse in March 1990 and opened the way for a process that resulted in elections in December 1990.

By an overwhelming majority Haitians chose a charismatic ordained priest, Jean-Bertrand Aristide, as president in what was regarded by most observers as the nation's first modern election. The 1990 elections presaged a period of intermittent euphoria as well as a succession of spectacular failures that has lasted well into the new century in what might now be termed the Aristide Presidencies.

The Aristide Presidencies and Global Politics

Aristide is a powerful political persona and by all accounts the principal variable in Haiti since 1990. Born in Haiti's south and brought up in Catholic schools, he early acquired a rapport with Haiti's large and overwhelmingly poor population. He speaks their social and political language and has been able to convey a message of hope. This has been coupled with vivid images of change clearly directed at the elite, encapsulated most dramatically by *Lavalas,* the cleansing flood. In Aristide's powerful words, the latter will bring his fellow countrymen "from misery to poverty with dignity."

Aristide is a survivor, having escaped death several times since the late 1980s. A very complex personality, he displays an almost mystical vision of his country. What began as a liberation-theology-based political movement anchored in Port-au-Prince's slums was catapulted into national prominence in the late 1980s at a time when the nation's military leadership was providing neither stability nor growth. Often accused of holding a questionable commitment to the western-based notions of representative democracy, Aristide sprung into the 1990 elections late in the game.

The 1990–2005 period includes three presidential elections, two won by Aristide (1990 and 2000) and another won by a close ally (René Préval in 1995). The period also is composed of two constitutional interruptions (late 1990 and early 2004), both involving Aristide. This underscores the uncertain verdict of Haiti's steps toward democratic governance, let alone coherent management of national policy issues. It also suggests the deep chasm that now frames Haitian political dynamics and the unique role played by Aristide in this regard.

In 1990 Aristide was chosen by the Haitian electorate to achieve justice, address the concerns of Haiti's poor, and provide a clear break with the recent Duvalier era. He survived an early coup attempt and seemed to be reestablishing some level of national confidence and peace, but within eight months was ousted in a coup whose causes continue to be debated. Whether it was the army's paranoia, Aristide's inflammatory rhetoric, or the pockets of violence directed at the opposition, the crisis that ensued has continued in varying ways for over a decade.

Aristide was succeeded in 1995 by his protégé, René Préval, who in the end governed weakly but concluded a complete five-year mandate. A major impediment was the inability of the government and the national assembly to work together to pass laws, approve budgets, or sign off on appointments (notably for prime minister), all of which led to political paralysis and a festering crisis that previewed tensions during the next cycle of elections in 2000. The hopes triggered initially by Aristide's election in 1990, the near-crusade for his return in 1994, and the succession of Préval were mostly disappointed by zero-sum political dynamics. The distrust between Aristide's *Lavalas* movement and the rest of the political community not only deepened but in turn brought about conflict within *Lavalas*. This generated break-away groups and ultimately formed the basis of an enlarged political opposition. By the late 1990s some of Aristide's early allies had become his opponents.

As predicted, Aristide returned to office in early 2001 following elections the previous year whose credibility was questioned by the international community, notably the OAS in the case of the May 2000 parliamentary races. What was a serious but manageable dispute instead triggered a deepening mistrust among

Haitian political actors, as well as with the international community. Diplomatic mediation by the OAS failed, and by 2003 the political atmosphere between the Aristide government and multiple opponents had deteriorated close to the point of no return. Pockets of violence erupted, with some of Aristide's tactical allies turning against him and aligning themselves with an assortment of gangs, former military, and renegade police. In tandem, increasingly large segments of Haiti's urban civil society began to mobilize against Aristide. The ensuing stand-off in early 2004 was broken under pressure from Paris and Washington. Facing a violent rebellion, Aristide left the country, ultimately to exile in South Africa.

The backdrop to these domestic dynamics is a never-ending cycle of ultimately unproductive external interventions. Following the September 1990 coup Aristide went into exile, first to Venezuela, then the United States, from where he returned in October 1994. This period was anchored by an increasingly tough economic and diplomatic embargo of Haiti to strangle what became known as the de facto military-led regime. This came to an end in September 1994 with a U.S.-led and UN mandated military intervention.

Almost ten years later the international community once again intervened in the wake of a rebellion against Aristide's second presidency. An initial joint U.S.-French-Canadian diplomatic and military initiative midwifed a transition to an interim government led by Gerard Latortue, whose mandate was to hold elections by late 2005. This intervention was ultimately folded into a UN mandate operating under the Charter's more forceful Chapter 7 terms of reference and a multinational military and civilian police force with a majority Latin American composition.

Throughout the Cold War Haiti generally stayed away from Third World politics and most North-South disputes, and in this respect alone differed from that of its English-speaking Caribbean neighbors. Yet one constant that remains is Haiti's relationship with the United States. Successive U.S. administrations have been disposed to reassess ties with Haiti, and periods of cooperation have followed. In retrospect, much of this has been built on exaggerated expectations in Washington and suspect political foundations in Haiti itself. The record is one of economic downturn and troubles with foreign aid, intervals of political upheaval and refugee crises, bouts of bloody violence, and a gradual internationalization of Haiti's problems.

Haitian Challenge

Notions of establishing a modicum of democratic governance have turned out to be a long-term and frustrating campaign. Neither Haitian leadership nor various international actors have had very realistic conceptions of what is involved. This led, for example, to a succession of electoral exercises

(1987, 1990, 1995, 1997, 2000) whose imperfections cumulatively resulted in the 2004 collapse of Haitian governance and a further narrowing of Haiti's political options. Haiti's limited modern civil society and nongovernmental organizations have gotten squeezed also by a socioeconomic environment dominated increasingly by corruption and violence.

The extensive international financial commitments (over $1 billion) promised upon Aristide's return in 1994, and undergirding a remarkable goodwill in the development assistance community toward Haiti, were either wasted or went unused. To compound matters the collapse of government economic development policies in the late 1990s gave further prominence to the influence of narcotics trafficking and contraband trade in all forms. The intersection of political and economic instability with organized crime and a dramatic decay of already fragile national institutions has been an unhappy outcome to the hopes of a democratic transition.

A nation in desperate socioeconomic condition with almost no track record of purposeful government faces limited choices. Haiti has a reservoir of individual skills and political acumen, but the challenge lies in the pooling of these human resources and the development of relevant economic and political organizations. Although there are egalitarian and cooperative features in the nation's peasant environment, Haiti's traditional political culture and linguistic bifurcation are profound obstacles to the development of a modern democratic government. In addition, the dubious interest of portions of the elite in collaborating in the economic, political, and cultural integration of the nation renders near-term national development problematic at best.

Given all this and the nation's catastrophic social and ecological collapse since the late 1980s, any future Haitian government faces a daunting task. Quasi-humanitarian concerns are likely to predominate, and fears of political crisis will continue to attract external interest. This is particularly true for Washington, whose vision of regional Caribbean strategic interest has been amplified by a concern that any crisis in Haiti will affect the United States directly through refugee flows. Foreign governments and agencies will therefore continue to set priorities in the hope of generating a basis for technocratic development and socially relevant and politically responsible governance in Haiti. The degree to which Haiti's political culture, leadership, and decayed institutions have learned from the frustrations of the past decade represents the fragile basis upon which Haiti's future is to be built.

Suggestions for Further Reading

Abbot, Elizabeth. *Haiti: The Duvaliers and Their Legacy.* New York: McGraw-Hill, 1988.

Aristide, Jean-Bertrand. *Dignity*. Charlottesville: University Press of Virginia, 1996.

Arthur, Charles, and Michael Dash, eds. *Libete, A Haiti Anthology*. Princeton, NJ: Markus Wiener, 1999.

Bell, Madison Smartt. *All Soul's Rising*. New York: Penguin, 1995.

Dandicat, Edwidge. *The Farming of the Bones*. New York: Soho, 1998.

Dayan, Joan. *Haiti, History, and the Gods*. Berkeley: University of California Press, 1995.

Diederick, Bernard, and Al Burt. *Papa Doc: The Truth About Haiti Today*. New York: McGraw-Hill, 1969.

Farmer, Paul. *The Uses of Haiti*. Monroe, ME: Common Courage, 1994.

Fass, Simon M. *Political Economy in Haiti: The Drama of Survival*. New Brunswick, NJ: Transaction, 1988.

Fatton, Robert. *Haiti's Predatory Republic: The Unending Transition to Democracy*. Boulder, CO: Lynne Rienner, 2002.

Fauriol, Georges A. *Foreign Policy Behavior of Caribbean States: Guyana, Haiti, and Jamaica*. Lanham, MD: University Press of America, 1984.

Fauriol, Georges A., ed. *Haitian Frustrations, dilemmas for U.S. policy*. Washington, DC: Center for Strategic and International Studies, 1995.

Gibbons, Elizabeth D. *Sanctions in Haiti: Human Rights and Democracy Under Assault*. Westport, CT: Praeger/CSIS Wash Papers #177, 1999.

Girard, Philippe R. *Clinton in Haiti: The 1994 U.S. Invasion of Haiti*. New York: Palgrave Macmillan, 2004.

Greene, Graham. *The Comedians*. New York: Penguin, 1965.

Healy, David. *Gunboat Diplomacy in the Wilson Era: The U.S. Navy in Haiti, 1915–1917*. Madison: University of Wisconsin Press, 1976.

Heinl, Gordon Debs Jr., Nancy Gordon Heinl, and Michael Heinl. *Written in Blood: The Story of the Haitian People 1492–1995* (Revised and expanded). Lanham, MD: University Press of America, 1996.

Herskovitz, Melville J. *Life in a Haitian Valley*. Garden City, NY: Doubleday, 1971.

Laguerre, Michel. *The Military and Society in Haiti*. Knoxville: University of Tennessee Press, 1993.

Langley, Lester D. *The Americas in the Age of Revolution 1750–1850*. New Haven, CT: Yale University Press, 1996.

Leyburn, James G. *The Haitian People*. 2nd ed. New Haven, CT: Yale University Press, 1966.

Logan, Rayford W. *The Diplomatic Relations of the United States with Haiti, 1776–1891*. Chapel Hill: University of North Carolina Press, 1941.

Lundhal, Mats. *Politics or Markets? Essays on Haitian Underdevelopment*. London: Routledge, 1992.

Malone, David. *Decision-making in the UN Security Council: The Case of Haiti, 1990–1997*. New York: Oxford University Press, 1998.

Nicholls, David. *From Dessalines to Duvalier: Race, Colour, and National Independence in Haiti*. Cambridge: Cambridge University Press, 1979.

Ott, Thomas O. *The Haitian Revolution, 1789–1804*. Knoxville: University of Tennessee Press, 1973.

Plummer, Brenda Gayle. *Haiti and the United States: The Psychological Moment*. Athens: The University of Georgia Press, 1992.

Preeg, Ernest H. *The Haitian Dilemma: A Case Study in Demographic, Development, and U.S. Foreign Policy*. Washington, DC: Center for Strategic and International Studies, 1996.

Renda, Mary A. *Taking Haiti: Military Occupation and the Culture of U.S. Imperialism, 1915–1940*. Chapel Hill: University of North Carolina Press, 2001.

Rotberg, Robert I. *Haiti: The Politics of Squalor*. Boston: Houghton Mifflin, 1971.

Schmidt, Hans. *The United States Occupation of Haiti, 1915–1934*. New Brunswick, NJ: Rutgers University Press, 1971.

Shacochis, Bob. *The Immaculate Invasion*. New York: Viking, 1999.

Stotzky, Irwin P. *Silencing the Guns in Haiti: The Promise of Deliberative Democracy*. Chicago: University of Chicago, 1997.

Trouillot, Michel-Rolph. *Haiti: State Against Nation: The Origins and Legacy of Duvalierism*. New York: Monthly Review Press, 1990.

United Nations. *Les Nations Unies et Haiti 1990–1996*. New York: United Nations Blue Book Series, 1996.

Wilentz, Amy. *The Rainy Season*. New York: Simon and Schuster, 1989.

Williamson, Charles T. *The U.S. Naval Mission to Haiti 1959–1963*. Annapolis, MD: Naval Institute Press, 1999.

Notes

1. Compare among others, David Nicholls, *From Dessalines to Duvalier: Race, Colour, and National Independence in Haiti* (Cambridge: Cambridge University Press, 1979); Robert I. Rotberg, *Haiti: The Politics of Squalor* (Boston: Houghton Mifflin, 1971); and Robert Fatton, *Haiti's Predatory Republic: The Unending Transition to Democracy* (Boulder, CO: Lynne Rienner, 2002).

2. Rayford W. Logan, *The Diplomatic Relations of the United States with Haiti, 1776–1891* (Chapel Hill: University of North Carolina Press, 1971).

PART IV

Conclusion

26

Latin America and the Future

A Living Laboratory

Latin America has long been one of the world's most exciting "living laboratories" of economic, social, and political change. Historically it has been a hotbed of conflict between democracy and authoritarianism; mercantilism, capitalism, and socialism; First- and Third-World perceptions; change and continuity; the traditional and the modern. These conflicts have often torn Latin America apart and hindered its progress.

By now some of these earlier conflicts have faded, although they have not disappeared. By the early 1990s and continuing into the new millennium a new consensus seemed to have emerged between the United States and Latin America on the desirability of (1) democracy in the political sphere, (2) open markets and liberalization in the economic sphere, and (3) an international order focused on free trade. Under this rubric a large number of changes have occurred in Latin America and much of the area is freer and more democratic than it was a decade or two ago. But the various chapters of this book also make clear how limited, incomplete, and perhaps even reversible these changes are. History has not yet "ended" in Latin America.

It is both the common trends and the differences among the countries that make Latin America such a fertile laboratory for studying comparative economic, social, and political change. Few areas of the world offer such rich conditions for study and research on the processes of comparative change and modernization. Here we have countries with a common historical background, colonial experience, law, language, religion, sociology, and politics. All were cast five hundred years ago in a common feudal and medieval setting and relationship to the mother countries of Spain and Portugal. Yet because of geography, topography, resources, ethnic mix, and history, each country has developed differently and now has its own system of values, sociology, politics, and national identity. Moreover, the countries of the area, although retaining

583

many common traits, are becoming more and more unlike rather than alike. As President Ronald Reagan once told the reporters who accompanied him on a trip to Latin America (and knew no more about the area than he did): "There really are different countries down there."

These common background features, combined with increasingly diverging trends among the countries of the area, are what make Latin America such an interesting "laboratory" for study. Here we have countries with similar backgrounds and yet very different developmental patterns. How do we explain why some countries have become democratic, others remain authoritarian, still others a mixture of authoritarianism and democracy, and Cuba pursues a Marxist-Leninist course? How can we account for why some countries have developed economically while others remain mired in poverty? In answering these questions, once again the living laboratory metaphor comes into play. Latin America is like a laboratory in which we can hold some variables constant (law, language, religion, colonial experience), while we examine other variables (such as resources, social structure, or political institutions) to help account for why and how some countries succeed and develop economically and politically while others do not. There is probably no other area in the world that offers both so many individual country cases combined with such a clear delineation of converging/diverging variables as does Latin America.

Looking at Latin America comparatively, it is clear that almost all the countries conform more or less closely to the general model set forth in the introductory chapters of this book. There were colonial experiences and institutions common to most of the countries, similar patterns (as well as differences) in the interrelations of the races, and common problems of organization and underdevelopment to overcome. All the countries remained locked in a medieval and semifeudal colonial experience for three centuries; all had common problems of instability, rigid class structure, lack of viable political institutions, and economic underdevelopment in the nineteenth century.

However, the strength of the Spanish model was stronger in some places (Mexico and Peru) than in others (Costa Rica, Chile, Uruguay), and accordingly their developmental patterns were different.

In the twentieth century all the countries experienced accelerated economic development, greater social change, industrialization, and more rapid political change. Yet even in colonial times the differences (geographic, resource-wise, ethnic makeup, value to the monarchy) among the several colonies were apparent, differences that were accentuated in the nineteenth and twentieth centuries. It is in this context of similarities and widening differences that we can begin to explain national variations, developmental success or the relative lack thereof, and why some countries became democratic and others did not. Hence the imperative in studying Latin America is that we know and understand the general pattern of the region as a whole while also comprehending the individual country variations. That is what this book, with the substantive general introduction followed by detailed treatment of all the countries, seeks to provide.

Change and Continuity

Although the main structures and institutions of Latin American society and politics remained remarkably stable through three centuries of colonial rule and even on into the postindependence nineteenth and early twentieth centuries (the "twilight of the middle ages"), in recent decades the process of change has been greatly accelerated. In the introduction we identified six broad areas of change and asked the authors of our individual country chapters to assess these as well: changes in the political culture and values, changes in the economy, changes in social and class structure, changes in political groups and organizations, changes in public policy, and changes in the international environment. Now it is time to assess and pull all these themes together, to link the general propositions set forth in the introduction to the concrete cases provided in the individual chapters, to see what general trends and conclusions apply.

The country chapters make clear the degree to which Latin American political culture is undergoing transformation. New values and ideologies—democracy, participation, liberalism, capitalism, and socialism—have challenged the traditional belief system of fatalism, elitism, hierarchy, and resignation. New communications and transportation networks are increasingly breaking down traditional beliefs and isolation. The hold of the traditional Catholic Church and religion on Latin America is also decreasing as Protestantism, secularism, a changed Catholic Church, and other belief systems make serious inroads. Although varying from country to country, the older authoritarian assumptions are being questioned and the older bases of legitimacy are being undermined. Latin American political culture is changing rapidly.

However, many of the old beliefs linger on, particularly in the backward rural areas and in the more traditional and poorer countries, but by no means exclusively there. For example, although Latin America prefers democratic rule, it tends to define that as "strong government." It wants regular democratic elections but often wants spoils, patronage, and government favors in return for the vote. It believes in separation of powers but still vests strong authority in an all-powerful executive. Hence, although formal democracy has been established throughout the region (except in Cuba), a genuinely egalitarian and participatory democracy is still weak in most countries. Most of the countries lack a well-developed "civil society"—a network of independent interest groups that mediate between the citizen and the government.

The economic structure has also been dramatically changed in recent decades even while many problems remain. These are no longer sleepy, traditional, backward "banana republics"; rather, the Latin American economies have become much more dynamic and diversified. The older subsistence agriculture and one-crop economies are increasingly giving way to industry, manufacturing, commerce, business, tourism, and services. Latin America is now far more integrated into the world economy; feudalism and semifeudalism have given way to capitalism and neoliberalism. All these changes have put more money into the economies of the area; provided new jobs, including jobs for women; quickened the way of life; and increased general prosperity.

Yet these changes are very uneven. Much of Latin America remains poor, backward, and Third World. Some countries and some people are "making it" into the developed world, but others lag behind. Moreover, even with the new wealth Latin America has the worst distribution of income of any area in the world. In addition, although some markets have been freed up, the temptation to return to the older mercantilism and statism is still powerful. So although there has been economic progress, many problems remain.

One of the most serious is the continuing social dualism that exists with a few very wealthy people and a large number of abjectly poor ones. This led to Brazil being referred to as "Belindia": one part modern and wealthy like Belgium and another part traditional and poor like India. This dualism exists in all Latin American countries, with the possible exception of Cuba, and in some countries—Peru, Bolivia, and Guatemala, most notably—the dualism is accentuated by the fact that the traditional, poor sector also contains Indians who do not even speak Spanish. Hugo Chávez in Venezuela claims to speak and govern for the marginalized sectors of the population.

Economic development has given rise to widespread social changes in all the countries. Latin America has gone from 70 percent rural to 70 percent urban, from 70 percent illiterate to 70 percent literate; life expectancy is up from sixty to seventy years; and per capita income has significantly increased. In addition, the once feudal, two-class societies of Latin America now have business, industrial, commercial, banking, and other elites along with the traditional landholding oligarchy. All the societies now have sizable middle classes ranging from 20 to 40 percent of the population. Trade union movements, peasants, women, indigenous elements, and the urban poor are all being organized for the first time. There are new community groups, social movements, and NGOs. These social changes have made Latin America far more pluralistic than in the past and have thus provided a more solid base for democracy.

However, these gross figures are often deceiving. Poverty, malnutrition, illiteracy, and disease are still often endemic in Latin America in both the rural and urban areas. Most of the wealth has remained in the hands of the elites and middle classes; little has trickled down to the poor. In most countries these same elites still rule; despite elections power is still mainly in the hands of the social, economic, and political elites. The social system is still unbalanced: As compared with the elites, the trade unions, peasant leagues, women's groups, indigenous movements, and other mass organizations tend to be weak, divided, and with limited power. As pointed out in Chapter 3, traditionally interest groups could exist only if given permission by the elite. Today there seems to be a change in this, as new groups and civil society can survive even if the government does not grant them recognition. Yet it is unclear to what extent the change from a system of government sanction of groups to a new one of de facto liberal, pluralist legitimacy has been made. In addition, although Latin America is undoubtedly more pluralist than before, the mass of the population is still excluded from effective participation in decisions that affect them most closely. Nor does Latin America, despite the greater pluralism, have the kind of counterbalancing interest group competition and lobbying characteristics of U. S. democracy.

Many of the same problems are characteristic of political institutions. Nineteen of the twenty Latin American countries hold elections regularly and are at least formally democratic, and that is encouraging. Similarly, the human rights situation is significantly better in most countries than it was twenty years ago. But the cultural and institutional bases of many of these new democracies are still fragile. Polls indicate that democracy's popularity is actually declining in Latin America, that the public doesn't think democracy has delivered on its promise. Cronyism and patrimonialism are still widely practiced rather than egalitarianism and advancement for merit. Corruption, violence, and crime are increasing. At the same time political parties, local government, and political institutions in general are not held in high esteem by the public. Latin America seems to practice democracy at election time but in the intervening years presidents rule almost as constitutional dictators.

If we look at public policy, many of the same disclaimers apply. Economic growth is occurring, but the gap between rich and poor is widening. Liberalization, privatization, and economic reform are going forward, but ever so slowly. Agrarian reform is all but dead as an issue, and where there is urban reform, the problems seem to mount up faster than the solutions. There are new social reforms, but they seldom seem to reach those most in need. In the areas of education, housing, health care, and employment, important steps have been taken, but the difficulties seem to outstrip government's capacity to cope with them.

The final area of major change in Latin America is in the international realm. It is clear that Latin America no longer lives in isolation. Globalization has come to the area. Global television and movies bring in new styles of taste and comportment: blue jeans, dating, McDonald's, Coca Cola, freedom, consumerism. Globalization also brings with it the requirements of democracy and human rights and, if these are abused, international sanctions on the country involved are likely to follow. Globalization also means economic competition, requiring that Latin America lower its protective tariffs and be prepared to compete with the world's most efficient economies. Competition has major political implications as well, requiring state downsizing, privatization, lessened patronage, and the likely going out of business of thousands of small, inefficient, "mom-and-pop" stores and businesses.

So the balance sheet on Latin America politics and development is still a mixed one: lots of progress on economic growth, social change, and democratization, but all of these with major weaknesses and problems as well. The gross figures sound wonderful—nineteen of twenty countries democratic—but the deeper we probe into the individual countries, the more problems we see.

What overall conclusions emerge from these considerations? First, most of Latin America is now in a transitional stage: It is in the process of breaking the back of the past but is not yet fully modern or developed. Second, we need to recognize that sustained development, whether in Africa, Russia, or Latin America, requires several generations, not just a few years. Third, modernization is uneven: Urban areas are affected more rapidly than rural ones. Fourth, the benefits of development are also uneven: Some groups benefit more than others, and there is always a tradeoff between growth and equity. Fifth, it is clear that those countries that have ample resources, strong institutions, and good public policy—Brazil, Chile, and Costa Rica—are doing better than those that lack these features.

Latin America today represents a dynamic, ever-changing mix of traditional and modern. Abject poverty exists alongside gleaming skyscrapers and the most modern, high-tech industry. Widespread corruption and patronage coexist with efficient firms and new public policy agencies. Latin America has embraced democracy, but it is sufficiently concerned about instability, chaos, and ungovernability to retain authoritarian features. The countries, their businesses, their governments, and their unions all recognize the need to streamline and eliminate waste, but that is hard to do if it is job, business, agency, or family that will be hurt in the process. Given these conditions it is probably no accident that we get such leaders as Chávez in Venezuela, Fujimori in Peru, Menem in Argentina, or the Revolutionary Institutional Party (PRI) in Mexico, that appear to combine democratic with authoritarian and populist tendencies. It is in the bridging of these gaps between traditional and modern, authoritarian and democratic, statism or mercantilism and liberalism that the genius of Latin American politics and politicians often shines through.

The future now looks brighter in Latin America than it has previously. On both the political (democracy) and economic (development) fronts, even with all the problems here enumerated Latin America seems to be doing better than at any time in its history. Although there may be reversions to authoritarianism in some of the poorer, weakly institutionalized countries, the possibility of a continent-wide reversion to authoritarianism as occurred in the 1960s and 1970s seems unlikely. Over time the social, economic, and political base for authoritarianism is being eroded by greater literacy, affluence, middle-classness, and democracy, but its attractiveness in some countries has not yet entirely disappeared.

Among the most important questions remaining to be answered are which Latin American countries can succeed in consolidating and institutionalizing their still-fragile political systems; whether they can adapt rapidly enough to globalization; whether they can combine economic growth with equity and social justice; and whether they can reconcile their recently reviewed democratic precepts with their own past historical traditions that are often authoritarian, corporatist, and patrimonialist. On the answers to these and other important questions hang not only the possibilities for Latin America's future success but also why Latin America remains such a fascinating area.

Common Currents and Distinctive Situations

Although the Latin American countries have become increasingly diverse over time, the common currents that emerge from this book remain equally interesting. These include the continued decline of the traditional semifeudal order in all countries, the emergence throughout the region of greater social and political pluralism, the continued weakness of modern institutions including those necessary for democracy, and the ongoing power of elite groups. The balance of power within Latin American politics is changing as the Roman Catholic Church, the armed forces, and the landed oligarchy lose power relative to the expanded influence of commercial, banking, manufacturing, and political elites and middle classes. Similar changes are occurring at the international level, with the United States being less interested in the domestic politics of Latin America but more interested in trade and commercial relations.

Although Latin America as a whole is undoubtedly more democratic than it was three or four decades ago, democracy is often limited, partial, and blended with authoritarian and corporatist features. Similarly, in the economic sphere greater liberalization has occurred but with persistent mercantilist and statist features. If we were to rank order the twenty Latin American countries in terms of the strength of democracy, the list midway through the first decade of the new millennium would be as follows:

1. Most democratic: Chile, Costa Rica, and Uruguay
2. Democratic but not fully consolidated: Argentina, Brazil, Dominican Republic, and Panama
3. Democratic in the past but now threatened: Colombia and Venezuela
4. Formally democratic but with weak institutions: Bolivia, Ecuador, El Salvador, Guatemala, Honduras, Nicaragua, Paraguay, and Peru
5. Moving from authoritarianism to democracy: Mexico
6. Having some fragile democratic institutions but lacking a democratic base: Haiti
7. Marxist-Leninist, undemocratic: Cuba

Note that very few of the countries are fully consolidated democracies; most are in transition where democracy is still weak and may still be precarious. Remember the injunctions of the introduction: Elections are a good start on the route to democracy, but many other criteria—human rights, civil liberties, genuine pluralism, freedom and equality, civic consciousness and participation, civilian supremacy over the military, separation of powers—must also be met before a country can be considered fully democratic.

Most of Latin America made an impressive transition to electoral democracy during the 1980s when the region's economies were in severe recession and plagued by foreign debt. In the 1990s most of the economies of the area began to recover, to show positive growth, and to begin a process of economic reform to go with the earlier political reforms. Economic reform helped to free up what had been overly statist and inefficient economic systems just as democratization had challenged the older authoritarianism; increasingly liberalism in the economic sphere was seen as related to democracy in the political sphere. More recently globalization has laid down the imperative that Latin America must continue with both political and economic reform if it wishes to be a significant player in the world of the twenty-first century.

Latin America has made great strides in recent decades but many problems and uncertainties remain. Both the progress and the problems provide good reason for students of the area to remain fascinated by it. We hope that some of our enthusiasm for the area has rubbed off on you!

Index